MULTICULTURAL LAW ENFORCEMENT

Strategies for Peacekeeping in a Diverse Society

Robert M. Shusta
Deena R. Levine
Philip R. Harris
Herbert Z. Wong

PRENTICE HALL, Englewood Cliffs, New Jersey 07632

Library of Congress Cataloging-in-Publication Data
Multicultural law enforcement : strategies for peacekeeping in a
  diverse society / Robert M. Shusta. . . .[et al.].
     p. cm.
   Includes bibliographical references (p.   ) and index.
   ISBN 0-13-554080-1
   1. Public relations—Police—United States.   2. Discrimination in
law enforcement—United States.   3. Multiculturalism—United States.
   4. Intercultural communication—United States.   I. Shusta, Robert M.
HV7936.P8M85   1994
363.2—dc20

94-20986

CIP

Acquisitions Editor: *Robin Baliszewski*
Production Editor: *Janet McGillicuddy*
Director of Manufacturing & Production: *Bruce Johnson*
Manufacturing Buyer: *Ed O'Dougherty*
Editorial Assistant: *Rose Mary Florio*
Formatting/page make-up: *Impressions, a division of Edwards Brothers, Inc.*
Printer/Binder: *R. R. Donnelley*

©1995 by Prentice-Hall, Inc.
A Simon & Schuster Company
Englewood Cliffs, New Jersey 07632

Printed in the United States of America

10 9 8 7 6 5 4 3 2 1

ISBN 0-13-554080-1

363.2
M961
1995

Prentice-Hall International (UK) Limited, *London*
Prentice-Hall of Australia Pty. Limited, *Sydney*
Prentice-Hall Canada Inc., *Toronto*
Prentice-Hall Hispanoamericana, S.A., *Mexico*
Prentice-Hall of India Private Limited, *New Delhi*
Prentice-Hall of Japan, Inc., *Tokyo*
Simon & Schuster Asia Pte. Ltd., *Singapore*
Editora Prentice-Hall do Brasil, Ltda., *Rio de Janeiro*

To the many law enforcement professionals who contributed to this book and, by their actions, have demonstrated the professionalism that is required in our multicultural society.

And to our families whose tolerance and support made it possible for us to reach our goal.

CONTENTS

PREFACE

Managing Multicultural Law Enforcement: Strategies for Peacekeeping in a Diverse Society is a textbook designed to assist all levels of law enforcement officials, to understand the pervasive influences of culture, race, and ethnicity in the workplace and the communities they serve. This book focuses on the cross-cultural contact that police officers and civilian employees have with citizens, victims, suspects, and co-workers from diverse backgrounds. Throughout the book we stress the need for awareness, understanding of cultural differences, and respect toward those of different backgrounds. We encourage all representatives of law enforcement to examine preconceived notions that they might hold of particular groups, and we outline for police executives why they should build awareness and promote cultural understanding and tolerance within their agencies.

An increasing number of leaders in law enforcement agencies and their employees have accepted the premise that greater cross-cultural competency must be a key objective of all management and professional development. Demographic changes have had a tremendous impact not only on the types of crimes committed, but also on the composition of the law enforcement workforce. To be effective, police executives must understand their workforces and communities. Professionalism today, includes the need for greater understanding across cultures and improved communication with members of diverse groups.

The public is exposed almost daily to instances of cross-cultural and interracial contact between law enforcement agents and citizens. So, too, have community members become increasingly sophisticated and critical with regard to how members of diverse cultural and racial groups are treated. Employees of police departments and other agencies entrusted with law enforcement find that they are now serving communities that carefully observe them and hold them accountable for their actions.

This book provides practical information and guidelines for law enforcement managers, supervisors, officers, and instructors. With cross-cultural knowledge, sensitivity, and tolerance, those who are charged with the responsibility of peacekeeping will demonstrate greater professionalism, both within the multicultural workforce and in the changing community.

Robert Shusta
Deena Levine
Phil Harris
Herb Wong

ACKNOWLEDGMENTS

The authors appreciate the insightful foreword provided to this book by Police Chief Willie L. Williams of the Los Angeles Police Department.

We are also grateful for the invaluable services rendered by Mrs. Midge Shusta, editorial coordinator, Dr. Hillel B. Levine, graphic artist, Ms. Robin Baliszewski, Executive Editor, for Criminal Justice, and Janet McGillicuddy, Production editor at Prentice Hall's Criminal Justice College Division.

In addition, we value the important contributions to our book from the following people and organizations:

Susan Haake, Beverly Short, David Spisak, and Russ Kindermann of the Center for Leadership Development, Commission on Peace Officers Standards and Training, Department of Justice, State of California

Paul Harman, California POST, formerly, Lt. Los Angeles Sheriff's Department

Lieutenant Ondra Berry, Reno, Nevada Police Department

Deputy Superintendent William Johnston, Boston, MA Police Department

Sergeant Mitchell Grobeson, Los Angeles, CA Police Department

Lt. Rodney Jackson, Lt. Alfred Castagna, Lt. Philip Banks, Jr., Sgt. Michael Hurley, Sgt. Edgar De Leon, Sgt. Jerry Kocik, and Detective Baron Marquis, New York City Police Department

Darrell Stephens (now chief of police of St. Petersburg, Florida) and Karin Schmerler of Police Executive Research Forum, Washington, D.C.

Black Families Association of Concord, CA, in particular, Carrie Frazier, a clinical social worker

ACCESS staff and community members (Arabic Community Center for Economic and Social Services), Dearborn, Michigan

Chung Chuong, Associate Professor of Asian American Studies, San Francisco State University, CA.

L. Philip Guzman, Ph.D., Director of Ethnic Minority Affairs, American Psychological Association, Washington, D.C.

George Simons, Ph.D., President, George Simons International, Santa Cruz, California

John Levelle, Executive Director and Co-Founder of the [American Indian] Center for the Spirit, San Francisco, California

And the following individuals:

Alfredo Aguirre, CA.
David Barlow, Ph.D. Wisconsin
Professor Danilo Begonia, CA.
Officer Mohamed Berro, Michigan
Officer James Caggero, CA.
Sylvia Castillo, Colorado
Gregory Chen, Massachusetts
Darrell Standing Elk, CA.
Robert Flint, Ph.D. CA.
Rafael Gonzalez, CA.
Inspector E. Grandia, B.C.
Steve Hanamura, Oregon
Captain Mary Harrison, CA.
Gregory Jones, CA.
Jim Kahue, Hawaii
Lawrence Katz, Judge, CA.
Thomas Kochman, Ph.D., Illinois
Juan Lopez, CA.
Char Miller, Ph.D., Texas
Alixa Naff, Ph.D., Wash. D.C.
Chief Alicia Powers, CA.
Oscar Ramirez, Ph.D., Texas
Officer Damien Sandoval, CA.
Audrey Shabbas, CA.
Stanley Sue, Ph.D., CA.
Director Fred Taylor, Florida
Sigfrido Urtecho, CA.
Norita Jones Vlach, Ph.D., CA.
George Woo, CA.

John Zogby, Ph.D., New York
Sgt. P. Andrash, British Columbia
Major David Barton, Missouri
Sgt. Guy Bernardo, CA.
Deputy Lori Brimmage, CA.
Joe Canton, Ph.D., CA.
Morris Casuto, CA.
Chief James Cox, Oklahoma
Officer Steve Fajardo, CA.
Yuko Franklin, CA.
Officer Darrell E. Graham, CA.
Chief Thomas Hall, Virginia
Sgt. Brian Harris, Texas
Sgt. Mark Jabour, Michigan
Sgt. Sue Jones, CA.
Sari Karet, CA.
Jean Kim, Ph.D., Connecticut
Hank Koehn (dec.), CA.
Officer Darryl McAllister, CA.
Sarah Miyahira, Ph.D., Hawaii
Dinh Van Nguyen, CA.
Ted Radke, CA.
Officer Jose Rivera, CA.
Victoria Santos, CA.
Jane Singh, Ph.D., CA.
William Tafoya, Ph.D., FBI, CA.
George Thompson, New Mexico
Reverend Onasai Veevalu, CA.
Steven Wallace, Ph.D., CA.
James Zogby, Ph.D., Wash. D.C.

We would also like to thank the following individuals for reviewing our manuscript: Darrell Stephens, Police Chief, City of St. Petersburg, Florida; Major Craig Masterson, New York State Police Academy; Wayne Madole, Ed.D., Broward Community College, Ft. Lauderdale, Florida and T.F. Adams, Rancho Santiago College, Santa Ana, California.

FOREWORD

Societies worldwide, especially within the United States, are increasingly multicultural in composition. No where is this more evident than in the cosmopolitan county of Los Angeles, a keystone urban center of the Pacific Basin. As the citizens in our communities become more diverse, pluralism and tolerance of cultural differences need to become the norm of human behavior. In a civilized society, these are the qualities that America has espoused, incorporating such ideals into Civil Rights legislation applicable throughout the nation. Although some individuals of all backgrounds may practice bigotry, intolerance, and racism, the majority of our citizens believe in justice for all, fair play based on ability, not on the basis of gender, race, religion, or sexual orientation. Most of our citizens respect the Bill of Rights, and translate it into their daily lives by "doing unto their neighbors what they would wish done unto themselves." With increasing multiculturalism, we interface regularly with peoples of diverse backgrounds and perceptions, many of whom do not speak our language or speak English as a second language. In terms of human relations, this becomes a communication challenge for all of us.

The Criminal Justice System reflects such social changes and attitudes. Law enforcement throughout the country is itself becoming more multicultural in its make-up, as well as more open and pluralistic in its outlook. In the professional development of its personnel, officers are better prepared to cope with cultural differences and to acquire cross-cultural skills. Only then can they be effective public servants and maintain the peace. Another factor encouraging these changes is the trend toward community-policing. If the community is more diverse, then peace officers must be capable of interacting effectively with various ethnic and minority groups, especially if law enforcement is to combat and contain rising hate crimes.

Multicultural Law Enforcement: Strategies for Peacekeeping in a Diverse Society, is a useful tool enabling law enforcement to meet such challenges. It should not only prove helpful as a text in criminal justice courses or police academies, but also its contents should be useful to a variety of practitioners in the justice system nationwide. The text combines both the theoretical and the practical in reviewing for peace officers such subjects as diversity, cultural understanding, and communication effectiveness.

The authors are themselves a unique multicultural writing team for this enterprise. The four contributors are diverse in their own gender, cultural and educational backgrounds. They represent both the private and public sectors and all have had experience in law enforcement and corrections, one as a police administrator and three as consultants and researchers in the justice system. They have compiled what experts predict will become a classic text in multicultural law enforcement. The extensive appendices and instructors manual provide a variety of useful resources for both students and teachers and those officers concerned about career development. I hope the readers will find this book a ready reference, one to draw upon frequently, so as to enhance problem-oriented policing and community relations across all cultures.

Willie L. Williams, Chief
LOS ANGELES POLICE DEPARTMENT

PART ONE

Impact of Cultural Diversity on Law Enforcement

1 MULTICULTURAL COMMUNITIES: CHALLENGES FOR LAW ENFORCEMENT
2 THE CHANGING LAW ENFORCEMENT AGENCY: A MICROCOSM OF SOCIETY
3 MULTICULTURAL REPRESENTATION IN LAW ENFORCEMENT: RECRUITMENT, RETENTION, AND PROMOTION

Part One introduces readers to the implications of a multicultural society for law enforcement, both within and outside the police agency. In Chapter 1 the changing population with whom law enforcement representatives have contact is described and differing views on diversity are discussed. Using three case studies, Chapter 1 exemplifies how the existence of different cultures can affect the very nature of crime itself. The authors present the subject of prejudice and its effect on police professionalism, providing specific examples of the consequences of prejudice in law enforcement. The chapter ends with suggestions for improving law enforcement in multicultural communities.

In Chapter 2 demographic changes that are taking place within law enforcement agencies are discussed, as are racism in the workplace and responses to it. In addition to data on ethnic and racial groups, information on women as well as on gays and lesbians in law enforcement institutions across the country is presented. The authors illustrate the realities of the new workforce and point out the corresponding need for flexibility in leadership styles.

In Chapter 3 challenges in recruitment, retention, and promotion of police personnel from various racial, ethnic, and cultural backgrounds are discussed. The authors present strategies for recruitment, emphasizing the commitment that must exist on the part of the law enforcement chief executive. In addition, the need to look inward is discussed: that is, what level of comfort and inclusion are minorities experiencing in a given agency? If the levels are not high, hiring, retention, and promotion will be difficult to achieve. The pressing need facing all agencies to build a workforce representing highly qualified individuals of diverse backgrounds, and one in which all people have equal access to the hiring, retention, and promotion processes, is described in Chapter 3.

Each chapter ends with discussion questions and a list of references. The following appendices correspond to the chapter content in Part One:

1

MULTICULTURAL COMMUNITIES:

Challenges for Law Enforcement

OVERVIEW

In this chapter we discuss some of the challenges facing law enforcement related to the growing multicultural population in the United States. Chapter 1 begins with the need for improved understanding of the diverse populations with which law enforcement officials interact. The discussion of two concepts, the "melting pot" and the "mosaic," incorporates a brief historical perspective on immigration. Three "mini-case studies" illustrate the points of contact between a person's culture and a particular crime or offense. Practical reasons are presented as to why officers should have an understanding of the cultural backgrounds of the groups they commonly encounter. Next, we discuss the subject of prejudice, specifically with reference to law enforcement and professionalism. The chapter ends with eight tips for improving law enforcement in multicultural communities.

COMMENTARY

The word *multicultural* has taken on multiple connotations. Throughout the book, *multiculturalism* refers to a society that is made up of many different ethnic and racial groups and does not refer to a "movement" or political force. Increasing multiculturalism or diversity creates new challenges and complexities for law enforcement officials who must protect and serve people different from themselves.

> Contemporary Issues in Law Enforcement: Cultural Awareness Training by Richard Kirkland, Chief of Police, and Lieutenant Ondra Berry, Reno, Nevada Police Department, 1992.

Law enforcement is under a powerful microscope in terms of how citizens are treated. . . . Minority communities are becoming more competent in understanding the role of law enforcement, and as a result their expectations of law enforcement are elevated from previous years.

Denver Post, "Diversity—when will we get it?" by Tomas Romero, Dec. 16, 1992.
We can view the furor over issues of diversity as an emerging, hopeless conflict—or we can view it as America renewing, reinvigorating itself and positioning itself for the next century.

INTRODUCTION

Our nation has experienced demographic changes this past decade that are the greatest in U.S. history and are virtually unparalleled in any other nation in the world. Reactions to these changes range from appreciation and even celebration of diversity to an absolute intolerance of differences. In its extreme form, absolute intolerance resulting in crimes of hate is a *major* law enforcement and criminal justice concern. From this perspective alone, multiculturalism cannot be ignored. Yet beyond hate crimes, peacekeepers are faced with other challenges related to diversity that require knowledge and skills to handle cultural barriers. With the trend toward community-based policing in the United States, law enforcement professionals are increasingly viewing communities in partnership roles. In doing this, many are now acknowledging that understanding diversity can play a significant and positive role in law enforcement's effectiveness in multicultural communities.

There is growing resistance to the ever-increasing diverse population and an attitude characterized by the following sentiments: "They're here now . . . they should do things 'the American way,'" or "the law is the law and must be applied equally to all." For a new immigrant, "knowing" the system and the "American way" is not something that happens the minute he or she sets foot on American soil. Furthermore, equal enforcement takes on a new meaning in a diverse society. To begin, officers need to recognize the fact of poor police–minority relations historically, including *unequal* treatment under the law. Many officers and citizens are defensive with each other because their contact is tinged with negative historical "baggage."

The strategies used to enforce the law with one's own cultural group may very well result in unsuspected difficulties with another group. The acts of approaching, communicating, questioning, assisting, and establishing trust with members of different groups require special knowledge and skills that have nothing to do with the fact that "the law is the law" and must be enforced equally. Acquiring sensitivity, knowledge, and skills leads to sensitivity that will contribute to improved communication with members of all groups. It does not imply preferential treatment of any one group. The goals on a personal level in multicultural law enforcement are to become more comfortable with groups and communities different from one's own and to treat people fairly and with respect. The more professional a peace officer is, the more sophisticated he or she is in responding to people of all backgrounds and the more successful he or she is in cross-cultural contact.

The Melting Pot: A Valid Notion?

For some, *multiculturalism* or *cultural pluralism* violates what they consider to be the "American way of life." In an interview on attitudes toward immigrants and ethnic minorities, a 57-year-old ex-marine said, "I want America to be for Americans, like it used to be" (*Contra Costa Times,* Feb. 10, 1992, p. 10). This statement represents a failure to understand a central reality of our American past. From the time our country was founded, we were *never* a homogeneous society. First, the indigenous peoples of America (the ancestors of the American Indians) were here long before Christopher Columbus "discovered" them. There is even strong evidence that the first African Americans came to this country as free people, 200 years before the slave trade from Africa began (Rawlins, 1992). Furthermore, the majority of people in this country can claim to be the children, grandchildren, or great-grandchildren of people who have migrated here. Americans did not originate from a common stock.

Did the melting pot ever exist in the United States? The answer is that it never did. Yet people still refer to the belief, which is not much more than a romantic myth about the "good old days." African Americans, brought forcibly to this country between 1619 and 1850, were never part of the early descriptions of the melting pot. Native American peoples, also, were not considered for the melting pot. It is not coincidental that these groups were nonwhite and were therefore not "meltable." Furthermore, throughout our past, great efforts were made to *prevent* any additional diversity. Most notable in this regard was the Chinese Exclusion Act in 1882, which denied entry to Chinese laborers. Early in the twentieth century the Japanese and Korean Exclusion League was formed by organized labor to "protest the influx of 'Coolie' labor and in fear of threat to the living standards of American workingmen" (Kennedy, 1986). Immigration was discouraged or prevented if it did not add strength to what already existed as the majority of the population (Handlin, 1975).

In the late nineteenth century, New York City exemplified how different immigrant groups stayed separate from each other, with little of the "blending" that people often imagine took place (personal communication, Char Miller, U.S. Historian, Dec. 23, 1992). Three-fourths of New York City's population consisted of first- or second-generation immigrants (including Europeans and Asians); 80 percent did not speak English and there were 100 foreign language newspapers. The new arrivals were not accepted by those who were already "settled" and many found comfort in an alien society by choosing to remain in ethnic enclaves with people who shared their culture and life experiences.

The first generation of every immigrant and refugee group seeing the United States as the land of hope and opportunity has always experienced obstacles in their own acculturation (i.e., integration) into the new society. In many cases, people resisted "Americanization" and kept to themselves. For example, the Italians, the Irish, the Eastern European Jews, the Portuguese, the Germans, and virtually every other group tended to remain apart when they first came. Most previously settled immigrants were distrustful of each newcomer group. "Mainstreaming" only began to occur with many of the children's children. The belief in the melting pot holds that when everyone arrived, they very quickly lost their own cultural identities and blended smoothly into one society.

Despite the reality of past multicultural disharmony and tension in the United States, the notion of the melting pot prevailed. History has *never* supported the metaphor of the melting pot, especially with regard to the first and second generations of most groups of newcomers. One of the earliest uses of the term was in 1914, when a famous American playwright, Israel Zangwill, referring to the mass immigration from Europe, said, "America is God's crucible, the great Melting-Pot where all the races of *Europe* are melting and re-forming . . . Germans and Frenchmen, Irishmen and Englishmen, Jews and Russians—into the Crucible with you all! God is making the American!" (Zangwill, 1908). The melting-pot notion was not designed to incorporate anyone except Europeans. The melting never did take place among Americans of all backgrounds; "pressure cooker" may be a more accurate term for this society.

Reactions to Diversity, Historically and Today

Accepting diversity has always been a difficult proposition for most Americans (personal communication, Char Miller, U.S. Historian, Dec. 23, 1992). Approaching the twenty-first century, we find people becoming increasingly uncomfortable with the numbers of immigrants, refugees, and ethnic minorities in our society in ways that are not much different from times past. Today, typical criticisms of recent immigrants include: "They hold on to their cultures. They won't learn our language. Their customs and behavior are strange. They stick to themselves." Yet, as noted previously, many newcomers have historically resisted "Americanization" and kept to ethnic enclaves and, in addition, were not usually accepted by the "mainstream."

Are the reactions to newcomers today so totally different from people's reactions to earlier waves of immigrants? Let's look at reactions to the Irish who by the middle of the nineteenth century became the largest group of immigrants in the United States, making up almost 45 percent of the foreign-born U.S. population. Approximately 4¼ million people left Ireland, mainly because of the potato famine. Most of these immigrants were from rural areas but ended up in cities on the east coast. Most were illiterate; some spoke only Gaelic (Kennedy, 1986). Their reception in America was anything but welcoming. (One could frequently see signs saying, "Jobs available, no Irish need apply.")

> The Irish . . . endure[d] the scorn and discrimination later to be inflicted, to some degree at least, on each successive wave of immigrants by already settled "Americans." In speech and in dress, they seemed foreign; they were poor and unskilled and they were arriving in overwhelming numbers. . . . The Irish found many doors closed to them, both socially and economically. When their earnings were not enough . . . their wives and daughters obtained employment as servants." (Kennedy, 1986)

If this were rewritten without specific references to time and cultural group, it would be reasonable to say that the reception to America's earlier immigrants was not that different from contemporary reactions to newcomers. One could take this quote on the Irish and substitute Jew, Italian, or Polish at various points in history. Today, it could be Chinese, Vietnamese, Mexican, or Haitian.

Comparing immigration today with earlier periods in U.S. history, one finds many similarities. Yet there are significant differences as well. In the past few decades, we have received people from cultures more dramatically different than those from Western Europe. For example, many of our "new Americans" from Southeast Asia bring values and languages not commonly associated with or related to the mainstream American values and language. Middle Easterners bring customs unknown to many U.S.-born Americans. (For cultural specifics, refer to Chapters 6 to 10.) Many Central Americans bring scars of political persecution, the nature of which most Americans cannot even fathom. The relatively mild experiences of those who came as voluntary migrants do not begin to compare with the horrors and tragedies of many of the more recent refugees. True, desperate economic conditions compelled many European immigrants to leave their countries (therefore, leaving was not *entirely* voluntary), but torture and brutality were not part of their experience as is the case for recent refugees from Central America and Southeast Asia.

Despite the differences, some of the same sentiments expressed toward the Irish are said today of the "new Americans" from Cuba, Mexico, Laos, Cambodia, Afghanistan, and elsewhere. Disparaging comments were once made toward the very people whose descendants would, in later years, constitute much of mainstream America. Many of the fourth- and fifth-generation immigrants have forgotten their history (personal communication, Char Miller, U.S. Historian, Dec. 23, 1992). Those who are intolerant of the "foreign ways" of various groups need to keep in mind this historical perspective. *Every* new group seems to be met with some suspicion and, in many cases, hostility. Adjustment to a new society is and has always been a long and painful process and the first-generation immigrant group suffers, whether Irish, Jewish, Polish, Afghani, Laotian, or Filipino. It must also be remembered that many groups did not come to the United States of their own free will but were, rather, victims of a political or economic system that forced them to escape their homelands and abruptly cut their roots. Although grateful for their welcome to this country, newcomers did not want to be uprooted. Many of our "new Americans" did not have any part in the creation of events that led to the flight from their countries.

CHOICES IN A CULTURALLY PLURALISTIC SOCIETY

In a report of The Attorney General's Commission on Racial, Ethnic, Religious and Minority Violence, (1986), California Judge Alice Lytle is quoted: "Someday we must learn to value the richness and beauty of our diverse racial, ethnic, and cultural heritage. We will all be the better and safer for it." Most people in law enforcement would agree that we *would* all be safer if citizens and the nearly 560,000 police officers of this country learned to appreciate diversity rather than fear it. Hate crimes and all other religious, racial, and ethnic incidents are the extreme manifestation of economic and social competition as well as intolerance, xenophobia (i.e., fear of strangers or foreigners), and racial supremacist attitudes. Perpetrators of hate crimes have contributed to the lack of success that our society has had in creating a melting pot of its many peoples.

To ignore diversity or to minimize its importance will not cause it to vanish. In its extreme form, when people attempt to strip others of their cultural identity, they do not allow them the right to be themselves. The consequences of this can be serious and even tragic. A San Francisco Bay Area police officer of Native American descent admitted to knowing very little about his roots. He said that his mother and grandmother were denied the opportunity to learn about their culture and, therefore, nothing was passed on to him. He admitted to feeling both an emptiness within himself and an intense anger toward those who had the power to decide that certain cultural traditions and beliefs were not worth preserving. He sees the alcoholism and suicide in some American Indian communities as a collective response to domination and forced denial of ethnicity. The only positive aspect of his cultural experience (or lack thereof) is the fact that he appreciates the cultures of other ethnic and minority groups (even to the point of envy). He feels that his "appreciation comes across in his contact with citizens and this contributes to better relationships with members of minority groups."

The cultural pluralism that has always characterized the United States is not going to reverse itself. For some, insisting on a melting pot may be a way to minimize or cover up differences, resulting in the rejection of diversity. It is possible that a culturally monolithic society (a rare phenomenon in this world) runs more smoothly, but that is not and has never been the reality of society in the United States. The more culturally diverse groups there are, the greater the magnitude of "we/they" thinking. "They" are changing the face of our society. "They" refuse to let go of their cultures. "Our culture is better." "They" only want to speak their languages. "They" are taking our jobs. "We are now the new victims." "They" are bringing more violence into our society. In other words, "We" can't and shouldn't be criticized. But, we can look to others and find fault.

A diverse society obviously makes any law enforcement officer's or manager's job more difficult. In a 1988 article, Alpert and Dunham concluded that "ethnicity seemed to complicate every police procedure and every encounter between the police and the public." It would be naive to "preach" to law enforcement officers, agents, and managers about the value of diversity when day-to-day activities are complicated by diversity. But the longer it takes to understand the influences of culture and ethnicity on behavior, the longer every police procedure and every encounter between the police and the multicultural public may remain complicated. At a minimum, there must be a basic acceptance of diversity as a precursor to improving interpersonal relations and contact across cultural, ethnic, and racial lines. Acceptance by law enforcement professionals should contribute to the establisment of more trust, safety, cooperation, and ultimately, more effectiveness.

Replacing the Melting Pot: The Mosaic

One way to begin to accept diversity is to view society as a mosaic in which all races and ethnic groups are displayed in a form that is attractive because of the very elements of which it is made. Each group is seen as separate and distinct but still contributes its own color, shape, and design to the whole, resulting in an *enriched* society. The terms *Mexican American, Asian American, Arab American, African American,* and so on, reflect a dual identity merged into one. "The term 'Asian American' defines [me] as being from America, but being Asian as well. When I call myself Asian American, I don't think that sets me off. I see it as integrating two parts of myself" (academician in an Asian American studies department, San Diego Union, *Currents,* Mar. 9, 1989, p. F-3). Having a dual identity is not un-American and does not imply separatism. On the contrary, it is the essence of being American. Although *multicultural* has been used as such, it is not a buzz word or a fad. The term *mosaic* puts a positive value on multiculturalism and carries it one step further to imply acceptance of our society as a culture of cultures.

In many areas across the country, one in every two or three Americans will be a "minority" by the year 2000. If people in general, and law enforcement in particular, do not view America's mosaic positively, the outcomes will be increased isolation, divisiveness, and fear. All of this will translate into a heavier burden for law enforcement.

Changing Population

Between 1980 and 1990, the population of the United States increased by 23 million people. Of this number, 40 percent (9.6 million) fell into the white/non-Hispanic category. The remaining 60 percent was comprised of (1) Hispanics (with a 6.4 million increase), (2) blacks (with a 4.3 million increase), and (3) Asians and other races (with a 3.4 million increase). Demographers estimate that the birthrate for Hispanics and Asians will continue to outpace that of other races. By the year 2020, a majority of children in New Mexico, California, Texas, New York, Florida, and Louisiana will be "minorities," comprised of African Americans, Asians, and Hispanics (Trojanowicz and Carter, 1990). Exhibit 1.1 shows the overall percentage increase of minorities between 1980 and 1990.

The group that showed the largest overall percentage increase from 1980 to 1990 is the Asian/Pacific Islander group. Exhibit 1.2 shows a breakdown of the groups included in this category. The group with the second largest overall increase was the Hispanic origin group. Exhibit 1.3 provides a partial breakdown of the various groups within that category. Exhibit 1.2 and 1.3 by no means provide a comprehensive list of Asian, Pacific Islander, or Hispanic groups but rather, a breakdown of some of the major groups that comprise the broad categories listed above. There are many other Asian and Pacific Islander groups that are not listed in Exhibit 1.2, evidence of the great diversity that exists within groups. Other groups of Hispanic not included in Exhibit 1.3 include people whose origins are from the various Spanish-speaking countries of the Caribbean, Central or South America, or from Spain (U.S. Department of Commerce News, Economics and Statistics Administration, 1991).

The Minority Becomes the Majority

What the growth rate means, according to demographic predictions, is that minorities will become the majority by the year 2010. This demographic "about-face" has

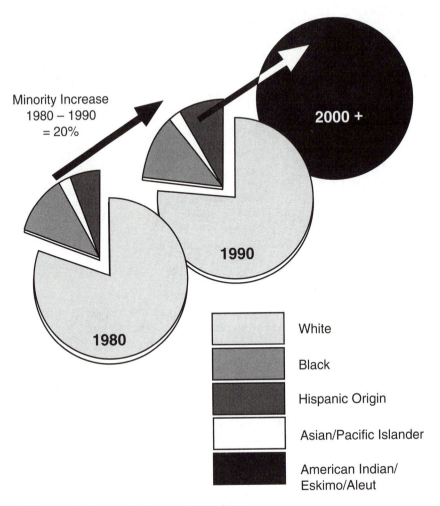

Minority Increase
1980 – 1990
= 20%

2000 +

1990

1980

White

Black

Hispanic Origin

Asian/Pacific Islander

American Indian/
Eskimo/Aleut

Exhibit 1.1 Minority Population Trends in the United States.

already occurred in some large cities across the country and in a number of areas in California. This change has had an impact on many institutions in society, not the least of which is law enforcement. The nation's diversity is affecting peacekeeping and law enforcement agencies in many direct and indirect ways.

Immigrants

As mentioned earlier in this chapter, immigration is not a new phenomenon in the United States. Virtually every citizen except for indigenous peoples of America can claim to be a relative or descendent of someone who migrated (whether voluntarily or not) from another country. However, immigration reached peak levels in 1990 (see Exhibit 1.4), when the number of immigrants surpassed 1.5 million. In addition, immigrants in the 1980s and 1990s came from many *more* parts of the world than those who arrived at the turn of the century (see Exhibit 1.5).

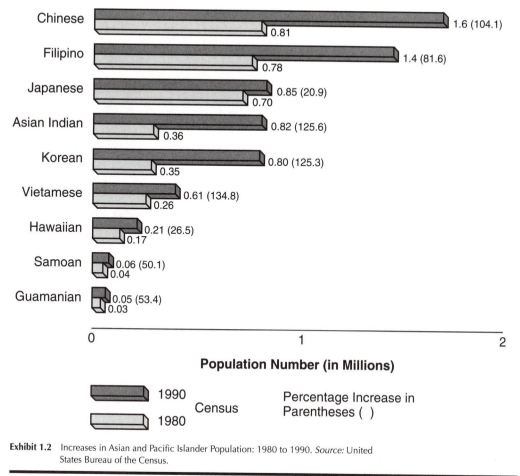

Exhibit 1.2   Increases in Asian and Pacific Islander Population: 1980 to 1990. *Source:* United States Bureau of the Census.

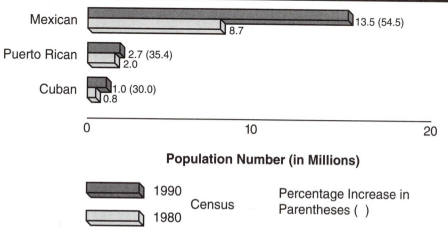

Exhibit 1.3   Increases in Hispanic Population: 1980 to 1990. *Source:* United States Bureau of the Census.

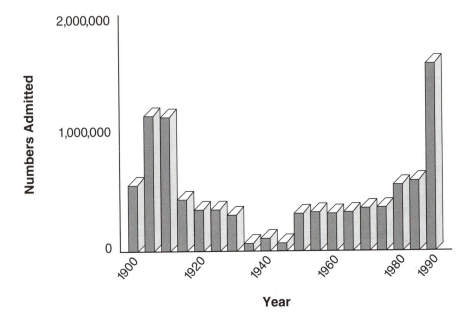

Exhibit 1.4   Immigrants Admitted into the United States: Fiscal Year 1990. *Source:* United
                   States Bureau of the Census.

In law enforcement, as in other professions, it is not uncommon to hear anti-immigrant sentiment. Especially in a time of recession, many people, including some police officers, perceive that immigrants are taking away jobs from "real Americans" (forgetting that legal immigrants are also "real" Americans). However, the issues surrounding immigration are not as clear-cut as they may appear at first. Along with the problems that are inevitably created when large groups of people have to be absorbed in the society, immigrants also stimulate the economy and often revitalize neighborhoods and also eventually become fully participatory and loyal American citizens. Nevertheless, if an officer has an anti-immigrant bias, it would not be unreasonable to expect that negative attitudes may surface when that officer interacts with immigrants, especially in stressful circumstances. When an officer is stressed, negative attitudes become apparent and his or her communication may become unprofessional. Indeed, some immigrants with language barriers and a lack of understanding of the "system" have claimed that officers with whom they have been in contact do not attempt to understand them or that officers demonstrate little patience in communicating or finding a translator. (See Chapter 5 for a fuller discussion of communication problems.)

In addition, officers must be aware of "racial flashpoints" that are created when immigrants move into economically depressed areas where large minority populations reside. Some people feel that immigrants moving into certain urban areas displace economically disadvantaged minorities or deprive them of access to work. (It is beyond the scope of this chapter to discuss the validity or lack thereof of this sentiment.) Thus law enforcement representatives will see hostility between,

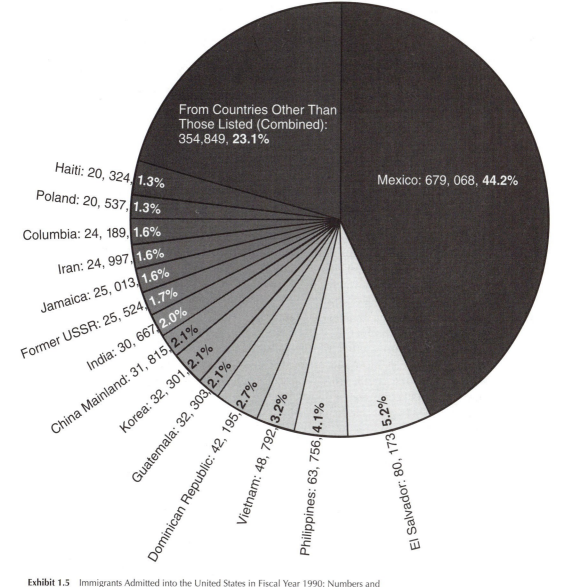

From Countries Other Than Those Listed (Combined): 354,849, **23.1%**

Mexico: 679, 068, **44.2%**

Haiti: 20, 324, **1.3%**

Poland: 20, 537, **1.3%**

Columbia: 24, 189, **1.6%**

Iran: 24, 997, **1.6%**

Jamaica: 25, 013, **1.6%**

Former USSR: 25, 524, **1.7%**

India: 30, 667, **2.0%**

China Mainland: 31, 815, **2.1%**

Korea: 32, 301, **2.1%**

Guatemala: 32, 303, **2.1%**

Dominican Republic: 42, 195, **2.7%**

Vietnam: 48, 792, **3.2%**

Philippines: 63, 756, **4.1%**

El Salvador: 80, 173 **5.2%**

Exhibit 1.5   Immigrants Admitted into the United States in Fiscal Year 1990: Numbers and Percentages by Countries of Birth. *Source:* United States Bureau of the Census.

for example, blacks and Korean immigrants and blacks and Arab immigrants in such cities as Los Angeles, New York, and Detroit. Although officers cannot be expected to solve these deep-seated problems, they will find themselves in situations where they can serve as cultural mediators, helping each group to understand and tolerate the other more than they currently do. To exemplify, police can point out that when a Korean grocer does not smile and greet the customer warmly, it is not necessarily a sign of hostility but rather, is a cultural trait. (Of course, the behavior may also be an expression of distrust, but it is not *always* this.) Or when a person complains that an Arab liquor store owner does not hire outside his or her community, the officer can explain that it is usually because the business is a small family-run operation in which the "employees" are family members. (See Chapters 6 to 10 for cultural specifics.) Not all problems are cultural, but with an understanding of immigrants' backgrounds, the officer can help explain points of tension to members of other ethnic groups.

Undocumented Immigrants

There are two major groups of undocumented immigrants: those who entered U.S. borders without having been "inspected" and those who entered the country with legal documents as temporary residents but have violated their legal admission status by extending their stay. The U.S. border patrol apprehends approximately 900,000 people every year (Kondracke, 1989). Initially, Mexicans and other Latin Americans come to most people's minds when they hear the terms *illegal alien* or *undocumented worker*. Over 60 to 70 percent of the illegal population does come through Mexico, including those from Central American countries such as El Salvador and Guatemala (personal communication, Edward Fernandez, Population Division of the U.S. Bureau of the Census, Jan. 1993). In addition, people from the Dominican Republic enter through Puerto Rico; since Puerto Ricans are U.S. citizens, they are considered legal. Therefore, officers may be in contact with "Puerto Ricans" who are actually from the Dominican Republic. People from other parts of the world may come to the United States on a tourist visa, then decide to remain permanently (e.g., Canadians, Irish, and other Europeans). In addition, there are those who enter the United States at its southern borders: namely, people from Pacific Rim countries and the Caribbean (Trojanowicz and Carter, 1990). Undocumented immigrants lack documents that would enable them to obtain legal residence in the United States. The consequences are far-reaching. Law enforcement officials, politicians, and social service providers, among others, have had to deal with many concerns related to housing, education, safety, employment, and health care.

Some undocumented aliens come to the United States hoping to remain legally by proving that they escaped their homeland because of political repression, and if they were to return, they would face persecution or death. People who are often deported as undocumented arrivals are those who come as "economic refugees" (i.e., their economic status in their home country may be desperate). Undocumented aliens generally have few occupational skills and are willing to take menial jobs that many American citizens would not accept. They fill economic gaps in various regions where there are needs for low-wage labor.

People in law enforcement need to be aware of a tendency to stereotype immigrants as illegal. Outer appearances are not an accurate guide to who has legal status and who does not. Both illegal and legal immigrants may live in the same neighborhoods. Many formerly undocumented aliens from Mexico were legalized through the Immigration Reform and Control Act (IRCA) in 1986, which reduced the size of the undocumented population from about 3 million in 1986 to nearly 2 million in 1988 (Woodrow, 1990). Through IRCA, aliens who offered proof to the Immigration and Naturalization Service (INS) that they had been "continuously resident in an unlawful status since before January 1, 1982" could apply for legalization (Woodrow, 1990).

The illegal segment of the immigrant population is particularly difficult for law enforcement officials. Trojanowicz and Bucqueroux (1990) state:

"[They] pose a difficult challenge for police, because fear of deportation often makes them reluctant to report crimes committed against them—which also makes them easy prey. They can also fall victim to crimes related to their vulnerability—scams including extortion, fees for phony documentation. . . . Because so many arrive with little or no money and have difficulty making a living, undocumented aliens often cluster in low-income, high-crime areas."

According to research sponsored by the Coalition for Immigrant and Refugee Rights, the fear of being deported has left many illegal immigrant women, in particular, victims of domestic violence (*Contra Costa Times,* Mar. 8, 1991, p. 9a). Many of the women who were the subject of the coalition's survey came to the United States to escape repression or poverty in their country of origin, but live with abuse constantly in their new life. The survey found that 34 percent of Hispanic women and 20 percent of Filipino women reported suffering some form of domestic violence, either physical, emotional, or sexual. According to the study's co-author, "the results [of the study] are significant because the issue of domestic violence is a real secret that nobody wants to talk about and the issue of being undocumented is also a secret" (*Contra Costa Times,* Mar. 8, 1991, p. 9a). Many of the women in the study became employed, whereas their spouses did not, creating a volatile domestic situation. This change in family roles whereby the wife works (along with other factors) often creates desperate and violent home environments.

According to an official of the U.S. Bureau of the Census, "The decision was made that local police priorities must override concerns about status. Basically, this means the police will leave the job of assessing the person's immigration status to INS, since that is their job, while the police concentrate on their crime and disorder concerns. Only in cases where the perpetrators prove to be undocumented aliens will the individual's immigration status become an issue" (Woodrow, 1990).

The principal barrier to establishing trust with undocumented immigrants concerns their fears about being reported to the INS. The argument supporting leaving illegal immigrants alone (unless they have committed a criminal act or are a disturbance) has to do with the fact that tracking down and deporting illegal workers is strictly the job of the INS and not the police. This is a decision that many police department managements have had to consider, weighing the benefits of gaining the trust of entire communities against any negative outcome of detaining illegal immigrants.

For law enforcement, most immigrants, whether legal or illegal, present challenges to the average officer working the streets. There is a great deal that immigrants have to learn about U.S. laws, about the system in general, and about the role of the police officer. Many immigrants fear the police because in their native countries police engaged in arbitrary acts of brutality in support of repressive governments (e.g., Central America). In other countries, citizens disrespect police because they are poorly educated, inefficient and corrupt, and have a very low occupational status (e.g., in Iran). The barriers that immigrants bring to the relationship with police suggest that American officers have to double their efforts to communicate and to educate. A further challenge for law enforcement is that for reasons mentioned above (not knowing the system and the laws, fear of police), new immigrants often become victims of violent crimes. Most new immigrants face hurdles when it comes to dealing with law enforcement. Their acculturation and ultimate success in this society depend in part on how they are treated when they are still ignorant of the social norms and laws. Most important is that others grant them the time and patience that every human being needs in times of difficult transitions.

INTERPLAY BETWEEN CULTURE AND POLICE INCIDENTS

With communities changing, not only have the concerns of law enforcement and criminal justice changed but so has the nature of some crime. Police in today's society witness crimes and other incidents that can be baffling. Consider the following example:

> In Los Angeles, a Thai man allegedly sprayed a group of four Laotians with gunfire after one of them sat with the soles of his feet bared at the defendant while the Thai sang in a nightclub. The gesture is considered highly insulting by some Asians. One of the Laotians was killed and another injured. . . . [A member of the Los Angeles Police Department's Asian Task Force] said the foot gesture may have been insulting, but "not to the point of murder." The head of the task force said, "As far as we're concerned, in serious crimes cultural ignorance is no defense," adding that police "have a certain amount of discretion" when it comes to making arrests in lesser crimes. (*San Francisco Chronicle,* "Culture clash and violence," Oct. 14, 1986, Sec. 1, p. 21)

In interviews with a deputy public defender and a deputy district attorney, a legal journal posed the following question: Should our legal system recognize a "cultural" defense? The deputy district attorney's response was: "No. You're treading on shaky ground when you decide something based on culture, because our society is made up of so many different cultures. It is very hard to draw the line somewhere, but [diverse cultural groups] are living in our country, and people have to abide by [one set of] laws or else you have anarchy." The deputy public defender's response to the question was: "Yes. I'm not asking that the [various cultural groups] be judged differently, just that their actions be understood according to their own history and culture" (Sherman, 1986).

If law enforcement's function is to "protect and serve" citizens from *all* cultural backgrounds, it becomes vital to *understand the cultural dimensions of crimes.* Obviously, behaviors or actions that may be excused in another culture must not go unpunished if they are considered crimes in this country (e.g., spouse abuse). Nevertheless, there are circumstances in which law enforcement officials at all levels of the criminal justice system would benefit by understanding the cultural context in which a crime or other incident occurred. Law enforcement professionals must use standard operating procedures in response to specific situations and the majority of these procedures cannot be altered for different groups based on ethnicity. In a multicultural society, however, an officer can modify the way he or she treats a suspect, witness, or victim given knowledge of what is considered "normal" in that person's culture. When officers suspect that an aspect of cultural background is a factor in a particular incident, they may earn the respect and, therefore, cooperation from ethnic communities if they are willing to evaluate their arrests in *lesser* crimes. (See "Police Knowledge of Cultural Groups" later in this chapter.)

Before looking at specific case studies of incidents and crimes involving cultural components, it is necessary to understand the concept of culture and the tremendous impact it has on the individual. All people (except for very young children) carry "cultural baggage." To varying degrees, this includes members of cultural and racial groups who constitute "minorities" in a given society (the degree is determined by their own conscious and unconscious identification with their group and their relative attachment to their cultural group's traditional values). Being influenced by cultural baggage is a natural human phenomenon. Much of who we are is sanctioned and reinforced by the society in which we have been raised. According to some experts, culture influences approximately 80 percent of an individual's personality (Hall, 1959), and often this influence is unconscious. Of course, there are other influences: age, gender, personality, and socioeconomic status. But culture apparently has a stronger influence than the others just listed, and for this reason it is virtually impossible to "drop" one's culture when interacting in another cultural environment.

The Definition of Culture

Although there are many facets of the term *culture,* we define culture as beliefs, values, patterns of thinking, behavior, and everyday customs that have been passed on from generation to generation. Culture is learned (i.e., it is not genetic) and is manifested in largely unconscious and subtle behavior.

With this definition in mind, consider that most children have acquired a general cultural orientation by the time they are 5 or 6. This is why expecting one to change behavior to accommodate a new culture is difficult. Many layers of cultural behavior and beliefs are subconscious. Additionally, many people assume that what they take for granted is taken for granted by all people ("all human beings are the same") and they do not even recognize their own culturally influenced behavior. Anthropologist Edward T. Hall, says (1959): "Culture hides much more than it reveals and, strangely enough, what it hides, it hides most effectively from its own participants." In other words, people are blind to their own deeply embedded cultural behavior.

To understand the hidden nature of culture further, picture an iceberg (Ruhly, 1976). The only visible part of the iceberg is the tip, which typically constitutes only about 10 percent of the mass. Like most of culture's influences, the remainder of the iceberg is submerged beneath the surface. What this means for law enforcement is that there will be a natural tendency to interpret behavior, motivations, and criminal activity from the officer's cultural point of view. This is due largely to an inability to understand behavior from alternative perspectives and because of the inclination toward *ethnocentrism* (i.e., an attitude of seeing and judging all other cultures from the perspective of one's *own* culture). In other words, an ethnocentric person would say that there is only one way of being "normal" and that is the way of his or her own culture. When it comes to law enforcement, there *is* only one set of laws that must be adhered to by all citizens, whether native born or not. However, the following case studies will illustrate that culture does affect interpretations, meaning, and intention.

MINI-CASE STUDIES: CULTURE AND CRIME*

All of the following mini-case studies involve descriptions of crimes or offenses with a cultural component. If the crime is a murder or something similarly heinous, most people will not be particularly sympathetic, even with an understanding of cultural factors involved. However, consider that understanding other cultural patterns gives one the ability to *see* and *react* in a new way. The ability to withhold judgment and to interpret a person's intention from a *different* cultural perspective is a skill that will ultimately enable a person to identify his or her own cultural blinders.

Mini-Case Study 1: A Tragic Case of Cross-Cultural Misinterpretation

In parts of Asia, there are medical practices unfamiliar to many law enforcement officials (as well as medical practitioners) in the West. A number of these practices result in marks on the skin that can easily be misinterpreted as abuse by people who have no knowledge of these culturally based medical treatments. The practices include rubbing the skin with a coin ("coining," "coin rubbing," or "wind rubbing"), pinching the skin, touching the skin with burning incense, or applying a heated cup to the skin ("cupping"). Each one of these practices leaves highly visible marks, such as burns and bruises. The following is an account of a serious misreading on the part of school authorities and law enforcement officials in the United States of some very common Southeast Asian methods of traditional folk healing.

A young Vietnamese boy had been absent from school for a few days with a serious respiratory infection. His father, believing that "coining" would help cure him, rubbed heated coins on specific sections of his back and neck. The boy's condition seemed to improve and he was able to return to school. Upon noticing heavy bruising on the boy's neck, the teacher immediately informed the school principal, who promptly reported the "abuse" to the police (who then notified Child Protective Services). When the police were notified, they went to the child's home to investigate. The father was very cooperative when questioned by the police and admitted, in broken English, that he had caused the bruising on his son's neck.

---

*Discussion questions corresponding to each case study are found following the summary of this chapter.

The man was arrested and incarcerated. While the father was in jail, his son, who was under someone else's custody, apparently relapsed and died of his original illness. Upon hearing the news, the father committed suicide in his jail cell. Of course, it is not known whether the father would have committed suicide as a response to his son's death alone. The tragic misinterpretation on the part of the authorities involved, including the teacher, the principal, and the arresting police officers, provides an extreme case of what can happen when people attribute meaning from their own cultural perspective.

Cultural understanding would not have cured the young boy, but informed interaction with the father could have prevented the second tragedy. All of the authorities were interpreting what they saw with cultural "filters" based on their own belief system. Ironically, the interpretation of the bruises (i.e., child abuse) was almost the opposite of the intended meaning of the act (i.e., healing). Even after some of the parties involved learned about this very common Southeast Asian practice, they still did not believe that it existed as an established practice and they could not fathom how others could believe that "coining" could actually cure illness. Their own conception of medical healing did not encompass what they perceived as such a "primitive treatment."

Ethnocentrism is a barrier to accepting that there *is* another way, another belief, another communication style, another custom, or another value that can lead to culturally different behavior. Ethnocentrism often causes a person to assign a potentially incorrect meaning or to attribute an incorrect motivation to a given act. Had only one person in the chain of authorities in contact with the Vietnamese child been able to view the bruises and consider something other than abuse, the spiral of serious cultural misunderstanding might have been averted.

Mini-Case Study 2: Statements of Sentiment versus Statements of Intent

This next example describes the case of *McPherson* v. *Rankin* (1986, Houston, Texas) involving an African American woman and a captain at a sheriff's office in Houston, Texas (personal communication, Thomas Kochman, Kochman Communications Consultants Ltd., June 19, 1992). The woman, a clerk in the sheriff's office, made a statement to her boyfriend at lunch that was overheard by a captain. The couple had been talking about recent federal cutbacks in social services for African Americans when the news of President Reagan's assassination attempt came over the radio. When the woman heard that the president had survived the assassination attempt, she said to her boyfriend, "I hope the next time somebody tries that, they get him." The captain who overheard the remark later reported this to the sheriff, who questioned her about her statement. He asked two questions, "Did you say it?" and "Did you mean it?" To the first question, the woman answered, "Yes"; and to the second question, she also answered, "Yes." The sheriff fired her and called in the Secret Service to investigate.

Alleging that the negative publicity about this incident prevented her from finding employment for at least six months, the woman sued the sheriff's office.

At issue was whether people could wish aloud for the president's death. The sheriff defended his actions by explaining that his office was often required to protect the lives of public dignitaries visiting Houston. Although the woman was not involved directly in protecting public officials, she did have access to information (such as schedules of politicians' visits) that could conceivably be useful in an assassination plan. The sheriff felt that; knowing her feelings, it would be risky for him to keep the woman as an employee. The federal district judge accepted the sheriff's argument and ruled against the plaintiff.

The Fifth Circuit Court (Houston) reversed the trial court and remanded the case, declaring that the trial judge had not investigated the woman's intent. At this point, Thomas Kochman, expert in black–white communication pattern differences, was asked to testify before the trial judge on behalf of the ACLU. In his testimony, Kochman discussed a cultural assumption that exists among many African Americans, in which there is a clear understanding that verbal threats and aggressive language can be expressed without any intention of imminent action to follow. Kochman's contention was that the "fighting words" doctrine of the Supreme Court is based on the assumption that everyone is assimilated to "white" standards whereby verbal aggression can be viewed as potentially inciting to violence. Nevertheless, the trial court again upheld the sheriff's actions. The circuit court overturned the trial judge's ruling because they did not see a private lunch conversation (in which the woman made her statement) as public discourse.

Additional background information for Mini-Case Study 2. In an interview with Dr. Thomas Kochman, author of *Black and White Styles in Conflict,* the following question was posed: What aspect of the black style of communication has great potential for misunderstanding among nonblacks and is of special significance to law enforcement officials? Clearly, his response had to do with "fighting words" and how threats are understood (see Chapter 7). Kochman explained that for many African Americans, threats are intended to arouse an image in the other person and signify a "feeling state." (He explained that this may possibly apply more to older blacks, but is understood by most people who understand the culture). Kochman added that the function of verbal threats in African American culture is similar to the use of threats in Arabic and Iranian culture. Supporting this statement, an Iranian psychologist explains: "I can think of a situation where an Iranian man would say, 'I get so angry that I could kill my boss.' . . . An American therapist might just call the police. It's difficult for him to know that this is the way the man expresses himself" (*Contra Costa Times,* June 16, 1993, p. 5.A). In other words, the manner in which a person can express a threat or verbal aggression (i.e., with intensity and rage) does not necessarily equal the potential for action. Yet some people from different cultural backgrounds would interpret such a threat differently.

To further illustrate Mini-Case Study 2, Kochman cited the words of Leanita McLain, the late African American editorial writer for the *Chicago Tribune.* After the election of Chicago's first African American mayor (early 1980s), Harold Washington, McLain wrote an article entitled "How Chicago Taught Me to Hate

Whites." In the article she discussed her rage over racism and, among other things, how she reacted when she heard whites on a bus talking about "*the* blacks." Her remark that elicited the greatest reaction was: "'*The blacks.' It would make me feel like machine-gunning every white face on the bus. Why couldn't these people just say 'blacks,' letting it roll from the tongue" (Kochman's 1989, p. 57).* Kochman explained that a white politician wondered whether the readers of the *Chicago Tribune* knew that one of the editorial writers on the staff "hates whites and now has publicly stated that *she'd like to* machine-gun them." McLain's statement "would make me feel like," Kochman pointed out, was understood as "would like to" (and in the minds of some people interpreting this: "will do").

(While making sure that an officer takes all necessary safety precautions upon hearing a verbal threat, he or she can also keep in mind that threats can function in culturally different ways. Although a cultural generalization will never apply to all people in one group, an officer is better prepared to deal with a variety of citizens when he or she has an understanding that the use of certain types of language can have different meanings for different groups of people.)

Mini-Case Study 3: Latino Values as a Factor in Sentencing

In a court of law, a cultural explanation or rationalization (i.e., a cultural defense) generally does not affect a "guilty" or "not guilty" verdict. It would be a rare occurrence for a cultural explanation or rationalization to affect the operation of law when it comes to assigning guilt or innocence. Nevertheless, there are cases when culture may affect sentencing. Consider the next case, where according to California Superior Court Judge Lawrence Katz (personal communication, June 8, 1992), somewhat milder sentencing than what might have otherwise occurred resulted in part because of cultural considerations.[*]

A Mexican woman living in the United States became involved in an extramarital affair. Her husband became outraged when the wife bragged about her extramarital activities at a picnic at which many extended family members were present. At the same time, the wife also made comments about her husband's lack of ability to satisfy her and how, in contrast, her lover was far superior. Upon hearing his wife gloat about her affair, the husband left the picnic and drove 5 miles to purchase a gun. Two hours later, he shot and killed his wife. In a case such as this, the minimum charge required in California would be second-degree murder. However, because the jury took into consideration the cultural background of this couple, the husband received a mitigated sentence and was found guilty of manslaughter. It was argued that his wife's boasting about her lover and her explicit comments made specifically to emasculate him created a passion and emotion that completely undermined his "machismo," pride and honor. To understand the

---

[*]This mini-case study involves homicide. In pointing out how the judges and jury were influenced, in part, by the defendants' cultural background (i.e., with regard to sentencing), the authors do not imply, in any way, that the crime was justifiable on cultural grounds. The purpose of this example is to illustrate, yet again, how culture plays a part in decision making at various levels in the criminal justice system.

severity of her offense, the law enforcement officer and the prosecutor must understand what it means to be humiliated in the context of the Latino culture in such a manner *in front of one's family.*

The purpose of these three mini-case studies is not to discuss the "rightness" or "wrongness" of any group's values, customs, or beliefs but to illustrate that the point of contact between law enforcement and citizens' backgrounds must not be ignored. Officers must be encouraged to consider culture when investigating and presenting evidence regarding an alleged crime or incident involving people from diverse backgrounds. Once again, *this does not mean that standard operating procedures should be changed nor does it imply that heinous crimes such as murder or rape should be excused on cultural grounds.* However, as a matter of course, officers need to count "culture" as a significant variable in understanding, assessing, and reporting certain kinds of incidents and crimes.

POLICE KNOWLEDGE OF CULTURAL GROUPS

Law enforcement representatives have the ultimate authority to arrest or admonish someone suspected of a crime. According to Katz, "discretion based on cultural knowledge at the police level is much more significant than what happens at the next level in the criminal justice system (i.e., the courts)." Any individual police officer has the possibility of creating positive public relations if he or she has demonstrated cultural sensitivity and respect toward members of an ethnic community. Judge Katz cited the example of police contact with the San Francisco Bay Area Samoan community, in which barbecues and parties can include a fair amount of drinking, resulting in fights. In Judge Katz's opinion:

> The police, responding to neighbors' complaints could come in with a show of force and, the fighting would cool down quickly. However, word would spread that the police officers involved had no cultural understanding or respect for the people involved. This would widen the gap that already exists between police and many Pacific Islander and other Asian groups and would not be a way to foster trust in the Samoan community. Alternatively, the police could locate the leader or the "chief" of this group and let that person deal with the problem in the way that he would have handled the conflict in Samoa. There is no question about the "matai's" (chief's) ability to handle the problem. He has a prominent role to play and can serve as a bridge between the police and the community.

The heads of Samoan communities are traditionally in full control of members' behavior, although this is changing somewhat in the United States. Furthermore, according to traditional Samoan values, if a family member assaults a member of another family, the head of the family is required to make sure that punishment takes place. (National Office of Samoan Affairs) Given the power entrusted to the chiefs, it is reasonable to encourage officers first to go through the community and elicit assistance in solving enforcement problems.

The awareness of and sensitivity to such issues can have a significant impact on the criminal justice system, where police have the power either to inflame or calm the people involved in the particular incident. According to Judge Katz,

"Many cases, especially those involving lesser offenses, can stay out of court." He asks, "Do you always need a show of force? Or can you counsel and admonish instead?" In certain types of situations, such as the one described above, officers can rethink traditional police methods in order to be as effective as possible. This involves knowledge of ethnic communities and a desire to establish a positive and trustworthy image in those communities.

PREJUDICE IN LAW ENFORCEMENT

The following questions were asked of police officers participating in a cultural diversity program:

"Raise your hand if you are a racist." Not a single officer raised a hand.
"Raise your hand if you think that prejudice and racism exist outside this agency." Most officers raised their hands.
The instructor (Lt. Ondra Berry, Reno, Nevada, Police Department) then asked with humor: "Then where were you recruited from?"

When discussing the implications of multicultural diversity for police officers, it is not enough simply to present the need to understand cultural background. Whenever two groups are from entirely different ethnic or racial backgrounds, there is the possibility that prejudice exists (i.e., because of fear, lack of contact, ignorance, and stereotypes). To deny the existence of prejudice or racism in any given law enforcement agency would be to deny that it does not exist outside the agency.

What Is Prejudice?

Prejudice is a judgment or opinion formed before facts are known and it usually involves negative or unfavorable thoughts about groups of people. Discrimination is action based on the prejudiced thought. It is not possible to force people to abandon their own prejudices in the law enforcement workplace or on the streets. Because prejudice is thought, it is private and does not violate any law. However, because it is private, it can also be that a person is not aware when his or her judgments and decisions are based on prejudice. In law enforcement, the expression of prejudice as bias discrimination and racism is illegal and can be tragic. All police must consider the implications of prejudice in their day-to-day work as it relates to equal enforcement and professionalism.

In workshops in law enforcement agencies addressing prejudice and discrimination, the authors of this book have heard some participants say: "We've already had this training (i.e., on prejudice) . . . why do we need to go over it again and again?" As with other training areas in law enforcement, such as self-defense and tactics, the area of prejudice needs to be reviewed on a regular basis. One only has to read the headlines that appear periodically to see that the problem of prejudice and racism in law enforcement is not yet a phenomenon of the past. For example, in 1993, black state troopers in an eastern state alleged that fellow officers had distributed racist fliers, including cartoons of Ku Klux Klansmen tying a rope around the neck of a black man. In addition, the cartoons depicted black police officers with watermelon faces. It is not our intention to single out any particular department but to state directly that prejudice has not yet disappeared from law enforcement.

Although police chiefs cannot *mandate* that their officers banish prejudicial thoughts, this subject should be dealt with seriously. While some police officers say that they have every right to believe what they want, the chief of every department must be able to guarantee, with as much certainty as possible, that no officer will ever act upon his or her prejudices. All officers must know whether they are capable of crossing the fine line between prejudice and discrimination, whether in the law enforcement agency with co-workers or with citizens. It becomes eminently clear that prejudice in the law enforcement agency must be addressed before it turns into racism and discrimination. Indeed, an agency cannot be expected to treat its multicultural population fairly if people in it are likely to act on their prejudiced thoughts.

How Prejudice Influences People

Prejudice is encouraged by stereotyping, which is a shorthand way of thinking about people who are different. The stereotypes that form the basis of a person's prejudice can be so fixed that he or she easily justifies his or her racism (sexism, etc.) and even makes such claims as, "I'm not prejudiced, but let me tell you about those ___ I had to deal with today." Coffey et al. (1982) discuss the relationship between selective memory and prejudice:

> A prejudiced person will almost certainly claim to have sufficient cause for his or her views, telling of bitter experiences with refugees, Koreans, Catholics, Jews, Blacks, Mexicans and Puerto Ricans, or Indians. But in most cases, it is evident that these "facts" are both scanty and strained. Such a person typically resorts to a selective sorting of his or her own memories, mixes them up with hearsay, and then overgeneralizes. No one can possibly know all refugees, Koreans, Catholics and so on. (p. 8)

Indeed, individuals may be so convinced of the truths of their stereotypes that they claim to be experts on "those people." One of the most dangerous types of prejudice can be subconscious. This type of prejudice (sometimes referred to as character-conditioned prejudice) usually runs deep and the person with this character deficiency may hold hostile attitudes toward many ethnic groups (not just one or two). People who tend to mistreat or oppress others because of their prejudices often were mistreated themselves, and this experience can leave them extremely distrustful of all others. In addition, people who have strong prejudices can be insecure and frustrated because of their own failures. Consequently, they blame or scapegoat others. They have a great deal of stored-up anger which frequently began in childhood because of dysfunctional relationships with their parents. Quite often, people in racial supremacist organizations fit the description of the *extremely* prejudiced person for whom mistrust and hate of all others is a way of life.

Another type of prejudice is acquired during "normal" socialization. This type of prejudice results when a person belongs to a group that holds negative views of other specific groups (e.g., southern whites and blacks, Arabs and Jews, Chinese and Japanese, Puerto Ricans and Mexicans, etc.). When there is a pattern of prejudice within a particular group, the "normal" person is the one who conforms to the prejudice. From childhood, parents pass on stereotypes of the "outgroup" in the child's mind because of their "normal" prejudices. By adulthood, the person who has learned prejudice against a particular group can justify the prejudice with rationalizations (Coffey et al., 1982).

However, not everyone in a given group holds prejudices common among the rest of the members of the group. According to Coffey et al., some people are more susceptible than others to learned (or "culture-conditioned") prejudice. Those who are more likely to be prejudiced include (1) older people, (2) less educated people, (3) farmers and unskilled or semi-skilled workers, (4) residents of rural areas or small towns, (5) people uninterested in civic affairs, and (6) people of low socioeconomic status.

Prejudice and Police Culture

Many different types of groups, including occupational groups, develop and pass on prejudices against some other out-groups. One out-group in police culture is citizens (think of all the labels officers use to describe citizens). In addition to viewing citizens as the "other" group (i.e., the "we/they" syndrome), some officers view *ethnic* citizenry as very much "other." Southgate, describing race relations in Britain, observed how the problem of prejudice is embedded in the nature of the police culture. He discusses some of the same pressures to conform and to achieve membership in the police subculture as one would find in any ethnic or cultural group:

> The police culture as a whole was fairly critical and unsympathetic towards minorities, particularly West Indians [in Britain]. This was illustrated in the language used to describe and refer to [dark-skinned minorities]. Terms used ranged from "the coloreds," to "our colored brethren," " . . . young black bucks," "coons" and "niggers." On paper or spoken . . . most of these are very offensive, but some were used in quite lighthearted ways by police officers with minimal malice. Officers claimed that even though not personally prejudiced, they tended to adopt such language and the views it implies because this was one way to be part of the group. This language was therefore presented as being merely one way of emphasizing the group solidarity of the police force. (Southgate, 1982)

Thus expressions of prejudice in police departments go unchallenged because of the need to conform or to fit into the group. Police officers do not make themselves popular by questioning peers or challenging their attitudes. It takes a nonconformist to voice an objection or not to go along with group norms.

Is there a *particular* problem with prejudice in law enforcement today? The answer would have to be both *yes* and *no. Yes,* because (as indicated earlier) there is a serious problem in society with prejudice and any group of officers or civilian employees as a group reflect general social attitudes. The answer is *yes,* because law enforcement representatives have more power than the average citizen, and therefore the potential to abuse this power exists. Police officers are inescapably brought into contact with people they do not like. Officers often have to get involved in situations where there is a high potential for failure and, therefore, it becomes easier to blame someone else for the failure (i.e., a scapegoat). Individuals from virtually all races and ethnic groups repeatedly abuse officers verbally and physically to an extent that no other professional experiences. Therefore, the provocation to act on one's prejudices exists more than it does for most people.

On the other hand: *No*, there is not a *particular* problem with prejudice in law enforcement, because officers are held to a higher standard of conduct than most citizens. In police work, today, the notion of professionalism is *beginning* to replace older, more traditional attitudes and methods whereby the manifestations of prejudice (differential treatment, discrimination, etc.) were more common. Furthermore, according to police psychologist Robert T. Flint (personal communication, Jan. 10, 1993), most officers are able to control their impulses, even in high-stress situations. Law enforcement has come increasingly to see, especially in the early 1990s, that prejudices unchecked and acted upon can result not only in lawsuits, loss of jobs, and long-term damage to police–community relations, but in personal tragedy as well.

Many of today's officers have learned a code of ethics vis-à-vis exhibiting their prejudices in the form of discrimination. Most of the time, training can be successful for some in changing behavior and possibly attitudes. Consider an example provided by Flint regarding departmental changes in policies regarding the firing of warning shots. According to Flint, most officers have retrained themselves to refrain from this action because they have been mandated to do so. They have gone through a process of "unfreezing" normative behavior (i.e., what is customary) and have incorporated desired behavior. Thus explicit instruction and clear directives from the top can result in profound changes of police actions. Flint's observations of the success of "mandated" change are supported by Fletcher Blanchard, a social psychologist at Smith College, who conducted and published research findings on fighting acts of bigotry (*New York Times*, Sept. 16, 1991, pp. C-1 and C-8.). His contention is that clear policies that *unequivocally* condemn racist acts or forms of speech will prevent most manifestations of prejudice. For example, Chief Willie Williams of the Los Angeles Police Department has told officers explicitly not to stop African American citizens in predominantly white neighborhoods *when there has been no provocation*. The question, "What are you doing here?" just because a person is of a different background than those of a particular neighborhood is not reason enough to make contact. Officers will listen to these specific and unambivalent directives coming from the top, even if their personal biases do not change. As Blanchard explains: "A few outspoken people [e.g., in an organization/agency] who are vigorously anti-racist can establish the kind of social climate that discourages racist acts. . . . It's very hard to change the stereotypes that underlie the prejudice. It's better to focus instead on discouraging racist acts" (*New York Times*, Sept. 16, 1991, p. C-8).

Other studies have shown that peer behavior in groups reinforces acts of racial bias. For example, "hearing someone in a group make ethnic slurs led others in the group to express the same hostile attitudes more freely" (*New York Times*,

Sept. 16, 1991, p. C-8). This is particularly relevant in law enforcement agencies given the nature of the police subculture and the strong influence of peer pressure. Thus law enforcement leaders must not be ambiguous when directing their subordinates to control their prejudice in the form of discrimination. Furthermore, according to some social scientists, the strong condemnation of any manifestations of prejudice can at times have an effect on the person's feelings: "Using pressure from the authorities or peers to keep people who are prejudiced from acting on those biases can, in the long run, weaken the prejudice itself . . . especially if the prejudice is not virulent. People conform. Even if they are still prejudiced, they'll be reticent to show it. If national authorities were more vocal in disapproving of prejudice, you'd have less of it shown" (*New York Times*, Sept. 16, 1991, p. C-8).

A process of socialization takes place when change has been mandated by top management and a person is forced to adopt a new standard of behavior. When a "mistake" is made and the expression of prejudice occurs, a police department will pay the costs (e.g., adverse media attention, lawsuits, citizen complaints, human relations commissions involvement, dismissal of the chief or other management). Government officials are subject to a great deal of scrutiny with regard to what they express in public places. Berry-Wilkinson, a lawyer and expert on harassment issues, cited the case of a prosecutor who was publicly reprimanded for a hallway comment to another lawyer during a murder trial: "I don't believe either of those chili-eating bastards." The court stated: "Lawyers, especially . . . public officials, [must] avoid statements as well as deeds . . . indicating that their actions are motivated to any extent by racial prejudice" (*People v. Sharpe,* 789 P.2d 659 [1989], Colorado, in *The Labor Beat,* Jan. 1993). Berry-Wilkinson's concluding statement following the reporting of this case reads: "What once may have been acceptable is now definitely not and may bring discipline and monetary sanctions. While public employees may be free to think whatever they like, they are not free to say whatever they think. A public employee's right to free speech is not absolute" (Berry-Wilkinson, 1993).

When officers in a police department are not in control of their prejudices (either their speech or in their behavior) the negative publicity affects the reputation of all police officers (i.e., reinforcing the popular stereotype that police are racists or bigots). Yet because of publicized instances of discrimination, officers become increasingly aware of correct and incorrect behavior toward ethnic minorities.

Beginning in 1990, a California police department was besieged by the press and outraged citizens for over two years because six police officers had exchanged racist messages on their patrol car computers, using the word "nigger" and making references to the KKK. The citizens of the town in which the incident took place ended up conducting an investigation of the department to assess the degree of racism in the institution. In their report, the committe members wrote that the disclosure of the racial slurs was "an embarrassment and a crushing blow" to the image and credibility of the city and police department. In addition, citizens demanded the chief's resignation. Some of the officers still believe that the entire incident was overblown and that there was no "victim" (personal communication with officers of department during cultural diversity workshop, Apr. 13, 1993). These officers fail to understand that the use of the derogatory terms alone is offensive to minority communities and to some white community members as well. Officers who do not grasp the seriousness of the matter may not realize that minority citizens feel unprotected knowing that those entrusted with their safety and protection are capable of using such hateful language. While the language is offensive, the problem is more with the attitude it conveys. Incidents such as these are extremely costly from all points of view—it can take a department years to recover from one incident connected to an officer's prejudice or racism.

Officers need to be aware that anything they say or do with citizens of different backgrounds that even *hints* of prejudice automatically creates the potential for an explosive reaction (personal communication, Wendell Lipscomb, African American psychiatrist, Jan. 15, 1993). Here the experience of the minority and the nonminority do not even begin to approach each other. An officer can make an unguarded casual remark and not realize that it is offensive. For example, an officer can offend a minority-group member by saying, "You people" (accentuating a we/they division) or implying that if a member of a minority group doesn't fit a stereotype, he or she is exceptional (e.g., "She's Hispanic, but she works hard," or, "he's black, but very responsible.")

Members of culturally diverse groups are up against the weight of history and tradition in law enforcement. Ethnic groups have not been represented traditionally in police work (especially in top management), nor have citizens had reasons to trust the police. The prejudice that might linger among officers must be battled constantly if they are to increase trust with ethnic communities. The perception of many ethnic minorities is that police will treat them more roughly, question them unnecessarily, and arrest them more often than they will nonminorities. Awareness of this perception is not, however, enough. The next step is to try harder with ethnic groups to overcome those barriers. Lipscomb, who himself experienced biased treatment from officers in his younger years, advises officers to go out of their way to show extra respect to those very citizens who least expect it. He suggests "disarming" the citizen who has traditionally been the object of police prejudice and who *expects* rude or uncivil behavior from the officer.

Beyond eliminating the prejudice manifested in speech, police management can teach officers how to eliminate or reduce acts of bias and discrimination. A large metropolitan police department hired several human relations consultants to help assess community–police problems. The chief insisted that they ride in a police car for four weekends so that they would "appreciate the problems of law officers working in the black ghetto." Every Friday to Sunday night, the consultants rode along with the highway patrol, a unit other officers designated as the "Gestapo police." When the month ended and the chief inquired as to what the consultants had learned, they replied, "If we were black, we would hate the police." The chief, somewhat bewildered, asked why. "Because we have personally witnessed black citizens experiencing a series of unjust, unwarranted intimidations, searches and series of harassments by unprofessional police." Fortunately, that chief, to his credit, accepted the feedback and introduced a successful course in human relations skills. After this training, the officers demonstrated greater professionalism in their interactions with members of the black community.

When it comes to expressions of prejudice, people are not powerless. No one has to accept sweeping stereotypes (e.g., "You can't trust an Indian," "All whites are racists," "Chinese are shifty," and so on). To eliminate manifestations of prejudice, people have to begin to interrupt biased and discriminatory behavior at all levels. Officers have to be willing to remind their peers that ethnic slurs and offensive language, as well as differential treatment of certain groups of people, is neither ethical nor professional. Officers need to change the aspect of police culture that discourages speaking out against acts or speech motivated by prejudice. An officer or civilian employee who does nothing in the presence of racist or other discriminatory behavior by his or her peers becomes a silent accomplice.

SUMMARY

Dramatic changes in the ethnic and racial makeup of the population has created new challenges at all levels of police work. Willingness to gain cultural information about the new communities that one serves will ultimately benefit officers in their interactions with people of different backgrounds. The officer's knowledge of cultural differences, coupled with an ability to demonstrate respect for those differences, can result in increased rapport and effective communication with people from various ethnic and racial backgrounds. Trust and cooperation in many ethnic communities have to be earned because of the cultural "baggage" that community members bring to their relationships with the police. Members of the law enforcement profession have to examine their words, behaviors, and actions to evaluate whether they are conveying professionalism and respect to all people, regardless of their race, culture, religion, or ethnic background. Finally, law enforcement agencies must be free of all expressions of prejudice on the part of their officers or civilian employees. An agency cannot be expected to treat its multicultural population fairly if personnel within it are likely to act on their prejudices.

EIGHT TIPS FOR IMPROVING LAW ENFORCEMENT
IN MULTICULTURAL COMMUNITIES*

- Make positive contact with minority-group members. Don't let them see you only when something negative has happened.
- Allow the public to see you as much as possible in a nonenforcement role.
- Make a conscious effort in your mind, en route to every situation, to treat all segments of society objectively and fairly.
- Remember that *all* groups have some bad, some average, and some good people within them.
- Go out of your way to be personable and friendly with minority-group members. Remember, many don't expect it.
- Don't appear uncomfortable or avoid discussing racial/minority issues with other officers and citizens.

*Tips and quote are from Lieutenant Ondra Berry, Reno, Nevada Police Department.

- Take responsibility for patiently educating citizens and the public, in general, about the role of the officer and about standard operating procedures in law enforcement. Remember that citizens do not understand "police culture."
- Don't be afraid to be a change agent in your organization when it comes to improving cross-cultural relations within your department and between police and community. It may not be a popular thing to do, but it is the right thing to do.

"Remember the history of law enforcement with all groups and ask yourself the question, Am I part of the past, or a part of the future?"

DISCUSSION QUESTIONS AND ISSUES*

1. *Views on the Multicultural Society.* The following viewpoints regarding our increasingly multicultural population reflect varying levels of tolerance, understanding, and acceptance. Discuss these points of view and their implications for law enforcement:

- Diversity is acceptable if there is not too much of it, but the way things are going today, it is hard to absorb and it just may result in our destruction.
- They're here now and they need to do things our way.
- To advance in our diverse society, we need to accept and respect our differences rather than maintaining the myth of the melting pot.

2. *Police Work and Ethnicity.* In the Alpert and Dunham (1988) study entitled *Policing Multi-ethnic Neighborhoods* the authors say that ethnicity complicates every police procedure. In your experience, is this correct? Explain why or why not.

3. *Dealing with Illegal Immigrants.* Does the police department in which you work have a policy regarding undocumented immigrants? Are officers instructed not to inquire into their status unless there has been a crime committed? How do you think police officers should deal with illegal immigrants?

4. *Mini-Case Study 1:* Reread, then discuss.

A Tragic Case of Cross-Cultural Misinterpretation.

(a) Do you think this case would have proceeded differently if all the authorities involved understood the cultural tradition of the medical practice ("coin rubbing") that caused the bruising? Explain your answer.

(b) Discuss whether you think Southeast Asian refugees should give up this medical practice because it can be misinterpreted.

5. *Mini-Case Study 2:* Reread, then discuss.

Statements of Sentiment versus Statements of Intent.

(a) Discuss the captain's reaction to what he overheard the African American woman saying. Do you feel that he was justified in the actions he took? Explain your answer.

(b) Discuss how officers can utilize the cultural information regarding threats and verbal aggression without creating unsafe situations for themselves.

---

*(See Instructor's Manual accompanying this text for additional activities, role-plays, questionnaires and projects related to the content of this chapter.)

6. *Mini-Case Study 3:* Reread, then discuss.

Latino Values as a Factor in Sentencing.

(a) Discuss whether in violent crimes such as murder or rape, culture should play any part in influencing the sentencing of the criminal. Was the lighter verdict in this case justified? Explain your answer.

(b) According to Superior Court Judge Katz, culture did influence the sentencing in this case. In your opinion, if the husband involved were not Latino, would the sentencing have been the same?

7. *Prejudice and Discrimination in Police Work.* In your own words, define prejudice and discrimination. Give examples of (a) discrimination in society in general; (b) discrimination against police officers; and (c) discrimination toward minorities by police officers.

REFERENCES

ALPERT G.P. AND R.G. DUNHAM (1988). *Policing Multiethnic Neighborhoods: The Miami Study and Findings for Law Enforcement in the United States,* Greenwood Press, Westport, Conn.

Attorney General's Commission on Racial, Ethnic, Religious and Minority Violence (1986). Sacramento, Calf., Apr., p. 14.

BERRY-WILKINSON, ALISON (1993)."Be careful what you say when . . .," *Labor Beat,* Vol. 5, No. 1, p. 16.

COFFEY, ALAN, ET AL. (1982). *Human Relations: Law Enforcement in a Changing Community,* 3rd ed., Prentice Hall, Englewood Cliffs, N.J.

HANDLIN, OSCAR (1975).*Out of Many: A Study Guide to Cultural Pluralism in the United States,* Anti-Defamation League of B'nai B'rith, published through Brown & Williamson Tobacco Corporation.

HALL, EDWARD T. (1959). *The Silent Language,* A Fawcett Premier Book, Greenwich, Conn.

KENNEDY, JOHN F. (1986). *A Nation of Immigrants,* Harper & Row, New York.

KOCHMAN, THOMAS (1981). *Black and White Styles in Conflict,* The University of Chicago Press, Chicago.

KONDRACKE, MORTON (1989). "Borderline Cases," *The New Republic,* Apr. 10.

National Office of Samoan Affairs, Inc. (1984). *Samoan Family Care, Child Abuse and Neglect Prevention: A Service Provider Handbook,* Grant 90CA923-01 from the National Center on Child Abuse and Neglect, San Francisco.

RAWLINS, GARY H. (1992). "Africans came 200 years earlier," *USA Today,* Oct. 8, p. 2a.

RUHLY, SHARON (1976). *Orientations to Intercultural Communication: Modules in Speech Communication,* Science Research Associates, Chicago, p. 4.

SHERMAN, SPENCER (1986). "When cultures collide," *California Lawyer,* Vol. 6, No. 1, p. 33.

SOUTHGATE, P. (1982). *Police Probationer Training in Race Relations,* Research and Planning Unit Paper 8, Home Office, London.

TROJANOWICZ, ROBERT, AND BONNIE BUCQUEOUX (1990). Community Policing: A Contemporary Perspective, Michigan State University, Anderson Publishing Co., Cincinnati, Ohio.

TROJANOWICZ, ROBERT, AND DAVID CARTER (1990). "The changing face of America," *FBI Law Enforcement Bulletin,* Vol. 59, 6–12.

U.S. Department of Commerce News, Economics and Statistics Administration (1991). CB 91-215, Bureau of the Census, Washington, D.C., June 12.

WOODROW, KAREN A. (1990). Speech given to the American Statistical Association of America, Anaheim, Calif., Aug.

ZANGWILL, ISRAEL (1914). *The Melting Pot:* Drama in Four Acts, The Macmillan Company.

2

THE CHANGING LAW ENFORCEMENT AGENCY:

A Microcosm of Society

OVERVIEW

The ethnic, racial, gender, and even lifestyle composition of law enforcement agencies is changing in the United States. In this chapter we address the transformation of the workforce in terms of its being more pluralistic. We provide examples of racism and cultural insensitivity within the law enforcement workforce and present suggestions for defusing racially and culturally rooted conflicts. Issues related to minorities, women, and homosexuals in law enforcement are discussed and we include recommendations for the employee, supervisor, and manager on working within a diverse workforce.

COMMENTARY

The changing law enforcement environment, both internal and external, is increasingly evident in today's diverse society:

> *Washington Post,* "FBI, DEA nearer to accord with minority agents," Apr. 30, 1991, p. 3.
>
> The Federal Bureau of Investigation and the Drug Enforcement Administration are grappling with charges of discrimination in their ranks—charges that culminated recently in a meeting at FBI headquarters in Washington between Director William S. Sessions and the bureau's 56 field office heads to discuss discrimination. . . .
>
> *San Francisco Chronicle,* "Ex-police officer sues over alleged gay bias," Dec. 31, 1992, p. A-3.

San Rafael—A San Francisco woman is suing [the city of] San Anselmo for allegedly forcing her out of her job as a police officer because she is a lesbian. In a civil suit in Marin [she said] . . . her supervisor repeatedly harassed her and that other officers made deprecating remarks about women and homosexuals.

INTRODUCTION

In Chapter 1 the evolution of multicultural communities and the demographic changes that we have witnessed in recent decades in the United States were discussed. Two of the most notable demographic changes mentioned involve the increases in minority and immigrant populations in our country. The range of reactions found in society are no different from what one sees within the law enforcement agency. Members of police communities across the country have demonstrated both tolerance and resistance toward the changing society and workforce. Some officers do not view the multicultural workforce positively and resent the new multicultural/racial employee because of their own personal prejudices or bias. This resentment is, in part, due to perceived or actual advantages others receive when competing for law enforcement positions. In addition, because of past incompetent affirmative action hiring (i.e., management rushed to fill quotas but did not focus on competence), some officers perceive that affirmative action means lowering standards. Indeed, where standards have been lowered, everyone suffers, especially the minority employee. (This is discussed further in Chapter 3.) Officers must understand that affirmative action does not mean the hiring of incompetent women and minorities, even if they know of specific cases in which that has happened. No officer wants to work with an incompetent co-worker, especially in life-threatening situations. Where this has happened in law enforcement agencies, officers have become extremely critical of affirmative action hiring. Chief executives and managers must find ways to address this issue; relationships with minority co-workers can suffer greatly because of these perceptions about affirmative action hiring. Personnel must receive guarantees from their management that standards will not be lowered and that competence is the key criterion.

Leading positively and, further, valuing the diversity that is within the agency is the key to meeting the challenge of policing multicultural communities. As was discussed in Chapter 1, racial and ethnic tensions still exist in the law enforcement community. Agency personnel must first address the conflicts in their own organizations before dealing with community racial and ethnic problems. Action or inaction of police departments is crucial to resolution of social problems that manifest themselves in law enforcement agencies. Across the United States there have been numerous cases, which made the national press, where inaction or the wrong action was taken. Whether we like it or not, the police are a primary role model for citizens and are judged by a higher standard of behavior than are others.

As stated in Chapter 1, those concerned with peacekeeping and enforcement must accept the realities of a diverse society as well as the heterogeneity in their workforce. It is ironic, however, when those very peacekeepers who are to uphold and enforce the law as it pertains to acts of bigotry and bias themselves become the perpetrators, even with their own peers. If our departments are to be representative of the populations served, changes have to be initiated by police executives. These changes have to do with treatment of peers as well as recruitment, selection, and promotion of employees who have traditionally been underrepresented in law enforcement in the past. Just as there has been an argument (Chapter 1) that the United States has never really been a "melting pot," the same dispute occurs in the law enforcement community. In some cases relationships within the law enforcement workplace, especially as diversity increases, are characterized by disrespect and tension. While many in the "police subculture" would argue that membership implies brotherhood (and, therefore, belonging), this membership has excluded women and minorities in both subtle and obvious ways.

CHANGING WORKFORCE

As microcosms of their communities, law enforcement agencies increasingly include among their personnel more women and ethnic and racial minorities. While still far from *parity* (the state or condition of being the same in power, value, rank, etc; equality) in most agencies in the United States, advances have been made (see Chapter 3). In many regions of the country, the law enforcement workforce differs greatly from the way it was in the past and women and ethnic and racial minorities have brought profound changes to law enforcement.

Law Enforcement Diversity: A Microcosm of Society

The Bureau of Justice Statistics (BJS) in their 1990 Law Enforcement Management and Administrative Statistics report concluded that overall, minority-group representation among full-time sworn:

- Local police officers increased from 14.6 percent in 1987 to 17 percent in 1990—a 2.4 percent increase.
- State police agencies increased from 11.3 percent in 1987 to 12.9 percent in 1990—a 1.6 percent increase.
- Sheriffs' agencies increased from 13.4 percent in 1987 to 15.5 percent in 1990—a 2.1 percent increase.

As these increases occurred, a corresponding reduction in the numbers of whites in law enforcement workforces followed. While the numbers of white males decreased, the numbers of white females in the workforce increased. Exhibits 2.1 and 2.2 provide more details on the percentages by ethnic and racial group as of 1990 in state, local, and sheriffs' departments.

Some major law enforcement agencies have achieved parity in terms of the percentage of minorities in their workforce compared to the percentage in the community; others have not. Law enforcement is still a predominantly white male occupation and there must be an expansion of efforts in the recruitment, hiring, and promotions of minorities and women nationwide. This is discussed further in Chapter 3.

Measuring responsiveness to diversity. A manual produced by the Canadian Association of Chiefs of Police includes a 10-question checklist and scoring

Exhibit 2.1   Characteristics of full-time sworn personnel in local police departments, by size of population served, 1990

Population served	Total	PERCENT OF FULL-TIME SWORN EMPLOYEES[a]								
		White		Black		Hispanic		Other	
		Male	Female	Male	Female	Male	Female	Male	Female
All sizes	100	77.5	5.5	8.5	2.0	4.7	0.5	1.2	0.1
1,000,000 or more	100	65.4	7.0	12.4	4.2	8.4	1.5	0.9	0.1
500,000–999,999	100	62.9	5.7	15.6	4.4	5.6	0.5	5.0	0.4
250,000–499,999	100	68.0	6.8	13.0	3.2	7.2	0.7	1.0	0.1
100,000–249,999	100	76.7	6.0	9.1	1.8	4.1	0.4	1.9	0.1
50,000–99,999	100	84.2	4.9	5.7	0.8	3.4	0.2	0.7	—[b]
25,000–49,999	100	85.8	4.4	5.6	0.5	2.9	0.1	0.6	—[b]
10,000–24,999	100	89.4	4.3	3.5	0.3	2.1	0.2	0.3	0.1
2,500–9,999	100	88.2	4.6	3.6	0.4	2.6	—[b]	0.5	0.1
Under 2,500	100	87.6	3.8	4.5	0.2	2.4	0.3	1.2	0

[a]"Black" and "white" categories do not include Hispanics. "Other" category includes American Indians, Alaskan Natives, Asians, and Pacific Islanders. Detail may not add to total because of rounding.
[b]Less than 0.05%.
*Source:*A LEMAS Report, February 1992, U.S. Department of Justice, Office of Justice Programs, Bureau of Justice Statistics, Washington, D.C.

Exhibit 2.2   Characteristics of full-time sworn personnel in sheriffs' departments, by size of population served, 1990

Population served	Total	PERCENT OF FULL-TIME SWORN EMPLOYEES[a]								
		White		Black		Hispanic		Other	
		Male	Female	Male	Female	Male	Female	Male	Female
All sizes	100	72.6	11.9	7.2	2.6	3.9	0.8	0.9	0.1
1,000,000 or more	100	64.0	14.2	6.8	2.9	8.2	1.9	1.9	0.2
500,000–999,999	100	68.9	9.7	11.8	4.0	4.1	0.5	0.9	0.1
250,000–499,999	100	74.7	10.6	6.1	2.0	5.0	1.0	0.6	0.1
100,000–249,999	100	72.7	12.4	8.1	3.1	2.3	0.5	0.8	—[b]
50,000–99,999	100	78.8	12.1	5.6	2.2	0.8	0.2	0.3	0.1
25,000–49,999	100	77.7	11.4	5.4	1.5	2.0	1.0	0.8	0.2
10,000–24,999	100	79.5	11.5	4.6	1.0	2.3	0.2	0.8	0.1
Under 10,000	100	76.4	14.0	4.7	0.9	2.9	0.4	0.5	0.2

[a]"Black" and "white" categories do not include Hispanics. "Other" category includes American Indians, Alaskan Natives, Asians, and Pacific Islanders. Detail may not add to total because of rounding.
[b]Less than 0.05%.
Source: A LEMAS Report, February 1992, U.S. Department of Justice, Office of Justice Programs, Bureau of Justice Statistics, Washington, D.C.

Exhibit 2.3   How Responsive Is Your Organization?

Check off and count the number of initiatives that your police service has undertaken. See how you rate.

(   )   1. Are members of ethnic/cultural communities participating in your community and crime prevention programs?

(   )   2. Do your programs provide for community input into the development and implementation of local policing programs?

(   )   3. Does your organization have a race relations policy that is integrated into your overall mission?

(   )   4. Do your patrol officers use foot patrols in areas of high concentrations of ethnic minorities?

(   )   5. Do you use translators or interpreters from within your police department or from local immigrant service agencies or ethnic community organization in your contacts with linguistic minorities?

(   )   6. Are your ads and brochures multilingual, and do they depict a multicultural community?

(   )   7. Do you have a recruitment campaign that actively targets ethnic and visible minorities?

(   )   8. Have your hiring and promotional practices been evaluated to see if they recognize and value knowledge and skills related to community policing, especially with ethnic/cultural communities?

(   )   9. Have your in-service training programs dealt with the issue of diversity?

(   )   10. Have your officers participated programs for in multicultural or race relations training for trainers?

Scoring:

0–3,   Don't panic. The fact that you did the checklist shows that you are interested. Start small, but start today!

4–6,   Good start. You are part of a community-based policing movement. You beginning to tackle some of the issues that face police services in a multicultural environment.

7–9,   Well done. It is obvious that you understand and value the benefits of ethnoculturally sensivtive and community-based policing. You're on the right track, keep up the good work!

10,   Congratulations. Your challenge is to maintain the momentum and evaluate the effectiveness of your initiatives.

Source: Police Race Relations: Raising Your Effectiveness in Today's Diverse Neighborhoods through Community Policing, The Canadian Association of Chief's of Police. Place de Ville, Tower B, 112 Kent St., Suite 1908, Ottawa, Ontario KIP 5P2, Canada.

method for law enforcement organizations to determine how responsive they are in adapting to diversity. It is reproduced here (Exhibit 2.3) for your use in rating your own agency.

Ethnic and Racial Issues within the Workforce

Racism.   Racism within law enforcement agencies has been a documented fact for decades. An African American history display at the New York

Police Academy in October 1992 contained this written account of the experiences of one of the first New York Police Department's black officers:

> Seven years before the adoption of the charter creating New York City, Brooklyn, then an independent city, hired the first black policeman. Wiley G. Overton was sworn in March 6, 1891. . . . His first tour of duty was spent in civilian clothing because fellow officers breaking with tradition refused to furnish him with a temporary uniform. . . . Officers in his section refused to sleep in the same room with him. . . . The officers in the precinct ignored him and spoke only if it was necessary in the line of duty.

Unfortunately, 100 years later, the actions of a few New York officers, most off duty, showed that the problem of racism and bigotry still exists. On September 16, 1992, 10,000 rank-and-file New York police officers gathered at city hall in what became an unruly protest of a proposed independent civilian complaint review board. New York City Mayor Dinkins, an African American, had been considering changing the composition of their civilian review board from half civilian/half police, to a board consisting of all civilians. According to news media reports and interviews of a few persons present, including officers, some of the police protesters blocked traffic on the Brooklyn Bridge for over an hour. Some jumped on parked cars, harassed and assaulted passersby, and left city hall littered with beer cans. A few officers were accused of using racist language, carrying racist signs and calling Mayor Dinkins, a "nigger." Although the Patrolmen's Benevolent Association (PBA) and other officers challenged whether police had used racial slurs or assaulted civilians, there was evidence that a few such incidents did occur.

Two officers, including one charged with using a racial slur, were suspended without pay and 40 others, including a captain, faced internal department charges and discipline following the investigation. Every one of the mostly white officers interviewed in New York expressed disgust with those few, unruly colleagues who they felt had disgraced all of them by their actions (personal communications New York City Police Department officers, Oct. 1992). Acting Police Commissioner Raymond Kelly said: "The fact that any New York City Police Officer would feel free to flaunt the law and spew racial venom publicly gives each and every member of the department reason to pause and reflect on how much more we need to do to achieve tolerance, understanding and harmony" (*New York Daily News*, Sept. 29, 1992, p. 2).

The incident divided the department, although not totally along racial lines. The division centered not only on the civilian review board issue, but also on the events at city hall and the Brooklyn Bridge. Some black officers came out in support of the mayor, which angered white colleagues and leaders of the Benevolent Association. The PBA accused the mayor of putting a "racial spin" on the police protest. The results were polarization of officers from each other and some from the city and department administration. This incident and its aftermath damaged relations among officers, and the public's view of the police department.

The New York Police Department is not alone. Racism can occur in police departments regardless of size or region. The Dallas police strike in 1992, characterized by racial overtones, polarized the department—cop versus cop. The *New Jersey Daily News* in 1993 had bold headlines: "Racism on the Job: Black N.J. Troopers

Charge Harassment, Bias and Discrimination." (*New York Daily News,* Apr. 22, 1993, p. C-3). Unfortunately, racism has been an issue in many communities and departments for decades. As long as racism exists in society, the potential exists for police agencies to reflect these attitudes.

The present authors spoke with several officers from different states about racism in their department. Those interviewed requested that their names not be included, as they felt that there could be repercussions against them. One African American officer recounted almost coming to blows with a white officer who used a racial slur against him. For the white officer, the use of such slurs was commonplace for him and his friends. A Cuban American officer recalled when a nonresisting Latino suspect was caught in the commission of a minor crime. The white arresting officers beat the suspect and used racial epithets. One major city in Massachusetts suspended a deputy superintendent of police for using the word *nigger* directed toward one of his own officers. An African American officer in a large city in Florida was fired after using racial epithets against other blacks in violation of a strict citywide policy. In this particular case, the African American officer's conduct was reported by another officer at the scene. In yet another city, an African American officer was overheard telling a white prisoner, "Wait until you get to Central Booking and the niggers get a hold of you."

City and state police and county sheriffs have not cornered the market on racism. Between 1985 and 1991, within the FBI a total of three agents and eight managers were disciplined for racial harassment of an African American former agent. In August 1991, the chairperson of the U.S. Commission on Civil Rights called for an investigation into what he described as pervasive race discrimination against black service personnel and civilian employees in the armed forces. According to newspaper accounts, the charges ran counter to the widespread view among sociologists and others that the U.S. military is relatively free from the racial tensions that divide the rest of society (*New York Times,* Aug. 24, 1991, p. A-12).

Defusing racially and culturally rooted conflicts.   One of the greatest challenges of society and for the police is dealing with racism. It must be acknowledged that racism does exists within our law enforcement organizations; police are not immune from social ills. The first step in addressing the problem is for police department personnel, on all levels, to admit that it exists rather then denying it. One can read an account, for example, of an African American police officer, off duty or on plain clothes assignments, who is an instant suspect in the eyes of some white officers. If this occurs in one city or county, it can occur in another. Police researcher, David Shipler, after two years of interviews across the country, maintained that he encountered very few black officers (including those out of uniform) who had not been "hassled by white cops." He was quick to point out that not every white police officer is a bigot and not every police force a bastion of racism—that some agencies have made great strides in improving race relations.

Shipler, (*New York Times,* May 26, 1992, p. A-17) advocated that law enforcement should combat and defuse racism by using the U.S. Army model developed during a time of extreme racial tension in the military in the early 1970s. Obviously, no model of training will bring guaranteed success and alleviate all acts of prejudice and racism. However, professional groups can build on each other's attempts, especially when these attempts have proven to be fairly successful. Shipler agrees that police officers are not identical to soldiers, as the former have constant contact with the public, where they see the worst and must use personal judgment in dangerous and ambiguous situations. Nevertheless, he suggests that some military approaches are adaptable to law enforcement. For example, the following constitute the basic framework for combatting and defusing racism in the military:

- **Command commitment:** The person at the top sets the tone all the way down to the bottom. Performance reports document any bigoted or discriminatory behavior. A record of racial slurs and discriminator acts can derail a military career.
- **Training:** Military personnel are trained at the Defense Equal Opportunity Management Institute in Florida. They are placed through courses to prepare them as equal opportunity advisers. The advisers are assigned to military units with direct access to commanders. They conduct local courses to train all members of the unit on race relations.
- **Complaints and monitoring:** The advisers (see above) provide one channel for specific complaints of racial and gender discrimination, but they also drop in on units unannounced and sound out the troops on their attitudes. Surveys are conducted and informal discussions are held to lessen racial tensions.

Exhibit 2.4   Tips for Conflict Resolution

Sondra Thiederman, cultural diversity consultant and author, provides 10 tips that will help the organizational manager/leader identify and resolve conflicts that arise because of cultural, and not necessarily racial, differences in the workplace. She says that these guidelines are applicable no matter which cultures, races, religions, or lifestyles are involved.

1. Bring together the workers who are involved in the conflict (include informal group leaders if appropriate).
2. Give each party the opportunity to voice his or her concerns without interruption.
3. Attempt to obtain agreement on what the problem is by asking questions of each party and by finding out specifically what it is that upsets each person.
4. During this process, stay in control and keep the employees on the subject of the central issue.
5. Establish if the issue is indeed rooted in cultural differences by determining:

   - If the parties are from different cultures or subcultures
   - If the key issue represents an important value in each person's culture
   - How each person is expected to behave in his or her culture as it pertains to this issue
   - If the issue is emotionally charged for one or both of the parties
   - If similar conflicts arise repeatedly and in different contexts

6. Summarize the cultural (racial, religious, or lifestyle) differences that you uncover.
7. State the negative outcomes if the situation is not resolved (be specific).
8. State the positive outcomes if the situation is resolved (be specific).
9. Negotiate terms by allowing those involved to come up with the solutions.
10. Provide positive reinforcement as soon as the situation improves.

Source: S. Thiederman, *Bridging Cultural Barriers for Corporate Success,* 1991.

Thiederman's approach is based on conflict resolution and crisis intervention techniques training that many police and correctional officers receive either in their academy or in in-service training. Police department command must encourage the use of conflict resolution techniques by officers of all backgrounds as a way of handling issues prior to their becoming "flash points." With professionalism and patience, conflict resolution techniques used to reduce racial and ethnic problems will work within both the workforce and the neighborhoods.

As a result of allegations of racism against them, the Alameda, California police department developed a series of general orders as one approach to remedy the problem. Violation of the department general orders (D.G.O.) carries disciplinary ramifications up to and including termination. The general orders deal with control of prejudicial conduct based on race, religion, ethnicity, disability, sex, age, or sexual orientation and are as follows (used by permission of Chief Robert Shields, 1993):

1. *Code of Ethics:* commits to personal suppression of prejudice, animosities, malice, and ill will as well as respect of constitutional rights of *all* persons.
2. *D.G.O. 80-1:* requires courtesy and civility in the performance of duties.
3. *D.G.O. 80-1:* requires avoidance of conduct that would bring the department into disrepute.
4. *D.G.O. 80-1:* specifically addresses discrimination, racial remarks, and requires courtesy and respect to all persons. It states: "Discrmination or racism in any form shall never be tolerated."
5. *D.G.O. 80-1:* requires courtesy in dealing with the public.
6. *D.G.O. 80-1:* requires impartiality toward all persons and guarantees equal protection under the law. Prohibits exhibition of partiality due to race, creed, or influence.
7. *D.G.O. 90-3:* deals with harassment in the workplace based on race, religion, color, national origin, ancestry, disability, marital status, sex, age, or sexual preferences.

The Alameda Police Department also produced the following as an in-service training guide and a posted announcement within the agency:

ALAMEDA POLICE DEPARTMENT MORTAL SINS
1. Racism, racial slurs, racial discrimination
2. Sexism, offensive sexual remarks, sexual harassment, sexual discrimination
3. Discrimination/harassment for sexual orientation
4. Religious discrimination
5. Untruthfulness/falsifications
6. Unnecessary/excessive force
7. Use of illegal drugs
8. Violations of the law

This department has sent a clear message to its employees that its leaders will not tolerate discriminatory behavior. The same department adapted a San Diego, California Police Department attitude assessment survey instrument on perceptions regarding contact with the multicultural community and workforce. The survey instrument is reproduced in Appendix A.

Minority police fraternal organizations.   Police fraternal, religious, and ethnic organizations are used by members for social activities, counseling, career development, as a resource, and for networking with persons of common heritage, background, or experience. The New York Police Department, for example, has many clubs, societies, and associations to address the needs of their pluralistic organization. The Irish are represented by the Emerald Society; African Americans by the Guardians Association; Christian religious officers by Police Officers for Christ; those of Asian–Pacific Islander heritage (which includes Chinese, Japanese, Korean, Filipino, and Asian Indian officers) by the Asian Jade Society; Italian officers by the Columbia Association, and so on. The police subculture can be a stressful environment, so it is only natural that persons different from the majority workforce members seek emotional comfort zones with those of similar background. These memberships provide emotional sanctuary from stereotypes, hostility, indifference, ignorance, or naiveté that members encounter within their organizations and communities.

Occasionally, one hears of criticism within a department or by the public that such organizations actually highlight the differences between groups of people. At a 1992 NOBLE (National Organization of Black Law Enforcement Executives) conference, a white female (nonattendee) asked one of the authors the meaning of the acronym NOBLE. When given the answer, she asked: "Is it ethical for blacks to have their own organization? Could whites have an organization called 'The National Organization of White Law Enforcement Executives' without being referred to as racists? Why can't the multicultural, social, and professional organizations that already exist satisfy the needs of everyone?"

The woman's concern was brought up directly with one of the conference participants, Sergeant Thomas Hall, an African American, who is a Virginia state trooper. Sergeant Hall explained (personal communication, Oct. 1992):

> In America, we need independent black institutions . . . to foster cultural pride, and have a place where we can go and feel comfortable. We cannot express ourself in society. We cannot assimilate in society. We cannot even assimilate like some Hispanic groups can because of their complexions. I can't assimilate on a bus. As soon as I step on the bus, you are going to realize there is a black guy on the bus. I can't assimilate in a police organization . . . so without these black institutions, I cannot survive. We all have survival mechanisms. I have cultural needs and I have to be around people that share my needs and frustrations. I cannot do that in organizations that are predominantly white. The whites don't suffer from the racial pressures and tensions that I suffer from. So how can they [mostly white organizations] meet my interests and needs. It is impossible.

Hall (now Chief of Police at Virginia State University, VA) stressed that African American law enforcement organizations provide him with a network of persons with similar interests, concerns, and background.

The ethnic organizations within law enforcement are not meant to divide but rather, to give support to groups who traditionally were not accepted in law enforcement fully and had no power in the organization. Yet the sentiment expressed by the white female who inquired into the meaning of NOBLE is a common sentiment among some police officers. Police command officers as well as supervisors must not ignore this debate (whether expressed or not). They must address the issues underlying the *need* for the support groups within the department and they must ensure that there will be dialogue and shared activities between all formalized groups within the organization. All officers must hear from the minority officers' point of view what benefit they receive from membership in the groups. Officers must be willing to discuss ways to guard against divisiveness, either real or perceived, with their agencies.

Assignments based on diversity.   There has been limited research on the assumption that an increase in the proportions of any minority in a police agency would have a "positive" effect within the minority community where they work. For example, the belief of some scholars, minority advocates, and minority citizens is that an increase in Hispanic, African American, or Asian officers in a neighborhood of the same race/ethnicity will improve police–community relations; that there would be a more sensitive response of "like folks" who are aware of needs and issues of "their kind." In fact, historically, immigrants (Irish, Italian, and German) were hired by police departments because they could communicate and operate more effectively than could nonindigenous officers in neighborhoods with immigrants.

Although citizens, according to surveys, appreciate having officers of their own color or national origin work their area, there can be an unfairness in this deployment strategy. Studies (Benson, 1992; Ross, Snortum, and Beyers, 1982; Wells, 1987) have concluded that this can result in a career path for minorities that may be a very different path than that of white officers in agencies that follow this practice. For example, instead of receiving specialized assignments in traffic, investigations, SWAT, and so on, the minority officer who is working effectively in the minority community may have an extended tour of duty in that function. In addition, the area to which the minority officer is assigned is often a tougher, high-crime area, which means that the officer of color or ethnicity is exposed more frequently to violence.

Even officers who are of the same background as the predominant ethnicity in the neighborhood, do not necessarily make the best "crime fighters" or problem solvers there. It should not be assumed that all minority officers have the skills or desire to work with their own cultural or racial group. Assignments based on diversity alone, therefore, are generally unfair and may be a disservice to both the officer and the neighborhood. Officers should not be restricted to work in specific areas based on the notion that police–community relations will improve automatically. In addition, it cannot be assumed that an officer of the same background as the citizens will *always* show sensitivity.

Ron Hampton, a Washington, D.C. peace officer and executive director of the National Black Police Officers Association, illustrated this point at a 1992 NOBLE conference when he discussed the reasons why a new African American recruit wanted to work the black areas of Washington, D.C. The recruit said that he could tell people of his own race what to do and couldn't always do so in predominantly white neighborhoods. Hampton noted that the young recruit "called people from his neighborhood 'maggots'" (Hampton, 1992). Hampton made the point that supervisors must hold subordinates accountable for their conduct, and the chief executive must make it known that inappropriate behavior will be disciplined no matter what the neighborhood. We present this example here also to illustrate how *some* minority officers may have internalized the hatred that society has directed toward them and that, consequently, they are not automatically going to be the most effective in certain neighborhoods.

Like many other law enforcement executives, Chief Burgreen of the San Diego, California Police Department does not deploy officers according to color or ethnicity, but based on the best fit for the neighborhood and related to an officer's competence and capabilities. Chief Burgreen does, however, have four community relations sergeants, one for each major group in the city: Hispanic, African American, Asian, and gay/lesbian. He describes them as his "eyes and ears" for what is going on in the various communities. Some cities use cultural affairs committees made up of people from the diverse groups in the community and the officers who provide them service.

Women in Law Enforcement

Historically, women have always been part of the general workforce in American society, although usually in jobs that fulfilled traditional female employment roles: as nurses, secretaries, schoolteachers, waitresses, and flight attendants, to name a few. In 1845, New York City hired its first police "matron." Until the 1970s, most women in law enforcement occupations were referred to as "policewomen" or "matrons," not "police officers." In 1888, Massachusetts and New York passed legislation making it mandatory for communities with a population over 20,000 to hire police matrons to care for female prisoners. In 1922, the International Association of Chiefs of Police passed a resolution supporting the use of policewomen. Barriers to female entry into the police field included separate entrance requirements, limits on the number of women that could be employed, and lower pay (More, 1992). Women police officers were given duties that did not allow or require them to work street patrol. Assignments or roles were limited to positions such as juvenile delinquency and truancy prevention, child abuse, crimes against women, and custodial functions (Bell, 1982).

The first major enclave of women into the general workforce occurred during World War II. With men off to war, women entered the workforce in large numbers and occupied many nontraditional employment roles and performed admirably. Postwar, U.S. prosperity and growth still saw 30 percent of all women working outside the home (*Business Week,* Sept. 19, 1991, p. 112). By 1990, almost 55 percent of women in the United States worked outside the home. It is predicted that by the year 2000, that number may be as high as 75 percent (Naisbitt and Aburdene, 1986).

Considering how long organized police departments have existed in the United States, women have entered relatively late into sworn law enforcement positions within them. It was not until the early 1970s that women were assigned to patrol duties in some departments. According to police research studies, as of 1992, female officers comprised less than 10 percent of the total sworn police workforce nationwide. This fact stems, in part, from role perceptions. Along with the predominant belief that law enforcement agencies function to exercise authority and use force is the accompanying belief that women are not capable of performing the necessary functions. According to More, (1992, p. 123) during the first half of the nineteenth century, a number of police practices were challenged, and this served as the basis for the initial entry of women in the police field. Also, the law played an important role in opening up police departments to women. Passage of the 1972 Equal Employment Opportunity (EEO) Act applied to state and local government the provisions of Title VII of the Civil Rights Act of 1964, prohibiting employment discrimination on the basis of race, color, religion, sex, or national origin. Selection procedures, criteria, and standards were changed or eliminated and/or made "job related." Affirmative action also played a role in bringing more women into law enforcement. A 1986 Police Foundation study reported the following findings: "In those agencies under court order to increase the representation of women and minorities, women made up 10.1 percent of the sworn personnel in 1986; in those with voluntary affirmative action policies, women made up 8.3 percent of the personnel; and, in those without affirmative action plans, women constituted only 6.1 percent of the personnel" (Martin, 1990).

The U.S. Department of Justice, Bureau of Justice Statistics (BJS), in a 1990 Law Enforcement Management and Administrative Statistics (LEMAS) Report concluded that sworn representation of women nationwide:

- Within sheriffs' departments increased from 12.5 percent in 1987 to 15.4 percent in 1990—a 2.9 percent increase.
- Within state and local police departments increased from 4.2 percent in 1987 to 4.6 percent in 1990—only a 0.4 percent increase.

A 1991 Police Foundation study of the six largest cities in the United States examined the percentage of women officers employed by those police departments (Exhibit 2.5).

Exhibit 2.5   Percentage of women officers

CITY	PERCENT
Detroit	20.8
Philadelphia	16.5
Chicago	16.5
New York	15.5
Los Angeles	14.0
Houston	10.2

Researchers have made various predictions of the numbers of women expected to be in law enforcement professions by the turn of the century and they range from 47 to 55 percent of the workforce. In 1992, the Los Angeles City Council passed a resolution, backed by Chief Willie Williams, requiring the LAPD to boost the number of women in its ranks from 14 percent to 44 percent (*Los Angeles Times,* June 5, 1993, p. A1.) As of 1993, however, the vast majority of women police officers in the United States were still in entry-level positions.

Women are slowly advancing to supervisory, management, and executive police positions. The BJS data on women in law enforcement does not distinguish between the numbers of women in supervisor and manager positions and those at the entry level. A study completed by the Police Foundation in 1990 reports on the results of a 1986 Foundation survey of all state police agencies and municipal departments serving populations over 50,000. The findings show: "Data on the number of officers by rank indicate that women make up only 3.3 percent of all supervisors (i.e., persons at the rank of sergeant or above) in municipal agencies and 0.7 percent of supervisors in state police agencies" (Martin, 1990).

Although women are making gains, they still only constitute a minuscule proportion of police managers. Marrujo and Kleiner (1992) reached conclusions about women in the corporate world that are applicable to women in law enforcement:

> Women are faced with the dilemma of fighting traditional values that have been ingrained into the male executives running today's corporations. These executives were raised since birth to believe that the man is responsible for being the breadwinner, whereas the woman is to stay at home and raise the family. Unfortunately, these stereotypes/attitudes that these male executives possess blind their business judgement and inhibit competent and talented women from making it to the top. These men believe women will eventually quit their careers to raise a family; therefore, they view women as uncommitted to their careers.

One could speculate that some law enforcement executives hold these same attitudes and beliefs, which keep women from obtaining important promotions. Watts has written that a woman must learn certain executive qualities to fit into male-dominated corporate ranks: "She has to be a risk taker but consistently outstanding; she has to be tough but not macho; she has to be ambitious without expecting equal treatment; and she has to take responsibility while still able to follow others advice" (Watts, 1989). These corporate qualities for women also apply to the woman aspiring to rank within the criminal justice system.

McCoy (1992) conducted enlightening research useful to law enforcement executives. He addressed one primary topic and four related subissues (p. 64).

PRIMARY TOPIC: What will be the organizational structure that will support a positive work environment for policewomen by 2001?

Conclusion: The research suggests that the majority of policing executives have not created the organizational culture that values the diversity of women within law enforcement. The organizational structure that will support a positive work environment for policewomen is one that values the complex role and competing interests which policewomen face within both a societal and workplace environment. An organizational culture must be developed which does not view women as an intrusion into the male-dominated profession of law enforcement.

SUBISSUE 1: What will be the effect of increasing women in law enforcement? on the organizational culture.

Conclusion: The research indicates that the personal traits that women bring to law enforcement will foster a greater service-oriented approach to the organizational culture; that increased numbers of women within law enforcement will provide a more flexible approach to the policing ranks.

SUBISSUE 2: What will be the effect on job assignments and methods due to the increasing employment of women in law enforcement?

Conclusion: Police agencies will have to explore a restructuring of traditional work methods. Such options as job sharing and flex-time will have to be considered to assist women officers with family responsibilities and career development.

SUBISSUE 3: What kind of support programs should be provided for women in law enforcement?

Conclusion: Women in policing need support programs to assist in family responsibilities, including child care. The development of mentoring and network programs as well as specific programs for women to discuss gender-related issues to reduce unnecessary stress. The researcher suggests that department-wide diversity and awareness training programs include issues of women in law enforcement.

SUBISSUE 4: What will be the effect of legal mandates on the organizational structure?

Conclusion: The research, as well as the history of women in policing, has shown that legal actions have driven the work environment for women in policing. His research concluded that legal mandates may continue to drive change of the organizational structure until police executives take a proactive, leadership role to support a positive work environment for women.

McCoy made the following recommendations:

- A committed chief executive must create a positive work environment for police-women by establishing it as a priority in their organizational mission and values statement, and through policies and procedures.
- Agencies must provide awareness training that values the diversity of the workforce to all members of the organization.
- To maintain a positive work environment, employees must be held accountable for actions which are harmful to any segment of the workforce.
- Problems within the organizational structure that inhibit a positive work environment for women must be sought out and corrected.
- Agencies must develop and employ mechanisms that allow women to express concerns without "spotlighting" gender.
- Agencies must demonstrate their support of a positive work environment for women by actively providing opportunities for career development.

Still, the integration of women into policing has led many departments to grapple with gender issues such as sexual harassment and discrimination, family leave, and pregnant-officer policies.

Gender issues.   Research on gender issues confronting women in law enforcement focus on discrimination/sexual harassment, role barriers, the "brotherhood," and career versus family.

DISCRIMINATION/SEXUAL HARASSMENT: Although sexual harassment exists in both private and public sectors, the authors contend that it is particularly a problem in law enforcement—an occupation that is still mostly male. The predominantly male makeup and macho image of law enforcement lends to problems of sexual harassment in the workforce. Harassment on the basis of sex is a violation of Section 703 of Title VII of the Civil Rights Act [29CFR Section 1604.11(a)(1)] and is defined as unwelcome or unsolicited sexual advances, requests for sexual favors, and other verbal or physical conduct of a sexual nature when:

1. Submission to such conduct is made either explicitly, or implicitly, a term or condition of an individual's employment; or
2. Submission to, or rejection of, such conduct by an individual is used as the basis for employment decisions affecting such individual; or
3. Such conduct has the purpose, or effect of unreasonably interfering with an individual's work performance or creating an intimidating, hostile, or offensive working environment.

The majority of women officers interviewed for this book (who requested that their names not be used) said that they had been sexually harassed in the workplace. Most of them indicated that when they were exposed to offensive male-officer behavior, they remained quiet for fear of negative male backlash. Sexual harassment occurs at all levels of an organization and is not limited to male harassment of women. Women, too, can be offenders when they initiate sexual jokes or innuendos and use provocative language with men. This usually results in men countering in a similar fashion, which contributes to and escalates the problem. In these instances, women must be held accountable. The questions of what is offensive and where the line should be drawn frequently are the central issues and must be addressed. Command officers, rather than simply stating, "We don't have a harassment problem here," must first model acceptable behavior and then set very clear guidelines as to acceptable behavior.

When harassment takes place, the results for the employees involved can be devastating in terms of their careers, the internal environment of the organization, and the public image. The importance of training *all* law enforcement employees (sworn and nonsworn) on the issues of sexual harassment cannot be stressed enough. The need for training was recognized by the city of Los Angeles when the new chief of police was appointed in 1992: "Los Angeles Police Chief Willie Williams has called for development of a department-wide training program on sexual harassment that for the first time would include the LAPD's top brass, including Williams himself" (*Los Angeles Times,* Jan. 13, 1993, p. B-4).

As sexual harassment complaints and lawsuits have increased in law enforcement, training and policies against harassment have also. With training and awareness, sexual harassment is expected to decrease in the law enforcement workforce as the once male-dominated occupation makes its transition to mixed-gender, multiethnic, and multilifestyle organizations—a microcosm of the society served. Discrimination/sexual harassment training should not only deal with legal and liability issues, but also address deep-seated attitudes about differences based on sex.

ROLE BARRIERS: Barriers based on gender have diminished, not only in the general population but also within law enforcement. For example, ideas about protection differ by gender—who protects whom? In American society, women may protect children, but it has been more socially acceptable and traditional for men to protect women. In the act of protecting, the protectors become dominant and the protected become subordinate. This gender-role perception takes time to break down, especially in the law enforcement and corrections workforce. It is a difficult transition for many veteran police and correctional officers to make as women come into the dangerous, male-dominated occupations that men felt required "male" strength and abilities. The result has been described as a clash between cultures: between the once male-dominated workforce and one where women are becoming integral parts of a new organizational environment. The veteran male police or correctional officer, socially conditioned to protect women, often feels that in addition to working with inmates or violent persons on the streets, they have the added responsibility of protecting the women officers. These feelings, attitudes, and perceptions have made men and women in law enforcement positions uncomfortable with each other. Women sometimes feel patronized, overprotected, or merely tolerated rather than appreciated and affirmed for their work.

It appears that many in the new generation of male officers are more willing to accept women in law enforcement. Numerous interviews with veteran officers conducted by the authors of this book indicated that with few exceptions, the women were generally accepted by the men, but the acceptance was related to how well a specific woman performed her duties. Those who favored women in law enforcement recognized that even some men were not suited for such an occupation.

The Christopher Commission report, commissioned in Los Angeles to investigate the LAPD in the wake of the Rodney King beating, had quite a few conclusions and recommendations pertaining to critical issues within the department. One of their conclusions, of significance to our discussion of women, was that women officers are better equipped to resolve *peacefully* situations of potential violence. In the report it was noted that none of the 120 LAPD officers who were most frequently charged with excessive use of force were women. (Although it may be true anecdotally that women officers resolve situations without resorting to force more often than do male officers, more research on this conclusion is need to support this claim definitively.) The commission also observed that although female officers were performing effectively, they were still not fully accepted as part of the workforce on an equal basis (Independent Commission, 1991). To overcome barriers to women in law enforcement, departments, mentors, and trainers would need to take action, including:

- Increased training focusing on physical conditioning and self-defense
- The use of role playing to prepare for violent confrontation
- More rigorous supervision of backup officers
- Sensitivity training to modify the male-oriented environment of the police department
- Commitment by top management
- Affirmative action programs with formal goals and guidelines

THE BROTHERHOOD: Women who are accepted into the "brotherhood" of police or correctional officers have generally had to "become one of the guys." (Refer to Chapter 5 for more information on how language used in the brotherhood excludes women.) However, a woman who tries to act like one of the guys on the street or in a jail or prison sometimes overreacts and is considered too hard, too cold-hearted, or too unemotional and may be criticized by peers and supervisors. Karen Kimball, the LAPDs Women's Coordinator, says that she has seen some "'Jane Waynes' in the department who swagger, spit and are so aggressive they make many testosterone-charged men seem tame" (*Los Angeles Times,* June 5, 1993, p. A-12).

If she is too feminine or not sufficiently aggressive, men will not take her seriously and she will not do well in either police or correctional work. Women are confronted with a dilemma—they must be aggressive enough to do the job, but feminine enough to be acceptable to male peers and also be able to take different approaches to problems. Different approaches mean that women will use communication skills (verbal and nonverbal) in situations where men might resort to force. Women should not feel compelled to behave like men in the workplace. When women do, the results can be counterproductive and can even result in discipline. To succeed, women have to stay within narrow bands of acceptable behavior where they may exhibit only certain traditional masculine and feminine qualities. Walking this fine line is difficult.

A DOUBLE STANDARD: Interviews of women officers determined that the majority felt that they had to perform better just to be measured as being equal to male officers—a double standard. These women spoke of how they had to impose pressures on themselves to perform up to or better than expectations of their male peers. (Note that the minority employees often express the same sentiment.) One woman officer explained how many women were using a community policing philosophy long before it became the practice of their agency. She described how when she tried to do problem solving, she was "dinged" in her evaluations. Her supervisor rated her negatively for "trying too hard to find solutions to complainant's problems"; "spends too much time on calls explaining procedures"; and "gets too involved" (personal communication, Susan Jones, Sergeant, Concord, California, Police Department, Feb. 1993). The more senior women interviewed indicated that as their careers progressed, their confidence increased and the pressures and stress lessened.

CAREER VERSUS FAMILY: Women in law enforcement are faced with another dilemma—trying to raise a family and have a successful career, two goals that are difficult to combine. Women, especially single parents, who had children when they entered law enforcement frequently find that they do not have enough time for both family and work. If they had children after entering the occupation, they may be confronted with difficult maternity-leave policies. In both cases, women often have a sense of guilt, stress, and frustration trying to do well in a job and maintain a family. Progressive criminal law enforcement organizations have innovative work schedules, child care programs, mentoring/support groups, and a positive work atmosphere for women. Such programs benefit all employees within the organization. Today, men are taking a more active role in parenting and family; therefore, child care, creative work schedules, and even maternity leave should be of importance to them.

The hostile or traditional work environment. A hostile work environment, sometimes the result of men treating women officers as inferiors or insisting on "traditional" roles (pouring coffee, taking notes, etc.), can be overcome. Adria Libolt, Deputy Warden at the Riverside Correctional Facility in Ionia, Michigan, provides the following helpful hints for law enforcement executives (Libolt, 1991):

- Recognize that all employees bring different gifts and talents to the workplace. Both genders know that protecting society is important, but methods to achieve this goal may differ since we all have unique gifts to contribute. Managers need to embrace inclusiveness—they cannot afford to exclude talented, creative individuals who try new approaches.
- Focus on the quality of the work environment. Good conditions are essential for all employees.
- One way to minimize gender differences is to view maleness and femaleness as concepts and points on the gender continuum. Characteristics frequently associated with one sex should be viewed as human qualities that exist in both men and women. Each gender may overlap the other on the continuum by possessing certain characteristics at any given time, depending on the circumstances. To use our example of protection, even though men often protect women in our society, women may also protect men.

Mentor and support programs. A national study of women in law enforcement concluded that policewomen have a significantly higher rate of divorce than male officers and have a lower rate of marriage as a group than the national female rate (Pogrebin, 1986). Research also determined that while both male and female officers were affected by burnout, females were associated with higher levels of emotional burnout, while males showed higher levels of depersonalizing citizens (Johnson, 1991). Issues of child care, maternity leave, family responsibilities, flexible work schedules, job sharing, mentoring/support programs, and promotional opportunities are all important to the woman peace officer and must be addressed adequately by law enforcement agencies or frustration and stress results. Many of these issues are seen as barriers to women and their ability to work in and advance in law enforcement. As a result, women's performance and attitudes can be enhanced if they have access to support and mentoring programs.

Why are mentors important? Marrujo and Kleiner's (1992) research found that "women who had one or more mentors reported greater job success and job satisfaction than women who did not have a mentor." A mentor is described as an experienced, productive supervisor or manager (usually 8 to 10 years older than the employee) who relates well to a less experienced employee and facilitates his or her personal development for the benefit of the individual as well as that of the organization. Usually, this occurs in a "one-on-one" coaching context over a period of time through suggestions, advice, and support on the job. (Mentors and networking are discussed in more detail in Chapter 15.)

It is crucial that law enforcement managers recognize the differences between men and women employees and embrace the talents both contribute. Old traditions, beliefs, and attitudes can frequently surface, especially during times of stress. Although there has been progress, changing men's attitudes toward women in law enforcement is a slow process, and women, too, must develop confidence. As older, male supervisors, managers, and executives retire, their male replacements will be younger men who are more accustomed to working with women. Research on police performance has clearly shown that male and female peace officers are comparable in their performance and that women are perceived by the public as equally effective. The only exception mentioned in some studies is the handling of violent or confrontational situations, wherein the physical strength of women to subdue the suspect was questioned (Cordner and Hale, 1992). However, most studies indicate that with "a less authoritarian, more open style of women, they are less likely to trigger showdowns" (*Los Angeles Times,* June 5, 1993, p. A-1). Progress has been made in recent years. Women are now working street patrol assignments in almost all agencies, regardless of department size. Women also have "nontraditional" job assignments such as participating in special weapons and tactics teams, bomb units, hostage negation units, training, motorcycle traffic enforcement, and community relations. Thus women are beginning to see that opportunities are starting to open up to succeed in law enforcement careers within many jobs and ranks with their organization.

Gays and Lesbians in Law Enforcement

In a precedent-setting case, a Florida jury ruled March 9 [1992] in favor of a deputy fired because he is gay. The case is ultimately expected to go all the way to the Florida Supreme Court, where it will set the stage for a landmark ruling on the privacy rights of gays. . . . (*Frontiers,* Mar. 27, 1992)

The San Diego County Sheriff's Department announced Thursday that it will officially forbid discrimination or harassment against lesbians and gay men based on sexual orientation, settling a suit brought by a lesbian graduate of a recent department training academy. (*Los Angeles Times,* Dec. 4, 1992, p. B-1)

Milwaukee—Homosexuals are actively being recruited by the city's Police and Fire Commission as police officer candidates. . . . It is estimated that nearly 200 gay or lesbian officers are on the Milwaukee Police Department. The department has more than 1,900 officers. (*Bay Area Reporter,* June 18, 1992, p. 18)

The California Highway Patrol is reviewing its affiliation with the Boy Scouts because the group ousted a gay police officer from an Explorer post (advisor position). . . . San Diego police announced that they would sever ties with the Boy Scouts of America because of the group's decision to suspend El Cajon police officer [name] [from his advisor position] after he said publicly that he was homosexual. (*Los Angeles Times,* Aug. 18, 1991, p. A-31)

Texas Sodomy Law Ruled Unconstitutional—An appellate court in Texas on February 10 [1993] affirmed a lower court ruling that struck down the state's sodomy law, while barring the City of Dallas and its police department from using it to reject lesbian and gay applicants. (*Frontiers,* Mar. 12, 1993, p. 19)

Although still a silent minority in most police departments, many gay and lesbian officers are no longer willing to lie to conceal their sexual orientation. As of 1993, most law enforcement agencies did not knowingly hire or retain homosexuals. As late as 1992, a 20-year FBI agent was fired when he "came out of the closet" ("60 Minutes" report, Sept. 13, 1992). [Several federal class action law suits were pending in 1993-4 wherein employment barriers for gays and lesbians in sensitive federal law enforcement agencies were being challanged. The issue by the federal government was whether discrimination against homosexuals might have a basis when security considerations were part of the rational.] Predictions from research on gays/lesbians in law enforcement are that over the next decade there will be increased pressure from (McMahon, 1990):

- The homosexual community to have more officers who are openly gay and lesbian within law enforcement agencies
- Homosexuals to become officers and be openly gay
- In-service officers to be able to be honest about their sexual orientation

If these trends are not addressed on a timely and adequate basis, employing agencies will be ill prepared to deal with the complex, controversial issues involved. If not addressed proactively, there will probably be increases in litigation to enforce or legislate rights and proper treatment of gays and lesbians.

In Los Angeles, for example, a gay sergeant was awarded $208,250 for wrongful discharge and was offered reinstatement. LAPD Sergeant Grobeson claimed in a 1988 lawsuit that years of harassment forced him to resign. As a result of the settlement, LA's city council also promised to adopt new provisions that would make discrimination against gays and lesbians grounds for dismissal from employment. This settlement, occurring in 1993, involved two other LAPD officers who resigned for the same reasons as Sergeant Grobeson. All three former LAPD members were offered reinstatement and the total cost of the settlement for the three was $770,000 (personal communications, Mitch Grobeson, 1993).

Forced changes are usually uncomfortable and can be costly for all involved. Law enforcement leaders must address the pressing issues involving homosexual recruitment, hiring, retention, promotions, and nondiscrimination. In San Francisco, the sheriff and the chief both actively recruit homosexuals. In that city, gay and lesbian deputies and officers are so common that it is almost a nonissue. In Los Angeles, Chief Daryl Gates in 1992 had said his department should not specifically seek homosexual recruits since the law had not recognized gays and lesbians as a minority group. Gates, during his administration, banned off-duty officers from wearing uniforms at police information booths during street fairs in neighborhoods populated by gays. The chief's policy caused mixed reactions in the community and police department. This was about the same time that other major law enforcement agencies were actively seeking improved relations with gays and lesbians.

GAY PRIDE CELEBRATION OPENS WITH POLICE OFFICERS, WITHOUT CONTROVERSY

About 2,500 attend Orange County event. For the first time, uniformed members of the CHP [California Highway Patrol] and local law enforcement agencies participate . . . [with] informational booths representing several city police departments and the California Highway Patrol. (*Los Angeles Times,* Aug. 18, 1991, p. A-31)

Those chiefs who have encouraged gays and lesbians to apply to their respective departments understand that they cannot discriminate or restrict opportunities to these applicants. These chiefs are keenly aware that to be effective, they must represent the diverse community they serve. Many chief executives are reviewing their policies and procedures to ensure that neither they nor the organizations they affiliate with discriminate. As indicated in the opening quote of this section, the California Highway Patrol decided to review its affiliation with the Explorers Scouts program because agency policy prohibits discrimination based on sexual orientation. The San Diego Police Department severed its ties with the Boy Scouts of America because of that group's suspension of an El Cajon homosexual police officer from his position as an advisor. Most of the scouts' parents wanted the officer to continue as an advisor. San Diego Police Chief Bob Burgreen explained: "'It breaks my heart to have to do this. . . . however, this department cannot continue to affiliate with an organization that discriminates against a group of people.' . . . Burgreen angrily compared the Boy Scouts' decision to oust [officer] to the racial segregation of the 1960's. The group forbids association with homosexuals because it mistakenly equates homosexuals with child molesters" (*Contra Costa Times,* Oct. 22, 1992, p. B-7).

The controversy. In 1993, President Clinton, against the wishes of his commanders, ordered an end to the ban on gays and lesbians in the military. The U.S. Military Joint Chiefs of Staff argued against repealing the 50-year-old ban, maintaining that allowing homosexuals in the armed forces was certain to shatter morale, hasten the spread of AIDS among heterosexual troops, undercut recruitment, and force devoutly religious service members to resign. Similar arguments have been heard in the law enforcement community. Canada lifted its ban on homosexuals in the military in late 1992 under court order. According to Canadian authorities, there were no resignations, no open declarations of homosexuality, no reported morale problems, and no reduction in recruitment numbers as a result of the new policy (*Contra Costa Times,* Jan. 30, 1993, p. A-1).

In the United States, a federal judge in Los Angeles in 1993 ruled in the case of a navy petty officer that the military's ban on homosexuals was unconstitutional. The judge cited the Pentagon's own studies going back to the 1950s that showed no foundation for the commonly held belief that gays and lesbians disrupt morale, good order, discipline, or are more of a security risk than their heterosexual counterparts. The proposed overturn of the military's antigay policies were watched and advocated by gay-rights leaders. For gay-rights advocates, there is an enormous symbolic importance to the movement because the ban was seen as an official stamp of discrimination; of setting a national tone of how gays and lesbians are to be treated in American society, especially the workforce.

Translated to law enforcement, researchers reported that urban police departments adopting nondiscrimination statutes and actively recruiting homosexual officers have not reported a drop-off in morale within the organization. The San Francisco Police Department was among the first major agencies to take these steps. San Francisco Police Chief Anthony Ribera wrote General Colin Powell, chairman of the joint chiefs of staff, to express concern over Powell's opposition to lifting the military ban. In his letter he declared: "'In 1979, before the first openly gay and lesbian officer entered our department, I had doubts about the propriety of hiring gays as police officers.' . . . Today the San Francisco Police Department has approximately 85 openly gay and lesbian officers. Their performance, professional conduct and loyalty to the department has been exemplary" (*Contra Costa Times,* Jan. 30, 1993).

Concerns about homosexuals in the military or law enforcement include a belief that gay soldiers or officers will walk around hand in hand, dance together at clubs, make a pass at or "watch" nongay colleagues, and seek benefits for their gay marriage. These arguments for bans are not based in reality. In the military and the criminal justice system, the majority of gays, just like the majority of "straight" officers, are extremely work-oriented. They want to accomplish the mission, make the rank, work special assignments, and avoid harassment or "spotlighting" their sexuality. They do not want to provoke "straights" or the system. These persons are no different from others in wanting to support the disciplinary processes. They believe any inappropriate conduct should be handled with proper discipline.

When conjuring up images of homosexuals, some police officers visualize only extremist militant types who publicly display their sexuality in offensive and socially unacceptable ways. Extreme groups such as "Dykes on Bikes" and "Queer Nation," to name two, do not represent the majority of the homosexual population. The majority of gays and lesbians cause no problem for law enforcement and live private lives without drawing attention to themselves. It should also be pointed out that some researchers believe that there is evidence that homosexuality is something that a person is born with rather than a choice that one makes in later life (*The Economist,* Dec. 5, 1992). Although this is still a controversial issue in research, many gays would support this claim. For example, Sergeant Mitchell Grobeson of the LAPD, in a course presented to a group of northern California police officers, said the following: "Why would anyone *choose* a lifestyle for which their parents are likely to disown them, their church reject them, society discriminate against them and individuals harass them? Would not most people be more likely to *choose* the easy path and be heterosexuals? You must consider that for the majority of gay men, this is no choice."

The transition. There will inevitably be problems during the transition within the police organization or correctional facility as gay and lesbian officers "come out of the closet." For some organizations and employees, this is a major change and involves attitudes that are not easily or quickly altered, if at all. Obviously, if any homosexual displays his or her sexuality unacceptably, they must be subject to progressive discipline (counseling, oral reprimand, written reprimand, suspension, demotion, and discharge) just as any heterosexual would. Organizational policies—rules and regulations—providing penalties for inappropriate actions must be applied to *all* officers.

A suspected or known gay or lesbian may encounter discriminatory or biased treatment due to negative stereotypes and attitudes and may even encounter hostility from other employees. There may be fear of AIDS transmission unless proper education occurs. Gay men, in particular, will have an even more difficult time assimilating into departments than ethnic or racial minorities. In interviews conducted by the authors of this book, some heterosexual officers stated that they did not view gay males as being "masculine" and therefore felt that they could not rely on them for "backup" in dangerous situations. By necessity, patrol officers must be able to count on their partners; trust is the most crucial element in law enforcement relationships. The gay or lesbian officer is often placed in a position of having to prove him or herself on the job. This may take the form of a physical confrontation with an arrestee, or being tested with confidential information regarding personal conduct of patrol officers. As openly gay or lesbian officers are recruited and hired, there may be a change in the comfort level within the organization. Individual and group prejudices and assumptions will have to be challenged. There may be resistance at many levels unless measures are taken to smooth the change. The progressive organization will have plans in place assisting the homosexual officer's transition into the department and gain employee acceptance.

It is beneficial for gays and lesbians to have support groups or homosexual peer counselors from their own or neighboring police agencies. In the early 1980s, openly homosexual officers formed networks of support within the San Francisco Sheriff's Department. The San Francisco and New York City Police Departments and a few other agencies assisted homosexuals in forming support groups in the late 1980s. Besides networking, the groups do public presentations and provide mentoring and support for their members. Support can also be necessary for heterosexual employees who promote or defend the rights of the homosexual officer. For example:

POLICE CHIEF BACKS GAYS, GETS THREATS TO HIS LIFE

Rarely a week goes by that Tom Potter does not receive either a death threat on the phone or a nasty letter in the mail. As police chief of Oregon's largest city [Portland], Potter said he had come to expect that a small number of people would always hate police officers. What has been somewhat of a surprise to him was to learn how many people also profess to hate homosexuals. (*Contra Costa Times.* Oct. 4, 1992, p. B-2)

"Coming out of the closet" and having the support of straight officers can also have negative consequences, as this example illustrates. Here the chief's daughter is a lesbian officer in the Portland, Oregon Police Department. The chief supported her and other gays and lesbians by marching in two gay pride events in Portland.

If the state does not have one, the city/county or law enforcement agency should enact a specific policy of nondiscrimination against homosexuals in the workplace (as of 1993, seven states had enacted legislation). City or county administration officials must support and possibly even champion such legislation. The policy must establish that:

- Sexual orientation is not a hindrance in hiring, retention, or promotion.
- Hiring is done solely on merit as long as the individual meets objective standards of employment.
- Hiring is not on a quota basis, but on the basis of the identical, job-related standards and criteria for all individuals.

The chief executive must establish departmental policies and regulations dealing with gay and lesbians in the workforce. These policies must make it clear that harassment or failure to assist fellow gay or lesbian officers shall result in discipline. The chief executive should obtain the support of his/her supervisors and managers to ensure that the intent of these rules, policies, and procedures are carried out. Strict disciplinary procedures for violations of such laws or policies is crucial.

Cultural awareness programs that train department personnel on diversity in communities and the workforce must also educate employees on gays and lesbians, addressing the stereotypes and myths. Legal rights must also be covered, including discussion of statutes and department policies of nondiscrimination and penalties, including liability, for acts of harassment. Often, best results are achieved by involving openly gay officers (from other agencies, if necessary) in the awareness training programs (see Chapter 4). Ideally, this training will enable employees to come to know the gay or lesbian person and fellow officer as a human being deserving of respectful treatment. Training can help reduce personal prejudices and false assumptions among employees and thus begin to change behavior. This type of training furthers the ideal of respect toward all people. The obvious secondary benefit is the decreased likelihood of personnel complaints and lawsuits by homosexuals.

Successful training programs in California have been completed at the Alameda and Sacramento Police Departments, the Santa Clara Sheriff's Department, and the San Francisco Police Department. Officer Lenora Militello of the San Francisco Police Department teaches about gay and lesbian issues at the SFPD Police Academy. She tells each class: "I'm not expecting that eight hours of training is going to change anyone's mind. But I am expecting that when you put on your uniforms, you will leave your prejudices behind and do your job professionally" (*San Francisco Chronical*, September 11, 1992, p. 83).

Police officers are the protectors of individuals in a diverse society that includes gay and lesbian persons. Police officers who are prejudiced against homosexuals must still guarantee the rights of gays and lesbians. Those same officers also must maintain a good working relationship with peers who may be homosexual.

LEADING IN A PLURALISTIC SOCIETY AND WORKFORCE

Most managers and supervisors will need to change their leadership style to meet the challenges and requirements of a culturally diverse society and workforce. Management experts suggest that the modern leader will have to have two important traits: *vision* and the ability to *communicate* that vision to others. The challenge for the manager or supervisor will be to communicate visions and values to others who are from different ethnic, racial, religion or lifestyle backgrounds within the workforce and the community.

The Chief Executive

The chief law enforcement executive should follow specific guidelines to meet the challenge of policing a multicultural and multiracial community. Of course, as stressed previously, he or she must first effectively manage the diversity within his or her own organization. Progressive law enforcement executives are aware that before employees can be asked to value diversity in the community, the diversity within the organization must be valued. Managing diversity in the law enforcement workplace is therefore given a high priority.

Executive leadership and teambuilding are crucial to managing a diverse workforce and establishing good minority–community relations. The chief executive must take the lead in this endeavor by:

- Demonstrating commitment
- Developing strategic, implementation, and transition management plans
- Managing organizational change
- Developing police–community partnerships (community-based policing)
- New leadership models

Demonstrate commitment. The organization must adopt and implement policies that demonstrate a commitment to policing a diverse society. Policies must be developed with input from all levels of the organization and community representatives. Valuing diversity and treating all persons with respect must first come from the chief executive. His or her personal leadership and commitment is viewed as the keystone to implementing policies and awareness training within the organization and building a bridge successfully with the community. One of the first steps is the development of a "macro" mission statement for the organization that elaborates the philosophy, values, vision, and goals of the department to foster good relationships with a diverse workforce and community. The following is an example of a *macro mission statement* satisfying step one above:

> We constitute an organization whose very existence is justified solely on the basis of community service. Our mission must be clearly expressed to both members of the Department and to the community. . . .
>
> Our broad philosophy must embrace a wholehearted determination to protect and support the doctrine of individual rights while providing for the security of persons and property in the community. . . .
>
> People are the community's most valuable asset. . . . The community has demonstrated this in its demand for a well-trained, cooperative, responsive, humanistic

and professional police department. The Department, therefore, has a continuing obligation to demonstrate to the community that it is worthy of such trust and to provide the type of police service expected. [Concord Police Department, California, *Regulations Manual*]

All policies and practices of the department must be reviewed to see how they may affect ethnic/racial minorities as well as gays and lesbians. This would include a review of recruitment, hiring, and promotional practices to ensure that there are no institutional barriers to them. The chief executive stresses, via the mission and values statements, that the agency will not tolerate discrimination, abuse, or crimes motivated by hate against protected classes within the community or within the agency itself. The policy statements would also include references to discrimination or bias based on physical disability, gender, or age.

The executive must use every opportunity to speak out publicly on the value of diversity and to make certain that people inside and outside the organization know that upholding those ideals is a high priority. The chief executive actively promotes the policies and programs relating to improved community relations. These executives use marketing skills to sell their program, both internally and externally. Internal marketing is accomplished by involving senior management and the police association in the development of the policies and action plans. The chief or sheriff uses this opportunity to gain support for the policies by demonstrating the value of having community support in terms of the departments effectiveness and officer safety. External marketing is accomplished by involving community-based organization representatives in the process.

Police leaders institute policies that develop positive multicultural beliefs and attitudes even as early as the selection process. During background interviews, polygraphs, and psychological exams, candidates for law enforcement employment must be carefully screened. The questions and processes would determine the candidates' attitudes and beliefs and, at the same time, make him or her aware of the agency's strong commitment to a multicultural workforce.

Develop strategic, implementation, and transition management plans. Textbooks and courses that teach strategic, implementation, and transition management planning are available to the law enforcement leader. The techniques, although not difficult, are quite involved and will not be elaborated on in this book. Such techniques and methodologies are planning tools providing the road map that the organization uses to implement programs and guide the agency through change. An essential component consists of action plans that identify the specific goals and objectives expected to be achieved. Action plans include budgets and timetables and establish accountability—who is to accomplish what by when. Multiple action plans involving the improvement of police–community relations in a diverse society would be necessary to cover such varied components as policy and procedures changes; affirmative recruitment, hiring, promotions; cultural awareness training (see Chapter 5); and community involvement—community-based policing.

Manage organizational change. The department leadership is responsible for managing the change processes and action plans. This is an integral part of implementation and transition management discussed above. The chief executive must ensure that the policies, procedures, and training implemented result in increased employee responsive and awareness of the diversity in their community and within the organization workforce. The chief executive must require that management staff continually monitor progress on all programs and strategies to improve police–community relations. The chief must ensure that all employees are committed to those ideals. Managers and supervisors need to ensure accountability to these established philosophies and policies of the department and they must lead by example. When intentional aberrations of the system are discovered, retraining and discipline should be quick and effective. Employees must be rewarded and recognized (especially patrol officers) for their ability to work with and within a multicultural community. The reward systems for employees, especially first- and second-line supervisors, would be for those who foster positive gender and ethnic/racial relations within and outside the organization. As we have illustrated, the chief executive, management staff, and supervisors are role models and set the tone for the sort of behavior and actions that they expect of employees.

Develop police–community partnerships. Progressive police organizations are adopting community-based policing as one response strategy to meet the needs and challenges of a pluralistic workforce and society. The establishment of community partnerships is a very important aspect of meeting the challenges. For example, a cultural awareness training component will not be as effective if police–community partnerships are not developed, utilized, and maintained. The chief executive establishes and maintains ongoing communications with all segments of the community. This is best accomplished by community-based policing (discussed in detail in Chapter 15).

New Leadership Models

Historically, all methods or models of management and organizational behavior have been based on implicit assumptions of a homogeneous, white male workforce. Even best-sellers such as *The One-Minute Manager* and *In Search of Excellence* that have been, and still are, useful tools for the manager are based on that traditional assumption. Managers must learn to value diversity and overcome personal and organizational barriers to effective leadership, such as stereotypes, myths, unwritten rules, and codes (one of those being that the organizational role model is white male). New models of leadership must be incorporated into law enforcement organizations to manage the multicultural/racial workforce.

Jamieson and O'Mara (1991) have addressed the topic of motivating and working with a diverse workforce, explaining that the leader must move beyond traditional management styles and approaches. They indicate that the modern manager must move from the traditional "one size fits all" management style to a **"flex-management"** model. They describe flex-management as not just another program or quick fix but one that is "based on the need to individualize the way we manage, accommodating differences and providing choices wherever possible" The flex-management model they envision involves three components:

1. **Policies:** published rules that guide the organization
2. **Systems:** human resources tools, processes, and procedures
3. **Practices:** day-to-day activities

The model is based on four strategies: matching people to jobs, managing and rewarding performance, informing and involving people, and supporting lifestyle and life needs. Five key management skills are required of the modern manager to accomplish this:

1. Empowering others
2. Valuing diversity
3. Communicating responsibly
4. Developing others
5. Working for change

The leader not only knows his or her own ethnocentrism, but also understands the cultural values and biases of the people with whom he or she works. Consequently, leaders can empower, value, and communicate more effectively with all employees. Developing others involves mentoring and coaching skills, an important tool for the modern manager. To communicate responsibly means that the leader understands the diverse workforce from a social and cultural context and flexibly utilizes a variety of verbal and nonverbal communication strategies with them. The leader is also familiar with conflict mediation in cross-cultural disputes.

Jamieson and O'Mara (1991) explain that the manager, to establish a flex-management model, must follow a six-step plan of action which includes:

1. Defining the organization's diversity
2. Understanding the organization's workforce values and needs
3. Describing the desired future state
4. Analyzing the present state
5. Planning and managing transitions
6. Evaluating results

They contend that to be leaders in the new workforce, most managers will have to "unlearn practices rooted in old mindsets, change the way their organization operates, shift organizational culture, revamp policies, create new structures, and redesign human resource systems."

The vocabulary of the future involves leading employees rather than simply managing them. Hammond and Kleiner (1992) wrote about the distinction between the two:

> One of the first things companies must look at in multicultural environments is the leadership vs. management issue. Leadership, in contrast to management, deals with values, ethics, perspective, vision, creativity and common humanity. Leadership is a step beyond management; it is at the heart of any unit in any organization. Leadership lies with those who believe in the mission and through action, attitude, and attention pass this on to those who have to sustain the mission and accomplish the individual tasks. People want to be led, not managed; and the more diverse the working population becomes the more leadership is needed.

Hammond and Kleiner explain that in a multicultural/racial society and workforce, "the genius of leadership" is:

- Learning about and understanding the needs of the diverse people you want to serve—not boss, not control—but serve.
- Creating and articulating a corporate mission and vision that your workers can get excited about, participate in, and be a part of.
- Behaving in a manner that shows respect to and value for all individual workers and their unique contributions to the whole. Those you can't value, you can't lead.

Management, to build positive relationships and show respect for a pluralistic workforce, needs to be aware of differences, treat all employees fairly (and not necessarily in completely similar ways), and they must lead. The differing needs and values of a diverse workforce require flexibility by organizations and their leaders. Modern leaders of organizations recognize that employees' needs not only differ but also change over time. The goal of law enforcement leaders is to bridge *and not close* the cultural as well as racial gaps within the organization.

SUMMARY

The officer who traditionally worked in a predominately, all white, male workforce, must learn to work with increasing numbers of women and minorities. In many communities the officer also works within a society that is becoming more pluralistic. The chapter suggests that to be effective in this new environment, officers must have a knowledge of conflict resolution techniques to reduce racial and ethnic problems.

The chapter focused on concerns and issues of minorities, women, and homosexuals in law enforcement. The importance of support and mentor programs for women and minorities was stressed. Such programs help them make transitions into organizations, cope with stress, and meet their workplace challenges more effectively.

In the chapter we provided suggestions for the law enforcement executive whose jurisdiction is pluralistic and whose workforce is diverse. Law enforcement leaders must be committed to setting an organizational tone that does not permit bigoted or discriminatory acts and must act swiftly against those who violate those policies. They must monitor and deal quickly with complaints both within their workforce and from the public they serve.

DISCUSSION QUESTIONS AND ISSUES*

1. *Measuring Responsiveness to Diversity.* Using the check off and scoring sheet (Exhibit 2.1), determine how responsive your police department has been to the diversity of the jurisdiction it serves. If you are not affiliated with an agency, choose a city or county police department and interview a command officer to determine the answers and arrive at a score. Discuss with the command officer what initiatives his or her department intends to undertake to address the issues of community diversity.

*See Instructor's Manual accompanying this text for additional activities, role-plays, questionnaires and projects related to the content of this chapter.

2. *Defusing Racially and Culturally Rooted Conflicts.* What training does the police academy in your region provide on defusing racially and culturally rooted conflicts? What training does the city or county law enforcement agency in which you live or work provide to officers? What community (public and private) agencies are available as referrals or for mediation of such conflicts? Discuss what training should be provided to police officers to defuse, mediate, and resolve racially and culturally rooted conflicts. Discuss what approaches a law enforcement agency should utilize.

3. **Women in Law Enforcement.** How many women officers are there within the law enforcement agency in which you work or the city or county in which you live? How many of those women are in supervisory or management positions? Are any of the women assigned to nontraditional roles such as SWAT, motorcycle enforcement, bomb unit, hostage negotiations, or community relations? Have there been incidents of sexual harassment of women employees, and how were the cases resolved? Has the agency you are examining implemented any programs to increase the employment of women, such as flex-time, child care, mentoring, awareness training, or career development? Discuss your findings in a group setting.

REFERENCES

HAMMOND, TERESA, AND BRIAN KLEINER (1992)."Managing multicultural work environments," *Equal Opportunities International*, Vol. 11, No. 2.

HAMPTON, RON (1992). *Unfinished Business: Racial and Ethnic Issues Facing Law Enforcement II,* NOBLE and PERF sponsored conference, Reno, Nev., Sept. 27–29.

Independent Commission on the Los Angeles Police Department (1991). *Summary, Racism and Bias,* The Commission, Los Angeles, pp. 7–8.

JAMIESON, DAVID, AND JULIE O'MARA (1991). *Managing Workforce 2000: Gaining the Diversity Advantage,* Jossey-Bass, San Francisco.

JOHNSON, L. (1991). "Job strain among police officers: gender comparisons," *Police Studies,* Vol. 14, No. 1, pp. 12–16.

LIBOLT, ADRIA (1991). "Bridging the Gender gap," *Corrections Today,* Vol. 53, No. 7, Dec., p. 138.

MARRUJO, ROBERT, AND BRIAN KLEINER (1992). "Why women fail to get to the top," *Equal Opportunities International,* Vol. 11, No. 4, p. 1.

MARTIN, SUSAN (1990). *The Status of Women in Policing.* Police Foundation, Washington, D.C. Sept.

MCCOY, DANIEL (1992). *The Future Organizational Environment for Women in Law Enforcement,* California Command College, Peace Officer Standards and Training, Sacramento, Calif.

MCMAHON, BROOK (1990). *"How Will the Role of Law Enforcement Change by the Year 2000 as It Deals with Suspected or Openly Gay Police Officers?"* Command College Class X, Peace Officers Standards and Training, Sacramento, Calif., June.

NAISBITT, JOHN, AND PATRICIA ABURDENE (1986). *Re-inventing the Corporation,* Warner Books, New York, p. 243.

WATTS, P. (1989). "Breaking into the old-boy network," *Executive Female,* Vol. 12, (No. 32.)

ROSS, RUTH, SNORTUM, JOHN, AND BEYERS, JOHN (1982). "Public priorities and police policy in a bicultural community," *Police Studies,* Vol. 5, No. 1, pp. 18–30.

BENSON, KATY (1992). "Black and white on blue," *Police,* Aug. p. 167.

WELLS, JAMES (1987). *Crime and the Administration of Criminal Justice,* "A common destiny: blacks and American society," pp. 491–97.

MORE, HARRY (1992). "Male-dominated police culture: reducing the gender gap," *Special Topics in Policing,* Anderson Publishing Company, Cincinnati, Ohio, pp. 113–137.

BELL, DANIEL (1982). "Policewomen: myths and reality," *Journal of Police Science and Administration,* Vol. 10, (No. 1) p. 112.

POGREBIN, MARK (1986). "The changing role of women: female police officer's occupational problems," *Police Journal,* Vol. 59, No. 2, p. 131. April/June.

CORDNER, GARY AND HALE, DONNA (1992). "Women in Policing" (in) *What Works in Policing: Operations and Administration Examined,* Anderson Publishing Company, Cincinnati, Ohio, pp. 125–142.

3

MULTICULTURAL REPRESENTATION IN LAW ENFORCEMENT:

Recruitment, Retention, and Promotions

OVERVIEW

In this chapter the reader is introduced to the recruitment crisis that currently exists and will inevitably be a challenge into the next century. A brief historical perspective of women and minorities in law enforcement is provided, including a profile of their numbers in state and local agencies across the country. We discuss reasons for recruitment difficulties and lead into recommended strategies for success. Selected case studies provide insight into the recruitment and promotion challenges facing law enforcement. Case laws and federal legislation on civil rights and discrimination are reviewed with a discussion on reverse discrimination issues. The retention and promotion of minorities and women and the issue of quotas are addressed in the final section of the chapter.

COMMENTARY

The information contained in the following quotes draws attention to the importance of minority recruitment, hiring, and promotion for law enforcement agencies and the community:

FBI Law Enforcement Bulletin, "Police recruitment: today's standard—tomorrow's challenge," by Ralph Osborn, June 1992, p. 21.

According to Trojanowicz and Carter, "By 2010, more than one third of all American children will be black, Hispanic, or Asian." The Caucasian majority of today will become a minority within America in less than 100 years. Obviously, this change in society will have a tremendous impact on the recruiting process of the future.

USA Today, "NYC ranks worst in ratio of black officers," Oct. 8, 1992, p. 3A.

New York City has the worst ratio of black police officers to black residents, a survey of the USA's largest cities shows. "It's atrocious," said Sam Walker, a criminal justice professor at the University of Nebraska at Omaha, who conducted the survey of the 50 cities with the highest population in the 1990 census.

"Occasional Paper" published by the Center for Applied Urban Research. "Employment of Black and Hispanic Police Officers, 1983–1988: A Follow-up Study" by Samuel Walker, professor of criminal justice, University of Nebraska at Omaha, No. 89-1, February 1989.

Police departments in the 50 largest cities in the United States made uneven progress in the employment of black and Hispanic officers between 1983 and 1988.

Washington Post, "Racial preferences produce change, controversy," by Thomas B. Edsall, *Washington Post* staff writer, Jan. 15, 1991.

In the harsh battleground over jobs, college education and access to the promotion ladder, the issues of quotas and racial preferences can come to dominate, if not supersede, the national struggle to achieve equity in the workplace and on the college campus. Take, for example, the core of city government: the police and fire departments. In many communities well into the 1960's, these departments were white male enclaves, controlled by such European ethnic groups as Irish, Italian and Polish Americans.

INTRODUCTION

Diversity is becoming so commonplace in communities that talking about a majority or a minority group borders on the obsolete. In California, demographers predict that by the year 2005 there will be no single racial or ethnic group constituting the majority. That trend is occurring in major United States cities as well. Some demographers say that the coming reality is that every group will be a minority.

To recruit and retain a representative staff and provide effective services, therefore, law enforcement executives must have a clear understanding of their community and their own workforce. The recruitment and retention of qualified "protected classes" and women have become a concern and a priority of law enforcement agencies nationwide. Many agencies are having difficulty finding qualified applicants, whether minorities or not, and a crisis has developed. The recruitment pool of eligible and qualified candidates is diminishing. The crisis is multidimensional and is discussed in detail later in this chapter. It is maintained by researchers that more than 90 percent of new entrants into the labor pool will be women, minorities, and immigrants by the year 2000.

HISTORICAL PERSPECTIVE OF MINORITIES IN LAW ENFORCEMENT

The recruitment and retention of qualified ethnic and racial minorities (male and female) have been a concern and a priority of law enforcement agencies nationwide for a few decades. This is not a new issue in the history of U.S. law enforcement. A President's Crime Commission Report in 1967 recommended that more minorities be hired and that they receive opportunities for advancement. Soon after the Watts riot in Los Angeles, the 1968 Kerner Commission Report identified the underrepresentation of blacks in law enforcement as a serious problem. The report recommended improved hiring and promoting policies and procedures for minorities. The Kerner Commission also concluded that white racism in communities and within law enforcement organizations was a dominant factor related to civil disorders. The Warren Christopher Commission report on the Los Angeles Police Department, directly after the 1992 riots, cited the problems of racism and bias within the LAPD and recommended improved hiring and promotions processes for minorities. It is incumbent on law enforcement to take action on many of these recommendations now.

Profile of Local and State Law Enforcement Agencies

The U.S. Department of Justice, Bureau of Justice Statistics (BJS), collects information on law enforcement agencies and produces a report every three years profiling the demographic makeup of departments in the United States (see Exhibit 3.1). According to the 1990 LEMAS (Law Enforcement Management and Administrative Statistics) Report, there were nearly 17,000 publicly funded state and local law enforcement agencies operating in the United States. This included 49 general-purpose state police departments; 12,288 general-purpose local police departments and 3100 sheriffs' departments. The profiles were:

- Local departments, sheriffs' agencies, and state police collectively employed 741,000 full-time persons, a decrease of 16,508 individuals since 1987.
- Sworn female employees in sheriffs' agencies represented 15.4 percent of the workforce (12.5 percent in 1987); in local agencies women represented 8.1 percent (7.6 percent in 1987); in state police departments, 4.6 percent were women (4.2 percent in 1987)
- Sworn personnel in local police agencies were 83 percent white (down 2.4 percent from 1987); 10.5 percent black (up 1.2 percent from 1987), and 5.2 percent Hispanic (up 0.7 percent from 1987).
- Sworn personnel in sheriffs' agencies were 84.5 percent white (down 2.1 percent from 1987); 9.8 percent black (up 3.3 percent from 1987), and 4.7 percent Hispanic (up 0.9 percent from 1987).
- Sworn personnel in state police agencies were 87.1 percent white (down 1.1 percent from 1987); 7.5 percent black (up 1.0 percent from 1987); and 4.4 percent Hispanic (up 0.6 percent from 1987).

These numbers show that women and minorities are not yet represented to any great degree in the law enforcement workforce.

Samuel Walker, professor of criminal justice, completed a five-year study of racial minority employment in the 50 largest U.S. cities (Walker, 1989). Forty-seven out of 50 of those states responded, or 94 percent. The study, published in 1989, determined that there had been uneven progress in the employment of black (Exhibit 3.2) and Hispanic officers between 1983 and 1988. A synopsis of his findings for the 47 big-city police agencies responding are:

Exhibit 3.1 Characteristics of full-time sworn local and state police and sheriffs' departments, 1990 and 1987

Category[a]	1990		1987	
	Percent	Number	Percent	Number
Local police departments				
Officer total	100.0	363,001	100.0	355,290
Male	91.9	333,598	92.4	328,288
Female	8.1	29,403	7.6	27,002
White	83.0	301,291	85.4	303,418
Black	10.5	38,115	9.3	33,042
Hispanic	5.2	18,876	4.5	15,988
Other	1.3	4,719	0.8	2,842
Sheriffs' departments				
Deputy total	100.0	141,418	100.0	122,544
Male	84.6	119,640	87.4	107,103
Female	15.4	21,778	12.6	15,441
White	84.5	119,498	86.6	106,124
Black	9.8	13,850	8.3	10,171
Hispanic	4.7	6,647	4.3	5,269
Other	1.0	1,414	0.8	980
State police departments				
Officer total:	100.0	52,372	100.0	50,498
Male	95.4	49,976	95.8	48,354
Female	4.8	2,396	4.2	2,144
White	87.1	45,590	88.7	44,825
Black	7.5	3,928	6.5	3,285
Hispanic	4.4	2,315	3.8	1,942
Other	1.0	539	0.9	446

[a]"Black" and "white" categories do not include Hispanics. "Other" category includes American Indians, Alaskan Natives, Asians, and Pacific Islanders.
Source: U.S. Department of Justice, Bureau of Justice Statistics, Washington, D.C. 1992.

- 45 percent made significant progress in the employment of black officers and 42 percent made progress in hiring Hispanic officers.
- 17 percent reported a decline in the percentage of black officers employed and 11 percent a decline in the number of Hispanics employed.
- 17 percent reported no change.

Walker commented: "The 1988 data suggest guarded optimism with respect to racial minority employment in policing. Progress toward a theoretical ideal level of minority employment in many cities has been offset by lack of progress or an actual decline in other cities" (Walker, 1989).

The decline in minority employment for some agencies has been a cause for concern. Conjecture about the decline had to do with departments making progress in recruitment and then losing their gains when minority members se-

Exhibit 3.2   Percentage of blacks in a few major U.S. cities compared with percentage of black officers on their police forces

City	Blacks in city	Black police
Five Highest		
Honolulu	1.3	1.4
Washington	65.8	67.8
Los Angeles	14.0	14.1
Fresno	8.3	8.0
Toledo	19.7	18.8
Five lowest		
Kansas City, Mo.	26.6	13.4
Minneapolis	13.0	5.5
Long Beach, Calif.	13.7	5.6
Sacramento	15.3	6.3
New York	28.7	11.4

Source: Sam Walker, University of Nebraska–Omaha, 1990.

cured jobs in non–law enforcement occupations. Walker (1989) speculated that the decrease in numbers might also have been due to "covert institutional racism that, among other things, blocks career advancement"; that those employees became disgruntled and left. Of course, other factors such as the financial situation in many cities may also have contributed to the decline in minority employees (i.e., layoffs due to the recession of the early 1990s). Clearly, more research is need to explore the degree to which institutional racism may have led to the decline.

The downsizing of departments through layoffs most often affects the last hired. Women, ethnic, and racial minorities, having been the last hired, are usually the first fired or laid off. Therefore, the gains made in terms of a multicultural workforce, including women, are lost. Progressive agencies still try to fill vacancies due to retirements, resignations, and dismissals with new hires, many of whom could be minorities and women. The fact is that law enforcement is still a predominantly white male occupation. Although there has been some improvement in the recruitment of minorities and women, more must be done for departments to reflect the makeup of their local community.

Recruitment Crisis

Gordon Bowers (1990) wrote: "There is a crisis developing in recruitment that will change law enforcement as it is known today. For each year over the next decade, the number of new police officers needed and the minimum qualifications will be raised, but both the number and percentage of high school graduates in the normal age range of police applicants will decrease. The shortage of qualified applicants may be so severe that some departments will be dissolved."

A number of factors have contributed to the reduction of the once substantial law enforcement applicant pool. A primary explanation is offered by the futurists Cetron, Rocha, and Luckins (1988). They indicate that "the percentage of the population between 16 and 24 years old will shrink from 30 percent of the labor force in 1985 to 16 percent in the year 2000" (p. 64). The same researchers predict that "during the next decade, white men will account for only one in four new workers" (p. 34). Therefore, law enforcement will attempt to recruit from an applicant pool that is not only shrinking but expected to be largely minorities and women. There is an additional reason for fewer numbers of applicants within the typical age range eligible for careers as peace officers. According to annual FBI Uniform Crime Reports, millions of young people between the ages of 15 and 29 are arrested each year, many for crimes that would disqualify them for police work.

Law enforcement competes with private industry and the armed forces for this reduced pool of qualified and eligible applicants, especially for minorities and women, resulting in an even more critical shrinkage for police agencies. The lack of a qualified pool of applicants is a problem of special concern to small departments, which simply do not have the resources for extensive recruiting efforts.

However, there are those who are not convinced that there is a recruitment pool problem and that there are sufficient numbers of qualified minority candidates. William Shackelford, president of Industry Education Connection Enterprises in Atlanta, said, "If you can't find them [minorities], you're not looking in the right places. You are not doing the right things" (Micari, 1993). He maintains that "companies that say [that they are] homogeneous because they just can't find qualified minority and women candidates are either relying on a defense as dissembling as it is tired or—often naively—taking recruitment efforts in the wrong direction."

According to Barbara Parker, associate professor at the School of Business at Seattle University, there is no question that there are enough properly trained, diverse candidates for jobs. She echoes other diversity recruitment specialists, explaining: "The companies that are looking for women and minorities are finding them" (Dettweiler, 1993). Furthermore, in the future the argument "There are no qualified minorities" will become less of a defense as increased numbers of women and minorities are earning college and university degrees. *Cultural Diversity at Work* (September 1993 issue), a diversity newsletter, contains a list of the 10 most frequent causes of the failure to attract and retain high-level minority and female employees (Micari, 1993). A brief synopsis of those most pertinent to law enforcement include:

1. **Senior management isn't sending the "diversity message" down the lines.** Senior management does not always demonstrate commitment in the form of "value" statements and policies emphasizing the importance of a diverse workforce.

2. **Informal networking channels are closed to outsiders.** Women and minorities often experience discomfort within the traditional, all-white, all-male informal ca-

reer networks, including extracurricular activities. For example, women police officers are uncomfortable in most police association activities that involve recreational gambling, fishing, sports activities, or the roughhousing that can take place at meetings.

3. **In-house recruiters are looking in the wrong places.** Recruiters must use different methods and resources than those they have traditionally used to find diverse candidates.

4. **Differences in life experience are not taken into account.** Some applicants, both women and minorities, will have had life experiences that differ from those of the traditional job candidate. For example, the latter has typically had some college experience, a high grade-point average, and is often single (i.e., without the many responsibilities that accompany marriage and children). On the other hand, many minority job candidates frequently have had to work through school and are married and possibly had children. Therefore, their grade-point average may have suffered.

5. **Negative judgments are made based on personality or communications differences.** Although not everybody's style reflects cultural, racial, or gender characteristics, there are distinct differences in communication style and personality between women and minorities and the traditional, white-male job applicant. As far as communication style differences, this is especially true when English is the applicant's second language. Women are, generally, not as assertive as men in communications style. Sometimes these factors can affect the outcome of a preemployment interview and be a barrier to a job offer.

6. **The candidate is not introduced to people who are like him or her.** It is important that the candidate or new hire meet people of the same gender, race, or ethnicity within the agency. A mentor or support group may be crucial to a successful transition into the organization.

7. **Organizations are not able or willing to take the time to do a thorough search.** Recruitment specialists indicate that searches for qualified minority and women candidates take one to one-and-a-half months longer than others. It takes commitment, resources, and time.

8. **Early identification is missing from the recruitment program.** Programs that move students into the proper fields of study early on and that provide the education required for the job are essential. Examples of these include internships, scholarships, and police programs (e.g., police athletic league) that bring future job candidates into contact with the organization.

Law Enforcement Recruitment Difficulties

The Police Executive Research Forum (PERF) created a nationwide task force addressing the issue of decreasing numbers of qualified police applicants. Some of the findings of the task force, which completed its study via surveys in 1987, are as follows:

1. **Identification of recruiting problems.** The problem most frequently reported were:

   - A decreasing number of qualified applicants
   - The inability to offer competitive compensation
   - Difficulty in recruiting minorities

   Those responding to the survey who perceived a decline in the number of qualified applicants attributed it to lack of education, use of drugs, and limited life experience.

2. **In which testing areas are police officer candidates most likely to fail?** The top three in rank order were the written, background investigation, and polygraph.

3. **Higher education (college) contributes to the success of a police officer candidate.** Slightly over 93 percent felt that college contributes to the success of a candidate.

The decreasing pool of candidates (regardless of gender, ethnicity, or race) often includes candidates rejected because they have abused substances and therefore can not meet the department standards. In addition, lack of education, lack of life experience, physical or weight problems, crime-related backgrounds, and psychological problems considerably narrowed the number of eligible candidates.

Bowers (1990) concluded that law enforcement agencies will have to utilize alternatives to the traditional applicant pool to secure qualified candidates. He suggests that it is possible to develop a recruitment strategy that would target people not usually recruited. Bowers defined the "alternative applicant pool" as those people who are qualified but who have no current intention of pursuing law enforcement as a career.

RECRUITMENT STRATEGIES

With regard to building a diverse workforce, recruitment strategies used in the past will not be sufficient and will not provide agencies with high-quality applicants. Specific goals, objectives, and timetables must be established at the top level of the organization, and at the same time, management must commit to not lowering standards for the sake of numbers and deadlines. The philosophy and procedures required are discussed below.

Commitment

The law enforcement chief executive must commit to hiring, promoting, and retaining minorities and women. This genuine commitment must be demonstrated both inside and outside the organization. Internally, this involves developing policies and procedures that emphasize the importance of a diverse workforce. Affirmative action programs will not work in a vacuum. Chief executives must integrate the values that promote diversity and affirmative action into every aspect of the agency from its macro mission statement to its roll-call training. Externally, the police executive should publicly delineate the specific hiring and promotion goals of the department to the community through both formal (media) and informal (e.g., community-based policing, networking with minority organizations) methods.

Although the chief executive is the champion for the philosophy, policies, and procedures, they are carried out by committed staff who are sensitive to the needs for affirmative hiring and promotions. The executive should also build a partnership with personnel officials so that decisions better reflect the affirmative action goals of the department.

Although the chief may be genuine in his or her efforts to champion diversity and affirmative action hiring, care must be taken. The chief must make sure that in doing so, none of the policies and procedures violate Title VII of the Civil Rights Act of 1964. Policies and procedures should be reviewed by a knowledgeable personnel department and/or legal staff.

Planning

Action plans should be developed that commit the objectives, goals, budget, accountability, and timetables for the recruitment campaign to paper. Demographic data should form one of the foundations for the plans which must take into account the current political, social, and economic conditions of the department and the community. A sample action plan for such a recruiting effort in the Concord, California Police Department is contained in Appendix C.

Resources

Adequate resources, including money, personnel, and equipment, must be made available to the recruitment effort. Financial constraints challenge almost every organization's recruitment campaign. The economic condition of a particular city or county is an important factor when budgeting for recruitment. Due to the size or financial condition of the agency, it may be necessary to use less expensive, innovative approaches. For example, many small law enforcement jurisdictions can combine to implement regional testing. One large county on the west coast successfully formed a consortium of agencies and implemented regional testing three times per month for law enforcement candidates. To participate, each agency pays into an account based on the population of its jurisdiction. Alternatively, each agency can pay according to how many applicants it hired from the list. The pooled money, then, is used for recruitment advertising (e.g., billboards, radio, television, newspapers) and the initial testing processes (e.g., reading, writing, and agility tests, including proctors). The eligibility list is provided to each of the participating agencies, which then continue the screening process of those applicants in whom they have interest. Police agencies should not see others as adversaries with respect to recruiting. By combining their efforts, they:

- Save money (consolidate resources)
- Develop a larger pool of applicants
- Are more competitive with private industry and other public agencies
- Test more often
- Reduce the time it takes from application to hire

In terms of recruiting a diverse workforce, the second benefit listed—developing a larger pool of applicants—is central to reaching beyond the traditional applicant pool.

Selection and Training of Recruiters

A recruiter is an ambassador for the department and must be selected carefully. Full-time recruiters are a luxury most often found only in the larger agencies. The benefit of a full-time recruiter program is that usually the employees in this assignment have received some training in marketing techniques and salesmanship. They have no other responsibilities or assignments and can therefore become focused on what they do and do it well. They develop the contacts, resources, and skills to be effective. Whether full time, part time, or assigned on an "as needed" basis, the following criteria should be considered when selecting a recruiter.

Recruiters should be selected who are:

- Committed to the goal of recruiting
- Believers in a philosophy that values diversity
- Able to work well in a community policing environment
- Like salespersons who believe in and market a product—law enforcement as a career
- Comfortable with people of all backgrounds who know how to communicate this comfort
- Able to discuss the importance of minority representation in police work and the advantages to the department without sounding patronizing

The recruiter must be provided resources (e.g., budget and equipment) and must have established guidelines. He or she must be highly trained with respect to organizational values and ethics, the recruiters' job, market research, sales and public relations, and cultural awareness. With few exceptions, in the United States there is no recruiting course for law enforcement. For instance, the military, which has had tremendous success at recruiting, has a state-of-the-art two-month recruiting course. The military uses a weeding-out process for those with natural sales skills, and they place their best recruiters into those assignments. In the military, there are many incentives attached to recruitment responsibilities. Typically, if they have full-time recruiters at all, most law enforcement departments have chosen them for perhaps the wrong reasons. Typically, recruiters do not have many sales and marketing or human relations skills. Most are simply assigned the task and are provided with little if any direction or training. Few agencies can afford to send a recruiter to a two-month course.

To respond to the lack of skill associated with recruitment, the Commission on California Peace Officer Standards and Training has completed the development of a 24-hour course entitled "Techniques and Methods of Recruitment." Other state POST commissions may follow the example. Progressive large agencies (or a consortium of agencies), in the absence of action at the state POST level, could develop an in-house course patterned after the program described in Appendix D. The recruitment course objectives are to:

- Foster a positive image of law enforcement
- Promote intraagency cooperation and commitment in the recruiting mission
- Develop an awareness of various cultures and subcultures
- Identify target groups

- Make effective use of agency resources in recruiting
- Identify proven recruitment techniques
- Review legal and ethical issues in recruitment

The course covers subjects such as:

- **The role of the recruiter:** knowing department needs; marketing the job and department
- **Ethics:** personal, professional, and organizational values
- **Recruitment skills:** time management; developing recruitment presentations
- **Cultural awareness:** developing an awareness of cultural diversity
- **Recruitment methods:** ideas; POST recruitment survey
- **Legal issues:** employment and discrimination (federal and state laws; consent decrees and hiring quotas; local agency rules)
- **Recruitment resources:** agency resources; external resources; multiagency efforts

Agencies that cannot afford the luxury of a recruiter(s) should develop incentive programs to encourage officers to recruit bilingual whites, women, and minorities, informally, while on or off duty.* One possible incentive program would be to give officers overtime credit for each person in those categories they recruit who makes the eligibility list; additional credit if that same applicant is hired; and additional credit for each stage the new officer passes until through probation. For example, the San Jose, California Police Department has a "Recruiting Incentive Program." "The program authorizes an award of 10 to 40 hours compensatory time to any department member, sworn or non-sworn, who recruits a 'protective class,' bi-lingual (Spanish or Vietnamese) or female Police Officer candidate. Protected class individuals include the following, as designated by the City Affirmative Action Office: Black, Asian, Hispanic, Native American and Filipino." The time is awarded in 10-hour increments at a "straight-time" rate based on the following phases of employment:

1. Candidate is hired   10 hours
2. Candidate completes basic academy (or equivalent)   10 hours
3. Candidate completes the FTO program   10 hours
4. Candidate completes probation   10 hours

Another agency awards $250 to the employee who recruits an applicant (whether minority or not) who is hired and completes all phases of the background process and starts the academy. The same department awards $250 to an employee who recruits a lateral police officer candidate once he or she completes all phases of the background process, is hired, and reports for duty. When either recruit makes it through probation, the employee receives $250 as an additional incentive. Encouraging all members of the department to be involved in the recruitment effort and in selling a career with their agency is healthy and usually effective.

---

*The authors acknowledge that there may be some controversial aspects to recruitment incentives that target only women and minorities. Each agency will need to decide the appropriateness of such strategies.

Job-Related Selection Process

Every aspect of the recruiting, applicant testing, pre-employment counselling, and promotions processes should be reviewed continually to make certain they are up-to-date, relevant, and free from bias or discrimination. All testing processes must be evaluated objectively. Selection criteria should be streamlined and job related. Agencies that do not have a streamlined system will lose applicants to other departments. Departments that do not use job-related/validated testing processes are subject to legal challenges that could stop the entire process, resulting in long delays in hiring. The selection process must not be counterproductive to the goals of the department's affirmative hiring program.

The need for creative thinking on building a pluralistic workforce came from the chief of police Louis Cobarruviaz of San Jose, California. He was asked the following question by an Asian Indian whose religion was Sikh: If he were hired into the department, would he be permitted to wear the turban representative of his Sikh religion? The chief told him yes, as long as it was blue and as long as the department could place their official emblem on it. Many tradition-bound executives might tell him to seek another job. In December 1992, the Federal Equal Opportunity Employment Commission ruled that a Jewish postal worker could wear a "yarmulke" (skullcap) uncovered by a postal service cap while delivering mail, despite the opposition of his supervisors. In law enforcement, strict dress codes have been part of tradition for generations; in some cases the strict codes may have to be broken to accommodate a multicultural workforce.

Community Involvement

A pluralistic community must have some involvement early in the recruitment effort of candidates for police work. Representatives from different ethnic and racial backgrounds should be involved in initial meetings to plan a recruitment campaign. They can assist in determining the best marketing methods for the group they represent and can help by personally contacting potential candidates. They should be provided with recruitment information (brochures, posters, etc.) that they can disseminate at churches, civic and social organizations, religious ceremonies, schools, and cultural events. Community-based policing also offers the best opportunity for peace officers to put the message out about a recruiting campaign.

Minority community leaders should also be involved in the selection process, such as sitting on oral boards for applicants (regardless of the applicants' background). The San Francisco Police Department utilizes community leaders in all the processes listed above. Many progressive agencies have encouraged their officers to join community-based organizations, where they interact with community members and are able to involve the group in recruitment efforts for the department.

Satisfaction Level of Minority Employees

The first step before outreach recruitment can take place should be to look inward. Are any members, sworn or nonsworn, experiencing pain because of their color, nationality, religion, or sexual orientation? If the environment of the organization is hostile, it is difficult to make progress in hiring, retaining, and promoting minorities. (See Appendix A, a survey that can help your department determine the overall environment with regard to minority employees.) Managers must talk with minority persons within the organization on a regular basis to find out if there are issues that are disturbing them. Mangers must then demonstrate that they are taking steps to alleviate the source of discomfort for the employee, whether it involves modifying practices or discussing behavior with other employees.

The field training program for new recruits should be reviewed and evaluated to ensure that new officers are not being arbitrarily eliminated or subjected to other forms of prejudice or discrimination. By the time a recruit has reached this stage of training, much has been invested in the new officer; every effort should be made to see that he or she completes the program successfully. Negligent retention is a liability to an organization. When it is well documented that the trainee is not suitable for retention, release from employment is usually the best recourse regardless of race, ethnicity, lifestyle, or gender.

Role models and mentoring programs should be established to give recruits and junior officers the opportunity to receive support and important information from senior officers of the same race, ethnicity, and gender. There are many successful programs, however, where role models are of different backgrounds than the recruit. A department offering careers to minorities and women cannot have internal problems, either real or perceived, related to racism or discrimination. The department must resolve any such internal problems before meaningful recruitment can occur.

Recruitment Programs and Strategies

1. **Role model/mentor program.** Implement a role model/mentor program which involves police officers working or spending leisure time in positive ways with youth during their formative years. Encourage youths to stay drug free, not commit crimes, and to complete high school. These are major reasons applicants for law enforcement fail to qualify. Drug Awareness Resistance Education (DARE) is a good example of such a program which can be found in most communities. The age-old Police Athletic League (PAL) can also serve an important role in this type of effort.

2. **Vocational law enforcement education.** An example of this is the magnet program at Santa Teresa High School in San Jose, California. The program involves minority youth from grades 9 through 12. The students carry the regular high school course work and, in addition, are enrolled in specialized police subjects which include classes on report writing, first aid, law, self-defense, and a police cadet program. Approximately 25 percent of their classwork is law enforcement related. The first class graduated in 1992 and many of the students were attractive candidates for agencies without a two-year college/60-unit requirement. Those students found it easy to continue in that agency's cadet program, wherein they worked part time at the department while attending college.

3. **Cadet/Explorer Scout/Intern programs.** Many departments have work–study (apprenticeship) programs where, for pay or as volunteers, young people interested in law enforcement attend school full time (high school or college) while working part time at the agency. Such programs are designed to develop young people into prospective police officers and to help them determine career goals. This is an excellent vehicle to "grow your own cop." The New York City Police Department recruits college students for their cadet corps program. The city loans the cadet $3000 toward the last two years in college. The cadet is paid for part-time work during the school term, where he or she gains valuable work experience. The department is also able to evaluate the cadets' suitability for a law enforcement career. Upon graduation and the completion of at least two years with the department, the loan is considered paid in full. If they decide not to continue in police work or do not complete the two years, they must repay the loan with interest.

4. **Deactivated military.** The military is an excellent source for recruitment. Tests for law enforcement positions should be advertised at bases where military personnel complete their tours of duty. Since few military persons make the service a career, the department who hires such candidates often gets the advantage of well-trained, well-educated, and highly disciplined persons who enhance the professionalism of the agency. Many of these service men and women are minorities.

5. **Minority community networking and educating.** Recruiters and community-based policing strategies should include programs (networking) to help change any negative attitudes and perceptions of ethnic community members toward police. As discussed further in the culture-specific section of this book, many people from different countries carry extremely bad memories of police in their country of origin. They associate police with corruption, torture, and repressive governments. No recruiting effort could succeed in these communities without reeducating citizens (especially parents of candidates) first as to the positive functions that officers perform in the United States.

6. **Night and weekend recruitment.** Seeking only those candidates without jobs does not always result in finding the best employee. Successful recruitment programs include contacting and testing recruits on weekends and nights when those already employed are available.

7. **Testing seminars.** Some agencies provide seminars on the various testing devices (written, physical agility, etc.) so that candidates (regardless of race, gender, etc.) are better prepared and guided through the stages of the selection process.

8. **Task force.** Many agencies have formed recruitment task forces comprised of minority-group members targeted for employment. The task force typically consists of both community and agency persons of the race or nationality the department is trying to reach.

9. **Minority schools.** Some law enforcement agencies have been successful at recruiting in high schools and colleges or universities in areas that have high numbers of minorities. For example, police from Pasadena, California performed outreach recruitment at black colleges and universities in southern states. The department placed recruiting advertisements in predominantly black college newspa-

pers, displayed posters, sent information (including a video) to student organizations and professional fraternities and sororities, and had a toll-free (800) number for interested applicants. The agency compacted their testing and background processes into the fewest days possible. Those who came to California for testing were hosted by local minority families who made them feel more comfortable and welcome. This effort resulted in a significant number of qualified candidates who are still with the department. This is a good example of expanding the locale from which a pool of candidates are typically found.

10.   **Job and career fairs.** There are many job and career fairs in communities and regions across the United States. Some are organized by the private sector, some by colleges and universities, but today, many are sponsored by a consortium of law enforcement agencies. Recruitment efforts at job and career fairs by agencies are usually successful. Departments, however, must be prepared to "fast track" applicants (through the testing and screening processes) or they will lose qualified candidates, especially minority, to competitors from the private or public sector.

11.   **Contracts.** In the future there may be experimentation with contracts between law enforcement agencies and college/university students, particularly minorities and women. The contract would involve a student, majoring in something other than criminal justice, having a large part of his or her college/university education costs paid by the city or county. In exchange, the student would work a specified number of years in the police department of the sponsoring agency. If the student does not fulfill the contract, he or she must repay the loan with interest. The merits of this approach still have to be studied. It takes a minimum of two to three years following in-service training for a police officer to reach a degree of effectiveness. The contracted employee may not remain with the department long enough to become an effective member. (The New York City Police Department is experimenting with this approach and may be a source of information.)

12.   **Older workers.** Law enforcement employers should look within their organization for sworn and nonsworn positions that could be filled by the growing pool of older workers, especially if qualified minorities. Recall the earlier discussion of the aging American society and workforce and the shortage within the traditional age range (16 to 29 year olds) for police recruits. The need to keep, and in some cases retrain, older workers is particularly acute and could be useful in some agencies in highly skilled jobs. For example, there are few reasons why a retired scientist could not be trained to work in a forensic crime lab or a computer expert trained to work on police computers; healthy individuals (especially military or athletes) have even been trained for sworn officer positions as a second career.

13.   **High schools, colleges, and universities.** Recruiters must be involved not only in recruitment at campuses but also in vocational programs and counseling. They must provide genuine information about what it takes to earn a job in public safety, and they must explain clearly how people can be disqualified for such work.

14.   **Police fraternal organizations/associations.** Fraternal groups or police associations that represent the diversity of the agency must be involved in the recruitment effort.

The most successful minority recruitment program, wherein applicants are solicited to apply for a career in law enforcement (excluding those who "walk-in" already interested), involve innovative techniques that reach out to targeted groups. They also involve police managers who are outspoken in support of affirmative recruitment and hiring methods. Aggressive recruitment efforts must be followed up immediately by a streamlined system to handle the new flow. If not brought into the system quickly, good recruits usually accept other employment. Successful programs will vary by community. If recruitment efforts result in a large enough pool of qualified applicants, the pool will contain persons of all backgrounds who can then be screened to determine the most qualified. It must be stressed that aggressive recruitment program should be accompanied by equal emphasis on retention and remediation of applicants. Desirable applicants must be developed to succeed. This could include training or coaching in:

- Physical development, from being taught skills to pass the preemployment physical fitness exam and the academy fitness tests to in-service defensive tactics
- Assertiveness
- Mock orals
- Training techniques
- Language skills
- Introduction to stress management and discipline

Some applicants need remediation during the various phases of preemployment screening and then some after employment. They need to be eased into what will be a totally different environment—the police subculture.

LAWS AND COURT DECISIONS

Title VII of the Civil Rights Act of 1964 (Act) prohibits employment discrimination based on race, sex, color, national origin, or religion. The prohibitions within the Act makes it unlawful for an employer: "(1) to fail or refuse to hire or to discharge any individual, or otherwise to discriminate against any individual with respect to his compensation, terms, conditions, or privileges of employment, because of such individual's race, color, religion, sex, or national origin . . . " (42 U.S.C. secs. 2000e–2000e-17, 1972).

Most challenges to personnel practices and procedures that might be discriminatory are brought under either the Equal Protection Clause of the Fourteenth Amendment or the Equal Employment Opportunity Act of 1972. The latter extended to public agencies the "antidiscrimination in employment" provisions of the Act. There have been many court decisions in the private and public sector that have tried to provide guidance on matters of equal employment opportunity. The intent of such laws and court decisions was to eliminate discrimination in the public and private sectors against protected classes and women. There is evidence that since the passage of the Act in 1972, overt employment discrimination, such as formal employment policies that discriminate, have become relatively rare.

The same interpretations have been applied to alleged reverse discrimination cases. In a case involving the Memphis, Tennessee Fire Department, the

Supreme Court in 1984 ruled that an affirmative action plan cannot disrupt seniority systems to save jobs of "protected classes"—provided that the seniority system was unbiased. The arrival of reverse discrimination cases resurrected the discrimination impact issue and the courts were wrestling with an appropriate legal conclusion for these cases during the 1990s. More discussion on this issue follows later in this section.

Court decisions established some narrow exceptions that allow race, sex, color, national origin, or religion to be considered in employment actions. An employer cannot look at those factors except in two instances. The two lawful exceptions are the bona fide occupational qualifications (BFOQ) exemption and the affirmative action exception.* Each permits employment actions based on consideration of some or all of the otherwise forbidden criteria; however, both are strictly interpreted and may be used by employers only where absolutely necessary. A BFOQ is difficult to establish and has been used most often where an absence of the requirement would "destroy the essence of the business or would create serious safety and efficacy problems" [653 F.2d at 1276-77 (9th Cir. 1981)]. In fact, race and color are specifically excluded from the exception and cannot be used lawfully as BFOQs.

The second exception, which allows consideration of the forbidden criteria in employment actions, is the "affirmative action" exception. Courts have ruled that this exception be strictly limited and held permissible only as a necessary remedy for prior discrimination. Under certain circumstances, employers, may therefore, extend preference to a particular race, religion, or sex of persons of a particular national origin or color in an effort to correct for past discrimination. Courts have ruled that employers may legitimately use employment practices having disparate impact if they serve, in a significant way, the legitimate employment goals of the employer. Courts have also directed that the preference cannot be overbroad, cannot unnecessarily frustrate the legitimate aspirations of those not receiving the preference, and must have a termination point—usually when the effects of prior discrimination have been reduced or eliminated.

John Sauls, attorney, special agent of the FBI, and legal instructor at the FBI Academy, researched the issues of employment discrimination. Regarding "disparate impact discrimination," he wrote:

> Employers may also be held to have engaged in illegal employment discrimination where they use employment practices that although apparently unbiased on their face, operate to the disadvantage of groups of persons based upon race, color, sex, religion, or national origin. This is true, even where no intent on the part of the employer to discriminate illegally is shown. This "disparate impact" theory of Title VII liability is based upon a judicial recognition that uniform standards have potentially unequal impact. It is also based on judicial recognition that the use of subjective employment standards may shield discriminatory intention from judicial scrutiny. For example, a written aptitude or achievement test on which a significantly higher percentage of whites achieve passing scores than minorities is a potential instrument of illegal discrimination. So too is a subjective promotional

---

*This exception was created through court decision. See, for example, Johnson v. Transportation Agency. [Santa Clara County, 107 S.Ct. 1442 (1987)].

process that advances a substantially higher percentage of whites than minorities. . . . (Sauls, 1991)

Sauls indicates that cases of disparate impact discrimination are proven by statistical comparisons utilizing any one or combination of:

- Actual success rates of one group versus another
- The composition of the employee group in question versus the composition of the relevant qualified labor pool available
- Testimony of discriminatory words or actions on the part of the employer

He recommends that employers assess their employment practices for potential legal problems. Through self-examination, corrective measures can be made in employment practices before an employer is accused of discrimination.

The laws discussed point out that, on the one hand, public and private entities cannot discriminate on the basis of race, sex, color, national origin, or religion. On the other hand, organizations must have an affirmative action plan, responding to the need to hire minorities and women. Consequently, the numbers of whites hired and promoted are substantially reduced in many organizations.

Integration of the lower ranks of the nation's police departments is often opposed by nonminorities and is sometimes achieved at a cost. There have been times when the use of hiring practices and procedures did not strictly follow civil service selection of those who perform best on tests. When this happens, there are always multiple negative consequences for everyone involved (discussed previously in Chapter 2).

RETENTION AND PROMOTION OF WOMEN AND MINORITIES

Efforts to recruit a more multicultural department reflecting the diversity of the community served is just one of the important challenges of law enforcement agencies. Retention and promotion are equally important.

Retention and Promotion

Retention of any employee is usually the result of good work on the part of the employee and a positive environment wherein all employees are treated with dignity and respect by every member of the workforce. Retention is more likely in organizations where the basic needs of the employee are met, along with reasonable opportunities for career development. Employees who are provided opportunities to rotate through various assignments within the organization and have career development opportunities are more inclined to remain. In fact, once an agency earns a reputation for fairness, talented men and women of all ethnicities and races will seek out that agency and will remain longer.

The lack of promotions of protected classes and women to supervisor and command ranks has been cited by scholars and police researchers as a severe problem in policing for at least two decades (see Goldstein, 1977, and Guyot, 1977). Authors and advocates for the promotion of women and minorities have used the term *glass ceiling* to describe an imaginary barrier that inhibits those officers from reaching ranks above entry level. It has been established that the glass ceiling has not been broken to any significant extent in most organizations, including law enforcement agencies. Police executives and city or county managers cannot afford to minimize the consequences of this problem. Failure to promote minorities and women can result in the continued distrust of the police by the communities they serve. Underrepresentation of protected classes within police departments aggravates tensions between the police and the minority communities. Some scholars and criminal justice experts argue that underrepresentation of minorities at *all* levels within law enforcement agencies hurts the image of the department in the eyes of the community (Walker, 1989).

Within the organization, minorities and women employees are frustrated when promotional opportunities seem to be the advantage of white males. The disenchantment that often accompanies frustration often leads to low productivity and morale, early burnout, and resignation because opportunities appear better elsewhere. In addition, court-ordered promotions can result from lack of attention to equal opportunity promoting practices. Court orders have a negative impact on a department's operations and relationships, both internally and externally, and often lead to distrust and dissatisfaction.

A study by Lanam (1993) involved discussions with police professionals, civic leaders, POST consultants, ethnic minorities, and educators. These experts concluded:

> Most felt that their respective police department's administrators were progressive in hiring ethnic minorities, but felt that most of the same administrators were hesitant and almost resistant toward achieving ethnic diversity within their own police command ranks. Some stated that they have heard the explanation from several police administrators that minority recruitment is a relatively new issue and more time is needed to promote officers through the ranks. However, this explanation was viewed as implausible or at best, inaccurate since the Civil Rights Act, Affirmative Action, and the Equal Opportunity Act all are over 20 years old. It was felt that it should take less than 20 years to recruit, train, and promote ethnic minorities into the police command ranks. (Lanam, 1993)

Affirmative action and consent decrees have been only moderately successful in achieving parity in the hiring of ethnic and racial minorities and women, and there has been even less success with their promotions to command ranks. There is no denying the strong negative internal reaction in an organization associated with court orders mandating promotions. Many nonminority employees feel anger or frustration with consent decrees or affirmative action–based promotions. In these cases the minority candidate promoted feels that he or she suffers from a loss of credibility. Peers may subtly or overtly imply that the promotion did not result because of competence. Consequently, employees can experience strained relationships and lowered morale. Clearly, preventive work must be done to avoid the problems just described.

Captain Lanam's research suggests that departments perform strategic planning to provide direction and objectives on ethnic diversity in command ranks. Such plans help determine available resources and capabilities of an organization to achieve their objectives and goals as they pertain to the promotion of women and minorities. An implementation and transition management plan is then formulated; if it is done well, it will help the agency achieve ethnic/racial diversity within the police command staff within the time frame decided upon. Specifically, Lanam's study recommended a strategy that involved the establishment of an office of management review and the formation of a cultural affairs committee. The function and composition of each would be:

- **Cultural Affairs Committee:** comprised of command personnel, civic leaders, community minority representatives, business leaders, and police officers representing all major ethnic groups in the department. The purpose of the committee is to provide an open, direct line of communication between the department and the minority community. The committee would be allowed input on all department policies and practices as they pertain to the recruitment, screening, hiring, and promotion of a diverse workforce.
- **Office of Management Review and Equal Opportunity:** a unit (staffing dependent on size of agency and need) within the police department with a command officer in charge who is accountable only to the chief. The purpose of the office is to provide an ongoing review of demographic changes, recruitment, promotions, minority representation within the department, training as it relates to cultural issues, and legal requirements as they relate to equal opportunity. The office would also be charged with the implementation and follow-through on action plans, policies, or procedures recommended by the cultural affairs committee and accepted/adopted by the department. The office would also direct the implementation of the cultural affairs committee.

The executive must be the overall "champion" for achieving diversity in his or her command staff. To be effective, he or she must carefully balance the public interests of equity with the interests of the department. The executive must strive to secure the best qualified persons to serve the public while meeting the goals of hiring and promoting protected classes and women. He or she is ultimately responsible. According to Lanam, the chief executive must take the following action steps:

1. Review symptoms or conditions which suggest that change is required with staff (includes environmental scan of demographics, economics, sociopolitical issues, and legal concerns).
2. Conduct an assessment of current department policy.
3. Establish an office of management review and equal opportunity and establish its goals and objectives.
4. Designate a "champion" or "change agent" to implement the program during the transition phase (preferably from the command ranks).
5. Develop action plans for each aspect of the strategic and implementation plans, which includes timelines, budget, and accountability.
6. Meet with all concerned groups and convey his or her vision, philosophy, goals, and timetables pertaining to promotions of minorities.

Most police executives will need to consult personnel department and legal experts for guidance on affirmative action promotion issues.

Quotas and Compliance

In some communities, federal judiciary oversight of law enforcement hiring and promotional practices has been the catalyst for the removal of selection criteria that operated to exclude minorities and women. Federal court decisions required that obvious disparate hiring and promotions practices (in the private and public sectors) be eliminated. Police departments now must prove that a selection procedure can be "scientifically linked" to job performance, and if not, they must restructure the selection process. For example, tangible evidence of job-related competence, such as the ability to handcuff, has been tested in some agencies through the use of a handcuffing simulation machine that requires a scientifically established amount of upper body strength to operate.

City and county affirmative action plans have played a significant role in police employment trends in agencies across the nation. In the 50 largest United States cities, nearly two-thirds (63.8 percent) of the police or sheriffs' departments reported operating under an affirmative action plan at some point between the dates surveyed, 1983 and 1988. Twenty-three of those plans were court ordered, and seven were voluntary (Walker, 1989). There are many police departments operating under a consent decree lawsuit to hire and/or promote more minorities. Therefore, while quotas are technically prohibited, in effect they are required, which makes compliance very difficult. Police executives and personnel department officials have been slow in designing procedures to meet the judicial standards being set. There have been difficulties in determining exactly what directions the court wanted followed because the judiciary applied different legal reasoning to the various civil rights, hiring, and promotions cases. Many persons confuse affirmative action with quotas—the terms are not synonymous.

Another source of compliance is the requirement of the federal government that to do business with them, the entity must have an affirmative action plan and be an affirmative action employer. Virtually all cities and counties (the private sector as well) must therefore have annual affirmative action plans (usually part of a five-year plan). These plans, submitted to the government, are in the form of numerical goals and timetables for increasing the employment of women and minorities within the agency.

Other forces for changes or improvement in affirmative hiring and promotions have been elected minority officials. There appears to be a direct correlation between the hiring and promotions of minorities and the level of political influence and pressure from the minority community and minority political officials.

REVERSE DISCRIMINATION ISSUES

There is often frustration and anger by some employees who perceive hiring and promotions of minorities as preferential treatment or reverse discrimination. This is especially true in law enforcement agencies, where, typically, the employees tend to be highly competitive and place great importance on the concept of merit.

The Merit System

The resistance to affirmative action is often due to the belief, even by some police executives, that only a true merit system produces a professional police force (Moran, 1988). They argue that the merit system is fair and effective, produces the best and brightest candidates, and does not discriminate. A system that involves the rank ordering of individuals based on combined scores on tests results in one list, with the scores sequenced from best to worst.

There has been, however, major debate and controversy over the validity of the traditional, standardized written tests used for hiring and promotions of persons in the private and public sectors. According to minority advocates and some scholars, even overtly equal procedures have covert unequal impact. They maintain that there is a reason for the statistical differences between the average performance of whites, blacks, and Hispanics on such written tests. They say that the tests are "racially unfair" in that they are based on culture, experiences, values, and education of white males. T. Kenneth Moran, a professor of criminal justice at John Jay College in New York, lists additional arguments against merit exams and ranking (Moran, 1988):

- With the exception of low-level skills, this type of hiring cannot meet the legal standard of job relatedness.
- To date, no police recruit exam has withstood the job-related test when the rank ordering of the scores is related to a rank ordering of field performance.
- Rank ordering of test scores as an employment device has proven to be unreliable for all persons.
- "Contrary to popular belief, the likelihood that scores on any particular aptitude test will correlate significantly with performance on any particular job is very slim indeed".

For several reasons, then, the "merit" system presents difficult issues for the law enforcement agency in general and for the minority candidate in particular. Does he or she think the promotion was because of having the best qualifications (merit) or because he or she is Asian, Hispanic, African American, or American Indian? Do nonminority co-workers stigmatize them as not worthy of the position, or allege reverse discrimination? Agencies doing affirmative hiring and promoting must address these difficult issues.

The use of quotas (or parity figures) to increase the percentage of jobs and promotions for minorities and women has had some negative results. For example, a number of white employees have seen opportunities go to competing applicants whose raw score ranking on written tests was lower than their own. How does one rationalize this to a nonminority, usually male, job applicant who perceives that the position was rightfully his? One minority deputy sheriff, hired by the Los Angeles Sheriff's Department, told an unsuccessful, white male applicant: "It is too bad that our [minority] misfortune (the lack of parity) has become your [male white] misfortune" (personal communication, Paul Harman, Lieutenant, Los Angeles Sheriff's Department, Jan. 7, 1992). Frankly, there is nothing more demoralizing to a workforce than a poorly administered affirmative action program.

There has been a massive backlash to affirmative action across the country. This was especially true during the early 1990s, when policies and practices were being questioned and tested in the courts and on the political front. There was widespread disagreement over what role traditional affirmative action policies should play. The debates became even more heated when President Bush vetoed the civil rights bill of 1990, which Congress had passed to redress discrimination in the workplace. Opponents said it would have set quotas for minority hiring. At about the same time, the U.S. Department of Education ruled that the practice of earmarking college scholarships specifically for minorities would not continue. The national mood on affirmative action made it difficult for companies and governments to adopt stringent affirmative action plans (*Contra Costa Times,* Dec. 30, 1990, p. A-1).

In 1993, just days before the start of a federal lawsuit filed by 48 white Dallas police officers, an out-of-court settlement was reached. The officers, both male and female, claimed that they were passed over for promotion in favor of black and Latino candidates as part of an unlawful quota system. In combined lawsuits filed between 1988 and 1990, the officers challenged an affirmative action plan adopted by the Dallas Police Department in 1988. At issue was the department's policy of "skip" or "out-of-sequence" promotions, in which higher-ranking white candidates on promotional lists were passed over in favor of lower-ranking black or Latino officers. The settlement (besides calling for the promotion, backpay, and seniority of many of those passed over) called for the city and the department to adopt what is termed "a standard error of measurement" as part of a revised affirmative action plan. This limits how far down on the list the city can skip to promote to meet an affirmative action goal. The police department also agreed to seven administrative changes that spell out the criteria for promoting out of sequence, defines a "promotional profile" used in weighing candidates, and provides an oral interview for candidates passed over in an out-of-sequence promotion. Court decisions have held that scores may not be adjusted based on race.

Law enforcement chief executives must anticipate a negative reaction on the part of their white employees when it appears that minorities and women are mainly the ones who are hired or promoted. As mentioned earlier, having a cultural affairs committee is highly valuable because its members are able to respond directly to this type of internal issue. The committee is charged with the task of providing information that will create a climate of understanding at all levels within the organization. Issues involving perceptions of reverse discrimination and preferential treatment cannot be avoided or ignored, and in fact, *should be addressed in advance to avoid a crisis.*

In a study reported in the *Washington Post* (1991), the Urban Institute concluded that the fear or claim of reverse discrimination in hiring is not necessarily supportable by facts in the private sector. Michael Fix, attorney and researcher at the Institute and primary author of this study, pointed out: "In general, the level of reverse discrimination that we found was limited, was certainly far lower than many might have been led to fear, and was swamped by the extent of discrimination against black job applicants. . . . These findings then refute, we believe, the notion that hiring practices for entry level jobs in these two cities either favor minorities or are color blind" (*Washington Post*, May 15, 1991, p. A-3). According to the 1990 census, blacks made up 10.6 percent of the U.S. civilian workforce but held only 6.3 percent of the executive, administrative, and managerial jobs (*Contra Costa Times*, Sept. 27, 1993, p. C-5). Based on a review of research mentioned earlier in this chapter, there appears to be a relationship between these private-sector findings and trends that have taken place in the public sector in the United States. Radelet (1986) suggests that if actions to strengthen affirmative hiring in law enforcement are not productive, there is a risk of "re-igniting the flames of violence—the communication of despair."

SUMMARY

Affirmative recruitment, hiring, and promotions will continue to be a law enforcement issue for the remainder of this century and into the next. Too many of the issues of equity and diversity have not been resolved in the law enforcement workplace, by the courts, or even in the congressional or executive branches of the U.S. government. The number of persons available and qualified for entry-level jobs will be smaller than it is today; more employers, both public and private, will be vying for the best.

With changes in the hiring, screening, and promotional policies and practices of law enforcement agencies come an unprecedented opportunity to build a future in which differences are valued and respected in our communities and our workforces. The progressive law enforcement executive must strive to secure the best qualified persons, including minorities and women, to serve the public. To do so, he or she must not only be committed to the challenges of affirmative hiring but must be capable of educating and selling his or her workforce on the legitimate reasons, both legal and ethical, for such efforts. In this chapter we presented effective strategies to implement changes and successful programs of recruitment and promotions of minorities. Law enforcement will have to use innovative and sophisticated marketing techniques and advertising campaigns to reach the population of desired potential applicants. It should be remembered by both community and law enforcement that serving multicultural/racial neighborhoods can never *solely* be the responsibility of minority employees in law enforcement agencies. In most jurisdictions, their limited numbers make this unrealistic. All staff should be prepared to understand and relate to diverse groups in a professional and sensitive manner, whether the persons contacted be responsibles, victims or witnesses.

While contributing to better police–minority community relations, improvement in protected class representation in law enforcement and other criminal justice professions, will not in and of itself resolve misunderstandings. The increased numbers of minority staff provide only the possibility of improved dialogue, cooperation, and problem solving both within an organization and with those whom the organization serves.

DISCUSSION QUESTIONS AND ISSUES*

1. *Institutional Racism in Law Enforcement.* Law enforcement agencies typically operate under the pretense that all its members are one color; that the uniform or job makes everyone brothers or sisters. Many minorities, particularly African American, do not agree that they are always treated with respect and that there is institutional racism in law enforcement. Caucasians clearly dominate the command ranks of law enforcement agencies. Discuss if you or class members believe that this disparity is the result of subtle forms of institutional racism or actual conscious efforts on the part of the persons empowered to make decisions? Consider whether tests and promotional processes unfairly give an advantage to white applicants' inherent attributes and whether they discriminate against ethnic/racial minorities. Do ethnic/racial minority officers discriminate against other minorities from different cultures?

2. *What Promotional Practices Will Be Used by the Year 2000/2005/2010?* Will seniority and "time in grade" promotional systems be a practice of the past? Will there be more lateral movement allowed between police department's command staff in the future?

3. *What Is the Impact of Ethnic/Racial Minority Chiefs/Sheriffs on Police Practices?* Do minority chief executives create significant change in the racial composition of the department at all levels and alter official policy? Does a good ethnic/racial mix of employees within a law enforcement organization have any effect on the informal police subculture and in turn affect police performance?

4. *Minority Employment and Police Practices.* What has been the impact of minority employment on police practices in your city or county? Is there evidence that significant change in the ethnic/racial composition of the department alter official police policy? Can the same be said of gay and lesbian employment? Does employment of protected classes have any significant effect on the informal police subculture and, in turn, affect police performance? Provide examples to support your conclusions.

5. *Marketing a Law Enforcement Career.* What approaches can the law enforcement recruiter use to market a career at his or her agency? How can the recruiter involve the entire staff of the department in the marketing program? What steps could be employed to improve the image of the agency? How can schools be involved early in marketing/recruiting efforts?

REFERENCES

BOWERS, GORDON A. (1990). "Avoiding the recruitment crisis," *Journal of California Law Enforcement,* Vol. 24, No. 2, p. 64.

CETRON, MARVIN J., WANDA ROCHA, AND REBECCA LUCK-INS (1988). "Into the 21st century: long-term trends affecting the United States," *The Futurist,* July/Aug. p. 64.

DETTWEILER, JOSH (1993). "Women and minorities in professional training programs: the ins and outs of higher education," *Cultural Diversity at Work,* Vol. 6, No. 1, Sept., p. 3.

GOLDSTEIN, HERMAN (1977). *Policing a Free Society,* U.S. Dept. of Justice Law Enforcement Assistance Administration, Washington, DC, Chapter 10.

GUYOT, DOROTHY (1977). "Bending granite: attempts to change the rank structure of American police departments," *Journal of Police Science and Administration,* Vol. 3, pp. 253–284.

LANHAM, MICHAEL (1993). *Achieving Ethnic Diversity in the Police Command Ranks by the Year 2001,* Command College Class XV, Peace Officer Standards and Training, Sacramento Calif., Jan.

*See Instructor's Manual accompanying this text for additional activities, role-plays, questionnaires and projects related to the content of this chapter.

MICARI, MARINA (1993). "Recruiters of minorities and women speak out: why companies lose candidates," *Cultural Diversity at Work,* Vol. 6, No. 1, Sept., p. 1.

MORAN, T. KENNETH (1988). "Pathways toward a nondiscriminatory recruitment policy," *Journal of Police Science and Administration,* Vol. 16, No. 4.

RADELET, LOUIS A. (1986). *The Police and the Community,* 4th ed., Macmillan, New York, p. 214.

SAULS, JOHN GALES (1991)."Employment discrimination: a Title VII primer," *FBI Law Enforcement Bulletin,* Dec., p. 23.

WALKER, SAMUEL J. (1989). *Employment of Black and Hispanic Police Officers 1983–1988: A Follow-Up Study,* Occasional Paper 89-1, Center for Applied Urban Research, University of Nebraska, Omaha, Neb.

None given (1993). "Don't bang that gavel! Dallas reverse-bias suit settled before trial," *Law Enforcement News,* Vol. 19, No. 379, Apr. 30, p. 7.

PART TWO

Training in Cultural Understanding for Law Enforcement

4 PREPARATION AND IMPLEMENTATION OF CULTURAL AWARENESS TRAINING
5 CROSS-CULTURAL COMMUNICATION FOR LAW ENFORCEMENT

In Part Two readers are presented with information on multiple aspects of cultural awareness training and cross-cultural communication in law enforcement. Chapter 4 is of particular significance to police executives and managers and to officers who are also instructors in cultural awareness/diversity programs. The chapter provides examples of successful police training program designs and methods and outlines several specific city, county and state models and lists guidelines for chief executives, trainers and officers. We list assumptions related to officer resistance that need to be explored in any cultural awareness training program for law enforcement. Information on the selection of external consultants is provided, along with key training phases and issues that cultural awareness curriculum should encompass. We emphasize the role of the chief executive who must demonstrate strong support for the training and develop action plans, in addition to implementing courses. The chapter summary includes a review of suggestions for the cultural awareness instructor as well as for the training participant.

Chapter 5 provides practical information highlighting the dynamics of cross cultural communication in law enforcement. We present typical styles of communication that people sometimes display when they are uncomfortable with cross-cultural contact. The chapter includes a discussion of the special problems involved when officers must communicate with citizens who are limited English speakers. In addition, it emphasizes sensitivity to nonverbal differences across cultures and to some of the communication issues that arise between men and women in the law enforcement agency. Skills and techniques for officers to apply in situations of cross-cultural contact are presented.

The following appendices correspond to the chapters content in Part Two:

4

PREPARATION AND IMPLEMENTATION OF CULTURAL AWARENESS TRAINING

OVERVIEW

Every human resource development program for those in the criminal justice system should have a substantial component that deals with culture and its impact on human behavior, both lawful and deviant. In this chapter we describe assumptions about cross-cultural understanding that must be examined before cultural awareness training can be effective. We then present designs, and methods of cultural awareness training for police officers. In this chapter specific city, county and state models are outlined, as are guidelines for chief executives, trainers, and officers. Information is included on the selection of cultural awareness trainers and instructors.

COMMENTARY

The importance of cultural awareness training for law enforcement employees is evident from the following quotations:

> California Attorney General's Commission on Racial, Ethnic, Religious and Minority Violence, *Final Report,* Apr. 1986, p. 51.
>
> Law enforcement officials, police officers, and prosecutors are essential in efforts to respond to and prevent hate violence but, often they are not trained to handle situations involving violence motivated by bigotry. Lack of training produces inadequate and inappropriate responses that exacerbate community tensions. *Law enforcement basic academies, field training programs, and advanced officer and*

management courses should include training on cultural differences and hate crimes.
[emphasis added]

"Law enforcement in a culturally diverse society," by Gary Weaver, *FBI Law Enforcement Bulletin,* Sept. 1992, p. 2.

Law enforcement professionals need to develop *cultural empathy*. They need to put themselves in other people's cultural shoes to understand what motivates their behavior. By understanding internal cultures, they can usually explain why situations develop the way they do. And if they know their own internal cultures, they also know the reasons behind their reactions and realize why they may feel out of control. Law enforcement officers should remember that racial and cultural perceptions affect attitudes and motivate behavior.

"The need for human relations training in law enforcement," by Gary Kusunoki and Hector Rivera, *The Police Chief,* July 1985, p. 32.

The "police subculture" has a tendency to be very opinionated and sometimes prejudicial in its dealings with others. This prejudice is often subconsciously directed at anyone who is not a "cop." The goal of any human relations training should be to raise the police department's awareness of the needs of its particular community as a whole, encompassing the needs of the minority and ethnic community.

"Police chiefs examine new training, policy," *Los Angeles Times,* May 3, 1992, p. B-7.

Many Southern California police chiefs, expressing disbelief at the Rodney G. King verdicts, say they will diligently move forward with sensitivity training and community outreach programs that have been cornerstones of reform since the case erupted 14 months ago.... As a result, many organizations have turned to new training techniques, scrutinized policies for reviewing brutality complaints and encouraged officers to loosen up and build stronger bridges to neighborhoods....

"Learning to manage a multicultural workforce," by Lennie Copeland, *California Police Recorder,* Jan. 1990, p. 16.

Diversity is emerging as one of the most serious issues in the workplace today, yet most employers are not prepared to deal with it, nor are their managers. Many managers grew up having little contact with other cultures. They are actually "culturally deprived," and their graduate school texts did not cover the kinds of situations that arise in today's multicultural settings.

INTRODUCTION

Throughout our nation's history, ethnic and racial minority groups and government have clashed; periodically, violence accompanied these clashes (as we witnessed in the late 1960s, early 1970s and in 1992). The public, scholars, and independent study commissions paid considerable attention to the causes of the strife, and much of the focus centered on law enforcement procedures and training. Some agencies reacted by implementing or revising community and human relations training; a few instituted "sensitivity" classes using outside facilitators. It appears, however, that law enforcement did not accomplish much more than that, especially following those earlier conflict years. The emphasis on community relations skills in law enforcement academies and in-service courses never materialized to any great degree. Many promising programs soon faded, giving the mistaken impression that such training was no longer needed.

Private organizations, governmental agencies, textbooks, and educators/trainers use various terms to describe such training: *human relations, cultural diversity, cultural awareness,* and *sensitivity* training. *Community relations* training traditionally provided for many law enforcement officers in academies or in-service courses since the 1970s has some similarities to the cultural awareness training that is taking place today. *Police community–relations* is "The process of developing and maintaining meaningful, two-way communications between the agency and specific populations served toward identifying, defining, and resolving problems of mutual concern" (Mayhall, 1985). Community relations is therefore, the process by which community members and police *work together* to identify and resolve problems that have caused or might cause difficulties between them. *Public relations* would include all activities engaged in by the police to develop or maintain a favorable public image.

Human relations is a rather ambiguous term applying to the interaction of people. It can mean everything from a study of organizational behavior and productivity of its employees, to the positive relationship skills an officer uses to provide services to the community. Human relations is an all-encompassing term and includes cross-cultural and race relations.

The term *sensitivity training,* used during the 1970s, had a negative sound for many law enforcement practitioners. Some officers resented and criticized what they referred to as "touchy-feely" training. Even some supervisors, managers, and instructors did not take the training seriously. The nature of the training was delicate and officers were unaccustomed to being confronted with police–minority group issues. They were uncomfortable dealing with issues of bias, prejudice, and/or racism. Officers, whose primary training and "bag of tools" was law enforcement (laws and procedures) and officer safety (crime fighter methods), were being exposed to human relations and sensitivity skills that made many uneasy. They were particularly uncomfortable discussing their own feelings and attitudes regarding those issues. David Barlow, on the faculty in the criminal justice program at the University of Wisconsin–Milwaukee, observed that the key buzzword, *sensitivity,* alienated officers in those 1970s courses and made them defensive. He elaborated: "'Sensitivity' is inherently accusatory, because the assumption is that officers are insensitive. The very concept of sensitivity runs counter to the image which many police officers hold of their role in society—as enforcers of the law. Police officers generally do not respond well to courses designed to give special treatment to minority cultures or to promote affirmative action" (Barlow, 1992).

Barlow explained that officers maintain that their job is to enforce the law uniformly and that, in their perception, they do so without regard to race, religion, ethnic background, sexual orientation, age, disability, or gender. For this reason it is important that the focus of training not be on any one group. Cultural awareness training must be presented as a universal issue that provides officers with skills to deal more effectively with all segments of the population that he or she serves.

Discrimination, violence, and prejudice still confront minority populations, sometimes at the hands of the police. Few law enforcement professionals today would dispute the important role that training plays in improving relationships between police officers and the community. The education of law enforcement officers is a vital component of any training approach that aims to reduce incidents of hate and bias toward an increasing and large ethnic and racial population. The education and training must start with understanding people, their culture, religion, race, and lifestyle, which is key to comprehending human behavior. Today in our multicultural society, cultural understanding on the part of the officer contributes to police professionalism. Law enforcement practitioners must embrace the idea that to be a professional, they need to understand and appreciate the diversity in their communities.

CULTURAL AWARENESS/CULTURAL DIVERSITY TRAINING

What Is Cultural Awareness? Assumptions and Resistance

Cultural awareness is the understanding that an individual has about different cultures. The term is often expanded to include race, religion, gender, age, physical disability, and gay/lesbian issues. We use the terms *cultural awareness* and *cultural diversity* interchangeably.

In terms of officers' receptivity to cultural awareness training, a number of assumptions and areas of resistance must be explored. The instructor must understand that he or she will encounter resistance to the training by some course participants. Gary Weaver, a professor of international and intercultural communications in the School of International Service at the American University, Washington, D.C., indicates that four assumptions, in particular, should be given consideration in order for the instructor to understand the law enforcement students mindset (Weaver, 1975).

Assumption 1: As society and the workforce become more diverse, differences become less important. Weaver maintains that simply mixing people will not cause conflict to disappear or resolve misunderstandings. Quite the contrary: as differences become more apparent, hostilities can actually increase between culturally diverse persons and groups. Individuals who associate only with those who share the same basic values, beliefs, and behaviors take their culture for granted. When those persons interact with people from different cultures, they see contrasts and make comparisons and therefore become more aware of their own culture. The best way to learn about other cultures therefore, is to leave your own and enter another. Some police cultural awareness training programs require recruits or veteran officers to spend time with members of minority communities in their environment. Two agencies with these types of programs are the Fresno, California Police Department and the San Bernardino County, California Sheriff's Department.

Assumption 2: "We're all the same" in the American melting pot. Weaver postulates that the notion that "we are all the same" is a spin-off of the "melting pot" hypothesis, or myth, as Weaver calls it. Those offering this hypothesis (also discussed in Chapter 1) would argue that America is a nation of immigrants who came from all parts of the world and threw their culture into the American melting pot. By doing so, and through their own individual efforts, they advanced economically. However, Weaver and others argue that, unfortunately, the notion is exaggerated, as "all cultures did not melt into the pot equally."

> What many immigrants found could be described as a cultural cookie cutter—a white, male, Protestant, Anglo-Saxon mold. Those who could fit in the mold more easily advanced in the socioeconomic system. The Irish, Italians, and Poles could get rid of their accents, change their names, and blend into the dominant white community. But, African Americans, American Indians, and Latinos couldn't change the color of their skin or the texture of their hair to fit the mold. They were identifiably different (Weaver, 1975).

Weaver also tells us:

> Along these same lines, all cultural, racial, and gender differences do not disappear when someone dons a uniform. Even though law enforcement asserts that everyone is the same when wearing blue, it becomes practically impossible to deny the diversity that shows itself in the ranks. *What law enforcement needs to do is to accept and to manage this diversity.* In the long run, this only strengthens law enforcement organizations. [emphasis added]

An African American Virginia state trooper described how when he was assigned to a coal miners strike in southwest Virginia, all the coal miners could pick him out because he was the only black trooper there. He also told of difficulties assimilating in society and within the law enforcement workplace because of his color (personal communication, W. Thomas Hall, Virginia State Trooper, Sept. 29, 1992). In Alameda, California, a black police officer told of his frustration when a citizen called his dispatcher saying that a police car had been stolen because a black was driving it. He was in uniform at the time.

Assumption 3: It's just a matter of communication and common sense. According to Weaver, 90 percent of the messages that people send are not communicated verbally, but by posture, facial expressions, gestures, eye contact, or lack thereof. Examples would include misinterpretation of the lack of eye contact; the reaction by some cultures to gesturing with the palm or fingers up; and the lack of facial expression, giving the appearance of being uncooperative or uncaring. These nonverbal messages can be very different across cultures. Nonverbal communication is not taught in any culture. Therefore, how are people of different cultures suppose to understand each other, especially police officers? It is not just a matter of communication or using common sense when interacting with people from different cultures!

Assumption 4: Conflict is conflict, regardless of the culture. Among members of certain ethnic groups, words and gestures are sometimes for effect and not intent. In some cultures, inflammatory or "fighting" words are used to get attention and communicate feeling, whereas in the mainstream American culture, the actions and words would demonstrate a threat (examples are provided in Chapters 5 and 7). Police officers must understand these differences in order to be effective in their interactions with persons of other cultures and races. Understanding different emotional styles across cultures, particularly in conflict situations, can help an officer know how to defuse tension and confrontation.

As society and the law enforcement workforce become more diverse, the ability to manage cultural diversity becomes essential. The law enforcement community needs to weave cross-cultural awareness into all aspects of training.

Why Cultural Awareness Training?

An overview. At no time has the need for cultural understanding and ethnic/race relations been more important than as we complete the twentieth century and enter the next. Media headlines during the late 1980s and 1990s have continually showed that racism, hate violence, community tensions and conflict are on the rise in the United States. There has been an increased demand for improved police–community relations from the public and from government. The problem can no longer be ignored or be addressed in a haphazard, short-term, or unilateral basis. Incidents originally simple in nature cannot be allowed to escalate because of ethnic/racial or cultural misunderstanding or hostility. It is no longer a matter of agencies doing the minimum to protect themselves and reduce liability exposure. It is time for all law enforcement employees to work with and understand the pluralistic society they serve. The broad goals of cultural awareness training contribute to this understanding. In a successful training program, officers learn about:

- Various cultures and subcultures and become more effective in providing services to all "customers"
- The impact of diversity on interdependent relationships and develop skills for communicating with those who are different
- The ramifications of demographic and sociological changes on law enforcement
- The influence of perceptions, culture, and prejudices on behavior
- Public and private agencies that provide assistance to members of the community, such as immigrants
- The reduction of citizen complaints, lawsuits, agency–customer friction, negative media, and liability
- Officer safety skills
- Conflict resolution techniques
- Cross-cultural knowledge and skills as part of "real police work"

Cultural awareness training will effectively prepare academy students and officers to confront sensitive issues and interact more positively with fellow officers and the people they serve. For example, a police supervisor in a records bureau, excited about the productivity of one of his Vietnamese office clerks, acknowledged her and thanked her profusely in front of her co-workers. He assumed that she would appreciate his overt praise. In fact, she felt that he overdid it as he went on and on with his compliments. She was so uncomfortable with the attention, that she called in sick for one day. She later confided that she felt that her peers would think that she was trying to rise up faster in the organization than they were. Her main concerns had to do with breaking harmony in her interpersonal relations with her co-workers. Another example involved an officer working a case involving a female Middle Eastern crime victim. The officer continually patted the victim on the back and placed his arm around the victim, intending to demonstrate sensitivity and empathy just as he was taught in recruit school. The Arab female hated being touched and became distant and uncooperative. No strange male in her culture would ever touch her. Thus, in these examples, the "standard" ways of motivating and showing concern were counterproductive in these cross-cultural interactions.

The complex problems arising in diverse neighborhoods where officers work also demand that they think differently about their law enforcement role. Officers must understand the importance of their role as sensitive and caring agents of the people they serve, not just as "crime fighters" who travel from one call to another. (Police officer role and image are discussed further in Chapter 15). The ultimate goal of cultural awareness training is to have law enforcement personnel become more comfortable with diverse ethnicities, races, religions, and cultures different from themselves. With increased comfort on the part of the officer comes the ability to establish rapport and help put other people at ease. Each improved interaction with citizens slowly leads to overall improved police-community relations. Further, cross-cultural communication skills enhance officer safety. Knowledge of words, gestures, and labels offensive to particular groups is the first step to controlling one's use of them. Responding positively to an individual's cultural style of communicating and knowing not to imitate that style (discussed further in Chapter 5) can contribute to the successful defusing of potential confrontation. The application of cultural knowledge on the streets must be treated as "real police work."

Perspective.   In the early 1990s, there was a dramatic increase in the range of courses and training materials developed by public agencies (including criminal justice) and private organizations and individuals addressing race relations, diversity in the workforce and community, prejudice, and discrimination. Now a wide variety of courses are taught on these subjects in each state. Although many such training courses had already been in place, some organizations turned to new training techniques as a result of widespread antipolice sentiment in the wake of the Rodney King case. The government, communities, and the criminal justice system viewed the King episode as a catalyst for improvements in law enforcement training. Similar events during the 1980s in Metro–Dade County Florida, Philadelphia, Washington, D.C., and New York City were also driving forces for change.

In many U.S. cities, agencies scrutinized their policies and procedures following the King case and similar police–related incidents. Departments modified how brutality complaints were handled and tightened up supervision of their officers. Some agencies encouraged their officers to "loosen up" and build stronger bridges to the neighborhoods—a task compatible with a community-policing philosophy. Other agencies introduced their officers to "verbal Judo" (George J. Thompson, president of the Verbal Judo Institute in Albuquerque, New Mexico, 1-800/448-1042; for more details on verbal judo, refer to Chapter 5) and other methods of communication leading to nonconfrontational ways of handling escalating situations. Some departments have experimented with the installation of videocameras in patrol cars, intended to protect both the officers and the people pulled over. Other agencies installed cameras in areas of their departments, such as in booking rooms, jails, and interview rooms, where suspect and officer contacts were potentially violent. However, as indicated previously, most agencies turned to a re-examination of police training with the goal in mind of restoring public confidence in law enforcement and improving the morale of officers.

The June 1988 issue of *Crime Control Digest* contained a study that found that "training is the best way to reduce police–citizen violence." The Police Foundation in 1989 completed a study on police training and also concluded that courses can reduce the possibility of confrontation for police officers. According to this study, the right training improves an officer's ability to defuse possible violence. Cultural awareness training contains components that deal directly with face-to-face interaction with citizens and therefore can be linked to conflict resolution training. The importance of training, as stressed in a number of studies, should be a call to action by police executives, training certification commissions, and legislatures in every state.

The Metro-Dade Police–Citizen Violence Reduction Project which began in 1987, was a joint effort between the Metro-Dade Police Department in Dade County and the Police Foundation. Its purpose was to discover ways to increase an officer's ability to minimize violence and the need to use force. The study involved one group of officers receiving three days of interactive classroom and scenario training to increase and improve their interpersonal relationship skills, emphasizing methods of defusing and managing hostility and potential violence. A control group of officers received no special training. The results of the study showed that the trained officers handled potentially violent encounters with citizens significantly better than the control group. They found that when officers have several possible courses of action in a volatile situation, they rely less on the use of force and arrest. The interpersonal skills taught in the above-mentioned program include communications (verbal and nonverbal), police–community relations, and intercultural awareness. Jan Torres, vice president of human resources for Inter-American Management Consulting Corporation in Miami, Florida, states:

> The abilities to speak without seeming to attack, to listen effectively and non-defensively, and to analyze non-verbal behavior accurately are important for police officers. They increase an officer's chance of calming a situation. Officers who are aware of the interdependent relationship between law enforcement and the community are usually more successful in dealing with difficult people. Good police-community relations occurs when police get to know their area and people with the community [community-oriented policing]. Knowledge of other cultures in the community is necessary to understand the behavior of citizens from these cultures. An officer needs to be aware of the impact that biases and prejudices have upon their own and others' behaviors (Torres, 1989).

Proper training can increase an officer's ability to reduce tensions in his or her interactions with citizens. The responsibility for providing such training belongs to everyone involved in police training.

It is not clear which training approaches are most effective, if effective at all, or if some are even counterproductive. Some training programs in the private and public sectors have been conducted by confrontational trainers who accuse employees of bigotry or pit them against each other on issues or discussions of stereotypes. Some executives, both private and public, have hired diversity trainers thinking that training sessions alone are adequate. Neither training nor education is a panacea for correcting the ills that exist within society or law enforcement. Training is only a part of what should be a holistic approach to problem solving. Too often, when a police officer has deviated from acceptable behavior, training is blamed or is used to "correct" the problem. Effective supervision and management is also an integral part of providing direction and exerting control over employees. There are limits as to what training can achieve; even less can be accomplished if objectives and approaches of a training program are not integrated with the values, philosophy, and mission of the law enforcement organization.

Cultural training for the criminal justice community (especially peace officers) can be informative, interesting, and pragmatic. The case for including cultural training as part of their professional development can be summed up best in the following quote from Weaver (1992):

> Because of naive assumptions, the criminal justice community seldom views cross-cultural awareness and training as vital. Yet, as society and the law enforcement workforce become more diverse, the ability to manage cultural diversity becomes essential. Those agencies that do not proactively develop cultural knowledge and skills fail to serve the needs of their communities. More importantly, however, they lose the opportunity to increase the effectiveness of their officers. Unfortunately, cross-cultural training in law enforcement often occurs after an incident involving cross-cultural conflict takes place. If provided, this training can be characterized as a quick fix, a once-in-a-lifetime happening, when in reality it should be an ongoing process of developing awareness, knowledge, and skills. (p. 6)

Cultural awareness and diversity training must be ongoing and interwoven into the fabric of every agency training venture, but especially in the basic academy program. Large law enforcement agencies with in-house training staff and training academies must increase the number of female and ethnic/racial minority trainers. Agencies that use qualified females and minorities as trainers in teaching defensive tactics, pursuit driving, physical fitness and firearms courses, to name a few, can do much to change attitudes positively within the white male–dominated law enforcement culture.

What is to be gained by an organization that introduces cultural awareness training? David Tullin, president of Tullin DiversiTeam Associates, has identified 24 reasons for making such a human resources development investment. Those that have particular significance for law enforcement agencies include:

- More problems are solved as cooperation increases and law suits decrease.
- The working environment becomes more positive and safer with less conflict.
- Managers become more effective in leading a diverse workforce thus allowing them to focus on other activities.
- Employees become more tolerant and motivated as morale improves.

- Performance becomes the focus of success, and more suitable job assignments and evaluations result.
- Client or community relations improve as more information is shared.
- Personnel become more committed to professional growth, while better mentoring/coaching emphasizes potential and performance.

DESIGN AND EVALUATION OF CULTURAL TRAINING

To be most effective, cultural awareness training must be agency and community specific and must encompass all aspects of multicultural relations, both internal and external to the organization.

Agency- and Community-Specific

Joyce St. George, a cultural awareness trainer, in a 1991 article advocated that course design must:

- **Be multidimensional.** Students must learn via such courses to assess what he or she encounters from several perspectives: organizational, community, and legal, to allow the totality of the circumstances encountered to be considered.
- **Be relevant.** Training programs must be structured to satisfy the specific interests and needs of the audience and the community. Needs, goals, demographic and cultural information, and issues participants currently face should be specific to the training audience.
- **Be behavior-based.** The course should focus on how the student expresses their attitudes through their actions and behaviors, which are governable and can be legally and departmentally controlled.
- **Be empathetic.** The program must ask the student to empathize with the feelings and concerns of minority community members, but it should also address the feelings and concerns of the student(s).
- **Be practical.** Programs must offer officers practical ways to assess and confront human dynamics—the tools that he or she will need to handle persons from diverse backgrounds and lifestyles.
- **Allow for controversy.** Courses on such topics often stir up controversy from the students. The program design must allow students to question openly the materials presented, especially if they are being asked to evaluate their own beliefs and behavior.
- **Be experiential.** The use of exercises (role-playing, game playing, etc.) in a controlled workshop environment is important. It is a training medium that allows the student time to practice and/or refine their communication, conflict management and confrontation skills. Participants practice using the cultural specific information that he or she has received while following appropriate officer safety procedures.
- **Provide follow-up supports.** Organizations should implement follow-up training on an ongoing basis through briefings and the like.
- **Identify potentially hostile employees.** Trainers conducting these programs should identify employees who are aggressive and or adversarial toward members of the diverse community. Employees who might be a threat to good community relations should be identified. They should receive additional training and/or be made aware of the potential for discipline if their behavior is unacceptable.

Frum Himelfarb, of the training research section of the Royal Canadian Mounted Police, Ottawa, Ontario, Canada, identified six key principles of the role of training in promoting policing in a manner that is culturally sensitive and responsive (Himelfarb, 1991):

1. Respect for and sensitivity to the diverse communities served is essential for effective policing.
2. Respect for and sensitivity to ethnocultural communities can best be achieved through a broad-based multicultural strategy.
3. Training must be an essential element of such a strategy.
4. Training must be ongoing and built into the experience of policing; that is, it must be more than a course or two on multiculuralism.
5. A multicultural strategy and the training that supports it will be most effective if they are perceived to be integrated aspects of the philosophy and operations of policing.
6. A multicultural strategy and training program must be created in consultation with the ethnocultural communities served by the police.

Training with respect to multicultural policing should be a continuous and natural extension of community policing.

Training Delivery Methods

The cultural awareness instructor or facilitator should utilize a mixture of teaching approaches and strategies, such as combining lectures (academics) with skills development and self-appraisal techniques (simulations, role-playing, group exercises). The following is an overview of delivery methods and includes sample topics.

Lectures. Lecturettes and discussions on subjects (sandwiched between role-playing, simulations, and group exercises) would include:

1. Examination of diversity, including definitions and relevance to police–community relations.
2. *Local demographics.* The instructor should develop information about the audience's community in terms of local demographics and the trends or changes taking place. Sources of such information are:
   (a) City and county departments
   (b) Housing authorities and schools
   (c) State and federal census material
   (d) Refugee resettlement or service organizations
   (e) Community-based organizations and advocates
3. *The police subculture and role.* The police subculture should be discussed in terms of its existence (what it is) and how it affects behavior and image, both internal and external to the organization. The role of the police should be discussed as it pertains to the crime fighter image versus service provider.
4. Communication skills.

   (a) Knowledge of personal communication styles
   (b) Active listening skills
   (c) Verbal and nonverbal communications
   (d) Noncombative communications

    (e) Cultural specific information related to communications: differences; "in-group privileges" (i.e., communication that would be inappropriate if used by others)

    (f) Cultural influenced styles of communications

  5. How perceptions are developed/shaped.

    (a) Past experiences: positive/negative

    (b) Maturity/age

    (c) Gender: male/female role; behavior expectations; emotions

    (d) Mental condition

    (e) Emotional involvement

    (f) Race, cultural, and ethnic background; experiences are different

    (g) Values from parents, peers, and religious institutions

    (h) Prejudice, biases, and assumptions

  6. Personal prejudices and biases.

The instructor should not rely on lectures alone, as they do not involve the student, and the information from lectures often does not leave a lasting impression.

    Role-playing. Develop vignettes or scenarios to reinforce cultural awareness and diversity lectures. Role-playing should emphasize skills of communication while stressing officer safety practices and procedures.

- Role-playing is intended to create a realistic environment for participants.
- Role players must be trained and monitored during the exercises so that the learning objectives are achieved.

    An example of role-playing is based on experiences of the San Jose, California Police Department. Officers learned the hard way that cultural differences can produce dangerous situations for themselves and citizens. When the SJPD made felony arrests, they followed departmental training in placing the suspect in a kneeling position with his or her back turned to the officer, hands clasped behind the head. For some Southeast Asians, this position of arrest brought back frightening memories of the position used for executions performed by police in Vietnam. Some Southeast Asian suspects would flee or become overly anxious, causing police to draw their weapons. The SJPD modified their felony arrest position not only to maintain their safety but also to take into account the fears of some suspects. Another role-playing situation could involve an officer modifying his or her English so as to be able to communicate with limited English speakers.

    Simulations. The purpose of interactive experience (simulations) is that the participants are involved in a process of identifying their own attitudes and feelings and thereby also achieve a better understanding of others. Some of the game examples that follow should be attempted only by a skilled and experienced facilitator. Four examples of games are:

1. "Star-Power"—a role-reversal simulation commercially available from Simile II, P.O. Box 910, Del Mar, CA, 1-800/942-2900. The game stresses how power or lack of power influences behavior and feelings.

2. "Eye of the Storm"/"Brown Eyes–Blue Eyes"—a 25-minute/color/16mm film/videocassette/discussion guide available from the Anti-Defamation League. The material is from an ABC-TV News special on the effects of prejudice. The cameras record a unique two-day experiment conducted by a third-grade teacher in a midwest agricultural community. The teacher, on the first day, had separated her class into "superior" and "inferior" groups, based solely on eye color. Blue-eyed children were "superior," brown-eyed children were "inferior." On the second day the roles were reversed. Attitudes, behavior, and classroom performance were measurably changed as children suffered segregation, discrimination, and the effects of prejudice. The "Brown Eyes–Blue Eyes" simulation has been used successfully with adults.

3. "Inner/Outer Groups"*—two circles can be formed of different ethnic, racial, or gender groups (e.g., whites/Caucasians and blacks/African Americans; or Asian Americans, Hispanic Americans, Native Americans; or males/females, etc.). One group is placed on chairs in a center circle and given this assignment: "Discuss what you like as well as what you dislike about the other race or gender" (the directions can be modified to what you like/dislike about police officers of this type). . . . The other racial/ethnic/gender group is placed in a circle around the inner one and instructed: "You are observers—listen carefully to the oral communication, watch the body language, take notes, and be prepared to share what you have heard and seen." Using two columns for like/dislike, a facilitator may summarizes the opinions of each projector group on a blackboard, flipchart, or overhead projector sheet. After 10 minutes, the two groups switch places; the participants become observers while the former observers discuss the other group's strengths/weaknesses as they perceive them. Finally, after 10 more minutes, the facilitator invites both groups to form one large cluster, so each group may share how they felt, what they observed, and what they learned from the total experience. The facilitator closes the loop by reviewing the notes that he or she took on each group's perceptions of the other to clear up misunderstandings, to draw further learning, and to make larger applications.

4. "Diversophy"—a board game with dice, coins, and question cards that can be played by four to six players. The game was researched and jointly developed by Multus, Inc. and George Simons International (it may be ordered from 408/426-9608 or fax 408/457-8590). The game stimulates thought-provoking discussion, deals with critical attitudes, and teaches useful skills especially for the multicultural workforce. It is not personally threatening. Players confront facts about diversity, choose how to behave toward others, experience cross-cultural risks, and share personal experiences.

Work groups/presentations.

Small-group discussions properly planned, implemented, and controlled allow participants to discuss issues. For example, small groups are useful in encouraging par-

---

*This technique must only be used by an experienced facilitator or trainer who knows how to handle negative group dynamics. In addition, there must always be enough time to debrief this exercise. If time runs out before the postactivity discussion (i.e., the most important part), the instructor can create a hostile situation.

ticipants to discuss their own feelings of prejudice, anger, or stereotyping with openness. Small groups of people usually achieve a greater awareness and understanding of issues than do large groups, where many people feel inhibited.

Critical incidents/case studies. The training class or group is asked to clip and collect actual stories from newspapers or magazines that deal with racial/ethnic/gender/sexual orientation issues and conflict, especially related to police work. These are reproduced and circulated in advance so that trainees can read them and think about them. A group discussion is then held on the most critical incident(s) selected. Questions such as the following are asked: What are the implications, especially for the criminal justice system and in particular the police? How could this incident be prevented or managed more effectively? For example, then presidential candidate, Governor Bill Clinton, gave a speech at Jesse Jackson's Rainbow Coalition (June 1992). After praising the reconciliation efforts of the coalition, the Arkansas governor criticized rap singer Sister Souljah, in her presence, for the song lyrics concerning "taking a week to kill whites." In the *Los Angeles Times* follow-up story (June 17, 1992), the young singer replied that her words were misinterpreted out of context, adding:

> Any time an African man or woman takes a strong stand for the development and control of their own lives, white America has an insensitive and irrational reaction. America has a problem with African people, whether they are directing films, making records or controlling their own business.
>
> I am very familiar with police brutality. Police violence is a regular event in the black community. It's as regular as brushing your teeth. The police have a hostile attitude toward men in our community.

With an experienced facilitator (one with either the authority or ability to control and/or direct dialogue), a very informative discussion could center around such an incident to further cross-cultural learning.

Local culture video profiles/cross-cultural films. A police agency or the criminal justice department of a college/university might cooperate in the production of video training films. Those among the trainees or students who have access to a small video camcorder would be invited to prepare a short video recording on ethnic or minority groups in the local community. A team from the law enforcement agency or academy class might be formed to help the producer decide which aspects of that group's cultural life to present in a positive manner. (The instructor's manual for this book contains a cross-cultural relations inventory for peace officers which has categories that may be useful for this exercise.) Each video profile is then played to the training class, and a prize might be given to the best video "snapshot" of a community group. A similar strategy can be used with video recordings of other community subcultures, such as the neighborhood youth, the elderly, and the homeless. Law enforcement can also collaborate with local organizations in producing training videos, as did the Orange County, California Chiefs of Police and Sheriffs Association. They produced high-quality videos specifically on law enforcement contact with Vietnamese and Latino communities in that county. Information on the project may be obtained from the Orange County Human Relations Commission (1300 South

Grand, Building B, Santa Ana, CA 92705, 714/567-7470). Another example of an excellent cultural awareness film produced by the Fresno, CA Police Department is "A World of Difference," which addresses the issue of law enforcement contact with Southeast Asians. The Sacramento, CA Police Academy produced a series of vignettes that other training or video departments can produce for their Respective police departments. Each of six scenes shows a police department employee (whether officer, sergeant, lieutenant, captain, etc.) interacting with someone of a different background. Various degrees of racial/cultural jokes and slurs (both intentional and unintentional) are heard. Viewers are asked to comment on the interactions and to suggest what action steps should be taken.

Experiential assignments. Class participants are assigned to spend time in the minority community/neighborhood or work environment. For example, in east Los Angeles, a program entitled "Guess Who Is Coming to Dinner" involves veteran officers going to dinner in minority homes. In New York City, police academy recruit officers are assigned to attend cultural events and present reports to the class on their experiences and observations.

Interactive-computer video. Not available for cultural awareness subjects as of 1993 in any state, but probably the most innovative and futuristic method of training. Interactive computer video involves the student sitting at a laser disc computer which takes the participant through phases of training and tests understanding and retention. The student cannot progress through the course from one phase to another until he or she passes the tests on each phase. There is no need for an instructor to be present, and the training can therefore take place at any time.

Training Format

The following outline should be considered as a partial list of what must be accomplished before any training program can take place:

1. CEO/chief develops a mission statement incorporating his or her vision, values, and philosophy concerning police–community relations and cultural diversity awareness.
2. Research what and how other agencies and academies are teaching cultural awareness, including who the instructors are.
3. Appoint a cultural awareness training facilitator. He or she, with the approval of organization management, selects the cultural awareness trainers from within the organization/agency. The facilitator might also hire a cross-cultural communication specialist or consultant in the field of cultural awareness training from outside the organization.
4. Design, disseminate, and analyze training needs assessment survey form. Involve minority community representatives in design. (Appendix B contains examples of needs assessment forms.)
5. Select community-based organization representatives to become involved in cultural/racial specifics and police–minority/community relations topics. Get as much input as you can from them.
6. Develop and implement program using the following suggested format or phases.

First phase: The relationship between cultural awareness and police professionalism.   After an overview of topics are presented, the trainer provides (i.e., sells) the rational for such training. The objective is to emphasize that knowledge of diversity and good police–community relations is both professional and practical. It is important to emphasize that the knowledge and skills gained will improve officers' effectiveness in working with diverse communities as well as enhance officer safety and reduce complaints and law suits. The objective of the instructor during the first phase is to motivate the course participants to want to learn. Only an effective, prepared instructor is capable of accomplishing this objective. Many instructors' experience has shown that achieving this objective is best facilitated by small-group discussion and exercises.

The class can be divided up, separated, and assigned to list the reasons why cultural diversity (police–community relations; human relations) awareness and skills training is important to the participants. Each group returns and the spokesperson for each records their list on flipcharts at the front of the room. Discussion is generated by the instructor on those items that reinforce the training objective. If an instructor does not successfully convey the importance of the training, officers may remain skeptical throughout the sessions.

Second phase: Recognizing personal prejudices.   One of the most difficult and sensitive aspects of the training course deals with the participants' awareness and acceptance of their own personal prejudices and biases. Once the student has an awareness, the instructor can develop the participants' understanding of how those prejudices and biases affect behavior—their own as well as others. This instruction should take place through a brief lecture, small-group exercise, then open class discussions when the small groups report back to the entire class. Police participants resent and react negatively to confrontational instructional approaches; this method must always be avoided. The instructor and/or facilitator must be highly skilled and sensitive in this aspect of training and demonstrate how the skills learned are important to the participant in the performance of his or her job. That is, the instructor must approach the material from a practical perspective rather than a moralistic one (i.e., in a preaching manner).

Third phase: Police–community relations.   This block of instruction is critical to the success or failure of the training. It involves the instructor and/or community member(s) who can provide the participant with past and present information on the perceptions of the minority community about the police. Some instructors may have the ability to lecture on what community perceptions are, but if they do so, they must not alienate the class. Some courses have effectively used minority community members to discuss cultural or racial specific information, but this must be closely monitored and controlled. The same is true of classes on the gay/lesbian community. Community member presenters must be carefully selected. Many community people are unable to handle the defensiveness of police officers during cultural awareness training classes. Some do not understand police behavior and tactics. The community member selected should work together with the police trainer/facilitator in the development of their lesson plan so that there are no surprises.

Outsiders must receive guidance so they will become familiar with the precise goals and objectives of the human relations course before they participate. This will ensure that their involvement contributes to, rather than detracts from, the overall intent of the training and curriculum. A healthy discussion of issues between police and minority spokespersons is useful; however, the intimidation of officers is nonproductive. Minority instructors who are hostile toward police will alienate the audience and should therefore not be utilized. Using community representatives must not become an opportunity for them to vent their frustrations by berating officers for their own or their department's alleged insensitivity. Community members who have had a negative experience with the police may not be able to transcend their feelings. Community-based organization representatives who want to assist will avoid confrontation and can provide valuable interaction and discussion on relevant topics. They must be prepared for officers to be direct, critical, and even confrontational if the officers feel even slightly attacked. If this forum is used, the training facilitator is encouraged to have ongoing meetings with the minority/community-based presenters to ensure that the goals and objectives of the course are being met. Modification of presentations are appropriate if problems are identified from evaluations or observations of the trainers and presenters.

Fourth phase: Interpersonal relations skills training. This section of training deals with the development or review of the interpersonal relations skills that can help the participant reduce tension and conflict in their interaction with community members. The goal is to improve the students' verbal and nonverbal communications skills. The approach is based on the idea that students learn how their behavior affects the feelings and, in turn, the behavior and response of persons with whom they come in contact. Through lecturettes, role-playing (videotaped with discussion), and exercises (individual and/or in groups), participants can learn how to appropriately control their own verbal and nonverbal behavior and can affect the response they receive. The training can cover such subjects as barriers to effective communications, conflict resolution skills, the power of words (slurs, abusive, racial, etc.), and problem solving. Most participants will actually be eager to receive "tools for the job"—those immediate and practical skills that will help them deal more effectively and safely with minority community members.

Cultural awareness training courses involve a great deal of information and skills being imparted to the participant in a short period of time. For learning and maximum retention to occur, the instructor or facilitator, in addition to using a variety of proven teaching methods, must provide the class with several basic principles to remember at the end of each session. The basic principles should be related directly to things they can use in their job assignment. This is accomplished by overheads or flipcharts with brief sentences emphasized with an asterisk (*) to summarize the key points they have learned. The best approach to cultural awareness training is to link it to other curriculum, such as officer safety and legal update classes. By using case studies and role-playing exercises, the skills are reinforced.

Training Evaluation

Cultural awareness courses must be evaluated on an ongoing basis to ensure that learning objectives are being met. Some trainers survey the participants before training to assess their knowledge of the subject and then after each class to assess how much information was gained. This type of survey also helps the facilitator or instructor evaluate change in the student. If the participant is required to evaluate the training six months after the course is completed, such a survey could be designed to determine how the information learned has been applied to job performance in the real world of the work environment. Other evaluation alternatives are:

- Community survey before and after training
- Random follow-up survey by phone to victims, witnesses, and even suspects who have come into contact with the employee(s) who have received the training
- An analysis of citizen complaints of all types against the agency/organization before and after the training
- Outgoing examination and/or course critique of all participants

DIVERSITY CONSULTANTS

What Does a Diversity Consultant Do?

According to Simons (1991), most consultants hired by organizations follow a four-stage pattern:

1. **Needs assessment.** The consultant, depending on the size and scope of the task, may conduct meetings and interviews or initiate an extensive in-depth assessment with instrumentation designed for the situation or circumstances in which the organization operates. The consultant may also be able to assist the organization leader with the "internal selling" of the project.
2. **Project design and pilot.** In collaboration with his or her clients, the consultant produces a design or sequence of events and activities which are aimed at achieving the results that the needs assessment has found critical. The design is customized to meet the needs of the organization and is normally tested in a "pilot" program with a limited group of people to determine whether the results aimed at can actually be achieved by the proposed design. The pilot program process may be repeated until the program is fine tuned and ready for full presentation. Packaged programs should be chosen carefully to ensure that the material meets the training objectives and needs of the organization.
3. **Implementation, program delivery, and administration.** The tested program is then put into service either by organizational trainers or by the consultant/consultant team. Consultants can also train organization trainers and evaluate the results for the agency employing them.
4. **Evaluation and follow-up.** The consultant can also assist in the design and implementation of an evaluation of the training program.

Consultant Selection

George Simons indicates that frequently, organizations are in a quandary as to how to select a consultant and whether the firm selected should include "minority" person(s). He believes that in a very mixed target population, it may be useful, at least at the outset or for longer-term programs, to employ a team that is at once visibly diverse and able to model working together successfully. According to Simons, whether to use internal or external consultants is usually dictated by two factors: (1) the resources of the organization and (2) the balance between objectivity toward the issues and the need for familiarity with the organization. To minimize the risks associated with hiring a consultant, Simons provides the following tips:

- Know roughly what objectives the organization intends to address through use of the training consultant.
- Interview thoroughly from a wide selection of candidates or services.
- Expect to pay for these services, including the expenses of the interviewing process.
- Watch how the potential consultant or team interacts with the diverse population of your interviewing team or your organization.
- Make sure that the candidate sees the relationship of diversity to the "big picture" of the organization and the community in which it operates.

There are many diversity/cross-cultural consultants throughout the United States. There are also organizations, such as the National Coalition Building Institute (NCBI), with 35 chapters in the United States, Canada, England, and Northern Ireland. According to the *Law & Order Journal,* this organization has had a good success record in creating and teaching effective prejudice reduction models for police departments (*Los Angeles Times Magazine,* Apr. 25, 1993, p. 22). They may also be able to provide information on creditable consultants in your area. We provide a partial list of individual consultants and organizations in Appendix K, although we are not personally familiar with each reference and therefore are not able to endorse each one.

LAW ENFORCEMENT AGENCY MODELS FOR CULTURAL TRAINING

Within the United States, various law enforcement agencies in many states have begun their own diversity training for their employees. The amount and scope of training varies considerably. See Appendix E for a description of four agencies' programs. One eight-hour course is for law enforcement executives regarding their:

- Leadership role as a change agent
- Managing organizational diversity
- Development of agency cultural awareness policy, value, and vision statements
- Selection criteria for cultural awareness facilitator
- Evaluation considerations for the entire training program

If a chief of police wants to send a staff member to the facilitator training course, he must have first attended the executive course. The executive also attends the first day of the train-the-trainer class to develop an agency training protocol with the training facilitator. This emphasizes the importance of the training and the facilitator position. During that first day, the chief receives an overview of the goals of cultural awareness training and makes a pledge to support the program actively. He or she is provided specific examples and models that can be modified and implemented at his or her agency.

The other 48-hour course ("train the trainer") for the agency's cultural awareness facilitator (CAF) consists of two modules. The first learning unit, in a classroom setting, covers skills and knowledge needed to:

- Understand the elements of culture, effective communications, and perceptions
- Perform an agency assessment using evaluation techniques
- Inventory the community
- Select and train community training mentors
- Design and implement a cultural awareness training plan that is customized to the local agency and community using effective instructional strategies and resources

During the final days of the classroom segment of the course, students apply what they learned by actually developing a needs assessment for their agencies and a cultural awareness training plan.

The second phase of training takes place at the agency and in the community where the CAF will:

- Conduct an agency and community assessment
- Select and train a community training mentor
- Design a cultural awareness training plan that is customized to the local agency and community

As mentioned previously, a large portion of the POST Commission February 1992 "Guidelines for Design of Cultural Awareness Programs" is contained in Appendix F. (More information is available from the State of California Commission on Peace Officer Standards and Training, 1601 Alhambra Boulevard, Sacramento, CA 95816-7083.)

ADMINISTRATIVE GUIDELINES FOR CULTURAL AWARENESS TRAINING

The Chief Executive

The key to successful diversity training in any police agency is executive leadership, which provides clearly stated cultural awareness goals. Two important steps, as they pertain to training, involve the executive:

(1) demonstrating commitment and,
(2) developing an action plan.

Demonstrating commitment. Commitment to cultural awareness training by the chief executive and the senior staff of an organization is crucial. They must be role models through attendance in training sessions as well as proactive leaders in all matters concerning diversity in the workforce and community. The chief's personal leadership is viewed as the keystone to successful training. Demonstrating commitment is, in part, accomplished via policy and practices (discussed in

Chapter 2) where the chief develops a "macro" mission statement about his or her philosophy, values, vision, and goals pertaining to valuing diversity. The chief also develops a "micro" mission statement prior to any diversity training taking place. For example, the following is an example of such a statement, in the form of a memorandum, from the chief executive to employees preceding training: "The demographics in our various jurisdictions are changing rapidly. To counter that change positively we have embarked on a new era of cultural awareness training for all sworn ranks. Our goals are to develop awareness and facilitate understanding in each of you as you deal with persons from different cultures. The end result will be an increased level of service to all citizens" (Harman, 1992).

The chief executive must ensure the continued commitment to ongoing training by making it a mandate for recruits, in-service officers including supervisors, managers, and executives, and nonsworn support staff. To be effective, cultural awareness training cannot be a one-time-only event but a continuous educational effort. The chief has repeatedly to set a positive tone for training if positive change is to take place in the organization. This then gets translated to better police–community relations.

Developing an action plan.   Action plans are part of strategic, implementation, and transition management planning (discussed in Chapter 2). An action plan for cultural awareness training identifies the specific goals and objectives expected to be achieved and includes a budget, accountability, and a timetable. Another essential element of designing cultural awareness training programs (part of the action plan) is that command officers and trainers involve community leaders in the planning. One strategy could involve the formation of a cultural awareness committee (CAC) with both internal and external membership. The CAC assists the law enforcement agency in the development of a survey instrument that could provide useful input from employees and/or the community in the design of a cultural awareness training program. The CAC also reviews and evaluates the cultural awareness training course and makes recommendations for improvement. The CAC also helps to identify the unique needs of each community or neighborhood that should be addressed in the training. An example of an internal survey is contained in Appendix B.

Cultural Awareness Trainer/Facilitator Selection

The in-service trainer/facilitator selection is crucial to the success of cultural awareness training programs. Successful programs have involved the chief executive appointing one person within the organization to be the cultural awareness facilitator. Smaller agencies have formed a consortium of departments, and one facilitator is selected, usually from the largest, to perform the required functions. The facilitator must be respected and have credibility with the organization(s) and be a good role model for the philosophies and values that will be taught. The facilitator must be trained on how to assess the agency and community; to select and train trainers, including community mentors; and to design an agency(ies) training plan. The facilitator may also be one of the cultural awareness trainers.

The selection of the trainer should be based on their ability as an effective communicator combined with good interpersonal skills. The trainer must be highly committed to the subject and a good role model for the philosophies and values that he or she is going to teach (i.e., the value of diversity). The facilitator may use a combination of approaches: trainers from inside the organization, community mentors/presenters, and/or a private consulting firm that specializes in cultural awareness training. Some agencies have effectively used police employees from other law enforcement agencies of different ethnic/racial, religious, or lifestyle backgrounds in discussion groups. They have credibility with police officers and are especially effective when discussing their own personal experiences with discrimination and bias directed at them.

Academy instructors and departmental, in-service trainers must attend technical course(s) to develop their teaching skills. A few states have developed a certified, train-the-trainer course for cultural awareness facilitators. The facilitator then trains instructors on the specifics of cultural awareness training. The instructors have to have the respect and gain the creditability of their audience.

Tips for the Cultural Awareness Facilitator and Trainer

Planning for cultural awareness training requires a great deal of forethought concerning the practical issues of audience, content, and delivery methods. The trainer of advanced officer or executive courses cannot be an amateur or come unprepared; otherwise, the instructor and the program will be "eaten alive" by police veterans. To have any level of success, the cultural awareness instructor must be able to cope with highly defensive, cynical, and jaded attitudes and actions, especially on the part of some veteran officers. The extremely negative attitudes found among some veterans are not generally found among basic academy students who tend to be much more receptive to training and the instructor.

It is important that the instructor know his or her audience well in terms of their professional identity and characteristic attitudes. A class of veteran police officers would be handled differently from a recruit academy class for the reasons mentioned previously. The trainer should understand the dynamics of the police subculture and be aware of and sympathetic toward the difficulties of the job. He or she also must create a nonthreatening training environment. This is accomplished by reassuring the participants that the purpose of the course is not to blame or condemn them for any negative incidents of poor agency–community relations. The same is true when the audience is made up of correctional officers. Their identity and particular problems must be considered in the design of the course.

Those involved in cultural awareness training observe that the instruction causes discomfort for some people. The discomfort may be based on the participants' dissatisfaction with the intended change that is expected. Some may truly believe that they do not need the training. Cultural awareness instructors hear: "I treat everyone with respect regardless of their ethnic or racial background—I don't need training." "Let them learn about our culture if they are going to live here—why do I have to learn about them?" "My job is to arrest criminals—I am not a social worker."

Another part of this reaction may be attributed to a backlash brought forth by white males who have historically been in the power positions and perceive themselves to be losing that position. They are therefore uncomfortable in training classes. Many white males have also felt that affirmative action hiring and promotion practices have reduced their opportunities and see ethnic/racial minorities and women as a threat. For this reason they may resist cultural awareness training. An instructor should not argue with a participant on these issues, but be willing to listen.

Tips for the Course Participant

Certain expectations should be understood by the course participant and trainer(s) prior to the beginning of the training. The participant:

- Must be able to express himself or herself openly in front of a group and not be afraid to do so
- Can offer constructive criticism of the information being taught
- Should keep an open mind and be willing to learn about other cultures, races, religions, and lifestyles
- Should attempt to make a positive effort to learn about the community/neighborhood(s) that he or she works
- Must make a positive effort to build an understanding of and with the diverse members of the community and workforce
- Will be open to learning about interpersonal and cross-cultural communications skills that make him or her more effective
- Will not take remarks by trainers or community presenters personally
- Will share factual knowledge and experiences about his or her own culture, race, religion, or lifestyle if appropriate
- Will accept the fact that the purpose of training is also to make their job safer

SUMMARY

In this chapter we dealt with cultural awareness training for law enforcement agencies in multiethnic/multiracial communities. The information was intended to provide the law enforcement executive and the trainer strategies and program ideas on cultural awareness training that can be implemented in any size agency and community. In the chapter we stressed that executives must take a leadership role in the development of community partnerships and of employees who are culturally aware and effective. Executives must look to policy and training to encourage their agencies to meet the unique community-oriented challenges of this decade and especially to prepare for the next. Agencies (POST) that certify state law enforcement training academies must take the lead in developing cultural awareness course guidelines and train-the-trainer classes. They must standardize and certify the core elements of cultural awareness training not only for police academies but also for advanced officer, supervisor, and executive courses.

Effective training models concentrate on cultural education, communications skills, interpersonal skills in relationships with minority-group members, and conflict resolution techniques. Courses must be designed to fit participant and community needs to be successful.

DISCUSSION QUESTIONS AND ISSUES*

1. *Personal Action Plan.* The student should complete a short- and long-term personal goals summary that makes use of concepts learned during cultural awareness training and how he or she will apply them at work.

2. *Instructors.* You are a cultural awareness trainer. What skill have you learned that will assist you in teaching others about prejudice reduction on the part of your audience? Make a list of teaching methods that you would utilize to teach about prejudice, bias, and their affect on behavior? How can prejudice be revealed in a nonthreatening way in a training course?

3. *Training Goals and Objectives.* You have been selected as the training facilitator for your agency. Make a prioritized outline of the steps and processes that you will need to complete to design and implement a cultural awareness training course. The course is now planned; now make a "to do list" of things that must be accomplished: three weeks before; one week before; and after the program.

4. *Chief Executive Officer.* You intend to implement cultural awareness training at your agency. List the steps you will need to take to ensure that an effective training course is prepared, implemented, and accepted. How will you determine what cultural/racial groups to include and/or discuss in the training sessions? How are you going to budget for the training? How are you going to remove patrol officers from their beats for the training sessions and still provide the level of services required for your community?

5. *Course Evaluation.* You are the cultural awareness trainer/facilitator. Make a list of the various methods you might employ to evaluate the effectiveness of the training class that is implemented at your agency or in your academy.

REFERENCES

Barlow, David, "Cultural Sensitivity Revisited," unpublished paper presented at the *NOBLE/PERF/Reno Police Department Conference,* Reno, Nev, Oct. 2–4, and at the *Academy of Criminal Justice Sciences Meetings,* Pittsburgh, Pa, Mar., p. 16.

Harman, Paul (1992). *Cultural Diversity Training for the Future,* California Police Officers Standards and Training Command College, Sacramento, Calif., June (Order 14-0274).

Himelfarb, Frum (1991). "A training strategy for policing in a multicultural society," *Police Chief,* vol. 5B No. 11, pp. 53–55.

Simons, George F. (1991). *"Diversity: Where Do I Go for Help—A Guide to Understanding, Selecting and Using Diversity Services and Tools,* George Simons International, Santa Cruz, Calif.

St. George, Joyce, (1991). "'Sensitivity' training needs rethinking," *Law Enforcement News,* Vol. 7, No. 347, Nov. 30, pp. 8–12.

Torres, Jane (1989). "Can Training Reduce Police/Citizens Violence?" *The Trainer.*

Weaver, Gary (1975). "American Identity Movements: A Cross-Cultural Confrontation," *Intellect,* Mar., pp. 377–80.

*See Instructor's Manual accompanying this text for additional activities, role-plays, questionnaires and projects related to the content of this chapter.

5

CROSS-CULTURAL COMMUNICATION FOR LAW ENFORCEMENT

OVERVIEW

This chapter begins with an overview of specific issues that people in law enforcement face with regard to communication in a diverse environment. The authors discuss several common reactions that people have when communicating with people from different backgrounds, including defensiveness, overidentification, denial of biases, and the creation of "we/they" attitudes. The next section provides information on language barriers and gives examples of *partial* solutions that several police departments have devised to compensate for large populations of limited English speakers. Following this is a discussion of commonly held attitudes about limited English speakers and an explanation of the challenges involved in second-language acquisition. The section on language barriers and law enforcement ends with a list of tips for communicating in situations where English is a second language. Following this is information on key issues and skills required for interviewing and gathering data, particularly across cultures. The next section covers nonverbal differences across cultures, emphasizing areas of contrast of which officers should be aware. The final section presents male–female communication issues, particularly within law enforcement agencies.

COMMENTARY

The challenge of communication across cultures for law enforcement personnel is multifaceted. Not only do officers have to consider the effect of limited English on their day-to-day work, they must also deal with the changing "culture" within their agencies and the sensitivities required in a multicultural workforce.

English language problems.   Interview with Vietnamese police officer (northern California department); reflections on his first few months in the United States.

> For the first few months of being here, I was always tired from speaking the language. I had to strain my ears all day long and all my nerves were bothered. It was hard work to make people understand my broken English and to listen to them. Sometimes, I just could not anymore and I just stopped speaking English. Sometimes I had to pretend I understood what they said and why they were laughing. But inside I felt very depressed. I am an adult and my language sounded worse than a child. Sometimes it was better not to say anything at all.

Limited-English citizens and crime.   "Speaking English—language barrier between police, crime victims—traumatic situation for crime victims," *San Francisco Chronicle,* July 20, 1992, p. 1.

> One night last January, Oakland resident "Anita C." was severely beaten by her husband. She called the police, who came, took a statement from her husband and told her to go back to bed. They didn't talk to her, they didn't make an arrest, they didn't try to ask, 'Do you want to press charges?' said . . . her attorney. She is so fearful now. Anita's complaint was ignored because she speaks little or no English.

Nonverbal behavior.   From "Law enforcement in a culturally diverse society," by Gary Weaver, *FBI Law Enforcement Bulletin,* Sept. 1992, p. 4.

> . . . The Nigerian [cab driver] then ignores the [officer's] command to "step back." Most likely, this doesn't make any sense to him because, in his eyes, he is not even close to the officer. The social distance for conversation in Nigeria is much closer than in the United States. For Nigerians, it may be less than 15 inches, whereas 2 feet represents a comfortable conversation zone for Americans.
>
> In Nigeria . . . people often show respect and humility by averting their eyes. While the officer sees the cabbie defiantly "babbling to the ground," the Nigerian believes he is sending a message of respect and humility. Most likely, the cab driver is not even aware of [what is perceived to be] wild gestures, high-pitched tone of voice, or rapid speech. But the officer believes him to be "out of control," "unstable," and probably "dangerous."

Communication sensitivity in the diverse work environment.   Comment from a female police officer made at a Women's Peace Officer Association conference, Concord, California, July 18, 1992.

> You have to go along with the kind of kidding and ribbing that the guys participate in otherwise you are not one of them. If you say that you are offended by their crass jokes and vulgar speech, then you are ostracized from the group. I have often felt that in the squad room men have purposely controlled themselves because of my presence, because I have spoken up. But what I've done to them is make them act one way because of my presence as a woman. Then they call me a prude or spread the word that I'm keeping track of all their remarks for the basis of a sexual

harassment suit down the road. I have no interest in doing that. I simply want to be a competent police officer in a professional working environment.

Good communication and officer safety. From the Los Angeles Sheriff's Department's explanation of its cultural awareness training in the academy.

Nothing about avoiding discrimination requires compromising officer safety . . . However, you should also remember that the misunderstandings and escalations which can be created by insensitive or discriminatory acts and words are also threats to your safety and your career advancement.

CROSS-CULTURAL COMMUNICATION IN THE LAW ENFORCEMENT CONTEXT

To understand the need for skillful communication with members of culturally and ethnically diverse groups, including women, the officer should recognize some of the special characteristics of cross-cultural communication in the law enforcement context (Exhibit 5.1).

To best protect and serve communities made up of individuals from many different racial and cultural backgrounds, officers as peacekeepers, crime fighters, and law enforcement representatives need to look beyond the "mechanics" of policing and examine what takes place in the process of cross-cultural communication. Communication, in general, is a challenge because it is "both hero and villain—it transfers information, meets people's needs, and gets things done, but far too often it also distorts messages, develops frustration, and renders people and organizations ineffective" (Harris and Moran, 1991). Why does communication pose this much of a challenge? Talking to others, making one's points, and giving explanations should not be so difficult. Yet every communication act involves a message,

---

Exhibit 5.1 Key Areas for Officers to Consider

- Officers have traditionally used styles of communication and language which at one time were considered acceptable. Now, because of diverse groups within the police agency and within our cities, the unspoken "rules" about what is appropriate and inappropriate communication are changing.

- For officers, communication can be, at best, tense in crises and culturally unfamiliar environments.

- The officer's perceptions of a cultural group may be skewed by the population that he or she encounters.

- The officer's communication will be enhanced when he or she is aware of:
  1. Perceptions
  2. Cultural filters
  3. Possible biases and stereotypes

- Through communication, officers have tremendous power to influence the behavior and responses of the citizens they contact. A lack of knowledge of the dynamics of cross-cultural communication will diminish this power.

- Improved communication with all citizens will also result in *safer* interactions for officers.

a sender, and a receiver and given that any two human beings are fundamentally different, there will always be a psychological distance between the two involved (even in the same culture). The more effective and professional police officer has learned ways of bridging the gap or psychological distance between two very different worlds of sender and receiver. In instances of *cross-cultural communication* (which includes cross-racial and cross-ethnic interactions) where the sender or the receiver are from different cultures, the officer has an even greater gap to try to bridge. Not only can the cultural influences affecting communication style contribute to misunderstanding and misperception, the "baggage" that goes along with police–minority relations sets people up for communication breakdown and conflict.

COMMUNICATION ATTEMPTS IN CROSS-CULTURAL ENCOUNTERS

It is usually much easier to interact with people who are like you than to communicate with those who are different. Communication can be strained and unnatural when there is no apparent common ground. The "people are people everywhere" argument and "just treat everyone with respect" advice both fall short when one learns that there are basic differences, especially in the area of values, which influence behavior and communication. Some police officers feel that an understanding of cross-cultural communication is unnecessary if respect is shown to every person. Yet many people, including some officers, have had limited contact with people from different backgrounds, and this can be obvious when certain types of statements are made or certain behaviors exhibited. In the next few paragraphs we answer questions concerning ways people attempt to accommodate or react to differences with citizens and in the culturally diverse work environment and ways in which some people cover up their discomfort in communication with people who are different from themselves. The final example (i.e., "You stopped me because I'm [fill in with any group]") describes a common reaction that some citizens have with police officers and offers suggestion for handling this response.

Using Language or Language Style to Become Just Like One of "Them"

BLACK OFFICER TO A WHITE OFFICER: "Hey, what kind of arrest did you have?"
WHITE OFFICER: "Well, man. I saw this bro and he was trying to jive me. . . ."

Officer Darryl McAllister, an African American, from the Hayward, California police department, used the example above in a cultural diversity workshop in response to the question: What do you never want other officers to say to you as an African American officer? His "pet peeve" was hearing other officers trying to imitate him in speech and trying to act like a "brother." He explained that this behavior, on the part of a white officer, was insincere and phony and made him feel as if people were going overboard to show just how comfortable they were with black people. He continued to say that he did not feel that this style of imitation was necessarily racist (although in some instances it could be), but that it conveyed an attitude to him that people were uncomfortable with his "blackness."

Similarly, officers attempting to establish rapport with citizens should not pretend to have too much familiarity with the language and culture or use words selectively to demonstrate how "cool" they are (e.g., using "senor" with Spanish-speaking people, calling an African American "my man," or referring to a Native American as "chief"). People of one cultural background may find themselves in situations where an entire crowd or family is using a particular dialect or slang. If the officer lapses into the manner of speaking of the group, it is very likely that he or she will appear to be mocking that style. Ultimately, the officer should be sincere and natural. "Faking" another style of communication can have extremely negative results.

Walking on Eggshells

When in the presence of people from different cultural backgrounds, some find that they have a tendency to work hard not to offend. Consequently, they are not able to be themselves or do what they would normally do. In a cultural diversity training workshop for employees of a city government, one white participant explained that he normally has no problem being direct when solicitors come to the door trying to sell something or ask for a donation to a cause. His normal response would be to say, "I'm not interested," and then he would promptly shut the door. He explained, however, that when a black solicitor comes to the door, he almost never rudely cuts him or her off, and most of the time he ends up making a donation to whatever the cause is. His inability to be himself and communicate directly stems from his concern about appearing to be a racist. It is not within the scope of this subsection to psychoanalyze this behavior, but simply to bring into awareness some typical patterns of reactions in cross-cultural and cross-racial encounters. A person must attempt to recognize his or her tendencies in order to reach the goal of communicating in a sincere and *authentic* manner with people of all backgrounds (Exhibit 5.2).

"Some of My Best Friends Are . . ."

In an attempt to show how tolerant and experienced they are with members of minority groups, many people often feel the need to demonstrate their tolerance strongly by saying things such as "I'm not prejudiced," or "I have friends who are members of your group," or even, "I know people . . . ," or worse, "I once knew

---

Exhibit 5.2   Key Areas for Officers to Consider

- Self-awareness about one's early life experiences that helped to shape perceptions, filters, and assumptions about people.
- Self-awareness about how one feels toward someone who is "different."
- Management of assumptions and discomfort in dealing with people who are different. For example, do we try to deny that differences exist and laugh differences away, or imitate "them" in order to appear comfortable?
- Ability to be authentic in communication with others while modifying communication style, when necessary.

someone who was also [for example] Jewish/Asian/African American." Although the intention may be to break down barriers and establish a rapport, these types of statements often sound patronizing. To a member of a culturally or racially different group, this type of comment comes across as extremely naive. In fact, many people would understand such a comment as signifying that the speaker actually does have prejudices toward a particular group. Minority-group members would question a nonmember's need to make a reference to others of the same background when there is no context for doing this. These types of remarks indicate that the speaker is probably isolated from members of the particular group." Yet the person making a statement such as, "I know someone who is [for example] Asian" is trying to establish something in common with the other person and may go so far as to go into detail about that other person he knows. As one Jewish woman reported in the aforementioned workshop, "Just because a person I meet is uncomfortable meeting Jews or has very little experience with Jews doesn't mean that I want to hear about the one Jewish person he met 10 years ago while traveling on a plane to New York!"

"You People" or the We/They Distinction

Former candidate for the U.S. presidency Ross Perot, in his first campaign appearance in front of the National Association for the Advancement of Colored People (NAACP), surprised and alienated his audience when he said "you people" and "your people" when singling out the unique problems of African Americans. In the same speech, Perot also quoted his father, who, referring to poor blacks who worked for him, said, "Son, these are people too, and they have to live" (*New York Times,* July 12, 1992, pp. 1, 17). People felt that the language he used not only was condescending and demeaning but emphasized a separation of blacks from whites. The president of the Los Angeles chapter of the NAACP explained: "He showed he had very little experience with black people. When he used the phrase 'your people,' he put up a big wall, and when he tried to tell us we're people, he made a big mistake. We know we're people" (*New York Times,* July 12, 1992, p. 17).

By deciding that a particular group is unlike one's own group (i.e., not part of "my people"), a person makes a simplistic division of all people into two groups: "we" and "they." (Chapter 1 introduces this concept.) Often, accompanying this division is the attribution of positive traits to "us" and the negative traits to "they." Members of the "other group" (the "out" group) are described in negative and stereotypical ("They are lazy," "They are criminals," "They are aggressive"), rather than neutral terms that describe cultural or ethnic generalities ("They have a tradition of valuing education," or "They have a communication style that is more formal than that of most Americans"). The phenomenon of stereotyping makes it very difficult for people to communicate with each other effectively because they don't perceive the person accurately. By attributing negative qualities to the "other" group, a person creates myths about the superiority of his or her own group. Cultural and racial "put-downs" are often attempts to make one's self feel better. (This is discussed further in Part Five in the context of police officer self-image.)

"You Stopped Me Because I'm . . ."

There are three types of situations in which an officer may hear the accusation: "You stopped me because I'm (black, Mexican, etc.) The first situation would be when citizens from a neighborhood with people predominantly from one culture may be suspicious of *any* person in their neighborhood from another background. Thus they may call 911 reporting a "suspicious character" and may even add such statements as "I think he has a gun" when there is no basis for such an accusation. In this situation the police officer must understand the extreme humiliation and anger citizens feel when they are the object of racist perceptions. Once the officer determines that there is no reason to arrest the citizen, it is most appropriate for the officer to apologize for having made the stop and to explain that department policy requires that officers are obliged to investigate all calls.

Indeed, there are many incidents all over the country where citizens call a police department to report a "suspicious character" just because he or she does not happen to fit the description of the majority of the residents in that area. Since there is a history of stopping minorities for reasons that are less than legitimate, the officer must go out of his or her way to show respect to the innocent citizen who does not know why he or she has been stopped and is caught totally off guard. Many people reported to be "suspicious" for merely being of a different race would appreciate an officer's final comment, which could be something like, "I hope this kind of racism ends soon within our community," or "It's too bad that there are still people in our community who are so ignorant." Comments such as these, said with sincerity, may very well get back to the community and contribute to improved future interactions with members of the police department. Of course, there will always be people who, after being stopped, will not appreciate any attempt that the officer makes to explain why the stop was made. Nevertheless, many citizens will react favorably to an officer's understanding of their feelings.

A second situation in which an officer may hear, "You stopped me because I'm. . . ." may occur not because of any racist intentions of the officer, but rather as a "reflex response" of the citizen (in other words, it has no bearing in current reality). Many minority members have been stopped for no reason in the past (or know people who have) and are carrying this "baggage" into each encounter with an officer. One police officer in a northern California police department explained: "I don't consider myself prejudiced. I consider myself a fair person, but let me tell you what happens almost every time I stop a black in City X. The first words I hear from them are 'You stopped me because I'm black.' That's bugging the hell out of me because that's not why I stopped them. I stopped them because they had a traffic violation. It's really bothering me and I'm about to explode."

Among the many multicultural challenges confronting peace officers, the situation in which an officer is accused of racially motivated stops is an area where officers truly need to remain professional and not escalate a potential conflict or create a confrontation. Law enforcement officials should not only try to communicate their professionalism, both verbally and nonverbally, but should also try to strengthen their self-control. According to Dan Martin, former police officer and current justice administration chairperson of Diablo Valley College (Pleasant Hill, California), who himself is African American, the best formula in dealing with these types of remarks from citizens is to work on your own reactions and stress level. His response to the police officer who made the previous remark was, "If you work in City X or any other city for that matter, you could be told on a daily basis, 'You stopped me because I'm black.' You have to develop a method whereby you don't internalize these things. You have to ignore these comments. People are reacting to you as a symbol and are taking their frustrations out on you" (personal communication, Dan Martin).

Let's assume that the officer did not stop a person because of his or her ethnicity or race and that the officer is therefore not abusing his or her power. George Thompson, founder and president of the Verbal Judo Institute, Inc. (1-800/448-1042) believes that in these situations, people bring up race and ethnicity in order to throw the officer off guard. (personal communication, July 1, 1992). According to Thompson (who is white and a former English professor and police officer), the more professional an officer is, the less likely the officer will let this type of statement become a problem. Newer officers, especially, can be thrown off by such allegations of racism when, in fact, they are simply upholding the law and keeping the peace as they have been trained to do. Thompson advocates using "verbal deflectors" when citizens make such remarks as "You stopped me because I'm. . . ." He recommends responses like "I appreciate that, but . . . (e.g., you were going 55 miles in a 25-mile zone)," or "I hear what you're saying, but . . . you just broke the law." The characteristics of "verbal deflectors" are (1) they are readily available to the lips, (2) they are nonjudgmental, and (3) they can be said quickly. Contrary to what Martin advocates, Thompson believes that statements from citizens should *not* be ignored because silence or no response can make people even more furious than they already are (i.e., because they were stopped).

> Pay attention to what citizens say, but deflect their anger. "You are not paid to argue with citizens. You are paid to keep the peace. If you use tactical language and focus every word you say so that it relates to your purpose, then you will sound more professional. The minute you start using words as defensive weapons, you lose power and endanger your safety. If you 'springboard' over their arguments, and remain calm, controlled and non judgmental, you will gain voluntary compliance most of the time. The results of this professional communication are that: (1) you feel good; (2) you disempower the citizen; and (3) you control them in the streets (and in courts and in the media). Never take anything personally." (personal communication, George Thompson, July 1, 1992)

Thompson adds that an officer should talk Friday night the way he or she wants to be quoted Monday morning in front of a jury. Finally, he emphatically asserts: "There's no one in America who can pull me into an argument." Thompson noted that since the Rodney King beating, many more officers in his classes have been wanting help in improving their responses to citizens.

The third and final situation in which an officer may hear "You stopped me because I'm (black/Latino, etc.)," is the situation in which the citizen is correct. Police department personnel are not immune from the racism that still exists in our society. Reflecting biased attitudes outside the law enforcement agency, some officers (and one assumes a minority of officers) do use their positions of power to assert authority in ways that can no longer be tolerated. Here we are not *only* referring to the white officer who subjugates minorities—it could be an officer of color who has internalized the hatred from the dominant society and may actually treat fellow minority members unjustly. (Such situations are exemplified in the movie *Boys of the Hood,* in which an African American officer shows no respect at all to African American citizens.) Alternatively, this abuse of power could take place between a minority officer and a white citizen.

Exhibit 5.3 is reproduced from a small town in northern California newspaper in which an African American citizen paid $1500 to buy a full-page ad telling others in his town of his experiences with the police. Antoine Blgirimana, one of the town's six African American residents in the early 1990s, was stopped for such violations as not having a bicycle license (he was riding his bicycle because his car had died) and because police thought he was riding a stolen bicycle. Bigirimana (an immigrant from Africa educated in Europe and owner of a California software company) could not understand the pattern of stops and arrests that he was experiencing. In the newspaper ad, he created mug shots from photos of himself (below) and entitled the ad: *What would you do if you saw this man riding a bike through your neighborhood?* His intention was to raise awareness in a humorous way of the treatment he had been receiving because of racial stereotypes. He felt that he must have fit a profile because he was stopped on a regular basis and, among other things, was accused of stealing a bicycle. After two days of searching for records indicating that Mr. Bigirimana had bought the bicycle, police were able to verify that the merchandise was not stolen. He concluded the explanation in his ad with the following:

> I am not a thief . . . it says so on a piece of paper the police gave me. I do not have a criminal record . . . Some of my friends say that any Black person is automatically considered a thief, a violent person, possibly a drug addict or a drug dealer. They ought to know, they are all white. I do not believe any of this; however I do not understand why all of these things are happening to me on a regular basis. If you know me, please call the Sonoma Police Department and let them know that I AM NOT A CROOK. (*Sonoma Index Tribune,* June 12, 1992, p. A-13)

One of the positive results from this publicity was that a cultural awareness committee was formed in the small town, consisting of police officers and citizens who began to address local racial and cultural concerns. However, officers and police departments would benefit from forward proactive thinking and professional behavior, rather than waiting for an incident (or incidents) that eventually force them into acting properly with citizens.

To conclude, officers must consider the reasons for "You stopped me because I'm . . . " and respond accordingly.* All three of the situations described above call for different responses on the part of the officer [i.e., (1) citizens call in because of racist perceptions and the "suspicious character" is innocent; (2) the citizen stopped is simply "hassling" the officer, and may or may not have been unjustly

---

*The Instructor's Manual contains discussion questions and role-plays on this aspect of communication.

WHAT WOULD *YOU* DO IF YOU SAW THIS MAN RIDING A BIKE THROUGH *YOUR* NEIGHBORHOOD?

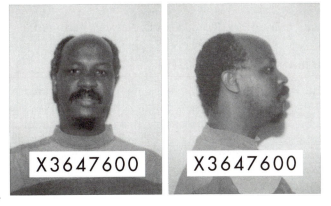

On Friday evening, just before Memorial Day week-end, my car, a ten year old Honda Civic, died. Despite all my CPR skills it refused to be resuscitated. Five years ago I had bought two bicycles from Toys R Us. They were sold disassembled in boxes and I assembled them into good-looking cheap bicycles, worth about $80.00 each. On this memorable Friday, with a dead car, it seemed the perfect opportunity to ride one of my bicycles from my home to my office on Broadway. It was around 9:25 pm. I walked the bike half of the way, briefly stopping to watch an angry conversation between a Sonoma police woman and a young Mexican man who was shouting in bad English that "This is discrimination." Thinking that the young Mexican must have done some terrible deed, I continued to walk my bike a few more blocks, until I reached MacArthur Street.

The straight portion of MacArthur between Fifth Street and Broadway seemed the perfect place to ride a bicycle at night: there are street lights, few dogs bark—I wonder what kind of strange presence they seem to resent—few cats attempt suicide by crossing the street. The perfect place to ride a cheap "Night Moves" by Murray . . . A Sonoma Police car approached me slowly from behind and forced me to stop. "Your bicycle has no lights." "Yes." "Do you have a bicycle license?" "NO! What kind of license is that? And is it really necessary?" "Yes, and I'm going to write you a fix-it ticket." "Thank you officer." I was starting to doubt my knowledge of the way this country works. Do you remember if a license is required before you take a little stroll after 9:00 pm? And then the bombshell: "Before you leave, I need to check if this bicycle is stolen." I suddenly understood that every time the Sonoma Police stop me (it happens very regularly and usually for no reason that I can think of) the last question is generally

whether I have been stealing from the businesses on Broadway. Should I really believe that this Police behavior has a logical pattern and *do I fit some kind of profile?*

The operator of the police computer came on-line, "The bicycle was stolen from Santa Clara County. Both the description (black and gray), the brand name (Night Moves) and the serial number X3647600 fit." I turned dark blue, then yellow, suddenly started glowing in the dark: I became allergic to my clothes, my body started emitting heat waves, and I felt that I was going to throw up.

"But officer, I bought this bike as a kit in a box, from Toys R Us in Santa Rosa. I assembled it myself. How can it be stolen? Did Toys R Us steal the bike and then sell it to me five years ago?"

Another police car slowly approached, and a police officer stepped out. I recognized him. He stopped me two years ago on Broadway, for no reason, looked in my car and asked me if I had been stealing. It was midnight, I was tired, and I tried to be as congenial as I could, but I felt humiliated. The new police officer stood there. I don't think he remembers the indignities he had inflicted on me. The voice of the police computer operator: "Confiscate the bike, it is stolen." I was very upset. I took a deep breath and managed to belt out my famous signature laugh: monstrously big, and for the circumstances, perfectly disharmonious.

"Here is the bike, it is all yours." My wife was away for the weekend, her car was at the SF Airport, my car was dead, my bicycle was stolen and I had a deadline to finish a software program by Tuesday afternoon. I had three days to prove that I was not a thief. "Your bike is confiscated until you can prove you did not steal it."

Saturday morning, Sonoma looked different. I wondered it the Tuesday Index-Tribune would have my name and address, and the ser-

ial number of the bicycle I stole? How was I going to explain to my wife and ten year old daughter that I stole a bicycle? To my bewildered eyes, everyone seemed to be pointing at me: "There is the thief, he steals bikes!" I looked around and started questioning anyone with a bicycle: "Do you have a receipt for your bike?" "No." "You don't have a light do you?" "No." "Do you have a bike license?" "No, I don't need one."

Out of 50 bike owners, one had a license and none had a light. I saw police cars driving around, none of these people were stopped. Why me? Why not them?

Sunday afternoon: "Hello, Toys R Us? You stole a bike and then you sold it to me. I am about to go to jail, can you help me?" "I'll transfer you to the manager . . ." The manager, a very competent and friendly lady, gave me the telephone numbers to the bike manufacturer and to Toys R Us inventory control. She insists that five years is a long time and they don't keep records for five years.

After two days of searching my records, I found the sales records, but they didn't contain the serial number of the bike. They showed that I bought merchandise worth $162.00 from Toys R Us on transaction #03013776 TOYS on 7/30/88. I still couldn't shake this criminal thief personality the police have caged me into.

Tuesday morning I was still a suspected thief. The bike was still warehoused at the Sonoma Police Department as stolen merchandise. My wife was back. I had to confess to her that I was a sleepwalking thief. She lent me her car. I drove to the Sonoma Police Department. I had sales records, telephone numbers, character references, my birth certificate, my teddy bear (just in case I needed comfort), and my best jeans.

How did this happen? My name is Antoine. I received the best education money can buy in Europe. I am a software engineer by profes-

sion. I own a software company in Sunnyvale. For the last five years, I've enjoyed a peaceful and happy life in Sonoma. For breakfast, I go to Homegrown Bagel or Scandia Bakery, and enjoy lots of laughter and pleasant conversations with the natives. For lunch, I like to go to Peterberry's Café, when I feel rich I got o Piatti or L'Esperance. For dinner I have a short list: for everyday, I like Happy Garden Chinese food; and for the special occasions that happen rather frequently, I love Winemaker Restaurant. For my desktop publishing, I go to Graphico and Copy Sonoma. I love Sonoma, the food, the wine, the people. BUT, HOW DID I BECOME A BICYCLE THIEF?

The police computer recorded the model number of a stolen bicycle instead of the serial number. The police officer who stopped me decided that the model number of my bike was the serial number. The manufacturer had to step in and inform the police about the situation of the serial numbers and model number. As of today, if you have a "Night Moves" bike by Murray, you can be arrested for stealing it from Santa Clara County. The police officer spent two more hours trying to find out if the manufacturer shipped these bicycles to Toys R Us in Santa Rosa. I am not a thief anymore—for the time being—it says so on a piece of paper the police gave me. I do not have a criminal record, but I have a case number (Case #48312).

Some of my friends say that any black person is automatically considered a thief, a violent person, possibly a drug addict or a drug dealer. They ought to know, they are all white. I do not believe any of this; however I do not understand why all of these things are happening to me on a regular basis.

If you know me, please call the Sonoma Police Department and tell them that I AM NOT A CROOK.

stopped in the past; and (3) the citizen making the accusation toward the officer is correct]. The officer would do well, in all three situations, to remember the quote included in the final section of Chapter 1: *"Remember the history of law enforcement with all groups and ask yourself the question, 'Am I part of the past, or a part of the future?'"* (Lieutenant Ondra Berry, Reno, Nevada Police Department).

LANGUAGE BARRIERS AND LAW ENFORCEMENT

Nationwide, law enforcement managers and officials need to respond sensitively to people in the increasingly large segment of the multicultural population who do not speak English, or who speak English as a second language. For limited English speakers who report crimes, for crime suspects who are arrested, and for victims, there are no absolute assurances that their words will be understood. On a "good day" some officers make a point to modify their English so that they will be better understood; while on a day that has been stressful, many officers are frustrated at having to slow down and listen more patiently. Some law enforcement officers are noticeably impatient when they deal with the limited-English speaker. As a result, a citizen with a language "handicap" is not successful at communicating even the minimum amount of necessary information. Perhaps most difficult is the situation in which a limited-English-speaking person finds him or herself traumatized, further affecting the victim's ability to speak English. Officers themselves are justifiably frustrated by language barriers and find it difficult to do their jobs the way they have been trained to do them.

Clearly, the more bilingual officers a department has, the more efficient and effective the contact. That is why many agencies subsidize foreign language training for their personnel or seek recruits with multiple language skills. When the resources are not available to do this, however, there can be serious and sometimes tragic consequences. Non-English-speaking citizens may not understand why they are being arrested or searched. They may not know their rights if they are unfamiliar with the legal system, as is the case with many recently arrived immigrants and refugees. Using the wrong translator can mislead officers, so much so that a victim and his or her translator may give two completely different versions of a story: for example, using the friend of a suspected child abuser to translate the allegations of the child who has been abused.

In some cases there is no sensitivity when it comes to language obstacles. For example, within a largely Spanish-speaking area in Los Angeles, a deputy, according to witnesses, asked a Hispanic male to get out of his car. The man answered in Spanish, "I'm handicapped," and he reached down to pull his left leg out of the car. The deputy apparently believed that the man was reaching for a weapon and, consequently, "struck him on the head with the butt of his gun" (*Los Angeles Times*, July 21, 1992, p. A-18). Insensitivity to language differences was also involved in the case of the officer who had been called to the scene of an accident in which a third-grade girl had died almost immediately after having been struck by a car that leaped a curb and hurled the girl 60 feet through the air. When the police investigator arrived, he tried to ascertain what had happened: "[The police officer] shouted out if anyone had seen what had occurred. No one responded because they had not actually been witnesses. The officer in apparent disgust and derision then remarked, 'Why don't any of you speak English?'" (Ogawa, 1990).

There are no easy answers to the problems described above. Clearly, sensitivity to the difficulties of those who do not speak English is in order, but that is only a partial solution to the problem. In attempting to cope with the problem of non-English-speaking citizens, suspects, and criminals, many departments have not only increased the number of bilingual officers in their forces but have also begun to utilize translation services such as "Language Line Services," a division of American Telegraph and Telephone Co., which provides translation services in almost 150 languages on a full-time basis. The 911 emergency line has interpreters 24 hours a day for some languages. Having access to translation services and referrals is a first step in addressing the challenge of communication with non- or limited-English speakers. Having bilingual officers or nonsworn personnel, however, constitutes a more direct method of addressing the problem. Some departments offer language classes on the job and pay their officers more for their skills. Some large departments have been making progress in increasing their bilingual hires: of the San Francisco police department's 1800-member force, in 1992 450 were certified bilingual officers, constituting 20 percent of the force. The San Jose, California Police Department has

---

Exhibit 5.4   Tips for Communicating Where English is a Second Language

1. Speak slowly and enunciate clearly.
2. Face the person and speak directly even when using a translator.
3. Avoid concentrated eye contact if the other speaker is not making direct eye contact.
4. Do not use jargon, slang, idioms, or reduced forms (*gonna, gotta, wanna, couldja*).
5. Avoid complex verb tenses. ("If I would have known, I might have been able to provide assistance.")
6. Repeat key issues and questions in different ways.
7. Avoid asking questions that can be answered by a "yes" or "no"; rather, ask questions so that the answer can show understanding.
8. Use short, simple sentences; stop between sentences.
9. Use visual cues such as gestures, demonstrations, and brief written phrases.
10. Use active rather than passive verbs. For example, "I expect your attention" (active) rather than "Your attention is expected" (passive).
11. Have materials duplicated in bilingual format.
12. Pause frequently and give breaks. Monitor your speed when you speak.
13. Use only one idea per sentence.
14. Respect the silence that limited-English speakers need to formulate their sentences.
15. Check comprehension by having the other speaker repeat material or instructions, and summarize frequently.
16. Encourage and provide positive feedback on the person's ability to communicate.
17. Listen even more attentively than you do with a native speaker of English.
18. Be patient. Every first generation of immigrants struggles with the acquisition of English.
19. Don't speak louder. It won't help.

approximately 850 members and (in 1992) 180 were bilingual (mostly in Spanish, with a only a few speaking Vietnamese and English) (*San Francisco Chronicle,* July 20, 1992, p. A-6). In Florida, officers are learning French to deal with Haitian refugees. Some community-based police programs use trained community volunteers to assist them in situations where English is not spoken. When there is not translation available, officers have no choice but to rely on English. In doing so, the tips listed in Exhibit 5.4 on modifying one's language will be helpful.

ATTITUDES TOWARD NON- OR LIMITED-ENGLISH SPEAKERS

Interestingly, whether society at large is concerned about a particular group's use of their native language seems to be directly related to the population size of that group. When large groups of Cubans or Puerto Ricans speak Spanish, there is often a higher level of anxiety among the dominant white population than when a few Armenians, for example, speak their native language. Virtually every immigrant group is said to resist learning English, yet the pattern of language acquisition among the generations of immigrants follows a predictable course: members of the second and third generations of an immigrant family almost always become fluent in English, while many of the first-generation immigrants (the grandparents and the parents) struggle, sometimes partly learning English and sometimes not learning it at all. Many immigrants, however, are extremely motivated to learn English and become productive members of society (e.g., there are four- and five-year waiting lists for English programs at Los Angeles community colleges). The newcomers are fully aware that without English, they will never be able to integrate into the society.

Nevertheless, people (including established immigrants) overgeneralize their observations about newcomers. It is true that some people do not want to learn English. Every population has its percentage of lazy people, including middle-class Americans who have not made efforts to improve their language abilities. How often does one hear that high school graduates (i.e., native English speakers) have not learned to write or speak well? Here laziness and or lack of high-quality education (or both) may have contributed to this aspect of illiteracy. In fairness, all groups have a percentage of lazy people, but people fall victim to the tendency to stereotype "others." While not all first-generation immigrants learn English, there is a great deal of mythology around the "masses" of immigrants who hold on to their native language.

The native language for an immigrant family is the language of communication for that family. It is not uncommon to hear comments such as, "They'll never learn English if they insist on speaking their native tongues at home." Imagine having been away from your family all day and coming home and interacting in a foreign language. Is it reasonable to expect that one could express affection, resolve conflicts, show anger, and simply relax in another language? Language is an integral part of a person's identity. During the initial months and even years of communicating in a second language, a person does not truly feel like him or herself. Initially, one often has a feeling of play acting or taking on another identity when communicating in a second language.

From a physiological point of view, speaking a foreign language can be fatiguing. As a child, when speaking one's own native language, one uses a set of muscles to articulate the sounds of a given language. Changing to another language, particularly as an adult, requires the use of an entirely new set of muscles. This causes mental strain and facial tension, which can result in a person "shutting down": after a point, the person cannot communicate in English (or whatever the new language is). It is no wonder that in the multicultural workforce, clusters of people from different ethnic groups can be seen having lunch together, taking breaks together, and so on. It is relaxing to be able to speak one's own language.

Sometimes police officers say: "I know they speak English because they speak it among themselves (i.e., when the group is culturally mixed). The minute I'm on the scene, it's 'No speak English.' Why do they have to play dumb? What do they think I am—stupid?"

It would be naive to say that this phenomenon does not occur. There will always be some people who try to deceive others and use or not use English to their own advantage. However, the perception that people "feign" not knowing English also exists in situations where there are other explanations. Several factors affect an immigrant's ability to use English at any given moment, and a few of these in particular are of special significance to law enforcement officers. Generally speaking, an immigrant's ability to express himself or herself in English is best when that person is comfortable with the officer. So the more intimidating an officer is, the higher the likelihood that anxiety will affect the speaker's ability in English. Language breakdown is one of the first signs that a person is ill at ease and stressed to the point of not being able to cooperate and communicate. It is in the officer's best interest to increase the comfort level of the citizen, whether victim, suspect, or simply person requiring help. Language breakdown in a person who is otherwise fairly conversationally competent in English can also occur as a result of illness, intoxication, fatigue, and trauma.

Finally, officers must realize that their attitudes about immigrants and non- or limited-English speakers, whether positive or negative, may very well affect their interaction with them. This is especially true when an officer is under pressure and negative attitudes are more likely to surface in communication.

INTERVIEWING AND DATA-GATHERING SKILLS

Interviewing and data-gathering skills form the basic techniques for communication and intervention work with multicultural populations. For the officer, the key issues in any interviewing and data-gathering situation are:

- Bringing structure and control to the immediate situation
- Establishing the interpersonal relationships with the parties involved to gain trust and rapport for continual work
- Gaining information about the problems and situations that require the presence of the law enforcement officer
- Giving information about the workings of the law enforcement guidelines, resources, and assistance available

- Providing action and interventions, as needed
- Bolstering and supporting the different parties' abilities and skills to solve current and future problems on their own

Listed in Exhibit 5.5 are helpful guidelines for giving and getting better information in a multicultural context.

In the area of data gathering and interviewing, the officer in a multicultural law enforcement and peacekeeping situation cannot assume that the key motivators and values for oneself are the same for the other parties involved. Recognizing such differences in motivation and values will result in greater effectiveness. For example, the values of saving face and preserving one's own honor as well as one's family's honor are extremely strong motivators and values for many people from Asian, Latin American, and Mediterranean cultures. An Asian gang expert from the Oakland, California police department illustrated this with a case of a niece who had been chosen by the police to translate for her aunt, who had been raped. The values of honor and face-saving prevented the aunt from telling the police all the details of the crime of which was the victim. Her initial story, told to the police through her niece's translation, contained very few of the facts or details of the crime. Later, through a second translator who was not a family member, the rape victim gave all the necessary information. Precious time had been lost, but the victim explained that she could not have revealed the true story in front of her niece because she would have shamed her family.

Exhibit 5.5 Interviewing and Data Gathering in a Multicultural Context

1. Be knowledgeable about who is likely to have information. Ask questions to identify who the head of a family is or who respected community leaders are.

2. Consider that some cultural groups have more of a need than others for rapport and trust building before they are willing to share information. Don't consider the time it takes to establish rapport a waste of time. For some, this may be a necessary step.

3. Provide background and context for your questions, information, and requests. Cultural minorities differ in their need for "contextual information" (i.e., background information) before getting down to the issues or business at hand. Remain patient with those who want to go into more detail than you think is necessary.

4. Expect answers to be formulated and expressed in culturally different ways. Some people tend to be *linear* in their answers (i.e., giving one point of information at a time in a chronological order); some present information in a *zigzag* fashion (i.e., they digress frequently); and others tend to present information in a *circular* style (i.e., they may appear to be talking in circles). And, of course, there are individual differences in ways of presenting information, as well as cultural differences.

5. It is important to speak simply, but do not make the mistake of using simpleminded English. Remember, listening skills are usually better than speaking skills.

6. "Yes" does not always mean "yes"; don't mistake a courteous answer for the facts or the truth.

7. Remember that maintaining a good rapport is just as important as coming to the point and getting work done quickly—slow down!

8. Silence is a form of speech; don't interrupt it; give people time to express themselves by respecting their silence.

Exhibit 5.6 Key Values or Motivators in Law Enforcement

1. Survival or injury avoidance
2. Control and structure
3. Respect and authority
4. Use of professional skills
5. Upholding laws and principles
6. Avoiding conflict and tensions
7. Harmony and peace keeping
8. Conflict resolution and problem solving
9. Self-respect and self-esteem

Exhibit 5.6 lists key values or motivators for police officers. In any given situation, these may be at odds with what motivates the victim, suspect, or ordinary citizen of any background. However, when the officer and citizen are from totally different backgrounds, there will often be additional cultural or racial variables in conflict with what is listed above.

Finally, when interviewing and data gathering in the area of hate incidents/crimes [as well as threats (phone calls, letters) targeted to individuals of particular backgrounds], the officer's need for control and structure may have to encompass possible hysterical or at least highly emotional reactions from other people of the same background. In the officer's attempt to be in control of the situation, he or she must consider that there will also be a community needing reassurance. For example, an officer will need to be willing to respond sensitively to heightened anxiety on the part of group members and not downplay their fears. Interviewing and data gathering may therefore last much longer when the officer is required to deal with multiple community members and widespread fears.

NONVERBAL COMMUNICATION

Up until this point in the chapter we have discussed verbal communication across cultures and its relevance to the law enforcement context. Consider the following examples of reactions to *nonverbal* differences across cultures and their implications for day-to-day police work:

> "He didn't look at me once. I know he's guilty. Never trust a person who doesn't look you in the eye." *American police officer*
>
> "Americans seem cold. They seem to get upset when you stand close to them." *Jordanian teacher*

In the case of the first example, if an officer uses norms of eye-contact as understood by most Americans, he or she could make an incorrect judgment about someone who avoids eye contact. In the second example, an officer's comfortable distance for safety might be violated because of a cultural standard defining acceptable conversational distance. The comments above demonstrate how people can misinterpret nonverbal communication when it is culturally different from their own. This can happen with two people from the same background, but it is more likely when there are cultural differences. Universal emotions such as happiness, fear, and sadness are expressed in similar nonverbal ways throughout the world. However, there are nonverbal variations across cultures that can cause confusion.

Take the example of the way people express sadness and grief. In many cultures, such as the Arabic and Iranian cultures, people express grief openly and out-loud. In contrast, in other parts of the world (e.g., in China and Japan), people are generally more subdued or even silent in their expressions of grief. In Asian cultures, the general belief is that it is unacceptable to show emotion openly (whether sadness, happiness, or pain). Without this cultural knowledge, one might, for example, observe a person who did not openly express grief and might come to the conclusion that he or she is not in emotional distress (Levine and Adelman, 1992). This would be an incorrect ethnocentric interpretation based on one's own culture.

The expression of friendship is another example of how cultural groups differ in their nonverbal behavior. Feelings of friendship exist everywhere, but their expression varies. It is acceptable for men to embrace and kiss each other (e.g., Saudi Arabia and Russia) and for women to hold hands (e.g., China, Korea, Egypt, among other countries). Russian gymnasts of the same sex have been seen on television kissing each other on the lips. This is apparently an acceptable gesture and does not imply that they are gay or lesbian. What is considered "normal" behavior in one culture may be viewed as "abnormal" or unusual in another.

The following areas of nonverbal communication have variations across cultures; the degree to which a person displays the nonverbal differences depends on how Westernized the person has become. Note that some people who are very Westernized in their thinking may still display traditional forms of nonverbal communication simply because they are unaware that the differences exist.

1. **Gestures.** There are a few gestures in American English that are offensive in other cultures [e.g., the O.K. gesture is obscene in Latin America, the good luck gesture is offensive in parts of Vietnam, and the "come here" gesture (beckoning people to come with the palm up) is very insulting in most of Asia and Latin America] (Levine and Adelman, 1992).

2. **Body position.** A police sergeant relaxing at his desk with his feet up, baring the soles of his shoes, would most likely offend a Saudi Arabian or Thai (and other groups as well) coming into the office. To show one's foot in many cultures is insulting because the foot is considered the dirtiest part of the body. This would also apply to an officer who makes physical contact with the foot when, for example, someone is lying on the ground.

3. **Facial expressions.** Not all facial expressions mean the same thing across cultures. The smile is a great source of confusion for many people in law enforcement when they encounter people from Asian, especially Southeast Asian, cultures. A smile or giggle can cover up pain, humiliation, and embarrassment. Some women (e.g., Japanese, Vietnamese) cover up their mouths when they smile or giggle. Upon hearing something sad, a Vietnamese may smile. Similarly, an officer may

need to communicate something that causes a loss of face to a person, resulting in the person smiling. This smile does not mean that the person is trying to be a "smart aleck" with you. It is simply a culturally conditioned response.

4. **Eye contact.** In many parts of the world, eye contact is avoided with authority figures. In parts of India, for example, a father would discipline his child by saying, "Don't look me in the eye when I'm speaking to you." An American parent would say, "Look me in the eye when I'm speaking to you." To maintain direct eye contact with a police officer in some cultures would be disrespectful.

5. **Facial expressiveness.** People in law enforcement have to be able to "read faces" in certain situations to be able to assess situations correctly. The degree to which people show emotions on their faces depends, in large part, on their cultural background. Whereas Latin Americans, Mediterranean, Arab, Israeli, and African Americans tend to show emotions facially, other groups, such as many of the Asian cultural groups, tend to be less facially expressive and less emotive. An officer may *assume* that this person is not being cooperative or would not make a good witness. This may be an entirely incorrect interpretation.

6. **Physical distance.** All people unconsciously keep a comfortable distance around them when communicating with others, resulting in invisible walls that keep people far enough away. Police officers are perhaps more aware than others of the distance they keep from people in order to remain safe. When someone "violates" this distance, a person often feels threatened and backs away, or in the case of an officer, begins to think about protective measures. Although personality and context also determine interpersonal distance, cultural background comes into play. In general, Latin Americans and Middle Easterners are more comfortable at closer distances than are northern Europeans, Asians, or the majority of Americans. An officer should not necessarily feel threatened if approached in a manner that feels uncomfortably close by, for example, an Iranian or a Greek. While maintaining a safe distance, the officer should also consider cultural background.

For the law enforcement professional, nonverbal communication constitutes a major role in all aspects of peacekeeping and enforcement. For multicultural populations, it is even more important that the officer be aware of the variety of nuances and differences that may exist from one group to another. Clearly, studies show that up to 50 percent of interpersonal communication is understood because of the nonverbal "body language" aspects of the speaker. Moreover, in many cultures, as is true for many ethnic minorities in the United States, greater weight and belief are placed on the visual and nonverbal aspects of communication. (Exhibits 5.7 and 5.8).

Officers must be authentic in their communication with people from various backgrounds. When learning about both verbal and nonverbal characteristics across cultures, officers do not need to feel that they must communicate differently each time they are in contact with someone of a different background. However, understanding that there are variations in communication style will help the officer interpret people's motives and attitudes more accurately and overall, assess situations without a cultural bias.

Exhibit 5.7 Nonverbal Communication: Key Points for Law Enforcement

1. Body language and nonverbal messages can override an officer's verbal content in high stress and crisis situations. For example, the officer's statement that he or she is there to help may be contradicted by a body posture of discomfort and uncertainty in culturally unfamiliar households.
2. For people of ethnic backgrounds, stress, confusion, and uncertainty can also communicate unintended messages. For example, an Asian may remain silent and look nervous and anxious at the scene of a crime. He or she appear to many as being "uncooperative" when in fact this person may have every intention of helping the officer.
3. For people with limited English skills, the nonverbal aspects of communication become even more important. Correct gestures and nonverbal cues help the English-limited person in understanding the verbal messages.
4. It is important for the officer to learn about and avoid offensive gestures and cultural taboos. However, it should be noted that the immigrant and international visitor are quick to forgive and to overlook gestures and actions made out of forgetfulness and ignorance. The officer should realize, too, that in time, the newcomer usually learns many of the nonverbal "ways" with which the officer is more familiar. Nevertheless, learning about offensive gestures can help the officer avoid interpersonal offenses.

Note: Each of the culture-specific chapters (Chapters 6 to 10) contains information about nonverbal characteristics of the particular groups.

Exhibit 5.8 Key Questions Concerning Nonverbal Communication Across Cultures

- When is touch appropriate and inappropriate?
- What is the comfortable physical distance between people in interactions?
- What is considered proper eye contact? What does eye contact and lack of eye contact mean to the people involved?
- What cultural variety is there in facial expressions? Does, for example, nodding and smiling mean the same in all cultures? If someone appears to be expressionless, does that mean that he or she is uncooperative?
- What are appropriate and inappropriate gestures for a particular cultural group?
- Is the person in transition from one culture to another and therefore lacking the knowledge of nonverbal communication with which the officer is familiar?

MALE–FEMALE COMMUNICATION IN LAW ENFORCEMENT

With the changing workforce, including increasing numbers of women in traditionally male professions, a host of new challenges in the area of male–female communication are presenting themselves. Within law enforcement, in particular, there is a strong camaraderie which characterizes the relationships mainly among the male members of a police force, although in some cases, women are part of this camaraderie. Women who are accepted into what has been termed the "brotherhood" have generally had to "become one of the guys" in order to gain acceptance into a historically male-dominated profession.

Camaraderies are formed when a group is united because of a common goal or purpose; the glue cementing the camaraderie is the easy communication between its members. The extracurricular interests of the members of the group, the topics selected for conversation, and the jokes that people tell all contribute to the cohesion or tightness of police department members. In some departments, women find that they or other women are the object of jokes about sexual topics or that there are simply numerous references to sex. Because certain departments within cities have consisted mostly of men, they have not had to consider the inclusion of women on an equal basis and have not had to examine their own communication with each other.

Young women who are new to a department feel that they must "take it" in order to be accepted. A female sheriff participating in a Woman's Peace Officer Association (WPOA) conference said that on a daily basis she confronts vulgar language and sexual references in the jail where she works. Her list was long: "I am extremely bothered about the communication of the men where I work. Without mincing words, I'll tell you—at the county jail, officers are very degrading to women . . . they sometimes make fun of rape victims, they are rude and lewd to female inmates and they are constantly trying to get me to join into the 'fun.' A woman is referred to as a 'dyke,' a 'cunt,' a 'douche bag,' a 'whore,' a 'hooker,' a 'bitch,' and I'm sure I could come up with more. The guys don't call me those names, but they use them all the time referring to other women" (WPOA, Concord, California, 7/18/92) This sheriff also noted that she did not experience the disrespectful verbal behavior in one-to-one situations with male deputies. She noted that many of her male co-workers became disrespectful when they were in a group. She wondered out loud, "What happens to men when they group with each other? Why the change?"

It is not only the male grouping phenomenon that produces this type of rough, vulgar, and sexist language. One study of a large urban police department conducted for California Law Enforcement Command College documented inappropriate communications from patrol cars' two-way radios and computers. The language on the official system was often unprofessional—rough, vulgar, offensive, racist, and sexist. Obviously, both discipline and training were needed in this agency.

This is not to imply that all men behave and talk like this, but the phenomenon is frequent enough that women in traditionally male work environments mention this repeatedly. Some women join in conversations that, in reality, make them uncomfortable; yet, they are unable to let it be known that their working environment is uncomfortable and is actually affecting their morale and productivity. Other women seem to be comfortable with the sexual comments of their male counterparts and may not object to the use of certain terms that other women find patronizing (e.g., "honey," "doll," "babe"). However, the percentage of woman who fall into this category may very well be decreasing. Through sexual harassment training, both women and men are learning that, for some, sexual innuendoes and patronizing terms can contribute to a "hostile working environment."

In male-dominated institutions, vocations, and professions, women find that speaking out against the type of talk and jokes creates discomfort for them and puts them in a double-bind. A female police officer at a workshop on discrimination in the workplace felt that women's choices regarding communication with fellow male officers were limited. She explained that when a woman objects or speaks up, she risks earning a reputation or label that is hard to shed. If she remains quiet, she must "put up" with a lot of verbal abuse and compromise her professionalism. This particular police officer decided to speak up in her own department, and indeed, she earned a reputation as a troublemaker. In fact, she had no interest in going any further than complaining to her supervisor, but nevertheless, was accused of preparing for a lawsuit. She explained that a lawsuit was the furthest thing from her mind and that all she wanted was professional respect.

Some women who have objected to certain mannerisms of their male counterpart's communication say that when they come in a room or office, the men stop talking. The result is that the communication that normally functions to "glue" a group together is strained and tense. The ultimate result is that the workplace becomes segregated by gender. When shut out from a conversation, many women feel excluded and disempowered; many men feel resentful about having to modify their style of communication.

Women in traditionally male work environments such as police or fire departments find that they are sometimes put in a position of having to trade their professional identity for their personal one. The woman officer who proudly tells her sergeant about the arrest she made finds herself slightly stunned when he, totally out of context, compliments the way she's been keeping in shape and tells her how good she looks in her uniform. This is not to say that compliments are never acceptable. But in this context, the woman is relating as a professional and desires reciprocal professional treatment. Men and women often ask, "Where do I draw the line? When does a comment become harassment? In terms of the legal definition of sexual harassment, when comments are uninvited and unwelcome (and the "harassee," whether male or female, must make this clear), the perpetuator of the

---

Exhibit 5.9   Inclusive Workplace Communication

- Use terms that are inclusive rather than exclusive.

  Examples: "police *officer*," "chair*person*," "*commendations* " instead of the informal "atta boys"

- Avoid using terms or words that many women feel diminish their professional status:

  Examples: "chick, babe"

- Avoid using terms or words that devalue groups of women or stereotype them.

  Example: Referring to women officers as "dykes"

- Avoid sexist jokes, even if you think they are not offensive (*Someone is bound to be offended; the same applies to racist jokes.*)

- Avoid using terms that "negatively" spotlight or set women apart from men.

  Examples: ""For a woman cop, she did a good job" (implying that this is the exception rather than the rule). This also applies to references about cultural minorities: "He's Latino, but he works hard." "He's black, but he's really skilled."

comments must be reasonable enough to stop making them. It is not within the scope of this chapter to detail sexual harassment and all the legal implications; however, it should be noted that everyone has his or her own limits. (See Chapter 2 for additional information on this subject.) What is harassment to one may be appreciated by another. When communicating across genders, each party must be sensitive to what the other party considers acceptable or insulting. It is also the responsibility of the person to make it clear to the other that certain types of remarks are offensive (this applies to both men and women).

SUMMARY

With regard to cross-cultural communication in law enforcement, be aware that officers' own filters and perceptions influence the assessment of each situation and the reactions the officers choose to exhibit. Each officer has unique "blind spots" and emotional "buttons" that may negatively affect the communication. To explore one's own skills in this regard, the reader is urged to undertake a self-evaluation by filling out the Peace Officers' Communication Inventory (in the Instructor's Manual accompanying this text).

Officers must keep in mind that rapport building is related to trust for many persons of different backgrounds. The more trust you earn with members of ethnic communities, the more helpful they will be with you when you need cooperation and information. To improve communication across cultures, it is essential that people in law enforcement understand the overall style of communication of different groups, including the special challenges facing men and women in the profession.

Finally, we would like to reiterate two points made earlier in this chapter regarding police officer communication:

- Officers have traditionally used styles of communication and language that at one time were considered acceptable, not only within the police agency but with citizens as well. Because of cultural diversity in the population and the accompanying need to respect all individuals, the unspoken "rules" about what is appropriate and what is not are changing.
- Through communication, officers have tremendous power to influence the behavior and responses of the citizens with whom they contact. This is true of all citizens, regardless of background. A lack of knowledge of the *cross-cultural* aspects of communication will diminish that power with people whose backgrounds are different from the officer's.

DISCUSSION QUESTIONS AND ISSUES*

1. *The Origins of Stereotypes.* In this chapter the authors say that officers need to recognize how their early experiences in life and later adult experiences shape their perceptions and "filters" about people from groups different from one's own. What do you remember learning about various ethnic and racial groups when you were

*See Instructor's Manual accompanying this text for additional activities, role-plays, questionnaires and projects related to the content of this chapter.

young? Did you grow up in an environment of tolerance or did you hear statements such as "That's the way they are . . . " or "You've got to be careful with those people . . . " or "They are lazy (or dishonest, etc.)? Discuss also your experiences as an adult with different groups and how those may be affecting your perceptions.

2. ***Police–Officer Interaction with Limited-English Speakers.*** The following dialogue illustrates a typical interaction between a police officer and a nonnative speaker of English, in this case a Vietnamese man. Judging from the English that the Vietnamese is speaking, how would you rate the officer's use of English? Analyze this interaction by being specific as to how the officer can improve:

SITUATION:	An officer pulls a car over, gets out of the car, and approaches the driver. The driver, who is Vietnamese, says, in poor English, "What happen? Why you stop me?"
OFFICER:	I pulled you over because you ran a red light.
CITIZEN:	(no response)
OFFICER:	This is a traffic violation (receives no feedback). Do you understand?
CITIZEN:	(Nodding) Yeh, I understand.
OFFICER:	I'm going to have to issue you a traffic citation.
CITIZEN:	(Staring at officer)
OFFICER:	Where's your driver license?
CITIZEN:	License? Just a minute. (Leans over to open glove compartment, but finds nothing. He gets out of car and goes to trunk.)
OFFICER:	(irritated and slightly nervous). HEY! (In a loud voice). What's going on here? I asked to see your driver's license. Are you the registered owner of this car?
CITIZEN:	Yeh. I go get my license.
OFFICER:	(Speaking much louder.) Wait a minute. Don't you understand? Are you not the owner of this car? Do you even have a license?
CITIZEN:	Wait. (Finds license in trunk and produces it for officer.)
OFFICER:	O.K. Would you mind getting back into the car now?
CITIZEN:	(Does nothing). Yeah, I understand.
OFFICER:	(Pointing to the front seat.) Back into the car!
CITIZEN:	(Does as told)

Note: The officer could make improvements in at least four areas: (1) choice of words, (2) manner of asking questions, (3) use of idioms (there are at least two or three that could be changed to simple English), and (4) tone and attitude.

3. ***Police Officers "Hot Buttons."*** Discuss how citizens (whether suspects, victims, complainants, etc.) affect your reactions in communication. Specifically, what words and attitudes do they use that break down your attempts to be professional? What emotionally laden language "sets you off"?

4. ***Professional Communication with Citizens.*** After you have discussed what affects your communication negatively (question 3), role-play with fellow officers situations in which you respond professionally to abuses you hear. (Refer back to the section on verbal judo if you need suggestions.)

5. ***Racially Derogatory Remarks.*** In late 1992, Marge Schott, 61-year-old owner of the Cincinatti Reds, was accused of making racist remarks over a period of years and she was accused of allegedly calling two Reds outfielders her "million dollar niggers"

and admitted to keeping a swastika armband in her desk drawer. She also told the *New York Times* that Hitler was "good" but that he went too far. One of the issues related to her racially and culturally insensitive remarks was that her comments were made in front of other people, but that no one said anything to her or objected. Some felt that she should have been confronted.

Try to answer the following questions truthfully. If you were with friends and one made an off-color remark similar to those of Mrs. Schott, what would you do? If you think that you would say something, what would it be? If you know that you would not say anything, does this mean that you condone it? Would things change if the remarks were made in the law enforcement agency or you overheard officers on the streets making such remarks? Explain your answer.

6. *Cultural Observations.* For each of the cultural groups with whom you have had a substantial amount of contact, make a list of your observations for each in the areas listed below. After you make your list, try to find someone from that culture with whom you can discuss your observations.

   (a) Display of emotions and expressions of feelings
   (b) Communication style: loud, soft, direct, indirect, etc.
   (c) Expressions of appreciation; conventions of courtesy (i.e., forms of politeness)
   (d) Need (or lack thereof) for privacy
   (e) Gestures, facial expressions, and body movements
   (f) Eye contact
   (g) Touching
   (h) Interpersonal space (conversational distance)
   (i) Taboo topics in conversation
   (j) Response to authority

7. *Discomfort with Unfamiliar Groups.* Try to recall a situation in which you found yourself in a culturally unfamiliar environment (e.g., responding to a call in an ethnically different household or being the only minority person of your background among a group of people from another cultural or ethnic group). How much discomfort, if any, did you experience? If the situation was uncomfortable, did you feel that this affected your communication effectiveness or professionalism?

8. *Accusations of Racially/Ethnically Motivated Stops.* Have you encountered, "You stopped me because I'm (any ethnic group)?" If so, how did you handle the situation? How effectively do you think you responded?

REFERENCES

BERRY-WILKINSON, ALISON (1992). "Confronting discrimination in the workplace," presentation for Women's Peace Officers' Association (WPOA), July 18, Concord, Calif.

HARRIS, PHILIP R. (1989). *High Performance Leadership,* Scott Foresman, Co. Carmel, Indiana.

HARRIS, PHILIP R. AND MORAN, ROBERT T. (1991). *Managing Cultural Differences: High Performance Strategies for a New World of Business,* Gulf Publishing Company, Houston, Texas.

LEVINE, DEENA, AND MARA, ADELMAN, (1992). *Beyond Language: Cross-Cultural Communication,* rev. ed., Prentice Hall, Englewood Cliffs, N.J.

OGAWA, BRIAN (1990). *Color of Justice: Culturally Sensitive Treatment of Minority Crime Victims,* Office of Criminal Justice Planning, Sacramento, Calif. pp. 5, 6.

PART THREE

Cultural Specifics for Law Enforcement*

Part Three Asian/Pacific, African American, Latino/Hispanic, Middle Eastern, and American Indian cultural backgrounds with regard to the needs of the law enforcement representative. The authors' decision to select the above-noted groups (as opposed to other groups not described in this book) is related *one or more* of the following reasons: (1) the group is a relatively large ethnic/cultural "minority" group in the United States; (2) the traditional culture of the group differs widely from that of mainstream American culture; or (3) typically and/or historically, there have been problems between the particular group and law enforcement officials.

In the chapters general information is presented on the following areas: historical background, demographics and diversity within the cultural group. Following the introductory information, the authors present specific details relevant to law enforcement in the following areas: communication styles (both verbal and nonverbal), group identification terms, offensive labels, stereotypes, and family structure. Each chapter ends with key concerns for officers related to the particular cultural group and a summary of recommendations for law enforcement officials.[†]

The following appendix corresponds to the chapters in Part Three:

Appendix G   Cultural Holidays and Religious Celebrations

*The names for groups used in the titles are explained in the chapters.

[†]Important note to the instructor: The instructor's manual contains a lecture to help you introduce the cultural specific chapters.

6

LAW ENFORCEMENT CONTACT WITH ASIAN/PACIFIC AMERICANS

OVERVIEW

This chapter provides specific ethnic and cultural information on Asian Americans and Pacific Islanders. The label *Asian Americans/Pacific Islanders* encompasses over 32 different ethnic and cultural groups. For ease of use, we will use the shortened version, *Asian/Pacific Americans,* to refer to members of these ethnic groupings. We will first define this very diverse group. A historical overview is provided to include information about direct and indirect examples that can affect the relationship between law enforcement personnel and citizens. The chapter presents demographics and diversity elements among Asian/Pacific Americans as well as issues related to ethnic and cultural identity. Aspects of the Asian/Pacific American family are discussed, including myths and stereotypes, assimilation and acculturation processes, the extended family and community, the role of the man and the woman, generational differences, and adolescent/youth issues. In the section "Cultural Influences on Communication" we discuss the subtle aspects of nonverbal and indirect communications often found troublesome to peace officers. The closing section presents several key concerns for law enforcement: dealing with the non-English speaker, Asian "closed" communities, use of translators, and gaining community cooperation. There is a review of recommendations for improved communication and relationships between law enforcement personnel and Asian/Pacific American communities.

Exhibit 6.1   Typology of Asian/Pacific Americans

TYPE	DESCRIPTION
I	Asian/Pacific refugee and most recent immigrants
II	Asian/Pacific immigrant (major life experiences in Asia or the Pacific Islands)
III	Asian/Pacific American (second generation, offspring of immigrant or refugee)
IV	Asian/Pacific immigrant (major life experiences in the United States)
V	Asian/Pacific American (third or more generations in the United States)
VI	Asian/Pacific National (anticipates return to Asia or to the Pacific Islands, to include visitors and tourists)
VII	Asian/Pacific National (global workplace and residence)

discuss how the motivational components within each of the groupings can affect the way that Asian/Pacific American persons may respond in a law enforcement situation.

HISTORICAL INFORMATION

The first Asians to arrive in the United States in sizable numbers were the Chinese in the 1840s to work on the plantations in Hawaii. Then in the 1850s they immigrated to work in the gold mines in California and later, the transcontinental railroad. The native populations in the Pacific Islands (e.g., Samoans, Hawaiians, Guamanians, Fijians, etc.) were there before the 13 colonies of the United States. The Chinese were followed in the late nineteenth and early twentieth centuries by the Japanese and the Pilipinos (and in smaller numbers by the Koreans and Asian Indians). Most immigrants in these earlier years were men, and most worked as laborers and at other domestic and menial jobs. Until the change of the immigration laws in 1965, the number of Asians and Pacific Islander peoples immigrating into the United States was severely restricted (families often had to wait over a decade or more before members of a family could be reunited). With the change in the immigration laws, large numbers of immigrants from the Pacific Rim came to the United States from Hong Kong, Taiwan, China, Japan, Korea, South Asia (e.g., India, Ceylon, Bangladesh), Philippines, and Southeast Asia (e.g., Vietnam, Thailand, Singapore, Cambodia, Malaysia). Following the end of the Vietnam War, large numbers of Southeast Asian refugees were admitted in the late 1970s and early 1980s.

Law Enforcement Interactions with Asian/Pacific Americans as Not "User Friendly"

Asian/Pacific Americans have found the passage and enforcement of "anti-Asian" federal, state, and local laws to be more hostile and discriminatory than some of the racially motivated community incidents experienced by this population. Early experiences of Asians and Pacific Islanders was that of the majority population wanting to keep them out of the United States and putting tremendous barriers in the way of those who were already here. It was the role of the law enforcement agencies and officers to be the vehicle to carry out these laws against Asian/Pacific American immi-

COMMENTARY

For many Asian/Pacific American groups, especially those who recently immigrated into the United States, the law enforcement system seems to be a mystery. As such, Asian/Pacific Americans may find it difficult to cooperate and to participate fully with law enforcement officers.

> To the Vietnamese immigrant, our law enforcement system doesn't seem to serve his community well. In Vietnam, if you are arrested, then the work of the attorney is to prove that you are innocent. You remain locked-up in jail until your innocence is proven. In the United States, a suspect, who is arrested, is released upon posting bail, usually within 24 hours. To the Vietnamese immigrant, it would seem that if you have the money, you can *buy* your way out of jail! (Vietnamese refugee's comments about a merchant's reluctance to cooperate with the police)

For some law enforcement officers, the diversity of customs, activities, behaviors, and values in the different Asian/Pacific American groups is not easily understandable. Many law enforcement officers do not know where to go to get such information without the fear of offending. Yet such cultural knowledge is vital to understanding and to effective peacekeeping in any Asian/Pacific American community.

> For some of the Asian groups, you just hear things that you're not sure about, but there's no one you can turn to to ask sometimes. For example, in our work, we hear that Sikhs always carry a sword or knife on their person (which they carry as a religious object), so is it insensitive to confiscate it? We also hear that if it is drawn, they must also draw blood—true or false? Moreover, what is the thing to do with their turbans? Would it be an insult to pat-search a turban while it's on the person's head?
>
> (Police officer's comments in a cultural awareness training session)

INTRODUCTION

For the past three decades, the Asian/Pacific American population has represented the largest proportional increases (over 100 percent growth in each decade) of any ethnic minority population in the United States. The population growth can be attributed to (1) higher immigration from the Pacific Rim countries, (2) greater longevity, and (3) higher birthrates. Growth in the major urban areas has been particularly striking, most exceptionally in San Francisco, New York City, Los Angeles, Boston, Denver, Chicago, San Jose, San Diego, Seattle, Houston, Philadelphia, and Phoenix. Growth in the population as a whole is most dramatically reflected in terms of increased numbers of Asian/Pacific Americans in politics, community leadership, business, education, and public service areas. Law enforcement contact with Asian/Pacific people has increased because of their larger number in the communities.

ASIAN/PACIFIC AMERICAN DEFINED

The phrase *Asian/Pacific Americans* is a contraction of two terms, *Asian Americans* and *Pacific Islander peoples*. Although used throughout this chapter, *Asian/Pacific*

Americans is, in fact, a convenient summary label for a very heterogeneous group. There certainly is not a universal acceptance of this labeling convention, but for practical purposes it has been adopted frequently with occasional variations (e.g., Asian and Pacific Americans, Asian Americans/Pacific Islanders, Asians and Pacific Islanders). It represents the self-designation preferred by many Asian and Pacific people in the United States and is preferred over the more dated (and to some, offensive) term *Orientals*. The U.S. government and other governmental jurisdictions usually use *Asian Americans/Pacific Islanders* to refer to members within any of the 32 or more groups.

At least 32 distinct ethnic and cultural groups would meaningfully be listed under this designation: (1) Bangladeshi, (2) Belauan (formerly Palauan), (3) Bhutanese, (4) Burmese, (5) Chamorro (Guamanian), (6) Chinese, (7) Fijian, (8) Hawaiian, (9) H'mong, (10) Indian (Asian, South Asian, or East Indian), (11) Indonesian, (12) Japanese, (13) Kampuchean (or Cambodian), (14) Korean, (15) Laotian, (16) Malaysian, (17) Marshallese (of the Marshall Islands to include Majuro, Ebeye, and Kwajalein), (18) Micronesia (to include Kosrae, Ponape, Truk, and Yap), (19) Nepalese, (20) Okinawan, (21) Pakistani, (22) Pilipino (preferred spelling to "Filipino"), (23) Saipan Carolinian (or Carolinian from the Commonwealth of the Northern Marianas), (24) Samoan, (25) Singaporian, (26) Sri Lankan (formerly Ceylonese), (27) Tahitian, (28) Taiwanese, (29) Tibetan, (30) Tongan, (31) Thai, and (32) Vietnamese. Although most of us are aware that there are marked differences among the 32 groups listed above, individuals within any of the 32 groups may differ in a vast number of ways as well.

From the viewpoint of law enforcement, it is important to recognize some of the differences that may cut across or be common to all Asian/Pacific ethnic groups: for example, (1) area of residence in the United States, (2) comfort and competence with the English language, (3) generational status in the United States (first, second, third generation, etc.), (4) degree of acculturation and assimilation, (5) education (number of years outside of the United States and in the United States), (6) native and other languages spoken and/or written, (7) age (what is documented on paper and what may be the "real" age), (8) degree of identification with the "home" country and/or region of self or parents' origin, (9) family composition and extent of family dispersion in the United States and globally, (10) extent of identification with local, national, and global Asian/Pacific social-political issues, (11) participation and embeddedness in the ethnic community network, (12) religious beliefs and cultural value orientation, (13) economic status and financial standing, and (14) sensitivity to ethnic/ cultural experiences and perceptions as an Asian/Pacific person in the United States.

It should be noted that the definition itself of the Asian/Pacific group points to and embodies an ever-emerging ethnic mosaic of diverse constituencies. Groups are added and removed based on self-definition and needs for self-choice. Clearly, the pooling of separate Asian and Pacific Islander groups under the label *Asian/Pacific Americans* emerged, in part, out of the necessity to have a collective whole when a larger numerical count may make a difference (especially in political and community areas). Merging these 32 ethnic groups into a collective entity al-

lowed for sufficiently large numbers with respect to meaningful repre the community and other arenas.

Other Key Definitions

Since a large proportion of Asian/Pacific Americans that law enforcem may encounter are born outside the United States, it is important to some of the key differences that relate to immigration status. One key d that which is found for Asian/Pacific Americans who are considered "ref those who are considered "immigrants." Some of the between-group (within the Asian community and among other ethnic minority commun been a result of not understanding the implication of having status in t States.

Refugees are sponsored into the United States on the authority o government. While there may be many ethnic groups who have come in i sponsorship of the federal government having "refugee" or "emigre" si larger numbers have been from Southeast Asia as a result of the upheaval on by the Vietnam War. Since they are sponsored into the United States by ernment, refugees are expected to utilize public support services fully [fare, ESL (English-as-a-second-language) programs, educational tuiti training programs, case management, etc.]. It is part of being a "good ref participate fully, and often, case managers are assigned refugee families to that family members are utilizing all possible services provided. Such partic in public programs can result in "dependency" and "learned helplessness" ing from having others help or interfere in what many could have done fo selves.

An *immigrant* enters the United States under the direct sponsorship person's family. The federal government allows immigrants to enter the States only if their families can completely support or establish work for the p In fact, one of the criteria for being able to attain permanent residence sta "green card") is that the immigrant will not become a burden to the govern which means that participation in any "public-funded" program may jeopa that person's chances for attaining permanent residence status (so, for immigr they try very hard to avoid getting involved in public/community programs services). In contrast to the refugee, being a "good immigrant" is to *avoid* parti tion in public service programs.

TYPOLOGY OF ASIAN/PACIFIC AMERICANS

As we look at Asian/Pacific American individuals, families, and communities, have developed a seven-part typology that will be useful in understanding and summarizing some of the differences among individuals within this group.

Our typology suggests that as law enforcement and public safety organiz tions prepare and train their personnel to work with the Asian/Pacific America communities, a focus on the key differences within each of the typological grouﾏ would be most effective. We will come back to this typology in a later section t

grants. From the beginning, the interactions of Asian/Pacific Americans with law enforcement officials were fraught with conflicts, difficulties, and mixed messages.

Anti-Asian Federal, State, and Local Laws

Almost all of our federal immigration laws were written such that their enforcement made the Asian newcomers feel unwelcomed and unwanted. Following the large influx of Chinese in the 1850s to work in the gold mines and on the railroad, many Americans were resentful of the Chinese for their willingness to work long hours for low wages. With mounting public pressure, the Chinese Exclusion Act of 1882 banned the immigration of Chinese laborers for ten years, and subsequent amendments extended this ban indefinitely. Because of this ban, and with the Chinese populations in the United States being primarily male, the Chinese population in the United States dropped from 105,465 in 1880 to 61,639 in 1920 (Takaki, 1989a). Since the Chinese Exclusion Act applied only to Chinese, Japanese immigration started around 1870 to Hawaii, with larger numbers to the mainland in the 1890s to work as laborers and in domestic jobs on the farms on the west coast. Similar to the Chinese, public pressure to restrict Japanese immigration ensued. In the case of the Japanese, the Japanese government did not want a "loss of face" and of international prestige through having its people "banned" from immigrating to the United States. Rather, the "gentleman's agreement" was negotiated with President Theodore Roosevelt in 1907, which resulted in the Japanese government voluntarily restricting the immigration of Japanese laborers to the United States. Family members of Japanese already in the United States, however, were allowed to enter. Under the gentleman's agreement, large numbers of "picture brides" began entering into the United States, resulting in a large increase in Japanese American populations: 25,000 in 1900 to 127,000 in 1940 (Daniels, 1988). Subsequent laws banned or prevented immigration from the Asiatic countries: the Immigration Act of 1917 banned immigration from all counties in the Pacific Rim except for the Philippines (a U.S. territory). The Immigration Act of 1924 restricted migration from all countries to 2 percent of the countries' national origin population living in the United States in 1890. This "2 percent" restriction was not changed until 1965. It was not until 1952 that most Asian immigrants were eligible to become naturalized citizens of the United States and, therefore, the right to vote. (African Americans and American Indians were able to become citizens long before Asian/Pacific Americans were given the same rights.)

While Pilipinos (preferred spelling over Filipinos) have been immigrating to the United States since the early 1900s, large numbers of Pilipino laborers began entering in the 1920s because of the need for unskilled laborers (and because of the unavailability of Chinese and Japanese immigrants who were restricted entry by law). Similar to previous Asian groups, Pilipino immigration was soon to be limited to a quota of 50 immigrants per year with the passage of the Tydings–McDuffie Act of 1934.

Anti-Asian immigration laws were finally repealed starting with the removal of the Chinese Exclusion Act in 1943. Other laws were repealed to allow immigration of Asians and Pacific Islanders, but the process was slow. It was not until 1965 that amendments to the McCarran-Walter Act opened the way for Asian immigrants to enter in larger numbers (a fixed quota of 20,000 per country, as opposed to the 2 percent of the countries of national origin living in the United States in 1890). The 1965 amendment also established the "fifth preference" category, which allowed highly skilled workers needed by the United States to enter this country. Because of the preference for highly skilled workers, a second major wave of immigrants from Hong Kong, Taiwan, India, Korea, Philippines, Japan, Singapore, and other Asiatic countries entered in the mid-1960s. With the upheaval in Southeast Asia and the Vietnam War, the third major wave of close to 1 million refugees and immigrants arrived in the United States from those Southeast Asian countries affected starting in the mid-1970s and lasting to the early 1980s (Special Services for Groups, 1983).

While many immigrant groups (e.g., Italians, Jews, Poles) have been the target of discrimination or bigotry, and prejudice, Asian/Pacific Americans have similarities with African Americans in that both groups have experienced extensive legal discrimination. This has hindered their ability to participate fully as Americans and has gravely affected their well-being and quality of life. Some states had laws that prohibited intermarriage between Asians and whites. State and local laws imposed restrictive conditions and taxes specifically on Asian businesses and individuals. State courts were equally biased: For example, in the case of *People* v. *Hall* heard in the California Supreme Court in 1854, Hall, a white defendant, had been convicted of murdering a Chinese man on the basis of testimony provided by one white and three Chinese witnesses. The California Supreme Court threw out Hall's conviction on the basis that state law prohibited blacks, mulattos, or Indians from testifying in favor of or against whites in court. The court's decision read: "*Indian* as commonly used refers only to the North American Indian, yet in the days of Columbus all shores washed by Chinese waters were called the Indies. In the second place the word *white* necessarily excludes all other races than Caucasian; and in the third place, even if this were not so, I would decide against the testimony of Chinese on the grounds of public policy" (California Supreme Court: *People* v. *Hall*).

This section of anti-Asian/Pacific American laws and sentiments cannot close without noting that Japanese Americans are the only immigrant group of Americans that have been routed out of their homes and interned without due process in the history of the American people. President Roosevelt's Executive Order 9066 resulted in the evacuation and incarceration of 100,000 Japanese Americans in 1942. For Asian/Pacific Americans, the internment of Japanese Americans represents how quickly anti-Asian sentiments can result in incarceration and punishment by law even if no one was convicted of any crime.

DEMOGRAPHICS: DIVERSITY AMONG ASIAN/PACIFIC AMERICANS

As we noted in the section defining Asian/Pacific Americans, this is an extremely heterogeneous population comprised of many different ethnic and cultural groups, generational differences within the United States, educational and socioeconomic diversity, and many other background/life experience differences.

Exhibit 6.2   1990 Asian/Pacific American population by groups

ASIAN/PACIFIC AMERICAN GROUPS	PERCENT OF TOTAL
Chinese	22.6
Pilipino	19.3
Japanese	11.6
Asian Indian	11.2
Korean	11.0
Vietnamese	8.4
Laotian	2.0
Thai	1.3
Cambodian	2.0
Hmong	1.2
Pakistani	1.1
Indonesian	0.4
All other groups	3.0

Source: U.S. Bureau of the Census, Racial Statistics Division.

Notwithstanding, Asian/Pacific Americans currently number about 7.3 million and represent approximately 3 percent of the U.S. population. The Asian/Pacific American population doubled with each census taking since 1970 (1.5 million in 1970, 3.5 million in 1980, and 7.3 million in 1990). While greater longevity and higher birthrates contribute to this population increase, the major contributor to the growth of Asian/Pacific Americans is immigration from the Pacific Rim countries. Since the 1970s, Asian/Pacific American migration makes up over 40 percent of all immigration to the United States (U.S. Bureau of the Census, 1990). As is evident in Exhibit 6.2, Chinese are the largest group with 22.6 percent of the total Asian/Pacific American population. Pilipinos are close behind with 19.3 percent of this population; in the next decade, Pilipinos will be the largest Asian/Pacific American group in the United States. Japanese, Asian Indians, and Koreans composed approximately 11 percent for each group of the Asian/Pacific Americans. Vietnamese Americans constitute 8.4 percent, and all other Asian/Pacific American groups amount approximately to 10 percent of this population.

For the law enforcement officer, the key Asian/Pacific American groups to understand would be these top six groups: Chinese, Pilipino, Japanese, Asian Indian, Korean, and Vietnamese (of course, one must consider local community trends and uniquenesses of populations). Knowledge of the growing trends among this Asian/Pacific American population would also be important for officer recruitment and for other human resource considerations. Current Asian/Pacific Americans involved in professional law enforcement careers are largely Japanese and Chinese Americans. To plan for the changing Asian/Pacific American population base, it is critical to recruit and develop officers from the Pilipino, Vietnamese, Korean, and Asian Indian communities.

As noted in Exhibit 6.3, the vast majority of Asian/Pacific Americans are not born in the United States. Most of the Japanese, Pilipinos, Cambodians, and

Exhibit 6.3   1990 Asian/Pacific American population by groups

ASIAN/PACIFIC AMERICAN GROUP	PERCENTAGE NOT U.S.-BORN	PERCENTAGE WHO DO NOT SPEAK ENGLISH WELL	PERCENTAGE IN THE WEST
Chinese	63.3	23.0	52.7
Pilipino	64.7	6.0	68.8
Japanese	28.4	9.0	80.3
Asian Indian	70.4	5.0	19.2
Korean	81.9	24.0	42.9
Vietnamese	90.5	38.0	46.2
Laotian	93.7	69.0	45.7
Thai	82.1	12.0	43.0
Cambodian	93.9	59.0	55.6
Hmong	90.5	63.0	37.4
Pakistani	85.1	10.0	23.5
Indonesian	83.4	6.0	56.2
All Asian/Pacific Americans	62.1	15.0	56.4

Source: U.S. Commission on Civil Rights (1992).

Indonesians reside in the western states. Chinese, Koreans, Vietnamese, Laotians, and Thais are fairly distributed in the large urban areas of the United States. Most of the Asian Indians and Pakistanis live in the eastern states (however, there are large numbers of Indians in California). Minnesota and Fresno, California have the largest Hmong populations (from mountain regions in Laos) in the country. Proficiency in the English language varies within groups, with those immigrants who have most recently arrived having the larger percentage of those not able to speak English well. Depending on their jurisdictions, law enforcement and peace officers, can use Table 6.3 to determine what additional languages and skills training might be appropriate in their work with Asian/Pacific American communities.

ASIAN/PACIFIC AMERICANS KEY MOTIVATING PERSPECTIVES

Earlier in this chapter we provided a typology for viewing Asian/Pacific Americans. We have provided in Exhibit 6.4 the same typology and have appended to it the key motivating perspectives for members in each group. By understanding some of these key motivating perspectives, the law enforcement officer might be better able to understand the behaviors exhibited by citizens from these groupings.

For example, for the most recent immigrants and refugee group (Asian/Pacific refugee, type I), the key to understanding this group's behavior is that members are in a "surviving" mode (see Exhibit 6.4). Many members from this category may remember that law enforcement and police officers in their country of origin were corrupt, aligned with a repressive government and the military, and subjected to bribes by those who were more affluent. All activities tended to be

Table 6.4   Key motivating perspectives in understanding Asian/Pacific American groups

MOTIVATION	GROUP
SURVIVING	Asian/Pacific refugee (and most recent immigrants)
PRESERVING	Asian/Pacific immigrant (major life experiences in Asia or the Pacific Islands)
ADJUSTING	Asian/Pacific American (second generation, offspring of immigrant or refugee)
CHANGING	Asian/Pacific immigrant (major life experiences in the United States)
CHOOSING	Asian/Pacific American (third or more generations in the United States)
MAINTAINING	Asian/Pacific National (anticipates return to Asia or to the Pacific Islands)
EXPANDING	Asian/Pacific National (global workplace and residence)

guided by this perspective to survive, to get through; this perspective also makes sense in terms of the traumatic ordeals faced by refugees in their journeys to the United States. Encounters by these people with law enforcement personnel usually involved saying and doing anything to discontinue the contact because of possible fears of personal harm (e.g., not speaking English, not having any identification, "Yes, I will cooperate!").

> Mr. Pok and Mr. Nguyen came in as part of the "boat people" in 1979. Although both of them are in their early-thirties, because of their size and informal dress, they look much younger. Both worked as building maintenance personnel for one of the high-technology companies on the west coast. One evening as they were driving home following their work at approximately 1:30 A.M., Mr. Pok and Mr. Nguyen found themselves pulled over by two police cars. Two officers approached their car and requested that they step outside. The officers were responding to a call about two young Asian males, driving a light-colored car, involved in an armed robbery of a nearby convenience store. Mr. Pok's and Mr. Nguyen's car was light-colored. When the officers asked both individuals to take a kneeling position while the officers conducted a search and verified DMV information, Mr. Pok fell to the ground and pleaded at the feet of one of the officers, "Please don't kill me!" It was Mr. Nguyen who finally explained that the kneeling position is the "execution position," and Mr. Pok saw many individuals executed that way in his escape from Cambodia. (Example cited by community organizer)

With regard to the Asian/Pacific immigrants (type II), understanding their behaviors should focus on "preserving" their "backhome" culture as the motivating perspective. Since the majority of their life experiences occurred in Asia or the Pacific Islands, members are trying to preserve as many of their traditional values and customs as they can. Many Asian business persons and investors in the United States are included in this category. Much intergenerational conflict between grandparents or parents and youths occur within this group. Members are inclined to keep to their ethnic communities (e.g., Little Saigons, Chinatowns, Korean-towns, Japantowns, Manilatowns, etc.) and have as little to do with law enforcement as possible. Many remember that the police have not served them well in the past (e.g., immigration laws, Japanese internment).

> Police officers, in a west coast city, were confused and wondered if a local "private bar" frequented by Japanese and Korean businessmen was a front for prostitution. They noticed that the bar had many Asian female "hostesses," and that companies

paid hundreds of dollars per bottle for the companies' liquor stock for entertaining guests (when the off-the-shelf price of these liquors was one-fifth of what the bar charged). Only after much exchange between members of the local Asian/Pacific American community and the community relations police officers was the understanding made that these "private bars" allowed many immigrant business persons to feel at home in this culture. Among their own peers and in keeping with their own customs and cultural practices, they were comfortable, and no prostitutes nor any other illegal activities were involved. (Police officer's anecdote in cultural awareness training session)

Asian/Pacific Americans (second generation, type III) tend to be what we often consider as the "image" in our mind of the "Asian American." For those of the second generation, individuals work very hard at being assimilated into the mainstream, adjusting and changing to be a part of mainstream "America." The expectations of second-generation parents are usually high; parents will sacrifice so that their offspring will "make it" in their lifetime. Members may interact primarily with non-Asians and take on many of the values and norms of the mainstream society. This group may be considered "marginal" by some (Sue and Wagner, 1973). They may try to become like the mainstream (become "white"), but their acceptance by others may still be one of considering them "Asian." Many from this group try to minimize their contact with law enforcement personnel and agencies primarily because of the immigration and other experiences relayed to them by their parents' generation. Individuals of the second generation were born in the United States before the mid-1960s and may have had relatives (or parents) who entered the United States by using "false papers." Fear of disclosures of such illegal entries have prevented many Asian/Pacific Americans from cooperating with peace officers and with other human and social service agencies and programs.

The Asian/Pacific immigrant (type IV), whose major life experience is in the United States, focuses much of his or her energies around changes (either through assimilation and/or acculturation) that have to be made to succeed. While these individuals have tended to continue to value the cultural and ethnic elements of their former homeland, most of the people in this group know that changes are necessary. Members in this group reflect the socioeconomic standings of the different waves in which each has entered into the United States. For example, people who had entered as part of the first wave of laborers and domestic workers (primarily Chinese and Japanese, with some Pilipinos and Koreans) represent one grouping. Others entered more as part of the second wave of immigration as "foreign students" and/or under the "fifth preference" as professional skilled workers. Asian/Pacific immigrants (type IV) who are designated under the "fifth preference" on the Immigration and Nationalization Service form are professionals with skills in short supply in the United States. Under the "fifth preference" it is considered in the best interest of the United States to allow these professionals to enter. This second group consists of very educated, professional individuals (e.g., the largest numbers of foreign-trained medical doctors/psychiatrists in the United States are from India, the Philippines, and Korea; President's Commission on Mental Health, 1978). Since the fall of Saigon in 1975 and the beginning of the immigration of Southeast Asians into the United States, this third wave includes over 1 million Asian/Pacific immigrants who suffered great trauma in their escape, with many of them in their young adulthood today. For the members of this group, reactions to law enforcement officials will vary depending on their wave of immigration and socioeconomic experiences. For the law enforcement officer, it is critical to understand the differences among the immigrant groups (i.e., do not confuse the professional Asian/Pacific immigrant with one of the other groups).

For Asian/Pacific Americans (third generation or more, type V), we are dealing with persons who are more able to choose which aspects of the old culture to keep and of the new culture to accept. Focus is on "choosing" activities, values, norms, and lifestyles that blend the best of that which is Asian/Pacific and that which is "American." The importance of being "bicultural" is a unique aspect of this group. Many may no longer have as much skill with their native language and may rely primarily on English as their primary or only language (thus a person can be bicultural but not bilingual). Contact by members of this group with law enforcement personnel would often be no more different than with any other American.

For the last two categories, the Asian/Pacific nationals, we make a key distinction between those who plan to return to their own country following a work assignment in the United States (type VI) and those whose work is truly global in which people may have several residences in different parts of the world (type VII). For the former (type VI, on a U.S. work assignment that may last five to seven years), the people are working to maintain their homebase cultural orientation and experiences, knowing that when the work assignment is over, they will be back to their home country again. Because they intend to maintain the native culture, many of the individuals may be inadequately prepared to understand some of the laws and practices of the United States. For this group, being able to stay in the United States to complete their assignments is of key importance. Sometimes, individuals may not be aware of the differences between "minor" violations (e.g., minor traffic violations, small claims) and more "major" violations and crimes. Let's look at this following example:

> Mr. Sato is a manager assigned to oversee a technical department in a joint U.S.–Japanese automobile plant in the midwest. One evening, while driving home from a late night at the plant, Mr. Sato did not see a stop sign and went right through it on a nonbusy intersection. A police officer in a patrol car saw the violation and pulled Mr. Sato over. The interaction with the police officer was a puzzle for the officer since Mr. Sato seemed very cooperative, but he kept asking the officer "to forgive him and to please let him go!" After much discussion and explanation, it was discovered that Mr. Sato thought that the officer would have to confiscate his passport because of the stop-sign violation (something that is done in many of the Asiatic countries) and that he might be "kicked" out of the country, and thus not be able to complete his work assignment. Upon clearing this misconception, Mr. Sato accepted the traffic citation "with appreciation."

For the second group of Asian/Pacific nationals (type VII), the key focus is their ability to "expand" their actions and behaviors effectively into different global environments. These people see themselves as being able to adapt in a variety of global environments; many may speak three or more languages (including English). People within this group pride themselves in knowing about the different laws, norms, values, and practices of the countries they encounter. Law enforcement personnel would find this group equally able to understand and to follow the laws and practices of a community.

LABELS AND TERMS

As we noted earlier, the term *Asian/Pacific Americans* is a convenient summarizing label used to refer to some very heterogeneous groups of people. The key to understanding which terms to use is based on the principle of "self-designation and self-preference." There is great sensitivity among Asian and Pacific Islander people about the fact that this population was, up until the 1960 census, relegated to the "other" category. With the ethnic pride movement and ethnic minority studies movement in the late-1960s, people of Asian and Pacific Islands descent began to designate self-preferred terms for group reference. The terms were chosen over the previous term *Oriental,* which is considered by many Asian/Pacific Americans to be offensive, because it symbolizes many of the past references, injustices, and stereotypes of Asian and Pacific people. It was also a term designated by "the West" (i.e., the *Occident,* the western hemisphere) for Asian people and reminds many Asian/Pacific Americans about the "colonial mentality" of foreign policies and its effects on the Pacific Rim countries.

In federal and other governmental designations, the label used is *Asian American/Pacific Islanders.* While very few Asian/Pacific Americans refer to themselves as such, the governmental designation is used in laws and regulations and in most reports and publications. For people within any of the groups, often the more specific names for the groups are preferred (e.g., Chinese, Japanese, Vietnamese, Pakistani, Hawaiian, etc.). Some people may prefer that the term *American* be part of their designation (e.g., Korean American, Pilipino American, etc.). For the law enforcement officer, the best term to use to refer to a person *is the term that he or she prefers to be called.* It is perfectly acceptable to ask people what ethnic or cultural group(s) they identify with and what they prefer to be called.

The use of slurs—"Jap," "Chink," "Gook," "Chinaman," "Flip," or other derogatory ethnic slang terms—are never acceptable in crime fighting and peacekeeping, no matter how provoked an officer may be. Other stereotypic terms, such as "Chinese fire drill," "DWO (Driving While Oriental)," "Fu Man Chu mustache," "yellow cur," "yellow peril," "Bruce Lee Kung Fu type," "slant-eyed," "Vietnamese bar girl," and "dragon lady" do not convey the kinds of professionalism and respect for community diversity important to law enforcement and peacekeeping, and need to be avoided in law enforcement work. Officers hearing these words used in their own departments (or with peers or citizens) should provide immediate feedback about the use of such terms to the other person. Officers who may out of habit routinely use these terms may find themselves (or their superiors) in the *embarrassing situation* (on the 6:00 o'clock news) of explaining to offended citizens and communities why the term was used and how they had intended no prejudice.

MYTHS AND STEREOTYPES

Knowledge and sensitivity to Asian/Pacific Americans' concerns, diversity, historical background, and life experiences will facilitate the crime fighting and peacekeeping mission of peace officers. It is important to have an understanding about some of the myths, environmental messages, and stereotypes of Asian/Pacific Americans that contribute to prejudice, discrimination, and bias encountered by this population. Many Americans do not have much experience with the diversity of Asian/Pacific American groups and learn about these groups only through the stereotypes, often perpetuated by movies and the media. These simplistic and often inaccurate views lead many people to lump all Asian/Pacific Americans into one stereotypic group. Often, the complexities of the diverse Asian/Pacific American groups in terms of language, history, customs, cultures, religions, and life experiences become confusing and threatening, and it is easier to deal with stereotypes. Notwithstanding, it is important for the law enforcement officer to be aware of the different stereotypes of Asian/Pacific Americans. The key to effectiveness with any ethnic/racial group is not that we do not have myths and stereotypes about these groups, but that *we are aware of the existence of these stereotypes and we can monitor our thinking and behavior with respect to the person with whom we are dealing.*

Some of the stereotypes that have affected Asian/Pacific Americans in law enforcement include the following:

1. *Viewing Asian/Pacific Americans as "all alike."* That is, because there are many similarities in names, physical features, and behaviors, many law enforcement officers may make comments about their inability to tell people apart or to deal with them in stereotypic group fashion (e.g., they are *all* "inscrutable," involved in gangs, etc.). Cultural awareness training and sensitivity will allow the officer the skills and knowledge to avoid a mistake such as the following:

> In Florida, Mr. Nguyen Ngoc Tieu, a Vietnamese defendant, was charged with murder and was awaiting trial at the county jail. At the time of the trial, Mr. Nguyen Hen Van, also of Vietnamese descent, was in jail charged with theft and was mistakenly transported to stand trial for murder. During the two-day trial, no one had noticed the difference, even though the defendant had continuously protested that he was the wrong person. Two testifying witnesses in the murder trial even identified the mistaken defendant as the murderer, and even the defense attorney (who previously had interviewed the alleged murderer two weeks ago) did not recognize that the wrong person was on trial. It was finally through the recognition of someone viewing the trial in the courtroom that called the court's attention to the fact that the wrong Mr. Nguyen was on trial and that a mistrial was declared. (*Seattle Times,* Oct. 26, 1985)

2. *Viewing Asian/Pacific Americans as successful, a "model minority," or a "super minority."* Some hold the stereotype that Asian/Pacific Americans are "all" successful, and this stereotype is reinforced by the media (Sue et al., 1975; Ramirez, 1986). Such stereotypes have resulted in intergroup hostilities and hate crimes toward

Asian/Pacific Americans and have served to mask true differences and diversity among the various Asians and Pacific Islanders groups. Clearly, no group of people are "all successful," nor are they "all criminals." Notwithstanding, the "success" and "model minority" stereotypes have affected Asian/Pacific Americans negatively. For example, because of their implied success, law enforcement organizations may not spend the time to recruit Asian/Pacific Americans for law enforcement careers (assuming that they are more interested in other areas, such as education and business pursuits). This stereotype also hides the existence of real discrimination for those who are successful, such as "glass ceilings" in promotional and developmental opportunities. The "success" stereotype has resulted in violence and crimes against Asian/Pacific persons:

> The murder of Vincent Chin, and the subsequent inability of the court system to bring the murderers to justice is now a well-known case among Asian/Pacific American communities. The perpetrators in this case, Ronald Ebens and Michael Nitz, were two white automobile factory workers who blamed Vincent Chin (a *Chinese American*) for the success of the *Japanese* automobile industry, which was, in turn, blamed for taking away American jobs in the automobile factory. (Takaki, 1989b)

3. *Perceiving Asian/Pacific Americans as "foreigners" and not as Americans.* It is not unusual for Asian/Pacific Americans to be asked by a stranger, "What country are you from?" or "How long have you been in the United States?" The implication conveyed by these questions is that the Asian/Pacific American is a "foreigner" and therefore could not possibly be an American. This perception of Asian/Pacific Americans as foreigners has resulted in consequences like the internment of Japanese Americans in the United States during World War II [at the same time, the most decorated World War II unit (fighting in Europe) was the U.S. Army 442nd Division, consisting entirely of Asian/Pacific Americans, the majority of whom were Japanese Americans]. Even at the highest level of the U.S. government, such stereotypes of Asian/Pacific Americans are pervasive:

> United States Senator Sparkie Matsunaga (from Hawaii) was at the White House as part of the United States delegation to welcome the delegation from Japan visiting President Reagan. When Senator and Mrs. Matsunaga arrived at the White House, the protocol officer immediately told them to go to the side of the room where the Japanese delegation was standing. As the Senator tried to correct the misperception that he was not from Japan (a "foreigner"), but that indeed he was a United States Senator from the state of Hawaii (and should be part of the American welcoming delegation to the visiting Japanese), Secretary of State Alexander Haig came over to insist that the Senator stand with the Japanese delegation and ushered him and his wife to stand with the group from Japan (on the opposite of the room), whereupon Mrs. Matsunaga said to the Senator, "Sparkie, we're on the wrong side of the room and in the wrong delegation. No other American in the room had noticed the error. It was not until Secretary of State Haig's introduction to Senator Matsunaga did he realize the error.

SECRETARY HAIG: "Welcome to the United States; I'm Secretary of State, Alexander Haig."

SENATOR MATSUNAGA: "I know, Mr. Secretary. I voted to confirm you as Secretary of State; I'm United States Senator Sparkie Matsunaga from Hawaii."

(Personal anecdote told to one of the authors)

From a law enforcement perspective, many hate crimes against Asian/Pacific Americans are related to the stereotype of the group as "foreigners" and not as "Americans." The case of Vincent Chin and the following case of Jim Loo in North Carolina are examples illustrating the consequences of this stereotype:

> Jim Loo had been in the United States for 13 years and had been working in a restaurant in Raleigh, North Carolina to save enough money to go to college. He had immigrated from China. Jim and several Vietnamese American friends were playing billiards in a local pool hall when Robert Piche and his brother, Lloyd, began calling them "Chinks" and "Gooks" and blaming them for American deaths in Vietnam: "I don't like you because you're Vietnamese. Our brothers went over to Vietnam and they never came back." In the ensuring physical attacks by the Piche brothers (one had a shotgun and the other a pistol), Jim Loo sustained injuries that resulted in his death. Jim Loo had nothing to do with Vietnam and had never been there; he had considered himself a Chinese *American*. (Effron, 1989)

4. *Misunderstanding Asian/Pacific cultural differences as threats to other Americans.* The more than 32 Asian/Pacific American groups encompass great differences in life experiences, languages, backgrounds, and cultures. It is easy to make mistakes and draw incorrect conclusions because of such cultural differences. Certainly, when one lacks information about any group, it is natural to draw conclusions based on our own filtering system, stereotypes, and assumptions. Most of the time, these incorrect assumptions and stereotypes are corrected by favorable contact and actual interpersonal relationships with Asian/Pacific American people. From a law enforcement perspective, the thrust of community policing, as well as cultural awareness training, is to provide opportunities to modify stereotypes and to learn about ethnic communities. Law enforcement agencies, however, have to intervene in situations in which individuals and/or groups view Asian/Pacific American cultural differences as perceived "threats" to themselves:

> On January 17, 1989, Patrick Edward Purdy entered the school yard at Cleveland Elementary School in Stockton, California firing an AK47 assault rifle. In the ensuing few minutes of fire, Purdy had killed five Southeast Asian children and wounded 30 other children. He then turned the rifle on himself and killed himself. More than 60 percent of the children at this school were Southeast Asians. The California Attorney General's Report noted that "it appears highly probable that Purdy deliberately chose Cleveland Elementary School as the location for his murderous assault in substantial part because it was heavily populated by Southeast Asian children. His frequent resentful comments about Southeast Asians indicated a particular animosity against them. (Mathews and Lait, 1989; Kempsky, 1989)

The misunderstanding of cultural differences that leads to stereotypic conclusions has resulted in law enforcement involvement between Asian/Pacific American communities and other ethnic/racial minority groups: for example, (1) the

Korean American and African American conflicts in the Los Angeles riots following the Rodney King verdict, (2) disputes among Vietnamese and Hispanic fishermen in Florida, and (3) the Flatbush boycott incident described below:

> While there are many conflicting stories to this incident, it is clear that aspects of cultural stereotyping and misunderstanding of cultural differences led to a more than a year of conflict between Korean Americans and Blacks in Flatbush, Brooklyn, New York with much involvement by law enforcement, city, state, Federal, and community parties. Specifically, on January 18, 1990, Ghislaine Felissaint, a Haitian American resident of Flatbush was shopping for a few small items at the Red Apple store, owned by Korean Americans. While the details are not clear about the ensuing altercation at the cash register, both the Black community and the Asian/Pacific American community began to be involved in a year long conflict which eventually resulted in the closing of two Korean American stores in the area. One of the reasons mentioned for the inability of the police to help solve this conflict was the lack of any police officers with the ability to speak Creole, French or Korean, at the time of the incident, to interview witnesses. (Goldstein, 1990; Kandel, 1991)

THE ASIAN/PACIFIC AMERICAN FAMILY

Obviously, with over 32 different cultural groups under the label of Asian/Pacific Americans, there are great subgroup differences when we look at how families operate within each subgroup. We would like to present some common characteristics shared among many Asian/Pacific American families that can be of value in crime fighting and community peacekeeping. Asian/Pacific American families generally exhibit very strong ties among extended family members. It is not unusual for three to four generations of the same family to live under one roof. Moreover, the extended family can even have ongoing close family contacts that span great geographic distance. For example, family members (all of whom consider themselves to be *one* family) can be engaged in extensive communications and activities with members of the same family in the United States, Canada, Hong Kong, *and* Vietnam, all simultaneously. It is not uncommon for an officer to come into contact with members of the extended Asian/Pacific American family in the course of servicing these communities. One key to the success of law enforcement officers in working with an extended family network is the knowledge of how best to contact an Asian/Pacific American family and whom within the family to speak to for information, help, and referral (to be discussed).

Culture Shock and the Asian/Pacific American Family

Because the traditional cultures of Asia and the Pacific Islands are so very different from those of the United States, many Asian/Pacific American families (be they refugees, immigrants, business persons, students, tourists, etc.) experience some degree of culture shock upon their entrance and residence in the United States. Culture shock results not only from differences in values and traditions but also from differences in urbanization, industrialization, and modernization from technology that may be different from their homeland. Peace officers need to be aware that Asian/Pacific Americans may cope with their culture shock by becoming "clannish" (e.g., Chinatowns, Koreatowns, etc.). Other survival mechanisms include avoiding contact and interaction with those who are different (to include police officers).

The Role of the Man and the Woman

In most Asian/Pacific American families, the relationship and communication patterns tend to be quite hierarchical, with the father as the identified head of the household. While many decisions and activities may appear to be decided by the father, many other people may come into the picture. Generally, if there are grandparents in the household, the father would still act as the spokesperson for the family, but he would consult the grandparents, wife, and others regarding any major decision. It is often important in any kind of law enforcement contact that requires a decision and/or choice to allow the parties time to discuss issues in, as much as possible, a "private" manner. Self-control and keeping things within the family are key values for Asian/Pacific Americans. As such, the officer may find that there is more control in a situation by allowing the Asian/Pacific American to come to the same conclusion and to exercise his or her own self-choice (which may be the same as what the officer would want the parties to do anyway). For example, the officer can explain an arrest situation to the father of a family member, and instead of saying directly to the family member to be arrested that he or she has to leave with the officer, the officer can allow the father to suggest to the family member that he or she leave with the officer. What may appear to be a minor consideration in this case can result in a higher degree of persuasion, control, and cooperation by all parties concerned.

Although there are no clear-cut rules as to whether one goes to the male head of the household or to the female head to make a law enforcement inquiry, the general rule of thumb is that one would not go too wrong if one starts with the father. It should be noted that for most Asian/Pacific American families, the role of the mother in discipline and in decision making is very important. While the household *may* appear to be "ruled" by the father, the mother's role in finances, discipline, education, operations, and decision making is major.

Children/Adolescents/Youth

Most Asian/Pacific American families involve at least two or more people within the same household working outside the home. To that extent, if young children are present, there is a high reliance on either family members or others to help care for them while the parents are at work. It is not uncommon for older children to care for younger children within a household. Moreover, "latchkey" children within an Asian/Pacific American home are common, especially for families who cannot afford external child care. In recent immigrant and refugee families, Asian/Pacific American children have a special role in being the intermediaries between parents and the external community because of the ability of the younger people to learn English and the American ways of doing things. Children often serve as translators and interpreters for peace officers in their communication and relations with Asian/Pacific American families involving recent immigrants and refugees. In such situations it is suggested that the officer review what role is expected of the youthful member of the family, how sensitive an area the translated content is to the different family members, and what consequences there might be if the content is incorrectly translated. As an example, asking a juvenile to translate to his or her parents that the juvenile had been involved in a sexual abuse situation at the school may result in significant omissions because of the embarrassment caused to both the juvenile and to the parents. In all cases, when a child is acting as a translator, the officer should direct all verbal and nonverbal communication to the parents (as one would normally do without a translator). Otherwise, the parents may view the officer's lack of attention to them as an insult.

CULTURAL INFLUENCES ON COMMUNICATION

While we do not wish to create any kind of stereotypes, there are key features of Asian/Pacific American verbal and nonverbal communication style that necessitate explanation. Misunderstanding resulting from style differences can result in perceptions of poor community services from police agencies, conflicts resulting from such misunderstandings, and safety and control issues for the peace officer.

Language Limitations

It is important that officers take the time to get information from witnesses, victims, and suspects even if the people have limitations on their English-speaking abilities (the use of officers who may speak different Asian/Pacific dialects/languages, translators, and language bank resources will help). Often, the Asian/Pacific American has not been helped in crime-fighting and peacekeeping situations because the officer could not or did not take information from a non or limited-English speaking person.

> Huang Jin Bao, a Chinese American who could read English but did not speak it well was being given a ticket for double parking. He tried to explain himself to the officer but was unsuccessful. While he sat in the car and waited for the ticket, the officer came back with two tickets for Huang, the original ticket for double parking, and another ticket. The officer left, but he also walked away with Huang's driver's license. When Huang followed the officer and asked for his driver's license back, the officer handcuffed him, pushed him around, and arrested him. Huang Jin Bao was charged with traffic violations, harassing a police officer, and resisting arrest. (New York *Nichibei,* Apr. 9, 1987)

Perception of Evasiveness

Asian/Pacific Americans tend to hold a more "family" and/or "group" orientation. The lack of the use of "I" statements and/or self-reference should not be evaluated as not being straightforward and/or being evasive about oneself or one's relationships. The officer may be concerned because an Asian/Pacific American may wish to use the pronoun "we" when the situation may call for a personal observation involving an "I" statement. For example, in a traffic accident, the Asian/Pacific American may describe what he/she saw and may tell the officer that "We saw. . . . " Such group statements to mean what the person saw are consistent with the family and group orientation of Asian/Pacific Americans.

Saying "No" and Losing Face

The officer must be aware that for Asian/Pacific Americans it is considered by many to be rude, impolite, and involve a "loss of face" to say "no" directly to an authority figure like a peace officer. Peace officers need to understand the following possibilities when an answer of "Yes" is heard from an Asian/Pacific American: It can mean,

- "Yes, I heard what you said (but I may or may not agree with you)."
- "Yes, I understand what you said (but I may or may not do what I understand)."
- "Yes, I can see this is important for you (but I may not agree with you on this)."
- "Yes, I agree (and will do what you said)."

Because the context of the communication and the nonverbal aspects of the message are equally meaningful, it is vital for the law enforcement officer to be sure of the "yes" answers received, as well as other language nuances from Asian/Pacific Americans. Two examples can illustrate this: (1) Especially for more voluntary events and situations (e.g., a community neighborhood safety meeting), if an Asian/Pacific American says that he or she will "try his or her best to attend," this generally means that he or she won't be there. (2) If an Asian/Pacific National says in response to a question, "It is possible," this generally means don't wait for the event to happen. Such communications, as noted above, may be more applicable to some Asian/Pacific Americans than others; however, sensitivity of the law enforcement officer to these language nuances will facilitate communication. It is not that specific rules for interacting with each Asian/Pacific American group on language are necessary in and of themselves but rather that a general understanding of language and cultural styles be addressed and considered. In a communication situation in which the response of "yes" may be ambiguous, it is suggested that the law enforcement officer rephrase the question so that the requested outcome action and understanding is demonstrated in the verbal response.

Ambiguous response:

OFFICER: "I need you to show up in court on Tuesday. Do you understand?"

ASIAN WITNESS: "Yes!"

Rephrasing of question to show understanding and outcome:

OFFICER: "What are you going to do on Tuesday?"

ASIAN WITNESS: "I will be in court on Tuesday. I must go there."

High-Context Communication

Asian/Pacific Americans tend to be "high context" in communication style. This means that the officer needs to provide both interpersonal and situational contexts for effective communications. Context for Asian/Pacific Americans means that members of the community know the officers in the community. Community members may previously have had working relationships with the officer (e.g., crime prevention meetings, police athletic league, etc.). Moreover, other members of the community may help to provide information and context for police cooperation based on past relationships. Context also means providing explanations and education to Asian/Pacific Americans about procedures, laws, and so on, before asking them questions and/or requesting their participation in an activity. By providing background information and by establishing prior relationships with Asian/Pacific Americans communities, the Asian/Pacific American person has a context for cooperating with law enforcement agencies and officers.

Nonverbal Nuances

Be aware of nonverbal and other cultural nuances that may detract from the effective communication of the officer. Many Asian/Pacific Americans find it uncomfortable and, sometimes, inappropriate to maintain eye contact with authority figures such as police officers. It is considered in many Asian/Pacific American cultures to be disrespectful if there is eye contact with someone who is of higher status, position, importance, or authority. Many Asian/Pacific Americans may look down on the ground and/or avert their eyes to avoid direct eye contact with a police officer. The officer should not automatically read this nonverbal behavior as a lack of trust or a dishonest response. Similarly, the police officer should be aware of possible nonverbal gestures and actions that may detract from his or her professional roles (e.g., gesturing with the curled index finger for a person to come forward in a manner that might be used only for servants or animals in that person's home culture).

Expression of Emotion

Asian/Pacific Americans may not display their emotionality in the same way that the officer expects. The central thesis guiding Asian/Pacific Americans is the Confucian notion of "walking the middle road." This means that extremes—too much or too little of anything—are not good. Asian/Pacific Americans tend to moderate their display of positive and/or negative emotion. Often, in crisis situations, nonverbal displays of emotions are controlled to the point that the Asian/Pacific American appears "flat." Under such circumstances, the officer needs to understand and interpret such displays of emotion appropriately. For example, when the parent of a murder victim does not appear emotionally shaken by an officer's report, this does not mean that the person is not experiencing a severe emotional crisis.

KEY ISSUES IN LAW ENFORCEMENT

Underreporting of Crimes

Because of their past experiences with some law enforcement agencies (e.g., anti-Asian immigration laws, health/sanitation code violations in restaurants, as well as perceived unresponsiveness by police) Asian/Pacific Americans are reluctant to report crimes and may not seek police assistance and help. Many Asian/Pacific Americans bring with them remembrances of how police in their home countries have brutalized and violated them and others (e.g., in Southeast Asian and other Asian countries). Many immigrants and refugees are simply not knowledgeable about the legal system of the United States and, therefore, avoid any contact with law enforcement personnel. Outreach and community policing perspectives will enhance the contact and relationship with Asian/Pacific American communities in the underreporting of crimes.

Differential Treatment

The U.S. Commission on Civil Rights (1992) highlighted several areas in which Asian/Pacific Americans may have received different treatment in police services as a result of their culture or ethnic heritage. Incidents reported included aspects of police misconduct and harassment. The commission reported the following two cases as examples:

> On June 1, 1991, a young Italian American man who had recently moved to Revere, Massachusetts was murdered. Witnesses said that he was brutally beaten and stabbed repeatedly by a group of Asian men. The Revere Police Department which has no Asian American police officers and has no access to interpreters, was unable to solve the case and apprehend the murderers quickly and came under increasing criticism from the victim's family.

> On July 1, in an attempt to force information about the murder to the surface, a team of 40 Revere police officers, along with representatives of the Immigration and Naturalization Service, made a 2-hour sweep through a Cambodian neighborhood in search of persons with outstanding warrants and possible illegal aliens. 'We wanted to break open the case,' said one of the police officers involved in the sweep. The Cambodian Americans living in Revere were frightened and angered by the police sweep. (U.S. Commission on Civil Rights, 1992)

> In September, 1987, A Korean student was stopped in Manhattan, New York for a traffic violation he committed while on his bicycle. According to a newspaper account, witnesses saw him being forced off his bicycle onto the ground by the police, who proceeded to beat his head against the pavement. The student was then arrested for traffic violations, disorderly conduct, and obstructing governmental administration. The witnesses followed the student to the police station, where, they claim, the police made a reference to the student's "Asian nose." (U.S. Commission on Civil Rights, 1992)

Increasing Asian/Pacific American Community Police Services

James Chin (1987), an officer with the Los Angeles Police Department Airport Police Bureau, describes the benefits and improved relationships as a result of a storefront outreach effort to better service the Asian/Pacific American neighborhood in the Korean area of Los Angeles (a second storefront has been established in the Chinese area as well).

> The Los Angeles Police Department has two storefronts serving Asian/Pacific Islander communities, one located in a Korean neighborhood; the other in a Chinese neighborhood. Both storefronts are the results of organized community demands for such operations and subsequent donations from individuals and organizations within the community helped provide space and needed materials. The storefronts are staffed by a police officer and a bilingual community person whose salary is paid by community donations and the police department. (Chin, 1985)

Another outreach approach is the use of Asian/Pacific American bilingual community service officers (CSOs), who are nonsworn officers holding badges and wearing uniforms to serve the Southeast Asian communities in San Diego,

California. The CSOs provide many of the supportive services available from the police department by using bilingual nonsworn personnel.

Increasing Asian/Pacific American Peace Officers

There is a noticeable underrepresentation of Asian/Pacific Americans in federal, state, and local law enforcement positions. The small number of Asian/Pacific American officers has prevented many departments in high-density Asian/Pacific American neighborhoods from effectively serving those communities with effective role models and bicultural expertise. A variety of reasons exist for such underrepresentations:

- Past history of law enforcement relationships with the Asian/Pacific American communities
- Interests of Asian/Pacific Americans in law enforcement careers
- Image of law enforcement personnel in Asian/Pacific American communities
- Lack of knowledge about the different careers and pathways in law enforcement
- Concern with and fear of background checks, physical requirements, and the application process
- Lack of role models and advocates for law enforcement careers for Asian/Pacific Americans

Crimes within the Asian/Pacific American Communities

Many of the crimes within Asian/Pacific American communities are perpetrated by others within the same group. This is particularly true among the Asian/Pacific refugee and immigrant groups. Law enforcement officials have often found it difficult to get cooperation from refugee and immigrant victims of extortion, home robbery, burglary, theft, blackmail, and other crimes against persons. In part, the fear of the Asian/Pacific American person in these cases relates to the retaliatory possibilities of the criminal who is within his or her own community. Other concerns of the Asian/Pacific American victim include:

- The perceived responsiveness of the peacekeeping officers and agencies
- Lack of familiarity and trust with police services
- Perceived effectiveness of the law enforcement agencies
- Prior stereotypes and images of law enforcement agencies as discriminatory (e.g., immigration laws) as well as unresponsive to crimes against Asian/Pacific Americans

The recent Asian/Pacific American refugees and immigrants are often prime targets, in part, because of their distrust of most institutions (e.g., banks as well as police departments, health departments, etc.). As a result, they are more inclined to hide and store cash and other valuables in the home. A key challenge for police agencies is to educate this group and to work cooperatively with Asian/Pacific Americans to reduce the crimes within these communities.

SUMMARY OF RECOMMENDATIONS FOR LAW ENFORCEMENT

1.   As a result of the early immigration laws and other discriminatory treatment received by Asian/Pacific Americans in the United States, the experiences of

Asian/Pacific Americans with law enforcement officials had been fraught with conflicts, difficulties, and mixed messages.

- Officers should realize that some Asian/Pacific Americans may still remember this history and carry with them stereotypes of police services as something to be feared and avoided. Law enforcement officials may need to go out of their way to establish the trust and to win cooperation to accomplish their goals to serve and to protect Asian/Pacific Americans.

2.   The label "Asian Americans/Pacific Islanders" encompasses over 32 different and very diverse ethnic and cultural groups.

- Law enforcement officials need to be aware of the differences among the 32 diverse ethnic groups (e.g., different cultural and language groups) as well as the differences that may result from the individual life experiences within any one of the 32 groups (e.g., generational differences). Since a key stereotype of concern for Asian/Pacific Americans is that they are regarded by mainstream Americans as very much "alike," it is important that peace officers not make such errors in their interactions with Asian/Pacific Americans.

3.   There is tremendous diversity among Asian/Pacific Americans, and one way to understand people within these communities is to look at some of the motivating forces that might affect decisions by Asian/Pacific American citizens. We have provided a seven-part typology that will assist the officer in viewing some of these motivational bases.

- Although there are many ethnicities, cultures, and languages among the 32 or more groups within the Asian/Pacific American communities, one way to understand the impact of their immigration and life experiences is by learning the motivational determinants of people within different generational and immigrant groups.

4.   The self-preferred term for referring to Asian/Pacific Americans varies with contexts, groups, and individual experiences.

- Law enforcement officials need to be aware of terms that are unacceptable and derogatory, and terms that are currently used. When in doubt, officers have to learn to become comfortable in asking Asian/Pacific Americans which term they prefer.
- Officers are advised to provide helpful feedback to their peers when offensive terms, labels, and/or actions are used with Asian/Pacific Americans. Such feedback will help reduce the risk of misunderstanding and improve the working relationships of officers with the Asian/Pacific American communities. Moreover, it will help enhance the professional image of the department for those communities.

5.   Many Asian/Pacific Americans are concerned with their ability to communicate clearly, and this is of particular concern among those Asian/Pacific Americans who are immigrants and refugees.

- Peace officers need to take the time and be aware that bilingual and English-limited-speaking persons want to communicate effectively with them. Maintaining contact, providing extra time, using translators, and being patient with the speaker will allow the Asian/Pacific American to communicate his or her concerns.

6.   Cultural differences in verbal and nonverbal communication often result in misinterpretation of the message and of behaviors.

- Officers need to be aware of nonverbal aspects of the Asian/Pacific American in his or her communication style, such as eye contact, gestures, and affect (show of emotions). Verbal aspects, such as accent, limited vocabulary, and incorrect grammar, may give the officer the impression that an Asian/Pacific American is not understanding what is communicated. It is important to remember that the listening and comprehension skills with English of Asian/Pacific American immigrants and refugees are usually better than their speaking skills.

7. Because of their past experiences with law enforcement agencies, along with their own concerns about privacy, self-help, and other factors, Asian/Pacific Americans are reluctant to report crimes and may not seek police assistance and help.

- It is important for law enforcement departments and officials to build relationships and working partnerships with Asian/Pacific American communities. This is often helped by outreach efforts such as community storefront offices, bilingual officers, and participation of officers in community activities.

DISCUSSION QUESTIONS AND ISSUES*

1. ***Law Enforcement as Not "User Friendly."*** Under the historical information section of this chapter, it was noted that many anti-Asian/Pacific American laws and events may leave Asian/Pacific Americans with the view that law enforcement agencies are not "user friendly." What are the implications of this view for law enforcement? What are ways to improve such possible negative points of view?

2. ***Diversity among Asian/Pacific Americans.*** The authors noted that Asian/Pacific Americans consist of over 32 diverse ethnic and cultural groups. Which groups are you most likely to encounter in crime fighting and peacekeeping in your work? Which groups do you anticipate encountering in your future work?

3. ***How Asian/Pacific American Groups Differ.*** A typology for understanding what motivates some of the behaviors of Asian/Pacific American people in terms of their generational and immigration status in the United States was provided. How might you apply this typology to better understand an Asian/Pacific American refugee involved in a moving traffic violation? An Asian/Pacific American immigrant involved as a victim of a house robbery? An Asian/Pacific national involved as a victim of a burglary? Southeast Asian youths involved in possible gang activities?

4. ***Choice of Terms.*** The term *Asian Americans and Pacific Islanders* is used in many publications and is used by people to refer to members from the more than 32 diverse groups included within this label. How might you find out which is the best term to use to refer to a person if ethnic and cultural information of this kind is necessary?

5. ***Offensive Terms and Labels.*** The authors strongly urge that offensive terms such as "Chinks," "gooks," and "flips" not be used in law enforcement work at any time. Give three practical reasons for not doing so.

6. ***Effects of Myths and Stereotypes.*** Myths and stereotypes about Asian/Pacific Americans have affected this group greatly. What are some of the Asian/Pacific American stereotypes that you have heard of or have encountered? What effects would these stereotypes have on Asian/Pacific Americans? Do you know of any examples (other than those provided in the chapter) of stereotypes that have affected law enforcement officials' interaction with Asian Americans?

*See Instructor's Manual accompanying this text for additional activities, role-plays, questionnaires and projects related to the content of this chapter.

7. *Verbal and Nonverbal Variations among Cultures.* How do you think the information in this chapter about verbal and nonverbal communication styles can help officers in their approach to Asian/Pacific American citizens? When you can understand the *cultural* components of the style and behaviors, does this help you to become more sensitive and objective about your reactions? Provide some examples of rephrasing questions in such a way that they elicit responses to show understanding and intended actions on the part of the Asian/Pacific American.

8. *Self-Monitoring and Avoidance of Law Enforcement.* Why do you think that many Asian/Pacific Americans keep to their own communities and express the desire for self-monitoring and community resolution of their problems? When are such efforts desirable? When are they ineffective? How can police agencies be of greater service to Asian/Pacific American communities in this regard?

REFERENCES

CHIN, J. (1987). "Crime and the Asian American community: the Los Angeles response to Koreatown," *Journal of California Law Enforcement,* Vol. 19, 52–60.

DANIELS, R. (1988). *Asian America: Chinese and Japanese in the United States since 1850,* University of Washington Press, Seattle, Wash.

EFFRON, S. (1989). "Racial slaying prompts fear, anger in Raleigh," *Greensboro News and Record,* Sept. 24.

GOLDSTEIN, L. (1990). "Split between blacks, Koreans widens in N.Y. court," *Washington Post,* May 8.

KANDEL, B. (1991). "Tensions ease year after NYC grocery boycott," *USA Today,* Jan. 4.

KEMPSKY, N. (1989). *A Report to Attorney General John K. Van de Kamp on Patrick Edward Purdy and the Cleveland School Killings,* State of California Attorney General's Office, Sacramento, Calif., Oct.

MATHEWS, J., AND M. LAIT, (1989). "Rifleman slays five at school: 19 pupils, teacher shot in California; assailant kills self," *Washington Post,* Jan. 18.

President's Commission on Mental Health (1978). *Report of the Special Population Subpanel on Mental Health of Asian/Pacific Americans,* Vol. 3, U.S. Government Printing Office, Washington, D.C.

RAMIREZ, A. (1986). "America's super minority," *Fortune,* Nov. 24.

Special Services for Groups (1983). *Bridging Cultures: Southeast Asian Refugees in America.* Special Services for Groups, Los Angeles.

SUE, S. AND WAGNER, N. N. (1973). *Asian-Americans: Psychological Perspectives,* Science and Behavior Books, Palo Alto; Calif.

SUE, S., D. W. SUE, AND D. SUE (1975). "Asian Americans as a minority group," *American Psychologist,* Vol. 30, pp. 906–910.

TAKAKI, R. (1989a). *Strangers from a Different Shore: A History of Asian Americans,* Little, Brown, Boston.

TAKAKI, R. (1989b). "Who killed Vincent Chin," in *A Look beyond the Model Minority Image: Critical Issues in Asian America,* G. Yun, ed., Minority Rights Group, New York.

U.S. Bureau of the Census (1990). *United States Population Estimates by Age, Sex, Race, and Hispanic Origin: 1980 to 1988,* Current Population Reports, Series P-25, No. 1045, U.S. Government Printing Office, Washington, D.C.

U.S. Commission on Civil Rights (1992). *Civil Rights Issues Facing Asian Americans in the 1990s,* U.S. Government Printing Office, Washington, D.C.

7

LAW ENFORCEMENT CONTACT WITH AFRICAN AMERICANS

OVERVIEW

This chapter provides specific cultural and historical information on African Americans, which can, both directly and indirectly, affect the relationship between law enforcement officials and citizens. This chapter presents demographics and diversity among African Americans as well as issues related to cultural and racial identity. Following this background information is a section on group identification terms and a discussion of myths and stereotypes. Aspects of the family are discussed, including the extended family, the roles of men and women, single-mother families, and adolescents. A section on cultural influences on communication deals with African American varieties of English, nonverbal communication, verbal expressiveness and emotionalism, and fighting words, threats, and aggressive behavior. The closing section presents several key concerns for law enforcement, including information on differential treatment, excessive force and brutality, interaction with poor urban communities, and needs of the inner city. The summary of the chapter reviews recommendations for improved communication and relationships between law enforcement officials and African Americans.

COMMENTARY

The history of intimidation of African Americans by police continues to affect the dynamics of law enforcement in black communities today.

Senator Robert Kennedy after visiting the scene of the Watts Riot, 1965.

There is no point in telling blacks to observe the law. . . . It has almost always been used against them.

Martin Luther King, 1964.
We must learn to live together as brothers or perish together as fools.

The Evolving Strategy of Police: A Minority View, by Hubert Williams and Patrick Murphy, National Institute of Justice, Jan. 1990, No. 3.
If . . . the more recent trends towards inclusion of African Americans and other minorities in policing and in the broader society are continued, then community policing might finally realize a vision of police departments as organizations that protect the lives, property, and rights of all citizens in a fair and effective way.

AFRICAN AMERICAN CULTURE

Americans of all races often gloss over the *cultural* differences between white and black Americans because of the overwhelming problems associated with the *racial* aspects of black–white relations. The effects that slavery and discrimination have had on the black experience in America are not to be downplayed, but in addition, African American *culture* must also be considered. African American culture is in part influenced by African culture and is significantly different from white culture. Many police executives have come to recognize that when there is an influx of immigrants from a particular part of the world, their officers are better equipped to establish trust, good communication, and mutual cooperation if they have some basic understanding of the group's cultural background. However, past history has shown when it comes to African Americans, cultural differences are seldom considered, even though they can cause serious communication problems between citizens and police officers. Failing to recognize the distinctiveness of black culture, language, and communication patterns can lead to misunderstandings, conflict, and even confrontation. In addition, understanding the history of African Americans (which is related to the culture) is especially important for law enforcement officials as they work toward improving relations and changing individual and community perceptions.

HISTORICAL INFORMATION

The majority of African Americans or blacks (the terms will be used interchangeably) in the United States trace their roots to West Africa. They were torn from their cultures of origin between the seventeenth and nineteenth centuries when they were brought here as slaves. Blacks represent the only migrants to come to the Americas, North and South, against their will. Blacks from Africa were literally kidnap victims, kidnapped by Europeans, as well as purchased as captives by Yankee traders. This has made African Americans, as a group, very different from immigrants, who chose to come to the United States to better their lives, and different from refugees, who fled their homelands to escape religious or political persecution.

The very word *slave* carries the connotation of an "inferior" being. Slave owners inwardly understood that treating people as animals to be owned, worked, and sold was immoral, but they wanted to think of themselves as good religious, moral people. Hence they had to convince themselves that their slaves were not really human, but a lower form of life. They focused on racial differences (skin color, hair texture, etc.) as "proof" that black people were not really people, after all. Racism began, then, as an airtight alibi for a horrifying injustice. The notion of the slave (and by extension, any African American) as less than human has created great psychological and social problems for succeeding generations of both black and white citizens. Slavery lead to a system of inferior housing, schools, health care, and jobs for black people, which persists to this day.

The institution of slavery formally ended in 1863, but the racist ideas born of slavery have persisted. These ideas continue even now to leave deep scars on many African Americans. Today, particularly in the lower-socioeconomic classes, many blacks continue to suffer from the psychological heritage of slavery, as well as from active, current discrimination that still prevents them from realizing the American dream.

Until recently, the "public" history that many Americans learned presented a distorted, incomplete picture of black family life (emphasizing breakdown) during the slave era, which had crippling effects on families for generations to come. This version of history never examined the moral strength of the slaves or the community solidarity and family loyalty that arose after emancipation. There is no doubt that these strengths have positively affected the rebuilding of the African American community.

> According to almost all witnesses, the roads of the South were clogged in 1865 [after emancipation] with Black men and women searching for long-lost wives, husbands, children, brothers and sisters. The in-gathering continued for several years and began in most communities with mass marriage ceremonies that legalized the slave vows. This was a voluntary process for husbands and wives who were free to renounce slave vows and search for new mates. Significantly, most freedmen, some of them 80 and 90 years old, decided to remain with their old mates, thereby giving irrefutable testimony on the meaning of their love. . . . (Bennett, 1989)

Despite slave owners' attempts to destroy black family life, some slaves did manage to form lasting families headed by a mother and a father, and many slave couples enjoyed long marriages. Although white slave masters would often do everything possible to pull families apart (including the forced "breeding" and the selling of slaves), there is evidence that slaves maintained their family connections as best as they could and produced stable units with admirable values. According to U.S. Historian Char Miller, "Despite the fact that slavery tore apart many families, blacks maintained links, loves and relationships just as anyone else would under these circumstances" (personal communication, Dec. 24, 1992).

The more accurate version of history counters the impression that all slave families were so helpless that they were always torn apart and could never reestablish themselves, or that their social relationships were chaotic and amoral. The resolve of large numbers of blacks to rebuild their families and communities as soon as they were freed represents an impressive determination in a people who survived one of the most brutal forms of servitude that history has seen. African American survival, and consequently, African American contributions to American society, deserve a high level of respect and testify to a people's great strength. It is not within the scope of this chapter to discuss African American contributions to society, but suffice it to say that frequently the perceptions of some people in law enforcement are often conditioned by their exposure to the black underclass, for whom crime is a way of life.

Law Enforcement Interaction with African Americans: Historical Baggage

In the United States during the late seventeenth and eighteenth centuries, following slave uprisings in a number of colonies, the colonists created strict laws to contain the slaves. Even minor offenses were punished harshly. This set the negative tone between law enforcement and blacks. American police were called on to form "slave patrols" and to enforce racially biased laws (Williams and Murphy, 1990). In many areas of the country, police were expected to continue enforcing deeply biased, discriminatory laws (including those setting curfews for blacks, and barring blacks from many facilities and activities). Today, segments of the African American population, especially the lower-socioeconomic classes, continue to struggle with "historical baggage" relating to law enforcement–police interaction. "The fact that the legal order not only countenanced but sustained slavery, segregation and discrimination for most of our Nation's history—and the fact that the police were bound to uphold that order—set a pattern for police behavior and attitudes toward minority communities that has persisted until the present day. That pattern includes the idea that minorities have fewer civil rights, that the task of the police is to keep them under control, and that the police have little responsibility for protecting them from crime within their communities" (Williams and Murphy, 1990).

Most police officers have had some exposure to the historical precedents of poor relationships between police and minority communities. The damages of the past give us no choice but to make a greater effort, today, with groups such as African Americans, for whom contact with law enforcement has long been problematic.

DEMOGRAPHICS: DIVERSITY AMONG AFRICAN AMERICANS

Currently, blacks comprise approximately 32 million people, or over 12 percent of the population of the United States. Until the last few decades, the vast majority lived in the south. Between 1940 and 1970, over 1.5 million blacks migrated initially to the north and then to the west coast, largely seeking better job opportunities. Over 85 percent now live in urban areas and are economically impoverished. Despite a growing black middle class, the black inner cities have been expanding rapidly since the 1950s. As whites have moved to the suburbs, urban cores were repopulated mainly by blacks, Hispanics, and various new immigrant groups. The most vivid example is the city of Detroit, where at least 60 percent of the population is black, while most whites and immigrant groups have settled in outlying areas. Similarly, other cities, such as Washington D.C., St. Louis, Chicago and Cleveland, are populated mainly by blacks and new immigrants, creating layers of tension where diverse groups with conflicting values and customs suddenly find themselves crowded into the same urban neighborhoods.

Between 1970 and 1980, 3 1/2 million blacks and Hispanics moved to cities that had been abandoned by more than 3 million white residents (Lohman, 1977). These population shifts have created "two Americas." One America is the world of the suburbs, where schools, recreational facilities, and community resources are far better. The other is the inner city, where many African Americans (and other minorities) have much poorer access to educational and job opportunities and where living conditions are often closer to those of ravaged Third World cities than to those of America's comfortable suburban environment.

Although many African Americans belong to the lower-socioeconomic classes, blacks are present in all classes, from the extremely poor to the extremely affluent. As with all ethnic groups, there are significant class-related differences among blacks, affecting values and behavior. It is no more true to say that a poor black has a great deal in common with an affluent black than to say that poor and rich whites are the same. (Later in this chapter we discuss stereotyping of all blacks based on the black underclass.) However, color, more so than class, often determines how the larger society reacts to and treats blacks. Therefore, the *racial* (as opposed to cultural) experience of many African Americans in the United States is similar, regardless of an individual's level of prosperity or education.

The *cultural* diversity that exists among African Americans is related to a variety of factors. Over the last 400 years, black families have come from many different countries (e.g., Jamaica, Trinidad, Belize, Haiti, Puerto Rico). By far, the largest group's forefathers came directly to the United States from Africa. In addition, there are cultural differences among African Americans related to the region of the country from which they came. As with whites, there are "southern" and "northern" characteristics as well as urban and rural characteristics.

Religious backgrounds vary, but the majority of American-born blacks are Protestant, and many are specifically Baptist. The first black-run, black-controlled denomination in the country was the African Methodist Episcopal church (which was created because churches in the north and south either banned blacks or required them to sit apart from whites). In addition, a percentage of blacks belong to the Black Muslim religion, including the "Nation of Islam" and "American Muslim Mission." (The term *Black Muslim* is often used but is rejected by some members of the religion.) There are also sizable and fast-growing black populations among members of the Seventh-Day Adventists, Jehovah's Witnesses, Pentecostals (especially among Spanish-speaking blacks), and especially among blacks of Caribbean origin, Santeria, Candomble, Voudun, and similar sects blending Catholic and West African (mainly Yoruba) beliefs and rituals. Rastafarianism has spread far beyond its native Jamaica to become an influential religious movement among immigrants from many other English-speaking Caribbean nations.

ISSUES OF IDENTITY

In the 1960s and 1970s the civil rights and Black Pride movements marked a new direction in black identity. The civil rights movement opened many barriers to educational and employment opportunities and to active political involvement. Some adults marched in the civil rights movement knowing that they themselves might never benefit directly from civil rights advances: They hoped that their efforts in the struggle would improve the lives of their children. The middle-class youths who attended community churches and black colleges became the leaders in the movement for equal rights (McAdoo, 1992)

Many blacks (both American-born and Caribbean-born), inspired by a growing sense of community identification and increased pride in racial identity, have determined to learn more about Africa. Despite the great differences in culture between African Americans and Africans, blacks throughout this hemisphere are discovering that they can take pride in the richness of their African heritage, including its high ethical values and community cohesiveness. Examples of African culture that have influenced American black culture or are held in high esteem by many African Americans are (Walker, 1982):

- Cooperative interdependence among and between people (contrasted with Western individualism)
- Partnership with nature and with the spirit world reflected in the approach to ecology and in communication with the spirit world (closer to Native American beliefs)
- Balance and harmony among all living things, reflected in the placing of human relations as a priority value (contrasted with the Western view of achievement and "doing" as taking priority over the nurturing of human relations)
- Joy and celebration in life itself
- Time as a spiral, focused on "now" (contrasted with the Western view of time as "money," and time running away from us)
- Focus on the group and not on the individual
- Giving of self to community
- Renewed interest in respecting elders

The combination of the Black Pride movement of the 1960s and 1970s and the current focus on cultural roots has freed many African Americans from the "slave mentality" that continued to haunt the African American culture long after emancipation. A new pride in race and heritage has, for some, replaced the sense of inferiority fostered by white racial supremacist attitudes.

GROUP IDENTIFICATION TERMS

Several ethnic minority groups, in a positive evolution of their identity and pride, have initiated name changes for their group, including African-American. This is not confusion (although it can *be* confusing), but rather represents, on the part of minority-group members, growth and a desire to name themselves rather than be named by the dominant society. Up until fairly recently, the most widely accepted term was "black," this term having replaced "Negro" (which in turn replaced "colored people"). "Negro" has been out of use for at least two decades, although some older blacks still use the term (as do some younger African Americans among themselves). In the 1990s, the usage "African American" has grown in popularity, because many feel that this term accurately and fairly describes their background. (It is the equivalent of, for example, Italian American or Polish American.) Many feel that the word "black" is no more appropriate in describing skin color than is "white." In the 1980s and early 1990s, the term *people of color* was briefly popular, but this catchall phrase has limited use for police officers. The following is some advice about correct terms to use, written by an African American sergeant in the late 1980s to his fellow police officers.

> Use the common term preferred and defined by black people (black male adult, black male juvenile, black female adult, black female juvenile) rather than NMA (Negro male adult), NMJ or NFA, etc. Use the preferred black term, especially in the presence of blacks. You may not get a violent reaction or even a mildly violent reaction, at least at the conscious level, from a black person if he or she hears the term Negro male. However, at an unconscious level, the inappropriate terms by which you are identifying the black person are registering and affect his or her behavior and opinion [towards you]. Inappropriate usage of terms can even affect the level of cooperation you will get from the individual. (Personal communication, Steve Odom, Sergeant, Berkeley, California, Police Department, Nov. 5, 1992)

Similarly, African American Lieutenant Berry of the Reno, Nevada Police Department says that he still hears that officers stop blacks and say into their radios, "I've got a Negro male here . . . " (personal communication, Ondra Berry, Lieutenant, Cultural Awareness Training Facilitator, Dec. 16, 1992). This usage is insulting in the 1990s because, to many, it symbolizes what the African American became under slavery. The replacement of "Negro" with "black" has come to symbolize racial pride. (The exception to the use of "Negro" and "colored" is in titles like "United Negro College" and "National Association of Colored People.") *African American,* a term preferred by many, focuses on positive historical and cultural roots rather than race or skin color.

The use of the words, "nigger," "boy," or "coon" are never acceptable at any time and especially in crime fighting and peacekeeping, no matter how provoked an officer may be. (Although you may hear black youths using "nigger" to refer to each other, the word is absolutely taboo for outsiders—especially outsiders wearing badges.) Police who do not like to be called "pigs" can certainly relate to a person's feelings about being called "gorilla." Officers hearing these types of labels used in their own departments, even when they are not being used to address somebody directly, should remind their peers of the lack of professionalism and prejudice that those terms convey. Officers who fall into the habit of using these words in what they think are harmless situations may find that they are unable to control themselves during more volatile situations with citizens.

MYTHS AND STEREOTYPES

Many of the impressions that people in the society (and consequently, in law enforcement) form about African Americans come from their exposure to or contact with the criminal element, usually representing America's underclass. Here the phenomenon of stereotyping is at much at work as it is when citizens see *all* police officers as repressive and capable of brutality. Stereotyping of police officers in regard to their treatment of minorities probably reached a peak in 1992, when there were three well-publicized incidents (in Los Angeles, Detroit, and Nashville) involving police brutality toward blacks. Police officers all over the country "took a beating" and felt, even more intensely than before, the consequences of citizens' stereotypes of *them—the officers.*

The white majority's view of blacks reflects the same problem. Those who are bent toward prejudice may feel that their racism is justified whenever a crime involving an African American makes the evening newscast. A suburban African American mother addressing a community forum on racism pointed out: "Every time I hear that there has been a murder or a rape, I pray that it is not a black who committed the crime. The minute the media reports that a black person is responsible for a crime, all of us suffer. When something negative happens, I am no longer seen as an individual with the same values, and hopes as my white neighbors. I become a symbol, and more so my husband and sons, become feared. People treat us with caution and politeness, but inside we know that their stereotypes of the worst, criminal element of blacks have become activated."

Even the fact of a crime rate that is disproportionately high among young black males does not justify sweeping statements about all African Americans. Certainly, 32 million African Americans cannot be judged by a statistic about the criminal element.

In the section on prejudice in Chapter 1 we discussed the phenomenon of grouping people into "we" and "they." When referring to "they," people justify their stereotypes by looking only at extreme examples in the "other group." Then they say: "Blacks do this . . . ," "Blacks are like this . . . ," "Blacks act this way." Unfortunately for the vast majority of the African American population, some whites do base their image of all blacks largely on the actions, including criminal behavior, of the black members of America's "underclass." It is well known that women clutch their purses harder when they see a black man approaching. Similarly, officers have been known to stop blacks and question them simply for not "looking like they belong to a certain neighborhood." (This is discussed and illustrated further in the chapter.) Many people, including whites and Asians, often harbor unreasonable fears about black people. Having never had a black friend or acquaintance, they feed such fears, instead of reaching out to meet or get to know people who look different from themselves.

African Americans have to contend with many myths and stereotypes that are central to a prejudiced person's thinking. For example, one myth, related to "raw and uncontrolled sex," leads people to believe that blacks have no morals, easily surrender to their "instincts," and can't practice self-restraint (Bennett, 1989). This type of thinking gives some people a sense of moral superiority over blacks for what they perceive to be black sexual habits. In a nationwide survey on sex practices of married couples, including adultery, it was found that blacks are no more likely (or, expressed differently, precisely as likely) as whites to commit adultery. Somehow, *white* sexuality never became a racial issue during the interlude of highly publicized "wife swapping" among middle- and upper-class suburbanites, nor did *white* sexuality become an issue during the 1960s and 1970s when many young people (e.g., white "hippies" in the 1960s and whites on the singles-bar scene a few years later) engaged in widespread sexual promiscuity. Although these practices were often criticized, the race of the people involved was ignored.

For African Americans, however, race has historically been connected to sexuality in ways that it would never occur to people to do with whites. This is another legacy of slavery and of the self-justifying racist thinking that arose from that institution. Many slave owners routinely and brutally raped their female slaves (often even before puberty), as well as forced their healthiest slaves to couple and breed regardless of the slaves' own attachments and preferences. (The fact that many African American's genetic background is part Caucasian is testimony to the slave owners' "tendencies" to violate slave girls and women.) While using slaves to indulge their desires, white slave owners convinced themselves that Africans had no morals and would couple indiscriminately like animals if left to do so. Like the myth of black inferiority, the white view of black sexuality was shaped by the need of slave owners to find an excuse for their cruel and unjust behavior.

Thornton et al. (1992) discuss several commonly held beliefs about blacks and counter their validity with research and results from polls. The following is of special interest to people in law enforcement:

Myth:
Blacks resent tough law enforcement. An 11-city survey of police in ghetto precincts taken after the 1960's riots showed that 30 percent of white officers believed "most blacks regard the police as enemies." The 1990 National Opinion Research Center (NORC) found that half of whites rated blacks as more violence-prone than whites.

Fact:
In the 1992 edition of *The Police in America* (Walker, 1992) it is reported that 85 percent of blacks rate the crime-fighting performance of police as either good or fair, which is not much different from the rating whites gave the police (i.e., just below 90 percent of the whites surveyed approved of police performance). A Los Angeles Times poll that was taken after the 1992 Rodney King riots revealed that 60 percent of local blacks (contrasted with 72 percent of whites) believed that police officers were effective in fighting crime. In addition, since the majority of victims of black crime are black, "blacks more than whites, . . . are likely to be afraid to walk alone or to feel unsafe at home." (Thornton et al., 1992)

Obviously, officers do encounter black citizens who display hostile attitudes toward police, and some officers have fixed their images of blacks based on these experiences. Still, according to Walker, in *The Police in America,* studies consistently show that white officers have "seriously overestimated the degree of public hostility among blacks." Since the majority of black crime victims are blacks themselves, it stands to reason that they feel unprotected and want to be able to rely on their communities' police departments. Walker states in *Policing in America* that African Americans are nearly as likely as whites to ask for additional police protection rather than less of it. *African Americans and other minorities strongly criticize law enforcement for underpolicing in the inner city.*

CROSS-RACIAL PERCEPTIONS IN LAW ENFORCEMENT

Prejudice, lack of contact, and ignorance lend themselves to groups developing perceptions about the other that are often based on biased beliefs. Unfortunately,

Exhibit 7.1   Are People Viewed in Equal Terms?

BLACK MALE	WHITE MALE
Arrogant	Confident
Chip on shoulder	Self assured
Aggressive	Assertive
Dominant personality	Natural leader
Violence prone	Wayward
Naturally gifted	Smart
Sexual prowess	Sexual experimentation

perceptions are reality for the individuals and groups who hold them. Perceptions are seen as the truth, whether or not they are the truth. Exhibit 7.1 illustrates differing perceptions that some members of the dominant society have toward black and white males. In this case, the media and popular literature have contributed to the differing perceptions.

How about perceptions that African Americans have developed of police officers' actions? Because of a past history of prejudice and discrimination toward blacks, police officers have used techniques that indeed *continue* to create perceptions among many African Americans. In other words, while some officers no longer exhibit racist actions, the perceptions remain.

The description of perceptions as listed in Exhibit 7.2 were presented by Al DeWitt, vice president of the Alameda, California NAACP chapter to northern California police officers.

According to Dewitt, over time, African Americans have formed perceptions about police behavior which often lead to a lack of trust, riots, and race

Exhibit 7.2   Perceptions of Police Officers' Actions by Some Blacks

POLICE ACTION	BLACK PERCEPTION
Being stopped or expelled from so-called "white neighborhoods."	Whites want blacks to "stay in their place."
Immediately suspecting and reacting to blacks without distinction between dope dealer and plainclothes police officer.	Police view black skin as itself as probable cause.
Using unreasonable force, beatings, adding charges.	When stopped, blacks must be submissive or else.
Negative attitudes, jokes, body language, talking down to people.	Officers are racists.
Quick trigger, take-downs, accidental shootings.	Bad attitudes will come out under stress.
Slow response, low priority, low apprehension rate.	Black-on-black crime not important.
Techniques of enforcing local restrictions and white political interests.	Police are the strong arm for the status quo.
Police stick together, right or wrong.	We against them mentality; they stick together . . . we have to stick together.

problems. Improving and preventing racial misperceptions will take time and effort on the part of the officer but will inevitably benefit him or her by way of increased cooperation and officer safety.

THE BLACK FAMILY

African American families generally enjoy very strong ties among extended family members, especially among women. Female relatives will often substitute for each other in filling family roles; for example, a grandmother or aunt may raise a child if the mother is unable to do so. Sometimes several different family groups may share one house. When there is a problem (i.e., an incident that's brought an officer to the house), extended family members are likely to be present and to want to help. An officer may observe a number of uncles, aunts, brothers, sisters, sweethearts, and friends who are loosely attached to the black household. Enlisting the aid of any of these household members (no matter what the relationship) can be beneficial.

The Role of the Man and the Woman

A widespread myth holds that black culture is a matriarchy, with one or more women heading the typical household. Historically, it is true that women did play a crucial role in the family, because of repeated attempts to break down black manhood (Bennett, 1989). However, in a true matriarchy (female-ruled society), women control property and economic activities. This is not generally true of black America, but outsiders often assume that black women are *always* the heads of the household. In the 1960s and 1970s, for instance, the media stereotyped the black mother as loud and domineering, clearly the boss. In addition, black women have, in a sense, been considered less of a threat to the status quo than the black male, and consequently have been able to be more assertive in public (personal communication, Steve Odom, Sergeant, Berkeley, California, Police Department, Nov. 5, 1992). Historically, in contacts with law enforcement, a black man may feel that, unlike a black woman, he risks arrest or at least mistreatment if he "talks back."

Black fathers, regardless of income, usually view themselves as heads of the household (Hines and Franklin, 1982), and thus any major decisions regarding the family should include the father's participation. It is insulting to the father when, with both parents present, officers automatically focus on the mother. An assertive mother does not mean that the father is passive or indifferent, and a father's silence does not necessarily indicate agreement. It is always worthwhile to get his view of the situation (Shusta, 1986).

The Single Mother

Feeding the stereotype of the female-headed black household is the fact that in many urban black homes, no father is present. In 1965, about 25 percent of black families nationally were headed by women; currently, that figure is at about 50 percent, and in certain urban core areas (particularly in housing projects) it can reach 90 percent.

The single mother, particularly in the inner city, does not always receive the respect that she is due; outsiders may be critical of the way she lives—or the way they think she lives. She is often stereotyped by officers who doubt their own effectiveness in the urban black community. For instance, an unmarried welfare mother who has just had a fight with her boyfriend should receive the same professional courtesy that a married suburban mother is likely to receive from an officer of the same background. In practice, this is not always the case. Some officers may mistakenly speak to the single black mother as if she were a slut, or treat her callously as though "She's seen it all and done it all; therefore, it does not matter how I [the officer] treat her."

"A complaint frequently heard in the . . . black community by black women is that non-black people, especially white men, treat the black woman poorly. This means that they feel comfortable using profanity in the woman's presence and treat them with little respect" (personal communication, Steve Odom, Sergeant, Berkeley, California, Police Department, Nov. 5, 1992).

Berry offers advice regarding relations between the peace officer and the single black mother. He advises officers to go out of their way to establish rapport and trust. Following are his suggestions for assisting the single mother (personal communication, Ondra Berry, Lieutenant, Reno, Nevada, Police Department, Dec. 16, 1992):

- Offer extra assistance to poor welfare mothers.
- Try to get the children into organized social, recreational, or therapeutic programs.
- Show warmth to the children (e.g., touch them).
- Offer the children something special, such as toy badges or other police souvenirs.
- Give your business card to the mothers in a professional manner.
- Make follow-up visits when there are *not* problems so that the mother and the children can associate the officer with good times.
- Carefully explain to the mother her rights.
- Use the same discretion you might use with another minor's first petty offense (e.g., shoplifting), simply by bringing the child home and talking with the mother and child, rather than sending the child immediately to juvenile hall.

All of these actions will build a perception on the part of the black single mother (and her children) that you can be trusted and that you are there to help. "Since you are dealing with history, you have to knock down barriers and work harder with this group than with any other group" (personal communication, Ondra Berry).

Children/Adolescents/Youth

Since so many homes, especially in the inner city, are absent a father, young boys in their middle childhood years (7 to 11) are beginning to be at real risk and school is often where serious behavior problems show up. According to Lieutenant Berry, many single mothers unwittingly place their young sons in the position of "father," giving them the message that they have to take care of the family. These young children can get the mistaken impression that they are the heads of the household, and in school situations, they may try to control the teacher—who is often female and often white. Berry observed that many young boys are placed in special education programs because they have been belligerent and domineering with the teacher. What these boys lack is an older male role model who can help them to grow into the appropriate behavior. An officer who refers these children to agencies that can provide such role models (even if only on a limited-time basis) will gain the family's and community's trust and respect. Eventually, he or she will win more cooperation from community members.

Among older black male children, especially in inner cities, statistics indicate a disproportionately high crime rate, stemming from the difficult economic conditions of their lives. Officers may have to remind themselves that the majority of black teenagers are law-abiding citizens (Shusta, 1986). Perfectly responsible black teens and young adults report being stopped on a regular basis by officers when they are in predominantly "white neighborhoods" (including those where they happen to live). A 19-year-old African American male living in an upper-middle-class suburban neighborhood in Fremont, California, reported that he was stopped and questioned four times in two weeks by different officers. On one occasion, the conversation went this way:

OFFICER:	"What are you doing here?"
TEEN:	"I'm jogging, sir."
OFFICER:	"Why are you in this neighborhood?"
TEEN:	"I live here, sir."
OFFICER:	"Where?"
TEEN:	"Over there, in that big house on the hill."
OFFICER:	"Can you prove that? Show me your I.D."

On another occasion, also when he was jogging, a different officer stopped him and asked (referring to the very expensive jogging shoes he was wearing), "Where did you get those shoes?" When the boy answered that he had bought them, the next question was; "Where do you live?" When the teen answered, "In that large house on the hill," the officer apologized and went on his way.

LANGUAGE AND COMMUNICATION

As mentioned at the beginning of the chapter, because of the *racial* conflicts between blacks and whites and other citizens, such as Asians, *cultural differences*, until recently, have been largely ignored or minimized. Yet many would acknowledge that cultural differences between, for example, a white officer and a Vietnamese citizen could potentially affect their communication as well as their perceptions of each other. Similarly, culture comes into play when looking at patterns of language and communication among many African Americans.

African American Varieties of English

"The use of black language does not represent any pathology in blacks. . . . The beginning of racial understanding is the acceptance that difference is just what it is: different, not inferior. And equality does not mean sameness" (Weber, 1991).

There are many varieties of English that are not "substandard," "deficient," or "impoverished" versions of the language. Instead, they may have a complete and consistent set of grammatical rules and may represent the rich cultures of the groups that use them. For example, Asian Indians speak a variety of English somewhat unfamiliar to Americans, while the British speak numerous dialects of British English, each of them containing distinctive grammatical structures and vocabulary not used by Americans. Similarly, some African Americans speak a variety of English that historically has been labeled as substandard by people who had no understanding of its origins.

It is estimated that over 80 percent of all African Americans use [or have used] what has been called "black English" at least some of the time (Smitherman, 1972). While some African Americans speak only a black variety of English, many enjoy the flexibility and expressiveness of speaking black English among peers, and switching to "standard English" when the situation calls for it (e.g., at work, in interviews, with white friends).

Most language and dialect researchers accept the notion that black English (which some linguists call "Ebonics") is a dialect with its own rules of grammar and structure (Labov, 1972). To many white people, black English merely sounds "southern." However, the fact that some of the same grammatical structures—spoken in a wholly different accent—are found throughout the English-speaking Caribbean (as far south as Trinidad, 8 miles north of Venezuela) points to an earlier, African origin for the grammar. Linguists have done years of research on the origins of black English and now believe that it developed from the grammatical structures common to several West African tribal languages. For example:

BLACK ENGLISH:	*You lookin good.*
STANDARD ENGLISH:	You look good *right now.*
BLACK ENGLISH:	You be *looking* good.
STANDARD ENGLISH:	You usually look good.

That is, the presence of the word "be" indicates a general condition and not something related only to the present. Apparently, some West African languages have grammatical structures expressing these same concepts of time. Nonetheless, many white people cling to an unscientific (and racist) view of language varieties of African Americans.

> One [view] says that there was African influence in the development of the language and the other that says there was not. Those who reject African influence believe that the African arrived in the United States and tried to speak English. And, [according to this first view], because he lacked certain intellectual and physical attributes, he failed. This hypothesis makes no attempt to examine the . . . structures of West African languages to see if there are any similarities. . . . when the German said *zis* instead of *this,* America understood. But, when the African said *dis* [instead of *this*], no one considered the fact that . . . *th* may not exist in African languages. (Weber, 1991)

Slaves developed black English to overcome the differences in their tribal languages and communicate with one another and with their English-speaking slave masters. They also developed a type of "code language" so that they could speak and not be understood by their slave owners.

Many people still assume that black English is "bad" English, and they display their contempt nonverbally, with their facial expressions or with an impatient tone of voice. They may interrupt and finish the speaker's sentences for him or her, as though that person were unable to speak for himself or herself. Acceptance of another person's variety of English can go a long way toward establishing rapport. People interacting with blacks who do not use standard English should realize that blacks are not making random "mistakes" when they speak and that they are not necessarily speaking badly. In fact, verbal skill is a highly prized value in most African-based cultures. (For example, the loser of the African American verbal-insult game called "The Dozens" is the person who gives up talking to start punching.)

Finally, in trying to establish trust and rebuild relations with a people who historically have not been able to trust the police, white officers shouldn't try to imitate black accents, dialects, and styles of speaking. Imitation (especially bad, inept imitation) can be very insulting and may give blacks the impression that you are making fun of them—or that you're seriously uncomfortable with them. (This is elaborated on in Chapter 5.) Don't try to fake a style that is culturally different from your own. You have to be authentic when you communicate with citizens, while remaining aware and accepting of differences.

Nonverbal Communication: Style and Stance

Black social scientists have been studying aspects of black nonverbal communication, which have been often misunderstood by people in positions of authority. Psychologist Richard Majors at the University of Wisconsin has termed a certain stance and posturing as the "cool pose," which is demonstrated by many young black men from the inner city. "While the cool pose is often misread by teachers, principals and police officers as an attitude of defiance, psychologists who have studied it say it is a way for black youths to maintain a sense of integrity and suppress rage at being blocked from usual routes to esteem and success" (Goleman, 1992).

Majors explains that while the "cool pose" is not found among the majority of black men, it is commonly seen among inner city youth as a "tactic for . . . survival to cope with such rejections as storekeepers who refuse to buzz them into a locked shop." The goal of the pose is to give the appearance of being in control. However, a storekeeper, a passerby, or a police officer may perceive this stance as threatening, so a negative dynamic enters the interaction (e.g., the officer seeing the "cool pose" feels threatened, and so becomes more authoritarian in response). This form of nonverbal communication may include certain movements and postures designed to emphasize the youth's masculinity. The pose involves a certain way of walking, standing, talking, and remaining aloof facially. It can include cultivating a certain style in appearance (e.g., an unbuckled belt and thick gold chains). The pose, writes Majors, is a way of saying, "[I'm] strong and proud, despite [my] status in American society" (Goleman, 1992).

A Harvard Medical School psychiatrist, Dr. Possaint, points out that because so many inner city male youths have no male role models in their families, they feel a need to display their manliness (Goleman, 1992). Problems occur when others read their nonverbal language as a sign of irresponsibility, apathy, defiance, and/or laziness. With the knowledge that for some black youths, the "cool pose" is not intended to be a personal threat, officers should be less on the defensive (and, consequently, less on the offensive) when observing this style.

In a *20/20* broadcast entitled "Presumed Guilty" (ABC News, 1992), the mother of an African American premed student referred to style and communication: "They don't have to be doing anything but being who they are, and that's young black men, with a rhythm in their walk and an attitude about who they are, and expressing their pride and culture by the clothes they choose to wear. . . ." This young man had been stopped on numerous occasions for no apparent reason. This is discussed in the section "Differential Treatment" later in this chapter.

Verbal Expressiveness and Emotionalism

Linguist and sociologist, Thomas Kochman has made it his life work to study differences in black and white culture that contribute to misunderstandings and misperceptions. Chicago's African American mayor Harold Washington passed out copies of Kochman's book *Black and White Styles in Conflict* (1981) to the city hall press corps because he believed that he was seriously misunderstood by the whites of the city. According to Kochman, "If a person doesn't know the difference in cultures, that's ignorance. But if a person knows the difference and still says that mainstream culture is best, that 'white is right,' then you've got racism."

Kochman explains that blacks and whites have different perspectives and approaches to many issues, including conversation, public speaking, and power. This notion is supported in the following advice to police officers: "Don't get nuts when you encounter [an African-American] who is louder and more emotional than you are. Watch the voice patterns and the tone. Blacks can sound militant [even when they are not]. Blacks have been taught to be outwardly and openly emotional. Sometimes we are emotional first and then calm down and become more rationale (personal communication, Lieutenant Ondra Berry, Reno, Nevada Police Department, Dec. 16, 1992). The lieutenant went on to say that often whites are rational at first but express more emotion as they lose control. This cultural difference has obvious implications for overall communication, including how to approach and react to angry citizens.

Kochman explains that "whites [are] able practitioners of self-restraint [and that] this practice has an inhibiting effect on their ability to be spontaneously self-assertive." (This would apply to many Asians as well, perhaps to an even greater degree.) He continues to explain that "the level of energy and spiritual intensity that blacks generate is one that they can manage comfortably but whites can only manage with effort." The problems in interaction come about because neither race understands that there's a cultural difference between them. Kochman states: "Blacks do not initially see this relative mismatch, because they believe that their normal animated style is not disabling to whites. . . . Whites are worried that blacks cannot sustain such intense levels of interaction without losing self-control [because that degree of 'letting go' of emotions for a white would signify a lack of control].” In other words, a white person or an Asian, for that matter, unaware of the acceptability in black culture of expressing intense emotion (including rage) may not be able to imagine that he, himself, could express such intense emotion without losing control. He may feel threatened, convinced that the ventilation of such hostility will surely lead to a physical confrontation.

While racism can also be a factor in communication breakdowns, differing conventions of speech do contribute in ways that are not always apparent. In several cultural awareness training sessions, police officers have reported that neighbors (non-African American), upon hearing highly emotional discussions among African Americans, called to report fights. When the police arrived on the scene of the “fight,” the so-called guilty ones responded that they were not fighting, just talking. While continuing to respond to all calls, officers can still be aware of different perceptions of what constitutes a fight. Although you can never make any automatic assumptions, an awareness of differences can and should affect the way you approach the citizen.

Berry illustrated how a white police officer can let his own cultural interpretations of black anger and emotionalism influence judgment. He spoke of a fellow officer who made the statement: “Once they [i.e., blacks] took me on, I wanted to take control.” This officer, working in a predominantly black area for a three-month period, made 120 stops and 42 arrests (mainly petty offenses such as prowling and failure to identify). He then worked in a predominantly white area for the same period of time, made 122 stops and only six arrests. The officer went on to say, “One group will do what I ask; the other will ask questions and challenge me.” His need to “take control” over people whom he perceived to be out of control was so extreme, it resulted in his getting sued. His perception of the level of threat involved was much higher in the black community than in the white. One of the factors involved was, undoubtedly, this officer’s inability to deal with being “taken on.” If he’d used communication skills to defuse citizens’ anger rather than escalate it, he might have been able to work situations around to his advantage rather than creating confrontations. Listening professionally, instead of engaging in shouting matches with citizens of other backgrounds, can require a great deal of self-control, but it will usually bring better results. (Once again, George Thompson of the Verbal Judo Institute reminds officers, “You are not paid to argue.” See Chapter 5.)

Threats and Aggressive Behavior

> “Sir, we are now in confrontation, but I do not see any violence.” [Malcolm X (as portrayed in a movie) responding to a white man asking a question equating confrontation and violence]

Related to verbal expressiveness and emotionalism is an area (touched upon in Chapter 1) having to do with threats and confrontations. Kochman, who conducts cultural awareness training nationwide (including for police departments) asks the question, “When does a fight begin?” Many whites, he notes, believe that “fighting” has already begun when it is “obvious” that there will be violence (. . . “when violence in imminent”). Therefore, to whites, a fight begins as soon as the shouting starts. According to whites, then, the fight has begun whenever a certain intensity of anger is shown, along with an exchange of insults. If threats are also spoken, many whites would agree that violence is surely on its way.

Kochman explains that while the situation described above (verbal confrontation, threats) may indeed be a prelude to a fight for blacks, many blacks have a clear boundary between their fighting words and their physical actions. Kochman includes a quote to show how fighting does not begin until one person does something physically provocative: "If two guys are talking loud and then one or the other starts to reduce the distance between them, that's a sign, because it's important to get in the first blow. Or if a guy puts his hand in his pocket, and that's not a movement he usually makes, then you watch for that—he might be reaching for a knife. But if they're just talking—it doesn't matter how loud it gets—then you got nothing to worry about" (Allen Harris quoted in Kochman, 1981).

Of course, officers who are trained to think about officer safety might have a problem accepting this dismissal (". . . then you got nothing to worry about"). Similarly, a threat in today's society, where anyone may be carrying semiautomatic weapons, may be just that—a very real threat that will be carried out. A threat must always be taken seriously by officers. However, there can be instances when cultural differences are at work and rage will be expressed without accompanying physical violence. When this is the case, an officer can actually escalate hostilities with an approach and communication style that demonstrates no understanding toward culturally/racially different modes of expression.

KEY ISSUES IN LAW ENFORCEMENT

Differential Treatment

> I think that African American males and other minority males are more prone to be stopped for small or frivolous reasons than non African American males in not just big cities like Los Angeles and Philadelphia, but small, suburban and rural and country towns. Statistically, it is a fact. [Chief Willie Williams, Los Angeles Police Department, in ABC News (1992)]

Contrary to popular belief in some segments of society, not all police officers are bigots. Still, some officers, being a reflection of society at large, do hold deep-seated prejudices without realizing it. When people work hard at denying their biases, they cannot admit when they are acting on them. (This is discussed in more detail in Chapter 1.) An officer loses credibility when he or she says "I am not prejudiced. Some of my best friends are black," but then arrests blacks for lesser offenses without arresting whites who have committed more serious crimes.

> My partner and I several years ago went to an all white night club. He found cocaine on this white couple. He poured it out and didn't make an arrest. Later we were at an all black nightclub. He found marijuana on one individual and arrested him. I was shocked, but I didn't say anything at the time because I was new to the department. African American policer officer (anonymous)

In the *20/20* television segment entitled "Presumed Guilty," an undercover investigation set out to answer the question "Are black men being singled out by police, pulled over even when they're doing nothing wrong?" Many officers will deny this and register the counterpart complaint (heard repeatedly in cultural awareness training sessions), "They're always saying that I'm stopping them because they're black when, in fact, I've pulled them over because they have violated the law." African American parents continue to complain that their teenage and young adult children are pulled over and questioned when there has been no violation. How are these two viewpoints reconciled? How can perceptions be so far apart?

The truth most likely lies between the categorical denial of some police officers and the statement, "We're *always* being stopped *only because we're black.*" Undoubtedly, there are police procedures of which citizens are unaware, and they do not see all the other people an officer stops in a typical day. However, the citizen is not getting paid to be professional, truthful, or even reasonable with the officer. Therefore, in this section we will not deal with citizens who are stretching the truth or being downright dishonest. (See Chapter 6 for tips on responding to these types of remarks.) Instead, the discussion will focus on the fact that some officers still discriminate in their practices without being aware of it.

The network investigation took place in Los Angeles, but according to many different accounts by individuals and citizens' groups, the phenomenon of differential treatment is still common throughout America. In the program "Presumed Guilty," the reporters cite the case of Al Joyner, Olympic track and field athlete who now "refuses to drive the streets of L.A. for fear of the police" (ABC News, 1992). He was stopped because it was believed that he was driving a stolen car. Joyner was asked to walk with his hands behind his head when he noticed about five or six police cars "out there, and all of them in their gun position with their guns out on me." Joyner was instructed to get on his knees while his license plate was being checked. When the police discovered that the car was registered in his wife's name (Griffith-Joyner) the officers realized their mistake and let Joyner go. Joyner then drove less than two blocks before he was stopped again by the same group of officers. This time he was told that he was a suspect in a hit and run: The officers were looking for "a burgundy RX7; a black man with a baseball cap." Joyner explained to the 20/20 reporters: "I didn't have an RX7, but I am black with a baseball cap."

MR. JOYNER:	"I felt violated, because when I was there, I felt like I was raped."
CHIEF WILLIAMS: OF THE LAPD:	"I understand what Al Joyner has said. My son, at 19, was driving my seven-year-old Lincoln, in Philadelphia [and] was stopped three times in a seven-hour period."
20/20 REPORTER:	For what?
CHIEF WILLIAMS:	Because he was a young man in a nice-looking car.
20/20 REPORTER:	And he was black.
CHIEF WILLIAMS:	. . . And he was black, and his dad was a police captain at the time. And dad followed up to see what the reasons were, and no traffic ticket."

Chief Williams makes the point that many black men are stopped simply because they are in white neighborhoods. He says that this alone is *never a justifiable reason to make a stop and that officers should never ask the question, "Why are you in this neighborhood?"*

Officers in cultural awareness training have said they've been surprised when suburban middle-class blacks express as much anger and outrage (but perhaps in a more constrained manner) about differential treatment as do poorer blacks in inner city areas. Many middle- and upper-class parents whose children have experienced the types of stops described above are, if anything, likely to be even less forgiving: Stops like these indicate painfully that despite all their hard-won social and economic success, their race is still the first thing that mainstream society perceives about them and their children.

Law enforcement agents need to recognize the validity of a percentage of the complaints made about unfair treatment toward African Americans and other minorities. While recognizing that many stops are perfectly justified (and the citizen may be unaware of the reasons involved), the issue is to wipe out all biased police actions.

Excessive Force and Brutality

> Patrolling the mean streets can be a dangerous and dehumanizing task for police officers. Drawing the line between necessary force and deliberate brutality is perhaps the toughest part of the job. . . . A career of confronting the vicious, conscienceless criminal-enemy frays the nerves. . . . (Morrow, 1991)

The year 1992 brought public attention to the fact that excessive force and brutality are still problems in America. The existence of brutality has been a problem that blacks and other minorities have asserted, but until the early 1990s with several highly publicized cases, including Rodney King, many whites either did not believe or closed their eyes to this reality. In December 1992, just one month after Detroit Police Chief Stanley Knox fired four officers charged in the fatal beating of African American motorist Malice Green, another incident attracted national attention. In Nashville, Tennessee, two white police officers were fired for using excessive force to subdue a black motorist who turned out to be an undercover officer working to break a prostitution ring (Associated Press, Dec. 9, 1992). Reggie Miller, the beaten officer, was working undercover in a high-crime area when he was ordered by another officer to pull over. To avoid exposing the undercover operation, Miller drove about three blocks from the main sting area before stopping. At this point, the officer who stopped him called for a backup. What followed was:

> When Miller stopped, he was ordered to show his hands. Officers pulled him from the truck and placed him on the ground. Miller, who was unarmed, said his eyes were gouged and he was choked and kicked in the groin and kneed in the back. After 20 seconds, other undercover officers arrived and intervened. . . . The beaten undercover officer said, "I feel I was treated like a piece of meat, thrown out to a pack of dogs." (Associated Press, Dec. 9, 1992)

The majority of police officers around the nation do not use excessive force. Nevertheless, the year 1992 showed the world that police brutality in

America is not yet a thing of the past. The three publicized incidents all involved African Americans; the message the incidents conveyed is that police are out to harm this group of people. Every time an incident of this nature occurs, all police officers suffer from citizens' stereotypes and anger. It is in the best interest of every department to address this problem directly and on a regular basis (*once a year is not enough*).

Controlling one's impulses, not acting out one's biases and prejudices must be a priority training issue in all departments across the country. (Chapter 1 deals with prejudices and biases.) Police departments need to recognize that reducing an officer's buildup of stress as he or she faces abuse (in some cases on a daily basis) has to be addressed as frequently and seriously as does self-defense. Finally, the individual officer must remember that even though abusive behavior from citizens constitutes one of the worst aspects of the job, it is *not* the citizens who have to behave like professionals. Remembering that apparently there was no abusive behavior from the undercover officer in the Nashville police department, those entrusted to keep the peace must examine their own assumptions and search their own motives to make sure they will not subject citizens to criminal brutality under cover of the law.

Law Enforcement Interaction with Poor Urban Black Communities

Many police officers feel that they are putting their lives in danger when going into certain black communities, particularly those in urban areas where poverty and crime go hand in hand. As a result, some segments of the black community feel police are not protecting them, and are extremely fearful of "black-on-black" crime. The increase in citizens' weapons in urban areas, including increased self-protective weaponry, contributes to defensive reactions among both the police and the citizens. Hence a vicious cycle continues to create and escalate hostilities (Cross and Renner, 1974). Police are often expected to solve the social ills of society, but have neither the resources nor the training to deal with problems that are rooted in historical, social, political, and economic factors. Blacks and police officers are often frustrated with each other and barriers seem insurmountable:

> Many policemen find themselves on the alert for the slightest sign of disrespect. One author has shown [McNamara] that the police [officer] is often prepared to coerce respect and will use force if he feels his position is being challenged. Likewise, the attitudes and emotions of the black citizen may be similar when confronted with a police [officer]. Intervention by police is often seen as an infringement on the blacks' rights and as oppression by the white population. Consequently many blacks are on the alert for the slightest sign of disrespect that might be displayed by the police [officer]. (Cross and Renner, 1974)

Cross and Renner go on to explain that fear of belittlement and fear of danger operate for both the black citizen and the officer, and these fears cause both sides to misinterpret what might otherwise be nonthreatening behavior. The problem often arises not from the reality of the situation but from the results of mutual fears. This is as true now in some parts of the country as it was in the mid-1970s when the article cited above was written.

African American social scientists have been studying the problems of inner city young men, in particular, since this group is most endangered. Consider the following (Goleman, 1992):

- About one in four black men aged 20 to 29 is in prison, on probation, or on parole.
- The unemployment rate for black men is more than twice that for whites.
- The leading cause of death among black youth is homicide.
- A 1991 report from the National Center for Health Statistics found that 48 percent of black males between 15 and 19 who died were shot, while the figures for white males was just 18 percent.
- For black men in Harlem, life expectancy is shorter than that for men in Bangladesh; nationally, black men die at a higher rate than any other group except those aged 85 and older.

Law enforcement officials alone cannot solve social ills but should realize that African Americans in disadvantaged communities desperately need excellent police protection. The perception that whites in middle-class communities are better served by the police forces naturally reinforces existing antipolice attitudes among the lower class. "Blacks are still far more likely than whites to identify race discrimination as a pervasive problem in American society, especially when it comes to police and the criminal justice system" (*U. S. News & World Report*). In a report entitled "The Victims' Profile", the U.S. Bureau of Justice Statistics (1990) found that black victims were more likely than white victims to be physically attacked during a violent crime. In aggravated assaults, black victims were more likely than white victims to be injured.

Addressing the Needs of the Inner City

Progress is definitely being made to improve relations between police and members of African American communities, particularly in inner cities. There are more African Americans officers and more African American police executives who are changing policy that directly affects police–black relations. Many departments (although by no means all) have put into writing strict rules regarding the use of excessive force, discourtesy, racial slurs, and aggressive patrol techniques. Police management in some locales is beginning to understand why many people in urban black communities believe they receive unequal police services. An African American police chief in Charleston, South Carolina, has said, "Black-on-black crime seems to be tolerated and even accepted as inevitable" (*USA Today*, Apr. 24, 1991).

Still, progressive police departments are moving forward. Hubert Williams and Patrick Murphy, former police director of Newark, New Jersey, and former commissioner of the New York City Police Department, respectively, speak of the progress that has been made and the challenges still facing law enforcement with regard to contact with citizens in the inner city:

> A number of improvements have occurred that have reduced the barriers between the police and the inner city. . . . A number of steps have been taken to ensure adequate patrol coverage and rapid response to calls for service from inner city areas.

> Open, impartial, and prompt grievance mechanisms have been established. Policy guidelines have been implemented to direct officers' discretion in potentially tense situations. . . . Although the police are better prepared to deal with residents of the inner city than they were 20 years ago, they are far from having totally bridged the chasm that has separated them from minorities—especially blacks—for over 200 years. (Hubert and Murphy, 1990)

SUMMARY OF RECOMMENDATIONS FOR LAW ENFORCEMENT

1. The experience of slavery and racism *as well as* cultural differences have shaped African American culture.

-   Patterns of culture and communication among black Americans differ from those of white Americans. In face-to-face communication, officers should not ignore or downplay these differences.

2. For many African Americans, particularly those in the lower-socioeconomic rungs of society, the history of slavery and later discrimination continues to leave its psychological scars.

-   Law enforcement officials, in particular, represent a system that has oppressed African Americans and other minorities. To protect and serve in many African American communities across the nation necessarily means that officers will need to *to go out of their way* to establish trust and win cooperation.

3. There is tremendous diversity among African Americans, which includes individuals at all socioeconomic levels, a number of religions, different regions of the country (rural and urban, as well), and various countries of origin.

-   Color and race, however, often determine how the larger society will react to and treat African Americans. Therefore, the *racial* (as opposed to the *cultural*) experience of many African Americans is similar.

4. The changing terms that African Americans have used to refer to themselves reflect stages of racial and cultural growth, as well as empowerment.

-   Respect the terms that African Americans prefer to use. "Negro" and "colored" are completely inappropriate and have been replaced by "black" for the purposes of many police communications. However, in speech, many people prefer the term "African American." Officers can learn to become comfortable asking a citizen which term he or she prefers if there is a need to refer to ethnicity in the conversation.
-   Officers are advised to stop each other when they hear offensive terms being used. Not only does this contribute to the first step of making a department free of overt prejudices, it will also help the individual officer to practice control when he or she is faced with volatile citizens. An officer in the habit of using offensive terms may not be able to restrain himself or herself in public situations. Therefore, officers monitoring each other will ultimately be of benefit to the department.

5. African Americans react as negatively to stereotypes that they hear about themselves as officers do when they hear such statements as, "Police officers are biased against blacks" or "All police officers are capable of brutality."

- Many of the stereotypes about African Americans stem from ignorance as well as an impression people receive from the criminal element. Law enforcement officers, in particular, must be sensitive to how their own perceptions of African Americans are formed. The disproportionately high crime rate among African American males does not justify sweeping statements about the majority of African Americans, who are law-abiding citizens.

6.   The predominance of households headed by women, particularly in the inner city, coupled with the myth of woman as the head of the household, has created situations where officers have dismissed the importance of the father.

- Despite common myths and stereotypes regarding the woman, officers should always approach the father to get his version of the story and to consider his opinions in decision making. If the father is ignored or not given much attention, he is certain to be offended.

7.   Young African American males, in particular, and their parents (of *all* socio-economic levels) feel a sense of outrage and injustice when officers stop them for no apparent reason.

- You will destroy any possibility of establishing trust (and later winning cooperation) for stopping youths (and others) because it "looks like they don't belong in a given neighborhood." Every time an instance of this nature occurs, police–community and police–youth relations suffer.

8.   The use of African American varieties of English does not represent any pathology or deficiency and is not a combination of random errors, but rather reflects patterns of grammar from some West African languages.

- Many people have strong biases against this variety of spoken English. Do not convey a lack of acceptance through disapproving facial expressions, a negative tone of voice, or a tendency to interrupt or finish the sentences for the other person.
- When it comes to "black English" or an accent, do not fake it in order to be accepted by the group. People will immediately pick up on your lack of sincerity; this, in and of itself, can create hostility.

9.   People in positions of authority have often misunderstood aspects of black nonverbal communication, including what as been termed the "cool pose."

- Police officers may interpret certain ways of standing, walking, and dressing as defiant. This can create defensive reactions on the part of the police officer. In many cases, the police officer need not take this behavior personally or feel threatened.

10.   *Cultural* differences in verbal communication can result in complete misinterpretation:

- Do not necessarily equate an African American's expression of rage and verbal threats with a loss of control that leads automatically to violence. Within the cultural norms, it can be acceptable to be very expressive and emotional in speech. This is in contrast to an unspoken white mainstream norm, which discourages the open and free expression of emotion, especially anger.

11. The existence of excessive force and brutality is still a reality in policing in the United States, even if it is only a minority of officers who commit these acts. When there is police brutality, everyone suffers, including officers and entire police departments.

- Every officer should be on the lookout for unchecked biases within themselves and others that could result in inappropriate force with citizens of all backgrounds. This also involves awareness of one's own level of stress and frustration and having the means and support to release tension before it breaks loose in the streets.

12. A dynamic exists between some officers and African Americans, particularly in poor urban areas, whereby both the officer and the citizen are on the "alert" for the slightest sign of disrespect.

- The fear that both the citizen and the officer experience can interfere with what may actually be a nonthreatening situation.
- The police officer can be the one to break the cycle of fear by softening his or her verbal and nonverbal approach.

13. In areas populated by African Americans and other minorities all over the United States, there is a need for increased and more effective police protection.

- Bridging the gap that has separated police from African Americans involves radical changes in attitudes toward police–community relations. Together with changes in management, even the individual officer can help by making greater efforts to have positive contact with African Americans.
- The task of establishing rapport with African Americans at all levels of society is challenging because of what the officer represents in terms of past discrimination. Turning this image around involves a commitment on the part of the officer to break with deeply embedded stereotypes and to have as a goal, respect and professionalism in every encounter.

DISCUSSION QUESTIONS AND ISSUES*

1. ***Racism: Effects on Blacks and Whites.*** Under "Historical Information" in this chapter, the authors state that the fact of African Americans having been slaves in this country has created great psychological and social problems for blacks and whites for generations to come. How is this true for both races? What are the implications for law enforcement?

2. ***Offensive Terms*** The authors advise refraining from using such offensive terms as "nigger" at all times, even where there are no African Americans present. Give two practical reasons for this.

3. ***"Cool Pose" and the Use of Threats.*** How do you think the information in this chapter about threats, emotional expression (including rage), and the "cool pose" can help officers in their approach to citizens? Describe or role-play how an officer would communicate if he or she did not feel threatened by such behavior. Describe or role-play how an officer might approach and interact with the citizen if he or she was threatened by the behavior.

4. ***Police Department Over-Reaction?*** When the movie *Malcolm X* came out in late 1992, many officers were afraid of how the movie would affect the public, and some po-

*See Instructor's Manual accompanying this text for additional activities, role-plays, questionnaires and projects related to the content of this chapter.

lice department managements felt that they needed to prepare themselves for the worst possible trouble that would result from the movie. Following is a description of how two San Francisco Bay Area police departments chose to react (personal communication, Darryl McAllister, Officer, Hayward, California, Police Department, Dec. 18, 1992). Discuss what can be learned from the different approaches.

- **Department A**: Management decided to place a number of uniformed officers in the theater where *Malcolm X* was playing. Officers were ready and prepared for the worst. This plan backfired in terms of public perception. Citizens going in and exiting from the theater expressed anger about the heavy police presence. Some of the movie goers made comments such as, "I just wanted to come here with my family to enjoy and learn. They are getting a bad message and we enjoyed the movie less because of the police presence."
- **Department B:** Management planned to have uniformed officers in lobby and to position a large prisoner police bus in front of theater. An African American officer convinced them first to send 10 officers to preview the movie to discuss possible consequences. After seeing the movie, the officers decided that the movie would probably not result in any confrontation. The resulting action was the placement of two or three undercover officers in the theater. There were no incidents.

5. *Inner Cities: Officers and Citizens' Reactions.* Towards the end of the chapter, the authors mention the vicious cycle that is created in urban areas, especially where citizens have become increasingly armed (with highly sophisticated weapons) and officers, consequently, have to take more self-protective measures. Each views the other with fear and animosity and approaches the other with extreme defensiveness. Obviously, there is no simple answer to this widely occurring phenomenon, and police cannot solve the ills of society. Discuss your observations of the way officers cope with the stresses of these potentially life-threatening situations and how the coping or lack thereof affects relations with African Americans and other minorities. What type of support do police officers need to handle this aspect of their job? Do you think police departments are doing their job in providing the support needed?

6. *When Officers Try to Make a Difference.* Many young African American children, especially in housing projects in inner cities, live without a father in the household. This means that they do not have a second authority figure as a role model and are, consequently, deprived of an important source of adult support. No one can take the place of a missing parent, but there are small and large things a police officer can do to at least make an impression in the life of a child. Compile a list of actions officers can take to demonstrate their caring of children in these environments. Include in your first list every gesture, no matter how small; your second list can include a realistic list of what action can be taken given resources available. Select someone to compile both sets of suggestions (i.e., the realistic and ideal suggestions). Post these lists as reminders of how officers can attempt to make a difference in their communities not only with African American children but with other children as well.

REFERENCES

ABC NEWS (1992). 20/20 ABC News Report, "Presumed Guilty," Transcript 1247, Nov. 6.

BENNETT, LERONE JR. (1989). "The 10 biggest myths about the black family," *Ebony*, Nov.

CROSS, STAN, AND EDWARD RENNER (1974). "An interaction analysis of police–black relations," *Journal of Police Science Administration*, Vol. 2, No. 1.

GOLEMAN, DANIEL (1992). "Black scientists study the 'pose' of the inner city," *New York Times*, Apr. 21, p. 21.

HINES, PAULETTE MOORE, AND NANCY-BOYD FRANKLIN (1982). "Black families," in *Ethnicity and Family Therapy*, M. McGoldrick et al., eds., Guilford Press, New York.

KOCHMAN, THOMAS (1981). *Black and White Styles in Conflict*, The University of Chicago Press, Chicago.

LABOV, WILLIAM (1972). *Sociolinguistic Patterns,* University of Pennsylvania Press, Philadelphia.

LOHMAN, D. L. (1977). "Race tension and conflict," in *Police and the Changing Community,* N.A. Watson, ed., International Association of Chiefs of Police, Washington D.C.

MCADOO, HARRIET PIPES (1992). "Upward mobility and parenting in middle income families," in *African American Psychology,* Sage Publications, Newbury Park, Calif.

MORROW, LANCE (1991). "Rough justice," *Time,* Apr. 1, pp. 16, 17.

SHUSTA, ROBERT (1986). *Cultural Issues Manual,* Concord Police Department, Concord, Calif., p. 5.

SMITHERMAN, GENEVA (1972). *Talkin' and Testifyin',* Houghton Mifflin, Boston, p. 2.

THORNTON, JEANNE, AND DAVID WHITMAN WITH DORIAN FRIEDMAN (1992). "Whites myths about blacks," *U.S. News & World Report,* Nov. 9, pp. 41–44

U.S. Bureau of Justice Statistics (1990). *Special Report: Black Victims,* U.S. Government Printing Office, Washington, D.C., Apr.

WALKER, ANNA (1982). "Black American cultures," in *California Cultural Awareness Resource Guide,* Chinatown Resources Development Center, San Francisco.

WALKER, SAMUEL (1992). *The Police in America,* McGraw-Hill, New York.

WEBER, SHIRLEY N. (1991). "The need to be: the sociocultural significance of black language," in *Intercultural Communication: A Reader,* 6th ed., Larry Samovar and Richard Porter, eds., Wadsworth Press, Belmont, Calif.

WILLIAMS, HUBERT, AND PATRICK MURPHY (1990). *The Evolving Strategy of Police: A Minority View,* National Institute of Justice, U.S. Department of Justice and the Program in Criminal Justice Policy and Management, Harvard University, Cambridge, Mass., Jan., No. 13.

8

LAW ENFORCEMENT CONTACT WITH LATINO/HISPANIC AMERICANS

OVERVIEW

In this chapter specific ethnic and cultural information is provided on Latino/Hispanic Americans. The label *Latino/Hispanic Americans* encompasses over 25 different ethnic and cultural groups from Central and South America and the Caribbean. For ease of use we will use the term Latino/Hispanic Americans to refer to members of these ethnic groupings. We first define this diverse group. Then a historical overview is provided which includes information about direct and indirect examples that can affect the relationship between law enforcement personnel and citizens. Demographics and diversity among Latino/Hispanic Americans are presented as well as issues related to ethnic and cultural identity. Aspects of the Latino/Hispanic American culture are discussed, including myths and stereotypes, assimilation and acculturation processes, the extended family and community, the role of the man and the woman, generational differences, and adolescent/youth issues. The section on cultural influences on communication discusses the subtle aspects of nonverbal and indirect communications often found troublesome to law enforcement personnel. The closing section presents several key concerns for law enforcement: contact with the non-English speaker, diversity of Latino/Hispanic American communities, use of translators, and gaining community cooperation. The chapter ends with a review of recommendations for improved relationships between law enforcement personnel and members of the Latino/Hispanic American communities.

COMMENTARY

In this chapter we refer to Latino/Hispanic Americans more in terms of the similarities they share across groups rather than in terms of the differences. Certainly, there are great differences among the many groups of Latino/Hispanic Americans with regard to customs, values, and behaviors. One of the first issues of diversity and a concern of many law enforcement officers is the use of appropriate terms for the different groups comprising Latino/Hispanic Americans.

> The term *Hispanic* means so many different things to so many different people. To the typical American, stereotypes of poverty, illegal aliens, laborers and uneducated come to mind. For those who are part of the "so-called Hispanic" group, there is really no agreement as to what we want to be called: Is it Latino, Hispanic or the people from the specific countries of origin like Mexican, Puerto Rican, Cuban, Salvadorean, Columbian, Dominican, Nicaraguan, Chilean, Argentinean, Brazilian, and other South and Central Americans? (Latino/Hispanic American community organizer)

Law enforcement officers are called to respond to concerns or complaints by community members against Latino/Hispanic Americans. Often, such complaints are made by persons who do not understand the Latino/Hispanic American community. Moreover, law enforcement officers, in response to community member's concerns and complaints, see only one side of a much more diverse group of people. As is evident by the two quotes below, the Latino/Hispanic American community reflects the full range of economic and cultural diversity.

> Every day, we get complaints from parents, merchants, and commuters, wanting the police to do something about the "Mexicans" and other "Latino/Hispanic" types waiting to be picked-up for a job around the freeway on-ramps. They stand there for hours waiting for a *patron*, a boss, to drive up and employ them for a day, a week, or a few hours. It's a community issue, yet the police are expected to solve it. We can ask them to disband and move on, but all that would do is to have them move around the corner. (Police officer's anecdote told at a cultural awareness training session)

> It is unfortunate that for the average American, the stereotypes of Latino/Hispanic Americans include the characteristics of poor, uneducated immigrants, and perhaps of illegal status. What is missing from the picture are the vast numbers of us who are successful in business, university educated, community leaders, and active in shaping the political future of our country. (Business owner's comment at a Hispanic Chambers of Commerce Conference in Denver, Colorado)

INTRODUCTION

Latino/Hispanic Americans are the fastest growing cultural group in the United States. Between the 1980 and 1990 Censuses, the population increased by 53 percent, from 14.6 million in 1980 to 22.4 million in 1990. Growth in all urban and rural areas of the United States has been most striking. The population growth can be attributed to (1) higher birth rates; (2) higher immigration from Mexico, Central and South America, and the Caribbean; (3) greater longevity since this is a relatively young population; and (4) larger numbers of subgroups being incorporated into the Latino/Hispanic American grouping.

LATINO/HISPANIC AMERICANS DEFINED

Hispanic is a generic term referring to all Spanish-surname and Spanish-speaking people who reside in the United States and in Puerto Rico (a U.S. territory). *Latino,* the preferred label on the west coast and on parts of the east coast and the southeast, is a Spanish word indicating a person of Latin American origins. *Hispanic* is preferred on the east coast primarily by the Puerto Rican, Dominican, and Cuban communities (although the members within each of the Puerto Rican, Dominican, and Cuban communities may prefer the specific term referring to their country of heritage). *Hispanic* is also the official term used in federal, state, and other local governmental documents and is used for demographic references. Objections to the use of the term *Hispanic* include the following: (1) *Hispanic* isn't derived from any culture or place (i.e., there is no such place as "Hispania"), and (2) the term was invented primarily for use by the U.S. Census. Sometimes, the term *Spanish speaking/Spanish surnamed* may be used to recognize the fact that a large number of Latino/Hispanic Americans may not speak Spanish (thus "Spanish surnamed"). *La Raza* is another term used, primarily on the west coast and in the southwest, to refer to all peoples of the western hemisphere who share the cultural, historical, political, and social legacy of the Spanish and Portuguese colonists and the native Indian and African people (it has its origins in the notions of the political struggles and the mixing of the races, *el mestizaje*). *Chicano* is a term that grew out of the ethnic pride and ethnic studies movement in the late 1960s and refers to Mexican Americans (used primarily on the west coast, the southwest, and the midwest, and in college communities that have an ethnic studies curriculum).

It should be noted that the definition itself of *Latino/Hispanic* is considered by many to be a "mega-label" that does not fit well with members included in the group. "Younger people in some cities, especially, find Hispanic archaic, if not downright offensive, much as "Negro" displeased a previous generation of blacks and African-Americans. They say it recalls the colonization by Spain and Portugal and ignores the Indian and African roots of many people it describes. Yet others, including business and political leaders, dismiss "Latino" as a fad. Still others use the terms "Hispanic" and "Latino" interchangeably" (Gonzalez, 1992).

HISTORICAL INFORMATION

The historical background of Latino/Hispanic Americans provides key factors that affect their interactions with and understanding of law enforcement and peacekeeping personnel. Clearly, this brief historical and sociopolitical overview can only provide highlights of the commonalities and some of the diversity of cultural experiences of Latino/Hispanic Americans. The largest numbers under the Latino/Hispanic groupings in the United States are from Mexico, Puerto Rico, and Cuba. Our historical review will focus on the larger Latino/Hispanic communities.

Under the declaration of "Manifest Destiny," the United States began in the nineteenth century the expansionist policy of annexing vast territories to the south, north, and west. As Lopez y Rivas (1973) noted, the United States viewed itself as a people chosen by "Providence" to form a larger union through conquest, purchase, and/or annexation. With the purchase (or annexation) of the Louisiana Territories in 1803, Florida in 1819, Texas in 1845, and the Northwest Territories (Oregon, Washington, Idaho, Wyoming, and Montana) in 1846, it was inevitable that conflict would occur with Mexico. The resulting Mexican–American War ended in 1848 with the signing of the Treaty of Guadalupe Hidalgo, in which Mexico received $ 15 million from the United States for the land that is now Texas, New Mexico, Arizona, and California, with more than 100,000 Mexican people living in those areas. As is obvious from this portion of history, it makes little sense for many Mexican Americans to be stereotyped as "illegal aliens," especially since more than a million Mexican Americans (some of whom are U.S. citizens and some of whom are not) can trace their ancestry back to families living in the southwest United States in the mid-1800s (Fernandex, 1970). Moreover, for Latino/Hispanic Americans (especially Mexican Americans), the boundaries between the United States and Mexico are seen as artificial: "The geographic, ecological, and cultural blending of the Southwest with Mexico is perceived as a continuing unity of people whose claim to the Southwest is rooted in the land itself" (Montiel, 1978). While one-third of Mexican Americans can trace their ancestry to families living in the United States in the mid-1800s, the majority of this group migrated into the United States after 1910 because of the economic and political changes that occurred as a result of the Mexican Revolution.

Puerto Rico was under the domination of Spain until 1897, at which time it was allowed the establishment of a local government. The United States invaded Puerto Rico and annexed it as part of the Spanish-American War (as were Cuba, the Philippines, and Guam) in 1898. While Cuba (in 1902) and the Philippines (in 1949) were given their independence, Puerto Rico remained a territory of the United States. In 1900, the Foraker Act was passed by the U.S. Congress, which allowed the president to appoint a governor, to provide an executive council consisting of 11 presidential appointees (of which only 5 had to be Puerto Rican), and to elect locally a 35-member chamber of delegates. In reality, the territory was run by the presidential appointed governor and the executive council. The Jones Act in 1917 made Puerto Ricans citizens of the United States. It was not until 1948 that Puerto Rico elected its first governor, Luis Munoz Marin. In 1952, Puerto Rico was given commonwealth status, and Spanish was allowed to be the language of instruction in the schools again (with English taught as the second language).

Following World War II, large numbers of Puerto Ricans began migrating into the United States. With citizenship status, Puerto Ricans could travel easily and settled in areas on the east coast, primarily New York City (in part, because of the availability of jobs and affordable apartments). The estimated number of Puerto Ricans in the United States is 2 million on the mainland and 3.3 million living on the island (Ramos-McKay et al., 1988).

Cubans immigrated into the United States in three waves. The first wave occurred between 1959 and 1965 and consisted of primarily white middle- or upper-class Cubans who were relatively well educated and had business and financial resources. The federal government's Cuban Refugee Program, Cuban Student Loan Program, and Cuban Small Business Administration Loan Program were established to help this first wave of Cuban immigrants achieve a successful settlement (Bernal and Estrada, 1985). The second wave of Cuban immigrants occurred between 1965 and 1973. This second wave resulted from the opening of the port of Camarioca, which allowed all who wished to leave Cuba to exit. Those who left as part of the second wave were more working class, and lower-middle class, primarily white adult men and women. The third wave of immigrants, leaving Cuba from Mariel, occurred from the summer of 1980 to early 1982. This third wave was the largest (about 125,000 were boat-lifted to the United States) and consisted primarily of working-class persons, more reflective of the Cuban population as a whole. Most immigrated to the United States with hopes for better economic opportunities. Within this group of *Marielito* were many of the antisocial, criminal, and mentally ill persons released by Fidel Castro and included in the boat-lift (Gavzer, 1993).

In addition to the three major groups that have immigrated into the United States from Mexico, Puerto Rico, and Cuba are the immigrants from the 21 countries of South and Central America and the Caribbean. Arrival of these immigrants for political, economic, and social reasons began in the early-1980s and has added to the diversity of the Latino/Hispanic American communities in the United States. Some groups, like the Dominicans, who are growing rapidly on the east coast, are difficult to determine in terms of numbers because of their undocumented entry status in the United States.

DEMOGRAPHICS: DIVERSITY AMONG LATINO/HISPANIC AMERICANS

As is evident from the historical background provided, Latino/Hispanic Americans are a very heterogeneous population comprised of many different cultural groups with significant generational, educational, and socioeconomic differences, varying relocation experiences, as well as many other life experience differences. While the Spanish language may provide a common thread for most Latino/Hispanic Americans, there are cultural and national differences in the terms and expressions used, including nonverbal nuances. Moreover, the language of Brazil is Portuguese, not Spanish, and thus the language connection for Brazilians is unique. Notwithstanding, the Latino/Hispanic American population number about 22.4 million and represent 9 percent of the U.S. population (these numbers do not include the 3.3 million people who live in Puerto Rico). The growth of the Latino/Hispanic American population is the fastest, with a 53 percent increase between the 1980 and 1990 censuses. Eighty-five percent of the Latino/Hispanic Americans trace their roots to Mexico, Puerto Rico, and Cuba, while the remaining 15 percent are from the other countries of Central and South America, the Caribbean, and Spain (Gonzalez, 1992).

Latino/Hispanic Americans are concentrated in five states: California (26 percent), Texas (21 percent), New York (11 percent), Florida (6 percent), and Illinois (5 percent). Some of the key demographic characteristics of this population include the following (the implications of the information below are presented in the "Key Issues in Law Enforcement" section):

Exhibit 8.1   Language spoken at home by Latino/Hispanic Americans (Percent)

LANGUAGE SPOKEN AT HOME	TOTAL	BORN IN THE U.S.	BORN OUTSIDE THE U.S.
Spanish dominant	56	18	78
Spanish/English equally	23	35	16
English dominant	21	47	6

1. **Age.** Latino/Hispanic Americans tend to be younger than the general U.S. population. The median age is 25.5 years, in contrast to the rest of America, with an average age of 30.
2. **Size of household.** The average Latino/Hispanic household consists of 3.6 people, which is nearly double that for the rest of the United States, at 1.9 persons per household.
3. **Purchasing power.** The estimated purchasing power of Latino/Hispanic Americans in the United States is $160 billion.
4. **Urban households.** Eighty-eight percent of all Latino/Hispanic Americans live in metropolitan areas, making this group the most highly urbanized population in the United States.
5. **Language.** Latino/Hispanic American self-identification is most strongly demonstrated in the use and knowledge of Spanish. The Spanish language is often the single most important cultural aspect endorsed to be retained by Latino/Hispanic Americans. The *Hispanic Monitor* (1991), based on research by Yankelovich Clancy Shulman and Market Development, Inc., summarized their findings regarding the use of Spanish in Latino/Hispanic American households (Exhibit 8.1).

   As might be expected, with the large number of Latino/Hispanic Americans born in the United States, English will soon be the dominant language as this population moves into successive generations.

LABELS AND TERMS

As noted earlier, the term *Latino/Hispanic American* is a convenient summarizing label referring to a very heterogeneous group of people. Similar to the case of Asian/Pacific Americans, the key to understanding which terms to use is based on the principle of "self-preference." As Cisneros noted in Gonzales (1992): "To say Latino is to say you come to my culture in a manner of respect," said Sandra Cisneros, the author of "Women Hollering Creek: And Other Stories," who refuses to have her writing included in any anthology that uses the word Hispanic. "To say Hispanic means you're so colonized you don't even know for yourself, or someone who named you never bothered to ask what you call yourself. It's a repulsive slave name."

While many Latino/Hispanic Americans may not hold as strong an opinion as the author noted above, sensitivity is warranted in the use of the term *Hispanic* with the Latino/Hispanic American community. For those who have origins in the Caribbean (e.g., Puerto Rican, Cuban, Dominican), the term *Latino* may be equally problematic for self-designation and identification.

In federal and other governmental designations, the label used is *Hispanic.* While only some refer to themselves as such, the governmental designation is used in laws, programs, and regulations and in most reports and publications.

For people within any of the groups, often the more specific names for the groups are preferred (e.g., Mexican, Puerto Rican, Cuban, Dominican, Argentinean, Salvadorean, etc.). Some individuals may prefer that the term *American* be part of their designation (e.g., Mexican American). For the law enforcement officer, the best term to use in referring to a person is *the term he or she prefers to be called.* It is perfectly acceptable to ask a person what term is favored.

The use of slurs such as "wetback," "Mex," "Spic," "Greaser," or other derogatory ethnic slang terms is never acceptable in crime fighting and peacekeeping, no matter how provoked an officer may be. Other stereotypic terms such as "Illegal," "New York Rican," "macho man," "Latin lover," "Lupe the virgin," and "low rider" do not convey the kinds of professionalism and respect for community diversity important to law enforcement and peacekeeping and need to be avoided in law enforcement work. Officers hearing these (or other similar) words used in their own departments (or with peers or citizens) should provide immediate feedback about the inappropriate use of such terms to the other officer. Officers who may out of habit routinely use these terms may find themselves (or their superiors) in the *embarrassing situation* of explaining to offended citizens and communities why the term was used and how they had intended no bias, stereotype, nor prejudice.

MYTHS AND STEREOTYPES

Knowledge of and sensitivity to Latino/Hispanic Americans' concerns, diversity, historical background, and life experiences will facilitate the crime fighting and peacekeeping mission of law enforcement officers. It is important to have an understanding about some of the myths and stereotypes of Latino/Hispanic Americans that contribute to prejudice, discrimination, and bias encountered by this population. Many law enforcement officers do not have much experience with the diversity of the Latino/Hispanic American groups and learn about these groups only through stereotypes, often perpetuated by movies and through the very limited contact involved in their law enforcement duties. Simplistic views of Latino/Hispanic Americans have led many Americans to lump members of these diverse groups into one stereotypic group, "Mexicans." The law enforcement officer should be aware of the different stereotypes of Latino/Hispanic Americans. The key to effectiveness with any ethnic/racial group is not that we do not have myths and stereotypes about these groups, but that *we are aware of the existence of these stereotypes and can monitor our thinking and behavior with respect to the person with whom we are dealing.*

Some of the stereotypes that have affected Latino/Hispanic Americans in law enforcement include the following:

1. *Viewing Latino/Hispanic Americans as illegal aliens.* While many argue over the number of Latino/Hispanic illegal and undocumented immigrants (see Ferriss, 1993), the vast majority of Latino/Hispanic Americans do not fall into this stereotype (i.e., the vast majority of Latino/Hispanic Americans in the United States are U.S. citizens or legal residents). While the issues of illegal aliens and undocumented immigrants are complex ones, cultural awareness training will offer the officer knowledge which can help him or her avoid the offensive situation of acting on the

stereotype of Latino/Hispanic Americans as "illegal." The following is not an unusual occurrence for many Latino/Hispanic Americans:

> Esteban Vasquez worked in the maintenance department of one the larger downtown hotels in southern California. While at work on his day shift, all "immigrant members" of his maintenance department were asked to go to Personnel. When he had arrived, he found himself (and others) questioned by several officers of the Immigration and Nationalization Services (INS) asking for identifications and "papers." Esteban was asked if he was an illegal and undocumented alien. He explained that he was a fourth-generation Mexican American, that he was born and grew up in Arizona, and that his family had lived for several generations in Arizona and Colorado. When Esteban was asked for proof of citizenship and/or permanent residency, he told the officers that he had a driver's license and car insurance papers. He further explained that he had grown children in college, and one was pursuing a master's degree. While the INS officers were finally satisfied with his explanations, Esteban felt very insulted and offended by the assumption made that he was an illegal alien and not a U.S. citizen. (Latino/Hispanic American community organizer anecdote)

In the October 1989 edition of *Badge 911,* an example of blatant discrimination and stereotyping of Latino/Hispanic Americans is present. We have provided Exhibit 8.2 which is a copy of a memorandum found on the wall of a sheriff's station.

Exhibit 8.2   Example Memorandum Containing Stereotypes About Latino/Hispanic Americans

To: All sworn personnel
          Sheriff's station

From: _____   Administrative Sgt.
          _____   Sheriff's station

Please inventory your assigned patrol vehicles for aliens.

The City of _____ has been generous enough to see that each vehicle is equipped with three (one tall, two short), and they should be alpha-numerically designated per your unit number, i.e., 495-a, -b, and -c.

Please check your vehicle and make sure all three aliens are present and properly numbered. They should also be fully equipped with baseball caps and plastic shopping bags.

In addition, these aliens are to be carried only in your vehicle's trunk, under no circumstances are they to be put in the console or glove compartment.

                              Thank you,

Note: As of October 8, 1989, this official memo from a sergeant was hanging on the briefing board at the Sheriff's Station. Information has it that this type of unprofessional communication is commonplace. Another example of this type of practice is a so-called "Mexican Day," where deputies are instructed to stop all vehicles with "Mexican-looking" people (and for no other reason).

  It is very unfortunate to hear that this type of activity exists and apparently is not only condoned but is initiated by some members of the supervisory staff.

---

2. *Viewing Latino/Hispanic Americans as lazy and as poor workers.* This is a stereotype that has been perpetuated in the workplace. Moreover, this stereotype of Latino/Hispanic Americans is often extended to Latino/Hispanic Americans as being a "party people." A workplace law enforcement example illustrates this stereotype:

> A flyer was sent out through interdepartmental mail announcing the retirement party for Sergeant Juan Gomez. The flyer showed a man (with sergeant's stripes) dressed in traditional Mexican garb (sombrero, serapé, sandals, etc.) sleeping under a large shade tree. While Sergeant Gomez did not appear offended by the stereotype, a Latina nonsworn departmental employee was deeply offended by this flyer and requested that it not be used to announce a party by the organization. The people planning the event said that she was being "overly sensitive" and ignored her request. (Police officer's anecdote told at a cultural awareness training session)

It is difficult to understand why this stereotype continues to be held or what factors continue to perpetuate it (given what we know about the Latino/Hispanic American workforce in the United States and globally). Harbrecht et al. (1993) noted that the Mexican workers (in Mexico) comprise a smart, motivated, and highly productive workforce and "a potent new economic force to be reckoned with." Latino/Hispanic American community advocates make the argument that it is difficult to imagine anyone being labeled as "lazy" or "poor workers" if they are willing to work as laborers from dawn to dusk in the migrant farm fields, day in and day out, year after year.

3. *Perceiving Latino/Hispanic Americans as uneducated.* Prior to 1948, many Latino/Hispanic American children were denied access to the educational system available to others, and instead, were relegated to "Mexican" schools. It was the challenge in the U.S. courts of segregated schools that improved and allowed the access of Latino/Hispanic children into the "regular" school system (see *Mendez* v. *Westminster School District,* 1945, and *Delgado* v. *Bastrop Independent School District,* 1948). This stereotype of "uneducated" relates to how Latino/Hispanic officers may be *inappropriately* stereotyped and seen in terms of being able to learn and to achieve in law enforcement and other professional training in peace keeping.

4. *Viewing Latino/Hispanic Americans as dishonest and not trustworthy.* Clearly, this stereotype would affect professionals in law enforcement and peacekeeping. Cultural understanding would allow the following shopkeeper (and peace officers as well) to avoid insulting situations as the following:

> "Angel Llano, a New York native of Hispanic descent who works for the State of California and lives in a Northern California city wrote in complaining about a local video store that fingerprints only male Latinos among its new customers. (A subsequent review of 200 membership cards found 11 with fingerprints—all those of men with Hispanic surnames.)" (Mandel, 1993).

5. *Considering Latino/Hispanic American young males as gang members and drug dealers.* Some hold the stereotype, especially among young males in the inner city, that Latino/Hispanic Americans are gang members and involved as drug dealers.

Latino/Hispanic cultures are group oriented, and people from young to old tend to congregate as groups rather than as individuals or couples. "Hanging out" as a group tends to be the preferred mode of socialization. However, given the stereotype of Latino/Hispanic American young males as being gang members, it is easy to perceive five young Latino/Hispanic males walking together as constituting "a gang." Such stereotypes have resulted in suspicion, hostility, and prejudice toward Latino/Hispanic Americans and have served to justify improper treatment (e.g., routine traffic stops) and poor services (e.g., in restaurants and stores). Such stereotypes can lead law enforcement officers to consider anyone associated with a criminal suspect to be a criminal, as in the following example: "Look through here," says Detective Don Benderhoff, one of four detectives in the special "Cuban task force" in NYPD's Bronx headquarters, leafing through an address book seized as evidence. "They have phone numbers with area codes 305 [Miami], 201 [New Jersey]. They have Hialeah addresses, St. Paul addresses, Queens addresses, Skokie addresses. You name the town, they have a contact. And it's all done by telephone" (Taft, 1982).

6. *Assuming that all Latino/Hispanic Americans speak Spanish.* As noted earlier in the chapter, 21 percent of the Latino/Hispanic Americans reported their families as speaking English as the dominant language in the home. Many Latino/Hispanic Americans have been in the United States for five generations or more and English is the only language they speak and write.

> George Perez is a Latino/Hispanic American cultural awareness trainer for many law enforcement, emergency service, and other public service organizations. As one of the outstanding trainers in his field, he is not surprised by the often heard stereotypical comment, "You speak English so well, without an accent. How did you do it?" His reply would usually be, "It's the only language I know! I'm a fifth-generation Latino/Hispanic American. I grew up in northern California and received my bachelor's and master's degree in the field that I teach." (Latino/Hispanic American law enforcement trainer)

THE LATINO/HISPANIC AMERICAN FAMILY

Obviously, with over 25 different cultural groups that make up Latino/Hispanic Americans, there are many differences existing between any one group with another group in this collective. We would like to present some characteristics related to family that are shared among many of the different Latino/Hispanic cultural groups that can be of value in community peacekeeping and crime fighting. *La familia* is perhaps one of the most significant considerations in working and communicating with Latino/Hispanic Americans (in places where we have used the Spanish term, we have done so to indicate that there are additional cultural meanings encompassed. The full extent of the Latino/Hispanic "*familia*," for example, is not captured in the English term "the family"). The Latino/Hispanic American family is most clearly characterized by bonds of interdependence, unity, and loyalty, which includes nuclear and extended family members as well as networks of neighbors, friends, and community members. Primary importance is given to the history of the family, which is firmly rooted in the set of obligations tied to both the past as well as to the future. In considering the different loyalty bonds, the parent–child relationship emerges as primary, with all children owing *respecto* to parents (*respecto* connotes additional cultural meanings than in the English term "respect"). Traditionally, the role of the father has been that of the disciplinarian, decision maker, and leader of the household. Father's word is the law, and he is not to be questioned. The father will tend to focus his attention on the economic well-being issues of the family and less the social-emotional issues. Mother, on the other hand, is seen as balancing the father's role through her role in providing for the emotional and expressive issues of the family. Extended family members such as grandmothers, aunts and uncles, and godparents (*compadre/comadre*) may supplement mother's emotional support. In the Latino/Hispanic American family, the older son is traditionally the secondary decision maker to the father and the principal inheritor (*primogenito*) of the family. Because of the central nature of the Latino/Hispanic American family, it is common for police officers to come into contact with members of the nuclear and extended family in the course of working with community members. One key to the success of law enforcement officers in working with the Latino/Hispanic American extended network is knowledge of how best to communicate in the family context and with whom to speak for information, observations, and questions.

The Role of the Man and the Woman

In many Latino/Hispanic American families, the relationship and communication patterns are hierarchical, with the father as the identified head of the household and held in high respect. When it comes to family well-being, economic issues, and discipline, the father may appear to be the decision maker; however, many other people may come into the picture. Generally, if there are grandparents in the household, the father may consult them, as well as his wife, on major decisions. In the case of law enforcement matters, it may be of great importance for officers to provide the father and the family some privacy, as much as possible, to discuss key issues and situations. With central values like *respecto* (respect) and *machismo* (see below) in the Latino/Hispanic American culture, it is critical for the father and other family members to demonstrate control in family situations. In this way, the law enforcement officers may find that there is more control in a situation by allowing the citizen to think through a decision, come to the same conclusion as that of the officer, and exercise self-control in behaving in the best interests of all parties concerned. In the training videotape "Common Ground" by the Orange County, California Sheriff's Department (1990), several examples are provided: (1) In a vignette in which the father of the family had to be arrested, the officers responded to the father's concern about being handcuffed in the presence of his children. The arresting officers were willing to wait until the father had left the house and gotten into the car before handcuffing the father (provided that he was willing to go peacefully). (2) In the scenario in which neighbors had complained about the noise of a wedding party and officers were dispatched to disband the party, the officer in charge allowed the father to tell everyone that the party was over and to bid his guests farewell (instead of the officers closing down the party).

Within the Latino/Hispanic American family, the sex roles are clearly defined, in which boys and girls, since childhood, are taught two different codes of male versus female behavior (Comas-Diaz and Griffith, 1988). Traditional sex roles can be discussed in the context of the two codes of gender-related behaviors: *machismo* and *marianismo*. *Machismo* literally means maleness, manliness, and virility. Within the Latino/Hispanic American cultural context, *machismo* means that the male is responsible for the well-being and honor of the family and is in the provider role. *Machismo* is also associated with having power over women as well as responsibility for guarding and protecting them. Boys are seen as strong by nature and do not need the protection required by girls, who are seen as weak by nature.

Women are socialized into the role of *marianismo*, based on the beliefs about the Virgin Mary, in which women are considered spiritually superior to men, and therefore able to endure all suffering inflicted by men (Stevens, 1973). Women are expected to be self-sacrificing in favor of their husbands and children. Within the context of the Latino/Hispanic American family, the role of the woman is in the home as the caretaker of children and the homemaker. In the current U.S. context, the traditional gender roles of women and men in the Latino/Hispanic American community have undergone much change and have resulted in major conflicts since women have begun to work, bring home a paycheck, and do many of the financially independent activities that men can do (e.g., go out and socialize with others outside the family).

While there are no clear-cut rules as to whether one goes to the male head of the household or to the female member, law enforcement officers would probably be more correct to address the father first in law enforcement inquiries. Consistent with the cultural values of *machismo* and *marianismo*, the Latino/Hispanic American household appears to be run by the father; however, in actual practice, the mother's role in discipline, education, finance, and decision making is also central.

Children/Adolescents/Youth

Within the Latino/Hispanic American family, the ideal child is obedient and respectful of his or her parents and other elders. Adults may at times talk in front of the children as if they are not present and as if the children cannot understand the adults' conversations. Children are taught *respeto* (respect), which dictates the appropriate behavior toward all authority figures, older people, parents, relatives, and others. If children are disrespectful, they are punished and scolded. In many traditional families, it is considered appropriate for parents (and for relatives) to discipline a disrespectful and misbehaving child physically.

In Latino/Hispanic American households, there is a high reliance on family members (older children and other adults) to help care for younger children. It is often the case that both parents of a Latino/Hispanic American family work. It is common for families to have "latchkey" children or have children cared for by older children in the neighborhood. As in other English-limited communities, Latino/Hispanic American children have a special role in being the intermediaries for their parents on external community matters because of their ability to learn English and the American ways of doing things more quickly than their parents. Children often serve

as translators and interpreters for peace officers in their communication and relations to Latino/Hispanic American families involved in legal matters, immigration
concerns, and community resources. While the use of children and family members
as translators is viewed as professionally and culturally inappropriate, it is often by necessity the only means available to the law enforcement officer. In such situations it is
suggested that the officer review what role is expected of the youthful member of the
family. The officer needs to see how sensitive an area the translation is for various
family members. Moreover, the consequence of an incorrect translation needs to be
evaluated (e.g., asking a juvenile to translate to his or her parents who speak no English that the juvenile has been involved in drinking and riding in a stolen vehicle may
result in significantly changed content because of the embarrassment caused to both
the juvenile and possibly to the parents). In all cases, when a child is acting as a translator to parents, the officer should direct all verbal and nonverbal communication to
the parents. Otherwise, the parents may view the officer's lack of attention to them as
an insult. Such sensitivity by the peace officer is particularly important for
Latino/Hispanic Americans because of the cultural value of *personalismo* which emphasizes the importance of the personal quality of any interaction. This cultural concept implies that relationships occur between particular individuals as persons, not as
representatives of institutions (e.g., law enforcement) nor merely as individuals performing a role (e.g., as a person who enforces the law).

CULTURAL INFLUENCES ON COMMUNICATION

Although we do not wish to create any kinds of stereotypes, there are key features
of Latino/Hispanic American verbal and nonverbal communication styles that necessitate explanation. Misunderstanding resulting from style differences can result
in perceptions of poor community services from police agencies, conflicts resulting
from such misunderstandings, and safety and control issues for the peace officer.

Group Orientation Style in Communication

Latino/Hispanic Americans high cultural value for *la familia* will result in a very
strong "family" and/or "group" orientation. The frequently seen behavior of "eye-
checking" with other family members before answering and the lack of the use of
"I" statements and/or self-reference should not be evaluated as not being straight
forward about oneself or one's relationships. The officer may be concerned because a Latino/Hispanic American witness may wish to use the pronoun "we" when
the situation may call for a personal observation involving an "I" statement. For example, a Latino/Hispanic American family member who witnessed a store robbery
may first nonverbally check with other family members before talking and then describe what he or she saw. Such verbal and nonverbal behavior is consistent with the
family and group orientation of Latino/Hispanic Americans.

Language Limitations

Speaking Spanish to others in the presence of a law enforcement officer even
though the officer had requested responses in English should not be interpreted

automatically as attempts to hide information from the officer nor should it be seen as an affront. In times of stress, speakers of English-as-a-second-language will automatically revert to their first and native language. In a law enforcement situation, many individuals may find themselves under stress and may speak Spanish, which is the more comfortable language for them. Moreover, speaking Spanish gives the citizen a greater range of expression (to discuss things with other speakers and family members) and thus provide more useful and clearer information to law enforcement personnel about critical events.

It is important for officers to take the time to get information from witnesses, victims, and suspects even if those involved have limitations in their English-speaking abilities (the use of officers who speak Spanish, translators, and language bank resources will help). Often the Latino/Hispanic American has not been helped in crime fighting and peacekeeping situations because the officer could not or did not take information from limited-English speakers.

Communicating Trust

While Latino/Hispanic Americans may show respect to law enforcement officers because of their authority, this does not mean that the person necessarily "trusts" the officers and/or the organization. *Respecto* is extended to elders and those who are in authority. This is certainly noted in the Spanish language, in which respect is shown by the use of *usted* (the formal "you") versus the use of *tu* (the informal "you"). Showing respect, however, does not mean trust. The cultural value of *confianza* (or trust) takes some time to develop. Like many from ethnic/minority communities, Latino/Hispanic Americans have experienced some degree of prejudice and discrimination from the majority community. Citizens with such experiences need time to develop trust with law enforcement officers, who are identified as being a part of the majority community.

"High Context" Communication

Because of the cultural value of *personalismo*, which emphasizes the importance of the "person" involved in any interaction, Latino/Hispanic Americans take into strong consideration not only the content of any communication, but also the context and relationship of the communicator. This means that it is important for the officer to provide information about why questions are asked, the person who is asking the question (i.e., information about the officer), and how the information will be used in the context for effective communications. Additionally, context for Latino/Hispanic Americans means taking some time to find out, as well as to self-disclose, some background information (e.g., living in the same neighborhood, having similar concerns about crime, etc.). Additional contexts, such as providing explanations and information to Latino/Hispanic Americans *about* procedures, laws, and so on, before asking them questions and/or requesting their help, will ease the work of the officer. By providing background information and by establishing prior relationships with members of the community, the officer has set the stage for members' future cooperation with law enforcement agencies.

Nonverbal Communication

Be cognizant of nonverbal nuances that may detract from effective communication with the officer. Many Latino/Hispanic Americans, especially younger people, find it uncomfortable and sometimes inappropriate to maintain eye contact with authority figures such as police officers. It is considered a lack of respect if there is strong eye contact with someone who is in a higher position, or is an authority figure. Many citizens from this background may deflect their eyes when they look at a police officer. It is important that the officer not automatically read this nonverbal behavior as a dishonest response.

Perception of Evasiveness

People may exhibit behaviors that appear to be evasive such as claiming not to have any identification or by saying that they do not speak English. In many of the native countries from which some Latino/Hispanic Americans have immigrated, the police and law enforcement agencies are aligned with a politically repressive government. The work of the police and of law enforcement in those countries is not one of public service. Many Latino/Hispanic Americans may have similar "fear" reactions to law enforcement officers in the United States. It is suggested that the officer take the time to explain the need for identification and the importance of reaching understanding and cooperating.

> Carlos and his family had escaped from one of the South American countries where he saw the police serving as part of the politically repressive force upon his community. He was aware of the role of some of the police as members of the "death squad." He and his family were admitted to the U.S. and given political asylum and lived in southern California. Although he speaks fluent English and Spanish and has been in the U.S. for over five years, he relates how on one occasion when he was pulled over by the police (for a broken taillight), he automatically had this fear reaction and had the thought of saying to the officer, "No habla English" in the hope of avoiding further contact. (Latino/Hispanic American trainer's anecdote told in a police cultural awareness training course)

Expression of Emotion

Another area where people may differ in communication style has to do with how much emotion is displayed through facial expressiveness, voice volume, and body gestures. A police officer may attempt to calm down a person whom he or she perceives as being overly emotional (or even hysterical) simply because of discomfort with the degree of emotionalism conveyed. Latino/Hispanic Americans tend to display feelings freely in everyday situations and even when reporting incidents that appear to be relatively minor. Mexicans have been known to refer to North Americans (from the United States) as "corpses," believing that they (i.e., Anglos) are devoid of feeling (Condon, 1985). In this case, Mexicans may be misreading the cues based on their own cultural norms. Similarly, officers who do not share a cultural background with Latino/Hispanic Americans need to assess the expression of emotionalism in its cultural context.

KEY ISSUES IN LAW ENFORCEMENT

Underreporting of Crimes

Because of their past experiences with some law enforcement agencies in their countries of origin (e.g., as part of the repressive military force in their native country, as well as perceived "unresponsiveness" by police) some Latino/Hispanic Americans, are reluctant to report crimes and may not seek police assistance and help. Many people bring with them memories of how police in their home countries have brutalized and violated them and others (e.g., as members of the "death squad"). Moreover, there is the perception among many that the police, no matter how "good" they are, will not be able to reduce crime in Latino/Hispanic American neighborhoods (Carter, 1983). Many immigrants and refugees are simply not knowledgeable about the legal system of the United States and avoid any contact with law enforcement personnel. Outreach and community policing perspectives will enhance the contact and relationship with Latino/Hispanic American communities and may help alleviate the underreporting of crimes. As Carter (1983) noted in his study in Texas, 98.8 percent of the Latino/Hispanic American respondents cited inadequate police protection as the reason for their fear of crime.

Victimization

The Bureau of Justice Statistics provided a special report on "Hispanic victims" (Bastian, 1990). The following are some key conclusions from the ongoing study of approximately 100,000 persons age 12 or older, interviewed twice a year in about 50,000 households:

1.   For the period 1979 to 1986, Latino/Hispanic Americans experienced higher rates of victimization from violent crime than all other populations. For every 1000 Latino/Hispanic Americans age 12 and over, there were 12 aggravated assaults and 11 robberies (as compared to 10 aggravated assaults and 6 robberies for all other populations).

2.   Latino/Hispanic Americans suffered a higher rate of household crimes (e.g., burglary, household larceny, motor vehicle theft) than all other populations. In the study (Bastian, 1990), there was an annual average of 266 household victimizations per 1000 households headed by a Latino/Hispanic American, as compared to 205 crimes per 1000 households for all other populations.

3.   The street was the most common place for violent crimes to occur: 45 percent of the robberies of Latino/Hispanic Americans occurred on the city streets. The higher victimization rate can be partly explained by some of the individual and environment characteristics of Latino/Hispanic Americans, that is, a younger, poorer population with a large urban area concentration.

4.   Latino/Hispanic American victims of violent crime were more likely to be accosted by a stranger (65 percent) than were African American victims (54 percent) or Caucasian or white victims (58 percent). Latino/Hispanic American victims (and African American victims) were more likely to face an offender with a weapon (57 percent for each group) than were Caucasian or white victims (43 percent).

Differential Treatment

In Bastian's (1990) study, Latino/Hispanic Americans said that one of the reasons for not reporting victimizations to the police was that "the police would not do anything." Among nonreporting Latino/Hispanic American (and African American) victims of robbery, personal theft, and household crimes, comparatively similar percentages said that they did not call the police or other law enforcement agencies because they felt that the police would think the incident unimportant or would do little to respond. Clearly, outreach and community efforts are needed to remove this stereotype. Many of the crimes within Latino/Hispanic American communities are perpetrated by others within the same group; however, for this community, a greater number of violent crimes are committed by strangers, that is, by someone whom the victim did not know (65 percent). Law enforcement officials have often found it difficult to get cooperation from Latino/Hispanic American crime victims. In part, the fear of the Latino/Hispanic American person in these cases relates to the retaliatory possibilities of the criminal who is within his or her own community. Other concerns of the Latino/Hispanic American victim include (1) the perceived nonresponsiveness of the peacekeeping officers and agencies, (2) lack of familiarity with and trust of police services, (3) perceived lack of effectiveness of the law enforcement agencies, and (4) prior stereotypes and images of law enforcement agencies as discriminatory. A key challenge for police agencies is to educate this group and to work cooperatively with the communities.

Increasing Latino/Hispanic American Community Police Services

As noted in Chapter 6, Chin (1985), a police officer with the Los Angeles Police Department of the Airport Police Bureau, describes the benefits and improved relationships as a result of a storefront outreach effort to better service for ethnic neighborhoods of Los Angeles. Such strategies would be equally appropriate for Latino/Hispanic American neighborhoods, given the high concentration of the population in the inner city. The outreach approach of using bilingual community service officers (CSOs) (i.e., nonsworn officers holding badges and wearing uniforms) to serve the ethnic communities in San Diego, California provides another feasible model for the Latino/Hispanic American community as a whole. The CSOs provide many of the informational, referral, educational, and crime-reporting services available through the police department. The use of bilingual CSOs provides the Spanish language to community members in an effective way. As many officers will attest, simple Spanish language training is not usually effective: "Crash courses are a waste of time," says Stephen Hrehus, Brighton Beach's Russian-speaking officer, who learned his Russian as a child. "It's like college Spanish. All I remember from my college Spanish is, '*Las montanas en Mexico son bonitas*'—the mountains in Mexico are pretty. All that in six weeks! In six weeks, you are not going to be able to learn much of anything" (Taft, 1992).

This is not to say that the willingness of the law enforcement officer to use Spanish phrases in their interactions with Latino/Hispanic Americans is not useful. The use of everyday greetings and courteous phrases in Spanish indicates the respect and positive attitude of the officer to the Latino/Hispanic American community and is viewed favorably.

Increasing Latino/Hispanic American Peace Officers

There is a significant underrepresentation of Latino/Hispanic Americans in federal, state, and local law enforcement positions. Police departments in states, cities, and community neighborhoods with large Latino/Hispanic Americans have been hampered in their attempts to serve those communities effectively by the small number of officers from similar backgrounds. A variety of reasons exist for such underrepresentation, including:

- Past history of law enforcement stereotypes and relationships with the Latino/Hispanic American communities
- Interests of Latino/Hispanic Americans with respect to law enforcement careers
- Image of law enforcement personnel in the Latino/Hispanic American communities
- Lack of knowledge about the different careers and pathways in law enforcement
- Concern with and fear of background checks and immigration status, physical requirements, and the application process
- Ineffective and misdirected law enforcement recruitment and outreach efforts in the Latino/Hispanic American community
- Lack of role models and advocates for law enforcement careers for Latino/Hispanic Americans

When John Garcia, a senior law enforcement executive, was traveling through some of the Latino/Hispanic American neighborhoods to do some research on how law enforcement agencies might better serve the community, he was constantly receiving comments from Latino/Hispanic American community residents like, "You must be very rich to be a police chief." "You must have been very famous to be a police captain." "Are you really a police chief? I've never seen anyone like you before" (Latino/Hispanic American law enforcement executive's anecdote in a cultural awareness seminar in Southern California).

Clearly, role models are needed to help clarify to the community what is required for a career in law enforcement.

SUMMARY OF RECOMMENDATIONS FOR LAW ENFORCEMENT

1. The experience of Latino/Hispanic Americans with law enforcement officers in the United States has been complicated by (a) the perceptions of Latino/Hispanic Americans regarding the enforcement of immigration laws against illegal aliens and by the discriminatory treatment received by Latino/Hispanic Americans in the United States, and (b) by community conflicts as well as perceptions of police ineffectiveness and unresponsiveness.

- Officers should realize that some citizens may still remember this history and carry with them stereotypes of police services as something to be feared and avoided. Law enforcement officials need to go out of their way to establish the trust, to provide outreach efforts, and to win cooperation in order to effectively accomplish their goals to serve and to protect Latino/Hispanic Americans. Building partnerships focusing on community collaboration in the fight against crime is important.

2.   The label *Latino/Hispanic Americans* encompasses over 25 very diverse ethnic, cultural, and regional groups from North, Central, and South America.

- Law enforcement officials need to be aware of the differences among the diverse groups (e.g., nationality, native culture, regional differences and perceptions, and language dialects) as well as the differences that may result from the individual life experiences within any one of the groups (e.g., social-political turmoils). Since key stereotypes of Latino/Hispanic Americans are regarded by mainstream Americans as more negative than positive, it is important that the peace officers make a special effort to extend respect and dignity to this community of very proud people with a culturally rich heritage.

3.   The preferred term for referring to Latino/Hispanic Americans varies with contexts, groups, and experiences of the Latino/Hispanic American individuals.

- Law enforcement officials need to be aware of terms that are unacceptable and derogatory, and terms that are currently used. When in doubt, officers have to learn to become comfortable in asking citizens which term(s) they prefer.
- Officers are advised to provide feedback to their peers whenever offensive terms, slurs, labels, and/or actions are used with Latino/Hispanic Americans. Such feedback will help reduce the risk of misunderstanding and improve the working relationships of officers with the Latino/Hispanic American communities. Additionally, it will help enhance the professional image of the department for those communities.

4.   Many Latino/Hispanic Americans are concerned with their ability to communicate clearly and about possible reprisal from the police as associated with the role of law enforcement in more politically repressive countries.

- Peace officers need to take the time and be aware that bilingual and English-limited speaking persons want to communicate effectively with them. Maintaining contact, providing extra time, using translators, and being patient with the speaker encourage citizens to communicate their concerns.

5.   Cultural differences in verbal and nonverbal communication often result in misinterpretation of the message and of behaviors.

- Officers need to be aware of nonverbal aspects of some Latino/Hispanic Americans in their communication style such as eye contact, touch, gestures, and emotionality. Verbal aspects, such as accent, mixing English with Spanish, limited vocabulary, and incorrect grammar, may give the officer the impression that the person does not understand what is communicated. As in all cases when English is the second language, it is important to remember that listening and comprehension skills with English are usually better than speaking skills.

6.   Because of their past experiences with law enforcement agencies, together with their own concerns about privacy, self-help, and other factors, Latino/Hispanic Americans are reluctant to report crimes and may not seek police assistance and help.

- It is important for law enforcement departments and officials to build relationships and working partnerships with Latino/Hispanic American communities. This is helped by outreach efforts such as community offices, bilingual officers, and participation of officers in community activities.

7.   Latino/Hispanic Americans tend to hold more severe punishment-oriented perceptions of law enforcement and corrections (Carter, 1983). That is, citizens have strong authoritarian views and an equally strong sense of "rightness" and of punishing the criminal. Because of this point of view, members from this community may view law enforcement as more severe than it really is.

- Law enforcement officials should be aware of this perspective. The *perceptions* of Latino/Hispanic Americans about what they might encounter in dealing with law enforcement officers can be more severe and punitive than what may actually be the case.

DISCUSSION QUESTIONS AND ISSUES*

1. ***Latino/Hispanic Americans Views of Law Enforcement as Insensitive.*** In the historical information section of this chapter, the authors noted many associations made about immigration law enforcement and events which may leave Latino/Hispanic Americans with the view that law enforcement agencies are not "sensitive, effective, and responsive." What are ways to improve such negative points of view?

2. ***Diversity among Latino/Hispanic Americans.*** The authors noted that Latino/Hispanic Americans consist of over 25 diverse regional, national, ethnic, and cultural groups. Which groups are you most likely to encounter in crime fighting and peacekeeping? Which groups do you anticipate encountering in your future work?

3. ***Choice of Terms.*** Use of the terms *Latino, Hispanic, Chicano, Mexican, La Raza, Puerto Rican,* and so on, are confusing for many people. How might you find out which is the best term to use if ethnic and cultural information of this kind is necessary? What would you do if a person reacts negatively to the term you use?

4. ***Offensive Terms and Labels.*** The authors state that offensive terms such as "wetbacks," "illegals," and "Spics" should not be used in law enforcement work at any time. Give three practical reasons for this. How would you respond to other officers who use these terms in the course of their work?

5. ***Effects of Myths and Stereotypes.*** Myths and stereotypes about Latino/Hispanic Americans have affected this group greatly. What are some of the Latino/Hispanic American stereotypes that you have heard of or have encountered? What effect would these stereotypes have on Latino/Hispanic Americans? What are ways to counter these stereotypes in law enforcement?

6. ***Verbal and Nonverbal Variations among Cultures.*** How do you think the information in this chapter about verbal and nonverbal communication styles can help officers in their approach to Latino/Hispanic American citizens? When you can understand the *cultural* components of the style and behaviors, does this help you to become more sensitive and objective about your reactions? In what ways might you use your understanding about the Latino/Hispanic American family dynamics in law enforcement?

7. ***Avoidance of Law Enforcement and Underreporting of Crimes.*** Why do you think that many Latino/Hispanic Americans keep to their own communities and underreport crimes of violence? When are such efforts desirable? When are they ineffective? How can police agencies be of greater service to Latino/Hispanic American communities in this regard?

*See Instructor's Manual accompanying this text for additional activities, role-plays, questionnaires and projects related to the content of this chapter.

8. ***The Future of Latino/Hispanic Americans and Law Enforcement.*** The Latino/Hispanic American population is the fastest-growing segment in the United States. What implications do you see for law enforcement in terms of services, language, recruitment, and training?

REFERENCES

BASTIAN, LISA D. (1990). "Hispanic Victims," Bureau of Justice Statistics, U.S. Department of Justice Reference number: NCJ-120507.

BERNAL, G., AND A. ESTRADA (1985). "Cuban refugee and minority experiences: book review, *Hispanic Journal of Behavioral Sciences,* Vol. 7, pp. 105–128.

BERNAL, G., AND M. GUTIERREZ, (1988). "Cubans" in *Cross-Cultural Mental Health,* L. Comas-Diaz, and E. E. H. Griffith, eds. Wiley, New York.

CARTER, D. L. (1983). "Hispanic interaction with the criminal justice system in Texas: experiences, attitudes, and perceptions," *Journal of Criminal Justice,* vol. 11, pp. 213–227.

CHIN, J., COMAS-DIAZ, L. AND E. E. H. GRIFFITH, eds. (1988). *Cross-Cultural Mental Health,* Wiley, New York.

CONDON, JOHN C. (1985). *Good Neighbors: Communicating with the Mexicans,* Intercultural Press, Yarmouth, Maine.

FERNANDEX, L. F. (1970). *A Forgotten American,* B'nai B'rith, New York.

FERRISS, S. (1993). "Racists or realists? All over California, forces are being mustered against undocumented immigrants," *San Francisco Examiner,* Mar. 21.

GAVZER, G. (1993). "Held without hope," *Parade,* Mar. 21.

GONZALEZ, D. (1992). "What's the problem with 'Hispanic'? Just ask a 'Latino'," *New York Times,* Nov. 15.

HARBRECHT, D., G. SMITH, AND S. BAKER (1993). "The Mexican worker," *Business Week,* Apr. 19.

HISPANIC MONITOR (1991). *Segmenting the Hispanic Market,* Yanklovich, Clancy Shulman and Market Development, Inc., New York.

LOPEZ Y RIVAS, G. (1973). *The Chicanos,* Monthly Review Press, New York.

MANDEL, B. (1993). "Black man's ad is the talk of the town," *San Francisco Examiner,* Jan. 24.

MARTINEZ, C., JR. (1988). "Mexican-Americans," in L. Comas-Diaz, and E. E. H. Griffith, eds., *Cross-Cultural Mental Health,* Wiley, New York.

MONTIEL, M. (1978). *Hispanic Families: Critical Issues for Policy and Programs in Human Services,* COSSMHO, Washington, D.C.

Orange County Sheriff's Department (1990). "Common Ground," videotape by the Orange County Sheriff's Department, Santa Ana, Calif.

RAMOS-MCKAY, J. M., L. COMAS-DIAZ, AND L.A. RIVERA (1988). "Puerto Ricans," in *Cross-Cultural Mental Health,* L. Comas-Diaz, and E. E. H. Griffith, eds., Wiley New York.

STEVENS, E. (1973). "Machismo and marianismo," *Transaction-Society,* Vol. 10, No. 6, pp. 57–63.

TAFT, P. B., JR. (1982). "Policing the new immigrant ghettos," *Police,* July.

9

LAW ENFORCEMENT CONTACT WITH ARAB AMERICANS AND OTHER MIDDLE EASTERN GROUPS

OVERVIEW

This chapter provides specific cultural information on the largest group of Middle Easterners to settle in the United States, the Arab Americans. We begin with an explanation of the scope of the term *Middle Easterner* as it is used in this chapter and provide information briefly on non-Arab Middle Eastern groups. This is followed by a summary of the two major waves of Arab immigration to the United States. The chapter presents demographics and the diversity among Arab Americans as well as information on basic Arab values and beliefs. The background information leads into a discussion of commonly held stereotypes of Arabs. A brief presentation of some aspects of the Islamic religion is included in the chapter, as a substantial percentage of Arab newcomers to the United States are Muslim. Elements of family life are presented, which includes a discussion of the role of the head of the household and issues related to children and "Americanization." The next section presents various cultural practices and characteristics, including greetings, approach, touching, hospitality, verbal and nonverbal communication, gestures, emotional expressiveness, and general points about English language usage. The final section describes several key concerns for law enforcement, including information on perceptions of police, women and modesty, Arab store owners in urban areas, and hate crimes against Arab Americans. In the summary of the chapter, recommendations for improved communication and relationships between law enforcement personnel and Arab American communities are reviewed.

COMMENTARY

Middle Easterners come to the United States for numerous reasons: to gain an education and begin a career, to escape an unstable political situation in their country of origin, and to invest in commercial enterprises with the goal of gaining legal entry into the country. People in law enforcement find themselves having increasing contact with Middle Easterners from a number of different countries:

> From *A Woman's Journey into the Heart of the Arab World,* by Laila Abou-Saif, Charles Scribner's Sons, New York, 1990, p. xiii.

> If you're riding in a cab in New York and you glance at the name of the cabdriver on the license [plate] in front of you, it might be something like Issa Mohammed (an Arab name) or Igall Nidam (an Israeli name). These drivers might be in their mid-thirties or early forties. You don't have to stretch your imagination too far to envisage them a decade or so before, facing one another across enemy lines in the Sinai desert or across the banks of the Suez Canal. Why are they here driving cabs in New York? The answer is simple. There is instability in the Middle East and the future is uncertain. . . .

Established Americans of Arab origin are sometimes treated as if they had just come from the Middle East and may be potential terrorists. Stereotypes, which have long been imprinted in people's minds, can result in Middle Easterners, whether third generation or recent refugees, receiving less than welcome treatment.

> From *1991 Report on Anti-Arab Hate Crimes: Political and Hate Violence against Arab-Americans,* American-Arab Anti-Discrimination Committee, ADC Special Report, Feb. 1992.

> The Arab world has long been perceived in the West in terms of negative stereotypes, which have been transferred to Americans of Arab descent. . . . Briefly put, Arabs are nearly universally portrayed as ruthless terrorists, greedy rich sheiks, religious fanatics, belly dancers or in other simplistic and negative images. When these stereotypes are coupled with the growing centrality of the Middle East in world politics and the increased political visibility of Arab-Americans, one result is that our community becomes more susceptible to hate crimes.

> Comment by Arab American community member about police reactions to Arab Americans:

> Police see Arab emotionalism as a threat. They see the involvement of our large families in police incidents as a threat. They don't need to feel overwhelmed by us and try to contain our reactions. We will cooperate with them, but they need to show us that they don't view us as backward and ignorant people who are inferior just because we are different. . . . (*Anonymous community member*)

MIDDLE EASTERNERS DEFINED

Among the general population there is considerable confusion as to who Middle Easterners are and, specifically, who Arabs are. Although commonly thought of as

Arabs, Iranians and Turks are not Arabs. What all Arabs have in common is the Arabic language, even though spoken Arabic differs from country to country (e.g., Algerian Arabic is different from Jordanian Arabic). The following countries constitute the Middle East and are all Arab countries with the exception of three:

- Aden
- Bahrain
- Egypt
- Iran (non-Arab country)
- Iraq
- Israel (non-Arab country)
- Jordan
- Kuwait
- Lebanon
- Oman
- Quatar
- Saudi Arabia
- Syria
- Turkey (non-Arab country)
- United Arab Emirates
- Yemen

There are other Arab countries that are not in the Middle East (e.g., Algeria, Tunisia, Morocco, Libya) in which the majority population shares a common language and religion (Islam) with people in the Arabic countries of the Middle East. In this chapter we cover primarily information on refugees and immigrants from Arab countries in the Middle East, as they constitute the majority of Middle Eastern newcomers who bring cultural differences and special issues requiring clarification for law enforcement. We only briefly mention issues related to the established Arab American community (i.e., the people who began arriving in the United States in the late nineteenth century). We begin with a brief description of the population from the three non-Arab countries (see Exhibit 9.1).

Iranians and Turks. Iranians use the Arabic script in their writing, but speak Farsi (Persian), not Arabic. Turks speak Turkish, although there are minority groups in Turkey who speak Kurdish, Arabic, and Greek. More than 95 percent of Iranians and Turks are Muslim,* which is the most common religion among people in many other Middle Eastern countries. However, many Iranians in the United States are Jewish and Bahai, both of which groups are minorities in Iran. Of the Muslim population in Iran, the majority belong to the Shi'ah sect of Islam, the Shi'ah version of Islam being the state religion. Persians are the largest ethnic group in Iran, making up about 60 percent of the population, but there are other ethnic populations, including Arabs, Armenians, and Assyrians (among others), all of whom can be found in the United States. During the Iranian hostage crisis in 1979, many Iranians in the United States were targets of hate crimes and anti-

Exhibit 9.1   Non-Arabic immigrants in the
United States from the Middle East

GROUP	NUMBER
Iranians	235,521
Turks	83,850
Israelis	81,677

Source: 1990 Census figures

Iranian sentiment: the same attitudes prevailed against other Middle Easterners (Arabs) and Asians (Indians from India) who were mistakenly labeled as Iranian. Iranians and Turks are not Arabs, but some of the cultural values related to the extended family with respect to pride, dignity, and honor are similar to those in the traditional Arab world. Many Iranian Americans and Turkish Americans came to the United States in the 1970s and are from upper class, professional groups such as doctors, lawyers, and engineers. Of the Iranian immigrant population in the United States, many are Jewish Iranians who left Iran after the fall of the Shah. In the United States, there are large Iranian Jewish populations in the San Francisco Bay Area, Los Angeles, and New York. Also, one can find populations of Muslim Iranians in major U.S. cities, such as New York, Chicago, and Los Angeles.

Israelis.   Israel is the only country in the Middle East in which the majority of the population is not Muslim. Approximately 20 percent of the population in Israel is made up of Arabs (both Christian and Muslim). Eighty percent of the Israeli population is Jewish, with the Jewish population divided into two main groups: Ashkenazim and Sephardim. The Ashkenazim are descended from members of the Jewish communities of Central and Eastern Europe. The majority of American Jews are Ashkenazi, while currently the majority of Israeli Jews are Sephardim, having come originally from Spain, other Mediterranean countries, and the Arabic countries of the Middle East. Israeli immigrants in the United States may be either Ashkenazi or Sephardic and their physical appearance will not indicate to an officer what their ethnicity is. An Israeli may look like an American Jew, a Christian, or a Muslim Arab (or none of these).

Most of the Israeli Arabs who live within the borders of Israel are Palestinians whose families stayed in Israel after the Arab–Israeli war in 1948, when Israel became a nation. The Six-Day War in 1967 resulted in Israel occupying lands that formerly belonged to Egypt, Syria, and Jordan, but where the majority of the population was Palestinian. Thus until the signing of the 1993 peace accord between Israel and the Palestine Liberation Organization (PLO), Israel occupied territories with a population of approximately 1 million Palestinians. The Palestinian–Israeli situation in the Middle East has created a great deal of hostility on both sides. The peace treaty represents progress, but there are still large factions of Israelis and Arabs (including Arabs in other Arab countries) who oppose the peace efforts.

*Also referred to as *Moslem*, but *Muslim* is the preferred term.

This conflict has consequences for law enforcement in the United States in areas where both Israelis and Palestinians reside in large numbers (e.g., Los Angeles, New York, Chicago) or where individuals and groups with extremist views are represented.

Public events such as Israeli Independence Day celebrations and Israeli or Palestinian political rallies have the potential for confrontation, although the majority of these events have been peaceful. Police presence is required at such events, but as with other situations, excessive police presence can escalate hostilities. Law enforcement officials need to be well informed about current events in the Middle East, as conflicts there often have a ripple effect across the world. Monitoring of world events and community trends, will be discussed in Chapter 12, will help police officers take a preventive posture, which can help to avoid confrontation between various Middle Eastern ethnic groups in this country.

HISTORICAL INFORMATION

Although many recent Middle Eastern immigrants and refugees in the United States have come for political reasons, not all Arab Americans left their country of origin because of these. There have been two major waves of Arabic immigrants to the United States. The first wave came between 1880 and World War II and were largely from Syria and what is known today as Lebanon (at the time these areas were part of the Turkish Ottoman Empire). Of the immigrants who settled during this wave, approximately 90 percent were Christian. Many people came to further themselves economically (thus these were immigrants and not refugees forced to leave their countries), but in addition, many of the young men wanted to avoid the military in the Ottoman empire (personal communication, Alixa Naff, Middle Eastern social and political historian, Jan. 25, 1993). A substantial percentage of these immigrants were farmers and artisans and became involved in the business of peddling their goods to farmers and moved from town to town.

Naff has recorded several conversations with older immigrants in which they have recounted their early experiences with and perceptions of American police at the time they were newly arrived immigrants. She explains that because the Arabs competed with local, native-born merchants, there were calls to the police requesting that the Arab peddlers be sent away. Naff has several accounts whereby Arab immigrants reported that they had positive views toward the American police. One immigrant from Syria said that he appreciated the way police treated him in the United States and that in his own country, the police (i.e., the Turkish military police) would have beaten him; there was no civilian police force at the time. This immigrant was impressed with the hospitality of the police . . . a police officer actually let him sleep in the jail! (personal communication, Alixa Naff, Jan. 25, 1993). In the way of crime statistics, not much is reported, partly due to the fact that in the Arabic immigrant community, people took care of their own. When there was a crime, the tendency would have been to cover it up.

In sharp contrast to the characteristics and motivation of the first wave of immigrants, the second wave of Arabic immigrants to the United States, beginning after World War II, came in large part as students and professionals because of economic instability and as political refugees. As a result, these groups brought a "political consciousness unknown to earlier immigrants" (Zogby, 1990). The largest group of second-wave immigrants is made up of Palestinians, many of whom came around 1948, the time of the partition of Palestine, which resulted in Israel's independence. In the 1970s, after the Six-Day War between Israel and Egypt, Syria, and Jordan, there was another large influx of Palestinians. In the 1980s a large group of Lebanese came as a result of the civil war in Lebanon. Yemenis (from Yemen) have continued to come throughout the century; Syrians and Iraqis have made the United States their home since the 1950s and 1960s because of political instability in their countries (Zogby, 1990). Thus these second-wave immigrants came largely because of political turmoil and have been instrumental in changing the nature of the Arab American community in the United States.

DEMOGRAPHICS

There are now approximately 2.5 to 3 million Americans of Arabic ancestry in the United States, constituting approximately 1 percent of the total population. The communities with the largest Arab American populations are in Detroit, Chicago, New York, and Boston. California, Texas, and Ohio have a number of smaller Arab American communities. Between 1980 and 1988, there were more immigrants originating from Arab countries than from any individual European country (Zogby, 1990).

The most dramatic example of how Arab immigration has affected a city is the Detroit area in Michigan. There Arabs began to arrive in the late nineteenth century, but the first huge influx was between 1900 and 1924, when the auto industry attracted immigrants from all over the world (Woodruff, 1991). The Detroit–Dearborn area now has the largest Arab community in the United States, with Arab Americans constituting about one-fourth of the population in Dearborn (personal communication, John Zogby, Arab American demographer, John Zogby Group International, Inc., Jan. 29, 1993). An example of a specific Arabic immigrant group whose population has undergone a tremendous increase since about 1970 is the Chaldeans (Iraqi Christians) in the Detroit area; their population increased from 3500 to about 50,000 (Woodruff, 1991).

DIFFERENCES AND SIMILARITIES

There is great diversity among Arab American groups. Understanding this diversity will assist officers in not categorizing Arabs as one homogeneous group and will encourage people to move away from stereotypical thinking.

Differences

Arabs from the Middle East come from at least 13 different countries, many of which are vastly different from each other. The governments of the Arabic countries also differ, ranging from monarchies to military governments to socialist republics (Nydell, 1987). Arab visitors such as foreign students, tourists, businesspeople, and diplomats to the United States from the Gulf states (e.g., Saudi Arabia, Quatar, Oman, Bahrain, United Arab Emirates) are typically wealthy, but their Jordanian, Lebanese, and Palestinian brethren do not generally bring wealth to the United States, and in fact, many are extremely poor. Another area in which one finds differences is clothing. In the Middle East in a number of countries, many older men wear headdresses, but it is less common among men who are younger and who have more education. Similarly, younger women in the Middle East may abandon the wearing of the head covering and long dress that covers them from head to toe. Yet traditional families even in the United States may still insist that their daughters and wives dress modestly. (This is discussed later in this chapter.)

The younger generation of Arabs, much to the disappointment of the parents and grandparents, may display entirely different behavior from what is expected of them (as is typical in most immigrant/refugee groups). In addition, there are Arab Americans who have been in the United States for generations who are completely assimilated into the American culture. They may even be almost completely unaware of their roots. Others, although they have also been in the United States for generations, consciously try to keep their Arabic traditions alive and pass them on to their children. As with Asian Americans who were born and raised in this country and are no less American than anyone else, officers should not treat the established Arab American as if he or she were a newcomer. This type of overgeneralizing would signal to the citizen that the officer's understanding was based on narrow and stereotypical images of an Arab.

There are broad differences among Arab American groups associated with social class and economic status. Although many Arab Americans coming to the United States now are educated professionals, there is a percentage who come from rural areas (e.g., peasants from southern Lebanon, West Bank Palestinians, Yemenis) who differ in outlook and receptiveness to modernization. On the other hand, despite traditional values, many newcomers are modern in outlook. For example, there is a stereotypical image that many people have of the Arab woman, yet the following description certainly illustrates that not all women of Arabic descent adhere to the image. For example, John Zogby has described many modern Arab women who defy the stereotype: "Among the upper class, educated Palestinian population here, you can find many women who are vocal and outspoken. You might see the young husbands wheeling the babies around in strollers while the women are discussing world events" (personal communication, John Zogby, John Zogby Group International, Inc., Jan. 29, 1993).

On the other hand, certain Arab governments (e.g., Saudi Arabia) place restrictions on women mandating that they do not mix with men, that a woman must always be veiled, and that she not travel alone or drive a car (*New York Times International*, Feb. 7, 1993, p. Y7). Women, then, from less restrictive Arab countries (e.g., Egypt and Jordan) might exhibit very different behavior from those who had fewer freedoms. Nevertheless, women in traditional Moslem families from *any* country typically have limited contact with men outside their family and wear traditional dress. Some implications of these traditions as they relate to Arab women and male police officers in the United States are discussed further in this chapter.

It is important to look at people's motivation for coming to the United States to help avoid thinking in stereotypical terms. Arab American police officer Mohamed Berro of the Dearborn, Michigan Police Department makes a distinction between immigrants (who have "few problems adjusting to the United States") and refugees. He explains that refugees, having been forced to leave their country of origin, believe that they are here temporarily because they are waiting for a conflict to end. As a result, they are usually more hesitant to change and may pose a greater challenge for the police officer (personal communication, Mohamed Berro, Officer, and Mark Jabour, Detective Sergeant, Dearborn, Michigan, Police Department, Dec. 5, 1992).

Similarities

Despite most differences, whether apparent in socioeconomic status, levels of traditionalism, or motivation for coming to the United States, there are values and beliefs associated with Arab culture that law enforcement officials should understand in order to establish rapport and trust. Officers will recognize that some of the information listed below does not apply *only* to Arab culture. At the same time, the following explains deeply held beliefs that many Arab Americans would agree are key to understanding traditional Arab culture.

Basic Arab Values

1. "A person's dignity, honor and reputation are of paramount importance and no effort should be spared to protect them, especially one's honor" (Nydell, 1987). Traditional Arab society upholds honor; the degree to which an Arab can lose face and be shamed publicly is foreign to the average Westerner. Officers recognize that dignity and respect should be shown to *all* individuals, but citizens from cultures emphasizing shame, loss of face, and honor (e.g., Middle Eastern, Asian, Latin American) may react even more severely to loss of dignity and respect than do other individuals. (Keep in mind that "shame" cultures have sanctioned extreme punishments for loss of face and honor, e.g., death if a woman loses her virginity before marriage.)

2. "Loyalty to one's family takes precedence over other personal needs" (Nydell, 1987). A person is *completely* intertwined with his or her family; protection and privacy in a traditional Arab family often overrides relationships with other people. Members of Arab families tend to avoid disagreements and disputes in front of others.

3. Communication should be courteous and hospitable. Harmony between individuals is emphasized. Too much directness and candor can be interpreted as extremely impolite. From a traditional Arab view, it may not be appropriate for a person to give totally honest responses if they result in a loss of face, especially for self or family members. From this perspective (i.e., this does not apply to most established Arab Americans) this is viewed as "adjusting" the truth (not lying) and is acceptable because there exists the higher goal of honor and face-saving. This aspect of cross-cultural communication is not easily understood by most Westerners

(and is often criticized). Certainly, officers will not accept an "adjusted truth" because of cultural ideals having to do with face and shame. However, it may lead an officer nowhere to point out a person's "lies" directly when the statements are not perceived by the person as such. The officer would be well advised to work around the issue of the "half-truths" rather than insisting upon proving the citizen a liar.

STEREOTYPES

The Western media have been largely responsible for representing Arabs in a less than human way. When one hears the word, "Arab," several images come to mind: (1) wealthy sheik (there are class distinctions in the Middle East as elsewhere between a wealthy Gulf Arab sheik and a poor Palestinian or Lebanese); (2) violent terrorist (the majority of Arabs *worldwide* want peace and do not see terrorism as an acceptable means for achieving peace); (3) sensuous harem owner; man with many wives ("harems" are rare and for the most part, polygamy or having more than one wife has been abolished in the Arab world); and (4) ignorant, illiterate, and backward (Arab contributions to civilization have been great in the areas of mathematics, astronomy, medicine, architecture, geography, and language, among others, but this is not widely known in the West) (Macron, 1989).

As with all distorted information of ethnic groups, it is important to understand how stereotypes interfere with a true understanding of a people. Laurence Michalak, cultural anthropologist and director of the Center for Middle Eastern Studies at the University of California, Berkeley, points out: "When we consider the Western image of the Arab—Ali Baba, Sinbad the Sailor, the thief of Baghdad, the slave merchant, the harem dancer, and so on—we have to admit that, at least in the case of Arabs, fiction is stranger than truth.... *The Arab stereotype, while it teaches us very little about the Arabs, teaches us a good deal about ourselves and about mechanisms of prejudice."* [Italics added] (Michalak, 1988)

Movies and Television

According to Michalak, the most offensive stereotyping of Arabs can be seen in children's television programs, in which Arabs are portrayed as evil and foolish. In his publication *Cruel and Unusual,* he mentions cartoons that include Arab villains, or "troublemakers who look vaguely Middle Eastern–swarthy, with a turban and curling mustache" (p. 7) He mentions that even "Sesame Street," a program noted for its sensitivity and respect toward people of all backgrounds, illustrated the word "danger" by using an Arab figure. Michalak points out further that via movies and television programs, Americans (and Westerners, in general) have "mass produced and marketed a negative stereotype." In analyzing more than 100 films produced since 1921 which include images of Arabs, Michalak (p. 32) finds the following themes (this is a partial list):

- 28 films involve sheiks
- 25 films involve harems
- 19 involve theft or thieves

Because many Americans do not know Arabs personally, these sorts of images become embedded in people's minds. A recent film involving the abduction of a child to Jordan (*Desperate Rescue*) can subtly influence decision makers in cases involving custody and Moslem and Arabic fathers, especially where the wives are non-Arabic and non-Moslem. Yet according to the State Department (Child Custody Division, statistics as of July 1992), nearly five times as many children were abducted to the United Kingdom as were abducted to Jordan. Apparently, while abduction to Arabic countries does occur and is a matter for concern, it is not as common as abduction to Europe.

Operation Abscam: The Government's Stereotype

Finally, it is worth noting how the U.S. government used a common stereotype of Arabs (that of the wealthy Arabic sheik) in an official capacity to try to stop white-collar crime and corruption. "Operation Abscam" ("Ab" for Abdul, the name used in the sting), which began in 1978, involved dressing up two Federal Bureau of Investigation (FBI) agents as rich oil barons in order to entrap politicians. Because the media have succeeded in portraying Arabs as terrorists or rich sheiks, the politicians "bought into" the trap, which involved the "sheiks" discussing Arab investments with the lawmakers. If the politicians had been more aware of Arabic culture and the distinctions between Arabic groups, they would not have fallen for the sting. For example, one of the "sheiks" was from Oman, a Gulf state. In Oman, a rich man is not known as a "sheik" but as "Sayeed" (Shaheen, 1988, p. 1). The other so-called "sheik" was from Lebanon. In Lebanon, however, there are no sheiks and there is no oil.

The media succeeded in fooling eight members of Congress into becoming entrapped in the FBI bribery sting. While law enforcement officials have been known to disguise themselves in order to make arrests (e.g., drug dealers and pimps), there are several issues to be aware of with regard to "Abscam." Despite the "success" of the law enforcement operation, the message sent to Arabs around the world, and to non-Arabs, was that of acceptance of one Arab stereotype, "a dehumanizing caricature that purposely widens the communications gap between their culture and ours" (Shaheen, 1988, p. 5). Twenty-four Congress members did call upon the FBI to publicly apologize to the Arab community in this country and to Arabs worldwide, saying: "We find this insensitive choice of ethnicity to be abrasive in spirit and intent, to perpetuate an unjust stereotype and to nurture an already firmly established prejudice" (p. 4).

Many people might respond to this by saying that the operation was one big joke and should not be taken seriously. However, whenever stereotypes are promoted, people's prejudice becomes more established and they become more convinced of the truth of their stereotypical beliefs. When a stereotype is promoted by a government agency, people believe that there is all the more reason to hold on to their stereotypical thinking.

Arabs, especially Muslims, in addition to being perceived as wealthy sheiks, are simultaneously labeled as illiterate and terrorists. Muslims have been described as "backward" and primitive by people who consider the West and Christianity to be the standard by which all other cultures should be evaluated (once again, ethnocentrism is operating). These stereotypes that many Westerners have mistakenly formed of Arabs, in general have extended to Arab Americans (even those who have been here for generations): "Although there are around three million Arab Americans, ninety percent of whom are Christian, our image has long been distorted and defamed. A great part of the distortion stems from American perceptions of Arabs of the Middle East, an image which suffers from a historic bias in Western culture which has treated the Middle Easterner as 'Other'" (Jabara, no date).

ISLAMIC RELIGION

Readers may recall the discussion in Chapter 1 of the we/they tendency. In cross-cultural interactions between Americans and Arabs or Arab Americans, the misunderstandings or discomfort can often be traced to religious differences and sometimes a lack of tolerance of these differences. Islam is practiced by the majority of Middle Eastern newcomers to the United States, as well as by many African Americans. Many Arab Americans (especially those from the first wave of Arab immigration) are Christian, however, and prefer that others do not assume they are Muslim simply because they are Arabs.

By and large, most Americans do not understand what Islam is and, because of stereotyping, wrongly associate Muslims with terrorists or fanatics. Many, but by no means all Arabic Muslims in the United States are deeply religious and have held on to the traditional aspects of their religion, which are also intertwined with their way of life. Islam means submission to the will of God and for traditional, religious Muslims, the will of God (or fate) is a central concept. The religion has been called "Mohammedanism," which is an incorrect name for the religion because it suggests that Muslims worship Muhammed rather than God (Allah). It is believed that Allah's final message to man was revealed to the prophet Muhammed. "Allah" is the Arabic word for God and it is used both by Arab Muslims and Arab Christians (Islamic Affairs Department, 1989).

The Koran and the Pillars of Islam

The Koran is the Islamic "Bible" and is regarded as the word of God (Allah). There are five "Pillars of Islam" or central guidelines that form the framework of the religion:

- Profession of faith in Allah (God)
- Prayer five times daily
- Alms giving (concern for the needy)
- Fasting during the month of Ramadan (sunrise to sunset)
- Pilgrimage to Mecca (in Saudi Arabia) at least once in each person's lifetime

There are several points where law enforcement officials can respect a Muslim's need to practice his or her religion. The need to express one's faith in God and to be respected for it is one area. Normally, people pray together as congregations in mosques, the Islamic equivalent of a church or synagogue. People, however, can pray individually if a congregation is not present. Religious Muslims in jails, for example, will continue to pray five times a day and should not be ridiculed or prevented from doing so. Remember that prayer, five times a day, is a "pillar" of Islam and that strict Muslims will want to uphold this "command" no matter where they are. Call to prayer takes place at the following times:

- One hour before sunrise
- At noon
- Midafternoon
- Sunset
- Ninety minutes after sunset

Taboos in the Mosque

A peace officer will convey respect to a Muslim community if he or she can avoid entering a mosque and interrupting prayers (obviously, emergencies may occasionally make this impossible). Religion is so vital in Arab life that law enforcement officials should always show respect for any Islamic customs and beliefs. Thus, other than in emergency situations, officers are advised to (personal communication, Mohamed Berro, Officer, Dearborn, Michigan, Police Department, Dec. 5, 1992):

- Avoid entering a mosque, or certainly the prayer room of a mosque, during prayers.
- Never step on a prayer mat.
- Never place the Koran on the floor or put anything on top of it.
- Avoid walking in front of people who are praying.
- Speak softly as you would in a church.
- Dress conservatively (both men and women are required to dress conservatively—shorts are not appropriate).
- Invite a person out of a prayer room to question him.

Proper protocol in a mosque requires that people remove their shoes before entering, but this must be left to the officer's discretion. Officer safety, of course, comes before consideration of differences.

Ramadan: The Holy Month

One of the holiest periods in the Islamic religion is the celebration of Ramadan, which lasts for one month. There is no fixed date because like the Jewish and Chinese calendars, the Islamic calendar is based on the lunar cycle and dates vary from year to year. During the month of Ramadan, Moslems do not eat, drink, or smoke from sunrise to sunset. The purpose of fasting during Ramadan is to "train one in self-discipline, subdue the passions, and give [people]. . . . a sense of unity with all Moslems" (Devine and Braganti, 1991, p. 28). On the twenty-ninth night of Ramadan, when there is a new moon, the holiday is officially over. The final fast is broken and for up to three days, people celebrate with a feast and other activities. On the last night of Ramadan, Muslim families pray in the mosque.

For Muslims, Ramadan is as important and holy as Christmas; this fact is appreciated when others (who are not Muslim) recognize the holiday's importance. One city with a sizable Arab American population put up festive lights in its business district during Ramadan as a gesture of acceptance and appreciation of the diversity that the Arab Americans bring to the city. The Arab American community reacted favorably to this symbolic gesture. Meanwhile, in the same city, at the end of Ramadan, while many families were in the mosque, police ticketed hundreds of cars that were parked in store parking lots across from the mosque, even though according to some Arab American citizens, the stores were closed. When people came out of the mosque and saw all the tickets, the mood of the holiday naturally was spoiled. The perception from the Arab American citizens was that "They don't want to understand us . . . they don't know how we feel . . . they don't know what's important to us . . ." (Readers will have a chance at the end of the chapter to analyze this situation from an enforcement and community relations point of view as well as to discuss whether the situation could have been prevented.)

Knowledge of Religious Practices

Knowledge of religious practices, including what is considered holy, will help officers avoid creating problems and conflicts. A belief in the Islamic religion that may occasionally arise in the course of police work will illustrate this point. In a suburb of San Francisco, California, a group of police officers and Muslims (from Tunisia, an Arab country in North Africa) were close to violence when, in a morgue, police entered to try to get a hair sample from a person who had just been killed in a car accident. Apparently, the body had already been blessed by an "Iman" (a religious leader) and, according to the religion, any further contact would have been a defilement of the body since the body had already been sanctified and was ready for burial. The police officers were merely doing what they needed to do to complete their investigation and were unaware of this taboo. This, together with a language barrier, created an extremely confusing and confrontative situation in which officers lost necessary control. In this case they needed to explain what had to be done and communicate their needs in the form of a request for permission to handle a body that had already been sanctified. If the citizens had not granted permission, the police would then have had to decide how to proceed. Most members of the Arab American community would comply with the wishes of police officers. As in many other situations involving police–citizen communication, the initial approach sets the tone for the entire interaction.

FAMILY STRUCTURE

Arab Americans typically have close-knit families in which family members have a strong sense of loyalty and fulfill obligations to all members, including extended family (aunts, uncles, cousins, grandparents). Traditionally minded families also believe strongly in the family's honor, and members try to avoid any behavior that will bring shame or disgrace to the family. The operating unit for Arab Americans (and this may be less true for people who have been in the United States for generations) is not the individual but the family. Thus if a person behaves inappropriately, the entire family is disgraced. Similarly, if a family member is assaulted (in the Arab world), there would be some type of retribution. For the police officer, three characteristics of the Arabic family will affect his or her interaction with family members:

- Extended family members are often as close as the "nuclear family" (mother, father, children) and are not seen as secondary family members. If there is a police issue, officers can expect that many members of the family will become involved in the matter. *Although officers might perceive this as interference, from an Arabic cultural perspective, it is merely involvement and concern. The numbers of people involved are not meant to overwhelm an officer.*
- Family loyalty and protection is seen as one of the highest values of family life. Therefore, shaming, ridiculing, insulting, or criticizing family members, especially in public, can have serious consequences.
- Newer Arab American refugees or immigrants may be reluctant to accept police assistance. Because families are tightly knit, they can also be closed "units" whereby members prefer to keep private matters or conflicts to themselves. As a result, officers will have to work harder at establishing rapport if they want to gain cooperation.

There is an important point of contact between all three of these characteristics and law enforcement interaction with members of Arab American families. Berro explains: "When we respond to a call at a home, the police car is like a magnet. Every family member comes out of the house and everyone wants to talk at once. It can be an overwhelming sensation for an officer who doesn't understand this background" (personal communication, Mohamed Berro, Dec. 5, 1992).

A police officer who is not trained in understanding and responding appropriately and professionally to cultural differences could alienate the family by (1) not respecting the interest and involvement of the family members, and (2) attempting to gain control of the communication in an authoritarian and offensive manner. The consequences may be that he or she would have difficulty establishing the rapport needed to gain information about the conflict at hand and would then not be trusted or respected. To do the job effectively, law enforcement officials must respect Arab "family values" along with communication style differences (which will be discussed shortly).

Head of the Household

As in most cultures with a traditional family structure, the man in the Arab home is overtly the head of the household and his role and influence are strong. The wife has a great deal of influence, too, but it can often be more "behind the scenes." An Arab woman does not always defer to her husband in private as she would in public (Nydell, 1987). However, as mentioned earlier in the chapter, there are women, even among recent newcomers such as Palestinians, who have broken out of the traditional mold and tend to be more vocal, outspoken, and assertive than their mothers or grandmothers. Traditionally, in many Arab countries, some fathers maintain their status by being strict disciplinarians and demanding absolute respect, thus creating some degree of fear among children and even among wives. Once again, Arab Americans born and raised in this country have, for the most part, adopted middle-class "American" styles of child-raising whereby children participate in some of the decision making and are as respected as each adult member would be. In addition, as with changing roles among all kinds of families in the United States, the father as traditional head of the household and the mother as having "second-class" status is not prevalent among established Arab Americans in the United States. Wife abuse and child abuse are not considered respectable practices by educated Arab Americans, but the practice still occurs, just as it does in mainstream American society (particularly, but not exclusively, among people on the lower-socioeconomic levels).

In traditional Arabic society, men do exert influence and power, *publicly*. According to Audrey Shabbas, Middle East educator and director of Arab World and Islamic Resources and School Services (AWAIR), "This power is usually seen by Westerners in a negative context, but [it is important to] caution against misinterpreting a husband's or father's behavior as merely *control*. He, and other male figures of importance, can be employed in securing the compliance of the family in important matters. . . . The husband/father can be a natural ally of . . . authorities (Shabbas, 1984). Officers would be well advised to *work with* both the father and the mother, for example, in matters where children are involved. On family matters the woman is the authority, even if she seems to defer to her husband. Communicating with the woman, even if indirectly, while still respecting the father's need to maintain his public status, will win respect from both the man and the woman.

Children and "Americanization"

"Americanization," the process of becoming more "American" in behavior, attitudes, and beliefs, has always been an issue with refugees/immigrants and their children. Typically, children are better able than their parents to learn a language and pick up the nuances of a culture than their parents are. In addition, peer influence and pressure in American society begins to overshadow parental control, especially beginning the preteen years. Arab children, who are sacred to and cherished by their parents, face an extremely difficult cultural gap with their parents if they reach a stage where they are more "American" than "Arabic." Children in Arabic families are taught to be respectful in front of parents and to be conscious of family honor. Parents do not consider "Americanized" behavior, in general, to be respectful or worthy of pride. When children exhibit certain behaviors that bring shame to the family, discipline can indeed be harsh.

In *extreme* and infrequent cases, shame to the family can result in crimes against the children, involving violence. Officer Berro and Sergeant Jabour of the Dearborn, Michigan Police Department (personal communication, Dec. 5, 1992) described three cases involving homicide. In one case, parents were having a discussion about how Americanized their children should become. In another, a father shot his daughter because she had a boyfriend (Arab women are not allowed to associate freely with men before marriage and are expected to remain virgins). Finally, the third case involved a brother who shot his sister when she returned late from a New Year's party. The cases above do not suggest that violent crime, in the Arabic cultural context, is an appropriate response, and mental problems (and/or drugs and alcohol) accompany most violent acts. However, when a child's (especially a girl's)

Americanized behavior involves what is seen as sexual misconduct, the family's "face" is ruined. When this happens, all members of the family suffer.

There is very little an officer can to do change the attitudes of parents who oppose their children's Americanized behavior. However, if an officer responds to calls where he or she notices that the family has become dysfunctional because of children's Americanized behavior, it would be a service to the family to initiate some sort of social service intervention or make a referral. If a family is already at the point of needing police assistance in problems involving children and their parents, then, more likely than not, they need other types of assistance as well. At the same time, newer immigrants and refugees will not necessarily be open to social service interventions, especially if the social workers do not speak Arabic.

CULTURAL PRACTICES

As with all other immigrant groups, the degree to which people preserve their cultural practices varies. The following descriptions of everyday behavior will not apply equally to all Arab-Americans, but they do not necessarily apply only to recent newcomers. Immigrants may preserve traditions and practices long after they come to a new country by conscious choice or sometimes because they are unaware of their cultural behavior (i.e., it is not in their conscious awareness).

Greetings/Approach/Touching

Most recent Arab American newcomers expect to be addressed with a title and their last name (Mr. _____; Miss _____), although in many Arab countries people are addressed formally by Mr./Mrs. + first name. Most Arabic women do not change their names after they are married or divorced. They, therefore, may not understand the distinction between a "maiden" name and a "married" name. The usual practice is to keep their father's last name for life (Boller, 1992).

Many Arab Americans who have retained their traditional customs shake hands and then place their right hand on their chest near the heart. This is a sign of sincerity and warmth. In the Middle East, Americans are advised to do the same if they observe this gesture (Devine and Braganti, 1991). Officers can decide whether they are comfortable using this gesture—most people would not expect it from an officer, but some might appreciate the gesture as long as the officer was able to convey sincerity. Generally, when Arabs from the Middle East shake hands, they do not shake hands briefly and firmly. (The expression. "He shakes hands like a dead fish *does not apply* to other cultural groups!) Arabs (i.e., not assimilated Arab Americans) tend to hold hands longer than other Americans and shake hands more lightly. Older children are taught to shake hands with adults as a sign of respect. Many Arabs would appreciate an officer shaking hands with their older children. With a recent immigrant or refugee Arabic woman, it is generally not appropriate to shake hands unless she extends her hand first. This would definitely apply to women who wear head coverings.

Many Arabs of the same sex greet each other by kissing on the cheek. Two Saudi Arabian men, for example, may greet each other by kissing on both cheeks a number of times. This does not suggest homosexuality, but rather is a common form of greeting. Public touching of the opposite sex is forbidden in the traditional Arabic world and officers should make every effort not to touch Arabic women, even casually (discussed further under "Key Issues in Law Enforcement").

Police officers should be aware that some Arab American citizens (e.g., Lebanese) who are new to the United States may react to a police officer's approach in an unexpected way. For example, an officer who has just asked a person to give his license may find that this person will then get out of his car in order to be able to talk to the officer. From the person's perspective, he or she is simply trying to be courteous (since this is done in the home country). An officer, always conscious of safety issues, may simply have to explain that in the United States, officers require citizens to remain in their cars.

Hospitality

"Hospitality is a byword among [Arabs], whatever their station in life. As a guest in their homes you will be treated to the kindest and most lavish consideration. When they say, as they often do, "My home is your home," they mean it" (Salah Said, as quoted in Nydell, 1987, p. 58). Hospitality in the Arab culture is not an option; it is more an obligation or duty. In some parts of the Arab world, if you thank someone for their hospitality, they may answer with a common expression which means, "Don't thank me. It's my duty." (Here the word "duty" has a more positive connotation than negative). Officers need to understand how deeply ingrained the need to be hospitable is and not to misinterpret this behavior for something that it is not. Whether entering a home or a business owner's shop or office, an Arab American may very well offer coffee and something to eat. This is not to be mistaken for a bribe and, from the Arabic perspective, carries no negative connotations. According to Berro, most people would be offended if you did not accept their offers of hospitality. However, given police regulations, you may have to decline. If this is the case, Berro advises that officers decline graciously (personal communication, Dec. 5, 1992). On the other hand, if the decision to accept the Arab American's hospitality depends on the officer's discretion, accepting can also be good for police–citizen relations. Audrey Shabbas of AWAIR points out that the period of time spent socializing and extending one's hospitality gives the person a chance to get to know and see if he or she can trust the other person. Business is not usually conducted among strangers. Obviously, on an emergency call, there is no time for such hospitality. However, with the move toward increasing community-based police organizations, officers may find that they are involved in more situations where they may decide to accept small gestures of hospitality, if within departmental policy.

Verbal and Nonverbal Communication

Arabs in general are very warm and expressive people, both verbally and nonverbally, and appreciate it when others extend warmth to them. There are some areas in the realm of nonverbal communication where Americans, without cultural knowledge, have misinterpreted the behavior of Arab Americans simply because of their own ethnocentrism (i.e., the tendency to judge others by one's own cultural standards and norms).

Conversational distance.   What is acceptable conversational distance between two people is often related to cultural influences. Officers are very aware of safety issues and keep a certain distance from people when communicating with them. Generally, officers like to stand about an arm's length or farther from citizens to avoid possible assaults on their person. This distance is similar to how far apart "mainstream Americans" stand when in conversation. Cultures subtly influence the permissible distance between two people. When the distance is "violated" a person can feel threatened (either consciously or unconsciously). Many, but not all, Arabs, especially if they are new to the country, tend to have a closer acceptable conversational distance with each other than do other Americans. In Arab culture, it is not considered offensive to "feel a person's breath." Yet many Americans, unfamiliar with this intimacy in regular conversation, have misinterpreted the closeness. While still conscious of safety, the law enforcement officer can keep in mind that the closer than "normal" behavior (i.e., "normal" for the officer) does not necessarily constitute a threat.

Devine and Braganti (1991) give the following advice to American travelers in the Middle East. There is application for police officers in the United States, especially in conjunction with communication with recent immigrants and refugees. "Don't back away when an Arab stands very close while speaking to you. He won't be more than two feet away. Arabs constantly stare into other people's eyes, watching the pupils for an indication of the other person's response [i.e., dilated pupils mean a positive response]. However, foreign men should never stare directly into a woman's eyes, either in speaking to her or passing her on the street. He should avert his eyes or keep his eyes on the ground."

Gestures.   There are gestures that Arabs from some countries use that are distinctly different from those familiar to Americans. In a section entitled "Customs and Manners in the Arab World," Devine and Braganti (1991, p. 13) describe some commonly used gestures among Arabs:

- **"What does it mean? or What are you saying?** Hold up the right hand and twist it as if you were screwing in a light bulb one turn.
- **Wait a minute.** Hold all fingers and thumb touching with the palm up.
- **No.** This can be signaled in one of three ways: moving the head back slightly and raising the eyebrows, moving the head back and raising the chin, or moving the head back and clicking with the tongue.
- **Go away.** Hold the right hand out with the palm down, and move it as if pushing something away from you.
- **Never.** A forceful never is signaled by holding the right forefinger up and moving it from left to right quickly and repeatedly."

As with many other cultural groups, pointing a finger directly at someone is considered rude.

Emotional expressiveness:

> When I came to my brother's house to see what the problem was [i.e., with the police], I asked, 'What the hell is going on?' I held my hands out and talked with my hands as I always do. I repeated myself and continued to gesture with my hands. Later (i.e., at a trial) the police officer said, _____* was yelling and screaming and acting wild, waving her arms and inciting observers to riot by her actions.

The Arab American involved in the above situation explained that Arab women, in particular, are very emotional and that police sometimes see this emotionalism as a threat. She explained that upon seeing a family member in trouble, it would be most usual and natural for a woman to put her hands to her face and say something like, "Oh, my God" frequently and in a loud voice. While other Americans can react this same way, it is worth pointing out that in mainstream American culture, there is a tendency to subdue one's emotions and not to go "out of control." The point of cross-cultural confusion here is that what some Americans consider to be "out of control," Arabs (like Mexicans, Greeks, Israelis, and Iranians, among other groups) consider to be perfectly "normal" behavior. In fact, the lack of emotionalism that Arabs observe among mainstream Americans can be misinterpreted as lack of interest or involvement.

Although a communication-style characteristic never applies to all people in one cultural group (and we have seen that there is a great deal of diversity among Arab Americans), there are group traits that apply to many people. Arabs, especially the first generation of relatively recent newcomers, do tend to display emotions when talking. Unlike many people in Far East Asian cultures (e.g., Japanese and Korean), Arabs have not been "taught" that the expression of emotion is a sign of immaturity or a lack of control. Arabs, as other Mediterranean groups, such as Israelis or Greeks, tend to shout when they are excited or angry and are very animated in their communication. They may repeatedly insert expressions into their speech such as "I swear by God." This is simply a cultural mannerism.

Westerners, however, tend to judge this "style" negatively. To a Westerner, the emotionalism, repetition, and emphasis on certain statements can give the impression that the person is not telling the truth or is exaggerating for effect. An officer unfamiliar with these cultural mannerisms may feel overwhelmed, especially when involved with an entire group of people. It would be well worth it for the officer to determine the spokesperson for the group, but to refrain from showing impatience or irritation at this culturally different style.

Swearing, the use of obscenities and insults.

Swearing, the use of obscenities and insults. Although one can find people in any culture who swear and shout obscenities, officers working in Arab American communities should know that for Arabs, words are extremely powerful, and some people, whether consciously or unconsciously, believe that words can affect the course of events and can bring misfortune (Nydell, 1987). If an officer displays

---

*The names of individuals and departments have been omitted even though permission has been granted to quote. The purpose of including these incidents is not to put undue attention on any one department or individual, but rather to provide education on police professionalism in interethnic relations.

any lack of professionalism by swearing at an Arab (even words like "damn"), it will be nearly impossible to repair the damage.

In one case of documented police harassment of several Arab Americans (names have been omitted in order not to single out this department), witnesses attest to officers' saying, "Mother-f_____ Arabs, we're going to teach you. Go back home!" One of the Arab American citizens involved in the case reported that officers treated him like an animal and were very insulting by asking questions in a demeaning tone such as, "Do you speak English? Do you read English?" (The man was a highly educated professional who had been in the United States for several years.) In asking him about his place of employment (he worked at an Arab American organization), the man reported that they referred to his place of employment as " . . . the Arab Islamic shit or crap? What is that?"

Officers who understand professionalism are aware that this type of language and interaction is insulting to all persons. The choice to use obscenities and insults, especially in conjunction with one's ethnic background, however, means that officers risk never being able to establish trust with the ethnic community. This can translate into not being able to secure cooperation when needed. Even a few officers exhibiting this type of behavior can damage the reputation of an entire department for a very long period of time.

English language problems. If time allows, before asking the question "Do you speak English?" officers should try and assess whether the Arab American is a recent arrival or an established citizen who might react negatively to the question. A heavy accent does not necessarily mean that a person is unable to speak English (although that can be the case). There are specific communication skills that can be used with limited-English-speaking persons (see Chapter 5) that should be applied with Arab Americans. When reading the Miranda rights to persons who are not fluent in English, it is a courtesy to take the time to explain them, preferably through a translator. Both the language of the rights and the concepts may very well be culturally alien for many people (and this applies to all newcomers). Officers should proceed slowly and nonaggressively with questioning and wherever possible, ask open-ended questions. An officer's patience and willingness to take extra time will be beneficial in the long run.

KEY ISSUES IN LAW ENFORCEMENT

Perceptions of and Relationships with Police

It is not possible to generalize about how all Arab Americans perceive the police. As mentioned earlier, the Arab immigrants who came in the late nineteenth century through World War II had the Turkish military police with whom to compare to the American police. Their experiences, then, in the United States were largely positive and they were cooperative with police. Since the majority of Arab Americans today are from that wave of immigrants, it is fair to say that a large part of the Arab American community does respect the police. On the other hand, some of the more recent immigrants, such as Jordanians and Palestinians, do not understand the American system and have an ingrained fear of police because of political problems in their own region of the world (personal communication, James Zogby, Director, Arab American Institute, Jan. 25, 1993). Since they distrust government, they are more likely to reject help from the police and this puts them at a decided disadvantage in that they can more easily become victims. Their fear, in combination with the interdependence and helpfulness that characterizes the extended family, results in families not wanting assistance from the police. Thus police will encounter some families who would prefer to handle conflict themselves even though police intervention is clearly needed. Some of the newer immigrants and refugees feel that it is dishonorable to have to go outside the family (e.g., to police and social service providers) to get help, and if given a choice, they would choose not to embarrass themselves and their families in this manner.

In the Arab world of the Middle East, there are major differences in the institution of policing and the manner in which citizens are required to behave with police. In Saudi Arabia there is more of a fear of police than in some other countries because the punishments are stricter. For example, if a person is caught stealing, he or she will have a hand removed if a repeat offender. A Saudi Arabian woman caught shoplifting in a San Francisco Bay Area "7-11" store begged a police officer on her knees not to make the arrest because she feared being sent back to Saudi Arabia and did not know what would happen to her there. As it turned out, the officer did let her go since this was her first offense. He felt that he had some discretion in this case and decided to consider the woman's cultural background and circumstances. This is something that each officer has to decide for himself or herself when it comes to interpreting cultural influences on police incidents and crimes, especially those of a lesser nature. (This aspect of law enforcement is discussed in Chapter 1.)

Women and Modesty

In the traditional Muslim world, women do not socialize freely with men and are required to dress modestly. However, the everyday practices in the various Arabic countries differ greatly. In some countries, such as Lebanon, Jordan, and Egypt, women dress more in the manner of people in the West, whereas in countries like Saudi Arabia, strict rules are maintained (e.g., the "morals police" tap women on the ankles with a long stick if their dresses are too short.)

Modesty for a traditional Arab Muslim woman may include the need to cover her head so that men will not see her hair. In some traditional Islamic societies, a man must not see a woman's hair, and officers should understand that asking a woman to remove a head covering (e.g., for the purpose of searching her or getting a photo identification) is analogous to asking her to expose a private part of her body. Arab American Officer Berro advises officers to approach this matter sensitively: "Don't overpower the woman, intimidate her or grab her head cover. Ask her to go into a private room and have her remove it or get a female officer to help with the procedure" (personal communication, Dec. 5, 1992).

American officers may not have a sense of the violation that a traditional Arabic woman feels when her head covering is taken away forcibly. Even if a woman is arrested for something like disorderly conduct, she will be offended by any aggressive move on the part of the officer to remove her head cover. When police procedures require that a head cover be removed, the officers should explain the procedure and offer some kind of an apology to show empathy. Having dealt with this same issue, the Immigration and Naturalization Service (INS) modified its regulations in the following way: "Every applicant . . . shall clearly show a three-quarter profile view of the features of the applicant with the head bare (unless the applicant is wearing a headdress as required by a religious order of which he or she is a member)" (INS Regulation 8 C.F.R. 331.1(a), 1992). Thus INS officials photograph Muslim women with their head coverings on. Because police departments deal with safety issues (such as concealed weapons), they may not have the liberty to accommodate this particular cultural difference, and thus it should be handled with extreme sensitivity.

Arab Grocers and Liquor Store Owners

> The ransacking of a North Richmond [California] liquor store reflects a growing racial tension between Middle Eastern store owners and their black customers. . . . It's a rift that has pitted Middle Eastern store owners, many of whom who shun alcohol for religious reasons but sell it, against some of their black customers who believe money is being made off of the misery of alcohol. "I don't want to be a racist . . . but the Arab people are coming into the black community and they're not putting anything back into it," said a Richmond resident. (*Contra Costa Times,* Jan. 9, 1993, p. 10A)

These types of comments can be heard across the United States where there are Arab grocers/liquor store owners in low-income areas (e.g., Detroit, Cleveland) The dynamics between Arab store owners and African Americans are similar to those between Koreans and African Americans in inner cities. The non-Arab views the Arab as having money and exploiting the local residents for economic gain. James Zogby explains that this perception is reinforced because one rarely sees a non-Arab working in an Arab-owned store. The local resident, according to Zogby, director of the Arab-American Institute, Washington, D.C., does not understand that the Arabs, for the most part, are political refugees (e.g., Palestinians) and have come to the United States for a better life. When they first arrive, the only work that they can do is operate small "marginal" businesses. Most of the small Arab-run grocery stores or liquor stores are family-operated businesses where two brothers or a father and two sons, for example, are managing the operation. It would not be economically possible for them to hire outside their family (the situation is similar to Korean family-run businesses). Police officers, in the midst of the conflicts between the store owners and the residents, can attempt to explain the position of the refugees, but of course, the explanation by itself cannot take care of the problem. Many poor American-born citizens harbor a great deal of animosity toward immigrants and refugees because of scarce resources.

Alcohol is forbidden in the Muslim religion, yet Arab liquor store owners sell it to their customers. There is currently a debate in the Arab American community as to whether Muslim immigrants and refugees should go into this type of business. For the majority of newcomers, the choices are very limited. Members of other ethnic groups have owned many of the mom-and-pop stores throughout the years and now some are asking: "Where did all these Arabs come from, and why is it all they want to do is sell alcohol to black folks?" (*Contra Costa Times,* Jan. 9, 1993, p. 10A). Some Arab liquor store owners, however, do set limits as to whom they will sell liquor. One Arab American owner in Richmond, California, explained, "Just this morning, I refused to sell wine to a lady and her husband with food stamps. I said, 'I'm not going to do it,' and she said, 'Oh you dumb Arab, we're going to come back and blow up the whole store'" (*Contra Costa Times,* Jan. 9, 1993, p. 10A).

Finally, there is another dimension to the problem of Arab store owners in inner cities. Many inner city residents (Arab Americans and African Americans included) do not feel that law enforcement officials take the needs of the inner city as seriously as they do elsewhere. A pattern in the Arab American community has emerged whereby Arab American store owners feel that they have to take on problems of crime in their stores themselves (personal communication, John Zogby, Jan. 29, 1993). If an Arab store owner is robbed and is treated in a nonsupportive or harsh way by the police, he feels that he has to defend himself and his store alone. In some cases, Arab store owners have assaulted shoplifters in their stores, then becoming the victims themselves because they then may get attacked. Like other minority-group members, some Arab shop owners in the inner city have given up on the police. Police officers cannot solve the social ills that plague the inner city, but at a minimum need to instill the confidence that they will be as supportive as possible when dealing with the crimes that immigrant/refugee store owners experience.

Hate Crimes against Arab Americans

In Chapters 11 to 13, hate crimes are discussed fully, while the following explanation deals only with the phenomena of the stereotyping and scapegoating of Arabs that is likely to take place when there is a crisis in the Arab world involving Americans. Arab Americans have a special need for protection during times of political tensions in the Middle East. "The number of racial incidents suffered by Arab Americans increased threefold in 1991 as the Persian Gulf War raged, the Arab American Anti-Discrimination Committee [AADC] reported. . . . The American Arab civil rights watchdog group said that there were 119 hate crimes nationwide [in 1991], compared to 39 in 1990. Twenty of those incidents took place in Michigan, according to AADC's Detroit regional director . . ." (*Detroit Free Press,* Feb. 21, 1992, p. 2).

Exhibit 9.2 shows only the *reported crimes*—the ADC points out that many cases do not come to their attention or "are never reported at all due to the unfortunate reality that many victims fear further repercussion" (*Detroit Free Press,* Feb. 21, 1992, p. 6).

Throughout 1991, violence against individual Arab Americans escalated more than it ever had before. The crisis in the Gulf began in August 1990 with "Desert Shield" and climaxed in January 1991 when the United States went to war with Iraq. Throughout this period, the number of hate crimes directed toward Arab Americans increased, with the largest number of attacks occurring during the

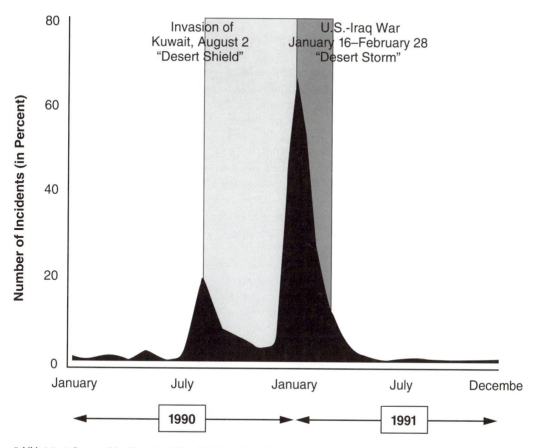

Exhibit 9.2   Influence of the Changing Political Crisis on Hate Crime Incidents against Arabs in the United States during 1990 and 1991. *Source:* American Arab Anti-discrimination Special Reports, 1992.

first few weeks following the war. The American-Arab Anti-Discrimination Committee (ADC) published a *1991 Report on Anti-Arab Hate Crimes*. The opening paragraph reads: "Significantly, a dramatic increase was recorded in acts involving physical violence such as arson, bombings, and physical assaults as Arab-Americans again became convenient scapegoats for a small minority of individuals seeking to vent their fears and frustrations by intimidating, harassing, and carrying out acts of violence against others. In short, Arab-Americans proved to be the domestic casualties of the war" (American-Arab Anti-discrimination Committee, 1992).

The ADC followed the Justice Department's guidelines on hate crime data collection in order to compile their report. (See Chapters 11 to 13, which deal extensively with hate crimes.) During the Gulf War, some people viewed all Arab Americans as "the enemy," even though the majority of Arab Americans supported President Bush's decision to invade Iraq.

Adding to an anti-Arab feeling was the FBI announcement to conduct investigations (extensive interviewing) into the Arab American community in order to gather information about domestic terrorism (*Washington Times*, Jan. 9, 1991, p. A-5). At least a few of the interviews took place with officers of local police departments such as in Los Angeles, where one Arab American described a visit of an FBI agent which was, "unannounced, unexpected and accompanied by a member of the Los Angeles Police Department's anti-terrorist squad" (*New York Times National*, Jan. 12, 1991). FBI agents interviewed at least 200 prominent Americans of Arab descent and offended them by their very insinuation that because they are Arab Americans, they must know of Arab terrorists in the United States.

A letter to President Bush (Jan. 9, 1993), Albert Mokhiber, president of the American-Arab Anti-discrimination Committee states: "To assume that Arab Americans as a community have special knowledge about potential acts of terrorism in the United States is offensive. Such an assumption is a throw-back to the dark days of our national history with the Japanese Internment camps during World War II." Mokhiber pointed out that Arab Americans are not known to be terrorists but rather, have been *victims* of terrorism and hate crimes. Arab American leaders acknowledged their appreciation of the fact that FBI agents investigated hate crimes against community members during the Gulf crisis. However, according to Mokhiber, the FBI's investigations (i.e., to locate terrorists) "gave the appearance that the Arab American community is 'suspect' . . . and will allow others . . . justification for their continued suspicion and acts of violence against us." James Zogby, referring to the FBI procedure and the general description of the Arab American community, pointed out, "Most of the Arab American community is assimilated and identifies themselves as Americans" (personal communication, Jan. 25, 1993).

As with relationships to all other groups, law enforcement officials must make distinctions among Arab American groups and not let stereotypes interfere with an understanding of Arab-Americans from diverse groups.

SUMMARY OF RECOMMENDATIONS FOR LAW ENFORCEMENT

1. There are several basic Arabic cultural values that officers should keep in mind when interacting with Arab American citizens:

- "A person's dignity, honor, and reputation are of paramount importance and no effort should be spared to protect them, especially one's honor" (Nydell, 1987).
- "Loyalty to one's family takes precedence over [other needs; thus an individual is completely intertwined with his family]" (Nydell, 1987).
- Communication should be courteous and hospitable; honor and face-saving govern interpersonal interactions and relationships.

2. Arab Americans have been wrongly characterized and stereotyped by the media, and as with all stereotypes; this has affected people's thinking on Arab Americans. Officers should be aware of stereotypes that may influence their judgments. Common stereotypes of Arabs include:

- Illiterate and backward
- Passive, uneducated women
- Thief
- Terrorist

3. Officers can demonstrate to Muslim Arabs a respect for their culture and religion by:

- Respecting the times when people pray (five times a day)
- Maintaining courteous behavior in mosques, such as not stepping on prayer mats, not walking in front of people praying, and speaking softly
- Working out solutions with community members regarding religious celebrations (e.g., parking problems, noise)

4. The basic unit for Arab Americans, especially recent arrivals and traditional families, is not the individual but the family (including the extended family).

- If a family member is involved in a police incident, officers should expect that other family members will become actively involved.
- Officers should not automatically assume that this involvement is an attempt to interfere with police affairs.
- The traditional Arabic family is used to working out their conflicts themselves; this is further reason for all members to become involved.

5. Traditionally and outwardly, the father is the head of the household and much of the conversation should be directed toward him. Officers should, however, keep in mind the following:

- Many Arab women are outspoken and vocal. Do not dismiss their input because men may appear to be, at least publicly, the ones with the power.
- Traditional Arab women who do not freely communicate with men may have difficulty expressing themselves to a male police officer. In their own families, however, they are often the real decision makers. Consider various ways of getting information (e.g., the use of a female translator, female police officer, and indirect and open-ended questions).

6. There are a number of specific cultural practices and taboos that officers should consider when communicating with Arab Americans who have preserved a traditional lifestyle (i.e., this does not apply to the majority of Arab Americans who have been in the United States for generations).

- Avoid even the casual touching of women. Be respectful of the need that some Arab women have to be modest.
- Never point the sole of one's shoes or feet at a person.
- Expect people to extend hospitality by offering coffee or food (this is not a bribe, from their cultural perspective).
- Arab Americans may stand closer to each other than other Americans do when talking. This is not meant to be threatening; it is largely unconscious and reflects a cultural preference for closer interpersonal interaction.

7. There are cultural differences in communication style that can affect officers' judgments and reactions:

- Becoming highly emotional (verbally and nonverbally) and speaking loudly is not looked down upon in the Arab world. Officers who may have a different manner of communication should not express irritation at this culturally different style. Nor should they necessarily determine that the people involved are being disrespectful.

Developing patience with culturally different styles of communication is a key cross-cultural skill.

- When a person speaks with an accent, it does not necessarily mean that he or she is not fluent in English or is illiterate. Many highly educated Arab Americans speak English fluently but with an accent, and would be insulted if they were treated as if they were not educated.

8. In areas where there are Arab American grocers and liquor store owners as well as poor residents, there is great potential for conflict.

- Arab American grocers and liquor store owners need to be able to depend on local police services. Many do not feel that they have the protection they need.
- Police officers may be in positions to explain to other residents why Arab-American store owners are usually not in positions to hire people from the community. This will not solve the conflicts, but at least officers can attempt to make some people understand the economic realities of life for refugees and immigrants.

9. During times of crises in the Middle East, Arab Americans become targets of prejudice and racism.

- Police departments need to monitor communities and keep informed of world events so that Arab American communities have more protection during times when they may be vulnerable to hate crimes.

DISCUSSION QUESTIONS AND ISSUES[*]

1. *Police–Ethnic Community Relations.* In the section entitled *"Islamic Religion,"* the authors mention an incident which took place at the end of the holy month of "Ramadan" whereby officers ticketed many cars parked across the street from the Mosque. According to community people, the stores adjacent to the parking lots were closed and although parking was technically for customers only, the Arab Americans did not anticipate that there would be a problem utilizing the parking lot after hours. From a community relations point of view, the mass ticketing created some very negative feelings and a collective perception that "They (meaning the police) don't respect us; they don't want to understand us." What is your opinion regarding the way things were handled? Do you have any suggestions as to how this situation could have been prevented? Comment on both what the community and the police could have done to prevent the problem.

2. *Who Is the Head of the Household?* The stated head of the household in most traditional Arabic families is the father, although the mother actually has a great deal of power within the family. Although in public many Arabic women will defer decision making to their husbands, a police officer should not totally discount what the woman might have to offer in various police-related situations. How can the police officer, while respecting the status of the father, still acknowledge the mother as well as get input from her?

3. *Nonverbal Variations across Cultures.* When Arab Americans greet each other, they sometimes shake hands and then place their right hand on their chest near their heart. This is a sign of sincerity. In your opinion, should officers greet Arab Americans using this gesture if a person greets them in this way? What would be the pro's and con's of doing this?

*See Instructor's Manual accompanying (this text for additional activities, role-plays, questionnaires and projects related to the content of this chapter.)

4. *Hospitality toward officers: A Cultural Gesture.* Hospitality is a virtue in Arabic culture and also functions to help people get to know (and see if they can trust) others with whom they are interacting. Given this cultural emphasis on being hospitable, what should an officer do if offered a cup of coffee and something to eat? If an officer has to decline the hospitality, how should it be done politely? Should department policy regarding the acceptance of hospitality be reexamined in light of this cultural tendency? Would your answer be different for departments that have adopted a community-based policing philosophy?

5. *"But It's the Custom in My Country."* In January 1991, the Associated Press reported that a Stockton, California man originally from Jordan was arrested for investigation of "selling his daughter into slavery" because he allegedly accepted $25,000 for her arranged marriage. After police officers had taken the girl to a shelter, a police lieutenant reported that the father protested that:"he was within his rights to arrange his daughter's marriage for a price. The father contacted us and quite upset, explained it was the custom in his country and is perfectly acceptable. Of course, we explained that you can't do that in this country. It is slavery. . . . The father then went to the shelter [where the daughter was] and was arrested after creating a disturbance." If you were investigating this case, how would you proceed? How might you assess the validity of what the father was saying? If you found out that the act was indeed, "perfectly acceptable in his country," how would you explain practices in the United States? Comment on the statement that the lieutenant made (" . . . It is slavery."). From the perspective of needing cooperation from this man, what type of approach should be taken?

6. *Officer Discretion: To Let Her Go?* In the section on the *perceptions of police,* the authors mention an incident involving a Saudi Arabian woman who was caught shoplifting in a "7–11." She begged the officer to let her go because she feared being sent home and there she would receive a harsh punishment (typically, in Saudi Arabia, a person's hand is cut off if he or she steals). The officer decided that since this was her first offense, he would let her go. What is your reaction to the officer's decision? What would you have done?

REFERENCES

American-Arab Anti-Discrimination Committee (1992). *1991 Report on Anti-Arab Hate Crimes: Political and Hate Violence Against Arab-Americans,* ADC Research Institute, Washington, D.C.

BOLLER, PHILIP J., JR. (1992). "A name is just a name—or is it?" *FBI Law Enforcement Bulletin,* Mar., p. 6.

DEVINE, ELIZABETH, AND NANCY L. BRAGANTI (1991). *The Traveler's Guide to the Middle Eastern and North African Customs and Manners,* St. Martin's Press, New York.

Islamic Affairs Department, The Embassy of Saudi Arabia (1989). *Understanding Islam and the Muslims,* Embassy of Saudi Arabia, Washington, D.C.

JABARA, ABDEEN (no date). "Time for a change," in *The Arab Image in American Film and Television,* ADC publication, supplement to Vol. 17, No. 1 of *Cineaste.*

MACRON, MARY (1989). *Arab Contributions to Civilization,* American–Arab Anti-Discrimination Committee, ADC Issue 6, Washington, D.C.

MICHALAK, LAURENCE (1988). *Cruel and Unusual: Nega-*

tive Images of Arabs in American Popular Culture, ADC Issue 15, American-Arab Anti-Discrimination Committee, Washington, D.C.

NYDELL, MARGARET K. (1987). *Understanding Arabs: A Guide for Westerners,* Intercultural Press, Yarmouth, Maine.

SHABBAS, AUDREY (1984). *Cultural Clues for Social Service Case Workers and Special Educators (unpublished monograph),* Arab World and Islamic Resources and School Services, Berkeley, Calif.

SHAHEEN, JACK (1988). *Abscam: Arabiaphobia in America,* ADC Issue 1, American-Arab Anti-Discrimination Committee, Washington D.C.

WOODRUFF, DAVID (1991). "Letter from Detroit: where the Mideast meets the Midwest—uneasily," *Business Week,* Feb. 4, p. 30A.

ZOGBY, JOHN (1990). *Arab America Today: A Demographic Profile of Arab Americans,* Arab American Institute, Washington, D.C.

10

LAW ENFORCEMENT CONTACT WITH AMERICAN INDIANS

OVERVIEW

This chapter provides specific cultural information on American Indians, including aspects of their history, which both directly and indirectly can affect the relationship between law enforcement officials and citizens. The chapter presents the question of American Indian identity, as well as group identification terms that may be confusing for law enforcement officials when identification is an issue. A brief explanation of the tribal system, reservations, and American Indian mobility is provided. The next section addresses the diversity that exists among American Indian groups, followed by a description of cultural similarities found among various Indian groups, including information on values and communication characteristics. Offensive labels, terms, and stereotypical statements are listed, followed by information relevant to law enforcement about family structure. The closing section outlines several key concerns for law enforcement, including information on perception of police, police jurisdiction problems, peyote, medicine bags, trespassing, violation of Indian sacred places, and problems related to fishing rights. In the summary of the chapter, there is a review of recommendations for improved communication and relationships between law enforcement personnel and members of American Indian communities.

COMMENTARY

The following quote is excerpted from an interview (Dec. 18, 1992) with retired Chief Jim Cox, a Comanche Indian and former chief of police at the Midwest City

Police Department, Oklahoma, who brought up the subject of officers' biased and prejudicial treatment. He described an incident during his youth in Oklahoma when he was riding with other American Indian teenagers in an old Nash automobile. Police officers stopped the car and discovered that the teens had been drinking. Instead of taking the appropriate action, which would have been to arrest the young people or at least to call the parents to pick up the kids, the officers let them go. Former Chief Cox recalls to this day having heard one of the officers say to the other: *"It's just a bunch of Indians—let them go!"* Cox's interpretation of this statement was that if they kill themselves, it did not matter because they were just Indians. This impression remained with him even after he became a police officer over 25 years ago.

> Interview with Jose Rivera, Native American California State Peace Officer, Sept. 11, 1992.

> When an officer contacts an Indian person, there is often 500 years of frustration built up. . . . The officer should be aware of the "baggage" that he or she [i.e., the officer] brings to the encounter.

> Preamble to 1991 Joint Resolution of Congress and Senate. Whereas the five hundredth anniversary of the arrival of Christopher Columbus to the Western Hemisphere is an especially appropriate occasion for the people of the United States to reflect on the long history of the original inhabitants of this continent and discover that the "discoverees" should have as much recognition as the discover.   Public Law 102-188, 102nd Congress, Dec. 4, 1991.

> Sitting Bull [Lakota], in *In the Spirit of Crazy Horse,* by Peter Matthiessen, Penguin Books, New York, 1992, p. 33

> What treaty that the whites have kept has the red man broken? Not one. What treaty that the white man ever made with us have they kept? Not one. When I was a boy the Sioux owned the world; the sun rose and set on their land; they sent ten thousand men to battle. Who slew [the warriors]? Where are our lands? Who owns them? What white man can say I ever stole his land. . . ? Yet, they say I am a thief. What white woman, however lonely, was ever captive or insulted by me? Yet they say I am a bad Indian. What white man has ever seen me drunk? Who has ever seen me . . . abuse my children? What law have I broken? Is it wicked for me because my skin is red?

(In this chapter, the terms *American Indian, Native American,* and *Indian* are used interchangeably.)

HISTORICAL INFORMATION AND BACKGROUND

Recorded history disputes the origins of the first "Indians" in America. Some researchers claim that they arrived from Asia more than 40,000 years ago; others claim that they did not arrive *from* anywhere else. In either case, despite their long history in North America and the fact that they are the first "Americans," traditional U.S. history books did not recognize their existence until the European conquests, beginning with Christopher Columbus in 1492. The subject of the native peoples as either nonexistent or simply as insignificant reflect an ethnocentric (in this case, a Eurocentric) view of history. Even the word "Indian" is not a term that native Americans originally used to designate their tribes or communities. Because Columbus did not know that North and South America existed, he thought he had reached the Indies (which then included India, China, the East Indies, and Japan). In fact, he arrived in what is now called the West Indies (in the Caribbean) and he called the people he met "Indians" (Los Indios). Eventually, this became the name for all the indigenous peoples in the Americas. However, before the White settlers came to North and South America, almost every "Indian" tribe had its own name, and despite some shared cultural values, native Americans did not see themselves as one collective group or call themselves "Indians." Most tribes refer to themselves in their own languages as "The People," "The Allies," or "The Friends." Some of the terms that whites use for various tribes are not even authentic names for that tribe. For example, the label *Sioux,* which means enemy or snake, was originally a term given to that group by an enemy tribe and then adopted by French traitors. In many cases, a tribe's real name is not necessarily the name commonly used (personal communication John LaVelle, executive director of the Center for the SPIRIT, San Francisco, California, Sept. 24, 1993).

Even today in public schools across the country, the nature of much of the contact with Native Americans in the early history of the United States is not discussed. Rather than being presented as part of the American people's common legacy, Native American cultural heritage is often presented as bits of colorful "exotica." Genocide or the killing of entire tribes is not a chapter in history that people have wanted to focus on. The reality is that Euro-American/Indian relations have been characterized by hostility, contempt, and brutality. The native peoples have generally been treated by Euro-Americans as less than human or as "savages," and the rich Native American cultures have been ignored or crushed. For this reason, the delight of Thanksgiving and the merriment of Christopher Columbus Day parades are not shared by all. To say that Columbus discovered America implies that Native Americans were not considered "human enough" to be of significance. Ignoring the existence of the Native Americans before 1492 constitutes only one aspect of ethnocentrism. American Indians' experience with the "white man" has largely been one of exploitation, violence, and forced relocation. It is this historical background that has shaped many Native American views of Euro-Americans and their culture. While the majority of people in the United States have a sense that Native Americans were not treated with dignity at some point in U.S. history, many are not aware of the extent of the current abuse toward them. This may be due to the fact that this group is a small and traditionally forgotten minority in the United States (constituting approximately 1 percent of the overall population).

It would not be accurate to say that no progress at all has been made in United States with regard to awareness and rights of our nation's first Americans. From an educational perspective, many people are discovering increasing opportunities to learn about the long history and rich culture of Indian tribes and communities. The federal government is at least verbalizing the need for understanding of and cooperation with Native American groups. In a joint resolution of the House and the Senate (Public Law 102-279, 102nd Congress) on May 9, 1992, the Congress resolved: "That 1992 is designated as the 'Year of Reconciliation Between American Indians and non-Indians.' The President is authorized and requested to issue a proclamation calling upon the people of the United States, both Indian and non-Indian, to lay aside fears and mistrust of one another, to build friendships, to join together and take part in shared cultural activities, and to strive towards mutual respect and understanding."

On the other hand, many Native Americans do not see that the spirit behind the foregoing sentiments have actually changed their lives. Indians have among the highest school dropout rates as well as unemployment rates of all minority groups. As for protection from the federal government, American Indians are still fighting legal battles over the retention of Indian lands and other rights previously guaranteed by U.S. treaties. They still feel abused by a system of government that has committed many treaty violations against tribes and individuals. Rights that have been guaranteed in the form of binding treaties have been disregarded by the federal government.

The history of American Indians has shown that the government has not always acted in good faith toward its Native American citizens and, consequently, many individuals and tribes are reluctant to trust the words of the government or people representing "the system." Knowingly or not, law enforcement agents carry this "baggage" into encounters with Native Americans. The police officer historically has been a very rigidly authoritarian part of governmental control that has affected nearly every aspect of an Indian's life, especially on reservations. Often, officers (like most citizens) have only a limited understanding of how the government (including the criminal justice system) caused massive suffering by not allowing Indians to preserve their cultures, identities, languages, sacred sites, rituals, and lands. Because of this history, officers have a special responsibility to educate themselves about the history of the treatment of Indian peoples in order to deal with them effectively and fairly today. Understanding Indian communities, plus making extra efforts to establish rapport, will increase law enforcement officials' success at winning cooperation and respect from people who never before had any reason to trust *any* representative of government.

THE QUESTION OF AMERICAN INDIAN IDENTITY

Law enforcement officials may find themselves confused as to who is and who is not an American Indian. Individuals may claim to have "Indian blood," but tribes have their own criteria for determining tribal membership. Because the determination of tribal membership is a fundamental attribute of tribal sovereignty, the federal government generally defers to tribes' own determinations when establishing eligibility criteria under special Indian entitlement programs. However, there are a number of Indian tribes which, for historical and political reasons, are not currently "federally recognized" tribes. Members of such tribes, although certainly Indian, are not necessarily eligible for special benefits under federal Indian programs. On the other hand, fraud in this area is quite rampant, whereby people falsely claim Indian ancestry to take unfair advantage of governmental benefits and other perceived opportunities.

Officers may find themselves in situations where someone claims to be Indian when he or she is not. *If officers have any doubt, they should inquire as to what tribe the person belongs and then contact the tribal headquarters to verify that person's identity.* Every tribe has its own administration and its own authority who will be able to answer questions of this nature. By verifying information with tribal authorities rather than making personal determinations of "Indianness," officers will help create a good rapport between tribal members and law enforcement officials (personal communication, John LaVelle, Sept. 24, 1993).

Federal census figures reveal that in 1990 there were approximately 2 million American Indians and Alaska natives living in the United States (U.S. Bureau of the Census figures). However, there is a great deal of numerical misinformation related to the census's lack of a method for verifying the accuracy of people's claims that they are Native American. The term *Native American* came into popularity in the 1960s and referred to groups served by the BIA, including American Indians and natives of Alaska. Later the term under certain federal legislation began to include natives from Hawaii. (*Native American,* however, has never been accepted by all Indian groups and is rarely used on reservations.) Alaska natives, such as Eskimos and Aleuts, are separate groups and prefer the term *Alaska Native.* To know by what terms individuals or tribes prefer to be called, officers should listen to the names they use for themselves rather than try to guess which way is "correct."

In the area of mislabeling, some Native Americans have Spanish first or last names (because of intermarriage) and may "look" Hispanic or Latino (e.g., the Hopis). Identification can be difficult for the officer, so he or she should not assume that the person is Latino just because of the name. Many Native Americans do not want to be grouped with Latinos because (1) they are not Latinos; (2) they may resent the fact that some Latinos deny their Indian ancestry and, instead, only identify with the Spanish part of their heritage; and (3) many tribes have a history of warfare with the "mestizo" populations of Mexico. As an aside, the majority population in Mexico and Central and South America is of "Indian" ancestry, but adopted or were given Spanish names by the "Conquistadores" (conquerors). Many Hispanics in U.S. border communities are really of Indian, not Spanish heritage, or at the very least, a mixture of the two.

TRIBES, RESERVATIONS, AND MOBILITY OF NATIVE AMERICANS

In the United States, there are over 500 "federally recognized" tribes (some of which use "tribe" and "nation" interchangeably), and these include native groups of Alaskans such as Aleuts. Federal recognition means that a legal relationship exists between the tribe and the federal government. There are about 100 tribes that do not benefit from federally recognized status. Some may be state recognized and/or in the process of seeking federal recognition, while others may not seek recognition at all. In a *New York Times* article (Sept. 6, 1992, p. 8y) the issue of the increasing rivalry among some Indian groups seeking recognition is raised: "Indians increasingly find themselves pitted against other Indians over a shrinking pie of government benefits. Those resources have become so small that allowing any new tribe to be recognized would only cause further hardship for other Indians . . ."

An Indian reservation is land that a tribe has reserved for its exclusive use through the course of treaty making. It may be on ancestral lands, or simply the only land available when tribes were forced to give up their own territories through federal treaties. A reservation is also land that the federal government holds in trust for the use of an Indian tribe. In the 1990 census, 314 reservations were counted. The Navajo reservation (and trust lands), extending into three states, was the largest. Since reservations are self-governing, most have tribal police. (The issue of jurisdiction will be presented later in the chapter.) Indians are not forced to stay on a reservation, but many who leave have a strong desire to remain in touch with and be nourished by their roots. For this reason and because of culture shock experienced in urban life, many do return to reservations (personal communication, John LaVelle, Sept. 24, 1993).

In general, the Indian population is characterized by constant movement between the reservation and the city and sometimes relocation from city to city. In urban areas, when officers contact an Indian, they will not necessarily know how acculturated to city life that person is. In rural areas it will be easier for officers to get to know the culture of a particular tribe. In the city, the tribal background may be less important than the fact that the person is an American Indian.

Since the early 1980s, more than half of the population of Native Americans have lived outside of reservation communities; many have left to pursue educational and employment opportunities, as life on some of the reservations can be very bleak. Although a large number return home to the reservations to participate in family activities and tribal ceremonies, many attempt to remake their lives in urban areas. A percentage of Indians do make adjustments to mainstream educational and occupational life, but the numbers are still disproportionately low.

DIVERSITY AMONG NATIVE AMERICANS

As with other culturally or ethnically defined categories of people (e.g., Asian, African American) it would be a mistake to lump all Native Americans together and to assume that they are a homogeneous group. For example, in Arizona alone, one finds a number of different tribes with varying traditions: there are Hopis in the northeast, Pimas and Papagos in the south, and Yuman groups in the west. All of these descend from people who came to what is now called Arizona. The relative "newcomers" are the Navajos and Apaches, who arrived about 1000 years ago. These six tribes represent differences in culture, with each group having its own history and life experiences.

Broadly speaking, in the United States, one finds distinct cultural groups among Native Americans in Alaska, Arizona, California, the Central Plains (Kansas and Nebraska), the Dakotas, the Eastern Seaboard, the Great Lakes area, the Gulf coast states (Florida, Alabama, Mississippi, Louisiana, Texas), the Lower Plateau

(Nevada, Utah, Colorado), Montana, Wyoming, New Mexico, North Carolina, Oklahoma, and the Northwest (Washington, Oregon, and Idaho). Every tribe has evolved its own sets of traditions and beliefs and each sees itself as distinct from other tribes, despite some significant broad similarities.

SIMILARITIES AMONG NATIVE AMERICANS

It is possible to talk about general characteristics of Native American groups without negating the fact of their diversity. The cultural characteristics that are described in the following section will not, of course, apply to all such Americans, but rather to many who are traditionally "Indian" in their orientation to life. While being aware of tribal differences, the law enforcement officer should also understand that there is a strong cultural link between the many worlds and tribes of Native Americans and their Indian counterparts throughout the American continent.

Philosophy toward the Earth and the Universe

"The most striking difference between . . . Indian and Western man is the manner in which each views his role in the universe. The prevailing non-Indian view is that man is superior to all other forms of life and that the universe is his to be used as he sees fit . . . an attitude justified as the mastery of nature for the benefit of man [characterizes Western man's philosophy] (Bahti, 1982). Through this contrast with Western philosophy (i.e., that people have the capacity to alter nature) the reader can gain insight into the values and philosophies common to virtually all identifying Native Americans. While acknowledging the character of each Indian tribe or "nation," there is a common set of values and beliefs involving the earth, nature, and the universe, resulting in a deep respect for nature and "mother earth." According to American Indian philosophy, the earth is sacred and is a living entity. By spiritual involvement with the earth, nature, and the universe, individuals bind themselves to their environment. The Indian does not see himself (i.e., a human being) as superior to all else (e.g., animals, plants, etc.), but rather as part of all of creation. Through religious ceremonies and rituals, the Indian is able to transcend himself such that he is in harmony with the universe and not separate from nature.

The inclination of many people who do not understand this philosophy would be to dismiss it as primitive and even backward. The costumes, the rituals, the ceremonies, the dances, are often thought of as colorful, but strange. Yet from an Indian perspective: "It is a tragedy indeed that Western man in his headlong quest for Holy Progress could not have paused long enough to learn this basic truth—one which he is now being forced to recognize, much to his surprise and dismay. Ever anxious to teach 'backward' people, he is ever reluctant to learn from them" (Bahti, 1982).

An Indian prayer:

Oh our Mother the earth, Oh our Father the sky,
Your children are we, and with tired backs
We bring you the gifts you love.

Then weave for us a garment of brightness. . . ;
May the fringes be the falling rain.
May the border be the standing rainbow.
That we may walk fittingly where birds sing . . . and where grass is
green, Oh our mother earth, Oh our father sky. (Author unknown)

When in contact with people who are celebrating or praying whether on a reservation or in a tribe or community, it is of vital importance to refrain from conveying an air of superiority because of an ethnocentric view that "those rituals" are primitive. American Indian prayers, rituals, and ceremonies represent ancient beliefs and philosophies, many of which have to do with the preservation of and harmony with the earth. An officer should try to avoid at all costs interrupting prayers and sacred ceremonies (just as one would want to avoid interrupting church services) and should never convey nonverbally or verbally that the practices or beliefs are "primitive." Many non-Indians now embrace certain Native American beliefs regarding the environment; what was once thought of as "primitive" is now seen as essential with regard to preserving our environment.

Acculturation to Mainstream Society

There are great differences among the cultures, languages, history, and socioeconomic status of Native American tribes, communities, and individuals. Nevertheless, in a study on suicide and ethnicity in the United States, the national Committee on Cultural Psychiatry (1989) concluded that there is still "a definitive pattern of self-destructive behavior which can be generalized to all [Indian] groups." However, it cannot be stressed enough that many of the origins of the psychosocial problems that some Indians experience in mainstream society are not as a result of their own weaknesses or deficiencies. The cause of the problems date back to the way government has handled and regulated Indian life. The dominant society in no way affirmed the cultural identity of Indians; thus many Indians have internalized the oppression that they experienced from the outside world. Furthermore, many young people feel the stresses of living between two cultural worlds. They are not fully part of the traditional Indian world (as celebrated on the reservation or in a community that honors traditions) and they are not fully adapted to the dominant American culture. People who are caught between two cultures and are successful in neither run the risk of contributing to family breakdown, often becoming depressed, alcoholic, and suicidal. Interestingly, according to the Committee on Cultural Psychiatry (1989) Indian groups that have remained tightly identified with their culture because of isolation from the mainstream culture and because of remaining on indigenous lands, do not exhibit the type of behavior described above. Tribes exemplifying healthier attitudes toward their identities and a lower suicide rate include the southwestern Pueblos and the Navajo.

Despite the persistence of many social problems, some progress has been made overall with respect to education and political participation. Law enforcement officials must not hold on to a stereotype of American Indians being uneducated. There is a growing population attending colleges and rising to high positions in education, entertainment, sports, and industry. In the early 1990s, there was only one Native American elected to the senate (from the state of Colorado). Many people are now working on revitalizing Native American culture rather than letting it die. This has resulted in the movement of "pan-Indianism" in which American Indians across the United States are celebrating their cultural heritage, while organizing politically. An American Indian culture is developing nationally, where members of tribes or communities with very different traditions are identifying as a group by following certain practices that are associated with Indians (personal communication, Don Brown, professor of sociology and specialist in Native American communities, Oklahoma State University, Aug. 13, 1992): for example, (1) males wearing long hair (long hair is a sign of a free man, not a slave); (2) the use of the sacred pipe (i.e., the pipestone pipe, sometimes referred to as the "peacepipe"); and (3) participation in sweatlodges, purification rituals, and the sacred sundance for purification. These rituals are not practiced by every tribe but are becoming symbols of a growing movement reflecting American Indian pride. It should be noted, however, that the pan-Indian movement is not necessarily viewed positively by all Indians, as some believe that there is a strong possibility of misusing a tradition or diluting the meaning of a ritual (personal communication, John LaVelle, Sept. 24, 1993).

LANGUAGE AND COMMUNICATION

It is possible to make some generalizations about the way a group of people communicate, even when there is great diversity within the group. The following contains information about nonverbal and verbal aspects of communication as well as tips for the law enforcement officer interacting with Native Americans. The paragraphs that follow describe patterns of communication and behavior as exhibited by some American Indians who are *traditional* in their outlook. No description of communication traits could ever apply to everyone within a group, especially one that is so diverse.

Openness and Self-Disclosure

Many Native Americans, in early encounters, will approach people and respond with caution. Too much openness is to be avoided, as is disclosing personal and family problems. This often means that the officer has to work harder at establishing rapport and gaining trust. In the American mainstream culture, appearing friendly and open is highly valued (especially in certain regions, such as the west coast and the south). Because different modes of behavior are expected and accepted, the non-Indian may view the Indian as aloof and reserved. The Indian perception can be that the Euro-American person, because of excessive openness, is superficial and thus untrustworthy. Mainstream American culture encourages speaking out and open expression of opinions, while American Indian culture does not.

Silence and Interruptions

The ability to remain quiet, to be still, and to observe is highly valued in Native American culture; consequently, silence is truly a virtue. (In mainstream American culture, it is said that "silence is golden," but this is probably more of an expression of an ideal than a description of a fact.) Indians are taught to study and assess situations and only act or participate when one is properly prepared. Indians tend not to act impulsively for fear of appearing foolish or bringing shame to themselves or to their family (Los Angeles Police Department Cross-Cultural Awareness tapes). When law enforcement officials contact Native Americans, they may mistake this reticence to talk as sullenness or lack of cooperation. The behavior must not be misinterpreted or taken personally. A cultural trait must be understood as just that (i.e., a behavior, action, or attitude that is not intended to be a personal insult). The officer must also consider that interrupting an Indian when he or she speaks is seen as very aggressive and should be avoided whenever possible.

Talking and Questions

Talking just to fill the silence is not seen as important. The small-talk that one observes in mainstream society ("Hi. How are you? How was your weekend?", etc.) is traditionally not required by Native Americans. Words are considered powerful and are therefore chosen carefully. This may result in a situation where Native Americans retreat and appear to be withdrawn if someone is dominating the conversation. When law enforcement officials question Native Americans who exhibit these tendencies (i.e., not being prone to talkativeness), the officer should not press aggressively for answers. (Aggressive behavior, both verbal and physical, is traditionally looked down upon.) Questions should be open-ended, with the officer being willing to respect the silence and time it may take to find out the needed information.

Nonverbal Communication: Eye Contact/Touching

With respect to American Indian cultures, people often make the statement that Indians avoid making direct eye contact. Although this is true for some tribes, it does not hold true for all. To know whether this applies or not, an officer can simply watch for this signal (i.e., avoidance of eye contact) and follow the lead of the citizen. In this section we explain the phenomenon of avoidance of eye contact from the perspective of groups who do adhere to this behavior. Some Indian tribes do have the belief that looking directly into one's eyes for a prolonged period of time is disrespectful (just as pointing at someone is considered impolite). The Lakota tribe, for example, has the belief that direct eye contact is an affront or an invasion of privacy (Mehl, 1990). Navajo tribe members have a tendency to stare at each other when they want to direct their anger at someone. An Indian who adheres to the unspoken rules about eye contact may appear to be shifty and evasive. Officers and other law enforcement officials must not automatically judge a person as guilty or suspicious simply because that person is not maintaining direct eye contact. To put a person at ease, the officer can decrease eye contact if it appears to be inhibiting the Native American citizen. Avoidance of eye contact with the officer can also convey the message that the officer is using an approach that is too forceful and demanding. Where such norms about eye-contact avoidance apply, and if an officer has to look at a person's eyes, it would help to forewarn the person (i.e., "I'm going to have to check your eyes").

With regard to their sense of space, most Native Americans are not comfortable being touched by strangers, whether a pat on the back or the arm around the shoulder. Either no touching is appropriate or it should be limited to a brief handshake. (Married couples do not tend to show affection in public.) Additionally, people should avoid crowding or standing too close. Keep in mind that many Indian relations with strangers are more formal than those of the mainstream culture; therefore, an officer might be viewed as overly aggressive if he or she does not maintain a proper distance.

Language

Some Native Americans speak one or more Indian languages. English, for many, is a second language. Those who do not speak English well may be inhibited from speaking for fear of "losing face" because of their lack of language ability. In addition, because of a tendency to speak quietly and nonforcefully, law enforcement agents will need patience and extra time; interaction must not be rushed. The Native American who is not strong in English needs to spend more time translating from his or her own language to English when formulating a response (this is true of all second-language speakers who are not yet fluent). As with all other languages, English words or concepts do not always translate exactly into the various Indian languages. Indian languages are rich and express concepts reflecting views of the world. It is mandatory that the utmost respect be shown when native Americans speak their own language. Remember that the Indians have a long history of forced assimilation into the Anglo society, in which, among other things, many were denied the right to speak their native languages.

Offensive Terms, Labels, and Stereotypes

In the interview mentioned in the opening of this chapter, retired chief of police Jim Cox, a Comanche Indian, described situations in which insensitive police officers told Indian jokes or used derogatory terms in his presence. He stated that he is proud of his heritage and is offended by commonly held stereotypes. Use of racial slurs (toward any group) are never acceptable in crime fighting and peacekeeping, no matter how provoked an officer may be. Officers hearing disrespectful terms and stereotypes about Native Americans (and other groups) should educate fellow officers as to the lack of professionalism and respect for community diversity that such terms convey.

There are a number of words that are offensive to Native Americans: chief (a leader who has reached this rank is highly honored), squaw (*extremely offensive*), buck, redskin, Indian "brave," and skins (some young Indians may refer to themselves using "skins" but would be offended by others using the term).

Other terms used to refer to Native Americans are "apple" [a slightly dated term referring to a highly assimilated Indian (i.e., red on the outside; white on the inside)] and "the people" (more commonly used by some groups of Indians to refer to themselves). In some parts, a reservation is called a "rez" by Indians; for example, in Oklahoma (where there is only one reservation), the term "reservation" is negative and the term "community" is used (personal communication, Donald

Brown, Aug. 13, 1992). It is also patronizing when non-Indians use certain kinship terms, such as "grandfather" when talking to an older man, even though other Indians may be using that term themselves.

Until recently, most public school children had the stereotypical picture of an Indian as being wild, savage, and primitive. In textbooks and other history books, recounting Native American history, Indians were said to "massacre" whites, whereas whites simply "fought" or "battled" the Indians (Harris, 1991). Other common stereotypes or stereotypical statements highly resented are: "All Indians are drunks" (despite the fact that there are a large percentage of alcohol-related arrests, not all Indians have a problem with liquor). Furthermore, the argument has been put forth that the white man introduced "fire water" (alcohol) to the Indian as a means of weakening him. "You can't trust an Indian," "Those damn Indians" (as if they are simply a nuisance), and "The only good Indian is a dead one" (this remark is traced back to a statement made by a U.S. general in 1869) (Harris, 1991).

Indians are often offended when non-Indians make claims (which may or may not be true) about their Indian ancestry: "I'm part Indian—My great-grandfather was Cherokee (for example). . . ." Although this may be an attempt to establish rapport, it rings of "Some of my best friends are Indians . . ." (i.e., to "prove" that one does not have any prejudice). In summary, a psychologist who has an extensive understanding of American Indians advises:

> "[People] should not assume some affinity [with American Indians] based on novels, movies, a vacation trip, or an interest in silver jewelry. These are among the most offensive, commonly made errors when non-Indians first encounter an American Indian person or family. Another is a confidential revelation that there is an Indian "Princess" in the family tree-tribe unknown, identity unclear, but a bit of glamour in the family myths. The intent may be to show positive bonding. . . , but to the Indian they reveal stereotypical thinking."
> (Attneave, 1982)

FAMILY-RELATED ISSUES

Respect for Elders

"Nothing will anger an Indian more than them seeing their grandmother or grandfather being spoken to belligerently or being ordered around with disrespect. [If that happens], that's a fire cracker situation right there" (personal communication, Jose Rivera, Native American California State Police Officer, Sept. 11, 1992). Unlike mainstream American culture, Indians value aging because of the respect they have for wisdom and experience. As this phase of life is highly revered, people do not feel that they have to cover up signs of aging. The elders of a tribe or the older people in Native American communities must be shown the utmost respect by people in law enforcement. This includes acknowledging their presence in a home visit, even if they are not directly related in the police matter at hand. In some tribes (e.g., the Cherokee) the grandmother often has the most power in the household and is the primary decision maker. It is advisable for people in law enforcement to include the elders in discussions where they can give their advice or perspective on a situation. The elders are generally respected for their ability to enforce good behavior within the family and tribe.

It should also be noted, however, that because of assimilation or personal preference among some Native Americans, the elders in any given household may tend to avoid interfering with a married couple's problems. And although the elders are respected to a higher degree than in mainstream culture, they may withdraw in some situations where there is police contact, letting the younger family members deal with the problem. If in doubt, it is advisable to begin the contact more formally, deferring to the elders initially. Then officers can observe how the elders participate and if the younger family members include them.

Extended Family and Kinship Ties

In mainstream society, people usually think of and see themselves first as individuals and only after that, may (or may not) identify with their families or various communities and groups with which they are affiliated. In traditional Native American culture, a person's primary identity is related to his or her family and tribe. Some law enforcement agents may be in positions to make referrals when there is a problem with an individual (e.g., an adolescent) in a family. A referral for counseling for that person *only* may be culturally alienating for two reasons: (1) Western counseling and therapy is a foreign way to treat problems; and (2) the person is an integral part of a group in which strong bonds and interdependence are emphasized (Mehl, 1990).

Unfortunately, today, much of the family and tribal cohesiveness has lessened because of forced assimilation, extreme levels of poverty, and lack of education and employment. However, for many Native Americans, there are still large networks of relatives who are in close proximity with each other. It is not uncommon for children to be raised by someone other than their father or mother (e.g., grandmother, aunts). When law enforcement officials enter an Indian's home and, for example, ask to speak to the parents of a child, they may actually end up talking to someone who is not the blood mother or father. Officers must understand that various other relatives can function exactly as a mother or father would in mainstream culture. This does not mean that Indian "natural" parents are necessarily being lazy about their child-rearing duties, even when the child is physically living with another relative (and may be raised by several relatives throughout childhood). The intensely close family and tribal bonds allow for this type of child-raising. The officer must not assume that something is abnormal with this type of arrangement or that the parents are neglecting their children.

Interestingly, from the perspective of a Lakota Indian who became a psychiatrist, the traditional mainstream way of raising children seemed odd to him. Referring to mothers in the 1950s, he said, "I could never understand how mothers could have their babies and then raise them alone and stay in boxes (i.e., their houses) all day!"

Children and Separation from Parents

It is crucial that peacekeepers understand the importance of *not* separating children from family members, if at all possible. Many families in urban areas and on reservations have been severely traumatized by the federal government's systematic removal of Indian children from their homes, where children were placed in boarding schools often hundreds of miles away. This phenomenon, including education for the children that stripped them of their language and culture, began in the late nineteenth century. Reports exist that say: "Until as recently as 1974, the Bureau of Indian Affairs (BIA) was operating 75 boarding schools with more than 30,000 children enrolled" (Ogawa, 1990).

Although for many families, the trauma of children being forcibly separated from parents took place years ago, the after effects still linger (personal communication, Jose Rivera, Sept. 11, 1992). In the early twentieth century there was a famous case in which Hopi Indian fathers were sentenced to years in high-security prisons and were subject to the fullest persecution. Their crime was hiding their children from the BIA officials because they did not want the children to be taken to boarding schools by the BIA. By hiding the children, the Hopi fathers violated federal law. This case is still talked about today (personal communication, Jose Rivera, Sept. 11, 1992). The memory of a "uniform coming to take away a child" is an image that can be conjured up easily by some Indians. It is this "baggage" that the law enforcement officer today brings into encounters; he or she may be totally unaware of the power of this baggage.

Since Native American parents can be very protective of their children, an officer would be well advised to let the parents know about any action that needs to be taken with regard to the child. Law enforcement officials can establish a good rapport with Indian families if they treat the children well.

KEY ISSUES IN LAW ENFORCEMENT

Perception of Police

The general distrust of police by Native Americans stems from a history of bad relations with "the system" (federal, state, and local governments). In their view, officers represent a system that has not supported Indian rights and their tribes or communities. Most of their contact with the police is negative contact. Thus many Native Americans (like other groups) usually have not had a chance to build a relationship of trust and cooperation with people in law enforcement.

Jurisdiction

Police officers are put into an unusual situation when it comes to enforcing the law among Indians. The following statement was made with reference to the difficulties officers face when an area that is considered to be "Indian land" (on which tribal police have jurisdiction) is adjacent to non-Indian land, sometimes forming "checkerboard" patterns of jurisdiction. "You've got to have a feel for a police officer when he makes arrests on Indian land (i.e., without realizing that it is Indian land). His bust may not be legal" (personal communication, Donald Brown, Aug. 13, 1992). In the case of an Indian reservation (on which tribal police may have authority), civil law enforcement agencies are challenged to know where their jurisdiction begins and where it ends. With multijurisdictional agreements that many tribes have signed with local and state officials, civil police officers may have the right to enter reservations to continue business (e.g., a criminal can be apprehended by a civil police officer on a reservation).

It is expected and desired (because it does not always happen) that civil law enforcement agents inform tribal police or tribal authorities when entering a reservation. Going onto reservation land without prior notice and contacting a suspect or witness directly is an insult to the authority of the tribal police (personal communication, Andrew Willie, BIA Law Enforcement, Ponga City, Oklahoma, Aug. 11, 1992). In other words, civil police should see themselves as partners with tribal police. Obviously, in dangerous or emergency situations, time may prevent civil authorities from conferring with the tribal police. Where possible, it is essential that the authority of the reservation be respected. When on the reservation, the police officer must refrain from using abusive language or mannerisms.

Levels of cooperation and attitudes toward civil and tribal law enforcement partnerships differ from area to area. The Sac and Fox Nation (originally from the midwest) is an example of a tribe that initiated a relationship with civil law enforcement resulting in a cooperative approach to law enforcement. The cross-deputization that resulted from the Sac and Fox Nation's efforts enables both sets of officers (i.e., from the tribal and civil police) to make arrests in each other's jurisdiction without being sued. Similarly, certain police departments have gone out of their way to work out relationships with local Indian tribes, Albuquerque, New Mexico being one of them. If there is a will to work cooperatively, police departments and Indian tribal departments can be of tremendous benefit to each other. Initiating this type of effort means, for both Indians and non-Indians, putting aside history and transcending stereotypes.

Police Stops

When Indians are driving large, poorly maintained cars (and especially when there are several Indians in a car together), there is the potential (and in certain locations the reality) that they will be stopped simply because they are perceived as suspicious and because negative stereotypes are operating (personal communication, anonymous Native American officer, police department in Oklahoma). While this phenomenon occurs with other racial and ethnic groups, negative biases against Indians are strong and have persisted for generations. A group of Indians in an old run-down car should not signal anything but what it really is (i.e., a group of friends driving around together). When there is *not* a legitimate reason to stop a car, the next step is for officers to check their stereotypes of who they think a criminal is. Like members of other minority groups, Indians have reported being stopped for no reason, and this obviously adds to their distrust of police.

Peyote

In the early 1990s approximately half of the states in the United States had specific laws exempting the traditional, religious use of peyote by American Indians from those states' drug enforcement laws. In a 1990 freedom of religion case, the

Supreme Court dealt a severe blow to traditional American Indians when the Court ruled that state governments could have greater leeway in outlawing certain religious practices. The ruling involved ritual use of peyote by some American Indians who follow the practices of the Native American Church (NAC). Until that time, the U.S. government allowed for the religious use of peyote among Native Americans based on the Bill of Right's "Free Exercise of Religion" guarantee; in other words, peyote use was generally illegal, except in connection with bonafide American Indian religious rituals.

From a law enforcement perspective, if drugs are illegal, no group should be exempt, and indeed, officers have to uphold the law. From a civil rights perspective, religious freedom applies to all groups and no group should be singled out for disproportionately burdensome treatment. The historical legal/illegal status of peyote is complex. There were many attempts to prohibit the use of peyote on the federal level, and many states passed laws outlawing its use. However, several states modified such prohibitions to allow traditional American Indians to continue using peyote as a sacrament. Moreover, in some states, such as Arizona, anti-peyote laws have been declared unconstitutional by state courts insofar as they burden the religious practice of American Indians. This historic ambiguity on the state level, together with the 1990 ruling on the federal level, causes confusion and resentment on the part of many native Americans. At the time of the completion of this book, Congress was considering legislation preempting state law that would protect numerous Indian ceremonies and ritual practices, including the traditional use of peyote by American Indians in bonafide religious ceremonies (i.e., Native American Free Exercise of Religion Act, 1993). If the bill becomes law, it would legalize the use, purchase, or transportation of peyote for bonafide religious reasons.

The use of peyote outside the Native American Church (NAC) is forbidden and regarded by church members as sacrilegious. If individuals are using peyote under the guise of religion, however, they are breaking the law. Within the NAC, there are very specific rules and rituals pertaining to its sacramental use. Establishing respectful communication with the leaders of the NAC would assist officers in determining whether peyote was being abused in certain circumstances.

Law enforcement officials should understand the importance and place of peyote in the culture from a Native American point of view. This understanding will lead to more effective officer–citizen contact in that the Native American will not be viewed as a simple drug user who is breaking the law. It is not the intent of the authors to recommend a particular course of action with regard to enforcement or lack thereof. If the use of peyote is understood from an Indian perspective, officers will communicate an attitude that shows respect for an ancient ritual which some researchers say dates back to 10,000 years ago. When police officers come in suddenly to a meeting or ceremony where peyote is being used (often along with prayers and drumming) and they *aggressively* make arrests, it will be very difficult to establish trust and rapport with the community. When peyote is an issue, officers must recognize their own ethnocentrism (i.e., unconsciously viewing other cultures or cultural practices as primitive, abnormal, or inferior). Appreciating the fact that cultures are acquired (i.e., they are not passed on through the genes) includes the realization that, "If I had been born in (any other culture), I would be doing things similar to those being done by the majority of other people in the culture." With this attitude in mind, it is easier to remain respectful of differences. Law enforcement personnel working in communities where peyote use is an issue should anticipate the problems that will occur and should discuss it with members of the Indian community.

The federal government has actively tried to suppress and change Native American cultures, from condemning traditional marriage practices as being "loose and barbaric" to condemning Indians "long-time tendency . . . to give too much time to dances, powwows, celebrations, and general festive occasions" (*1992 Report of the Commissioner of Indian Affairs*). The commissioner wrote in 1923: "To correct this practice a letter was widely circulated among the Indians last year . . . that they shorten somewhat the length of these gatherings and omit from them use of harmful drugs [peyote], intoxicants, gambling and degrading ceremonials." This explanation is given to illustrate to people in law enforcement that their peyote arrests symbolize official acts of condemning cultural practices. The banning of peyote was and is seen by Native American groups as a failure of the Bill of Rights to truly guarantee the freedom to practice one's own religion.

What is peyote? "Peyote is a small turnip-shaped, spineless cactus [containing] nine alkaloid substances, part of which, mainly mescaline, are hallucinogenic in nature; that is, they induce dreams or visions. Reactions to peyote seem to vary with the social situation which it is used. In some it may merely cause nausea; believers may experience optic, olfactory and auditory sensations. Under ideal conditions color visions may be experienced and peyote may be 'heard' singing or speaking. The effects wear off within twenty-four hours and leave no ill after effects. Peyote is non-habit forming" (Bahti, 1982).

There have been a variety of uses associated with peyote: (1) as a charm for hunting, (2) as medicine, (3) as an aid to predict weather, (4) as an object to help find things that are lost (the belief being that peyote can reveal the location of the lost object through peyote-induced visions; peyote was even used to help locate the enemy in warfare) and (5) as an object to be carried for protection. People have faith in peyote as a symbol and revere its presence.

The NAC, established in 1918, is linked directly to the formalized use of peyote, although peyote had been used thousands of years before the establishment of the church. The peyote users of the native American church claimed that "The White man had the Bible so that he could learn about God. The Indian was given peyote for the same purpose . . ." (Bahti, 1982). According to some peyote users, the white men read about God, but the Indian talked to him. (Brown, 1992). However, it should be noted that not all Indians who use peyote use it in the same way or have exactly the same beliefs about it. There are different rituals and cultural traditions associated with its use.

Peyote is carried in small bags or pouches and these can be "ruined" if touched. Police officers may need to confiscate peyote, but can do it in a way that will cause the least amount of upset. It is far better to ask the Native American politely to remove the bag in which the peyote is contained rather than forcing it away from him or her.

Medicine Bags

Native Americans from many tribes across the country wear small bags referred to as medicine bags which are considered extremely sacred. The medicine bags do not carry drugs or peyote but symbols from nature (e.g., corn pollen, cedar, sage, bark of a tree) which are believed to have certain powers. Law enforcement officers should handle these (if it becomes necessary) as they would handle any sacred symbol from their own religion. Ripping into the bags would be an act of desecration. The powerful medicine contained in the bags is often blessed and therefore must be treated in a respectful manner.

Trespassing and Sacred Lands

In a number of states, traditional Indian harvest areas or sacred burial and religious sites are now on federal, state, and especially private lands. Indians continue to go to these areas just as their ancestors did to collect resources or to pray. The point of concern with law enforcement is when conflicts occur between the ranchers, farmers, and homeowners on what Indians consider their holy ground. It is frequently how the officer reacts to these allegations of trespassing that determines whether there will be an escalated confrontation (personal communication, Jose Rivera, Sept. 11, 1992). When there is a dispute, the officer could choose an authoritarian method of handling the problem and simply say something aggressive like "You're going to get off this land right now," thereby alienating the citizen. Alternatively, he or she could acknowledge how the Indian must feel having had the land since time immemorial. If the officer is prepared to at least "hear" from an Indian perspective what it is like to have restrictions on what was once one's own land, the person may very well be more supportive of the officer's efforts to resolve the immediate conflict. If there is no immediate resolution, the officer can, at a minimum, prevent an escalation of hostilities.

Since police officers are truly in a situation where they cannot solve this complex and very old problem, the only tool available is the ability to communicate sensitively and listen well. "The officer is put between a rock and a hard place. If the officer is sensitive, he could try to speak to the landowner and describe the situation, although often the landowners don't care about the history [i.e., claiming, 'It's my land now']. However, there have been some people who have been sensitive [to the needs of the Native Americans] and who have worked out agreements" (personal communication, Jose Rivera, Sept. 11, 1992).

In California, Native Americans have initiated their own Indian Gathering Policy Act. When this problem arises in other jurisdictions (i.e., in other states), people might consider contacting the state of California (Assistant Director of Advisory Councils and Concessions, Office of the Director, California State Parks, Sacramento, California) and use its model as a point of negotiation for trying to resolve the conflict. One argument for working out a "win–win" situation is bringing up the perspective that Indians have often demonstrated that the way they harvest the resources while they are "trespassing" is beneficial to those resources in the long run.

Desecration and Looting of Native American Sites

For centuries there has been desecration and looting of Native American relics in the United States. Most often, the looting is done to make a profit on articles found in sites that have Native American artifacts. Native Americans see that there is vandalism on their archeological sites, but often no criminal prosecution.

Even more degrading to Native Americans is the taking of human remains (skulls and bones) from Indian reservations and public lands. Officers in certain parts of the country may enter non-Indian homes and see such remains "displayed" as souvenirs of a trip into Indian country. The Native American Grave Protection and Repatriation Act (NAGPRA) passed by Congress and signed by President Bush resulted as a response to such criminal acts. If an officer sees any human remains, he or she must investigate whether, indeed, foul play might be involved. Officers should contact state agencies established to enforce laws that protect Indian relics (e.g., in California, the Native American Heritage Commissions) to determine how to proceed in such situations.

Fishing

"If you ever want to get into a fight, go into a local bar [e.g., in parts of Washington State] and start talking about fishing rights. The fishing issue is a totally hot issue" (personal communication, Jose Rivera, Sept. 11, 1992).

> The wording of the treaties [i.e., with regard to the fishing rights of Native Americans] is clear and unequivocal in English as well as in the language of the specific tribes concerned. For example, the treaty with Indians of the Northwest regarding fishing rights on the rivers gives these rights to the Indians "for as long as the rivers shall flow." The rivers in the Northwest are still flowing, and the Indians are still struggling with the state of Washington about the state's violations of the treaty's terms, even on Indian property. (Association of Social Workers, 1972)

Indians in the 1990s *continue* to say, "We have treaties with the government allowing us to fish here." Commercial and sports fishermen, on the forefront of trying to prevent Native Americans from exercising their treaty rights, claim that Indians are destroying the industry. For the Indians, this is one way that they can provide sustenance to their families and earn extra money for themselves or their tribes to make it throughout the year. (For 150 years, there has been no industry on many, if not most, of the reservations.) Once again, the officer on the front line will be unable to solve a problem that has been raging for generations. The front-line officer's actions, in part, depend on the sensitivity of the commander who is in charge. Admittedly, the commander is in a difficult position. He or she is between the state fish and game industry and the people trying to enforce federal treaties. Nevertheless, the commander can communicate to officers the need for cultural sensitivity in their way of approaching and communicating with Native Americans. The alternative could be deadly, as has at least one situation illustrated when, in northern California, peace officers with flack jackets and automatic weapons resorted to pursuing Native Americans with shotguns up and down the river (personal communication, Jose Rivera, Sept. 11, 1992).

There are many complex dimensions to cases involving Native Americans "breaking the law" when, at the same time, the federal government is not honoring its treaties with them. Native Americans are frustrated by what they see as blatant violations of their rights. The history of the government's lack of loyalty to its American Indian citizens has caused great pain for this cultural group. Clearly, sensitivity and understanding on the part of the officer are required. The officer has to have patience and tact, remembering that history defines many aspects of the current relationships between law enforcement and American Indians. Being forceful and displaying anger will alienate many Native Americans and will not result in the cooperation needed to solve issues that arise.

SUMMARY OF RECOMMENDATIONS FOR LAW ENFORCEMENT

1. Those who are entrusted with keeping the peace in rural areas, in cities, or on Indian reservations should exhibit respect and professionalism when interacting with peoples who have traditionally been disrespected by governmental authority. It is important to remember that the U.S. government has violated many treaties with Americans Indians and that their basic rights as Americans have repeatedly been denied.

- Understand the initial resistance to your efforts to establish rapport and goodwill and do not take it personally.
- Make an effort to get to know the community in your particular area. Make positive contact with American Indian organizations and individuals. This behavior on your part will be unexpected but appreciated and will result in more cooperation.

2. The younger, more environmentally conscious generation of Americans have adopted much valuable ideology from the culture of America's original peoples.

- Convey a respect for Native American values. They are not alienating or "un-American," and many believe that those very values of preservation are necessary for our environmental survival.

3. Indians have been victims of forced assimilation whereby their languages, religions, and cultures have been suppressed. The negative effects have stayed with generations of Indians.

- The point of contact between a law enforcement professional and an American Indian can often involve issues related to poor adjustment to urban life. While the law must be upheld, consider the conditions that led some Native Americans toward, for example, alcoholism and unemployment. Having empathy for the conditions that lead to a person's circumstance need not make one any less effective in his or her line of duty.

4. Preferred mainstream American ways of communication often run counter to American Indian styles of communication. Keep the following in mind when trying to build rapport with citizens who are Indians:

- Do not take advantage of the American Indian just because he or she may be silent, appear passive, or not be fluent in English.

- Do not interrupt Indian people when they are speaking; it is seen as aggressive and rude.

5.   Many American Indians who favor traditional styles of communication will tend toward:

- Closed behavior and slow rapport-building with strangers. [*This does not mean that the person is aloof or hostile; rather, this can be a cultural trait.*]
- Silent and highly observant behavior. [*This does not mean that the person does not want to cooperate.*]
- Withdrawal if method of questioning is too aggressive. [*Remember to use time, patience, and silence, which will assist you in getting the response you need.*]
- Indirect eye contact for some tribes, but not all. [*Your penetrating or intense eye contact may result in intimidating the person and, consequently, in his or her withdrawal.*]

6.   The terms "chief," "redskin," "buck," "squaw," "braves," and "skins" are offensive when used by a non-Indian [sometimes younger Indians may use some of the terms themselves (e.g., "skins"), but this does not make it acceptable for others to use the terms].

- If you need to refer to the cultural group, ask the person with whom you are in contact whether he or she prefers the term Indian, Native American, or another tribal name. Your sensitivity to these labels can contribute to establishing a good rapport. If asking seems inappropriate, listen carefully to how the individuals refer to each other.

7.   The extended family is close-knit and interdependent among Native American peoples. Keep in mind the following:

- Be respectful and deferential to elders.
- The elders should be asked for their opinion or even advice, where applicable, as they are often major decision makers in the family.
- If there are problems with a child, consider other adults, besides the mother and father, who may also be responsible for child-raising.
- Whenever possible do not separate children from parents. This can bring back memories of times when children were forcibly taken from their parents and sent to Christian mission schools or government boarding schools far from their homes.

8.   With regard to key issues of law enforcement and contact with American Indians, particularly sensitive areas include:

- Use of peyote
- Allegations of trespassing
- Sacred sites violations
- Fishing

These all involve matters in which Indians feel that they have been deprived of their rights: in the case of peyote, the right to religious expression; in the case of trespassing, the right to honor their ancestors (e.g., when visiting burial grounds); and in the case of fishing, the ability to exercise their rights as guaranteed by treaties made with the U.S. government.

9. From an American Indian perspective, many people feel that they are abused by a system of government that is neither honest nor respectful of their culture. Many feel that the government degrades the land upon which all people depend. To a large extent, Indian rights are still ignored because members of the dominant society do not always uphold the laws that were made to protect Indians. This background makes it especially difficult for people in law enforcement vis-à-vis their relationships and interactions with Indians. For this reason, law enforcement officials need to go out of their way to demonstrate that they are fair, given the complexities of history and current law. In addition, chief executives and command staff of police departments have a special responsibility to provide an accurate education to officers on American Indian cultural groups (with an emphasis on government–tribal relations) and to address the special needs and concerns of the Indian peoples.

DISCUSSION QUESTIONS AND ISSUES*

1. *Popular Stereotypes.* What are some commonly held stereotypes of Native Americans? What is your personal experience with Native Americans that might counter these stereotypes? How have people in law enforcement been influenced by popular stereotypes of Native Americans?

2. *Recommendations for Effective Contact.* If you have had contact with Native Americans, what recommendations would you give others regarding effective communication, rapport building, and cultural knowledge that would be beneficial for officers?

3. *The Government's Broken Promises to American Indians.* The famous Lakota chief, Sitting Bull, spoke on behalf of many Indians when he said of white Americans: "They made us many promises . . . but they never kept but one: They promised to take our land, and they took it." There was a time when many acres of land in what we now call the United States were sacred to Native American tribes. Therefore, today many of us are living on, building on, and in some cases, destroying the remains of Indian lands where people's roots run deep. Given this, how would you deal with the problem of an Indian "trespassing" on someone's land when he or she claims to be visiting an ancestral burial ground, for example? What could you say or do so as not to totally alienate the Native American and thereby risk losing trust and cooperation?

4. *Fishing Rights: State Laws and Federal Treaties.* David Sohappy, Sr. was the leader of the effort to restore and protect treaty fishing rights of Columbia River Indians (state of Washington) and has been called the "Martin Luther King" for Indian fishing rights. His lifelong struggle on behalf of Indian fishermen led to the landmark federal court decisions assuring treaty fishermen of the Pacific Northwest the right to harvest up to one-half of the salmon returning to usual and accustomed fishing areas. Sohappy later became the target of a federal and state undercover "sting" operation, called "Salmonscam," in 1981 and 1982 that led to a five-year federal prison sentence for him, his son, and several other Columbia River Indians. Law enforcement agents from Washington and Oregon had spent over 20 years battling David Sohappy and the few remaining traditional Indians whose religion, the Seven Drum religion, claim a special relationship with the land where they

*See Instructor's Manual that accompanies this text for additional activities, role-plays, questionnaires and projects related to the content of this chapter.

were born, and with the salmon, wildlife, roots, and berries placed in their area "by their creator." There were years of bitter disputes throughout the Pacific Northwest when Washington state officials refused to enforce orders of the federal courts, and as a result, the federal government took control of the allocation of fishing opportunities to protect the Native Americans' treaty rights. In 1981, the U.S. State Commission on Civil Rights strongly criticized state officials for failing to protect treaty fishing rights and for falsely blaming Native Americans for salmon shortages in the region. (Letter from the Sohappy Family, Cooks Landing, Washington to "Interested Parties," May 7, 1991; Statement of David Sohappy, Sr. to U.S. Senate Select Committee on Indian Affairs, April 19, 1988)

Question: What are law enforcement agents (whose duty it is to uphold their state laws) supposed to do in situations such as the above whereby the state law is in conflict with a federal law based on treaties with Native Americans signed by the federal government? How can officers who are on the front lines win the respect and cooperation of Native Americans when they are asked to enforce something that goes against the treaty rights of the Indians?

REFERENCES

Association of Social Workers (1972). *Ethnicity and Social Work*, Vol. 17, No. 3, May.

ATTNEAVE, CAROLYN (1982). "American Indians and Alaska native families: emigrants in their own homeland," in *Ethnicity and Family Therapy*, M. McGoldrick et al., eds., Guilford Press, New York.

BAHTI, TOM (1982). *Southwestern Indian Ceremonials*, KC Publications, Las Vegas, Nev.

BROWN, DONALD (ed.) (1992). *Crossroads Oklahoma: The Ethnic Experience in Oklahoma*, Crossroads Oklahoma Project, Stillwater, Okla.

Committee on Cultural Psychiatry, Group for the Advancement of Psychiatry (1989). *Suicide and Ethnicity on the United States*, Brunner/Mazel, New York.

FORBES, JACK (1982). *Native Americans of California and Nevada*, Naturegraph Publishers, Happy Camp, Calif.

HARRIS, PHILIP R. AND ROBERT T. MORAN (1991). *Managing Cultural Differences: High Performance Strategies for a New World of Business*, Gulf Publishing Company, Houston.

LOCKLEAR, HERBERT H. (1972). "American Indian myths," in Special Issue on Ethnicity and Social Work, *Journal of the National Association of Social Workers*, Vol. 17, No. 3, May.

MEHL, LEWIS (1990). "Creativity and madness," presentation held in Santa Fe, New Mexico, sponsored by the American Institute of Medical Education.

OGAWA, BRIAN (1990). *Color of Justice: Culturally Sensitive Treatment of Minority Crime Victims*, Office of the Governor, State of California, Office of Criminal Justice Planning, Sacramento, Calif.

REDHORSE, J., A. SHATTUCK, AND F. HOFFMAN (eds.) (1981). *The American Indian Family: Strengths and Stresses*, American Indian Research and Development and Associates, Isleta, N. Mex.

PART FOUR

Response Strategies to Crimes Motivated by Hate/Bias

Part Four is a detailed explanation of strategies for preventing, controlling, reporting, tracking, and investigating crimes that are based on hate or bias because of the victim's race, ethnicity, religion, or sexual orientation. Criminal cases of these types have come to be known as "bias" or "hate crimes"; noncriminal cases are referred to as "incidents." Some agencies refer to these acts as civil rights violations. The chapters that follow contain policies, practices, and procedures for responding to these types of crimes or incidents. It is recognized that others, such as women, the elderly, and the disabled are sometimes victimized. However, in this book we only focus on hate crimes and incidents wherein the motivation was related to the aforementioned categories. The recommended policies, training, practices, and procedures outlined are currently in operation or are being adopted by many law enforcement agencies across the nation. Many of the policies and procedures are based on studies and recommendations by the U.S. Department of Justice, Community Relations Service. Another major source of materials has been the Commission on Peace Officer Standards and Training found in all states of the nation.

Statistical data useful in analyzing trends of hate violence have regretfully been lacking except in a very few states and in some progressive departments. Contained in Part Four are methods used to collect data on such crimes and/or incidents.

The following three chapters provide a framework for peace officers, students, and law enforcement agencies that want to develop sensitive and workable programs for handling these crimes and incidents in the community and in the law enforcement workplace. The type of policing/peacekeeping reviewed in this unit is a civilizing process that will contribute to multicultural coexistence and cooperation. All law enforcement professionals must have a good working knowledge of all the guidelines that follow.

The following appendicies correspond to the chapters in Part Four:

11

HATE/BIAS CRIMES:

Insights and Response Strategies

OVERVIEW

This chapter focuses on the hate/bias crime problem. First, the scope of the problem is discussed, including historical perspectives and examples. It is stressed that the law enforcement professional must have an awareness of the discrimination experienced by immigrants, persons of various ethnic, racial, and religious backgrounds, and persons of different sexual orientation. This chapter provides some brief insights on past and present experiences of certain groups, emphasizing anti-Semitism and homophobia. The chapter highlights the need for hate violence to be treated with the same concern as heinous crimes such as rape and sexual assault. It presents information on special statutes that provide for increased penalties for the perpetrator and specific response strategies within the criminal justice system. Also included are model hate/bias crimes response and management strategies and policies. Future trends are discussed which provide the law enforcement practitioner with what can be expected if society does not establish control of this insidious problem. The chapter considers the need for the community (religious institutions, schools, public agencies and private organizations, and neighborhood residents) to deal with the problem cooperatively as that this is not solely a law enforcement issue.

COMMENTARY

Violence motivated by racial, religious, ethnic, or sexual orientation hatred has existed for generations in the United States and all over the world and, increasingly, it seems to be on the rise:

National Institute against Prejudice Violence, *Forum,* Vol. 6, No. 1, Mar. 1992.

The institute estimates that a full 10 percent of the U.S. population is annually victimized by some form of ethnoviolence. That translates to more than 25 million victims [1991] year!

"Resurgence of racist violence: stimulus to anti-racist action," by Anne Braden, *Engage Social Action,* Vol. 15, No. 6, June 1987, p. 34.

"The most important development in 1987 is that large sections of the public are finally aware of the resurgence of racism and racist violence that has been occurring for at least the past decade in the United States."

"The cult of ethnicity, good and bad," by Arthur Schlesinger Jr., *Time,* July 8, 1991.

"But what happens when people of different origins, speaking different languages and professing different religions, inhabit the same locality and live under the same political sovereignty? *Ethnic and racial conflict*—far more than ideological conflict—*is the explosive problem of our times.* [emphasis added]

HISTORICAL PERSPECTIVES

As civilization and technology have progressed, it does not appear that human behavior toward other members of the human family has improved. Since the beginning of time people have gathered into tribes or groups with those of similar color, speech, and background for reasons of safety and commonality. Since that beginning, groups of people have been suspicious of others different from themselves. From such suspicions and discomfort about the new neighbor, conflict, crimes, and even killings occurred between the existing majority and the new minority "interlopers" and involved the old territorial imperative to protect oneself from the alien.

However, as civilization progressed, intermingling resulted in diverse mixtures of people in many countries. In the last decade, with advances in communications and transportation, there began cross-border migration of ideas, travelers, and even settlements. Locals became less ethnocentric and afraid of new arrivals, and thought more in terms of the human family. But suddenly in the process of creating a world culture and a "global village" mindset, the world witnessed the breakup of superpowers and even nation-states. The movement was then toward more local autonomy and separatism, often along the lines of ethnicity and religious fundamentalism—so Canada split into conflict between its Anglo and French citizens, the Soviet Union crumbled and broke into contending republics, former Central European satellite countries squabbled over borders and ancient rivalries flared, and Germany broke down the Berlin Wall in 1989 but experienced violence between neo-Nazis and those not in favor of their racist politics and actions. In Yugoslavia, this ethnocentricism and reversion to tribalism ended in civil wars among the former states with Serbs, Croats, and Bosnians, as well as Christians and Muslims engaged in wholesale slaughter of one another. By the end of 1992, 14,000 people had died in the former Yugoslavia, where so-called "ethnic cleansing" took pace to oust members of other ethnic groups from targeted areas. Street violence erupted in London in 1993 as riot police fought to keep more than 15,000 antiracism marchers away from an office of a racist political party that advocates expelling immigrants and Jews from England. What is important in terms of worldwide law enforcement is that its practitioners have some perspective on both the global and local situation when it comes to hatred and bias toward one another. Reality dictates that "peacekeepers" must be trained to counteract hate crimes and violence, as well as learn to cope with their inhumane impact.

Global Perspectives

Many ancient animosities that peoples have toward each other in Asia, Latin America, and Europe are brought with them when they relocate in North America. Instead of newcomers acculturating to their new opportunities and moving beyond past cultural biases and old country hatreds, the criminal behavior often simply gets transplanted. One sees this when Armenians, Turks, and Greeks in the United States keep alive ancient dislikes and distrusts, or when Chinese try to reestablish their tongs here. Thus, in the United States, the so-called "melting pot," society struggles not only with inhumanity toward new immigrants, but also with the imported hatreds and racism of those new immigrants. Elie Wiesel, Nobel Peace Prize winner, in a February 1992 interview at a Peace Prize Forum, said racism, fanaticism, and anti-Semitism are on the rise in many nations. They are certainly not unique to the United States.

A world conference assembled in 1992 by an international relief group based in Brussels, "Doctors without Borders," identified 11 minorities and nationalities it considered most threatened by the ultimate in racism—warfare and extreme oppression. In most cases the warfare and oppression was related to long-standing hatred due to religious and/or cultural differences among inhabitants of the crisis areas. The list included (*Contra Costa Times*, Nov. 23, 1992, p. B-4):

- **Muslims** in Bosnia-Herzegovina (former Yugoslav republics), where Serb and Croat forces were involved in ethnic purges or "cleansings" of this population. At least 24,000 from all ethnic groups had died in fighting.
- **Kurds** in northern Iraq, eastern Turkey, parts of Iran, Syria, and the Soviet Union. The Iraqi government has been involved in the organized "disappearance" of 180,000 Iraqi Kurds, and 4000 Kurdish villages were razed.
- **Rohingyas,** a Muslim group in Burma persecuted by the military government. In early 1992, 300,000 Rohingyas fled to neighboring Bangladesh.

The list did not include the Hindu–Muslim riots that broke out in Ayodhya, India, in December 1992 over a 430-year-old Muslim mosque. Rioters wielding hatchets, light bulbs filled with acid, and homemade bombs rampaged throughout India for days, creating war zones in areas where Hindus and Muslims lived in close proximity to each other. In New Delhi, India, the capital and a city of 12 million: "'The fires are everywhere,' said N. K. Batura, one of dozens of firefighters battling blazes that roared on almost every block around a burning timber market. 'All over. Can't count them. We put one out, they light another.' So far, at least 1,050 people have died in the riots, and the vast nation has divided on class, caste and religious lines over the challenge of maintaining a secular state in a country where Hindus (82 percent of population) far outnumber Muslims" (*Los Angeles Times,* Dec. 12, 1992, p. A-5). The importance of local law enforcement monitoring such world events is discussed in Chapter 12.

THE HATE/BIAS CRIME PROBLEM

The U.S. Attorney General's Commission on Racial, Ethnic, Religious, and Minority Violence (1986) has adopted a comprehensive definition of a hate/bias crime:

> "any act of intimidation, harassment, physical force or threat of physical force directed against any person, or family, or their property or advocate, motivated either in whole or in part, by hostility to their real or perceived race, ethnic background, national origin, religious belief, sex, age, disability, or sexual orientation, with the intention of causing fear or intimidation, or to deter the free exercise or enjoyment of any rights or privileges secured by the Constitution or the laws of the United States or of the State of California whether or not performed under the color of law."

Victims of hate/bias crime are particularly sensitive and unsettled because they feel powerless to alter the situation. That is, they cannot change their racial, ethnic, or religious background. Furthermore, the person is not the only victim, as often an entire group of citizens is affected due to fear. A physical attack on a person because of race, religion, ethnic background, or sexual orientation is a particularly insidious form of violent behavior. Verbal assaults on persons because of others' perceptions of their "differences" are equally distressing to both the victim and society. Often, the criminal justice system, especially local law enforcement agencies, become the focus of criticism if the attacks are not investigated, resolved, and prosecuted promptly and effectively. A hate/bias crime can send shock waves through a minority community at which the act was aimed. These acts create danger, frustration, concern, and anxiety in our communities.

Crimes and acts of hate serve as frightening reminders to minority citizens that their neighborhoods, streets, workplaces, and even their homes may not be safe. And unfortunately, these kinds of incidents can also occur in the law enforcement workplace among co-workers. Treating such occurrences seriously in law enforcement sends a message to the community that the local police agency will protect them. Doing the same within the law enforcement organization sends a vitally important message to all employees.

Despite the abundance of rhetoric deploring acts of bigotry and hate violence, few communities have utilized a holistic approach to the problem. Typically, efforts to prevent and respond to such crimes by local agencies have not been coordinated. Indeed, there are many effective programs that deal with a particular aspect of bigotry or hate in a specific setting. There are, however, few models for weaving efforts to prevent hate violence into the fabric of the community.

Community awareness of hate violence is growing rapidly in the United States. In the last few years, California, Maryland, and New York have commissioned special task forces to recommend ways to control such violence, and new legislation has been passed in a number of states. The timing for developing a model community approach to reduce hate violence has never been more apparent.

Crimes motivated by hate in the United States have occurred for generations; however, an unprecedented upward spiral began in the 1990s. Whether or not there was an actual increase or simply documentation is not known. In either case, the figures are disconcerting:

- Anti-Semitic incidents reached a 12-year high of 1685 (1990) (Anti-Defamation League, 1991).
- Gay–lesbian hate-related incidents rose 42 percent in the six major U.S. cities of New York, San Francisco, Los Angeles, Boston, Minneapolis, and Chicago (1990) (National Gay and Lesbian Task Force, 1991).
- The thirteenth annual County Human Relations Commission (Los Angeles) hate crimes report documented a record 736 incidents in 1992, up 11 percent from 1991. African Americans and gay men were the top two targets of hate crimes (*Los Angeles Times,* Mar. 23, 1993, p. B-1).

Hate crimes are one of the most extreme and dangerous manifestations of racism to which America has never been immune. The violence that erupted April 30, 1992, particularly in Los Angeles following the verdict in the trial of the four Los Angeles police officers in the Rodney King incident, was said by some to have been a reaction to increasing racism in America. The law enforcement professional, which includes the neighborhood police officer (the best source of intelligence information), must be aware of the scope of the hate/bias crime problem from both historical and contemporary perspectives.

The U.S. Commission on Civil Rights, (1990) identified several factors that contribute to racial intimidation and violence, including:

- Racial integration of neighborhoods, leading to "move-in violence" (explained later in the chapter)
- Deep-seated racial hatred played upon by organized hate groups
- Economic competition among racial and ethnic groups
- Insensitive media coverage of minority groups
- Poor police response to hate crimes

According to another study entitled "When Hate Comes to Town: Preventing and Intervening in Community Hate Crime" (Corporate, 1989), hate violence can be attributed to:

- A growing pattern of economic prejudice built on the stereotype that minorities are making economic gains that threaten the economic and social well-being of whites
- The unprecedented numbers of Latin American and Asian immigrants have drastically changed many neighborhoods that are unprepared for the social, economic, political, and criminal justice system consequences of multicultural living
- The higher visibility of gay men, often identified as "easy targets" who are unable to fight back, combined with the increasing national fear about AIDS
- The increasing lack of social preparedness of most young people when plunged into a multicultural school environment

Other factors contributing to social unrest in America have been the sudden, massive immigrations of both legal and illegal refugees from violence/political systems from Cuba, Haiti, Salvador, Vietnam, and Eastern Europe. In times of depressed economies and widespread unemployment in the United States, these masses have not been greeted with open arms, and their arrival certainly contributed to conflict and violence in many communities. Racism toward Latinos based on skin color and language is also based on perceptions that they take jobs and other benefits from those with whom they compete for needs. The experiences of the various peoples who came to America and became the victims of hate/bias crimes are presented in Chapters 6 to 10. In the following two sections of this chapter, we treat anti-Semitism and gay and lesbian victimization separately, as crimes against these groups constitute a large percentage of hate crimes overall. Chapters 6 to 10 covered cultural specific material on ethnic, cultural, and racial groups and included specific information on hate/bias incidents towards those groups.

Scope of the Problem Nationally

The psychocultural origin of hate crimes stems from human nature itself. To hate means to dislike passionately or intensely—to have an extreme aversion or hostility toward another person, idea, or object. Hate can have its normal manifestation, such as when one hates evil, or bad weather, or certain foods; or its abnormal expression when it becomes obsessive or when wrongly directed at someone who has done no harm. People can be culturally conditioned to hate those who are different from them—because of their place of origin, their looks, beliefs, or preferences. As the song in the musical "South Pacific" reminds us, "we have to be taught to hate and fear. We have to be taught from year to year. . . ."

An Associated Press release (1990) suggests the scope of the problem in this country:

- **Louisiana:** "Candidate cites racial hatred: The first black ever to make a runoff for mayor in Shreveport, Louisiana received anonymous calls threatening to kill him or his wife unless he dropped out of the race. Some callers identified themselves as Ku Klux Klan members."
- **California:** "Residents call for firing of racist-message cops: Outraged residents of Alameda want city to fire four white police officers who used mobile computer terminals to send racist messages while on patrol. The messages were derogatory references to blacks and jokes about dressing as the KKK."
- **New York:** "Racial violence flares up again in Brooklyn area: Racial violence flared for a third day in a Brooklyn neighborhood where blacks and ultra-Orthodox Hasidic Jews have a history of uncomfortable co-existence. It resulted in over three days of clashes between hundreds of blacks and Jews resulting in deaths, injuries, and significant property damage to stores and police vehicles. 61 arrests; 84 officers injured; 3 persons killed and 25 civilians hurt."
- **Indiana:** "Violence against homosexuals seems to be escalating in numbers and degrees: 5 gay men strangled this year. Police say the same person may be responsible for as many as 11 such murders."
- **Texas:** "McAllen, Texas: 5 gay men slain in a four-month period."
- **Washington D.C.:** "43 Protesters Cited as Clansmen March: Washington D.C.—about 30 Ku Klux Klan members marched through the Nation's capital . . . with about 4,000

police . . . on hand to keep the marchers and counter demonstrators separated . . . seven officers were hospitalized in disputes with counter demonstrators."

- **California:** "Slaying linked to Black–Korean racial tensions: Los Angeles—A Korean merchant slain by a black robber became the sixth victim this year of deadly blacks–Korean clashes that are increasing. . . ."

Tracking hate crimes, which have typically been underreported, did not begin in earnest until the 1990s.

BACKGROUND: URBAN DYNAMICS

The relationship between the clustering of new immigrant groups, the economy, hate/bias incidents, and violence in cities are well documented. It is important that the reader understand that hate incidents often do not occur in a vacuum but are rather part of a larger social and economic interchange.

Clustering and Target Zone Theory

Studies have shown that initially, new immigrants tend to locate or "cluster" where people of their own ethnic and racial background are already established. They tend to congregate in the same areas of the country or within the city to be near relatives or friends; to have assistance in finding housing, jobs, and in coping with language barriers; to find security of a familiar religion and social institutions. One study on new immigrant grouping was completed by Steven Wallace for the University of California, San Francisco. He stated that, generally:

> for the first generation or two, ethnic communities are helpful because they provide a sense of continuity for immigrants while easing subsequent generations into American values and society. . . . The existence of an ethnic or immigrant community is obvious evidence that a group has not assimilated. A community represents a place where immigrants are able to associate with others like themselves. An immigrant community provides a safe place to engage in these activities that deviate from dominant norms such as speaking a language other than English, honoring "foreign" symbols of pride, and exhibiting other non-Anglo behavior. Commonly located in low-rent districts, ethnic communities are functionally found where members can afford to live while they work at low wage jobs. (Wallace, 1987)

Wallace indicates that the rewards of better education and jobs come with assimilation into mainstream society. Further, that in ethnic communities, wealthier immigrants are just temporary inhabitants as they branch out and assimilate into society becoming more like Americans and gaining economic and educational advantages. When national demographic figures are compared with previous censuses, one sees that many immigrants leave the inner city for the suburbs. However, Wallace, now on staff at the University of California, Los Angeles, indicates that while some immigrant groups do move into the suburbs and assimilate, there are:

> other groups, such as blacks, having the same value structure and ideas as the dominant group (whites), yet have been kept segregated historically. There is a growing concern among policy analysts that this group of inner-city blacks (and some Latinos as well) is unable to work their way out of the inner-cities in the ways that earlier immigrants have. In part this is because of the loss of well-paying, low skilled

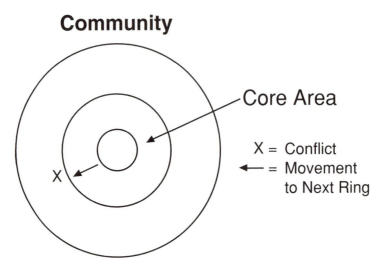

Community

Core Area

X = Conflict
⟵ = Movement
to Next Ring

X

Exhibit 11.1
Source: California Peace Officer Standards and Training Command College Independent Study:
A Model Plan for California Cities Experiencing Multicultural Impact by Robert Shusta, 1987.

jobs located in the inner cities (especially smoke-stack industries like autos, steel, etc.). (Personal communication, Steve Wallace, Nov. 9, 1992)

Ron Martinelli (a criminologist and former San Jose, California police officer) discusses a theory called *target zoning,* or as termed by sociologists the *concentric zone theory,* shown in Exhibit 11.1

This model of urban ecology explains in simple terms what takes place when new ethnic minorities settle in an existing core area ("inner city") that is often already economically depressed. These core areas are, typically, where lower-socioeconomic-class whites, blacks, Hispanics, and/or established immigrants have settled because housing is cheap (or government-subsidized), employment or welfare services are available, and there is some degree of comfort when living with people of one's own race or culture. (These areas are often impoverished ghettos, with substandard, older housing, and are frequently overcrowded with high incidents of social conflict and crime, including drug and gang activity.)

As the new minority/ethnic immigrants move into the core area, they come into conflict with existing members of that community—a phenomenon that has been going on for generations.

The newcomer and the established community member compete for housing, jobs, financial resources (welfare, food stamps, etc.), and education. When there is a collapse of affordable health services, lack of affordable housing, and reductions in benefits (cuts in social programs by federal and state authorities), as occurred in the 1990s, conflict intensifies between racial and ethnic groups. These circumstances magnify, and incidents of discrimination, bias, and hate violence increase (Shusta, 1987). Those established want to move out, not just to improve their lot, but to escape the conflict. Thus they move to the next ring out in the concentric circles. The whole process is then repeated as those in the next circle move to outer circles. The result in many cases is "move-in violence," discussed later in this chapter.

The concentric zone theory, while it works well to describe some cities, does not describe others. For example, in the past 20 years, "urban renewal" has further complicated the theory where inner city slums have been flattened and expensive condos, shopping centers, or civic center projects have been built in their places. Thus one sees a small but important return from the suburbs to areas to which the concentric zone theory would predict only poor immigrants would move. For example, the south central area of Los Angeles, which is thought of as poor black, is actually now half Latino immigrant. This area of comparatively low-cost housing is where most recent immigrants settled. On the other hand, Iranian immigrants, who are mostly business people and professionals, are heavily concentrated in west Los Angeles, which is an expensive housing market. Many from Hong Kong who have moderate means are settling in Monterey Park, a middle-class community that is now heavily Chinese.

The Economy and Hate Violence

Poor economic times contribute greatly to have violence (personal communication, Dennis Wynn, Justice Department, Community Relations Unit, Oct. 1987). In many areas of the country, when major industries such as steel and auto manufacturing have had downturns, go out of business, or relocate, the likelihood of economic distress among the low and unskilled increases. Scapegoating and blaming often results when blue-collar jobs are unavailable. The distress that accompanies unemployment and rising prices is often directed toward immigrants and minorities and manifests itself in harassment and violence. There seems to be a childlike tendency that exists within some people wherein they must blame others for their own misfortune or society's failings. New York City experienced an increase of 19 percent in reported hate crimes in 1988 (personal communication, New York City Police Department, Bias Investigation Unit, 1989) after a recession hit the region following the stock market crash of 1987 (*New York Newsday,* Jan. 14, 1991, p. 39). In 1990, the Massachusetts unemployment rate had risen to a level of 8.6 percent, one of the highest rates in the nation (*USA Today,* Mar. 11, 1991, p. B-4). For the same year, the Boston police reported 273 bias crimes, which was up from 202 the previous year (personal communication, Boston Police Department, Community Disorder Unit). In 1988, when the state's unemployment rate was 3.3 percent (*World Almanac and Book of Facts,* 1988), the city reported only 152 bias crimes. Los Angeles County reported an increase of 45 percent in bias crimes in 1990 after a nationwide recession caused unemployment in the state to jump up to 7 percent, from under 6 percent one year earlier. Thus the frequency and intensity of such acts are shown to increase when the economy deteriorates.

Sociologists indicate that hate frequently stems from being deprived or having one's needs unsatisfied—so the poor can despise the rich, the uneducated ridicule the intellectual, the poor envy the affluent, and the established ghetto inhabitant can hate the new immigrant/refugee who moves into the area. Social scientists argue that the government definition of poverty does not measure the real depths or the changes taking place in inner cities (i.e., that, not only have the number of ghetto poor increased but the severity of economic deprivation among them has risen as well). Ghetto poverty and concentrations of large numbers of a diverse population in one area often lead to conflict in those neighborhoods. The stresses of urban life, especially in inner cities, gives rise to increased incidents of violence, especially in depressed conditions and reduced space.

Move-in Violence

In 1987, Wallace Warfield, then director of the U.S. Department of Justice's Community Relations Service (CRS), reported that no less than 40 percent of the bias incidents reported to the CRS were cases of move-in violence. The New York State Governor's Task Force on Bias Related Violence (1988) issued the following finding: "Attempts to deprive minorities of equal access to housing through harassment, intimidation, threats, vandalism, arson, and other acts of violence persist and have intensified. This is true 20 years after the enactment of the Federal Fair Housing Act and the extension of the New York State Human Rights Law to non-public housing more that 25 years ago."

These same findings have been discovered in most states. The same New York State report concluded: "Young people in communities with exclusionary housing patterns often view themselves as guardians of the invisible walls that mark their community, and actively seek to drive away 'intruders' who are 'invading' their turf'." (The subject of gangs and turf wars is beyond the scope of this book.)

Move-in violence typically occurs when minorities or immigrants have sought housing in previously all-white suburbs or neighborhoods. Crimes directed at them range from threats and vandalism to arson and fire bombings. In most cases, racist whites attack their victims out of a desire to preserve racial segregation in their communities. Pat Clark, director of the Klanwatch Project and a leading expert on integration-generated violence, observed: "Of all the incidents of hate violence . . . the terrorism of minorities in white communities is probably the most common and the most devastating" *New York Times*, Apr. 28, 1990, p. 1).

New immigrants, especially if they look, act, and/or talk differently from the established community into which they move, regardless of whether that neighborhood is black, brown, or white, will probably meet with some resentment, biased treatment, and/or victimization. This is as true today as it has been over the past few centuries. Researchers and hate/bias enforcement officials have found that neighborhood integration, competition for jobs and services, and issues involving "turf" are the primary scenario for hate crimes (McDevitt, 1989; Southern Poverty Law Center, 1987). Social scientists and scholars from other disciplines have referred to "turf" as "the territorial imperative." This human drive describes how, since time began, all creatures seek to protect what they believe is their own (i.e., land, area, or family). When a relatively homogeneous group feels threatened by invasion of "others," be they refugees, job seekers, or immigrants looking for a better way of life, the human tendency has been suspicion, hostility, and even violence toward the "stranger."

Jack McDevitt of Northeastern University's Center for Applied Social Research, also found that over a five-year period, the majority of confirmed bias crime cases in Boston had to do with the victim being in a neighborhood where he or she "did not belong." The territorial imperative (this is my turf) dictates the violent actions of those with deep-seated prejudices of xenophobia (i.e., fear of strangers). However, no one group has a monopoly on hate crimes—perpetrators of such offenses come from all racial, ethnic and religious backgrounds.

Philadelphia Police Department conflict prevention and resolution team. The city of Philadelphia tested a way to prevent move-in violence in 1986 by utilizing a newly created police unit called the Conflict Prevention and Resolution Team (CPR). The unit has trained officers to investigate and prevent racial incidents. Their goal is to maintain a proactive posture in the enforcement of Pennsylvania's "Ethnic Intimidation Statute" (a law that deals with hate crimes). One of the more successful proactive programs undertaken by this unit is the Pre-Move Survey. The program involves officers of CPR performing a door-to-door canvas in the neighborhood to communicate with the "majority" population prior to a "minority" family assuming residence.

The program is predicated on the premise that potential conflict can be averted when persons residing in that community see that the police are interested in the welfare and rights of new neighbors. The survey gauges the sentiment of the established residents toward the ethnic or racial group in question. It also alerts the local police district hierarchy of the potential for trouble in a given location. This proactive approach serves notice to potential antagonists that the police department and city government are aware of the situation and will not tolerate any criminality perpetrated against the new neighbors. The sources of information about a pending minority move-in to a neighborhood whose backgrounds are ethnically or racially different are the Human Relations Commission, realtors, social service agencies, politicians, public servants, and other police officers. Certainly, many neighborhoods have been integrated without the unit's assistance and without incident. The Philadelphia Police Department is proud of the fact, however, that whenever the CPR unit has performed this procedure prior to the "move-in," there has not been an ethnically motivated criminal act perpetrated against the new neighbors. Philadelphia police officials do not claim that racial relations are significantly better because of the CPR unit, but they feel that their outreach approach has contributed to the reduction of racial violence in their city. (*Philadelphia Inquirer–Metropolitan,* June 14, 1987, p. A-3). The department has printed pocket guide cards to assist patrol officers and supervisors in explaining the ethnic intimidation laws to neighborhood residents. They have also produced and displayed multilingual posters within the community, explaining CPR's functions and responsibilities.

OTHER GROUP VICTIMS OF HATE CRIMES

Jews and Anti-Semitism

Jews belong to a religious and cultural group, although they have sometimes been incorrectly labeled as constituting a separate racial group. Jews have experienced discrimination, persecution, and violence throughout history because their religious beliefs and practices set them apart from the majority. Even where they have been totally "assimilated" (i.e., integrated into society, as was true in Germany early in the twentieth century), they were still not accepted as full citizens and eventually experienced the ultimate hate crime—genocide. The term *anti-Semitism* means "against Semites," which literally includes Jews and Arabs. Popular use of this term, however, refers to anti-Jewish sentiment.

European anti-Semitism had religious origins: Jews did not accept Jesus Christ as the son of God and were considered betrayers and even killers of Christ. This accusation gave rise to religious anti-Semitism and what others saw as justification for anti-Jewish acts. In the last three decades, there have been great strides by religious leaders to eliminate centuries of prejudice. This includes the 1965 Roman Catholic decree (the "Nastra Aetate"), which called for not holding Jews responsible for the death of Christ. The decree, written by the Second Vatican Council under the Pope, encouraged people to abandon the continual blaming of Jews and instead, work for stronger links between the religions and increase understanding. Despite some progress in ecumenical relations, there are still individuals who, 2000 years after Christ, believe that Jews today are responsible for his death.

Of more recent origin is another type of anti-Semitism which falls under what some would label as anti-Zionism (i.e., against the establishment of the state of Israel as a homeland for Jews). Although politically oriented, this type of anti-Semitism still makes references to "the Jews" and equates "Jews" with the suppression of the Palestinian people. Finally, racially based anti-Semitism originated in nineteenth-century pre-Nazi ideology, which claimed that Jews were an inferior race. In their attempts to eliminate the Jewish "race," the Nazis considered people as "unpure" if they had one grandparent or even great-grandparent in their family who was Jewish. Anti-Semitism is ancient in roots and worldwide in scope with religious, political, and racial origins.

Anti-Semitic groups and individuals.   Several different types of groups in the United States have exhibited anti-Semitic attitudes and a number of the more extreme groups have committed hate crimes against Jews. The most glaringly anti-Semitic organizations are white supremacist groups, such as the Ku Klux Klan (KKK), the Aryan Nations, White Aryan Resistance (WAR), the Order, the Posse Comitatus, the Covenant and the Sword, the Arm of the Lord, and neo-Nazi skinheads (discussed further in Chapter 13). These groups tend to hate all "others," but focus a great deal of attention on blacks and Jews. In addition, those who are vehemently pro-Arab and anti-Israel may exhibit strong anti-Jewish attitudes; however, it is not common for anti-Zionist attitudes to result in acts of violence against Jews in the United States (there have been terrorist acts against Jews in Europe). Some "Messianic" individuals who believe that "Armageddon" (the end of the world) is imminent have been known to threaten Jews verbally (by phone or mail), but rarely have these threats been actualized. These people believe that Jews need to repent and see themselves as instruments of God, connected to the coming of the end of the world. Additionally, Jewish Americans, like Arab Americans, can become targets during Middle Eastern crises, such as the Gulf War or after a terrorist attack takes place.

Finally, in times of recession, Jews are often blamed for the economic decline, and the notion of Jewish "influence" provides a convenient scapegoat (i.e., it is said that the Jews control the media, the banks, and even the world economy!). It is not within the scope of this section to delve into these myths but merely to point out that there is widespread harmful misinformation about Jews that anti-Semites continue to spread.

Jewish community concerns.   According to the Anti-Defamation League's (ADL) annual audit of anti-Semitic incidents, there has been a marked increase in anti-Semitic expressions and acts across the country since the late 1980s and into the 1990s. It is unclear whether there has been an actual increase or whether law enforcement officials, responding to hate crimes legislation, have simply tracked and investigated these incidents more effectively. In either case, those who lived through the Holocaust in Nazi Europe (in which 6 million Jews perished) may be more acutely sensitive to anti-Semitism, either real or perceived. On the other hand, younger families who may only have a distant connection to the Holocaust (i.e., none of their immediate family members died), still have concerns about their personal safety. Riva Gambert, associate director of the Jewish Community Relations Council (JCRC) of the Greater East Bay (California) noted that during the Gulf crisis in 1991, many Jewish parents who had children enrolled in Jewish schools were afraid that the Jewish institutions (i.e., Jewish community centers, Hebrew schools, and synagogues) would be attacked and, consequently, requested extra security precautions. Police officers must understand that different segments of the Jewish community feel vulnerable to anti-Semitism and, therefore, are advised to listen to and take seriously Jews' expressions of concern and fear.

Around the holiest days of the Jewish year (Rosh Hashanah and Yom Kippur, occurring in the early fall), there can also be heightened anxiety among some community members regarding security. Indeed, many synagogues hire extra security during times of worship over this 10-day holiday period. Acts of defilement can occur in synagogues and other Jewish institutions at random times as well. Community members affiliated with Jewish institutions have reported various acts of intolerance toward Jews, including swastikas painted on the doors or windows, bacon wrapped around the doorknobs (religious Jews do not eat pork products), hate mail, and bombs left next to Jewish institutions. In the fall of 1993, prior to the Jewish new year holiday period, a dead cat was left on the porch of a synagogue with a card attached, allegedly signed by the KKK. Such defilement and manifestations of prejudice bring back painful memories for Jews who experienced violent expressions of anti-Semitism in other countries; some of the memories and fears have been passed on to subsequent generations. At the same time, some people may overreact to an insensitive remark that stems from ignorance on the part of the speaker rather then malicious anti-Semitism. Some people may not understand that a swastika painted by teenagers on a building does *not necessarily* precede any acts of anti-Jewish violence. Yet a swastika almost always evokes a fearful reaction among many Jewish community members because of the past. The police officer needs to listen to and not dismiss these concerns as exaggerated hysteria. At the same time, he or she needs to explain to citizens that sometimes acts of vandalism are isolated and are not targeted at any group in particular (e.g., many skinheads or "thugs" are unhappy with their lot in life and tend to hate everyone). Finally, the officer who takes reports from citizens should reassure them that their local law enforcement agency views hate crimes and incidents seriously and that should the need arise, extra protection will be provided.

What law enforcement can do. By discussing concerns and fears of some Jewish community members, we do not imply that all Jewish citizens are overly concerned for their safety. In fact, a large percentage of American Jews do not even identify as Jews and do not share a collective or community consciousness with other Jews. At the other extreme are people who interpret events or remarks as anti-Semitic rather than as ignorance or insensitivity. Whatever the case, police officers should be aware that anti-Semitism has a long and active history and, even if some fears are exaggerated, they are still grounded in reality.

There are steps that officers can take to establish rapport and provide protection in Jewish communities when the need arises.

1. When an officer hears of an act that can be classified as a hate crime toward Jews, it should be investigated, tracked, and dealt with as such. Dismissing acts of anti-Semitism as petty crime will result in a lack of trust on the part of the community.

2. When hate crimes and incidents occur to other groups in the community (e.g., to gay, African American, Asian American groups), alert Jewish community leaders immediately. Their institutions may be the next targets.

3. Be aware of groups and individuals who distribute hate literature on people's doorsteps. Publications such as "Racial Loyalty," for example, target Jews and "people of color" and accuse Jews of poisoning the population. A book by the same publisher, entitled *On the Brink of a Bloody Racial War* has been left on many Jews' doorsteps. Even if no violence occurs, the recipients of such hate literature become very fearful.

4. In cooperation with local organizations (JCRC, ADL, etc.), provide information (through joint meetings) on ways that community individuals can heighten security of Jewish institutions (e.g., information on nonbreakable glass, lighting of facilities in evenings, etc.).

5. Be familiar with the dates of the Jewish calendar, especially when the High Holidays (Rosh Hashanah and Yom Kippur) occur. Some people are concerned about safety and protection during events at which large groups of Jews congregate.

6. Finally, contact a Jewish umbrella organization in the community that can assist you in helping to send necessary messages to the local Jewish institutions and places of worship. Two organizations in particular are worth noting. We list the national headquarters of each, which can provide addresses of local and regional offices (see Chapter 12 and Appendix I also):

   • The (National) Jewish Community Relations Advisory Council, 823 United Nations Plaza, New York, NY 10017, 212/490-2525 (referred to as JCRC)

   • Anti-Defamation League (ADL), 442 Park Avenue South, New York, NY 10016, 212/684-6950

The national JCRC has representative organization in almost every major city in the United States. This organization, the regional ADL organizations, or the Jewish

Federations can be of great assistance to law enforcement in disseminating information to members of the Jewish community.

Because of their history, some Jews expect anti-Semitic incidents and the reality is that there are still anti-Semites in our society. According to Riva Gambert (associate director of the JCRC of the Greater East Bay), whether or not the act was simply insensitive or whether it was indeed a hate crime, the officer still has to be responsive to the generated fears and community concerns. An officer's ability to calm fears as well as to investigate threats thoroughly will result in strong relations between law enforcement officials and Jewish community members.

Gay and Lesbian Victimization

Most of the discussion in this chapter, up until now, has centered around race, ethnic background, and religion in regard to hate/bias crimes and incidents. The motivation behind gay and lesbian hate crimes and incidents is unique because they are targeted against a group because of lifestyle and behavior rather than outer appearance or ethnicity. Gay and lesbian crimes and incidents are seriously underreported and deserve attention. The National Gay and Lesbian Task Force (NGLTF) defines antigay and antilesbian violence as: "any violence directed against persons because they are gay or lesbian, or perceived to be so. It is motivated by irrational fear and by the perception that gay people are easy targets, unable to fight back, or unwilling to risk exposure by reporting crimes against them to authorities" (Berrill, 1986).

Prevalence of homophobic crimes.   Studies presented to the U.S. House Judiciary Subcommittee on Criminal Justice indicate that homosexual victimization greatly exceeds that of the overall population (Berrill, 1987). A 1992 report from NGLTF indicates that "gay victim assistance agencies in Boston, Chicago, Minneapolis/St. Paul, New York and San Francisco documented 1,822 anti-gay incidents in 1991, *an increase of 31% over 1990.*"

A 1993 report from the NGLTF, studying the same communities listed in the quote above, determined that there was a 4 percent increase over the 1991 statistics in 1992 (*Contra Costa Times,* Mar. 12, 1993, p. B-5). This report established that in 1992, the percentage of gay and lesbian victims who did not report crimes to the police when they were the target ranged from 76 to 82 percent (National Gay and Lesbian Task Force, 1986).

Impact of hate crimes on gay and lesbian victims.   A hate-motivated attack is a psychological as well as a physical assault. For many gay and lesbian people, it is an attack on a part of their identity for which they have struggled to accept and value. According to doctors and to those working in the criminal justice system, gay male victims of hate crimes are often subjected to extreme brutality. Cases nationwide have involved torture, cutting mutilation (including castration), and even decapitations.

Gay and lesbian hate crimes perpetrators.   According to a 1984 NGLTF survey, one-third of the respondents had been either verbally or physically abused by family members. Otherwise, almost all of the perpetrators of antigay and antilesbian violence were strangers. The strangers tended to be adolescent or young adult males, often in groups. Unlike the offenders in other bias-motivated crimes or incidents, it is not uncommon for perpetrators to leave their own turf to hunt down gays or lesbians ("gay bashing").

One example involves four young members of a white supremacist group, barely out of their teens, who committed extreme antigay/lesbian violence in Salem, Oregon, in 1992. The four were accused of the firebomb murders of two persons when they lobbed a Molotov cocktail into the apartment where a black lesbian and a white gay male lived. According to the newspaper accounts, "The murder indictment said motive could be found in the 'defendants' perception of the race, color and sexual orientation of the victims" (Zuindlen, 1992).

Unacceptable is the allegation that many of the perpetrators of bias against gays and lesbians have been police officers. "The police have been cited as perpetrators in hundreds of cases reported to the NGLTF and they are frequently mentioned in the anecdotal evidence presented by other agencies serving the gay and lesbian communities. The reports have included verbal abuse, physical assault, entrapment, unequal enforcement of the law and deliberate mishandling of cases" (National Gay and Lesbian Task Force, 1992). When police officers, who are sworn to uphold the laws of the land, are the perpetrators of discrimination and even assaults upon gays and lesbians, the law enforcement community must take notice. For example, an off-duty Philadelphia police officer was accused of physically and verbally assaulting a man that he, and five companions, thought to be gay. The officer was suspended and then fired by the police commissioner. The officer was later acquitted in a nonjury trial. The judge wrote in his ruling that "'the [court] had enough evidence to establish a prima facie case. However, the [court] clearly did not have a strong case'" (*Au Courant,* July 17, 1989, p. 3). In Los Angeles, officers of the LAPD were accused of beating a gay man while yelling "'get out of the park you fucking queers'" (*Reactions,* Nov. 1, 1988). A 1984 National Gay and Lesbian Task Force (NGLTF) survey discovered that 23 percent of the gay men and 13 percent of the lesbians responding reported being abused in some way by the police. A similar study by NGLTF in 1988 indicated that of the 4835 harassment or violent incidents reported by gay or lesbian victims, 3 percent (205) were acts of police abuse. It comes as no surprise, then, that many gay people are reluctant to report assaults that are motivated by hate or bias or rely on the criminal justice system to protect them. Police professionals must treat gays and lesbians within the community and their own workforce with respect and dignity regardless of their own personal biases.

Some police departments have general orders that specifically state what is unacceptable conduct for their employees. For example, the Alameda, California Police Department has a general order [80-1 (A-1): 21:02] that specifically addresses discrimination, racial remarks, and requires courtesy and respect to all persons. It states, "Discrimination or racism in any form shall never be tolerated." Other general orders in that department deal with harassment in the workplace based on race, religion, color, national origin, ancestry, disability, marital status, sex, age, or sexual preferences. Violation of the orders carries disciplinary ramifications up to and including termination.

Police/gay and lesbian community relations.   Historically, in most cities and counties in the country, relations between the police and the gay and lesbian community have been strained. It is the perception of many homosexuals that the police regard them as deviants, criminals, and second-class citizens who are unworthy of protection or equal rights. Because of this fact or perception, many gay and lesbian crime victims do not report crimes to the police or cooperate with investigations. Even though negative attitudes and stereotypes will probably continue, progressive police departments have found that communication and mutual respect between the department and the gay and lesbian community are in the best interests of all concerned. Examples of police departments wherein outreach and communications have resulted in cooperation between the agencies and the homosexual community include San Francisco, Boston, New York, and Baltimore. Those departments have observed a noticeable difference in reporting by lesbian and gay crime victims, fewer complaints of police abuse, and a general improvement in police/gay relations.

Researcher Kevin Berrill (1992) observed that there are numerous ways to improve relationships between the justice system and gay/lesbian groups. One of the keys to good relations, according to Berrill, is regular, institutionalized communication at the department, in committees and councils, and in public forums. In addition, he mentions the following:

- The creation of task forces and councils to establish ongoing dialogue and networking on important issues.
- Public forums allowing police officials to meet the gay and lesbian community and help them to recognize that gays are a constituency with legitimate needs and concerns.
- The appointment of a police official to be a liaison with the gay/lesbian community to respond to complaints and requests.
- The involvement of prosecutors in development of policies, procedures, communications, and awareness training to improve relations between the criminal justice system and gay/lesbian groups and individuals.

When laws are violated by a gay or lesbian individual, whether acting alone or as part of a group, the usual criminal justice procedures should be followed—investigation, arrest, prosecution, and incarceration. Within almost every community there exists extremist and even militant segments and the gay community is no exception. These activist groups, often advocating AIDS related funding and research, may require additional attention and special interaction with area law enforcement. The goal of the agency liaison and management should be to avoid costly litigation and to have effective communication with persons representing such groups. Departments should have an assigned liaison officer meet with these groups in an attempt to agree on acceptable behavior *before* any public demonstration occurs. It must be recognized that some groups obtain press by orchestrating arrests by the police. In this case, liaison and close monitoring by field supervisors, a press relations officer, police video unit, and a department manager would be an absolute necessity. This methodology has been successful with agencies in the San Francisco Bay Area resulting in no use of force, no negative press or photos, and no legal action. However, even the best outreach efforts by the police may prove ineffective. For example, some members of the activist group "Queer Nation" have refused to communicate with police during their "actions." Nevertheless, police officers should not let negative publicity from previous incidents of this or any group stop them from attempting to make positive contact prior to scheduled public events. The willingness of the police to work with any community group, particularly gay activist groups, always results in positive publicity for police managers and their department.

WAR-RELATED HATE CRIMES

War-related hate crimes are not new in America—starting with the French–Indian War, to the Plains wars against Native Americans, to the Mexican American and Cuban American wars, to World War I ranting against the "Huns," to World War II with the "dirty Jap" campaigns and internment camps for Japanese Americans, and into our more recent wars against the "gooks" in Korea and Indochina. The Gulf War in Iraq in the early 1990s proved to follow the patterns of previous wars with respect to the perceived "enemy" (i.e., many Arab Americans were the targets of hate violence). Hatred directed toward the peoples living in the United States from "enemy" countries we have fought during these wars or "police actions" have been common. During the Vietnam War, however, war-related hate crimes were not common since there were not many Vietnamese living in the United States at that time. (Those prone to discriminate and hate "outsiders" expressed their sentiment after the Southeast Asians arrived in the United States.)

Asian American Experiences

Much hatred and discrimination characterized the experiences of Southeast Asians who immigrated to the United States following the war in their countries. Many had fought the same enemy alongside American forces. In a newspaper interview of Inh Sooksampan, director of the Richmond, California–based Refugee Center, he wondered why Americans seem to hate his people—the Laotians. He shared sorrowful tales of torment through name calling, beatings, rock throwing, and vandalism against Laotians. He explained that he, like members of other minority groups, has seen a marked increase in violence and hate crimes in the early 1990s. "I don't understand," Inh reflected, shaking his head. "I really don't understand. I've been here [America] 15 years and I've never been so scared as now" (personal communication, Inh Sooksampan, director, Laotian Refugee Center, Richmond, California, Apr. 4, 1992).

He and members of his cultural group speculate that maybe racism is the cause rather than the Vietnam War and confusion about who the enemy was "because we all look the same." Many Southeast Asians say that there is so much violence directed at them that they feel they are still living in a war zone.

Arab American Experiences

Scholars and cultural anthropologists indicate that Arabs and other Middle Easterners have been the targets of hate in the United States long before the recent

Gulf War. America's favorite enemies have had names like Arafat, Khomeini, and Gadhaffi. As mentioned in Chapter 9, the American stereotypes of Arabs in jokes, cartoons, and movies are, for the most part, negative. In addition to anti-Arab sentiment that exists generally, the American Arab Anti-Discrimination Committee indicates that an unfortunate trend usually follows any conflict in the Middle East, in that there is a corresponding backlash against Arab Americans in the form of hate crimes. The number of hate crimes reported against Arab Americans mushroomed during and immediately following the Gulf War. In a 1991 newspaper article the repercussions of hate toward the national "enemy" are presented:

> Hate crimes increased after Bush sent troops. Arab American organizations noted a rash of hate crimes in August and September [1990] after President Bush began sending troops to the Middle East, according to Khalil Jahshan, executive director of the National Association of Arab Americans. . . . The roughly 2 million Arab Americans in the United States brace themselves these days against looks of hatred, vandalism and other acts of violence by irrational people who direct their anger against people with dark skin and Middle Eastern accents. (*Contra Costa Times,* Jan. 27, 1991, p. A-6)

The hate crimes and incidents listed below illustrate how stereotypes are triggered during emotional times. The prejudiced person does not make distinctions among people whom he or she perceives as the "other" (or the enemy):

- **1/14/91—Dayton Ohio:** "*Multiple Incidents*—Two individuals threatened to shoot worshippers at a local Islamic Center. Later that night, several windows were broken at the mosque."
- **1/18/91—Tulsa, Oklahoma:** "*Shooting*—Shots were fired at the home of a local Muslim businessman."
- **1/21/91—Lakeland, Florida:** "*Bombing*—The *Washington Post* reported that a pipe bomb exploded at the garage door of a family believed to be Iraqi. The family, actually from India, received a threatening call one-half hour before the blast."
- **1/27/91—North Bergen, New Jersey:** "*Assault*—Three women in a department store attacked a woman wearing a Muslim headdress."

Japanese Americans Experiences

In 1992 in the United States, "Japan bashing" was resurrected. The Japanese prime minister made comments about lazy American workers. This, combined with the fiftieth anniversary of the Pearl Harbor bombing and the World War II Japanese internment order, brought increased threats to Japanese Americans as well as a stepped up "Buy American" campaign aimed at boycotting foreign, especially Japanese-made, products. The Japanese once again became a target of bias, in some cases, hate violence. This occurred despite the fact that others had, for the most part, learned to live peacefully with Japanese Americans.

Some Japanese American community members expressed anger about the "American bashing" that occurred in Japan in the early 1990s, saying that it placed them in an awkward position. "We still look Japanese; people can't distinguish between us and the national Japanese. But as citizens, we clearly identify ourselves as Americans" (*Contra Costa Times,* Jan. 27, 1991, p. A-6). For some American citizens, however, Asian populations have been hard to accept because of wars fought in

Asia (i.e., Japan, North Korea, Vietnam, and the cold war with China). Resentment of Asian nationals carries over. At the time of the 1940s internment, Japanese American citizens were just as American as any of their neighbors but were treated with extreme hate.

TRENDS IN HATE/BIAS CRIMES AND VIOLENCE

Futurists tell us that we are on the threshold of a "megachange" era, with major forces which will change the way America functions throughout the coming decade. The greatest impact on law enforcement is the mosaic society, that is, increased ethnic diversity in our communities and workforces. As indicated earlier, between the 1980 and 1990 censuses, the Asian American population more than doubled, growing by 108 percent, twice as fast as the Hispanic population, which grew by 53 percent, eight times as fast as the black population, which grew by 13 percent, and 15 times as fast as the white population, which grew by 6 percent (U.S. Bureau of the Census, Racial Statistics Division). As our society becomes more of a mosaic, there will inevitably be increases in hate/bias crimes and violence.

William Tafoya, an instructor, researcher, and agent for the Federal Bureau of Investigation, in a speech forecast that "major riots and civil disorders will dwarf the violence of the '60's [L.A. 1992?]. . . . By 1995, American white supremacists will have increased their terrorist acts by 50% over 1984 . . . that the threat from within the United States exceeds that of terrorists from outside the country. . . ." While Tafoya forecasts an increase in supremacist activity, other studies reveal that hate crimes are most frequently committed by individuals or small groups without ties to any organization. Criminal justice researchers Finn and McNeil (1988) report that fewer hate crimes are being perpetrated by organized hate groups, while more and more are being committed by individuals or small groups, predominately in the 16 to 25 age range. The youth population in the United States (people between 0 and 17 years of age) is projected to increase dramatically in the next decade, and the neo-Nazi movement, for example, has a predominantly youthful membership. Since hate crimes seem to correlate with youth and the numbers of young people are increasing, it is likely that supremacist movements will grow in numbers.

LAW ENFORCEMENT RESPONSE STRATEGIES

Public confidence and trust in the criminal justice system, and in particular, law enforcement, is essential for effective response to hate/bias crimes. Residents in communities where people of a different race, ethnic background, religion or sexual orientation reside, must be able to trust that they will be protected. They must believe that the police are not against them, that the prosecutors are vigorously prosecuting, that the judges are invoking proper penalties, and that parole, probation, and corrections are doing their share to combat crimes motivated by hate/bias. If people believe that they have to protect *themselves*, tensions build, communication breaks down, and people try to take the law into their own hands. For example, in Los Angeles in 1992 following the trial verdict of the four officers in the Rodney

King incident, Koreans were defending their property by shooting it out with looters. Many of the looters were stealing for personal gain, but there are indications that many were using the opportunity to take out their frustration and hatred for members of a different race during the turmoil of the riots.

In Massachusetts, Maryland, New York, and California, separate governors' commissions during the late 1970s and early 1980s discovered that relatively few law enforcement agencies had the expertise necessary to respond effectively to hate/bias crimes. Only a few had policies and procedures, and little or no training was taking place, even though there were signs that violence was increasing. The aforementioned states conducted hearings and recommendations, culminating in the adoption of policies and procedures that standardized responses to crimes motivated by hate/bias. Follow-up hearings since that time revealed that there was an increase in successful prosecutions in hate crime cases and a lessening of tensions between police and minority communities.

Model Management Strategy Policies

Mike Oliver, chief of police of Belmont, California, developed a hate crime management strategy in law enforcement as part of his Command College Independent Study Project for the state of California. The policies he recommended follow (Commission on Peace Officer Standards and Training, 1992).

Policy one. The establishment of an antiracist, antidiscrimination, pro-conflict-resolution posture on the part of law enforcement, including the following components:

1. **Police department mission statement.** The mission statement should articulate the department's antiracist, antidiscrimination, pro-conflict-resolution posture.
2. **Written hate crime policy.** A written policy should be developed that addresses the department's antiracist, antidiscrimination, pro-conflict-resolution posture; the departmental expectations regarding responses to hate crime incidents; and the departmental expectations regarding response to hate crime victims.
3. **Complaints.** Procedures should be instituted that ensure citizen complaints of bias and prejudice on the part of departmental employees are thoroughly and vigorously investigated.
4. **Formal resolution.** the police department management staff should encourage the mayor/council to issue a resolution that outlines the antiracist, antidiscrimination, pro-conflict-resolution posture of the city, and encourage the community to report all criminal and noncriminal hate-related incidents to the police department.

Policy two. The establishment of a workforce education program to include:

1. **Hate-crime.** To educate employees regarding the department's antiracist, antidiscrimination, pro-conflict-resolution posture, and the expected response to hate crime incidents and victims of hate crime.
2. **Cultural awareness.** To foster an understanding of and sensitivity toward the diverse cultures in the community.
3. **Conflict resolution.** To assist employees in managing the variety of disputes confronting them in performance of their duties.

Policy three. The establishment of a cooperative hate crime prevention effort with other law enforcement agencies to include:

1. **Intelligence gathering.** The police department should gather and maintain information regarding organized hate groups and local hate crime activity.
2. **Networking.** The police department should develop a program of regular meetings with other law enforcement agencies to share hate-crime-related information.

Policy four. The establishment of a cooperative hate crime prevention effort with the community using the following tactics:

1. **Community task force.** The police chief should appoint a task force of police department, community, religious, school, and victim advocate leaders that would meet regularly to share and discuss hate crime and related community concerns.
2. **Race relations officer (Community Relations Officer).** A command officer should be appointed to be the liaison between the police department and minority and community groups. This officer should serve on the community task force and should investigate all noncriminal hate-related matters as well as all complaints of bias made against police department employees.
3. **Recruitment.** The police department should make every effort to recruit qualified minority candidates and to promote qualified minority officers.
4. **Community activities.** The police department should develop a program encouraging all employees to become involved in community activities.

Policy five. The establishment of a cooperative hate crime prevention effort with the schools. The purpose is to develop and implement programs that educate students about hate crime and build bridges between the student population and the police department. Suggested programs include:

1. **Police and Community Together (PACT):** a program that couples a police officer and a social studies teacher at the middle and high school levels to instruct hate crime and cultural awareness issues.
2. **Adopt-a-Cop:** a program that involves classes of sixth-grade students who "adopt" a police officer volunteer for the school year. The officer spends one or two hours per month in the classroom, addressing hate crime and cultural awareness issues as well as other issues of importance. Since hate crime is perpetrated primarily by teenagers and young adults, this policy targets the majority of that population.

Policy six. The police department should ensure that the citizens of the community are informed of the positive and innovative hate crime strategy that has been developed and implemented. An understanding of the cooperative partnership formed among the police department, other law enforcement agencies, the community, and the schools is imperative for the strategy to be successful.

The Command College project of Robert Shusta, captain in the Concord, California Police Department, entitled "The Development of a Model Plan for Cities Experiencing Multicultural Impact," contained many of these same recommendations. It included the following important elements as well:

1. **Chief executive.** Police executives must speak out publicly on these issues and make certain that people inside and outside of the department know that hate/bias crimes, discrimination, and racism reduction or elimination is a high priority. The chief executive should create a *values statement* for the organization that

stresses the philosophy of the organization to protect and support the doctrine of individual rights.

2. **Human relations commissions.** Cities and counties should establish human relations commissions where they do not exist. Law enforcement agencies should report both criminal and noncriminal racial incidents to the local human relations commission, as they occur, and they should follow up with the final disposition of each incident.

3. **Dispositions.** Law enforcement should quickly and effectively communicate its investigative action and final disposition of racial crimes to victims of these crimes and to citizens who file complaints of police misconduct.

4. **Victim assistance.** Law enforcement and victim advocates need to provide immediate, practical assistance and support services to victims of hate violence.

5. **Interpreter programs.** Law enforcement must identify interpreters within the agency as well as community resources for language translations for emergency situations and planned interviews.

6. **Media utilization.** Marketing the reduction or elimination of discrimination and racism should involve use of the media. Law enforcement and the community should work with local newspapers, radio, and television to develop public education programs on cultural events, information exchange, and racial and cultural issues. The media must be sensitized to the minority communities, their culture, and their heritage. Sensationalistic journalism regarding persons of color, ethnic background, religion, and sexual orientation must be discouraged.

7. **Legislation support.** Criminal justice executives should become actively involved in supporting local, state, and national legislation to improve race relations, reduce crimes motivated by hate/bias, and assist victims in their recovery.

8. **Law enforcement computers.** Law enforcement should expand its utilization of computers to track hate/bias crimes, gangs, and crimes involving minorities/immigrants as victim(s) or responsible(s).

AGENCY RESPONSES TO HATE/BIAS CRIMES

In recent years, some progressive law enforcement agencies have developed strategies to address the problems of hate violence. Some of those strategies have become models for others in the criminal justice system, with the most successful approach involving the whole community. A few of the more notable contributions recognized as models by the U.S. Department of Justice have been the Boston, Massachusetts Police Department and the Baltimore, Maryland County Police Department.

Boston, Massachusetts Police Department

In 1978, after Boston had experienced several years of increasing racial tensions, the police commissioner established a Community Disorders Unit (CDU). The creation of the unit was based on a departmental policy that reads in part:

> It is the policy of this department to ensure that all citizens can be free of violence, threats, or harassment, due to their race, color, or creed, or desire to live or travel in any neighborhood. When such citizen's right are infringed upon by violence, threats, or other harassment, it is the policy to make immediate arrests of those individuals who have committed such acts. Members of the police force responding to these incidents will be expected to take immediate and forceful action to identify

the perpetrators, arrest them, and bring them before the court. . . . It will be the policy of this department to seek the assistance of state and federal prosecutors in every case in which civil rights violations can be shown. (Boston Police Department Departmental Policy)

This policy outlines procedures for handling "community disorders" and emphasizes the initial actions by the first responding police officer, who must notify his or her superior officer if a serious crime is involved. The CDU takes charge of the investigation after the responding officer completes an initial investigation.

CDU officers interview victims and witnesses, obtain evidence, and present the case for prosecution. Other duties include securing emergency housing for victims, making referrals to social service agencies, and arranging for additional security for victims. The unit is also involved in programs and liaisons with the minority community to improve relations between their members and the police department.

Since the inception of the CDU and the passage of the Massachusetts Civil Rights Act, Boston reports that there have been fewer incidents of violence and harassment of a racial, ethnic, and religious nature. The police department has been recognized nationwide for its aggressive attempts and model policy aimed at reducing crimes motivated by hate.

Baltimore County, Maryland Police Department

The state of Maryland has been acknowledged for its response to racially and religiously motivated violence and harassment. The policies of the Baltimore County Police Department have been used as a model in other states and localities. A Maryland law passed in 1981 required that every law enforcement agency in the state maintain a filing and reporting system on all acts of racially and religiously targeted violence and harassment. The result of this requirement has been greater awareness of the problem on the part of law enforcement officials. In addition, specific policies, practices, guidelines, and procedures to report and investigate hate violence incidents have been developed. The departmental guidelines instruct officers to report even those incidents which may not clearly be hate crimes (according to the strict definition) until further investigation proves otherwise.

These guidelines detail what each officer's role in the investigation will be, from the first officer on the scene to the supervisor and the investigator. The policy provides instruction on sensitivity to the feelings and needs of the victim(s). Under the guidelines, precinct commanders become involved in order to supervise the response and ensure that appropriate action will be taken. The policy also requires the area commander to contact community leaders concerning the progress of an investigation. This step is crucial in demonstrating that action is being taken to correct the problem immediately and to control rumors and/or negative media response.

HATE CRIME RESPONSE MODEL POLICY

The following is a compilation of successful departmental policies that could serve as models for those agencies yet to formulate their own. It is presented in a generic fashion and may not fit all departments because of size, staffing, or terminology usage differences. The model presented distinguishes between a hate crime and a hate incident. The U.S. Department of Justice model, as well as many other departmental models, do not make this distinction.

Policy (Concord PD policy: composite of Maryland and Boston)

1. This general order establishes a policy and department procedure for handling crimes and incidents that were motivated by hatred or prejudice arising from differences in race, religion, ethnic background, culture, or sexual orientation (RRES).

2. It is the policy of the [agency] to ensure that rights guaranteed by state laws and the U.S. Constitution are protected for all people regardless of their race, color, ethnic background, religion, or sexual orientation. When such rights are infringed upon by violence, intimidation, or other harassment, the department shall take all available steps to identify the responsible of criminal offenses, arrest them, and bring them before the courts.

3. All criminal offenses of violence, intimidation, or harassment based on racial, religious, ethnic background, or sexual orientation shall be viewed as serious, and an investigation shall be considered high priority. Such acts tend to generate fear and concern among victims and the public. They have a potential for recurrence and escalating to the point of counterviolence.

4. All reported incidents that are noncriminal (short of a criminal offense) that were motivated all or in part by race, ethnicity, religion, and/or sexual orientation shall be documented by a police report. An [administrative] follow-up and disposition will be made on appropriate incidents by the [community relations unit] or appropriate unit.

Definitions

1. A *reportable crime* is any act or attempted act to cause physical injury, emotional suffering, or property damage, which is or appears to be motivated, all or in part, by race, ethnic background, religion, and/or sexual orientation.

   (a) Committed acts having criminal sanctions are considered "hate crimes." Types of crimes could include threatening phone calls, hate mail, physical assaults, verbal abuse, vandalism, cross burning, fire bombing, physical attacks, and so on.

   (b) A commonsense approach should be taken toward this definition. If it appears that the crime was motivated by race, religion, ethnic background, or sexual orientation, it shall be reported under criteria established by this order. *Motivation* is the key element in determining if a crime is racially, religiously, ethnically, or lifestyle based.

2. A *reportable incident* is any noncriminal act directed at any person or group based upon race, religion, ethnic background, or sexual orientation.

   (a) The approach should be: Is this an incident that has potential to reoccur and escalate into a criminal offense?

Procedure The proper investigation of RRES crimes or incidents is the responsibility of all (agency) police officers and employees. *Each employee must be sensitive to the feelings, needs, and fears that may be present in the community as a result of acts of this nature.* The primary personnel responsible for investigating these types of crimes or incidents are:

1. **Uniform Division:** preliminary investigation of crimes or incidents, evidence collection, and, where appropriate, the arrest of the responsible
2. **Investigation Division/Specialized Unit:** follow-up investigation of crimes, arrest of responsible, filing of criminal complaints, records maintenance, and intelligence analysis
3. **Administrative Services Division (or Specialized Unit):** community liaison, resolution of appropriate noncriminal RRES incidents, records maintenance, and appropriate department and public training

Responsibilities All RRES crimes are priority 1 calls and shall require dispatch of a patrol officer to the scene, unless the complainant specifically requests that an officer not respond. In that case the call shall be dispatched to an officer, who shall make a phone call to the complainant for details for a report. All RRES incidents are priority 2 calls and shall require dispatch of an officer to the scene as soon as practical.

The International Association of Chiefs of Police (P.O. Box 6010, Gaithersburg, MD 20878; TL: 301/948-0922) created a model policy on racial, religious, and ethnic violence. It is intended to serve as a guide for the police executive who plans to implement such a policy for his or her department.

SUMMARY

Racism and crimes motivated by hate are two of the most challenging issues confronting the United States today. Our nation is one whose ancestry includes people from around the world who are guaranteed the rights to be free of discrimination and violence. Our society is one that continues to have incidents of hatred manifested in violence toward people perceived as "different." Racism and the resulting hate violence, bias treatment, and discrimination cause divisions between people and denies them their dignity. Racism is a disease that devastates society. Police officers should be at the forefront in the battle to combat such criminal behavior within society. Law enforcement must lead in the protection of human and civil rights of all citizens.

The presence of hate/bias crimes and incidents is often attributed to changing national and international conditions, immigration, and ethnic demographic change translated to a local environment. As immigrants, persons of color, or persons of different religious beliefs or sexual orientation move into previously unintegrated areas, increased threat of hate/bias crimes can be expected. The efforts of communities in the confrontation of these issues along with law enforcement agencies is critical. It is not just a problem for the criminal justice system, but rather must be addressed jointly by schools, business, labor, and social services. Taking the lead, law enforcement agencies can motivate other groups to join with them in their efforts to reduce hate violence.

Progress toward tolerance among peoples, mutual respect, and unity has been painfully slow in our country and marked with repeated setbacks. Criminal statutes and civil remedies to curb the problem in various jurisdictions across the nation have also been enacted slowly. Divisive racial attitudes, anti-immigrant sentiment, the increased number of hate/bias incidents, and the deepening despair of minorities and the poor make the need for solutions even more pressing and urgent.

DISCUSSION QUESTIONS AND ISSUES*

1. *Hate/Bias Crimes and Incident Reduction.* Make a list of how you would design a community-based program to reduce the number of hate/bias crimes and incidents in your area.

2. *Move-In Violence.* Discuss in a group setting what other strategies might be used by a community to reduce the impact of move-in violence on a new immigrant.

3. *Victims of Hate/Bias Crimes or Incidents.* Have you been the victim of a hate/bias crime or incident? Share the experience with others in a group setting: the circumstances, the feelings you experienced, how you responded, and what action was taken by any community-based agency or organization.

REFERENCES

Anti-Defamation League (1991). *1990 Audit of Anti-Semitic Incidents,* Anti-Defamation League of B'nai B'rith, Civil Rights Division, New York.

BERRILL, KEVIN (1986). Testimony before the House Judiciary Committee's Subcommittee on Criminal Justice: Second Session on Anti-Gay Violence, Oct. 9, Serial No. 132.

BERRILL, KEVIN (1992). *Dealing with the Criminal Justice System,* National Gay and Lesbian Task Force, Washington, D.C.

Commission on Peace Officer Standards and Training (1992). *Law Enforcement Tomorrow: A Journal of Command College Independent Study Projects,* Vol. 1, No. 1, Apr.

DEES, MORRIS (1987). "Gay-bashing prevalent among hate crimes," *Klanwatch Intelligence Report,* Dec. p. 5.

FINN, PETER, and TAYLOR MCNEIL (1988). *Bias Crime and the Criminal Justice Response: A Summary Report,* National Institute of Justice, Washington, D.C., May, pp. 2–3.

MCDEVITT, J. (1989). *The Study of the Character of Civil Rights Crimes in Massachusetts (1983–1987).*

National Gay and Lesbian Task Force (1986). *Anti-Gay Violence: Causes, Consequences, Responses,* a White Paper by the Violence Project of (NGLTF, Washington D.C.)

National Gay and Lesbian Task Force (1991). *Anti-Gay Violence, Victimization, and Defamation in 1990,* NGLTF, Washington, D.C.

National Gay and Lesbian Task Force (1992). *A Fact Sheet on Violence Against Lesbians and Gay Men,* NGLTF Policy Institute, Washington D.C.

New York State Governor's Task Force on Bias-Related

Crime (1988). *Final Report,* New York State Printing Office, Albany, N.Y., Mar. p. 242.

QUINDLEN, ANNA (1992). "Gay OK? Yes or no? Bigotry put to a vote," *Contra Costa Times,* Oct. 27, p. A-2.

SHUSTA, ROBERT M. (1987). *The Development of a Model Plan for California Cities Experiencing Multi-cultural Impact,* Class IV, POST Command College, Sacramento, Calif.

U.S. Attorney General's Commission on Racial, Ethnic, Religious, and Minority Violence (1986). *Final Report,* U.S. Government Printing Office, Washington, D.C., Apr. p. 4.

Southern Poverty Law Center (1987). *"Move-In" Violence: White Resistance to Neighborhood Integration in the 1980's,* Southern Poverty Law Center, Klanwatch Project, Montgomery, Ala.

U.S. Commission on Civil Rights, Intimidation and Violence (1990). *Racial and Religious Bigotry in America,* Clearinghouse Publication 96, Washington D.C., Sept.

WALLACE, STEVEN (1987). "Elderly Nicaraguans and immigrant community formation in San Francisco," unpublished doctoral thesis, University of California, San Francisco, pp. 88–89.

World Almanac and Book of Facts, (1988). World Almanac, Mahwah, N.J., p. 630.

Corporate Author, California Office of Criminal Justice Planning, Sacramento, CA. (1989). *Emerging Criminal Justice Issue: When Hate Come to Town: Preventing and Intervening in Community Hate Crime,* California Office of Criminal Justice Planning, Vol. 1, No. 4, p. 1.

Los Angeles County Commission on Human Relations (1990). *Report on Hate Crime in Los Angeles County.*

---

*See Instructor's Manual accompanying this text for additional activities, role-plays, questionnaires and projects related to the content of this chapter.

12

HATE/BIAS CRIMES:

Reporting and Tracking

OVERVIEW

This chapter discusses a nationwide reporting system and clearinghouse for hate crimes data collected from state and local police. Criminal justice leaders in every sector of the United States must have standardized and comprehensive statistics as one tool to analyze trends and direct their resources more effectively against crimes of hate/bias and civil rights violations. In the first section of the chapter we define the problem and establish why data collection is important. In the second section we examine reporting systems development by a few states and localities and the U.S. Congress Hate Crimes Statistics Act of 1990. The chapter continues with a discussion of the various organizations that monitor hate crimes and hate groups. In the fourth section we explore conditions in a community that should be monitored affecting the deployment of law enforcement and community resources (community-oriented policing) that will prevent or at least reduce hate/bias crimes and incidents. The final section examines the responsibility of law enforcement officers, supervisors, and managers in reporting and tracking these crimes and the usefulness of such data in forecasting and planning. Methods of forecasting are also presented. In the concluding section we discuss strategies of data collection, including definitions, forms, sources of information, and examples of reporting hate crimes.

COMMENTARY

The importance of reporting and tracking crimes motivated by hate and bias is evident in the following quotes:

The Adaptive Corporation, by Alvin Tofler, McGraw-Hill, New York, 1985.

In a society convulsing with change, the central need of management is for far more sensitive information . . . especially anticipatory information . . . about the environment in which the [organization]* must function. . . . It is important for [organizations] to know about social stresses, potential crises, shifts of population, changes in family structure, political upheavals and to know about these early enough to make adaptive decisions.

America on Fire: The Anatomy of Violence, by David Fritsche, The Dynamics Group, P.O. Box 11495, Reno, NV 89510, May 1992.

We can conclude that our environment contributes to our behavior. No social scientist would disagree. The issue becomes determining what social conditions contribute most to our behavior and to what degree "they" are responsible. Numerous studies show that the reduced space and increased stress of urban life give rise to increased incidence of violence. Economic levels have also been show as paralleling the incidence of violence.

"Rioting in the streets: déjà vu?" by William Tafoya, *C.J. the Americas,* Index Vol. 2, No. 6, Dec.–Jan. 1990.

Little has been written about the future of policing. What has been published are largely speculative personal images. A recent study offers the judgment of a panel of nationally recognized law enforcement experts concerning specific issues and specifies the year certain events are expected to occur (Tafoya, 1986). . . . Of the 25 forecasts outlined, one holds the potential for major social significance for America. The panel forecasts that by 1999 urban unrest and civil disorder (of the 1960's and 1970's variety) will take place throughout the United States. It is expected that this future rebellion will eclipse the past turbulence and violence in magnitude, intensity and duration.

DEFINING THE PROBLEM

Changing demographics in almost every part of the United States requires that all localities deal with issues of intergroup relations. The ideal of harmony in diversity and interracial and ethnic relations is offset by increased stress in the social fabric of a community that often leads to bigoted and/or violent acts. Newspaper headlines across the country provide convincing examples on a daily basis. Hate/bias crimes are not a new phenomenon; as pointed out in Chapter 11, they have been occurring for generations. The law enforcement need for documentation of such crimes is obvious.

The Southern Poverty Law Center in Alabama (see Appendix I for addresses of all organizations that follow) publishes *Klanwatch,* a project established in 1980 to conduct litigation, publish educational materials, and do monitoring of extremist groups, particularly the Ku Klux Klan. A release from that organization in 1987 contained the following: "Most hate violence attacks in the U.S. are perpetrated by whites against minorities. White-on-black incidents constitute the majority of such incidents, but white attacks on Hispanic, Asian and Jewish victims are also

---

*The authors have taken the liberty to change Tofler's word *corporations* to *organizations.* The word *organizations* in this setting is intended to refer to law enforcement agencies.

of serious proportions. Lately intergroup conflict between minorities, such as blacks and Asians, *has emerged as a growing facet of the overall hate violence problem*" [emphasis added] (Southern Poverty Law Center, 1987).

Demographer Lewis Butler, speaking about California, stated the following: "As this state becomes more Hispanic and Asian, it will test whether we can peacefully change from a European dominated society with minorities to a world dominated society where everybody is a minority" (*San Francisco Chronicle*, Feb. 26, 1991, p. A-7). Adelle Terrell, then acting director of the National Institute Against Prejudice and Violence (NIAPV), at a nationwide conference in Washington, D.C. in 1990, cautioned: "We know that we've got lots and lots of immigrants coming into this country and historically each and every wave of immigrants that has ever come into the United States has been greeted by violence" (*Contra Costa Times*, Feb. 23, 1991, p. A-3).

NIAPV also completed a study in 1986 showing that at least two-thirds of victims of hate/bias crimes had been subjected to a series of attacks. Studies show that bias attacks are more likely than nonbias criminal incidents to include multiple attackers. However, what is most frightening is that the vast majority of these offender groups tend to be informal associations and not members of organized hate groups. This type of "random unexplained violence" is more feared by victims and their affiliated group than are other types of crime where victims can take measures to protect themselves. For this reason, these crimes demand special treatment; the perpetrator often intends to send a brutally clear message of intimidation to victims and their communities. A forum in 1990 by NIAPV found that victims of bias crimes and incidents suffer 33 percent more traumatic symptoms than do nonbias victims.

Another study, by the National Organization of Black Law Enforcement Executives (NOBLE) in 1986, pointed out that bias crimes "not only bring suffering to the victims but may create tension and chaos within the community." Also of concern to the justice systems of cities, counties, and states is that some victims often fail to report such incidents, due to shock, embarrassment, guilt, or a distrust of police and prosecutors. Some simply choose not to become involved in the criminal justice process. In the workplace, the employee, who is a victim, often overlooks the incident(s) for fear of reprisal or to avoid additional alienation. The same is true of the community victim. Like a rape or child abuse victim, this person is often psychologically traumatized and, consequently, requires special handling and compassion on the part of the officers and all others in the criminal justice system with whom the victim comes in contact.

Data must be collected at local levels, then sent in a standardized fashion to the state and national clearinghouse so that proper resources may be allocated to hate/bias crimes investigations and victim assistance. Such a system provides the necessary information not only to the criminal justice system but also to public policy makers, civil rights activists, legislators, victim advocates, and the general public. The data provide a more reliable statistical picture of the problem. Agencies collecting the data have used it as arguments for new hate crime penalty enhancements. The information is used in criminal justice training courses and to educate communities on the impact of the problem. Energy must be devoted to tracking and analyzing these crimes: "A single incident can be the tragedy of a lifetime to its victim and may be the spark that disrupts an entire community" (New York State Governor's Task Force on Bias-Related Crime, 1988). As indicated, studies show that most hate/bias attacks are by people who are not members of an organized hate group. Yet there is evidence and data to suggest that white supremacist group membership is on the rise. [A white supremacist group is defined as any ongoing organization, association, or group of three or more persons, whether formal or informal, having as one of its primary activities the promotion of white supremacy through the commission of criminal acts (e.g., Ku Klux Klan).] For example, Klanwatch, reported: "A record number of white supremacist groups were active from coast to coast in 1991. . . . Totals surged from 273 in 1990 to 346 in 1991, a 27 percent increase" (Southern Poverty Law Center, 1992) and the Anti-Defamation League (1991) released a report which stated: "A ten year decline in the nationwide strength of the Ku Klux Klan came to a halt during 1990 and . . . [it] may be poised to gain new strength . . . especially if the current recession becomes lengthy and severe."

Therefore, increased public awareness of and response to such crime has largely been the result of efforts by community-based organizations and victim advocate groups. By documenting and drawing public attention to acts of bigotry and violence, these organizations laid the groundwork for the official action that followed. In addition to the aforementioned organizations that track these crimes, it became extremely important that hate groups across the United States be monitored (see Chapter 11) by criminal justice agencies. Documenting a problem does not guarantee that it will be solved, but is a critical part of any strategy to create change. Documenting and publicizing hate/bias crime and incidents raises the consciousness about the problem within the community and the criminal justice system. It is a simple but effective first step toward mobilizing a response.

HATE CRIMES DATA COLLECTION

Agencies that implemented policies to deal with hate/bias crimes in terms of reporting, investigating, treating the victim, and collecting and analyzing data during the 1980s were leaders in the field. The policies and procedures of the police departments of Boston, New York, San Francisco, Los Angeles, and the Maryland State Police have been used as models of how to deal with hate/bias crimes or, as Boston refers to them, civil rights violations.

As indicated in Chapter 11, the Boston Police Department began recording and tracking civil rights violations in 1978 when that agency created its Civil Disorders Unit. Boston was probably the first law enforcement agency in the United States to record and track such crimes. The Maryland State Police was also a forerunner when it began to record incidents on a statewide, systematic basis as a part of a pioneering government-wide effort to monitor and combat hate violence in 1981.

Numerous governmental initiatives have been tested to establish effective governmental response to crimes motivated by hate/bias. But as of 1992, only 13 states and the District of Columbia maintained a system where hate crime data were officially collected on a mandated statewide basis. Because most communities still do not record hate crimes, it gives the often false impression that hate/bias crimes or incidents are nonexistent there. Thus victimization continues and the problems intensify. The police or sheriff's department either refuses to recognize these crimes or they need training to identify, prevent, and investigate such occurrences.

Establishing a good reporting system within public organizations (human relations commissions, etc.) and the justice system is essential in every locality in the country. The collection of hate/bias crime data offer the following benefits:

- Help police identify current and potential problems.
- Assist police in responding to the needs of minority communities.
- Help with minority recruiting.
- Provide information for training of criminal justice personnel on the degree of the problem and reason for priority response.

Simply, if the police have more information about crime patterns, they will be able to better direct resources to prevent and resolve problems. The data can provide the information needed to develop preventive and investigative strategies. Tracking hate/bias incidents and crimes allows criminal justice managers to deploy their resources accordingly when fluctuations occur. Hopefully, it will allow an agency to deploy its resources to prevent such crimes. Aggressive response, investigation, and prosecution of these crimes demonstrate to the minority community that the police are genuinely concerned and that they see such crimes as a priority. As departments demonstrate their commitment to addressing hate/bias crime, minorities will be more likely to see policing as sensitive to their concerns. (A secondary benefit for the agency is that minorities would be more apt to consider law enforcement as a good career opportunity.) Agencies must also make it a priority to provide training to all department personnel on hate violence and civil rights violations, including such topics as victims' needs, effective responses, and investigation methods. This education would raise awareness and hopefully lead to more apprehensions, arrests, and discipline of the perpetrators.

There have been two primary concerns about implementing a hate/bias data collection system expressed by some law enforcement executives. Despite the benefits, these concerns are that:

- establishing a reporting system would be time consuming and expensive
- collecting and publicizing hate crime data (especially with increases normally attributed to more reporting) would make their city or county look bad

Those departments in the United States that have implemented a reporting policy in fact found few problems and associated costs. In these cases the reporting was incorporated into an existing Uniform Crime Reporting (UCR) system to which they already submitted data. The training of police personnel to identify, report, investigate, and resolve such crimes was the only additional expense. Furthermore, the community's image was not damaged by the typically large numbers of hate/bias crimes being reported. First, those agencies collecting data utilized local media to explain the implementation of the reporting system. It was explained that since the department encourages victims to document these crimes, there would be an associated increase in the numbers. The increase did not necessarily mean that more community members are being victimized, but that their reporting of the crimes and incidents simply made them known. Departments should always stress to the public that they need the information to assist them in allocating resources to address the problem effectively.

Congressional Directive: Federal Hate Crime Legislation

In response to a growing concern about hate/bias crimes, the U.S. Congress enacted the Hate Crimes Statistics Act of 1990. The Act required the Attorney General to establish guidelines and collect data "about crimes that manifest evidence of prejudice based on race, religion, sexual orientation, or ethnicity, including, where appropriate, the crimes of murder, non-negligent manslaughter; forcible rape; aggravated assault, simple assault, intimidation; arson; and destruction, damage or vandalism of property" (U.S. Department of Justice, 1990).

The U.S. Attorney General delegated his agency's responsibilities under the Act to the FBI. The Uniform Crimes Report (UCR) Section of the FBI was assigned the task of developing the procedures for, and managing the implementation of, the collection of hate crime data. According to the Act, the types of bias to be reported to the FBI's UCR Section are limited to bias based on race, religion, sexual orientation, or ethnicity.

The national clearinghouse for hate/bias crimes data enables the criminal justice system to monitor and respond to trends in those localities that voluntarily submit the information. States and/or localities enacting legislation involving hate crime reporting in the 1970s, 1980s, and early 1990s responded more effectively and reduced the numbers of incidents of hate/bias in their communities.

Uniform Crime Reports System

The approach adopted by the U.S. Department of Justice incorporated a means of capturing hate crime data received from law enforcement jurisdictions into the already established nationwide UCR program. The FBI had begun the process of upgrading the UCR program to collect and publish much more comprehensive data on the victims, offenders, and the circumstances of crime. Modifying the program only required the addition of a single new data element to the National Incident-Based Reporting System (NIBRS), which had the capability to flag criminal incidents as bias/hate motivated. The U.S. Department of Justice assigned a coordinator between NIBRS and the FBI's UCR Section to carry out the data collection.

In 1991, regional training conferences on the reporting system were conducted all across the United States. U.S. Department of Justice and FBI UCR Section staff trained top state UCR Section representatives and delegates from the largest 300 police and sheriffs' departments in the nation. According to Bob Lamb, regional director of the Community Relations Service (CRS), U.S. Department of

Justice (personal communication, July 31, 1992), local agencies were encouraged to follow the spirit of the federal legislation and voluntarily collect data "in house" until reporting procedures were established.

Only 2771 law enforcement agencies of the approximately 16,000 in the United States that participate in the UCR program submitted hate crime data voluntarily in 1991. FBI Director William Sessions said in a statement accompanying the first report covering 1991, "While these initial data are limited, they give us our first assessment of the nature of crimes motivated by bias in our society" (*Contra Costa Times,* Jan. 5, 1993, p. A-9). Of the 4558 hate crimes reported, racial bias accounted for 62.3 percent of the total, with blacks the main target. Religious bias accounted for 19.3 percent, most with anti-Jewish motives. Ethnic bias accounted for 9.5 percent, and sexual bias 8.9 percent, almost all aimed at homosexuals. The most prevalent hate-related crime was intimidation, which was 33.9 percent (1614 incidents); vandalism, 27.4 percent (1301 incidents); and there were 796 simple assaults (17.5 percent) and 773 aggravated assaults (16.9 percent) (*Contra Costa Times,* Jan. 5, 1993, p. A-9).

Objective Evidence: Bias Motivation

The following is intended to assist officers in making decisions on whether a crime is bias motivated. Motivation is subjective and therefore it may be difficult to know with certainty whether a crime was the result of the perpetrator's bias. Because of this difficulty, bias, per the Act, is to be reported *only if* investigation reveals sufficient objective facts which lead a reasonable and prudent person to conclude that the offender's actions were motivated, in whole or in part, by bias. The specific types of bias to be reported are (U.S. Department of Justice, 1990).

RACIAL BIAS

    Anti-white
    Anti-black
    Anti-American Indian or Alaskan Native
    Anti-Asian/Pacific Islander
    Anti-multiracial group

RELIGIOUS BIAS

    Anti-Jewish
    Anti-Catholic
    Anti-Protestant
    Anti-Islamic (Moslem)
    Anti-other religion (Buddhism, Hinduism, Shintoism, etc.)
    Anti-multireligious group
    Anti-atheist/agnostic/etc.

ETHNICITY/NATIONAL ORIGIN BIAS

    Anti-Arab
    Anti-Hispanic
    Anti-other ethnicity/national origin

SEXUAL ORIENTATION BIAS

    Anti-male homosexual (gay)

    Anti-female homosexual (lesbian)

    Anti-homosexual (gays and lesbian)

    Anti-heterosexual

    Anti-bisexual

To help the investigator(s) determine if an incident has sufficient objective facts to classify it as a hate/bias crime, the UCR provides guidelines which stress that no single fact may be conclusive. The guidelines indicate that facts such as the following, particularly when combined, support a finding of bias (U.S. Department of Justice, 1990):

- The offender and the victim were of different racial, religious, ethnic/national origin, or sexual orientation groups. For example, the victim was black and the offenders were white.
- Bias-related oral comments, written statements, or gestures were made by the offender which indicate his or her bias. For example, the offender shouted a racial epithet at the victim.
- Bias-related drawings, markings, symbols, or graffiti were left at the crime scene. For example, a swastika was painted on the door of a synagogue.
- Certain objects, items, or things that indicate bias were used (e.g., the offenders wore white sheets with hoods covering their faces) or left behind by the offender(s) (e.g., a burning cross was left in front of the victim's residence).
- The victim is a member of a racial, religious, ethnic/national origin, or sexual orientation group that is overwhelming outnumbered by members of another group in the neighborhood where the victim lives and the incident took place. This factor loses significance with the passage of time (i.e., it is most significant when the victim first moved into the neighborhood and becomes less and less significant as time passes without incident).
- The victim was visiting a neighborhood where previous hate crimes had been committed against other members of his or her racial, religious, ethnic/national origin, or sexual orientation group and where tensions remain high against his or her group.
- Several incidents have occurred in the same locality, at or about the same time, and the victims are all of the same racial, religious, ethnic/national origin, or sexual orientation group.
- A substantial portion of the community where the crime occurred perceives that the incident was motivated by bias.
- The victim was engaged in activities promoting his or her racial, religious, ethnic/national origin, or sexual orientation group. For example, the victim is a member of the NAACP, participated in gay rights demonstrations, and so on.
- The incident coincided with a holiday relating to, or a date of particular significance to, a racial, religious, or ethnic/national origin group (e.g., Martin Luther King Day, Rosh Hashanah, etc.).
- The offender was previously involved in a similar hate crime or is a member of a hate group.
- There were indications that a hate group was involved. For example, a hate group claimed responsibility for the crime or was active in the neighborhood.
- A historically established animosity exists between the victim's group and the offender's group.

- The victim, although not a member of the targeted racial, religious, ethnic/national origin, or sexual orientation group, is a member of an advocacy group supporting the precepts of the victim group.

Examples of Reporting Hate Crime Incidents

The U.S. Department of Justice's report *Summary Reporting System: Hate Crime Data Collection Guidelines* (which was generated due to the 1990 act) contains a series of examples related to the reporting of hate crime incidents. These examples are intended to ensure uniformity in reporting data by the locality to the state and the FBI's UCR Section.

Example 1. While driving through a predominantly Mexican American neighborhood, an African American male stopped his car to repair a flat tire. A group of Mexican Americans leaving a bar across the street accosted the driver and then attacked him with bottles and clubs. During the attack, the offenders called the victim by a well-known and recognized epithet used against African Americans and told him that he was not welcome in the neighborhood. This incident would be reported as anti-African American because the victim and offenders are of different races, the offenders used a racial epithet, and the facts reveal no other reason for the attack than the stated one (i.e., to keep African Americans out of the neighborhood).

Example 2. Overnight, unknown persons broke into a synagogue and destroyed several religious objects. The perpetrators left a large swastika drawn on the door and wrote "Death to Jews" on a wall. Although valuable items were present, none was stolen. Report this incident as anti-Jewish because the offenders destroyed religious objects, left anti-Semitic words and graffiti behind, and theft did not appear to be the motive for the burglary.

Example 3. A 29-year-old Chinese American male was attacked by a 51-year-old white male wielding a tire iron. The victim suffered severe lacerations and a broken arm. The incident took place in a parking lot next to a bar. Investigation revealed that the offender and victim had previously exchanged racial insults in the bar, the offender having initiated the exchange by calling the victim by well-known Japanese epithets and complaining that the Japanese were taking away jobs from "real" Americans. An anti-Asian/Pacific Islander offense would be reported based on the differences in race of the victim and offender, the exchange of racial insults, and the absence of other reasons for the attack.

Example 4. An adult white male was approached by four white teenagers who requested money for the bus. When he refused, one of the youths said to the others, "Let's teach this (epithet for a homosexual) a lesson." The victim was punched in the face, knocked to the ground, kicked several times, and robbed of his wristwatch, ring, and wallet. When he reported the crime, the victim advised that he did not know the offenders and that he was not gay. The facts are ambiguous. Although an epithet for a homosexual was used by one of the offenders, the victim was not gay, such epithets are sometimes used as general insults regardless of the target person's sexual orientation, and in this case the offenders' motivation appeared to be limited to obtaining money. Therefore, the incident would not be designated bias motivated.

Example 5.   A small neighborhood bar frequented by gays burned down after being closed for the night. Investigation revealed that the fire was deliberately set, but there were no witnesses or suspects. Although the fire was deliberately set, the fact that the bar was frequented by gays may have been coincidental. Therefore, the incident is not reported as bias motivated. Two weeks later, three white adult males were arrested on a tip from an informant. They admitted burning down the bar, saying they did it to keep gays out of the neighborhood. As a result, this incident should now be reclassified as a bias crime.

Example 6.   Six African American men assaulted and seriously injured a white man and his Asian male friend as they were walking through a residential neighborhood. Witnesses said that the victims were attacked because they were trespassing in an "African American" neighborhood. An anti-multiracial group bias incident should be reported because the victims and offenders were of different races and witnesses reported that the victims were attacked because they were not African American.

Additional Guidelines and Examples

1. **Need for case-by-case assessment of the facts.** The aforementioned guidelines and examples are not all-inclusive of the types of objective facts that evidence biased motivation. Therefore, reporting agencies must examine each case for facts which clearly prove that the offender's bias motivated him or her to commit the crime.
2. **Misleading facts.** Agencies must be alert to misleading facts. For example, the offender used an epithet to refer to the victim's race, but the offender and victim were of the same race.
3. **Feigned facts.** Agencies must be alert to evidence left by the offenders which is meant to give the false impression that the incident was motivated by bias. For example, students of a religious school vandalize their own school, leaving antireligious statements and symbols on its walls, in the hope that they will be excused from attending class.
4. **Offender's mistaken perception.** Even if the offender was mistaken in his or her belief that the victim was a member of a racial, religious, ethnic/national origin, or sexual orientation group, the offense is still a hate crime as long as the offender was motivated by bias against the group. For example, a middle-aged man walking by a bar frequented by gays was attacked by six teenagers who mistakenly believed the victim had left the bar and was gay. Although the offenders were wrong on both counts, the offense is a hate crime because it was motivated by the offenders' anti-gay bias.
5. **Changes in findings of bias.** If, after an initial incident report was submitted, a contrary finding regarding bias occurs, the national file must be updated with the new finding. For example, if an initial finding of no bias was later changed to racial bias or a finding of racial bias was later changed to religious bias, the change should be reported to the FBI's UCR Section.

These guidelines are from the U.S. Department of Justice's *Summary Reporting System: Hate Crime Data Collection Guidelines.* The quarterly hate crime report format, instructions, and forms for reporting hate crimes to the FBI's UCR Section can be obtained from the U.S. Government Printing Office, Washington, D.C.

MONITORING HATE/BIAS CRIMES AND INCIDENTS

Importance of Monitoring Hate Groups

Monitoring extremist groups is an extremely important obligation of law enforcement. Activities by all these groups are tracked through a homogeneous, nationwide criminal justice reporting system. There are also sources of hate/bias crime data other than those agencies that voluntarily collect it; however, the statistics are not comprehensive. But the data these organizations do collect confirm that bias incidents and violence are on the rise against a wide assortment of peoples. A few of those organizations (see Appendix I for addresses) are discussed below.

Klanwatch

Klanwatch, a project of the Southern Poverty Law Center (Montgomery, Alabama), considers its primary responsibility to monitor white supremacist groups on a national scale and keep track of hate crimes. They disseminate this information to law enforcement agencies through a bimonthly publication, the *Klanwatch Intelligence Report.*

Anti-Defamation League

The Anti-Defamation League (ADL), mentioned briefly in Chapter 11, has been a leader of national and state efforts and has assisted in the development of legislation, policies, and procedures to deter and counteract hate-motivated crimes. The ADL developed a recording system that has served as a model since it was launched in 1979. In 1981, ADL's Legal Affairs Department drafted a model hate crimes bill for introduction in state and local legislatures. The model statute was intended to assist state and local governments in the enactment of their own hate crimes laws. By 1991, more than half of the states that had enacted hate crimes laws based their statutes on ADL's model, and 46 of the 50 states had enacted some form of hate crimes laws.

National Gay and Lesbian Task Force and NGLTF Policy Institute

The National Gay and Lesbian, Task Force (NGLTF) works to eradicate discrimination and violence based on sexual orientation and HIV status. The NGLTF was also founded in 1973 to serve its members in a manner that reflects the diversity of the lesbian and gay community. In 1991 the Task Force was restructured into two organizations—the NGLTF and the NGLTF Policy Institute—to improve its lobbying efforts and expand its organization and educational programs. Both groups are headquartered in Washington, D.C. The Task Force has consistently reported increases in homophobic attacks, which they track.

The Center for Democratic Renewal

The Center for Democratic Renewal (CDR; formerly the National Anti-Klan Network), another organization that tracks bias activity, reported that there were

50,000 active hate group members and 150,000 supporters nationwide in 1990 and their numbers are rising (*Fresno Bee,* Nov. 12, 1990, p. A-1). Since 1982, CDR's strategy to end bigoted violence has not only concentrated its efforts in tracking bias activity, but also in educating society through publications and assisting victims by way of various programs. They have been active in pushing law enforcement and government agencies to use existing laws to protect people from hate violence and/or helping to build coalitions to educate the public of the need for new legislation that would punish perpetrators.

HATE CRIME LAWS

Federal laws provide criminal and civil causes of action for victims of hate crimes in the United States whether they are citizens or not. (State and local laws are not discussed in this book. Specific federal laws are contained in the Instructors Manual.)

The U.S. Congress has provided criminal and civil remedies to victims of racially motivated violence. Not all acts of hate violence are prohibited by federal law. Federal statutes forbid violence by private parties only when there is an intent to interfere with a federally protected right, that is, one specifically guaranteed by a federal statute or the U.S. Constitution. Nevertheless, these rights are broad when a perpetrator's motive is tainted by racial hatred. Similar protection is provided victim(s) of crime and incidents when motivated by sexual orientation.

A victim of a hate/bias crime that violated a federal law can initiate criminal prosecution of the perpetrator by reporting it to a local office of the Federal Bureau of Investigation (FBI). That office then assigns an investigator to the case. A victim may also contact the local U.S. Attorney's office or the criminal section of the Civil Rights Division at the U.S. Department of Justice in Washington, D.C. In addition to criminal prosecution, a victim can also prosecute civilly if the facts support a civil action under the federal statutes. The victim can seek both damages and injunctive relief in a civil action against the perpetrator of violence motivated by racial hatred.

In general, the federal criminal statutes are intended to supplement state and local criminal laws. Procedurally, the U.S. Justice Department will not become actively involved in prosecuting a particular action until local authorities have concluded their case. After a person is convicted or is acquitted in state courts, the Justice Department evaluates the end result before determining whether to prosecute under federal statutes. There is no set time within which the Justice Department makes its decision.

Why Special Legislation?

Some law enforcement leaders argue that there is no need for special legislation dealing with hate/bias crimes because there are already statutes and laws covering the specific crime(s) committed by the perpetrator. For example, an assault by one person upon another is prosecutable in all jurisdictions. Therefore, the argument is made, why would such an assault be prosecuted differently even if it was motivated by a person's hate or bias toward victims because of their color, ethnic background, religion, or sexual orientation? Those localities and states have no system for identifying, reporting, investigating, and prosecuting hate/bias crimes. Thus there are deficiencies in the very way most law enforcement agencies and prosecutors process hate crimes.

First, incidents are not classified by racial, ethnic, sexual orientation, or religious motivation, making it virtually impossible to tabulate hate violence acts, spot trends, and perform analyses. Second, an inaccurate characterization of certain types of hate violence crimes occurs. For example, cross burnings are variously classified as malicious mischief, vandalism, or burning without a permit. Swastika paintings are often classified as graffiti incidents or malicious mischief.

Many states have legislation that adds penalty enhancements to crimes motivated by hate/bias. Enhancements send a clear message to the perpetrator and the public that these crimes will not be tolerated and will be treated as serious offenses. The U.S. Supreme Court in April 1993 upheld the constitutionality of Wisconsin's state hate crime law and enhanced sentences. In upholding the law, the U.S. Supreme Court made a clear distinction between freedom of thought versus conduct in the commission of a hate crime. The Supreme Court's decision means that hate crime laws that impose tougher sentences are constitutional. The test case, *Wisconsin* v. *Mitchell,* involved a young black man who admitted he assaulted a white teen solely because of his race. Mitchell was convicted of aggravated battery, which carries a maximum two-year prison sentence in Wisconsin. But prosecutors invoked the state hate crimes law, which permits a seven-year sentence and Mitchell was sentenced to four years. Mitchell appealed and the Wisconsin Supreme Court rejected the extended sentence, maintaining that the hate crime law was unconstitutional because it infringed on First Amendment rights of free thought. The court had further reasoned that an assault is the same whether the victim is "attacked because of his skin color or because he was wearing British Knights tennis shoes." In reversing the Wisconsin decision, U.S. Supreme Court Justice Rehnquist acknowledged that the only reason for the longer prison sentence was Mitchell's discriminatory motive in choosing the victim, but that judges have long been permitted to examine motive to determine what sentence to impose.

The U.S. Supreme Court reaffirms that crimes committed against a person or property because of race, religion, or sexual orientation will be dealt with sternly. As discussed in Chapter 11, an attack of any kind on a person because of prejudice and bigotry is reprehensible and deserves special attention and enhanced penalties. There are some key differences that make hate/bias crimes more serious than standard offenses. Crimes of this sort deny the free exercise of civil rights, sometimes frightening the victim from exercising freedom of speech, association, and assembly. Furthermore, these crimes tend to be more violent than non-bias crimes. Often, the attacks are acts of terrorism intended to punish the victim for being visible (i.e., a person who looks or acts different is easy to single out by a bigoted person). Finally, these acts against individuals are also often meant to terrorize entire communities.

ROLE OF COMMUNITY HUMAN RELATIONS COMMISSIONS

Cities and counties nationwide have established community human relations commissions (HRCs). Created as independent agencies, they are responsible for fostering equal opportunity and eliminating all forms of discrimination. These objections are accomplished by means of investigating, mediating, and holding public hearings on problems that arise from discrimination prohibited by state, federal, and local laws. Most HRCs will not investigate incidents of discrimination where such a function is preempted or prohibited by state or federal legislation. In cases where there is a violation of state or federal law, the HRC refers the complainant to the appropriate local, state, or federal agency. They will then monitor the progress of the complaint but will not conduct any formal investigation. Each HRC has established procedures that govern how they receive, investigate, hold hearings, and mediate/resolve complaints. Confidentiality is a protected right of the complainant in discrimination cases reported to HRCs of civil rights violations. As established by state or federal law, the names of the parties may not be made public without the written consent of both, with few exceptions. Human relations commissions should also be part of the community–police partnership, in which they all take responsibility for educating their community about its ethnic makeup. This includes efforts to bring people together for dialogue.

TREND MONITORING IN MULTICULTURAL COMMUNITIES

Monitoring conditions in a community provides useful information for forecasting potential negative events and preparing accordingly. Futurist William Tafoya (1990) has suggested that responsible forecasting should go beyond issue identification. He and other social forecasters contend that the framework for evaluating any predictions should be done within a structure that includes an analysis of economic circumstances, social and cultural conditions, and the political environment. Tafoya warns:

> It is a grave error for law enforcement executives to dismiss social maladies as being not within their purview. These conditions constitute the setting within which police officers must daily cope. They not only exacerbate but are breeding ground for crime, drug use and violence. It is also a mistake to sweep aside such concerns as a function of bias and bigotry alone. Indeed, racism is a major component of the problem. But there are other ingredients in the witches' brew that transforms the essence of equity today. (Tafoya, 1990)

For this reason, many law enforcement agencies in the United States are establishing true forms of what most call *community-oriented policing* (COP). Enlightened police executives recognize that they have not been operating as partners with the communities and neighborhoods that they serve and must begin doing so; COP is the current means of accomplishing that objective.

IDENTIFYING AT-RISK COMMUNITIES

Community Profiling

Law enforcement agencies experiencing demographic changes in their communities are well advised to perform an analysis of what is taking place: *community profiling*. Profiling involves a demographic analysis of the community with regard to ethnicity/national origin, race, religion, and sexual orientation groups. Such a profile must include a sense of time (i.e., what can community and law enforcement personnel expect from profiled groups with regard to the observance of holidays and religious or cultural ceremonies? See Appendix G.) For example, during the U.S. observance of Pearl Harbor Day, more Japanese American students miss school than any other day of the year because they are or feel threatened.

Progressive agencies send out listings to their patrol officers of religious and cultural holidays and world crisis events that could affect the area they serve. If officers wait to identify at-risk communities until hate crimes are committed in their patrol neighborhood, they are not fulfilling their professional responsibilities. Knowing how to identify at-risk communities and then to commit resources to resolve problems is proactive police work and is crucial to preventing conflict. While this involves more departmental time and personnel initially, the final savings in terms of preventing and planning for possible incidents is well worth the time if community disruption is to be avoided.

Neighborhood and Police Partnership

Neighborhoods (citizens and all those institutions encompassed) and the police together are the best means of identifying communities "at risk": those having a high level of criminal activity or disorder and *usually a higher number of incidents of civil rights violations—hate/bias crimes, discrimination, and bigotry.* How does a city determine if a neighborhood is at risk? Who is responsible for the assessment? What strategies can be utilized to reduce the at-risk status? The best approach is community policing, described in Chapter 15, whereby police assist the community to protect itself and enhance the quality of life. Officers and citizens meet to discuss the neighborhoods' most serious problems and work together to resolve them.

Community policing strategies can certainly be applied to efforts to reduce racial tension. Mike Scott, director of administration at the Ft. Pierce, Florida Police Department, said: "Officers often recognize some kind of racial tension going on in a part of their city, but they can't seem to pinpoint it. 'They can feel it, they can see the incidents occurring on the streets, and people whispering about it, so there's a vague sense of tension. Unfortunately, that's where a lot of officers are left hanging' " (Parker, 1991).

Community policing encourages officers to delve into such observations and feelings to determine not only what is happening, but also who is involved, what is the motivation, where are they from, and so on. To be effective, officers who patrol areas where there are large numbers of racial and/or different ethnic concentrations must have some grasp of cultural awareness and cross-cultural communication. Morris Casuto, director of the San Diego Regional Office of the Anti-Defamation League and instructor at both the San Diego Police Academy and San Diego County Sheriff's Training Academy, stresses: "If officers are scrambling to understand communities only after a crime is committed, it is a terrible indictment of their lack of professionalism" (personal communication, Nov. 2, 1992).

Additionally, they must know neighborhood leaders and how to locate them quickly in the event that they are needed to help in rumor or people control and general assistance. Neighborhood leaders can be invaluable when it comes to victims who might distrust police. Officers should consider themselves as first-line intelligence assets for their community. One simple example would be that they watch for graffiti and/or other materials posted on walls, fences, telephone poles, buildings, and so on. This could be indicative of the operation of a person who is racist or a hate group active in the area.

Rana Sampson, a community policing training coordinator for the Police Executive Research Forum (PERF), stresses that the problem-focused approach provides officers with a better understanding of social, economical, and environmental problems in the community. Sampson stated: " 'When officers start understanding the problems of the community, it means they're starting to work with the community. . . . When they start working with the community, they realize that 80 percent of the people are really good. A much smaller percentage of people are actually engaged in negative behavior' " (Parker, 1991).

There are limits as to what the police can do without community help and they have a traditional role identification to overcome. However, when officers patrol neighborhoods daily, they can be the best resources to monitor, report, and determine occurrences while using problem-oriented policing strategies. Herman Goldstein, University of Wisconsin law professor and the architect of the Problem Oriented Policing (POP) concept, indicated: "The police department, more than any other agency of government, must have a bird's eye view of the dynamics within its community, including the demographics, agendas of various groups, and an in-depth understanding of the hopes, aspirations and frustration of various groups. . . . This will give the police a feel for the mood and tensions that exist within a community. That's the first step toward dealing with racial tension" (Parker, 1991).

Community Relations Service

About 1980, the Community Relations Service of the U.S. Department of Justice began preparing what became an annual appraisal report of racial tensions in a selective number of cities. The report identified the communities with the highest level of risk of serious civil disorder or other forms of racial violence. Julian Klugman, director of the service, at a conference in 1986, explained:

> Sometimes you can predict it, but usually not. At least you can pinpoint cities with serious problems, and that guides our apportionment of resources. When we identify a city as having a high risk or serious risk of racial disorder, we offer assistance to the police department so as to reduce the chance of a police related triggering incident. Almost always, a triggering incident is police related. . . . By and large we attribute the outbreaks of racial civil disorder to the presence of two tap roots. The first tap root is a perception that is clear and bold in the minority awareness of gross racial inequities in many aspects of the social structure. It is not necessary that this perception mirror reality, but it generally does. It is likely to be that the perception understates the real inequity; rarely is the real inequity exaggerated. The second tap root is the minority's lack of confidence in the interest or capability of government or other institutions that provide redress for grievances.

This Department of Justice service gathers data in seven areas: demographic balance, administration of justice (particularly police community relations), employment, education, housing, health and welfare, and community relationships. The statistical data are then used to assess six critical factors:

1. The relationship of minorities to the administration of justice system
2. The impact of the economy
3. The level of minorities inclusion and/or exclusion in the system, and the number of minorities serving as elected officials, as part of the system
4. The quality of intergroup relationships
5. The level of violence currently in the city
6. The basic demographic influence

It is time consuming to perform this type of analysis and develop a program based on the findings. Police departments have access to the same kind of data and a great deal of experience and expertise to complete the same type of analysis within neighborhoods if they choose to do so.

TRENDS TO MONITOR: STEEP TYPOLOGY

The acronym STEEP stands for "social, technological, environmental, economic, and political." As has been pointed out previously, there is a connection between economic, social conditions, and politics and the numbers of hate/bias crimes that occur. The relationship between poor economics, scapegoating, discrimination, bigotry, and violence against protected classes is explained in Chapter 11. It is important for agency personnel and officers involved in community-oriented policing to understand basic economic, social, and political issues as these factors contribute to social unrest.

Economic Circumstances

Communities monitoring economic conditions in the late 1980s and early 1990s saw a recession that touched all parts of the world. Unemployment and poor economic times were at an all-time high:

> A disquieting fact in the midst of mainstream economics is that the unemployment rate among blacks and hispanics continued to far exceed that of white Americans. (*Washington Post,* Nov. 3, 1988, p. A-1)

> A fuller accounting of the unemployed includes workers who cannot find more than a part-time job and discouraged workers who have quit looking. Last year (1991) the total of people in such distress was 40% of the U.S. labor force. (Gwynne, 1992)

> People were extremely frustrated. The distance between the "haves" and "have nots" increased and more children were living in poverty. (Wilson, 1987)

Several instances of crime, social unrest, riots, and disturbances in the United States have occurred during depressed economies. New, sudden massive immigrations (both legal and illegal) always affect the scramble for available jobs and services. Poverty, overcrowding, and wars have been pressuring more people to migrate than ever before, laying the conditions for what could become "the human crisis of our age," the United Nations reported in its 1993 annual report (*Contra*

Costa Times, July 7, 1993, p. B-1). In Florida, for example, waves of refugees from Cuba and Haiti flooded the state. Many areas experienced real conflict as those already struggling, established residents, now had masses of persons competing with them for services and jobs. California also experienced massive immigration (both legal and illegal), from Mexico, Central and South America, and Southeast Asia. The new immigrants (the weakest group) become the target for people's frustrations as their own personal well-being goes down. The established minorities in neighborhoods look at what they perceive as preferential treatment for the newcomers and react accordingly: "'People who come from other countries are welcomed and treated better than people who have lived here for many years,' says a black leader" (Preston, 1989).

Examples of immigrant/refugee settlement in economically depressed communities by the federal government are numerous. Frequently, placement of immigrants has taken place without regard to the capacity of local resources to handle the influx. Polls reflect an increase in anti-immigrant attitude—a backlash against all newcomers, especially in such economically depressed areas. Eventually, police–community problems evolve with immigrants brought in under well-meaning national policy, but policy that has not been thoroughly worked through. Tracking influxes into communities plus awareness of political decisions should alert law enforcement executives and officers to relocation and acculturation problems of newcomers into local communities. Tracking also provides an opportunity to work with the community to develop transition management plans as well as preventive programs for keeping the peace. National immigration policies and politics have a tremendous impact on cities and counties, and therefore criminal justice agencies must monitor them and plan accordingly.

Political Environment

The criminal justice system must monitor legislation and political events and decisions. Executives of criminal justice agencies must scan what is going on not only in the United States and the jurisdictions they serve, but also in the world. (Although *USA Today, Newsweek, and Time,* to name a few publications, are sources of information, *The Economist* offers a more comprehensive worldwide perspective). What occurs in Mexico, Haiti, and Bosnia–Herzegovina does affect us. For instance, during the 1992 conflict in the former Yugoslavia, there were attacks in the United States by Muslims on Serbs, both second-generation Americans. Awareness is crucial for prevention and conflict resolution. The criminal justice system can not operate as though it were in a vacuum.

Social and Cultural Conditions

There have been tumultuous events in major cities across the United States. In Howard Beach, New York, in 1986 two black men were chased from a "whites only" neighborhood and subsequently one was killed; in Forsyth County, Georgia, in 1987, a march by civil rights activists in a virtually all-white rural county protested racism as hooded Ku Klux Klansmen taunted them; in Shreveport, Louisiana, in 1988, a drug deal that went bad resulted in a white teenager shooting and killing an innocent black bystander, which unleashed two days of citywide rioting; in Miami, Florida, in 1989, a Hispanic police officer shot a black man who fled police on a motorcycle, which triggered two days of rioting. The major riots in Los Angeles and other cities following the initial acquittal of the four Los Angeles police officers who beat Rodney King were studied in depth. The social and cultural reasons, suggested by experts, that lead to explosive events due to an incident can be reduced to poverty, frustration with the system, perceptions of racism and unequal treatment, decline in the nuclear family, high divorce rates, and an explosion in the numbers of diverse peoples living in close proximity to each other. Another factor suggested is the younger generation: "Some authorities believe that an alarming proportion lack basic skills necessary to compete in an increasingly technologically-oriented job market. How will the frustration and joblessness of young people manifest itself tomorrow?" (Tafoya, 1990).

Some experts would not rule out the significance of gangs and/or drugs on society in general and on the neighborhoods specifically as a contributing factor. None of these elements alone, however, accounts for the violence manifested in the communities mentioned. But all factors in combination with political and economic conditions, contribute to the massive discontent found in society. Undoubtedly, decades of societal precursors set the stage for the upheavals.

Overreaction

Overreaction (and underreaction) by a city or county law enforcement agency is sometimes costly in terms of perception of the criminal justice system. In San Francisco, California, when a white truck driver was beaten and robbed in 1992, police flooded the neighborhood. The perpetrators were quickly arrested and no physical disturbance occurred in the aftermath. There was, however, an emotional reaction and cynicism by some members of the neighborhood (predominantly poor black) over the sudden police presence and anger over door-to-door police sweeps. "'A black girl was killed here and one police officer came,' said one resident, referring to the 1990 slaying of a 23-year-old murder witness.' But a white truck driver is beaten and everybody comes. They don't come when you need them,' said the resident . . . " (*San Francisco Examiner,* Oct. 11, 1992, p. B-1). Perceptions such as these must be changed. Community-oriented policing is one solution, combined with performing a neighborhood-at-risk analysis. (Forecasting techniques and processes are contained in the instructor's manual.)

SUMMARY

The changing demographics of our communities, coupled with a bleak economic environment, appear to be significant factors resulting in an increase in crimes motivated by hate/bias. Private organizations and law enforcement agencies monitoring these trends support this conclusion. It is clear that a national, standardized data collection process is essential in order that the criminal justice system and respective communities served will know the scope of the problem and be able to allocate resources accordingly. Such a system would enhance the prospects for developing an effective response to crimes motivated by hate/bias. Similar monitoring approaches must also be utilized by schools and businesses to ensure that acts of bigotry are tracked and resolved quickly and effectively.

Criminal justice executives must monitor and respond pro-actively to the negative conditions in the social, political, and economic environment. Police officers and all other representatives of the institution of law enforcement operate daily in environments characterized by extremely negative conditions. The criminal justice system represents one part of the community, and it alone cannot provide the answers and responses that would combat hate/bias crimes in society.

DISCUSSION QUESTIONS AND ISSUES*

1. ***Hate Crimes Monitoring Systems.*** Does your law enforcement agency (where you work or the community in which you reside) have a system in place for monitoring hate/bias crimes and incidents? If yes, get a copy of the statistics for at least five years (or as many years as are available) for the hate/bias crimes and determine the following.

   (a) What trends are noticeable in each category?

   (b) Do the categories measure essential information that will assist your law enforcement agency to recognize trends?

   (c) What would improve the data collection method to make it more useful in measuring trends and making predictions? (Use the ADL model in Appendix L as a guide.)

   (d) Determine if your law enforcement agency has actually used the data to track the nature and extent of such crimes and incidents and deployed their resources accordingly. Provide the class with example(s).

2. ***Trend Monitoring.*** Make a list of social, economic, and political conditions/events occurring within the law enforcement jurisdiction in which you work or live that are specific to that community and could potentially have a relationship to crimes motivated by hate. Next, for each condition listed, make a comments column that suggests what specific factors a peace officer/criminal justice practitioner should look for in the community that would assist the agency in forecasting trends and events.

REFERENCES

Anti-Defamation League (1991). *An ADL Special Report The KKK Today: A 1991 Status Report,* Anti-Defamation League of B'nai B'rith, New York.

GWYNNE, S.C. (1992). "The long haul," *Time,* Sept. 28, p. 36.

HATAMIYA, LESLIE (1991). *Walk with Pride: Taking Steps to Address Anti-Asian Violence,* Japanese American Citizens League, San Francisco, Aug. 1991, pp. 10–12.

KLUGMAN, JULIAN (1986). U.S. Department of Justice, Community Relations Service presentation at Sheraton Hotel, Concord, Calif., Dec. 1.

National Institute Against Prejudice and Violence (1986). *The Ethnoviolence Project Pilot Study,* Institute Report 1, NIAPV, Washington D.C., p. 5.

National Institute Against Prejudice and Violence (1991). *Striking Back at Bigotry,* NIAPV, Washington, D.C.

National Organization of Black Law Enforcement Officers (1986). *Racial and Religious Violence: A Law Enforcement Handbook,* NOBLE, Washington D.C., p. 23.

New York State Governor's Task Force on Bias-Related Crime (1988). *Final Report,* Albany, N.Y., Mar., note 13 at p. ES10.

*See Instructor's Manual accompanying this text for additional activities, role-plays, questionnaires and projects related to the content of this chapter.

PARKER, PATRICIA A. (1991). "Tackling unfinished business: POP plays valuable position in racial issues," *Police,* Dec., p. 19.

PRESTON, JULIA (1989). "Trouble spreads in troubled black areas," *Washington Post,* Jan. 18, p. A-1.

Southern Poverty Law Center (1987). *"Move-In" Violence: White Resistance to Neighborhood Integration in the 1980's,* Southern Poverty Law Center, Klanwatch Project, Montgomery, Ala. Feb. 5, p. 4.

Southern Poverty Law Center (1992). *Klanwatch Intelligence Report: Special Year End Edition,* Issue 59, Southern Poverty Law Center, Montgomery, Ala. Feb.

TAFOYA, WILLIAM L. (1990). "Rioting in the streets: deja' vu?," *C. J. the Americas,* Vol. 2, No. 6, Dec./Jan., p. 21.

U.S. Department of Justice (1990). *Summary Reporting System: Hate Crime Data Collection Guidelines,* U.S. Government Printing Office, Washington D.C., p. 1.

WILSON, WILLIAM J. (1987). "The truly disadvantaged: the inner city," in *The Underclass and Public Policy,* The University of Chicago Press, Chicago, p. 21.

13

HATE/BIAS CRIMES:

Investigations, Control, and Victimology

OVERVIEW

In this chapter we discuss the importance of hate crime investigations and treatment of the victim(s) and illustrate the need for departments' clearly establishing policies that specify responsibilities and procedures. This chapter contains a list of factors an investigator should examine to determine if an incident is hate motivated. The chapter covers information on the need for properly trained law enforcement officials to carry out investigations and prosecutions. We also discuss organized hate groups and the increase in hate activity. Finally the chapter presents model policies for follow-up investigations and concludes with community programs to reduce hate crimes and incidents.

COMMENTARY

The need for quick and effective investigation and prosecution of hate/bias crimes is exemplified in the following sentiment:

> National Organization for Black Law Enforcement Executives, *Racial and Religious Violence: A Law Enforcement Guidebook*, Landover, Md., 1985, p. 24.

> Victims of racially and religiously targeted incidents incur damage to their homes and property, injury to their bodies and sometimes death. In addition to physical suffering, being victimized because of one's race, religion, or national origin brings negative attention to one's differences, injures one's dignity and self-esteem, and makes one feel unwanted in the community, yet because most crimes against racial

and religious minorities are not extremely violent, victims are usually not given any special attention or assistance.

Richard Thornburgh, U.S. Attorney General, in *Hate Crime: A Training Video for Police Officers, Discussion Manual,* Anti-Defamation League of B'nai B'rith, New York, 1990.

Hate crimes are anathema to a free and democratic society. The destruction and fear that these acts cause, not just for the individual victim but for an entire group of citizens, have ramifications well beyond the actual crime itself. This is why we must vigorously investigate, indict and punish those who unleash their bigotry through cowardly acts of abuse, vandalism and violence. Local law enforcement agencies play a large role in combatting and deterring hate crimes. Police training in how to identify a hate crime and how to deal with a victim's trauma is essential for an effective law enforcement response.

INTRODUCTION

As mentioned in Chapters 11 and 12, criminal justice agencies must make hate/bias crimes and incidents a priority response from the initial report through prosecution. To ensure that such crimes receive priority and are treated seriously by all personnel, each agency must have a written policy that establishes what the procedures and responsibilities are within that organization. Only when policies and procedures are in place, combined with feasible community programs, will society begin to control and reduce hate crimes. Those policies and procedures define how a law enforcement agency will investigate hate/bias crimes and incidents. A "hate/violence pyramid" model (Exhibit 13.1-Source unknown) has been developed to show how hate and prejudice can evolve.

HATE/BIAS CRIME AND INCIDENT INVESTIGATIONS

The following provides a basic overview of general and specific procedures and protocol that should be utilized by law enforcement agencies and the district attorney's or prosecutor's office in response to crimes and incidents motivated by a person's race, religion, ethnic background, or sexual orientation (RRES).

General Procedures*

Assigned officer/first responder. When the assigned officer arrives on the scene and determines that the crime or incident may have been motivated by hate due to the victim's race, religion, ethnic background, or sexual orientation (RRES), the officer is to:

1. Stabilize the victim.
2. Apprehend the responsible.
3. Protect the crime scene and evidence.

---

*The ideas presented for the investigations of hate crime were compiled from multiple sources and are quoted only when extensively utilized from one document. Particularly helpful was Training Key 409 from the International Association of Chiefs of Police.

Exhibit 13.1   Hate/Violence Pyramid

Life-Threatening Acts

Violence

- Assassination
- Bombing
- Lynching

- Arson
- Genocide

Extermination

Acts of Violence

- Assault
- Vandalism

- Riots
- Terrorism

Physical Attack

Acts of Discrimination

- Harassment
- Exclusion of persons from:

Hate

  —Social privileges
  —Employment
  —Educational opportunities
  —Housing

Discrimination

Acts of Prejudice

- Members of disliked group are avoided at all costs

Avoidance

Acts of Indirect Prejudice

- Feelings about disliked groups are discussed with like-minded friends

Prejudice

- Antagonism is expressed
- Rumors and stereotypes form

Verbal Rejection

---

4. Request a field supervisor (follow department policy).
5. Conduct a preliminary investigation, including neighborhood survey for witnesses when appropriate.
6. Provide assistance to the victim and refer to the appropriate legal or service agency.
7. Collect and process evidence.
8. Complete an offense report form and code as an RRES.
9. Complete report with supervisor approval prior to end of the shift. Direct copies to required division commanders and follow-up unit.

Patrol field supervisor.   Upon arrival at the scene of an RRES crime or incident, the patrol field supervisor is to:

1. Assist in the stabilization of the victim.
2. Interview the officer receiving the complaint.
3. Verify that the crime or incident is an RRES.
4. Determine if additional personnel are necessary and ensure that evidence collection occurs.
5. Take steps to see that the situation does not escalate or reoccur.

6. Supervise the preliminary investigation.

7. Assure the victim that a total investigation will be conducted.

8. Ensure that all physical remains of the crime or incident are removed after processing as evidence is completed. If the remains cannot be removed (i.e., paint on walls), the supervisor will attempt to impress on building or property owners the need for complete restoration as soon as possible.

9. Notify the watch commander or senior supervisor on duty.

10. See that all reports are properly completed and submitted prior to the end of shift.

11. If appropriate, provide for increased patrol in the area for as long as necessary, but at least for several days following the crime or incident.

12. Identify training needs relative to RRES crimes or incidents.

Watch commander.   After being notified of an RRES crime or incident, the watch commander is to:

1. Report to the scene immediately if the crime or incident is determined to be serious.

2. Notify appropriate persons or units, such as the command duty officer, investigations, or specialized unit responsible for follow-up, depending on the nature and seriousness of the crime or incident(s).

3. Ensure that the chief of police/deputy chief is notified of serious crimes or incidents.

4. Determine whether press releases should be made or that the press information officer is notified.

5. Review all reports completed by patrol officers and/or field supervisors prior to their submission.

Assigned investigator (Crimes persons or specialized unit)

1. Check an extended neighborhood area to identify and interview witnesses when appropriate.

2. Coordinate investigative work and evidence analysis with the crime scene investigations unit.

3. Conduct surveillance and other techniques to identify and apprehend perpetrator(s).

4. Coordinate victim assistance with appropriate legal or service agency.

5. Maintain liaison with original reporting officer to keep him or her informed of the status of the case.

6. Keep the victim informed through personal contact regarding case status.

7. Prepare case for prosecution and refer to the district attorney's office.

Crime prevention/community relations/specialized unit

1. Perform appropriate administrative follow-up investigations to resolve noncriminal incidents that were motivated by RRES.

2. Conduct public meetings; meet with neighborhood groups, residents in target areas, and other groups to allay fears; reduce the potential for counterviolence; and provide safety and protection information.

3. Assist victims and their families.

4. Establish liaison with formal minority organizations and leaders.

5. Provide preventive programs, such as antihate seminars for schoolchildren.

Training unit

1. Include human and cultural relations training programs in both in-service and advanced officer training programs.
2. Use minority and community leaders' input for development of cultural awareness, human relations, hate/bias crimes, and so on, training programs.
3. Prepare bulletins pertinent to cultural and human relations subjects.
4. Ensure that all officers attend assigned cultural and human relations in-service courses. Those failing to attend shall be identified to division commanders and remedial training provided.
5. Review and revise training programs to reflect changes in the community and in society.
6. Assist field training officers in development of appropriate recruit training that deal with cultural awareness, human relations skills, and information.

Specific Procedures for Patrol and Investigative Officers

The preceding information is a generic listing of the responsibilities of each member of an agency that deals, in some capacity, with hate/bias crimes or incidents. What follows are some specifics points.

Patrol officer. When responding to calls involving hate violence/force, or where threatened use of force is involved, the patrol officer should remember the following:

1. Some perpetrators, especially members of hate groups that preach violence, are known to be well armed and capable of turning their hatred on officers.
2. There may be added problems in stabilizing the scene. The victim(s) and their friends, neighbors, and sympathizers are usually quite emotional. Crowds may develop and become unruly or riotous if there is not a timely and effective response by officers.
3. The victim's feelings and emotions may vary, as noted below, and the officer must be sensitive to this and react accordingly. When a person's identity—race, religion, ethnicity, or sexual orientation—is attacked physically or verbally, victims may exhibit a variety of responses:
   - Fear for themselves or their families; fear that the attacks could occur again or escalate.
   - Anger and/or hatred toward the perpetrator and/or the group the perpetrator represents. The victim and his or her support group may be prepared to retaliate or seek revenge. The actions of the first responding officer(s) under these circumstances is crucial to victim. The victim's subsequent reaction and actions will most likely have implications for the relationship of the officer's agency to the victim as well as the victim's racial, religious, ethnic, or sexual orientation group. It is vital, therefore, that the officer make a proper assessment of the situation and the resources required to control or manage it in an efficient and timely manner.
4. It is also vital that the officer(s) remain patient and express concern for the victim. Such statements as "I'm sorry that this happened to you" or "I'm glad that you are okay" will often calm the victim. The officer must remember to ask if the victim is in need of medical assistance. A simple, sincere: "Are you all right?" goes a long way to establish a positive relationship.

5. Since the responding officer is frequently of a different culture, nationality, race, and/or lifestyle than the victim, the officer, in some cases, can assist the victim by seeking a close friend, relative, or community resource to communicate with the victim to help the person deal with his or her emotions. If possible, the officer should not leave the scene until appropriate companionship or assistance has arrived.

6. Victim(s) must be allowed to vent their emotions. The officer should guide the victim(s) through the facts of the incident while also allowing him or her to express emotion. If the patrol officer does not have time to listen, he or she should utilize family, friends, neighbors, and/or community resources to provide that assistance.

7. The officer must inform victim(s) of the procedures that will be followed—the investigation, the involvement of the prosecutor, the process, names and telephone numbers, case number, and referrals.

Investigator.   After the patrol officer has finished the preliminary investigation, the report is forwarded to the investigations unit or a unit that specializes in crime motivated by hate/bias. In small departments where officers are generalists, usually the same officer, or the supervisor, handles the case to its conclusion and submits it to the prosecutor for complaint. Some departments permit the patrol officer, with the approval of a supervisor, to make a decision whether to classify the crime or incident as hate/bias motivated or as a civil rights violation. Some agencies only permit trained supervisor(s) or manager(s) of the unit to which the suspected crime or incident is referred to make that decision following established departmental guidelines. If a crime occurred, the case will be assigned to an investigator who will complete any investigation necessary and prepare the case for review by the district attorneys' office for a decision on prosecution. If it is determined that no crime occurred, an investigator will be assigned to contact the victim and explain why. In either event, an investigator must contact the victim(s) and inform him or her of the status of the case. At some law enforcement agencies, if the case turns out to be an "incident" (not a crime but still hate/bias motivated), the supervisor or manager will forward the case to a detective who has been trained to handle incidents. This person could be a detective or an administrative officer who works in the community relations/affairs unit.

As indicated previously, the investigator (regardless of the unit to which he or she is assigned) must maintain contact with the victim(s) and provide information on the status of the case. Keeping minority community leaders up-to-date can help stop false rumors and reduce tensions and fear for the victim and the surrounding community. The hate crimes investigating officer must coordinate and network with the department intelligence officer so that they are both aware of the existence of active organized hate groups in the area. Ideally, they will also attend local, regional, and state meetings dealing with hate groups. This is particularly helpful in relating offenses to the activities of these groups in their jurisdiction. Examples of hate/bias crimes and incidents tracking forms are contained in Appendix J.

Models for Investigating Hate/Bias Crimes

The following are suggested guidelines for law enforcement agencies without standardized protocol for follow-up of hate/bias crimes and incidents. The suggested formats are based on the size of the department.

Small department (agencies of 1 to 100 sworn).   A small department may not have the staffing depth to have a specialized unit or investigator who can deal solely with hate crimes. Officers in small departments are usually generalists, meaning that they carry any type of case from the initial report through the investigation and submission to the district attorney. Therefore, all personnel should receive cultural and racial issues awareness training and learn the requirements of handling crimes and incidents motivated by hate. The officer who takes the crime or incident report must have it approved by his or her supervisor. Some small departments have allowed patrol officers to specialize in the investigation of certain crimes and they might be involved in either providing advice and direction, or actually taking the case and handling it to its conclusion. Those officers are usually the ones allowed to attend training and conferences that will teach and update them on the investigations of these crimes and incidents. Some departments have a patrol supervisor perform the follow-up investigation and submit the case to the prosecutor's office. It is important that the officer and his or her supervisor keep command officers informed of major cases. Those small agencies with a detective follow-up investigations unit must be sure that they are trained in the aspects of dealing with crimes motivated by hate.

Medium sized department (agencies of 100 to 500 sworn).   The following is a model suggested for a medium-sized department with a crimes against persons investigations unit and an administration unit responsible for community relations or affairs. The format follows this protocol: The responding patrol officer takes the initial report and decides if what occurred was indeed a crime or incident motivated by hate/bias and then completes a preliminary investigation. After this, the officer documents the findings on the department offense report form and follows the policy and procedure as established by the agency. The report (which may or may not already be classified as a hate/bias or civil rights violation depending on department policy) is approved by the officer's supervisor and watch commander. Then it is forwarded to the investigations unit that follows up on such cases (usually the crimes persons unit). The report is reviewed by the investigations unit supervisor, who again evaluates whether a crime or incident did or did not take place. If it is decided that it is an RRES crime, the report is assigned to a crimes persons investigator who specializes in this type of investigation. The report is then forwarded (through the appropriate chain of command) to the administration and community relations/affairs unit for follow-up. The staff of the latter unit is also trained to handle hate/bias, civil rights violations investigations, and provide victim assistance. The administrative follow-up would include:

- Any investigation required
- Referrals and support for the victim
- Conducting public meetings to resolve neighborhood problems
- Conflict resolution
- Liaison with minority organizations in the community and victim advocates

Some cases may require that the criminal investigator and administrative officer work jointly to resolve the crime or incident under investigation.

Large departments (agencies of 500 plus sworn).   Most large departments have enough staff and the need for a specialized unit. There are many advantages to having a specialized unit that focuses on crimes motivated by hate/bias or civil rights violations. The investigators become familiar and experienced with the law and special procedures required and can handle more complex, sensitive cases. Investigators who are allowed to specialize can form networks with victim advocate organizations and other community-based agencies. They work closely with the district attorney's office (probably with a special bias unit within that agency), establishing working relationships and rapport important to successful prosecutions. The investigators develop a sense of pride in their efforts and a commitment to provide a competent investigative and victim assistance response. Since the primary function of the unit is hate/bias crime investigations, they can sometimes develop a knowledge of individuals and groups that commit such offenses as well as become more aware of where the incidents occur. Detectives in departments that handle a multitude of cases do not have the time to track and monitor these crimes and, therefore, may not spot trends. Specialized units can evaluate the field performance of the patrol officers who have handled such crimes and can provide suggestions for improvement or commendations when the response has been effective or innovative.

There are disadvantages to specialized units. Often, when there is a specialized unit, patrol officers believe that what is happening in the neighborhood in which they work is not their problem—it is the problem of the specialized unit. The officer takes reports and transfers responsibility for resolution of problems identified to the specialized unit. Patrol officers may be unaware of a problem or its magnitude or even what resources are being marshalled to resolve it unless there is good communication between them and the members of the specialized unit. The disadvantages are surmountable, however, especially if the department uses community-oriented policing strategies. Community-oriented policing usually involves a higher degree of communications between agency units and with the community.

Model Hate Crime/Civil Rights Violations Investigative Units

Boston, Massachusetts, Police.   The Boston Police Department established their Community Disorders Unit (CDU) in 1978. The unit has grown (as of 1992 the Boston Police Department had a total of 1960 sworn) from the initial two officers to a diverse staff of 12, which consists of a lieutenant, two sergeants, and nine officers. At that time there were also four part-time civilians who act as interpreters. Lieutenant Detective William Johnston, commander of the unit, explained (personal communication, Oct. 7, 1992): "staff for the unit are selected for their investigative and people skills and not for their ethnicity, race, or sexual orientation. They are police officers first!"

CDU investigators receive 2½ days of training on laws and procedures, then work within the unit reviewing policy, protocol, and cases before receiving a case load of their own. The unit has a "central file clipboard" which is mandatory reading for all members of CDU each workday, as it contains a summary of all civil rights violation cases received. The unit has two shifts covering 17 hours per day five days per week and are on call after hours and on weekends for major cases.

According to department policy, the uniformed officer taking the preliminary report does not make a decision as to whether or not the incident is a civil rights violation (hate/bias crime). He or she establishes what took place, gathers evidence, takes statements, makes an arrest if possible, then simply checks a box on the report form routing the case to the Community Disorders Unit. The officer must also notify the patrol supervisor, who in turn alerts his or her superiors. In major cases, the CDU is also apprised of an event that might be a civil rights violation. The decision as to whether the case involves this type of violation covered by their state statute is made by the supervisor of the CDU. Above Lt. Johnston's desk, however, is the following sign:

> Neither the victim, the perpetrator, the local detectives, the CDU investigator, the Commander of the CDU, the Police Commissioner, the Mayor, nor any other mortal creature determines whether an incident is a civil rights violation.

> Only the facts gathered during a competent, thorough investigation make that determination!

Johnston thinks it is unfair to have the officer make a decision because he or she has too many other responsibilities at the crime scene during the preliminary investigation and not enough time or expertise. "Let the experts do it," explains Johnston.

The Community Disorders Unit's primary function is to investigate thoroughly all cases involving an alleged civil rights statute violation. They may then seek complaints in court and assist in the prosecution of such cases. In the case where a responding patrol officer has made an arrest on another criminal charge unrelated to the civil rights violation, Community Disorders Unit personnel, after follow-up investigation, may seek additional complaints under the Massachusetts Civil Rights Law. CDU members are active in the community, attending various meetings and continually networking, and being aware of what is occurring in the neighborhoods.

The department has been in the forefront of designing innovative proactive strategies, many of which are described elsewhere in this part, to deal with civil rights issues. CDU members, and in particular Lieutenant Detective William Johnston, have been involved in training and/or providing their protocol to other agencies.

New York City Police. The New York City Police Department founded their Bias Incident Investigation Unit in 1980 due to anti-Jewish activities in the city (neo-Nazi demonstrations were also taking place worldwide). The bias unit is staffed seven days a week from 8 A.M. to midnight. The unit is assigned, organizationally, to the highest-level uniformed member of the Department (the Chief of Department Office) to provide the priority and emphasis on bias crimes and to "cut through all channels." In 1992, the staffing of the unit consisted of 1 inspector; 1 lieutenant (executive officer), 3 sergeants, 18 detectives, and 3 civilians. The department recognizes the importance of having diversity in the staff of the bias unit, but does not necessarily assign cases based on a match of the victim with a detective of the same background unless there is a particular reason to do so, such as language and cultural differences or the sensitivity needs involved. For example, a gay investigator is not just assigned gay and lesbian bias cases. The difference between how a bias crime is handled versus almost any other crime is that the investigation is intensified and enhanced. More investigators may be assigned and the case is given to an office much closer to the highest level of the police department. The staff in the bias unit also have had special training, provided by the sergeant, in assisting the victim.

If an officer in the field suspects that an incident was bias motivated, he or she assists the victim, secures the scene, then calls a supervisor. The supervisor responds to the scene, interviews the victim and performs an investigation. The supervisor then calls the patrol captain, who goes to the scene and makes the decision as to whether the incident was bias motivated. Only a captain and above can deem an incident to be bias motivated, and only the bias review panel can overturn the captain's judgment. The bias review panel consists of the chief of detectives, chief of patrol, deputy commissioner of community affairs, and department advocate (administers discipline within the NYPD). The bias review panel meets and makes the final determination on those cases where the decision is questioned. The operations unit is notified of the incident and that unit notifies the bias unit investigators. The local precinct in which the incident occurred has detectives who conduct a joint investigation with the bias unit. This demonstrates the mutual concern for what occurred both within the precinct or neighborhood and at headquarters level.

The human rights commission (HRC) is notified of bias crimes and their members work closely with the bias unit. Incidents that are not crimes are referred to the HRC and/or advocacy groups or other counseling agencies. The community affairs officer of the precinct where the offense took place is also alerted. The bias unit staff interacts with community-based groups, providing education on bias crimes and resolving neighborhood problems. The bias unit also networks with the department's "Good Neighbor Program," discussed later in this chapter, wherein neighborhood volunteers are trained to help victims of bias crimes.

The district attorney's office is automatically notified of criminal cases. According to bias unit statistics, if the crime was bias motivated, there is a greater likelihood that the convicted perpetrator will be incarcerated compared to other offenses of a similar degree. This sends a message to perpetrators and the community that such incidents are not tolerated.

In 1988, the mayor's office created the New York City Bias Response Coordinating Committee as one part of the mayor's bias response plan. The committee consists of members of the following city agencies:

- The mayor's office
- The police department
- City commission on human rights
- Mayor's community assistance unit
- Board of education

If necessary, the committee can call upon several secondary agencies or officials in the city, on an ad hoc basis, to assist in resolution of the problem at hand. When major incidents of bias or community unrest occur, the city, through its bias response coordinating committee, mobilizes a number of city agencies. Where appropriate, the committee will also call on the services of state or federal agencies, as well as private and voluntary organizations, to assist in the city's response. The role of agency personnel or officials constituting the committee is well defined, so that each knows what is expected when a major incident occurs. As soon as something does happen, the committee's process is activated. The plan is prepared to assist members of the NYC bias response coordinating committee and to provide operational guidelines during serious bias incidents and related periods of community unrest. The major functions are to [New York City Mayor's Bias Response Plan, BM 327-1 (Rev. 3-88)-30]:

- Coordinate and establish a systematic and orderly response to bias incidents so as to ensure restoration of calm and stability in affected communities.
- Establish contact with and gain cooperation of all units and outside agencies responding to the scene that are not members of the bias response coordinating committee.
- Evaluate the situation, develop strategies for stabilizing the area, identify possible criminal and civil violations, and prioritize the actions to be taken.
- Identify and develop community liaisons so that up-to-date and accurate information can be relayed to field personnel and community leaders.
- Analyze each agency's response and to determine follow-up procedures and programs to be implemented to prevent a "flare-up" and future disturbance following the stabilization of the area and its return to normalcy.
- Maintain an ongoing dialogue among agencies in order to amend responsibilities and response procedures, and reevaluate available resources.
- Debrief personnel and analyze each agency's response after an incident with a view toward adjusting the plan as necessary and identifying topics for exercises and drills.

HATE/BIAS CRIME PROSECUTION

District Attorney's Office

In the early 1990s, very few district attorneys' offices in the United States had attorneys or specialized units that targeted such offenses (although some had policies and procedures). There are compelling reasons for district attorneys to devote special attention and resources to these crimes. The chief of community services of the

Norfolk County, Massachusetts district attorney's office wrote: "A prosecutor has discretion to influence, if not determine, what might be called the public safety climate that citizens in the communities he serves will experience. . . . To establish a public safety climate that fosters the full enjoyment of civil and political rights by the minority members of our communities requires a focused political will directed to that end as well as resources and capacity" (Agnes, 1989).

The most effective and successful approaches that build a climate of public safety have been those that:

- Established specialized hate crimes or civil rights violations units
- Standardized procedures to prosecute hate crime cases; (this standardization should include vertical prosection of cases)
- Appointed attorneys to be the liaison with various ethnic, racial, religious, and sexual orientation groups in the community
- Provided all attorneys on staff with cultural awareness/sensitivity training

Prosecutors Offices That Target Hate/Bias Crime

District attorneys' offices with specialized hate/bias crime or civil rights units that can serve as models are:

> **San Francisco District Attorney's Office Hate Crimes Unit**
> Hall of Justice
> 850 Bryant Street
> San Francisco, CA 94103
> 415/552-6400

> **Suffolk County District Attorney's Office Civil Rights Unit**
> New Courthouse
> Pemberton Square
> Boston, MA 02108
> 617/725-8600

> **Queens County, New York District Attorney's Office, Anti-Bias Bureau**
> Anti-Bias Bureau
> 125-01 Queens Boulevard
> Kew Gardens, NY 11415
> 718/286-6598

Special Problems in Prosecuting Hate/Bias Crimes

The attorneys who handle hate/bias crimes indicate that there are four potential obstacles to successful prosecutions:

- Proving the crime was motivated by bias
- Uncooperative complaining witnesses
- Special defenses
- Lenient sentences

It is often difficult to identify hate-motivated crimes or incidents accurately. Usually, no single factor is sufficient to make the determination, and sometimes the incident is disguised by the perpetrator such that it does not appear to be a hate/bias crime. Even cases that have been well investigated may lack sufficient evidence to prove that the crime was motivated, beyond a reasonable doubt, by hate/bias. Generally, prosecutors follow established guidelines for determining if the crime was bias related. Criteria such as the following are assessed:

- Plain common sense
- The language used by the perpetrator
- The severity of the attack
- Lack of provocation
- Previous history of similar incidents in the same area
- Absence of any apparent motive

Special defense has been argued in some cases. One such example is the "homosexual panic" or "gay advance" defense, where the person charged with an attack claims self-defense or temporary insanity in response to a sexual advance. This sort of defense, on occasion, has resulted in lenient sentences or acquittals.

Despite some difficulties in these prosecutions, the experience of the above-mentioned district attorneys' offices suggests that targeting these cases is the most productive approach to combating crimes motivated by hate/bias. District attorneys can play a major role in educating judges to the nature, prevalence, and severity of hate violence crime and to encourage effective sentences for this offense. They can also be very effective in their working relationships with and encouragement of police officers investigating these crimes. The effort involves each member of the criminal justice system, but the prosecutor has one of the most important roles.

HATE/BIAS CRIME AND INCIDENT CONTROL

Hate/bias crime and incidents can only be controlled through the combined efforts of the community (schools, private organizations, government agencies, churches, service organizations, and families), federal and state legislatures, and the criminal justice system. This holistic approach is examined in Chapters 11 and 12. Additionally, it is essential to monitor and control organized hate groups (through aggressive prosecutions, tracking, and networking). It is also important to profile communities to determine if they are at risk of strife or conflict caused by social, economic, and environmental conditions that result in hate/bias crimes and incidents.

Organized Hate Groups

This chapter would be incomplete if it did not contain further discussion of hate groups.

> To those who are startled to hear that the KKK is alive and well, one can only ask, Where Have You Been? Have no doubt about it, the Klan—which lynched helpless black Americans, murdered civil-rights workers, burned its crosses and spread its divisive venom of prejudice across the land—has not disappeared. It continues to hawk its poison to anyone who will listen. To make matters worse, the Klan today

has been joined by other harbingers of hate such as the Skinheads, the Aryan Nations, Posse Comitatus, The Covenant, the Sword, and the Arm of the Lord, White Aryan Resistance (WAR) and the strident right-wing political cult of Lyndon LaRouche. (Bayh, 1989)

There are similarities between the abovementioned groups, not the least of which is the respective organization's bigotry and prejudice based on religion, race, ethnicity, and sexual orientation. The author of the foregoing, Birch Bayh (former senator, chairman of the National Institute Against Prejudice and Violence, and an attorney in Washington, D.C.), describes a terrifying fact—an increase of 41 to 100 percent in hate crimes committed by extremist groups in various communities across the country. Continuing from the same article:

- **Ridgedale, Missouri:** State trooper slain by a member of The Order extremists.
- **Bull Shoals Lake, Arkansas:** Officials uncover huge military cache at camp of Covenant, Sword, Arm of the Lord.
- **Reno, Nevada:** Black man allegedly shot to death by two adolescent skinhead supporters.
- **Coeur d'Alene, Idaho:** White supremacists bomb a federal building, a business, and a home.

Bayh reveals that similar incidents have occurred in hundreds of other communities in the United States, and that, according to the evidence, these are often not acts of older Americans (thus a dying vestige): that many of the perpetrators are young adults. Many sources confirm that white supremacism is, and continues to be, on the rise. The *Intelligence Report* by the Klanwatch indicated that "a record number of white supremacist groups were active from coast to coast in 1991 . . . totals surged from 273 in 1990 to 346 in 1991, a 27 percent increase" (Southern Poverty Law Center, 1992), and the Anti-Defamation League (1991) in a series of articles stated that "a ten year decline in the nationwide strength of the Ku Klux Klan came to a halt during 1990 and . . . [it] may be poised to gain new strength . . . especially if the current recession becomes lengthy and severe." Increased membership may also be the result of violent civil unrest and/or riots when some whites look for protection in numbers. In 1993 there were bombings at NAACP offices in Washington state and California by members of a skinhead organization. At about the same time, the FBI broke up alleged plots among white supremacists, one to launch a race war in Los Angeles by placing a bomb in a prominent black church and the other to kill Rodney King. Such ongoing incidents demonstrate the need to continually monitor, investigate, and prosecute the persons and organizations responsible. When hate crimes of this magnitude occur to other groups in the community, law enforcement must immediately alert other organizations, which may also be targeted. The Jewish community was critical of law enforcement when a synagogue in Sacramento, California, was firebombed. Community leaders felt that after a NAACP headquarters in Tacoma was bombed and another in Sacramento gutted by arson, warnings should have emanated. One synagogue president pointed out: "'Had we learned [about the NAACP bombing] . . . we would have notified all other congregations, the NAACP and other minority organizations. . . .

This was something that could have potentially been prevented, had law enforcement had the sensitivity, the direction and the competence to advise us'" (*San Francisco Chronicle,* July 29, 1993, p. A-20).

Defining the white supremacist movement. The Center for Democratic Renewal (CDR) in 1992 published *When Hate Groups Come to Town: A Handbook of Effective Community Responses,* wherein they define the white supremacist movement: "The white supremacist movement is composed of dozens of organizations and groups, each working to create a society totally dominated by white Christians, in which the human rights of lesbians and gay men and other minorities are denied. Some groups seek to create an all "Aryan" territory; others seek to re-institutionalize Jim Crow segregation."

Dozens of organizations have been identified as advocates of white supremacy. According to the CDR, white supremacist groups consist of only a few members, while others have tens of thousands. They estimated that as of 1993, while there were approximately 25,000 activists forming the hard core, another 150,000 to 200,000 people sympathize with the movement, either by attending meetings and rallies or making donations (Center for Democratic Renewal, 1992). There is no single organization or person that dominates a particular movement, and frequently individuals are members of several different groups at the same time. The major groups are the Ku Klux Klan, Aryan Nations, neo-Nazis, The Order, White Aryan Resistance (W.A.R.), the Christian Identity, The Christian Patriots, and the Skinheads. The ideology of the Klan, Aryan Nations, neo-Nazis, W.A.R., racist skinheads, and other white supremacists has been clear since their formation.

Skinheads. Membership by young adults in racist skinhead groups in the United States has mushroomed since 1986, "growing in membership from just 300 nationwide to a peak of perhaps 3,500 in 1991" (Center for Democratic Renewal, 1992, p. 46). Neo-Nazi skinheads have lately become one of the most violent segments of the hate movement, in fact, replacing the Ku Klux Klan in viciousness. In 1992 they were responsible for nearly *one-fourth of all bias-related murders* in the United States. They have committed murders and hundreds of assaults and other violent crimes. Adult white supremacist group influence on the neo-Nazi skinheads has been substantial. The youth participate in adult hate group rallies and show a great deal of solidarity with them. (*Southern Poverty Law Center Newsletter,* Sept. 21, 1993, p. 46).

The adult hate groups are seeking to replenish their membership ranks from the racist skinhead groups. According to the CDR, while most skinheads (easily recognized by their closely shaven heads) are explicitly racist, there are some skinheads who have banded together to oppose bigotry—Skinheads Against Racial Prejudice (S.H.A.R.P.). However, these skinheads do not represent the majority and have very little, if any, substantial influence on others.

Neo-Nazis and Klans. The CDR has identified many white supremacist groups and their leaders in the United States. A partial list of groups include (Center for Democratic Renewal, 1992, pp. 41–52):

NEO-NAZI-TYPE GROUPS:

SS of America
Christian Identity Skins
Confederate Hammer Skins
CASH
Haken Kreuz
American Front
Aryan National Front
Screwdriver Services
Eastern Hammer Skins
Northern Hammer Skins
National Socialist Skinheads
Bound for Glory
White House Network
White Vikings

KLAN-TYPE ORGANIZATIONS:

Knights of the Ku Klux Klan
National Association for the Advancement of White People
National Demo Front
Patriots Defense Foundation
C.A.U.S.E.
National States Rights Party
Christian Knights KKK
Dixie Knights KKK
Invisible Empire KKK
Invisible Empire—Klans
U.S. Klans
Confederate Knights of America

The quasi-theological movements of such groups as Christian Identity, the Christian Patriots, and the Church of the Creator deserve some mention.

Christian Identity.   Followers of this belief use the Bible as the source of its ideology. They form their views of diverse people based on a particular interpretation of the Bible. For example: "It teaches that people of color are pre-Adamic, that is not fully human and are without souls. Identity followers believe that Jews are children of Satan. . . ." (*Southern Poverty Law Center Newsletter,* Sept. 21, 1992, pp. 42–44).

Christian Patriots.   Followers belong to many different organizations, all of which espouse white supremacy. The core beliefs are (Center for Democratic Renewal, 1992):

- White people and people of color are fundamentally two different kinds of citizens, with different rights and responsibilities.

- The United States is not properly a democracy, but a republic in which only people with property should vote.
- Democracy is the same as "mobocracy" or mob rule.
- The United States is a Christian republic, with a special relationship between Christianity and the rule of law.
- Internationalists (usually identified as Jews) and aliens (sometimes identified as Jews, sometimes as immigrants and people of color) are attempting to subvert the U.S. Constitution and establish one-world socialism or, alternatively, the New World Order.
- The Federal Reserve banking system is unconstitutional and a tool of the "International Jewish Banking Conspiracy."

Church of the Creator. The members of the Church of the Creator have become (*The Southern Poverty Law Center Newsletter,* Sept. 21, 1992, pp. 42–44). "America's most dangerous white supremacist group. . . . Based in Florida and North Carolina, the Church of the Creator has been recruiting violent Skinheads from all across America. The group's rallying cry is 'Rahowa,' which stands for *RA*ial *HO*ly *WA*r."

It is members of this group who in 1993 plotted to start a race war in Los Angeles by machine-gunning parishioners of a major black church in southeast Los Angeles and planned an assassination of prominent civil rights leaders. The church's late founder, Ben Klassen, according to the Southern Poverty Law Center in a 1993

newletter, described Adolf Hitler as an "'astute' political leader and 'the greatest man the White Race has ever produced. . . . The most important step we can take is to cleanse our racially polluted society,' and that a race war is 'the only and ultimate solution' to the Jews and 'mud races' that he believed were a threat to the white race."

White Supremacists and the Political Arena

C. T. Vivian, 1992 chairperson of the Center for Democratic Renewal (CDR), stated that there has been an increase in the numbers of white supremacists attempting to gain political power through electoral campaigns—sponsoring and supporting candidates who advocate their beliefs. The most notable example was former klansman David Duke's bid for Louisiana Senate and governor in 1990 and then for president of the United States in 1992. Vivian expounded: "Even if they lose every election, their politics have gained a new currency that we long ago had hoped was forever devalued. It is important to remember that the white supremacists' commitment to the niceties of electioneering is tactical, not long term. Their goal is still to replace the hope of democracy and pluralism with the fear of racism and bigotry" (Vivian, 1992). Research by the CDR revealed that Duke and his organization, the National Association for the Advancement of White People, had raised and spent about $5 million on campaigns between 1989 and 1991.

The early 1990s witnessed leadership of the two largest Klans, instructing their followers to restrain from racist rhetoric and to avoid implication in violent crimes. They wanted to avoid criminal prosecution or civil lawsuits while selling their ideology and exploiting national issues such as affirmative action, immigration, drugs, and AIDS to their advantage (Boland, 1992). The more militant supremist groups, however, did not agree with the peaceful/political approaches and continue to advocate armed revolution and violence. They remain a threat and concern for law enforcement and communities.

The ADL and other authorities tie the economy to white supremacist movements and popularity in the United States. "The economy is the key. If it's bad, then everyone is looking for scapegoats, and the white supremacists are happy to oblige. They point to immigration, to affirmative action, and tell white people that is where the jobs have gone" (Rosenfeld, 1992). These authorities agree that when the economy is bad, middle-class, mainstream people seem to look for scapegoats and some listen to the white supremacist message and either sympathize or even, overtly or covertly, join the movement. This same phenomenon occurred before and during World War II in Germany, resulting in the extermination of 13 million "hate crime victims" (Jews, gypsies, gays, mentally ill, etc.). White supremacists, appearing respectable and reasonable, as we have seen in history, can gain support politically when large numbers of people are dissatisfied with the economy and believe that minority groups are responsible.

Response Alternatives to Organized Hate Groups

Departments must actively work to fight and control organized hate groups, tracking their activities, establishing when they are responsible for crimes, and assisting in their prosecution. Intelligence gathering, including networking and sharing hate group activities information with other criminal justice agencies, is crucial to efforts to reduce and prevent hate/bias crimes. Many have called this approach a cross-disciplinary coalition against racism. It involves state and regional commitments by criminal justice agencies with other public and private entities. All the institutions jointly develop and implement components of multitiered intervention strategies targeting enforcement, education, training, victim assistance, media relations, political activism/advocacy, and an ongoing self-evaluation. The fight begins with an understanding of the size and scope of the various supremacist groups, their movements and publications, and a knowledge of their leaders so that organized, multitiered responses can be developed. The CDR publication "When Hate Groups Come to Town: A Handbook of Effective Community Responses" offers some excellent material for understanding the various movements, their leaders, response strategies, and resources.

One example of networking on the west coast is the Bay Area Hate Crimes Investigators Association (BAHCIA), which provides training on hate crimes investigations and disseminates information on crimes, hate groups, and individuals active in their respective jurisdictions. Membership includes persons who specialize in hate crime cases from law enforcement, district attorneys, public agencies, and private organizations from the nine Bay Area counties. The association was formed *"to address the dramatic increase in the incidence of hate violence, and the special needs of law enforcement officers and investigators who work on hate crime cases."* The association by-laws mention that the mission of BAHCIA is to establish a cooperative effort among local, state, and federal agencies, with the purpose of eliminating hate crime in the greater Bay Area. Besides monthly meetings, it sponsors annual Hate Crimes Investigators' conferences. (Contact the S.F. Police Department Hate Crime Unit at 415/553-1133 for more information.)

Another response factor is that law enforcement leaders should consider the phenomenon of minority officers, who at times are required to provide protection to an organized hate group whose history of bigotry and violence have included the officers' own group. Those supervisors must be sensitive to the difficult and frustrating position into which these officers are placed.

Community Programs to Reduce and Control Hate/Bias Crimes

Some solutions to reduce hate/bias crimes involve back to basics issues. Programs or solutions must involve grass roots institutions: families, schools, workplaces, and religious organizations. When the criminal justice system can work in partnership with these institutions, crime reduction programs are often more successful. However, some institutions that once built positive values or exercised some control over people are no longer working. The dysfunctional family, for example, contributes to society's problems, including the increase in criminal activity.

An effort must be made to reinstitute values that reinforce noncriminal behavior; law enforcement must be an integral part of that movement. The *status quo* policing approach (reactive) will not work anymore. "'People have clearly begun to recognize that our strict law enforcement arrest approach isn't getting the job done,' says Darrel Stephens, executive director of the Police Executive

Research Forum and former chief in Newport News, Va. 'You've got a greater number of people in the police community who have come to realize that more is not the solution to this problem'" (*U.S. News & World Report,* May 11, 1992, pp. 27–35).

Progressive criminal justice executives and communities have arrived at the realization that crime has many complex causes and that police departments are not the first or only line of defense. They concluded that if crime is to be controlled, there must be a community alliance or partnership and that the causes must be attacked from multiple fronts.

Generic Community Resources and Programs

The sorts of community resources and programs that can be established would include some of the following:

1. **Hotline:** similar to those available for domestic violence and rape victims and suicide prevention. The staff is trained to provide victim assistance in terms of compassion, advise, referrals, and a prepared information package.

2. **Human Relations Commission:** established in many cities and/or counties that have staff available to assist victims of hate crimes or incidents and hold hearings and provide recommendations for problem resolution.

3. **United States/State Department of Justice Community Relations Unit** [Community Relations Service (CRS)]: has 10 regional offices and provides services to every state in the United States. The Justice Department has trained staff who, when notified of a problem, will participate and mediate in community meetings in an attempt to resolve conflicts. These units are not an investigative or enforcement body. Created by the 1964 Civil Rights Act, they are the only agency that Congress has assigned the task of providing direct help to communities to resolve disputes, disagreements, and difficulties relating to discriminatory practices based on race, color, or national origin. Their staff will respond when requested by state or local officials or citizens and organizations. They may also assist on their own initiative when they perceive that a community requires help. They occasionally get referrals from state and federal courts. The triracial, bilingual CRS staff have knowledge of, and experience in, techniques of racial and ethnic dispute resolution. They assume the role of a neutral third party and apply conciliation and remediation techniques to settle the problem. CRS has also effectively worked with state and federal correctional institutions, helping them to develop and train prison conflict response teams to mediate individual and group conflict. Many states have similar justice agencies that perform these services.

4. **Conflict resolution panels:** with specially trained staff of city or county employees who can assist agencies and/or victims (including groups) in the resolution of conflict, including that caused by hate/bias.

5. **The media:** cooperation in public awareness building on the problem of hate/bias violence via articles on causes and effects, resources, and legal remedies is essential.

6. **Multilingual public information brochures:** provided by government agencies on the rights of victims, services available, and criminal and civil laws related to hate/bias.

7. **Store fronts:** police substations established in the neighborhoods of communities having high concentrations of ethnic minorities which are staffed by bilingual officers and/or civilians. The staff takes reports and provides assistance to the members of that community.

8. **Community resource list:** list of organizations that specialize in victim assistance. Examples are the Anti-Defamation League of B'nai B'rith, Black Families Associations, Japanese-American Citizens Leagues, National Association for the Advancement of Colored People, Mexican-American Political Association, to name a few. National organizations that might be contacted as a resource are listed in Appendix I. *The importance of having established networks with minority leaders and organizations cannot be stressed enough.* These leaders are extremely important for criminal justice agencies and should be identified and cultivated in advance to assist in a timely fashion with investigations, training, victim(s) aid, and/or rumor control. If an agency experiencing serious hate/bias problems does not react quickly and effectively, this often results in the victim(s) and their community groups gaining media attention because they publicly question an inadequate response or resolution. Only when a system involving trust and respect is already in place will such a network prove its worth when violence occurs in the agency's community. The relationship with minority representatives is essential because it can help broaden the department's (sworn and nonsworn personnel's) understanding of different cultures and races. The same is true of members from gay and lesbian groups. When community members are utilized within departments, they can also help convince reluctant victims and/or witnesses to cooperate with investigators. Furthermore, they can encourage more victims to report incidents.

The key to a successful law enforcement response to hate crimes is building a partnership with victimized communities. There are many components and processes in building such a partnership. Other activities and events characterizing a joint effort would include:

9. **Educating the public at large:** Prejudice and bias, which can ultimately lead to violence against a racial, ethnic/national origin, religious, or sexual orientation person and/or group is often the result of ignorance about the group targeted. In many cases there has been little or no firsthand exposure by person(s) with bias to the racial, cultural, religious, and/or sexual orientation group from which to base their understanding; thus the bias may be due to learned stereotypes and negative media images.

One key to combatting ignorance is to educate the public at large as well as criminal justice system employees about the history, diversity, cultures, languages, and issues of concern of the various groups within the community. This can be accomplished through neighborhood forums, workshops, and "speaker's bureaus." The speaker's bureaus would be composed of groups of people prepared and well versed on the issues who would be able to speak at community meetings, schools, and other forums. Criminal justice employees, of course, would be trained in the workplace and/or in training courses offered in service or at an academy. Most cities and counties have organizations that represent community-based groups that can assist in developing and implementing such education at local elementary and secondary schools, churches, and college and university campuses. The education presented (via speakers, videos, pamphlets, etc.) should be factually correct and should not stereotype or caricature the community. (To check the accuracy of material presented, organizers of educational programs should have at least two or three minority community members provide input on the content of the program delivered. Preferably, they would represent the different subgroups within the community.) Neighborhoods and communities should be encouraged to observe their various heritages through the celebration of holidays and other special days via fairs and festivals. A look at a calendar will show that there are more holidays for different religions and cultures in the United States than anywhere else in the world: Chinese New Year, St. Patrick's Day, Cinco de Mayo, and Kwanzaa, to name a few (refer to Appendix G for a list and explanation of holidays and celebrations).

10. **Organizational networking:** National and local organizations must network to share information, resources, ideas, and support. A few of the organizations would include the National Association for the Advancement of Colored People (NAACP), the Anti-Defamation League of B'nai B'rith (ADL), Committee Against Anti-Asian Violence, the National Gay and Lesbian Task Force, and the National Institute Against Prejudice and Violence. (See appendix I for a comprehensive list of resources.) Such advocacy organizations can furnish an invaluable bridge to victim populations, and assist in urging citizens to come to the police with information about hate crimes. Many of these organizations have conducted research on hate violence laws, law enforcement models, statistics on hate violence, and can provide legal assistance and emotional support to victims of hate violence. Most of these organizations have also published books and reports covering such topics as how to respond to bigotry, trends in racism, and community organizing. Through networking, organizations or groups know who their allies are, increase their own resources and knowledge about other minority groups, and can form coalitions that make a greater impact on the community and the criminal justice system. They can also assist criminal justice agencies in dealing with community reactions to hate violence plus help the victims of violence cope with the experience.

11. **Monitoring the media:** Minority organizations and the criminal justice system must monitor the media. The media can be a foe or an ally. The media must be used strategically for education and publicity about hate/bias crimes and incidents, about multicultural/racial workshops, and about festivals and other cultural events. They must be monitored in terms of accuracy of reporting and must submit corrections when necessary. Negative editorials or letters to the editor pertaining to an affected group should be countered and rebutted by an op-ed piece from management within the involved criminal justice agency. Organization leaders or their designate should become a primary source of information for reporters to contact.

The police executive must often take the lead within the community in the ambitious endeavor to implement special programs to reduce and control hate/bias crimes. Special programs must involve line officers and the average citizen in solving problems in the areas where they live and work. The message to law enforcement and communities is that the *status quo* simply will not do anymore.

Communities with Special Programs

Some jurisdictions have used a community approach to decrease the numbers of crimes and incidents of all types, including those motivated by hate/bias. Some of those programs include:

1. **Block Watch Volunteers Program.** The Northwest Victim Services (NVS) is a nonprofit organization created in 1981 in Philadelphia, Pennsylvania. NVS and the police of the highest-crime-rate districts in Philadelphia (the 14th and 35th) formed a partnership that utilizes the organized block watch program in that city. Carefully selected, screened, and trained block watch volunteers not only perform the usual functions of neighborhood watch (crime prevention) but also perform a vital victim assistance role. They provide emotional support for victims, who are often frightened or unfamiliar with the criminal justice process and accompany them to the various trial stages—arraignment, preliminary, and so on.

2. **Task Force on Police Asian Relations.** In localities that have large Asians populations, task forces have been created which consist of criminal justice members, educators, victim/refugee advocates, and volunteer agencies, plus a representative of each Asian group living or working in the community. The purposes are several: to train criminal justice employees on communication techniques that improve relations and make them more effective and efficient in dealing with the Asian community; to prepare Asians on what might be expected from and by the various criminal justice components, especially the police; to open lines of communication between law enforcement and Asians; and to encourage Asians to report crimes and trust the police. Agencies in California that have created such tasks forces and that could be contacted for additional details are the San Francisco PD, Westminster PD, Garden Grove PD, Anaheim PD, Fresno PD, San Jose PD, and Huntington Beach PD. These task forces could certainly be expanded to include other ethnic and racial groups as well. The city of Boston and other cities have effectively used the task force approach to resolve neighborhood problems. The results are similar to those discussed above with regard to Asian task forces (i.e., they exchange information and curtail rumors; they identify problems and work on solutions; and perhaps most important, they allow citizens to help with and approach problems on a joint basis).

3. **Rapid Response Strategy.** The Boston Police Department has a program to address any problem that has a pattern. The strategy has been particularly effective in preventing and reducing civil right violation crimes. The police department first identifies the problem from police reports, interviews with known victims, attendance at community meetings, and in discussions with informants. If a pattern

exists that includes a particular day and time for the incidents, the department gathers a group of area residents together where the incident is occurring. They are asked to observe (they can remain anonymous) the vicinity in which the incidents are taking place. They are provided with a special "hotline" number to report activities rather than the usual police emergency line. A police officer or civilian is utilized to staff the "hotline" (with an interpreter available if necessary), who is equipped with a walkie-talkie. One or more unmarked police vehicles are strategically placed on the periphery of the "target area," plus any other officers needed, depending on the seriousness of the crime or activity expected. Calls coming from the observer to the base station are logged and the officers are dispatched when necessary via the walkie-talkies. Response time is generally less than 2 minutes; thus many crimes are prevented and/or the perpetrator is caught in the act or shortly thereafter. The effectiveness of this approach is due to the minimum amount of police staffing required for maximum coverage and the fact that some of the burden is placed on community members, who should share (a partnership) in their own protection.

4. **Citizens' Patrol.** Following a series of attacks, including one fatal, on gays and lesbians in the Hillcrest community of East San Diego, California, the police responded by appointing a task force to investigate the crimes and provided more officers to patrol the area's streets. They also organized a citizens' patrol, whose volunteer members began driving Hillcrest's streets, watching for and reporting suspicious activity. Even when the task force was disbanded after the arrest of the suspect, the citizens' patrol remained. The patrol's membership even increased and two-citizen teams, with a cellular telephone, regularly drive problem-area streets. Both police and community leaders say that there has been a noticeable decrease in violent street crimes and a feeling that Hillcrest is safer.

5. **Mobile Crisis Unit.** In 1984, San Joaquin County (the first of many now in California) organized a mobile crisis unit modeled after a pioneering program in Arizona. The unit is available 24 hours a day to counsel victims at crime scenes, transport victims, console families, make referrals to social service agencies, and provide instant information on the criminal justice process. The staff monitor police/sheriff's radio frequencies and respond when requested.

6. **Network of Neighbors.** The human relations commission in Montgomery County, Maryland, has a "memorandum of understanding" with the police that when a hate crime occurs, the police department immediately notifies the commission. The commission in turn contacts the volunteer of the Network of Neighbors who lives closest to the victim. The network member visits the victim as soon as possible to assure the person of community support and to assist with other needs. The volunteers receive training on victim assistance and referrals. The New York City Police Department modeled a similar Good Neighbor Program after Montgomery County, Maryland's Network of Neighbors.

7. **STOP Program.** The Montgomery County, Maryland, office of the Human Relations Commission (OHRC) has a program that educates juvenile perpetrators of hate violence about the impact of their behavior on victims and the entire commu-

nity. The program, which began in 1982, sends first offenders to the STOP program instead of through the court system. The OHRC staff requires that juvenile perpetrators and their parents attend five two-and-a-half-hour sessions. Sessions include written and experiential exercises, discussions, films, and homework relating to their specific incident and the impact of hate and violence in general. Juveniles are also required to perform 40 hours of community service. For information on STOP, call OHRC at 217/468-4260.

8. **Hate Violence Reduction Task Force.** The Contra Costa County, California, Human Relations Commission received a San Francisco Foundation grant to design a countywide integrated plan for reducing hate violence. The Contra Costa County Hate Violence Reduction Task Force was created under the auspices of the grant. The task force was comprised of:

- All human relations commissions in the county
- All police departments and the sheriff's department
- County probation
- District attorney's offices
- County health department
- All housing authorities in the county
- California Department of Justice
- Fair Employment and Housing Commission
- Unified school districts from the county
- Parent–teachers associations
- California Teachers' Association
- NAACP Racial Intolerance Task Force
- Black Families Association
- Hispanic Roundtable
- GLAD (a gay/lesbian organization)
- Japanese American Citizens League
- Asian Law Caucus
- Center for New Americans
- Filipino-American Association
- Churches and synagogues
- Crisis hotlines
- Contra Costa Conflict Resolution Panel

Three working committees (criminal justice, education, community) were charged with drafting appropriate models for preventing and responding to hate violence in Contra Costa County. A steering committee, composed of representatives from each working committee, was responsible for molding the separate models into an integrated county system. This is an excellent example of a holist approach to the problem.

Community models, such as those mentioned above, can play a vital role in reducing violence in neighborhoods. Successfully implemented programs can reduce individual violence, ranging from street crime to domestic abuse to drug-related crimes. Civil unrest, which can often include gang violence and open confrontations among various segments of society, can also be reduced.

> Building bonds of trust between the police and the community also allows community policing to contribute to the goal of promoting color-blind policing, where people and their police form new partnerships that offer the promise of reducing the potential for civil unrest. By allowing citizens the opportunity to hold the police accountable, community policing restores an important check on police behavior that has been just in the process of "professionalizing" the police by isolating them in patrol cars, where the system encourages them to interact primarily with each other. (*FBI Law Enforcement Bulletin*, May 1992, p. 11)

HATE/BIAS CRIME AND INCIDENT VICTIMOLOGY

The Criminal Justice System Response

Interest in victims of crime has increased markedly in recent years. Meaningful assistance to victims of major crimes only became a priority in the 1980s. The growth of a body of "victimology" literature and the emergence of numerous victim advocate and rights organizations began at about that time, reflecting a growing concern about crime, the victims of crime, and their treatment by the criminal justice system. The public mood or perception had become (and may still be) that the criminal justice system cares only about the defendant. The perception was that the defendant's rights were a priority of the system, while the victim was neglected in the process.

Possibly one of the forerunners of the movement to improve the system was the Victims of Crime task force created by President Reagan in April 1982. The task force made 68 recommendations in their final report for addressing the problems of victims. The recommendations called for action by police, prosecutors, judiciary and parole boards in making specified improvements in their respective operations. The preface included a statement of the task force chairman, Lois Haight Herrington, that reads:

> Victims who do survive their attack, and are brave enough to come forward, turn to their government expecting it to do what a good government should—protect the innocent. The American criminal justice system is absolutely dependent on these victims to cooperate. Without the cooperation of victims and witnesses in reporting and testifying about crime, it is impossible in a free society to hold criminals accountable. When victims come forward to perform this vital service, however, they find little protection. They discover instead that they will be treated as appendages of a system appallingly out of balance. They learn that somewhere along the way the system has lost track of the simple truth that it is supposed to be fair and to protect those who obey the law while punishing those who break it. Somewhere along the way, the system began to serve lawyers and judges and defendants, *treating the victim with institutionalized disinterest.* [emphasis added] (President's Task Force on Victims of Crime, 1982)

In 1982, the Omnibus Victim and Witness Protection Act was signed into law, which, among other features, requires use of victim impact statements at sentencing in federal criminal cases. The legislation also provided, in federal cases, greater protection of victims and witnesses from intimidation by defendants or their associates, restitution by offenders to victims, and more stringent bail laws. In 1984 the Comprehensive Crime Control Act and the Victims of Crime Act authorized federal and state victim compensation and victim assistance programs. By 1987 more than 35 states had enacted comprehensive legislation protecting the interests of the victim, compared with four before 1982.

As a result of the task force recommendations, state and federal legislation and other research (most notably by the National Institute of Justice) by public and private organizations, improvements were made in victim services and treatment as well as in the criminal justice system.

Law Enforcement and the Victim

In the law enforcement field, courses in recruit academies and in-service, advanced officer programs typically include training about victimization. The training usually covers such topics as social–psychological effects of victimization, officer sensitivity to the victim, victim assistance and advocacy programs, and victim compensation and restitution criteria and procedures for applying. Classes normally stress the importance of keeping the victim informed of their case status and of the criminal justice process. It was recognized that the manner in which patrol officers and investigators of such crimes interact with victims affects the victims' immediate and long-term physical and emotional recovery. Proper treatment of the victim also increased a victim's willingness to cooperate in the total criminal justice process. Due to this training, the victims of hate crimes began receiving special attention and assistance in progressive cities and counties all over the country.

Victims of hate/bias violence generally express three needs: (1) to feel safe, (2) to feel that people care, and (3) to get assistance. To address needs 1 and 2 law enforcement agencies and all personnel involved in contacts with the victim(s) must place special emphasis on victim assistance in order to reduce trauma and fear. Such investigations sometimes involve working with people from diverse ethnic backgrounds, races, and/or sexual orientation. Many victims may be recent immigrants with limited English who are unfamiliar with the American legal system or have fears of the police rooted in negative experiences from their country of origin.

> How immigrant and refugee communities generally perceive the criminal justice system is a principal factor in determining how best to serve those communities. These perceptions are often based upon the experiences of these groups with the criminal justice systems in their native lands. In many Asian countries, for example, there is a history of police corruption. The reporting of a crime may not only be futile but could invite unwanted and costly attention. The turmoil of war and the instability of political leadership have also dissuaded many from depending upon government institutions. (Ogawa, 1990)

The officer or investigator, therefore, must not only be a skilled interviewer and listener but must also be sensitive to and knowledgeable of cultural and racial differences and ethnicity. The officer/investigator must have the ability to show compassion and sensitivity toward the plight of the victim while gathering evidence required for prosecution. As with other crime victims, those involved in the investigation must (Concord, California, Police Department, 1988):

- Approach victims in an empathic and supportive manner. Demonstrate concern and sensitivity.
- Attempt to calm the victim and reduce the victim's alienation.
- Reassure the victim that every available investigative and enforcement tool will be utilized by the police to find and prosecute the person(s) responsible for the crime.
- Consider the safety of the victim(s) by recommending and providing extra patrol and/or providing prevention and precautionary advice.
- Provide referral information such as counseling and other appropriate public support and assistance agencies.
- Advise the victim of criminal and civil options.

The stress experienced by victims of hate/bias crime or incidents may be heightened by a perceived level of threat or personal violation. Just like the victims of rape or abuse, many become traumatized when they have to recall the details of what occurred. Sometimes transference takes place whereby the victim, due to what happened to him or her, transfers his or her anger or hostility toward the officer. The officer must be prepared for this and be able to defuse the situation professionally without resorting to anger himself or herself. It is imperative that every effort be made by officers and investigators to treat hate crime victims with dignity and respect so that they feel a sense of justice. Insensitive, brash, or unaware officers or investigators may not only alienate victim(s), witness(es), or potential witnesses, they may even create additional distrust or hostility and cause others in the community to distrust the entire police department.

To address need 3 (to get assistance) requires that the community have established resources that can assist the victim and the victim group (e.g., gays, Hispanics, etc.). Few communities have resources necessary to offer comprehensive victim services, and this became especially apparent during the recession of the early 1990s. Even where resources are available, victims are often unaware of the services due to poor public awareness programs or the failure of the criminal justice system to make appropriate referrals because of a lack of training or motivation. A key resource would be available interpreters for non-English-speaking victims and witnesses. Ideally, jurisdictions with large populations of non-English-speaking minorities should recruit and train an appropriate number of bilingual employees. If the jurisdiction does not have an investigator capable of speaking the same language, a prearranged interpreter system should be in place for immediate callout. Victims must be informed that services for hate crime victims are available in areas where those resources are present. Victims of hate-motivated incidents are encouraged to report the circumstances to the National Hate Crimes Hotline: 1-800/347-HATE.

SUMMARY

The degree to which the criminal justice system, especially law enforcement agencies, responds to acts of hate and bias intimidation, violence, or vandalism sends a message to the victim, the community (especially the group to which the victim belongs), and the perpetrator. If the criminal justice system reacts (or acts proactively) swiftly and effectively, perpetrators will know that their actions will result in apprehension and prosecution and that such acts will not be tolerated. Those sympathetic to the perpetrator may be deterred from similar hate/bias actions. The fears of the victim's group will be calmed and trust towards the criminal justice system will be established. Other members of the community who are sensitive to the impact of hate/bias crimes and incidents will also react favorably when state and federal laws are vigorously enforced. Where this occurs, trust and goodwill are generated between the community and the criminal justice system, leading to long-term benefits for all.

DISCUSSION QUESTIONS AND ISSUES*

1. ***Resources***   Find out what resources exist in your community to assist victims of hate/bias crimes.
   (a) Which groups provide victim assistance?
   (b) Which coalition groups exist, and what types of community outreach programs are offered?
   (c) What types of pamphlets or other written materials are available?
   (d) Which groups have speakers' bureaus?
   (e) Which groups are working with local law enforcement agencies with regard to response programs or cultural awareness training?
   (f) Which groups are working with the district attorney's office?
   (g) What types of legislative lobbying efforts are taking place, and who is championing the work?

2. ***Role of Human Relations Commissions.*** What is the role of the human relations commission if one exists in your area?
   (a) Does it have a specific task force on hate crimes?
   (b) Does it have any type of tracking system for recording statistics on hate crime?
   (c) What is its relationship with local law enforcement agencies and district attorneys' offices regarding hate crime?
   (d) What is its relationship with community organizations concerned with hate crimes?
   (e) Has it produced any brochures/pamphlets or other materials on hate crimes?
   (f) Does it provide multicultural workshops or sensitivity training regarding different minority or lifestyle groups?
   (g) Have there been occasions when the HRC has gone beyond the scope of its charter or stated goals which resulted in negative exposure or media attention? Describe the circumstances.

3. ***Role of Your District Attorney's Office.*** Assess the role of your district attorney's/prosecutor's office by determining the following.
   (a) Does it have a special hate crimes or civil rights unit?
   (b) Do hate crime cases receive special attention?
   (c) Are misdemeanor and felony hate crimes processed differently?
   (d) How does the office determine if it will prosecute a hate crime case?
   (e) What types of training do assistant district attorneys receive regarding hate crimes?
   (f) What types of community outreach does it do regarding hate crimes?

*See Instructor's Manual accompanying this text for additional activities, role-plays, questionnaires and projects related to the content of this chapter.

(g) Does the office take civil as well as criminal action regarding hate crimes? Does the office file for injunctions on behalf of the victim?

(h) What is the office's relationship with other community groups and agencies, such as the local human relations commission?

4. *Victim Assistance.* Identify avenues of victim assistance in your area. Research and document the following.

(a) Does your state have a crime victims' assistance program? Does it offer victim compensation? What about a victims' bill of rights?

(b) What services does the local department of mental health offer?

(c) Do any community groups, rape crisis centers, or crime victim services agencies in the area offer counseling to hate crimes victims?

(d) Are there any mental health care professionals willing to donate their services to victims of hate crimes?

A good resource for victim assistance networks in your area is the National Organization for Victim Assistance (NOVA), based in Washington, D.C. (202/393-6682).

REFERENCES

AGNES, PETER S. (1989). "Public safety in the 80's: new cultural dimensions in society. A modern prosecutor's response to the challenges posed by cultural diversity," unpublished paper, Norfolk County, Massachusetts District Attorney's Office, p. 3.

Anti-Defamation League (1991). *Law Enforcement Bulletin,* Issue 7, Anti-Defamation League of B'nai B'rith, New York, Spring.

BAYH, BIRCH (1989). "Let's tear off their hoods: the increasing violence by the KKK and other right-wing hates adds up to a record of shame," *Newsweek,* Apr. 17, p. 8.

BOLAND, MIRA (1992). "'Mainstream' hatred," *Police Chief,* June, pp. 30–32.

Center for Democratic Renewal (1992). *When Hate Groups Come to Town: A Handbook of Effective Community Responses,* Center for Democratic Renewal, Atlanta, Ga., p. 41.

Concord, California, Police Department (1988). "Response to racial, religious, ethnic, or sexual orientation complaints," *Concord, California, Police Department Training Bulletin,* Vol. VII, No. 27.

OGAWA, BRIAN (1990). *Color of Justice: Culturally Sensitive Treatment of Crime Victims,* Office of the Governor, State of California, Sacramento, Calif., pp. 215–216.

President's Task Force on Victims of Crime (1982). *Final Report,* U.S. Government Printing Office, Washington, D.C., Dec. preface.

ROSENFELD, HENRY O. (1992). *Establishing Non-traditional Partnerships to Mitigate the Future Impact of White Supremacist Groups,* Peace Officer Standards and Training, Sacramento, Calif., June 1992 (Order 14-0284); from interview of Hedy Immoos, Criminal Intelligence Specialist III, California Department of Justice.

Southern Poverty Law Center (1992). *Klanwatch Intelligence Report: Special Year End Edition, 1991,* Vol. 59, Southern Poverty Law Center, Montgomery, Ala., Feb.

VIVIAN, C. T. (1992). "Bullets and ballots in South Africa and USA," *The Monitor,* No. 25, May, p. 2.

PART FIVE

Cultural Effectiveness for Peace Officers

Part Five, the concluding section of the book, highlights some of the themes from previous chapters, while discussing broad concepts of the peace officer and cultural diversity. The chapters begin with an analysis of the changing role image in law enforcement and its impact on behavior. We examine why those who serve the public are expected to be more tolerant and less ethnocentric in their outlook and dealings with citizens. Chapter 14 reinforces the meaning of cultural sensitivity and provides a model for understanding cultural differences. We end the chapter with a section that focuses on law enforcement leadership and issues of diversity in the community.

Chapter 15, which considers peace officer professionalism and peacekeeping in a diverse society, first defines and presents the interwoven concepts of leadership, professionalism, and synergy. The next section links professionalism to ethics and interactions with minorities, emphasizing the special obligation that peacekeepers have in upholding respect for human dignity. In "Career Development and Training for Professionalism," we present ideas for advancing in one's career in law enforcement, and we stress the value of training that contributes to professionalism. We then cover networking and mentoring, with an emphasis placed on the mentoring of employees who have typically been excluded from law enforcement. The last section, which builds upon earlier chapters, presents two trends that some private-sector organizations exhibit which reflect a positive value on diversity. Finally, the conclusion of the book reiterates the need for police officer professionalism, tolerance, and understanding of diversity. It stresses the responsibility that leaders in law enforcement have for demonstrating a leadership style that respects the pluralism in our society.

The following appendices correspond to the chapters in Part Five:

Appendix K   Listing of Consultants and Resources

14

PEACE OFFICER IMAGE AND CULTURAL SENSITIVITY

OVERVIEW

This chapter considers the changing role image of peace officers that will result in increased cultural awareness and effectiveness in law enforcement. Given the impact of greater diversity on both peacekeeping and enforcement, we explore how cultural understanding can be translated into more effective community policing. To be more culturally aware, readers are provided with a simple model for quick analysis of differences in various cultures, ethnic groups, and generations. The content strengthens the case that improved police performance and professionalism are dependent on cross-cultural skills and understanding among officers.

COMMENTARY

Diverse images of law enforcement are evident in the following quotes:

> *Law Enforcement: A Human Relations Approach,* by A. Coffee, Prentice Hall, Englewood Cliffs, N.J., 1990, p. 245.

> In the sense that image has a profound impact on the actual human interactions, sensitivity to how people perceive police is a very positive indicator. . . . The alternative available to police, which is to isolate themselves from public opinion, is to seek more favorable public opinion. . . . If the police and general community were to agree that keeping the peace was the law enforcement job, the problem would continue in that reality dictates that police arrest law violators and enforce laws in general, not merely keep the peace.

Texas Police Sergeant Brian Harris on the charges against officers in the Rodney King case (Dec. 1992 letter to authors):

We can all learn from the incident, but remember the public has never seen the whole tape. . . . The public forgets that police officers are afforded the same rights as the victim. The media and the public assumed the officers were guilty, instead of presumed innocent. There was definite abuse, but nobody but the defense and the jury analyzed the tape and the evidence. . . . Do not think I condone the officers actions—they were wrong, but intent is the big issue. When those officers started their shift, they did not intend to hurt someone. When they encountered Rodney King, they did not intend to hurt him. But the issue was control—once the officers were threatened, and they saw their activities were not stopping him, I bet their intent was to stop him, but the crowd mentality set in. The help in training would be to control emotions when the adrenalin takes over!

IMPACT OF PEACE OFFICER IMAGE ON HUMAN BEHAVIOR

Peace officers today are both knowledge and service workers who must focus on effective performance, according to Norman Boehm, director of the California Commission on Peace Officer Standards and Training. Thus he believes their departments must become learning as well an enforcement agencies. Boehm maintains that the latter have the responsibility to provide officers with the new knowledge, skills, and behaviors to be effective on the job. "Smart cops," in every sense of that adjective, are becoming the norm. This is why so many justice agencies are mandating for entrance, a two- or four-year college degree for recruits, and why the report of the Police Executive Research Forum on *The State of Police Education: Policy Direction for the 21st Century* (Carter et al., 1992) describes in detail the benefits of an educated officer. Brainpower, not brawn, is what will make for effectiveness in this vastly, changing world. Exhibit 14.1 differentiates between perceptions of the disappearing and emerging police work culture. Contrasting the two views helps to explain why, within the criminal justice field, a new image of law enforcement must be created of the peace officer and then projected to the public. This is but a synopsis of the transition under way in the world of work and law enforcement, which in turn alters our images of various justice roles. In the latter, the shift and trends seem to be away from the traditional approaches—from reactive to proactive; from just enforcement and crime fighting toward prevention and detection of criminal activity, toward preserving the public peace and service, toward protecting life and property; from just public sector policing to synergistic security services by both public and private sectors working in cooperation (Mayhall, 1985).

Darrel Stephens former director of the Police Executive Research Forum (PERF) put the situation quite simply: Mechanically bean counting of arrests and putting squad cars on the street is no longer enough. Now as chief of St. Peterburg, Florida, he will be able to demonstrate his position on preventive, community-oriented policing. In a graduation address to police executives (Jan. 15, 1993) Stephens stated his conviction that citizens are the first line of defense in preventing and fighting crime, not the crime fighter who reacts after the crime is committed. Therefore, he advocates a problem-solving type of law enforcement that collaborates with the varied communities within departmental jurisdiction.

Exhibit 14.1 Law Enforcement Role Transitions

TRADITIONAL WORK CULTURE	EVOLVING WORK CULTURE
Attitude	
Reactive; preserve status quo	Proactive; anticipate the future
Orientation	
Enforcement as dispensers of public safety	Enforcement and peacekeeping as helping professionals
Organization	
Paramilitary with top-down command system; intractable departments and divisions; centralization and specialization	Transitional toward more fluid, participative arrangements and open communication system; decentralization, task forces, and team management
Expectations	
Loyalty to your superior, organization and buddies, then duty and public service; conformity and dependency	Loyalty to public service and duty, and to one's personal and professional development; demonstrate leadership competence and interpersonal skills
Requirements	
Political appointment, limited civil service; education—high school or less	Must meet civil service standards; education—college and beyond, lifelong learning
Personnel	
Largely white males, military background and sworn only; all alike, so structure workload for equal shares in static sharply defined slots	Multicultural without regard to sex or sexual preference; competence norm for sworn and unsworn personnel; all different, so capitalize on particular abilities, characteristics, potential
Performance	
Obey rules, follow orders, work as though everything depended on your own hard efforts toward gaining the pension and retirement	Work effectively, obey reasonable and responsible requests; interdependence means cooperate and collaborate with others; ensure financial/career future
Environment	
Relatively stable society where problems were somewhat routine and predictable, and authority was respected	Complex, fast-changing, multicultural society with unpredictable problems, often global in scope, and more disregard of authority, plus more guns/violence even among juveniles.

Within this larger context, comprehending the significance and power of *image* and its projection becomes critical for would-be peacekeepers. Image is not a matter of illusion or mere public manipulation of appearances. Behavioral scientists have long demonstrated the vital connection between image and identity. Realists among us have always known that life's "losers," many of them convicted felons, lack an adequate sense of identity and suffer from feelings of poor self-worth. Some people, raised in dysfunctional families, go so far as to engage not only in self-depreciation and abuse, but in self-mutilation. In contrast, one state established a special commission to promote self-esteem among school youth, so as to curb crime and delinquency.

Multiple Images

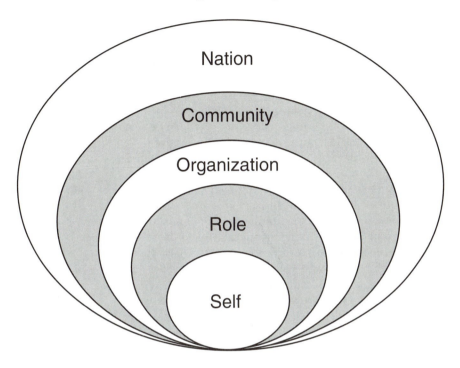

Figure 14.2   Multiple Images

Behavioral communication may be viewed in terms of senders and receivers of messages. Exhibit 14.2 suggests that we view image in terms of concentric or spiraling circles, centered around the all-important *self-image* at the core. As we see ourselves, we project an image to which people respond. Normally, we set this receiver up, more often than not, for the reactions and treatment we receive—the exception being when the receiver is biased or prejudiced toward certain types or races of people. Our self-concept has been long in development, the outcome not just of life experience, but the input of others to us. If a child continuously receives negative feedback from parents and teachers, he or she begins to believe in personal worthlessness. Usually, these young people fail to achieve unless there is an intervention that calls into question the distorted concept of one's self. Such a person is likely to project a weak image which often prompts others to take advantage of them. On the other hand, if the person has self-confidence and projects a positive image, both verbally and nonverbally, an acceptable response from others is probable. (Again, except for bigoted persons, who reflect an inner bias and refuse to accept people different from themselves, the problems and conflict are within themselves, as is the case with frustrated youth known as "skinheads.") *The best antidote to underachievement or even racism is for a person to have a healthy self-image.*

Furthermore, if a person is confused about self-identify, as is often the situation with adolescents, people tend to respond in an uncertain way toward that person. Therefore, in the selection of police candidates, law enforcement officials seek those with a strong self-image and appreciation; police academy training should reinforce, not undermine, this self-confidence. Police supervisors are well advised to provide regular positive reinforcement of their officers' sense of self.

We play many roles in the course of life—male or female, married or single, child or parent, student or mentor. However, our concern is specifically upon vocational roles in terms of the criminal justice system and the changing images projected by its practitioners. In terms of behavioral communication theory, *as police see themselves, they project an image to the public, and citizens respond to that image.*

Now to two cases in point, one old, one new. In 1829, Sir Robert Peel established the London Metropolitan Police, projecting an image of a paid, professional force to which the British public positively responded, calling them "peelers" or "bobbies." Rejecting the old adage "employ a thief to catch a thief," he recruited these new police from the military rather than from criminal backgrounds, and compensated them with adequate salaries so they would be less inclined to accept bribes or indulge in other irregularities (Gilbert, 1990).

Since then the role of police has evolved as society has changed in its perceptions of values and priorities, justice and criminality, law and enforcement. Currently, for example, the average citizen seems less concerned about police enforcement of vice and traffic laws and more concerned about their combatting gang violence and domestic violence, especially physical abuse of children, spouses, and the aged. Understandably, the American public today, particularly among minorities and the disenfranchised, has higher expectations about being treated humanely and fairly when encountering police in an economically developed country. However, new arrivals in the United States and Canada, whether legal or illegal entries, bring "cultural baggage" from their homeland, including negative images of police there, which may be that of oppressors and bribe-takers.

Modern media has a powerful influence on how the public perceives police. It began with novels and mystery fiction, expanded to newspapers and magazines, even radio broadcasting; today U.S. movies and television "cop shows" are viewed internationally. The range of media impact on images of law enforcement extends from the eighteenth century, when Charles Dickens wrote an essay about the Bow Street Flying Squad, founded in 1753, observing: "As Preventative Police they were utterly ineffective, and as Detective Police, they were very loose and uncertain in their operations."

With the age of television and media globalism, the ultimate diminishment of law enforcement's image occurred in 1991. This is the "watershed case" that took place with the beating of Rodney King by a few members of the Los Angeles Police Department. This unfortunate event was captured on videotape and played repeatedly over the airways around the world. It underscores another new reality—criminal justice representatives are now subject to extra scrutiny and accountability when citizens use camcorders to capture their activities for possible review.

Even police themselves and "ex-cop"-authored novels and film or television scripts do more to undermine than enhance the police image. It is no wonder that law enforcement agencies in this century have appointed community relations officers and established press units in attempts to keep the public informed of their activities while promoting a more positive image of their departments. The problem is that such personnel assigned to such posts frequently lack professional skills in public and media relations.

Adopted in various states, the term *peace officer,* which we have utilized in this book, is a concept that could possibly reverse negative publicity if law enforcement personnel would take pride in the term and internalize its meaning, while projecting this image to the citizens. Interestingly, it is terminology that was very popular in the Old West and often used in cowboy movies. Such national usage is based on terminology from the U.S. Department of Justice. For example, the California code (section 830) defines a peace officer as including sheriffs, police, marshals, constables, inspectors, and investigators of district attorneys, state highway patrol and police division, state university and college police, and designated personnel in the departments of justice/corrections/fish and game/parks and recreation/forestry. This broad designation applies to members of the national guard when on duty during states of emergency, as well as to U.S. federal marshals. It can encompass a wide range of related criminal justice occupations, such as arson investigators, park rangers, coroners, investigators of child support and fraud, security officers in municipal and public utilities, as well as harbor, port, and transportation, and public housing security. Similarly, in the state of Texas the term *peace officer* is in widespread use; the Commission on Law Enforcement Standards and Training uses the term for constables, sheriffs, city police, specialized police, and the Texas Rangers. But have practitioners internalized the full meaning of the term?

Within this wide spectrum of peace officers, the image is strengthened by their being "sworn" to uphold the law, their adherence to standards and training, their badge and weapon, and sometimes their uniforms and insignia. But the true significance of these two words has yet to be fully realized by most who are covered by this umbrella term. Do most so engaged really perceive themselves as peacekeepers? Does their training regularly include developing skills in conflict resolution and facilitation, in human relations and the managing of cultural differences, in group dynamics and crowd control? Yet those who officially uphold the law are increasingly being asked to intervene and resolve domestic/neighborhood conflicts, to maintain order during protests and civil disobedience, to manage youth gangs and limit their criminal behavior, and to assist runaway adolescents, the homeless, and those who would do harm to themselves. Society asks those in law enforcement to fulfill a multiplicity of roles, from apprehension of criminal offenders and participation in court proceedings, to preserving civil order, controlling traffic, and coping with accidents and emergencies of all sorts. Essentially, these functions come down to keeping the peace and enforcement of law—the emphasis placed on either or both aspects is interpreted by the individual department and officer.

Psychologists remind us that the image we have of our role affects not only our behavior but the behavior of those to whom we project this image. The U.S. Marine Corps, for example, is currently undergoing a change of image from warriors to peacekeepers and humanitarians. What if all those described previously under the definition of peace officers really saw themselves as such, authentically projecting that image to the public? What if they were actually to become peace practitioners rather than symbolic enforcers of authority? That implies functioning as preservers of equal justice under the law. What if such professionals, by their attitude and behavior, manifested that keeping the peace truly was the job of law enforcement? Then such a change in role image and actions among agents of the law might prompt the majority of the law-abiding community actually to perceive them as peace officers in fact as well as in name.

"COSMOPOLITAN" PUBLIC SERVANTS

Cosmopolitan is defined as "common to or representative of all or many parts of the world; not national or local; not bound by local or national habits or prejudices." The use of the term *cosmopolitan* is carefully chosen with reference to "public servants" in general and peace officers in particular. The public sector at all levels has long referred to its employees as public servants. Although the term *public servant* is not highly regarded by many police officers, it is still used commonly in American society. The term is communicated on some city police cars by the motto emblazoned on their sides, "To protect and serve." At issue for police officers is what type of public servant is desirable in terms of attitudes, values, and actions. Among public employed personnel, a "cosmopolitan" is more multicultural in perspective and open to people from throughout the world, in contrast to one who is full of local prejudices.

The differences can be illustrated in the consulting experience of one of the authors. Some years ago the U.S. Customs Service utilized him as a consultant because of a problem with the first promotions of minorities and woman as managers. Some employees within the agency who were racially biased so resented the upward mobility of Hispanics, African Americans, Asians, and female personnel into the ranks of supervision that they initiated a campaign of intimidation to force the resignation of these new supervisors. The harassment included writing demeaning graffiti inside their lockers, slashing their car tires parked on federal property, and making threatening telephone calls to their spouses. Since the promotions occurred as a result of federal equal employment opportunity legislation, this deviant behavior was not just un-American and criminal, it was not the image of a public service employee which that agency wished to project. To counteract the situation, a series of cultural diversity workshops were introduced and data were collected on employee attitudes in that region. The information demonstrated that only a minuscule number of enthnocentric personnel might be classified as "bigots" and were responsible for the un-American and unacceptable behavior. Eventually, the "silent majority" in the workforce were challenged to assert more wholesome American values; to confront the small, prejudiced minority; to establish more positive organizational norms concerning equality for all personnel.

A cosmopolitan officer would have a more accepting, pluralistic view of people and their differences. He or she would be the opposite of someone who is provincial or ethnocentric—that is, locked into the cultural conditioning of one's own upbringing. Although enthnocentricism was discussed in Chapter 1, we review the definition again here: "Belief in the inherent superiority of one's own group and culture; it may be accompanied by feelings of contempt for others who do not belong; it tends to look down upon those considered as foreign; it views and measures alien cultures in terms of one's own culture." It is this attitude that is found in the antisocial, white aryan movements like the KKK, skinheads, and other fascist groups worldwide, most of whose members themselves suffer from low self-esteem and lack self-confidence. These groups of hate-mongers somehow give the participants a feeling of belonging, of power.

The cosmopolitan officer is not put off by new immigrants or groups that are "foreign" to his or her own background. Instead, he or she strives to understand the differences from a positive perspective. These new immigrants, ethnic, or racial groups offer an opportunity for peace officers to expand their own view of life by altering personal perceptions, attitudes, and knowledge of human beings.

The law enforcement employee who is cosmopolitan demonstrates openness, tolerance, flexibility, and sensitivity with regard to cultural diversity among individuals and groups. Such a person is curious to learn about people's similarities and differences. Thus, when working in an ethnic neighborhood (i.e., when not responding to calls for service), these officers listen, observe, and ask questions about the citizens' cultural preferences, dislikes, and lifestyles (Alpert and Dunham, 1988). This contributes to establishing trust and rapport with citizens. For example, an officer might:

- Sample the ethnic food in local restaurants and show interest in its preparation.
- Seek to understand the family structure and childrearing practices in that ethnic group.
- Inquire about the local customs, values, myths, and taboos, and so on.

These suggestions can be carried out more easily in agencies that use community-based policing strategies.

With increased heterogeneity within local populations, many states and agencies have inaugurated training programs so that criminal justice personnel will learn to become more sensitive to cultural differences among the people they seek to serve. For example, the *Ohio Police Chief Magazine* (June 1992) reported on that state's Human Diversity Initiative, which includes an advisory committee that assists law enforcement trainers who orient officers on such matters. The committee includes representatives of police chiefs as well as of the Asian, African American, Hispanic, female, elderly, low-income, and homeless segments of the larger community. This type of approach is important for law enforcement today, when there is a trend back to community-based policing in increasingly diverse neighborhoods. This approach is more akin to Japanese-type policing—intensive, friendly, and more forgiving of petty misbehavior, but ruthless with presumed criminals (*The Economist*, April 16, 1994, pp. 38–40). The police in Japan are widely dispersed in neighborhoods for which they are responsible and expected to patrol while being helpful to citizens.

Cosmopolitan officers are comfortable with contemporary community policing, described as a problem-solving approach. It enables officers to work with civilians outside the conventional channels by meeting with community groups and learning of their concerns. It is more than a return to the old "beat cop" and traditional "crime fighting" approach. The strategy involves unconventional and creative ways of dealing with crime and peacekeeping at the neighborhood level (e.g., developing an aggressive neighborhood watch program). As a result of the Christopher Commission recommendations in 1991 relative to the Rodney King incident, the Los Angeles Police Department is again moving in this direction, trying to determine community, not just departmental, priorities. Given the negative image policing received by that incident and the riots that followed, it should be encouraging to the law enforcement community to know that under a new chief, LAPD is vigorously engaged in practices such as the following:

- A sergeant countered a string of bank robberies in the Wilshire district by cultivating relationships with local bank managers, having his picture taken with them, and placing the life-sized enlargement visibly in the banks, along with police hats on the managers' desks; the result was a dramatic decrease in robberies.
- An officer has learned to read neighborhood graffiti and the messages behind them, so as to thwart gang plans and activities.
- In the south central vicinity, 10 officers are engaged in "Operation Cul-de-Sac," which consists of barricading streets in a target area to cut down on drive-by shootings and drug peddling; they patrol the neighborhood on bicycles and develop rapport with the residents.
- In the Harbor Division, six officers are free from regular assignments to work with community leaders on alleviating a host of local problems, ranging from gang warfare to graffiti and removal of abandoned cars, to refuse dumping on the streets and evicting tenants involved in drug pushing.
- Officers visiting ghetto elementary schools to discourage students from joining gangs, to take them on ride-alongs, and to help them get away from the ghetto to summer camp.
- Officers working with local city council representatives and community associations to resolve community problems, such as rehabilitating a number of undesirable apartment houses (result—monthly complaint calls to police about drug and alcohol problems have dropped here from 30 to 0).

But those engaged in nonstandard peacekeeping confess that not all officers and the police bureaucracy are supportive of this community approach, for only a small percentage of the total force is involved directly in these innovative activities. UCLA professor James Q. Wilson, a recognized authority on the subject, observed: "When you allow officers to set their own hours and to work with community people, first-line supervisors become very nervous. They have a feeling their officers are becoming social workers, or as they sometimes put it, are 'carrying rubber bullets.' A strong, devoted police chief can gain support for it, but even those most enthusiastic . . . are not completely selling it to their departments" (*Los Angeles Times,* June 3, 1991, p. A-22).

Critics of community-based policing claim that fiscal constraints limit the number of personnel that can be devoted to this type of peacekeeping if regular emergency response calls are to be effectively answered. Their solution is to get taxpayers and government to provide more funding for law enforcement to undertake these additional duties and to train special units of community service officers.

In these transitional times when urban areas are swamped with substance abusers, mentally ill people, and escalating gang warfare and gun violence, it is not easy to convince law enforcement officials to change their traditional structures and practices, even in communities that are more multicultural. With resistance to change, the traditional image of the police officer cannot be expected to change. In an era of tight budgets, community-oriented policing, for example, ran into stiff resistance among the 4000-officer Houston police department. While a recent audit of that Texas department praised efforts toward neighborhood policing for encouraging innovation and initiative by officers, the auditors then criticized officers who stray too far from "bread-and-butter" policing, such as response time to emergency calls (*Los Angeles Times,* Aug. 27, 1991, p. A-20). Even a former chief admitted that neighborhood-oriented policing (NOP) is a "tough sell" within a semimilitary bureaucratic structure, agreeing that it may take a generation to transform such a large organization. Meanwhile, that agency has reduced the crime rate by providing more overtime for street officers to work their beats, meet and respond to residents, while transferring service calls to a department telephone unit. Under its new chief, Sam Nuchia, the Houston police department has contracted with another public agency, the Harris County Constables, to engage in neighborhood policing within that city. Each contract has a civilian security director who receives the local input from citizens about public safety concerns. "Citizens on Patrol" have direct contact with their contract deputy for their neighborhood. That deputy is totally involved with the people in that district, conducting crime surveys, vacation watchdog education programs, and other peacekeeping measures.

Though opening storefront police stations in shopping centers and minimalls may be popular with the locals, especially when businesses agree to pay the rent and utilities, such experiments are contrary to traditional police culture, which measures success in numbers of citations, arrests, and convictions. Nevertheless, advocates of community-oriented policing maintain that it is not just the next step in the evolution of law enforcement—it is its future. For such community emphasis is a way of regaining public trust in the tarnished criminal justice system. It projects a more positive image, especially in areas where officer-related negative incidents have been widely publicized.

Confidence building in police requires cooperation among public officials and civic leaders. Thus in San Diego, the mayor and city manager teamed up with the police chief to support a major reorganization of the latter's department. Among the increasing number of police executives with Ph.D's is their assistant chief, Norm Stamper, who is providing leadership in SDPD's renewal strategy. The aim is to reduce administrative layers while getting more police out on the street who are not only equipped with leading-edge technology but seek to get closer to the community. The alterations include creation of a division committed to dealing more effectively with family and domestic violence. This unit will utilize a new citywide computer system to track child abusers and juvenile criminals, attempting to break the cycle of violence that produces adult criminal behavior. While the department is understaffed and many personnel might fear such changes, cosmopolitan professionals welcome them.

Following the 1992 spring riots, a special commission under former FBI Director William H. Webster studied police response during those disorders and concluded that the Los Angeles Police Department failed to apply standard tactics that would have held the disorder to a relatively confined area. Since then, 16 hours of riot training have been provided officers in maneuvers by police squads to intercept convoys of gang cars, tips on rescuing hostages, and other techniques in crowd control. Thus later that same year, the image of LAPD as a professional police organization was somewhat improved because of preventive actions related to a protest rally on behalf of four south central gang members (arrested previously for the beating of truck driver, Reginald O. Denny, during the prior riots). This time the headline in the *Los Angeles Times* (Dec. 16, 1992) read: "LAPD Widely Saluted for Swiftly Quelling Incident." The public applause for the department resulted from the way officers handled a rock-and-bottle-throwing situation at the same flashpoint of the riots earlier that year. In the fragile social environment within the inner city, police were quickly placed on tactical alert, mobilized rapidly, and responded with strong force at the intersection of Normandie and Florence Avenues. As a result, there was public praise for LAPD's sensitivity to the volatile confrontation and their response, which demonstrated competent professionalism. Law enforcement's image can be revitalized and public confidence restored, as new Chief Willie Williams is demonstrating.

CULTURALLY SENSITIVE PEACEKEEPING

General Omar Bradley observed that the success of a leader is realized in the effectiveness of the lead. Perhaps the bottom-line message of the preceding section can best be summed up in the philosophy of Robert K. Greenleaf, who believed that to change society, its leaders must be first seen as servants[*] (Greenleaf, 1991). Public service does not mean subservience, but it does imply a willingness to help those and to show sensitivity to those who are in need.

Throughout this book we have implied that cultural understanding and skills can be a powerful aid in more effective policing. Those in any branch of the criminal justice system are essentially in the "people business." The more its practitioners can learn about human behavior, its motivation, and its deviance, the better they can accomplish their jobs. Cultural anthropology is one of the behavioral sciences that can contribute much insight. It reminds us, as we learned in earlier chapters, that culture is a distinctly human capacity for adapting to the circumstances in which we find ourselves, and that the knowledge gained from this experience can be transmitted to subsequent generations. Our cultural heritage conditions our thinking and affects our behavior, often unknowingly—that is, we are aware of only some of these cultural influences; much of it is in our unconscious mind. Within nationalities and ethnic groups in local communities, it is largely culture that sets the rules that govern behavior. Indeed, understanding human culture is a key to more effective enforcement and peacekeeping.

[*]For information and a newsletter on *The Servant Leader,* contact The Greenleaf Center, 1100 West 42nd Street, No. 321, Indianapolis, IN 46208.

Culture is our social environment, the way people cope or adapt to their physical or biological environments. Thus customs, practices, traditions, and taboos for survival and development are passed through generations among a particular people. Culture is the history of people in groups—what they believe and value, what they fear and exclude, how they learn and work, and how they create families and institutions to facilitate their lives. It preserves that group's cohesion and consensus, even its prejudices. Therefore, we tend to accept the common "lore" and myths of our unique community, practicing its "truths" about acceptable behavior and blocking out what is contrary to this wisdom from the past—unless we acquire knowledge from elsewhere, outside our own tradition. Experiencing "culture shock" when living in an alien environment often causes the expatriate to question some of his or her cultural inheritance (Furnham and Bochner, 1986). There is no doubt that culture helps us to make sense out of that part of the planet or space that we inhabit. It provides ready-made solutions to simple problems, establishing a pattern for living and forming relationships.

Anthropologist Edward Hall offers these insights, which may have special meaning for peace officers:

> Each cultural world operates according to its own internal dynamic, its own principles, its own laws—written and unwritten. . . . Any culture is primarily a system for creating, sending, storing, and processing information. Communication underlies everything. . . . Culture can be likened to an enormous, subtle, extraordinarily complex computer. It programs the actions and responses of every person, and these programs can be mastered by anyone wishing to make the system work. (Hall and Hall, 1987)

Those in law enforcement who would be culturally aware comprehend the characteristics of culture in general and are able to integrate these with specific cultures, whether of a foreign country, a minority group, or an organization. Those who would be leaders in this regard acquire knowledge of cultural influences on individuals and their patterns of behavior. Such astute officers are able to distinguish between cultural universals and cultural specifics. They can appreciate cultural themes and diversity. Sensitive peacekeepers translate awareness into effective relationships with people who are different, whether in their own agency or in the community.

Cultural insensitivity by agents of the criminal justice system can often lead to tragic consequences that may result in unjust harassment, civil disturbances, and even death. In an early chapter we discussed the dangers related to cultural "stereotyping" (false or fixed notions and myths about a type of person). Television reports in 1992 highlighted this problem in terms of undercover cops who may be of African American, Latino, or Asian heritage. The two cases in point occurred in the Nashville Police Department and the New York City Transit Authority Police, where in both incidents white policemen possibly fell into the "stereotyping trap"—in one case beating and in the other shooting a fellow officer carrying out his uncover duty because he looked suspicious merely because he was a black male. The outcome for the latter organization was that cultural awareness training was introduced for transit police. The problem is worldwide within the law enforcement culture. CBS's program *60 Minutes* broadcast a feature (Jan. 11, 1993) on inadequate policing by the British criminal investigative services. False arrests by London "bobbies," often on the basis of cultural misperceptions, had cost the government heavy payments to the victims of what appeared to be racial prejudice by police. Now retraining is under way to help the U.K. police cope better with a more multicultural society that is also becoming more violent.

To be culturally sensitive, one learns about differences in *macrocultures*—mainstream or majority cultures, such as Japanese, Russian, Mexican, French, or Italian. Even more critical for law enforcement officers is the need to then gather information and insight about the *microcultures* encountered in such societies within the course of daily life. These minority or ethnic cultures are found in abundance within local communities, such as American Indians, Irish Americans, African Americans, Asian Americans, or Mexican Americans. But the classification of subcultures may also be widely applied, as when we analyze the culture of youth or seniors, drug addicts or alcoholics, "white collar" professionals, or even criminals. Furthermore, like corporations or agencies, institutions have unique organizational cultures.

Vocational groupings worldwide have a commonality of culture, whether they are military, managers, or police officers. During the 1960s, the National Commission on the Causes and Prevention of Violence commented on the then U.S. police force as being for the most part white, upwardly mobile, lower middle class, conservative in ideology, and resistent to change. Therefore, the commissioners observed that young police officers of that decade, sharing the attitudes and biases of the majority culture, might experience (1) fear and distrust when dealing with minorities, and (2) mild cultural shock when working in the urban ghettos of America, especially if faced there with militant hostility.

Commenting on this disappearing law enforcement subculture, Coffee et al. (1982, 1990) confirm that it was largely Caucasian males of working or middle-class background, many with military service. Being of the conventional culture with limited minority contact, recruits experience a process of occupational socialization whereby they become identified with police associates and with their procedures, problems, and values. In other words, they adopt the cultural outlook or mind-set of their colleagues in law enforcement, developing their own secure miniworld or cultural oasis. Immersed daily in this police microculture with its humor and pathos, its peak energy highs and boredom, its stresses and dangers, this "culture" shapes their perceptions and attitudes, their role views and sense of responsibility, and their commitment to safeguard one another. Readers can decide for themselves whether this socialization process and outlook is still present among justice personnel in the 1990s. Furthermore, police constantly interact with the criminal subculture, the hazardous "underworld" of the unsavory, the deviant, and the brutal. Is it any wonder that some police retreat into a "we/they" isolation—"they" being not only the perpetrators of crime but also all the nonsworns or civilians. Thus many police are more comfortable with "their own kind," whether they come from another agency, another state, or another nation. However, with increasing professionalism and education, as well as the recruitment of more women and minorities, police culture everywhere is being altered rapidly. Peace officers are becoming more comfortable and skillful in interacting with a variety of peoples and cultures. In an article on "Taking Police Culture Seriously," law professor Andrew Goldsmith of Melbourne, Australia, makes these astute observations:

> Police culture tends to be seen negatively, as a contrary and perverse influence on 'proper' exercise of police discretion. It is seen as often subversive of the ideals and demands of legality. Yet most modern societies are essentially dependent upon rule-based forms of police accountability. Police culture needs to be approached more positively, as a potential *resource* in the formulation of rules governing police powers and practices. This requires that police administrators and officers participate in *negotiated rulemaking*, a process similar to collective bargaining, in which police cultural perspectives are drawn upon. (*Policing and Society*, an International Journal of Research & Policy, 1990, Vol. 1:2, pp. 91-114, published by Harwood Academic, STBS Ltd. PO Box 90, Reading, Berks, UK RG1 8JL.)

There are many ways to study a culture, such as a systems approach that might analyze kinship/educational/economic/political/religious/association/health/recreational systems. However, Harris and Moran (1991/92) provide a simple model that will enable those in law enforcement to get a grasp of a culture, whether it be macro or micro, irrespective of the grouping. (Harris and Moran, 1992) These 10 benchmarks can be used to better comprehend a foreign, organizational or local culture, especially minority or ethnic groups. Exhibit 14.3 summarizes these characteristics for cultural analysis, first in terms of cultures in general and then specifically in the context of police culture. A police officer, in emergency situations, is obviously not going to have the time to do an in-depth cultural analysis. However, especially in community-policing types of situations, the officer can do some preparation before beginning an assignment in a given area where citizens will largely be from unfamiliar ethnic groups. Most people have preconceived notions or only a stereotypical understanding of cultural groups with whom they have not previously had contact. The categories listed in Exhibit 14.3 are areas where one often finds predictable cultural variations. The more information an officer or agent can gather about the cultural patterns of a distinctive community group, the less likely he or she is to make false assumptions about people. Knowledge of these cultural patterns would help the officer understand the behavior and actions of groups and would contribute to an overall ability to establish rapport and gain trust.

Exhibit 14.3 offers only 10 general classifications for cultural analysis, be it a nation, an organization or profession, a group or a generation (e.g., youth or seniors), or an ethnic or racial group. There are other dimensions of culture, but the categories provided help peace officers more quickly and systematically comprehend cultures, such as those described in Part Three. The same approach can also be applied to study the "underworld" or criminal culture and its various subcultures (e.g., bank robbers, car thieves/hijackers, drug pushers, or sexual perverts). Further, during international travel, whether on duty or for vacation, these same 10 characteristics can be observed to make the intercultural experience more meaningful. When law enforcement officers from other countries visit, these guidelines are useful for getting them to talk about their national or police cultures. All of the

Exhibit 14.3 Characteristics for Cultural Analysis

1. **Sense of self and space.** Examine how people in this cultural group perceive themselves and distance themselves from others. Culture not only helps to confirm one's identity but provides a sense of space, both physical and psychological. Such cultural conditioning of behavior may dictate a humble bearing in one culture or macho posturing in another. Some cultures support rugged individualism and independent action, while others teach that self-worth is attained in group conformity and cooperation. In some cultures, such as American, the sense of space dictates more physical distance between individuals, while in Latin/Asian cultures, less distance is desirable. Some cultures are very structured and formal, while others are more flexible and informal. Some cultures are very closed and determine one's place very precisely, while others are more open and dynamic. Each culture validates self in unique ways.

Police culture, for example, expects officers to project a sense of authority and assertiveness, to be respected and in control, to be curious and suspicious, to act with social appropriateness and a sense of duty, to uphold the law, and to serve the common good. Sense of space is experienced in terms of a precinct or district, a patrol area ("beat"), or a neighborhood in community-based policing.

2. **Communication and language.** Examine the communication system in the culture, both verbal and nonverbal. Apart from the national or regional language that might be spoken, study the dialects, accents, slang, jargon, graffiti, and other such variations. For example, there are differences in the way the English language is spoken in England and within the British Isles and Commonwealth nations; in North America, between the Canadians and the Americans (and within the latter between regions and groups, such as black English). Levine reminds us to go *Beyond Language* to comprehend the full communication by seeking the meanings given to body language, gestures, and signals.

The *police culture* has its own jargon and code system for communicating rapidly within the field of law enforcement; organizational communications dictate a formal system for reporting, for exchanges with superior ranks, for dealing with public officials and the media. A code of silence may exist about speaking to outsiders concerning police business and personnel.

3. **Dress and appearance.** Examine the cultural uniqueness relative to outward garments, adornments, and decorations or lack thereof; the dress or distinctive clothing demanded for different occasions (e.g., business, sports, weddings or funerals); the use of color and cosmetics; the hair and beard styles, or lack thereof; body markings.

In *police culture,* policy, regulations and even custom may determine a uniform with patches and insignia of rank, plus certain equipment to be worn and even the length of hair permissible. Exceptions may be permitted for those in administration, detective, or undercover work.

4. **Food and eating habits.** Examine the manner in which food is selected, prepared, presented, and eaten. According to the culture, meat, like beef or pork, may be prized or prescribed, or even forbidden all together—one person's pet may be another's delicacy. Sample national dishes, diverse diets, and condiments for tastes do vary by culture (realize that cultural groups can be conditioned to accepting some food or seasoning that your own body would not tolerate without reactions. Feeding habits may range from the use of hands or chopsticks to the use of utensils or cutlery (e.g., Americans and Europeans do not hold and use the fork in the same manner). Subcultures can be studied from this perspective (as in soldier's mess, executive dining rooms, vegetarian restaurants, prescriptions for females, etc.). Even drinking alcohol differs by culture—in Italy, it is more associated with eating a meal, while in Japan and Korea it is ritualized in the business culture as part of evening entertainment and strengthening business relations, sometimes done to excess.

In *police culture,* the emphasis has been on fast foods, hearty meals (preferably "complimentary," although official regulations require payment by officers for all such services); customs include that the patrol car sets the eating time for both partners, as well as off-duty relaxation and comradery in a "cop's drinking hole," sometimes marked by too much alcoholic consumption. The new generation of police is more concerned about healthy foods, keeping physically fit, and stress management—including diet, exercise, no smoking, and no substance abuse.

5.   **Time and time consciousness.** Examine the time sense as to whether it is exact or relative, precise or casual. In some cultures, promptness is determined by age or status (e.g., at meetings—subordinates arrive first, the boss or elder last). Is the time system based on 12 or 24 hours? In tribal and rural cultures, tracking hours and minutes is unnecessary, for timing is based on sunrise and sunset, as well as the seasons, which also vary by culture (e.g., rainy or dry season vs. fall/winter/spring/summer). Schedules in the postindustrial work culture are not necessarily 8 hours; businesses may operate on a 24-hour basis because of telecommunications and electronic mail. Chronobiologists are concerned under such circumstances about the body's internal clock and performance, so analyze body temperature and composition relative to sleepiness, fatigue, and peak periods (e.g., as with jet fatigue when passing through time zones).

The *police culture* operates on a 24-hour schedule with sliding work shifts that do affect performance; some departments adopt the military time-keeping system of 24 hours. Normally, promptness is valued and rewarded; during police operations, timing is precise, with watch synchronization of all involved.

6.   **Relationships.** Examine how the culture fixes human and organizational relationships by age, sex, status, and degree of kindred, as well as by wealth, power, and wisdom. In many cultures, marriage and the family unit are the most common means for establishing relations between the sexes and among parents, children, and other relatives. In the Far East, this is accomplished through an extended family that may involve aunts, uncles, and cousins living in the same household. Many cultures also operate with the male head of household as the authority figure, and extend this out from home to community to nation, explaining the tendency in some countries to have dictators. In traditional cultures, custom sets strict guidelines about boy–girl relations prior to marriage, about treatment of the elderly (in some cultures, they are honored, in others ignored), about female behavior (wearing veils and appearing differential to males in contrast to being considered an equal). "Underworld" or criminal cultures sometimes adopt a family pattern with the "godfather" as the head and various titles to distinguish roles.

In *police culture,* organizational relations are determined by rank and protocol, as well as by assignment to different departmental units. Although policy may dictate that all fellow officers and citizens be treated equally, unwritten practice may differ. The partnership system usually forgoes close relations and trust between individuals whose life and welfare is dependent upon the other. Postindustrial policing is moving more toward developing team relationships.

7.   **Values and norms.** Examine how the culture determines need satisfaction and procedures, how it sets priorities, and values some behavior while decrying other practices. Thus cultures living on a survival level (e.g., homeless) function differently from those which are affluent. In some Pacific Island cultures, for instance, the more affluent one becomes, the more one is expected to share with the group. Cultural groupings with high security needs value material things (e.g., money and property), as well as law and order. In the context of the group's value system, the culture sets norms of behavior within that society or organization. Acting upon a unique set of premises, standards of membership are established affecting individual behavior—for example, the conventions may require total honesty with members of one's own group but accepts more relaxed behavior with those from other groups. Other standards may be expressed in gift-giving customs, rituals for birth/marriage/death, and guidelines for showing respect, privacy, and good manners. The culture determines what is legal or illegal behavior through a codified system or custom; what may be legal in one culture may be illegal in another.

In *police culture,* for instance, subordinates are expected to show respect for officers of superior rank, while the reverse may be tolerated for those who have broken the law. Publicly and by departmental regulations, a code of ethics is place in which bribery and corruption are punishable offenses. A department of internal affairs ensures that alleged transgressors of such norms are investigated and tried or exonerated. This culture also espouses traditional American values of duty, loyalty, patriotism, and so on.

8. **Beliefs and attitudes.** Examine the major belief themes of a people and how this affects their behavior and relations among themselves, toward others, and what happens in "their world." A cultural "universal" seems to be a concern for the supernatural, evident in religious adherence and practices, which are often dissimilar by group. "Primitive" or tribal cultures are described as "animists" because they experience the supernatural in nature (e.g., "Indians" or Native Americans)—a belief to which modern environmentalists resonate. The differences are apparent in the Western cultures with Judeo-Christian traditions, as well as Islamic, in contrast to Eastern cultures, dominated by Buddhism, Confucianism, Taoism, and Hinduism. Religion, or the lack of it, expresses the philosophy of a people about important realities of life's experiences. Some cultural groups are more fundamentalist and rigid in their religious beliefs, while others are more open and tolerant. The position of women in a society is one manifestation of such beliefs—in some, the female is enshrined, in others treated like an equal by the male; in others, she is subservient to the male and treated like chattel. A people's belief system is often dependent on their cultural stage of human development—hunting, farming, industrial, or postindustrial; advanced technological societies seems to substitute a belief in science or cosmic consciousness for more traditional beliefs.

In *police culture,* for example, there has been a strong belief in group loyalty, pragmatism, power, and public service. God and religion have been acknowledged in oaths, in religious societies of police officers, by appointment of department chaplains, and during burial ceremonies of officers who die in the line of duty. Until recently, the law enforcement culture tended to be "chauvinistic," but that is changing with the introduction of more female officers and education of the workforce on diversity issues.

9. **Mental processes and learning.** Examine how some cultures emphasize one aspect of brain, knowledge, and skill development over another, thus causing striking differences in the way their adherents think and learn. Anthropologist Edward Hall suggests that the mind is internalized culture and involves how a people organize and process information. Life in a particular group or locale defines the rewards and punishments for learning or not learning certain information or in a certain way. In some cultures, the emphasis is on analytical learning—abstract thinking and conceptualization, while in others it is upon rote learning or memorization; some cultures value logic, while others reject it; some cultures restrict formal education only to males or the wealthy, while others espouse equal education for all. While reasoning and learning are cultural universals, each culture has a distinctive approach. However, the emergence of the computer and telecommunications as learning tools are furthering the globalization of education.

In *police culture,* recruit academies and other forms of in-service training may differ by locality as to content, instructional emphasis, and method. Anti-intellectualism among some police is being undermined by professional development and standards established by the federal/state governments and their credentialing processes, as well as by criminal justice curricula in higher education. As a result, modern police are moving from a more reactive, pragmatic, action-oriented behavior based on feelings and experience toward a proactive, thoughtful, analytical, and informed response. Professional competence is judged now by high performance and level of learning, not just by years on the job and connections.

10. **Work habits and practices.** Another dimension for examining a group's culture is their attitude toward work, the types of work, the division of work, the dominant work habits and procedures, and the work rewards and recognitions that are provided. Some cultures adopt a work ethic that says it is desirable for *all* to be so engaged in worthwhile activities—even sports and the arts, while others preclude labor for income. Work worthiness is measured differently by cultures as to income produced, job status, or service to the community. In Japan, for example, cultural loyalty is transferred from the family to the organization, which is dependent upon the quality of individual performance. Classification of vocational activity is somewhat dependent on the culture's stage of development—a people can be characterized primarily as hunters, farmers,

or factory or knowledge/service workers, with the trend away from physical labor toward use of mental energy aided by new technologies. The nature of work, as well as the policies, procedures, and customs related to it, are in transition. In the postindustrial culture, there is more emphasis on the use of advanced technologies, such as automation and robotics, as well as upon quality of working life—from compensation and benefits to stress management or enhancement of one's potential on the job. In conjunction with work, a culture differs in the manner and mode of proffering praise for good and brave deeds, outstanding performance, length of service, or other types of accomplishment. Promotions, perks, and testimonials are all manifestations.

In *police culture,* a hierarchial structure has organized work into specializations, divisions, and other such operational units engaged primarily in law enforcement and crime fighting. Job performance varied from "workaholics" to those who just put in time. Today the trend is toward peacekeeping and crime prevention, toward teamwork and community-based policing, toward obtaining citizen cooperation. Rewards and recognitions in the past have been largely commendations, advancement in rank, and retirement dinners, but now are being expanded to include assignments for professional development, interagency exchanges, and even sabbatical leaves for educational advancement.

aspects of culture noted are interrelated; there is a danger in trying to compartmentalize this complex concept and miss the sense of the whole.

If the representatives of law enforcement are more culturally aware and sensitive, they are more likely to project to the public a positive image as peacekeepers. There are examples of actual newspaper headlines that affect the image of the department involved. Although the media does not always accurately report what has occurred, we know that there are still instances of police insensitivity. Some of those negative headlines have included:

- Report on Police Cites Racism, Excessive Force
- Law Enforcement: Officials Deny That Deputies Are Using Excessive Force as Agency Faces More Turmoil
- Policewomen Call Sex Harassment Endemic in Their Department
- On the Beat, Police March to a Changing Set of Rules
- Police Abuses Laid Bare, but Solutions Fall Short

On the plus side, there are numerous reports of law enforcement agencies that are engaged in constructive cross-cultural communication with the communities they patrol. One story concerned a special unit being established by the San Diego Sheriff's Department to patrol "Indian" reservations, which are being overrun from the outside by drugs and violence. Federal Public Law 280 transferred criminal jurisdiction and enforcement on reservations to some states. In this instance, the tribal chairman requested the deputies for their rural, remote areas, which have become a kind of "no-man's land." Four officers now make the East County reservations their sole focus, and the American Indians appreciate the improved service. The word has spread among the inhabitants that the "law is back in town and he's not so bad." As reported by the *Los Angeles Times* (June 17, 1991), analyze the following statement about deputy Terry Lawson's experience on the Barona Indian Reservation:

He's also taken a good look at how he carries himself, and has made a few changes. In his conversations with new Indian contacts, he noticed they rarely interrupted him. He now tries to return the favor. And he no longer relies on a handshake to make a good first impression—some Indians find that presumptuous, particularly from a stranger. 'You've got to make sure they offer their hands first,' Lawson said, sharing some hard-won knowledge. Also don't talk to one person about another person—many Indians are offended by that. . . . We're learning things the hard way, and I'm sure we're going to step on ourselves a lot more. When something bad happens, you're going to have a deputy who knows the tribal chairman by his first name, and who the Indians know by his first name. We're talking about personalized service.

But do the deputies have to learn about American Indian cultures the hard way? The issue is how much cross-cultural training was provided to the officers for this unique assignment? If they are culturally sensitized, it will facilitate their mission and interactions. For example, suppose that they had used the foregoing method of cultural analysis before and during their initial encounters with the local tribes?

Throughout this book the message has been not to patrol or observe on the basis of your own cultural background, or you may end up with distorted perceptions. Instead, peace officers should try to get into the unique world of the community being served. For example, gestures have different meanings in varied cultures. In India, men and women do not usually hold hands in public—men may hold hands, and women in some rural areas may walk behind the men; when asking questions of some people especially from southern India, the gesture of rolling the head side to side (which is similar to the "no" head movement in the West) signifies "I'm listening" or "I'm in agreement." Now transpose this into a North American urban area where a native of southern India is stopped by a police officer for running through a red light. The officer asks, "Did you see that red light?" If not yet acculturated to the ways of the United States/Canada, the response from the immigrant may be a head roll from side to side, the gesture for him which means "yes." This would probably confuse the officer, who may presume the Indian to be lying (i.e., the officer would interpret the Indian's head movement as "no"). Interpersonal interactions are complicated, especially when cross-cultural differences are present. Real peacekeeping requires cultural sensitivity if officers are to fully comprehend what is taking place.

SUMMARY

For professionals in any facet of the criminal justice system, change begins with the practitioners' image of their role, which is then projected to the public. In the evolving work culture, adhering to the image of peace officer is not only appropriate but requires that those in public service become more cosmopolitan in their outlook and approach. Effectively dealing with cultural issues within the field of law enforcement then becomes a means for exercising leadership which demonstrates that sensitive peacekeepers capitalize upon cultural uniqueness (Harris, 1989).

Since culture gives a people identity, the issue is how much of a person's cultural heritage is to be absorbed or retained in the process of acculturation to the new homeland. Author and consultant Janice Hepworth maintains that one of the greatest strengths of the United States is "its elasticity" in that regard. The challenges for law enforcement, in particular, are to recognize and appreciate diversity both within the community and workforce, while using such insights advantageously. Human diversity must become a source of renewal rather than intolerable conflict within our agencies, communities, and in society.

DISCUSSION QUESTIONS AND ISSUES*

1. *Cultural Impact.* Consider the long-term influence of the institution of slavery on the African American family in general and their male youth in particular. What is the implication of this negative heritage for today's black citizens in general, and within the subcultures of police officers and criminals? Identify hopeful trends that repair or redress the damage of slavery on this segment of the American population.

2. *Extended Families and the Law.* Many Asian cultures function with an extended rather than a nuclear family. When such immigrants come to North America, they attempt to carry on this family tradition (e.g., working hard in a family-owned businesses, remodeling and enlargening houses, acquiring several automobiles, intermarriage, etc.). Consider how such customs may possibly cause the new arrivals to violate local laws and regulations relative to child labor, multiple-family dwellings and occupancy, multiple-car parking on public streets, etc.). Have you observed anything in this regard about such refugees as Indo-Chinese, Cuban, Haitians, and natives from the subcontinent of India?

3. *Community-Based Policing.* Community-based policing is an attitude of mind as well as a change in strategies and techniques. Consider how you would apply this approach if, for example, you were a peace officer in California's Fresno Valley. After the Vietnam War, over 60,000 Hmong refugees were resettled there in appreciation for their services to their American allies, as well as to protect them from Communist retaliations. An aboriginal people coming from a tribal culture in the agricultural stage of development, these Laotians find it hard to adjust to a modern, technological society, even when relocated to a rural setting. However, their kids are soaring—studying hard, picking up English quickly, doing well in math. Adults suffer from "cultural shock," fearing their children are becoming too Americanized and losing too much of their own cultural heritage. What police challenges and problems would be found in a community with such a microculture? Can you identify other such refugee groups that have been suddenly relocated from a tribal culture to modern North America?

4. *Culture and Crime.* With inadequate border management and increased illegal entry, a criminal element slips into the United States and preys upon the vast majority of law-abiding immigrants from the "old country," particularly through extortion. Earlier in this century, such thugs and "crime families" were mainly from Europe; today they come in increasing numbers from the former USSR, Latin America, Caribbeans, and Asia. Consider how law enforcement nationally can share information and tactics to combat such threats (e.g., from Hong Kong triads, Salvadoran death squads, Russian black-marketeers, Jamaican mafia). At the same time, how can peace officers gain the confidence of the new émigré, many of whom have been culturally conditioned against police in their homelands? What insights can you share on these matters of concern to law enforcement?

---

*See Instructor's Manual accompanying this text for additional activities, role-plays, questionnaires and projects related to the content of this chapter.

REFERENCES

ALPERT, G. P., AND R. G. DUNHAM (1988). *Policing Multiethnic Neighborhoods,* Greenwood Press, Westport, Conn.

CARTER, D. L., AND OTHERS (1992). *The State of Police Education: Policy Directions for the 21st Century,* Police Executive Research Forum, Washington D.C.

COFFEE, A. (1990). Law Enforcement: *A Human Relations Approach,* Prentice Hall, Englewood Cliffs, N.J.

COFFEY, A., AND OTHERS (1982). *Human Relations: Law Enforcement in a Changing Community,* Prentice Hall, Englewood Cliffs, N.J.

FURNHAM, A., AND S. BOCHNER (1986). *Culture Shock: Psychological Reactions to Unfamiliar Environments, Methuen, New York.*

GILBERT, E. L. (ed.) (1990). *The World of Mystery Fiction,* Bowling Green State University Popular Press, Bowling Green, Ohio.

GOLDSMITH, ANDREW (1990). "Taking Police Culture Seriously," *Policing and Society,* an International Journal of Research and Policy, Vol. 1, No. 2, pp. 91-114, Harwood Academic, Reading, Berks, UK.

GREENLEAF, R. K. (1991). *Servant-Leadership: A Journey into the Nature of Legitimate Power and Greatness,* Paulist Press, Mahwah, N.J.

HALL, E. T., AND M. R. HALL, (1987). *Hidden Differences,* Anchor/Doubleday. Garden City, N.Y.

HARRIS, P. R., AND R. T. MORAN, (1991/92). *Managing Cultural Differences,* Gulf Publishing Company Houston, Texas.

LEVINE, D., AND M. ADELMAN, (1993). *Beyond Language: Cross-Cultural Communication,* Englewood Cliffs: N.J. Prentice-Hall.

MAYHALL, P. D. (1985). *Police–Community Relations and the Administration of Justice,* Prentice Hall, Englewood Cliffs, N.J.

15

POLICE OFFICER PROFESSIONALISM AND PEACEKEEPING STRATEGIES IN A DIVERSE SOCIETY

OVERVIEW

This closing chapter considers issues of professionalism and leadership as well as the future development of personnel within the criminal justice field. Given the trends toward greater multiculturalism within communities and the workforce, we examine specifically how this education and training can be directed toward creation of greater cultural cooperation within neighborhoods and local law enforcement agencies. We review professional development opportunities for peace officers in general. A section explores how networking, both personal and electronic, as well as mentoring, may contribute to career development. The chapter concludes with strategies for peacekeeping in a diverse society: community-based policing, curtailing litigation against peace officers, crime prevention techniques, and other innovative methods.

COMMENTARY

The following quotes reflect the importance of professional development of law enforcement officers:

> President's Commission on Law Enforcement and the Administration of Justice, Washington, D.C., 1967.

> In a paper presented to the Commission on "Recruitment, Selection, Promotion, and Civil Service, A. C. Germann outlined the criteria for a profession in general, and law enforcement in particular. These included being service-oriented; highly

competent, being allowed autonomy and authority in the exercise of that competence; utilization of scientific knowledge and specialized techniques; strong career commitment based on that competence and accomplishment; valuing of free inquiry and loyalty to the profession which relates more to the opinion of professional peers than to hierarchial supervisors; determination to influence change by actions to eliminate or ostracize all incompetent members of the organization. . . .

[The author of that national report in the late 1960s concluded that although there are many in these occupations of professional competence and character, American police service "does not meet the standards of a profession to the degree that it should, even though it be a professional activity."]

Police–Community Relations and the Administration of Justice, by P. D. Mayhill, Prentice Hall, Englewood Cliffs, N.J., 1985, pp. 194–195.

Numerous current studies clearly demonstrate that the training of American police is deficient. Many police academies have a training curriculum consisting of approximately 400 hours. . . . Even when an academy is well structured . . . the curriculum concentrates on the law enforcement task, which occupies a relatively small portion of the police officer's time. Although most of the officer's time is devoted to service activities, training in the service function is, for the most part, de-emphasized or ignored at police academies. . . . Dedicated and responsible officers may be placed on the street unprepared for the experience they will face. They do not have a clear understanding of the true attitudes of the public they are policing. They may not have an appreciation of the historical factors that shaped the larger community and its neighborhoods. They may not understand the sources of the fears and prejudices of the people in the community, including themselves. They may not be trained in the techniques necessary to defuse dangerous situations with finesse or to seek alternatives to arrest. Unfortunately, they are too often taught to respond to threats or hostility with force. Lack of training in such subjects as introduction to social theory, basic psychology, human development and behavior, constitutional law, minority history, ethnic studies, interpersonal relations and communications skills allows communication blocks to remain intact.

LEADERSHIP IN PROFESSIONALISM AND SYNERGY

Lack of professionalism and inadequate personnel development can be very costly to any organization. But when it occurs within the public sector, it can prove damaging to both individual careers and to society. The subheadings in this opening section contain three key concepts, which will be defined because of their implications for law enforcement and peacekeeping within a multicultural society.

Leadership

Leadership is exercised when one takes initiative and shows the way; guides or influences others in a direction; demonstrates how a process or procedure is performed. Leaders are said to possess a good mixture of conceptual, technical, and professional competence, and demonstrate judgment and people skills. Leaders are not only creative change agents but practical futurists, exercising foresight and the capacity for the "big picture" and the "long view" (McGregor, 1991). Today as we transition into a new information age and work culture, leaders need to be both transformational and transcultural. That is, such high performers innovate in:

- Transforming work environments from the "status quo" to the way it must be
- Renewing organizations, becoming a role model in terms of transmitting intellectual excitement and vision about their work
- Helping personnel to restructure their mind-sets and values

In terms of the transcultural, such a leader deals with persons equally, regardless of gender, race, color, religion, or cultural differences. Further, the transcultural leader cuts across cultural barriers while combatting prejudice, bigotry, or racism wherever found. The description of the cosmopolitan provided in Chapter 14 applies to such leaders. Police supervisors, for example, exercise this leadership through anticipatory thinking, strategic planning, sensitive decision making, and communications (Moran et al., 1993).

Professionalism

Professionalism means approaching an activity, such as one's occupation or career, with a sense of dedication and expertise. In contrast to an amateur, a professional is a committed high performer. A professional possesses integrity and demonstrates competence—regardless of the vocation, profession, or sport in which he or she is engaged. Some of the characteristics of professionalism, particularly with reference to law enforcement, were described in the opening commentary by A. C. Germann. When one possesses this quality, that person is concerned about:

- Doing an effective job or rendering an effective service
- Developing in one's skill level and career
- Ensuring ethical and sensitive behavior in one's self and other organizational members
- Capitalizing on diversity in people and organizations

Whether writing a report, conducting an investigation or an interview, or commanding a police action, a professional peace officer does it consistently well. Further, his or her performance observes the code of ethics expected of a public employee. With growing multiculturalism in both the community and workforce, law enforcement professionals support policies and programs that promote collaboration among people of diverse backgrounds. Furthermore, they curb among their colleagues or the community the first signs of divisiveness, intolerance, and discrimination.

Synergy

Synergy implies cooperation and the integration of separate parts to function as a greater whole and to achieve a common goal. Synergy occurs through working together in combined action, attaining a greater total effect than a sum of the parts. Cultural synergy builds on the very differences in people for mutual growth and accomplishment. Through such collaboration, similarities, strengths, and diverse talents are shared to enhance human activities and systems. In law enforcement, synergistic leaders (Parker, 1990):

- Create consensus, which enables disparate people and groups to work together by sharing perceptions, insights, and knowledge

- Promote participation, empowerment, and negotiation within an organization or community, so that members work to mutual advantage and are committed to teamwork and the common good over personal ambition or need
- Demonstrate skills of facilitating, networking, conflict resolution, and coordination
- Are open-minded, effective cross-cultural communicators

Thus leadership, professionalism, and synergy are three powerful concepts. When combined within the criminal justice system in general, or law enforcement and peacekeeping in particular, they may alter one's role image and performance. The following descriptions demonstrate the application of these concepts to real situations. Leadership, professionalism, and synergy are illustrated at both the organizational and individual levels in the context of the new work culture (Harris, 1995).

REGIONAL/STATEWIDE COOPERATION IN LAW ENFORCEMENT

Society and communities today are so complex and interdependent that individual departments can best deal with certain enforcement challenges and crime problems through cooperation among criminal justice entities at all levels of government. Although this is certainly more efficient and effective, for many traditional public safety agencies, this may require a "paradigm" shift in the thinking of its members. This means exercising a type of law enforcement leadership that actively promotes specific information interchanges, joint ventures, and task forces that operate on a statewide or regional basis. There are already in place many commissions, councils, and other structures for promoting interagency collaboration. Law enforcement leaders with a sense of professionalism and synergy would ensure that all officers were committed to such combined action. Thus many matters of police training are best dealt with at a regional level but with local agency input and participation. For example, there are regional and statewide programs with human or cultural diversity training for public-sector personnel. Again, in large metropolitan areas with several police jurisdictions, as is the case in many areas, a consortium might be established to deal jointly with ethnic gangs and juvenile delinquency in that locality. Similarly, a regional, collaborative approach in peacekeeping might involve joint problem solving and action on such matters as hate crimes or minority recruitment. In each of these instances, agency representatives come from differing *organizational cultures*. Therefore, any interagency collaboration requires the practice of the kind of cross-cultural communication skills described in Chapter 5.

Another illustration directly related to this book's theme would be in a border city with a twin urban area in another country. This could be along the northern border with Canada or the southern border with Mexico, and call for international cooperation among public agencies that have similar missions but different cultural contexts. In such situations, local police departments of both nations should routinely share information and cooperate in combatting crime and helping each other's citizen visitors. How much more could be accomplished if the police jurisdictions along the American/Mexican border were to enter into informal or formal arrangements to advance the professional development of each other? For example, within the two sister cities of Juarez, the Mexican police could be most helpful to their northern colleagues in terms of language and cultural training, particularly with reference to those of Mexican origin living within Texas. In return, the Texan peace officers might assist in the technical and professional preparation of their Mexican counterparts. This might contribute to more humane treatment of American citizens who break the "law" when south of the border, where the supposed "transgressor" is sometimes guilty until proven innocent. For American and Mexican police, there are numerous other ways to be mutually supportive, ranging from information exchanges on criminology to criminals, to promotion of better bilateral relations and border law enforcement management. Once the North American Trade Agreement is fully implemented, we can expect increased exchanges and transfers between the citizens of Canada, United States, and Mexico. When law enforcement in all three countries cooperate, that process is facilitated. To overcome cross-cultural barriers, police jurisdictions and their personnel in adjoining countries have more to gain by thinking in terms of synergy across borders. One place to begin is to learn about the differences in each culture's legal systems.

PROFESSIONALISM, ETHICS, AND MINORITIES

Police professionalism, according to Mayhill (1985), requires greater self-awareness and a positive self-image in an officer, such as was discussed in Chapter 14. For professionalism to grow in law enforcement, Mayhill advocates not only greater technical skill training, but higher educational attainments as well as the setting of goals for career development. To reduce stress within the working environment of modern police, this criminal justice professor advocates an atmosphere of improved intraagency communication as well as supportive relations with the community. What then seems to be the characteristics of a police professional? The answers provided throughout this book are:

- One who is properly educated and public service-oriented
- One whose behavior and conduct on the job is appropriate and ethical, avoiding clear conflict of interests
- One who respects the dignity and humanity of everyone contacted in the course of his or her work, attempting to treat all fairly and with equal justice
- One who is culturally sensitive to the differences and potential of others
- One who is aware of the impact of agency culture on the professional behavior of officers
- One who is a learner concerned about personal and career development for both one's self and others

The Florida Criminal Justice Executive Institute recently issued a monograph entitled *Against Brutality and Corruption*. It discusses how these evils can be countered within law enforcement by officers who demonstrate integrity, wisdom, and professionalism. Its author, Edwin J. Delattre (1991a) observes: "We tend nowadays to neglect the immorality of professional incompetence. Many people who discuss ethics in different walks of life, whether in business or public service or the traditional professions, seem to believe that behaving honestly on the job and having the 'right' attitudes about race, sexual orientation, and the environment are all that ethics requires. This view ignores our plain duty to be professionally competent and good at our jobs."

In the Teacher's Guide for another volume, Delattre (1991b) made the point to police academy instructors that all police training is directly relevant to ethics, which should include competent performance. The co-authors of *Multicultural Law Enforcement* not only reinforce that observation, but add to it—all police professional development should contain adequate education in culture and cross-cultural skills. Our position is that ethical behavior by law officers also encompasses a respect for human dignity, a concern for human rights, and tolerance for diversity in the human family. Unethical behavior is present when officers are deliberately racist, acting with prejudice, bigotry, and intolerance toward a fellow officer, citizen, or foreign visitor. Such actions by public employees are simply unprofessional and unacceptable. The public will no longer overlook or tolerate such behavior by peacekeepers.

At the core of professionalism should be one's sense of ethics. This may be manifested individually or through a group, such as society in general or a profession in particular, such as those "sworn" to uphold the law. Ethical practices are cultural expressions of a society or of organizations. *The Random House Dictionary* defines the term *ethics* as "a system of moral principles; the rules of conduct recognized in respect to a particular class of human actions of a particular culture as expressed by a group (e.g., medical ethics, police ethics, or Christian ethics), or by an individual (e.g., personal ethics)." The alternative definition is "a formal classification for study as a branch of philosophy dealing with values relating to human conduct, with respect to rightness and wrongness." Certain ethical standards are cultural universals, generally accepted by humankind; other ethical practices are culturally specific, dependent on the attitudes and traditions of a particular group. Some ethical expectations are overt or open, while others are covert or hidden. For example, in parts of rural India one of the authors discovered that if an automobile driver were to hit someone, the expectation was that the driver did not stop but proceeded to the nearest town, where the incident was to be reported to the police. The practice did not condone "hit-and-run driving" but faced a reality that in this developing country, the justice system was inadequate, so people might be tempted to take its administration into their own hands with immediacy. Thus the driver, whether at fault or not, escapes to police in the next village to admit the accident. In American culture, the legal and ethical action for those involved in a car accident is to exchange information and/or to call the police and report the matter immediately.

As a concept, ethics is closely associated with professionalism. Codes of ethics are vital to guide behavior of practitioners of the learned professions (e.g., law or medicine), to punish those who do not adhere to the agreed, enunciated conduct of behavior for those in such vocations. For peace officers, such codes promote self-regulation and discipline within a law enforcement agency. Often these codes are written and sometimes are summarized with an agency mission statement. To be a professional implies not only competence and expertness, but adherence to higher standards of professional conduct (Lewis, 1991; Bowman, 1991; Gellerman et al., 1990).

In the best sense, professionalism implies having more than technical skills and refers to the moral contributions that professionals make in a complex, democratic society—the ethic of the calling. The ethical person is perceived as someone who has courage and integrity, is willing to resist corruption and unprincipled people by upholding humanity, justice, and civility. Such a peace officer tries to be loyal to his or her own conscience and avoids unprofessional behavior (e.g., use of excessive force, expressions of bias and bigotry, or acceptance of bribery).

CAREER DEVELOPMENT AND PROFESSIONAL OPPORTUNITIES

A professional peace officer masters the basics of his or her discipline or field, then moves on to higher, more innovative performance. Such a person not only possesses a strong sense of mission and vision but has the capacity to bring out the best in others while coping with ever more complex situations (Block, 1991; Bolman and Deal, 1991). Professional development in the criminal justice system must be considered within realistic limits, however. For example, there are limitations on the officials in charge as to what education, training, and support services are possible. Departmental constraints include declining budgets, expanding service demands—including 911 calls—and the quality of personnel now employed. Individual officers face constraints on their career development caused by job demands, family requirements, educational/financial limitations, and personal motivation. For law enforcement organizations, human resource development starts with recruitment and selection of candidates. Apart from testing and basic qualifications, future peacekeepers must be chosen who have stable personalities, are educable and career-growth oriented, and are representative of the multicultural communities in which they serve. In previous chapters, especially Chapter 3, we have reviewed this challenge. The ideal recruit should possess the potential to become the police professional described earlier. Further, the academy curriculum must be relevant and constantly altered to prepare newcomers for the realities of their actual duties on the job in an ever-changing society. Just as a culture adapts, so do the laws that officers enforce and the duties they perform. For example, with the diversity of the New York City population, its police academy, like others in the east and midwest, devotes a third of the study to learning from the social sciences, a large part of which deals with cross-cultural issues. Once sworn, the new officers must be given ample opportunities to advance in their careers, whether through in-service training or external study, so as to be ready for promotions.

It is vital that those who rise into leadership positions within law enforcement be concerned about enhancing and capitalizing on the organization's human assets. Within law enforcement, it begins by actions to promote the career development of one's self and one's co-workers (Distelrath, 1988; Brooks, 1987; Terboch, 1987). Then this concern expands to learning about current concepts and practices not only in policing and peacekeeping, but in human relations and cross-cultural communications. Those assigned to agency specializations need additional training in those fields of expertise, which may range from criminology and management information systems to training and personnel functions. For many this continuing education may encompass new laws and technologies as well as cultural diversity skills and knowledge of equal employment legislation.

Apart from the FBI Academy and public service associations, there are several national organizations that peace officers may wish to utilize in terms of possible membership, publications, conferences, cultural diversity training, and other services. Appendix K provides lists for this purpose. For those with training responsibilities who are interested in becoming more professional in their people development activities within law enforcement, there is the American Society for Training and Development, which issues the *Training and Development Journal* as well as the *Human Resource Development Quarterly*. For those seeking to improve management skills, there is the American Society for Personnel Administration, while those involved in equal employment opportunity and diversity training would benefit from the Society of Intercultural Education, Training and Research. For police executives engaged in strategic planning, there is the Society of Police Futurist International.

We reviewed courses available only in New York, Florida, and California that deal with professional development. The California Commission on Peace Officer Standards and Training (POST), besides certifying basic and advanced officer courses, also has a Center for Leadership Development. California POST was a forerunner for executive-level training with their Law Enforcement Command College, which conducted its first classes in 1984. Although the catalog of POST-certified courses, including information on the Command College, is not available to the general public, it may be requested from POST by law enforcement officials.

In 1990 the state of Florida passed legislation establishing within its Department of Law Enforcement (FCJEI) a Florida Criminal Justice Executive Institute. The purpose of the institute is to foster professionalism among upper-level management. This is accomplished via ongoing executive seminars, workshops, and advanced operational programs, research into issues and publications of trends and results, and through enhanced systems of networking and mentoring. The FCJEI also offers the Senior Leadership Course, which is held at the Florida State University's Center for Professional Development. This program consists of 264 classroom hours where the participant attends 10 sessions of three- or four-day meetings every other month.

Neither the California Command College or Florida Leadership Course programs presently address emerging issues of a multicultural society and workforce and the skills to be acquired for that purpose by law enforcement leaders. In the private sector, for instance, the American Management Association (Appendix K) has a three-day program for Managing Cultural Diversity, which is for managers and human resource specialists. Its 1992–1993 catalog describes this course as aiming to develop the "synergy of diversity," so that within the organization the full energy of every talent and point of view is utilized. Among its objectives is to overcome barriers associated with difference in language, accent, ethnic background, age, gender, religion, and national origin. The content examines verbal and nonverbal communication; defines ethnicity/race/culture; analyzes participants' cultural orientations, including stereotypes, biases, prejudices, and values; explores how diversity contributes to common goals and objectives turning differences into assets; and describes how to be more creative, innovative, and competitive through a diverse workforce.

Networking and Mentoring

Law enforcement agencies and their officers have always, to some extent, shared information and cooperated in crime fighting, as well as in career advancement and for mutual benefit. Perhaps the latter motive was the basis for the emergence of the Police Benevolent Associations and ethnic police organizations. Other examples are the traditional "grapevine" and informal supportive camaraderie within the global police "brotherhood." What is proposed here is a cooperative strategy of networking and mentoring far beyond previous collaboration. This formal strategy would advance both professionalism and career development, especially among women, minorities, and new recruits in the criminal justice system.

The idea of people *networking* is as old as human beings; the first hunters and tribes shared information and skills in order to survive. With the United States becoming more complex and multicultural and tightknit communities and neighborhoods disappearing, the country is transforming itself into networks of consumers, environmentalists, and public-interest groups, to name a few. Citizens of like interest or concerns frequently form a homogeneous network around a central theme or cause (e.g., pro-choice or pro-life regarding abortion), and they are often connected by telephones, computers, or teleconferencing. A network society is more flexible and permissive, allowing for a greater range of behavior, including even deviancy and crime—local gangs, in a sense, are a form of networking. However, networks are usually formed for positive purposes to improve living conditions, solve problems, increase sales, or advance careers and fortunes. The "old boys' networks" have operated for the latter purposes; now women and minorities are learning to network to get jobs and promotions in management and the professions where they were formally excluded. Police women, for example, informally network to move ahead in a law enforcement bureaucracy and culture dominated by males. Other ethnic groups within the police establishment are also learning this valuable lesson, and thus there is the formation of black, Latino, and Asian associations of police officers. With the growth of electronic mail, the National Institute of Justice has a special free Electronic Bulletin Board for criminal justice exchanges and a network called Construction Information Exchange (Tel: 301 738-8895).

Obviously, when peace officers network they may not only help themselves and their organizations, but may make it easier for management or command to utilize their resources. Law enforcement networks can become powerful mechanisms for both professional development and more effective administration of the justice system. Consider the possibilities for such among the participants and graduates of the FBI National Academy, the Florida Criminal Justice Executive Institute described on page 375, or the POST Command College. Although these professionals came from diverse agencies and backgrounds and were at various levels of command, these peace officers began to network personally and informally with their own classmates and then with other alumni. In the course of their years of living and studying together through successive workshops, they created a shared mind-set, a futuristic orientation, and a new set of problem-solving techniques. They continue to network and help each other informally, gathering periodically for law enforcement updates. Now imagine if these many police executives were to establish a formal electronic computer network. As graduates of such elite programs, they could not only assist one another professionally but become a powerful force for law enforcement leadership and lobbying within their state or nation, a power to be reckoned with in public service.

A network has been defined as a web of free-standing, self-reliant participants linked by one or more shared values. It involves a system of interrelated people or groups, offices or workstations, that are linked together for information exchange and mutual support. Today this can be accomplished personally or electronically, informally or formally, locally or globally. Information networks are transforming not only society but also our organizations, replacing hierarchy. Networks provide not only data but also guidance and support to people. Networking is a strategy for performance improvement that is prominent in the emerging work culture. Advances in telecommunications have opened up undreamed of opportunities for networking, either within professional fields, multinational organizations, or among like-minded individuals, institutions, and systems, such as police worldwide. For example, persons working in the fields of cross-cultural communications or interested in diversity issues have formed two networks that publish their own newsletters:

- Cultural Diversity at Work, 13751 Lake City Way, Seattle, WA 98125, 206/362-0336
- Intercultural News Network, 16331 Underhill Lane, Huntington Beach, CA 92647, 714/840-3688

Creative police managers employ computers and other communication technology for networking by electronic mail and bulletin boards, teleconferencing, or videotext exchanges. Increasingly, management is subscribing to specialized, commercial networks that offer particular information and services that improve the effectiveness of their activities. As more information and knowledge is shared by this means at a faster pace, the nation, indeed the world, is moving toward a network marketplace. When person-to-person networks add electronic capabilities to their interchange, they enhance their potential for increasing human performance through cooperative action.

Personal networks of executives, professionals, scientists, and technicians help participants cope with high growth challenges and the turbulence of transition to the new work environment. One example formed for the purpose of management development is The Meta Network (Metasystems Design Group, Inc., 2000 North 15th Street, Suite 103, Arlington, VA 22201): when on-line, members engage in computer exchanges and conferencing on subjects such as leadership and organization development, economics and systems theory, cross-cultural communications, and social change.

Another illustration is a group of police administrators in a region who are concerned about a common problem. These officials might create an electronic network around the common theme to organize and store messages on the subject. This would include practices and procedures that have worked for those within the network. The same might be done for any police specialization or concern, from gang warfare to stress management, from community policing to cultural awareness training. Similarly, having to cope with the legal implications of rapid social changes, law enforcement command might wish to set up an electronic network for continuing exchange on their implications for their own workforce and the services performed. Thus, regarding the trend of "telecommuting" or working at home, these networkers might share such data and commentary on legal and regulatory news and on supervisory and technology issues. In fact, such a network exists and it spawned a newsletter entitled *Telecommuting Review* (Telespan Publishing Corporation, 50 West Palm Street, Altadena, CA 91001). Members share information on everything from security issues related to home work terminals to long-distance telecommuting from offshore offices.

Computer networks are spreading rapidly for the purposes of professional development or problem solving. The National Society for Performance Instruction reported in its *The Performance & Instruction Journal* that in the fields of science and technology alone there now exist over 1000 data bases used at least 2 million times a year by searchers. In addition, NSPI notes there are 530 bibliographic data bases with 70 million citations. To cope with the information explosion, managers and other professionals create their own prototype knowledge data base and networks, as is already happening within law enforcement. Colleagues join together to input, synthesize, and update this information; often, it is done monthly by a panel of experts. Thus if police management has a particular concern about leading-edge developments in departmental health services or advances in DNA technology or cultural diversity in law enforcement, a task force of volunteers can be formed to establish its own select computer network. As a case in point, Gulf Publishing (3301 Allen Parkway, Houston, TX 77019) has a *Multicultural Resource Databank and Directory* that is useful for anyone engaged in cross-cultural training and communication.

Another facet of commercial electronic networks serving new law enforcement management needs is PLATO. Founded originally to service schools through computer-assisted instruction, it now provides a note file on various academic subjects which can be entered into by users who wish to leave and receive messages on a category of information. There are many international and nationwide information exchanges that leaders already utilize, such as THE SOURCE and COMPUSERVE, for communication with special-interest groups for market research and other purposes.

Organizations invest considerable funds sending personnel to special meetings, workshops, seminars, and other information-gathering conferences or training. It has also been observed by the authors with their own clients that too many sponsors fail to get sufficient payback or return-on-investment with such expenditures. That is, there is not enough "follow-up" with individual employees or members so that the data obtained get internalized into organizational knowledge and become a force for innovation. One way of doing this is through some form of debriefing. That is an opportunity for the participant in continuing education to share his or her experience and information with colleagues, either orally in a group, in a report that is circulated, or through computer interaction. The other possibility is for personal or electronic networking to occur among the attendees in such programs. For example, officer "associates" who have benefited from the specialized training of the FBI's National Academy might report back to their commands on the learning acquired. Again, suppose that an agency sent a representative to a law enforcement association conference or an external cultural diversity workshop for executives. Obviously, there is need to pump back and distribute the information and insight attained at such gatherings into the agency that sponsored the participant, particularly the specific unit where it is most relevant.

In addition to resources cited in the text or in Appendix K, the following sources also provide further information on networking and data banks.

- Compuserve, 5000 Arlington Center Boulevard, Columbus, OH 43220 1 800 848-8199
- EasyNet, 134 North Narberth Avenue, Narberth, PA 19702
- Electronic Networking Association, 2000 North 15th St., Suite 103, Arlington, VA 22201
- International Association of Chiefs of Police (IACP) Net 1 800/227-9640
- Mead Data Central, P.O. Box 1830, Dayton, OH 45401 (Data base LEXIS for legal research; NEXIS for publications)
- National Center for Computer Crime Data, Suite 2113, Los Angeles, CA 90068
- Search Group, Inc. 916/392-4640
- The GEO Group, 5405 Alton Parkway, Irvine, CA 92714
- The Networking Institute, P.O. Box 66, West Newton, MA 02165
- The Source, 1616 Anderson Road, McLean, VA 22102

The ultimate form of networking is *mentoring*, where more experienced officers provide career guidance to recruits, minorities, and women, to newly "sworn," or even to civilian departmental personnel (Murray and Owen, 1991). Chapter 2 provided initial insight on this topic. Usually, it takes place on an informal basis, either individually or in small groups. Mentoring has always happened within law enforcement, but it takes on special meaning for professional development when it becomes a planned strategy to team up patrol partners or when it is organized to advance female, minority, and ethnic officers within an agency. The mentoring process discovers latent abilities and contributes to both professional and organizational effectiveness. It can be a single intervention or a life-long relationship that promotes change within the giver and the receiver. It is a sign of a true professional in law enforcement when one contributes to the growth and development of a fellow peace officer.

When a senior or more experienced officer shares him- or herself with a junior officer, both should benefit by the encounter and relationship. The mentor develops human potential, and this is important with persons (mentees) who have traditionally been denied admittance into a career field or into supervision and management opportunities. Some departments have developed internal peer counseling teams. These are sworn and nonsworn law enforcement personnel who have been trained to counsel and assist their peers in times of stress. Another source of help for officers is the local clergy. The clergy, on a volunteer basis, in any community are available to deal with stress among police officers and provide counseling—a form of mentoring.

The Professional Peace Officer

This chapter has reviewed numerous ways to further the professional development of those in law enforcement as a means for promoting effective human relations among its practitioners and through them with the communities in which they serve. The bottom line is that lifetime learning is essential and the "long view" is preferable (Schwartz, 1991). Yet some law enforcement organizations are not providing adequate in-service training, even for those promoted into management. For instance, Captain Ken Petersen discovered in a statewide survey of medium-sized police agencies in California that 65 percent have no management development programs (Petersen, 1991). Therefore, in such departments, self-motivated personnel seeking upward vocational mobility would have go outside for their management education. Thus many officers at their own expense seek graduate degrees in public administration or criminal justice.

Professionals do not stop with graduation from a school or program; that only begins the process for continuing education. High-performing peace officers take personal responsibility for this, utilizing the new educational and communications technology now available for this purpose (Lawler, 1992; Porter, 1991). If they are not media- and computer-literate, they take action to learn the necessary skills, even if it means overcoming their "cyberphobia" (fear of new technology). Self-learning opportunities abound, from correspondence courses to media learning packages that can be loaned, leased, or purchased. Apart from university extension programs, the open-university movement, and other distance tele-education opportunities described by Rossman, the following sources offer a few examples of the possibilities for justice personnel to explore.

- NRI Schools, McGraw-Hill Continuing Education Center, 4401 Connecticut Avenue NW, Washington, DC 20008—request catalog of their software programs, from computer programming to desk top publishing.
- The Teaching Company, P.O. Box 4000, Dept. 300, Kearneysville, WV 25430—request catalog of SuperStar Teachers' College Lecture Courses in audio- or videocassette format.
- National Technological University, 750 Center Avenue, Fort Collins, CO 80526—a delivery system and instructional television network of 40 universities offering advanced technical and management education.

Finally, we should be mindful that the last strategies discussed—networking and mentoring—are potent means for empowering not only ourselves but others, especially those who have historically been excluded from the knowledge and information so essential for law enforcement career growth. Professional officers who have taken advantage of career development opportunities will be better peacekeepers in a diverse society.

PEACEKEEPING STRATEGIES IN A MULTICULTURAL SOCIETY

Within multiracial communities struggling with myriad problems of transition and integration, economic constraints, and rising crime, representatives of the justice system cannot afford to act capriciously and prejudicially. If social order is not to be replaced by chaos, law enforcement representatives of all types need not only be culturally sensitive but also must actively avoid racist, sexist, and homophobic behavior that may trigger violent social protest. Police researcher Neil Lingle, in his futures study on ethnic minorities and culture, identified programs that can promote a cooperative and interactive relationship between peace officers and the community (e.g., coalitions and partnerships). His recommendations for law enforcement include (Lingle, 1992):

- More cultural awareness and sensitivity training of personnel
- More recruitment and promotion of minorities/ethnics with the help of police unions
- More information to officers on external factors affecting their performance (e.g., influence of wealth and economic power, as well as racial/ethnic political power)
- More study on how to confront institutional racism, and the impact of minority employment and promotion on police policies and practices in the future

Furthermore, the new generation of peacekeepers must not only increase their knowledge, they must promote positive law enforcement innovations (*Exhibit* 15.1). In this section we focus on a few strategies for agencies to consider in their efforts to keep community peace in a multicultural society.

Community-Based Policing The late 1980s and early 1990s brought new challenges to law enforcement. In the area of greater diversity in most communities, reduced budgets, increased illegal immigration, social disorder, all resulting in increased scrutiny of law enforcement. Progressive law enforcement executives embraced a strategy of policing to meet many of those challenges. Such change was encouraged in 1987 when the Philadelphia Police Commissioner's Council declared:

> A key concept . . . is that the police abandon the image of themselves as a "thin blue line," standing between the "good citizens" of the community on the one hand, and the "bad guys" on the other. Rather, they should favor an image of themselves as partners to the community in a joint effort to produce freedom from fear and victimization. . . . Finally, this concept acknowledges that unless the police work at establishing and maintaining a proper relationship with the community, they themselves can be seen as victimizers and troublemakers, rather than as peace-keepers. (*Philadelphia Police Commissioner's Report*, 1987, pp. 4–5)

Lee P. Brown followed this approach when chief executive for police in Houston and New York City. In the latter municipality, with a force of 29,000 police,

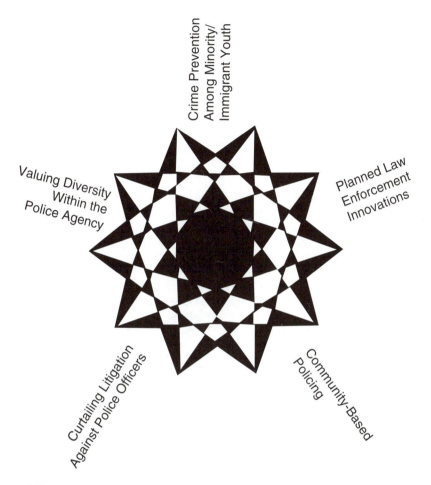

Crime Prevention Among Minority/ Immigrant Youth

Planned Law Enforcement Innovations

Valuing Diversity Within the Police Agency

Community-Based Policing

Curtailing Litigation Against Police Officers

Exhibit 15.1

Brown earned high marks for implementing a community policing program that quadrupled the number of officers on foot patrol while sponsoring a crime-fighting partnership with citizens which resulted in a 6.7 percent reduction in reported crimes in early 1992. When Brown resigned to become a criminal justice professor at Texas Southern University, New York's Mayor Dinkins praised him as among the world's best police administrators, who managed in 1991 to reduce crime in every category within the city "for the first time in some 36 years" (*Los Angeles Times,* Aug. 4, 1992, p. A-2). In the same year, similar recognition for his community-based police effectiveness was offered to police commissioner Willie L. Williams upon his resignation from the city of Philadelphia. As police chief of Los Angeles, he is introducing the same strategy involving community policing. Regarding LAPD, he observed: "We have to rebuild bridges between the police and the community and the government. The challenge is to take a very good department and just make it better" (*Los Angeles Times,* Feb. 29, 1992, p. A-3).

The law enforcement agency using this new strategy of community policing mes an advocate for the public. This changes the job of the police officer, espe- at the line level, in those cities and counties using community-based policing.

There are many terms for the various police programs that agencies across the nation are calling community-based policing (refer to Chapter 14). A few of the more common terms being used are problem-oriented policing (POP), community policing (CP), neighborhood-oriented policing (NOP), community-oriented polic- ing (COP), and innovative neighborhood-oriented policing (INOP). The Police Executive Research Forum (PERF) (1992) concluded that community policing had become the fastest-growing movement in policing in decades, both in theory and in practice.

The PERF research looked for commonalities among the various commu- nity policing programs and research on the subject. They discovered five different perspectives on community policing within agencies across the nation:

1. **Deployment perspective:** officers are placed in closer proximity to members of the community and thereby improve their knowledge of the area in which they work.
2. **Community revitalization perspective:** focuses on preventing deterioration of neighborhoods by police paying closer attention to fear-inducing characteristics of neighborhoods.
3. **Problem perspective:** maintains that the most critical element of CP is the prob- lem-solving efforts in which the police and community (residents, other govern- ment agencies, and private businesses) participate.
4. **Customer perspective:** focuses on developing proactive mechanisms for determin- ing the needs of the public relative to the police function. The approach uses rou- tine surveys of citizen and advisory groups to accomplish this.
5. **Legitimacy perspective:** an attempt by police, via CP, to be equitable and to be seen as equitable, especially in its relationships with the minority community. This per- spective involves opening a dialogue between the police and minority communities to identify their concerns and for the police to respond to them.

Departments typically mix varieties of community policing perspectives; however, the common thread within all approaches is that the police assist the community in policing and protecting itself. To do so, the police must engage the community in the task of policing. The police are actually dependent on a rela- tionship and partnership (some call it "building bridges") with the community to perform those tasks. Problems are identified by the community with the encour- agement and participation (direction) of the police. To accomplish this, methods must be developed to enter into a problem identification and solving dialogue. Mastrofski and Greene (1991) emphasized that "if police are to increase a neigh- borhood's involvement in determining how it is policed, then three issues must be addressed: (1) to what extent should the community be organized, (2) who should be represented, and (3) what should the community do?"

Critical to the success of any community-based policing program is resolu- tion of the following two issues: (1) How willing are citizens to accept some respon- sibility for community law enforcement? (2) How willing are police officers to relinquish the social isolation of police cars in order to be involved with neighbor- hood citizens in police–community programs? These issues must be a part of a strategic, long-term plan by the chief executive desiring to implement CP in his or her community. Executive director of the Police Executive Research Forum (now chief of St. Petersburg, Florida), Darrel W. Stephens, maintained that community- or problem-oriented policing is the future of law enforcement and is the next stage in the evolution of this profession.

How is the transition with the community to be made? Typically, it takes an agency five to seven years to go from traditional policing to community policing. As a start, some agencies have created citizen police academy programs that provide knowledge of CP and the requisite skills and resources to do problem solving. Other communities hold neighborhood forums to accomplish the same objective. As with change for most people, it takes time to change police officer attitudes. Some have the attitude that there are community-oriented police officers—and then there are the "real cops." Departments must recruit people who exhibit compassion, have good communications skills, and are problem solvers. Job de- scriptions and evaluations should be rewritten to emphasize and reward problem- solving abilities. It also requires obtaining personnel, whether sworn or not, who have the foreign language skills to reach out to new ethnic communities.

Community policing is not incident or technology driven. Officers work in the neighborhoods on a decentralized basis, stressing regular contacts with citizens. They report back to their supervisor, who in turn transmits the information to the chief executive and his or her staff so that additional resources can be deployed as necessary. In addition to tactical plans, the department has a plan that calls for con- sulting with key community leaders before merely reacting in the event of a racial crisis, for example. Too often a police reaction has been the triggering event for riots. Chief Willie Williams of the Los Angeles Police Department stresses: "'You just can't wait and look for the triggering mechanisms in the community. . . . Per- sonnel must be trained to understand that they live and work in a diverse commu- nity, and to understand the different values and nuances of those people'" (*Time*, Mar. 7, 1988, p. 24).

A medium-sized department in southern California exemplifies problems associated with not using COP. Management of the department (and the city) was unaware that the ethnic community had been changing dramatically. Two years later patrol officers drew this fact to their attention. Most of the changes had oc- curred suddenly following the fall of Saigon. After the withdrawal of American forces from Vietnam, the United States changed its immigration policy to relocate peoples in jeopardy from Southeast Asia. Police officers were performing their "crime fighter" role, but because there was no partnership with the community, there was no reason or incentive to monitor and report the changes they were noticing. This particular community, therefore, was not prepared for the increase in racial disputes and violence on the streets and in the schools, nor was it pre- pared for increasing needs in government, infrastructures, and social services. Captain Stan Knee of the Garden Grove Police Department, in a 1987 interview, observed that calls involving Vietnamese citizens took five times longer for an of- ficer to handle than in the Anglo community, due to language and cultural differ- ences. This lead to officer frustration and management concerns. Community policing would have had a plan in place for the changing events because the department (including all local government institutions) and the neighborhoods would have been working together closely.

However, community policing cannot function in a vacuum. It needs the support of other government agencies. Eldrin Bell, the African American chief of police of Atlanta, Georgia, declared at a conference hosted by the National Organization of Black Law Enforcement Executives, PERF, and the Reno Police Department in 1992: "We cannot get to community-oriented policing until we have community-oriented government" (Bell, 1992). Chief Bell suggested that government be decompartmentalized and cleaned up; made more community directed through use of community councils. He contends that by doing so, community members and government employees work together to solve problems. The police are a driving force in the process. (Berg, 1993)

Community-oriented policing is not reactive, it is proactive and based on the neighborhood and the police identifying problems and directing resources to solve them. For example, as the police move more into the world of high technology, we will see officers with laptop computers collecting and analyzing what is occurring in their neighborhood, including hate/bias crimes. Community-based policing will involve additional expenses in cities or counties with already tight budgets. Public administrators and legislators must support efforts such as community policing. In some cases it may be "Pay me now (budget for such strategies) or pay me later (the aftermath of riots, disturbances, distrust, etc.)."

Crime Prevention among Minority and Immigrant Youth

If it is to succeed, community-oriented policing must focus on positive relations, contact, and communications between young people and police officers. The challenge today is how to train officers to be successful models to benefit minority, immigrant, or "ghetto" young people, especially to make the case for law and order and eventually to attract some into law enforcement careers.

Some agencies contract with school districts to provide officers on a daily basis for security purposes, as well as to offer role models. Many officers get involved in educating youth on a voluntary basis in a variety of ways. Sworn officers are rightly proud of sponsoring projects such as the Police Athletic League (PAL) to involve neighborhood kids in constructive teamwork, or their Police Explorer Scout programs. Future studies by police executives propose a variety of youth strategies for this purpose, which range from a police high school curriculum to the usefulness of police cadet programs (Devore, 1990; Harding, 1989). In May 1992, the president of the United States publicly praised and advocated more efforts like the Los Angeles County Sheriff's Youth League, where off-duty police develop positive relations with the community's young people.

Perhaps the biggest challenges would appear to be in preventing or counteracting rising youth violence, especially among males between the ages of 12 and 24. The problem is critical in the nation's inner cities, where unemployed, disadvantaged youths seek identity and support through destructive gang participation (Huff, 1990; Kramer, 1987; Jackson, 1991; Thomas, 1990; Tognetti, 1991). As a case in point, the Los Angeles County district attorney, Ira Reiner, issued a May 1992 report on gang violence in that community, based on the mammoth county computer data base called GREAT (Gang Reporting Evaluation and Tracking). He estimated 150,000 members in 1000 gangs, made up largely of African Americans, Latinos, and some Asians. Although the figures may be less because of duplication in law enforcement agency data, misperception, or mislabeling of some young minority males, such groups are not the only cause of rising drug crimes and gun misuse. Yet gangs do account for a dramatic upswing in the murder rates (800 homicides a year), often through senseless drive-by killings. As such gangs declare truces and work together, or link up with gangs in other cities for criminal activity, they can become a real threat to community stability if members energies are not redirected. To manage the deteriorating situation, the district attorney's document recommended the usual remedies: improved education, job training, and gang prevention programs. Although the statistics may be controversial, the 235-page report of the district attorney does have proposals that have significance for urban communities elsewhere:

1. Develop a county-wide master plan for helping youth at risk of joining gangs, especially among minorities and immigrants.
2. Overhaul the juvenile justice system, which often serves as a recruitment/training program for the gangs.
3. Focus on the 10 to 15 percent hardcore criminal members in the gangs.
4. Develop cooperative private-industry programs to provide training and jobs for inner city youth (such as is being done by the organization previously cited, Rebuild L.A.).

Nationally, other solutions may be forthcoming in recent law enforcement studies, such as those on gang violence, Asian gangs, and antigang strategies (Hebel, 1990). Among the possibilities for law enforcement to explore are:

1. *Cooperation with local clergy, who maintain effective relations with gang members.* For example, a coalition of Protestant and Catholic churches have formed a Southern California Organizing Committee, promoting a "Hope in Youth" campaign: a five-year, public/private investment in a $20 million fund, with teams formed in their congregations—one would be an outreach worker with a caseload of 25 youths at risk, leading them from gang involvement to alternative education/training and drug rehabilitation; a second team member would work with individual parents of gang members, while a third develops parent unions to empower them with regard to their children's education; each church would sponsor and mentor gang members in transition.

2. *Assistance to local ethnic business organizations that wish to work with gangs in the community ventures and job development,* as is happening now between the Korean-American Grocers Association, with its 3600 members, and two Los Angeles African American gangs, the Bloods and the Crips. Although gangs will increasingly occupy law enforcement time, agencies must be more creative in devising nonarrest approaches to a community's disadvantaged youth, particularly in conjunction with other community organizations.

3. *Creation of ethnic police benevolent associations to provide role models and programs* for disadvantaged youth of similar cultural heritage who are in gangs or are potential recruits. Hence the black police groups get involved with young male African Americans, the Hispanic police officers' groups focus on young Latino males, while the police associations for Asian members attempt to serve the needs of young males from Chinese, Vietnamese, and Japanese backgrounds. The same strategy can be extended to ethnic police organizations for Italian Americans, Irish Americans, Polish Americans, and so on.

Forward-looking officers encourage and participate in a community task force that "gangs up" on the problem and brainstorms how to defuse the danger by providing positive places and group experiences for local young through social activities, sports, voluntary service, and other constructive mechanisms. The goal should be to convert present-day gangs into team programs engaging in community rebuilding, while offering a gang alternative to youth who have not yet joined gangs but seek some group identity. Community conservation or ecology corps are one example of how young adults can be involved constructively. The plan for National Youth Service is another. Junior Achievement has already proven what business persons can do to involve youth constructively. Even bored middle-class or affluent youth would benefit by such outlets for their energies, in contrast to hanging around or "mall hopping." Such endeavors take a combination of public/private investment and personnel in which peace officers could provide needed leadership.

Curtailing Litigation against Police Officers

Much innovation is necessary so that a police response will satisfy citizens, especially in multicultural communities, rather than provoke them to law suits against officers and their departments. Nonviolent peacekeeping is particularly critical in ethnic, immigrant, and minority communities, where misperception and miscommunication may occur because of language barriers, along with differences in body language and nonverbal interactions. The principal problem in this regard relates to the use of force by law enforcement at the time of arrest, whether it be perceived as excessive or deadly. Agencies that analyze citizen complaints against officers usually find that this is the arena which receives the most negative community feedback, especially from minorities. Exhibit 15.2 examines such allegations for the past decade and what it costs a city in terms of the Los Angeles Police Department. In 1991 that municipality had to pay $14,658,075 as a result of settlements, judgments, and awards related to excessive force litigation against its police. In 1994, a jury awarded Rodney King $3.8 million to compensate for the police actions.

If but a fraction of that sum were devoted to more creative training of officers in *improved* community relations, arrest tactics, and nonlethal, more peaceful apprehension, the taxpayers would be more appreciative of police services (McErlain, 1991; Rivetti, 1988).

Planned Law Enforcement Innovations

Attempts are being made by the new generation of law enforcement leaders to develop innovative strategies, structures, and services that meet the changing needs

Types of Complaints Against the Los Angeles Police Department

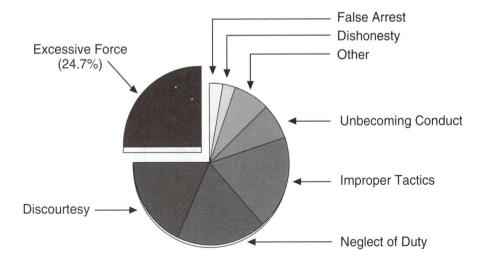

Frequency of Complaints Against the Los Angeles Police Department

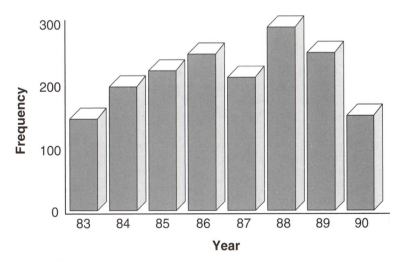

Exhibit 15.2   Excessive Force and its Costs Source: Los Angeles Times, May 28, 1992.

of communities (Allevato, 1989; Galvin, 1987; Jordan, 1992; Peavy, 1991; Riley, 1991; Schwab, 1992), as well as to improve interagency collaboration in serving those needs (Heller, 1992), or to evaluate effectiveness of delivery of these services (Jensen, 1992). Many innovative strategies have been described in this book. As one final example of an approach to serve better in a more pluralistic society, individual agencies might consider establishing an "innovation task force" made up of

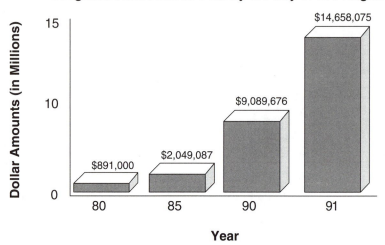

Judgments and Awards Paid by the City of Los Angeles

Exhibit 15.2 *(continued)*

the most creative officers from all units of a department. The chief asks this group to discover ways for police to encourage a "climate of understanding within the community, and combat a climate of fear" (words of President Bush after the 1992 U.S. riots). To that end, the "innovation team," along with community "focus groups" described next, might study together all new ideas of promise and develop action plans to implement them. Here are some examples of such innovations:

- Ongoing contact (both in the format of structured and unstructured meetings) with members of all minority community organizations (including church leaders, business and civic leaders, school officials, etc.)—*ongoing* must be emphasized because, typically, law enforcement only meets with community leaders after a crisis has taken place.
- Bicycle or scooter bike patrols in problem areas with officers who interact with community members, especially where there are large concentrations of minority and immigrant youth.
- Crises management strategies not only for emergencies and disasters but also for social unrest—identifying and working with neighborhoods at risk (see Chapter 13).
- Neighborhood or shopping mall store-front police substations.
- Police concentration on repeat offenders and repeat locations for criminal activities.
- Law enforcement strategies with the homeless (Brummer, 1988; Knuthson, 1989; Plummer, 1988).
- Teams consisting of officers from diverse backgrounds regularly meeting with inner city youth, engaging in such activities as sports, mentoring, and finding new ways to become role models.
- Programs with schools to reduce school violence.
- Development of neighborhood child protection plans to reduce incidents of child abuse; such plans should include constructive opportunities for youth to network with each other and with positive adult roles in their community; such plans should include business, civic, and religious organizations; the adoption of a particular

high-risk neighborhood that the police, community leaders, and family members make a commitment to protecting their youth (*Contra Costa Times*, Oct. 28, 1993, p. B-1).

Corporations have long invested in market research to ascertain consumer needs and their reactions to the goods and services being offered. Similarly, innovative municipalities and their law enforcement agencies are now utilizing the same survey methods and focus-group discussions to gauge taxpayer opinion about delivery of public services. Some advocate that police departments adopt a "marketing" approach to promoting crime prevention programs within communities.

The innovations described above are representative of what is happening throughout the field of law enforcement. The important point is that the agency or departmental culture must support creativity at both the institutional and individual level. Officers on their off-duty time can be encouraged to contribute their unique talents to community peace and diversity. Two such positive stories appeared on a single day in the *Los Angeles Times* (Aug. 8, 1992) about policemen doing just that through their avocations:

- LAPD's Dan Caldron works out of the 77th Street Division in South Central Los Angeles, and was at the center of the action when the violence broke out. To express his and other officer's frustration, Caldron completed a series of paintings about his riot experience which were exhibited in a Little Tokyo coffeehouse. The 12 black and white, expressionistic caricatures and various scenes of policing unrest also have painted narratives with dialogue detailing the sequence of events and laden with cop lingo.
- San Diego PD's Matt Weathersby has started a small business involving family members producing educational cards on the civil rights movement and African-American history, featuring both black and white personalities. Each 35 card set is available in flash card size for school use or "baseball card" size for hobbyists. Black and white photographs of a celebrity or historical figure appears on the front, and the biographical/historical information on the back. Matt and his wife are planning future series on Afro-American soldiers, scientists, artists, and women (MASS5 Educational Products, P.O. Box 620-711, San Diego, CA 92162).

The issue here is that police supervisors in their departments should be actively encouraging such innovators who contribute to cultural synergy and peace. Agencies, for example, might have an award for the "Innovative Officer of the Month" and display the person's picture in the squad room with a description of his or her innovative practice on or off duty.

Among the contemporary problems calling for law enforcement innovations is the escalation in juvenile intolerance, violence, and gun-related shootings. Since families, schools, and religious institutions are seemingly unable to provide adequate character education necessary to curb and contain these socially unhealthy trends, peace officers will seek, on or off the job, creative solutions. For some this will involve ensuring positive, leisure-time opportunities for inner city youth; for others, it may be encouraging the National Rifle Association to broaden its educational programs for youth on responsible use of guns; for still others, that strategy might be to promote greater utilization of the "teaching tolerance" learning materials offered by the Southern Poverty Law Center (400 Washington Ave., Montgomery, AL 36104).

ORGANIZATIONAL TRENDS

In concluding this book it is useful to present two organizational trends that have become increasingly visible in certain private-sector organizations. We return to the law enforcement agency itself, because change must come from within before all personnel can demonstrate effectiveness and sensitivity in the community.

**Trend One: Organizational Culture
Must Be Changed to Internalize the Diversity Concept**

In the past the law enforcement culture typically was dominated by white males, who were often military veterans principally from Irish and Italian ethnic backgrounds. With the influx of a multicultural workforce into the law enforcement field, system change will be necessary if the organizational culture is to reflect the needs and concerns of a new generation and a culturally diverse society.

One of the nation's leading diversity consultants, Elsie Cross, confirmed the reality of organizations' needing to change. Throughout 20 years of working with many large corporate clients, this consultant recognized that most corporate cultures have actually been white male cultures in which this majority controlled the power in the organization by dominating meetings, making all key decisions, establishing exclusive information loops, and choosing their own successors. To compensate for the past, Elsie Cross Associates recommends these strategies for managing diversity and valuing differences for organizational effectiveness (White, 1992):

- Introduce culture change to overhaul policies and procedures by means of focus groups and workshops that define basic assumptions, and unwritten codes and rituals, and revise the mission statement to a "culture vision and values" proclamation.
- Identify the barriers that block individual/group diversity goals and identify the "champions" capable of building broad, internal coalitions around cultural awareness and group action against discrimination and for change.
- Require that the top command make at least a five-year commitment of resources to redefining the agency culture toward more effective management of diversity.
- Hold managers accountable for implementing the diversity changes through regular evaluation of their efforts.
- Confront the pain of racism and sexism at the personal and group level in the organization.

This model has proven successful, and Cross, an African American woman (see Appendix K for her address), credits the National Training Laboratories for Applied Behavioral Sciences for helping her to develop it. The strategy is worthy of consideration by would-be law enforcement leaders in a multiracial/cultural society.

**Trend Two: Organizations Must Move beyond Awareness to Meet
Today's Multicultural Challenges**

When a law enforcement agency has provided the basic training in cultural awareness and inaugurated effective equal employment/affirmative action policies, it is time to adopt another strategic level. Diversity consultant George F. Simons* believes that we must move beyond mere avoidance of ethnic, racial, and gender discrimination or sexual harassment. Police supervisors and managers should not have to "walk on eggs" while at work trying not to offend women and minorities. For managing or training in a multicultural environment, this expert advises that:

- Diversity training be conducted which teaches people skills to communicate and collaborate effectively with each other as colleagues, especially through mixed gender and mixed ethnic/racial groups.
- Organizational policy be developed which supports productive partnerships and creative sharing with diverse membership of representatives from majority/minority groups.
- Executives and other leaders receive special coaching programs that include assessment, mind management, and communications which enable them to model behavior and values that inspire their associates to work ingeniously with differences.

To further promote police officer professionalism and peacekeeping strategies in a diverse society, officers must be able to look up to leaders who are not ethnocentric and biased in their manner of leading an organization and responding to the communities they serve. For a police officer to reflect tolerance and understanding of all peoples as well as apply the principle of fair treatment to every police action and communication, he or she must have role models all the way up the chain of command, especially at the police chief level. The police chief should explicitly demonstrate *pluralistic* leadership. Early in Chapter 14 we discussed the peace officer who would be cosmopolitan or pluralistic in approach. Attaining this outlook cannot happen consistently without direction set from the top.

MGH Consulting has developed a list of characteristics and attributes of a pluralistic leader (Exhibit 15.3).

SUMMARY

In this final unit and chapter, and throughout the book, the authors have shared information and insights with their readers about improving multicultural law enforcement. Our intention was to help the reader become more proactive with regard to the changing population and anticipate future developments in both the law enforcement agency and society. Our basic premise is that the personal and professional development of modern peacekeepers requires cultural awareness training as well as creative diversity policies and practices.

The first part of this book devoted three chapters to the impact of increasing cultural diversity on the community, peacekeeping, and the law enforcement agency. In the second part, the next three chapters centered on cross-cultural training and communication for peace officers. The third part reviewed cultural specifics relevant to officers when interacting with people from Native American, African American, Asian, Hispanic/Latino, or Middle Eastern backgrounds. The fourth part

---

*Based on his newsletter *Diversi-TIPs* and video-book package *Men and Women, Partners at Work* (see Appendix K for address).

Exhibit 15.3   Pluralistic Leaders

Pluralistic leaders:

1. Look for ways to serve as catalysts for changing the work environment and community to welcome and value diverse people

2. Are committed to eliminating all the various "isms" (racism, sexism, etc.) that exist in their immediate work environment or neighborhood and speak to the greater concerns for equality, fairness, and other democratic ideals

3. Help diverse people to be seen fairly and to be valued in the work environment and broader community

4. Accept feedback about how to improve their relationships with those who are different by remaining open to change and growth

5. Acknowledge their own prejudices or stereotypes and see the limitations that these will bring to their work

6. Take time to assess their individual progress toward achieving the qualities and characteristics of a pluralistic leader

7. Mentor others who need to gain sensitivity toward diversity

8. Value differences among people and cultures as one of the great treasures of the human family and global community

Source: MGH Consulting, © 1993, reprinted with permission of MGH Consulting, 2454 Cameron Drive, Union City, CA 94587.

examined the matter of culturally and racially motivated hate crimes and response strategies. Finally, in this fifth part, the last two chapters offered an overview of how peace officers can improve their effectiveness in a diverse workforce and community by practicing greater cultural sensitivity. Numerous concepts and methods were provided to promote innovative, futuristic professional development of sworn officers and their associates. With the human family everywhere in profound transition, and further social disturbances looming as a major threat, our analysis focused on *planned* changes in the image, operations, services, and skills of law enforcement practitioners within multicultural workforces and societies.

Readers are challenged to examine the concepts and techniques presented in these pages, as well as to implement those that are feasible within local agencies and communities. If the strategies proposed here are adopted, the law enforcement field will indeed provide diversity leadership within the public sector while presenting a positive model in that regard to the private sector. For the professionally minded who will go beyond the content of this book, several appendices and an instructor's manual complement the main text.

DISCUSSION QUESTIONS AND ISSUES*

1. *Police Culture.* Every group, whether ethnic, racial, vocational, or professional, has characteristics defining its "culture," and the police culture is no exception. People who do not belong to a particular "in-group" often develop myths and stereotypes

*See Instructor's Manual accompanying this text for additional activities, role-plays, questionnaires and projects related to the content of this chapter.

about another group in an attempt to categorize behavior they may not understand. Make a list of myths and stereotypes about police officers that exist among community members. After you compiled and shared your list with others, discuss the following.

(a) How did these myths or stereotypes arise?

(b) Is there any truth to the myths or stereotypes?

(c) Do they in any way affect communication with citizens or prevent you from doing your job well?

(d) Do any of the stereotypes or myths create special difficulties or challenges with people from diverse backgrounds? If so, how?

2. ***Community-Based Policing.*** Below are six topics for further discussion with your colleagues either on the job, in the police academy, or in a criminal justice class.

(a) Discuss community-based policing and its adoption and use by your police department. Focus on why and how it should be implemented if the strategy is not used now. Create a strategy for introducing CP into your department.

(b) Discuss how a manager or supervisor can encourage officers to be more humanistic in their interactions with the public.

(c) Discuss your perception of the police role now and in the future. Include how the "peacekeeping" role of the police can become more acceptable to those with the "crime fighter" mind-set. What strategies would you use to convince the traditionalist officer to change if you were the (1) chief/sheriff; (2) supervisor or manager; (3) a peer?

(d) Discuss why the success of the police mission depends largely on the support and involvement of the public/community.

(e) Discuss the problems of policing in a pluralistic/diverse society.

(f) Discuss ways in which the police can "humanize" their operations, internally as well as externally. Include a discussion of how supervisors, managers, and the chief executive can encourage and/or mandate the humanization of police services.

REFERENCES

ALLEVATO, S. (1989). *The Development of a Law Enforcement Plan for California Cities Committed to Quality Service through Community-Oriented Policing,* POST Commission, Sacramento, Calif. (Order 8-0133).

BELL, ELDRIN (1992). Keynote speech, NOBLE, PERF, and Reno Police Department sponsored conference, Reno, Nev. Sept. 28.

BERG, G. (1993). *What Will be the Status of Community-Based Policing in Large California Police Departments by the Year 2003?* Sacramento, CA: POST Commission (Order 16-0332).

BLOCK, P. (1991). *The Empowered Manager: Positive Political Skills at Work,* Jossey-Bass, San Francisco.

BOLMAN, L. G., AND T. E. DEAL (1991). *Reframing Organizations: Artistry, Choice, and Leadership,* Jossey-Bass, San Francisco.

BOWMAN, J. S. ed. (1991). *Ethical Frontiers in Public Management,* Jossey-Bass, San Francisco.

BROOKS, R. E. (1987). *What Is the Future of Incentive Programs for Mid-career Law Enforcement Officers,* POST Center for Leadership Development, Sacramento, Calif. (Order 4-0053).

BRUMMER, S. E. (1988). *How Will the Homeless Population Affect Services of a Medium Size Police Agency by the Year 2000?* POST Commission, Sacramento, Calif. (Order 6-0093).

DELATTRE, E. J. (1991a). *Against Brutality and Corruption: Integrity, Wisdom, and Professionalism,* Florida Department of Law Enforcement/Criminal Justice Executive Institute, Tallahassee, Fla.

DELATTRE, E. J. (1991b). *Character and Cops: Ethics in Policing,* American Enterprise Institute for Public Policy Research, Washington, D.C.

DEVORE, L. R. (1990). *The Purpose and Function of the Police Cadet Programs in Medium Sized Police Agencies by the Year 2000,* POST Commission, Sacramento, Calif. (Order 8-0138).

DISTELRATH, J. T. (1988). *What Will Be the Career Development Needs of Law Enforcement Managers by the 21st Century,* POST Center for Leadership Development, Sacramento, Calif. (Order 7-0115).

GALVIN, G. T. (1987). *Community Based Policing,* POST Commission, Sacramento, Calif. (Order 3-0037).

GELLERMANN, W., and others (1990). *Values and Ethics in Organization and Human Systems Development,* Jossey-Bass, San Francisco.

HARDING, J. W. (1989). *Organized Youth Programs in Middle Sized California Law Enforcement Agencies,* POST Commission, Sacramento, Calif. (Order 9-0165).

HARRIS, P. R. (1995). *The New Work Culture and HRD Transformational Management.* Amherst, CA: Human Resource Development Press, Inc.

HARRISSON, E. R. (1992). *What Municipal Police Services and Financial Support Considerations Will Exist by the Year 2002?* Sacramento, CA: Post Commission (Order # 15-0297).

HEBEL, M. S. (1990). *The Impact of Disadvantaged Youth on Large, Urban Law Enforcement Agencies by the Year 2000,* POST Commission, Sacramento, Calif. (Order 9-0166).

HELLER, S. (1992). *Addressing Community Problems through Interagency Cooperation,* POST Commission, Sacramento, Calif. (Order 13-0259).

HUFF, C. R. ed. (1990). *Gangs in America,* Sage Publications, Newbury Park, Calif.

JACKSON, K. D. (1991). *The Impact of Gang Violence on a Police Department Serving an Emerging, Urbanized City,* POST Commission, Sacramento, Calif. (Order 12-0234).

JORDAN, R. (1992). *Police Strategies that Address Community Needs in the 21st Century,* POST Commission, Sacramento, Calif. (Order 13-0257).

JENSEN, P. (1992). *Evaluating Police Effectiveness by the Year 2000,* POST Commission, Sacramento, Calif. (Order 13-0264).

KNUTHSON, C. V. (1989). *Family and Youth Homelessness: How Will It Impact California Law Enforcement by the Year 2000?* POST Commission, Sacramento, Calif. (Order 8-0141).

KRAMER, L. C. (1987). *How Will Changes in the Asian Population Impact Street Gang Related Crime in California,* POST Commission, Sacramento, Calif. (Order 3-0041).

LAWLER, E. E. (1992). *The Ultimate Advantage: Creating the High Involvement Organization,* Jossey-Bass, San Francisco.

LEWIS, C. W. (1991). *The Ethics Challenge in Public Service,* Jossey-Bass, San Francisco.

LINGLE, N. (1992). *People of Color and Culture:* The Future of California Law Enforcement, *POST Commission, Sacramento, Calif. (Order 13-0247).*

MASTROFSKI, STEPHEN D., AND JACK R. GREENE (1991). "Community Policing and the Rule of Law," in *The Changing Focus of Police Innovation: Problems of Law, Order, Community,* David Weisburd and Craig Uchida, eds., Springer-Verlag, New York.

MAYHILL, P. D. (1985). *Police–Community Relations and the Administration of Justice,* Prentice Hall, Englewood Cliffs, N.J.

MCERLAIN, E. J. (1991). *Deadly Force . . . An Age Old Problem . . . A Future Solution,* POST Commission, Sacramento, Calif. (Order 12-0237).

MCGREGOR, E. B. (1991). *Strategic Management of Human Knowledge, Skills, and Abilities,* Jossey-Bass, San Francisco.

MORAN, R. T., HARRIS, P. R., AND STRIPP, W. G. (1993). *Developing Global Organizations: Strategies for Human Resource Professionals,* Gulf Publishing Company, Houston, Texas.

MURRAY, M., AND M. A. OWEN (1991). *Beyond the Myths and Magic of Mentoring,* Jossey-Bass, San Francisco.

PARKER, G. M. (1990). *Team Players and Teamwork,* Jossey-Bass, San Francisco.

PEAVY, J. D. (1991). *Don't Call Us, We'll Call You: Strategies to Increase Police Service Usage by Ethnic Minorities,* POST Commission, Sacramento, Calif. (Order 12-0242).

PETERSEN, K. (1991). *Developing Managerial Resources in California Law Enforcement by the Year 1001,* POST Center for Leadership Development, Sacramento, Calif. (Order 12-0226).

PLUMMER, L. C. (1988). *The Development of a Law Enforcement Plan to Generate Support for and Solutions to the Problem of Homelessness,* POST Commission, Sacramento, Calif.

Police Executive Research Forum (1992). *Revisiting Community Policing: A New Typology,* PERF, Washington, D.C.

PORTER, A. C. (1991). *Forecasting and Management of Technology,* Wiley, New York.

RILEY, R. W. (1991). *How Will Law Enforcement Reduce Community Fear of Crime in Major Urban Areas by the Year 2000?* POST Commission, Sacramento, Calif. (Order 11-0214).

RIVETTI, D. J. (1988). *What Is the Future of Less Than Lethal Weapons in Law Enforcement?* POST Commission, Sacramento, Calif. (Order 5-0086).

SCHWARTZ, P. (1991). *The Art of the Long View: Planning for the Future in an Uncertain World,* Doubleday, New York.

SCHWAB, S. (1992). *Restructuring Small Police Agencies: A Transition Toward Customer Services,* POST Commission, Sacramento, Calif. (Order 13-0260).

TERBORCH, R. (1987). *Career Development: An Organizational Dilemma,* POST Center for Leadership Development, Sacramento, Calif. (Order 4-0070).

THOMAS, R. F. (1990). *A Response to Youth Gangs for a Mid-sized Police Department,* POST Commission, Sacramento, Calif. (Order 0-0175).

TOGNETTI, B. A. (1991). *Strategy for Addressing Illegal Youth Gang Activities by a Mid-size Police Department,* POST Commission, Sacramento, Calif. (Order 12-0230).

WHITE, J. P. (1992). "Elsie Cross vs. the suits: one black woman is teaching white corporate America to do the right thing," *Los Angeles Times Magazine,* Aug. 9, pp. 14–18, 38–42.

Appendix A

MULTICULTURAL COMMUNITY AND WORKFORCE:

Attitude Assessment Survey*

The first set of questions ask for your opinions about how certain segments of the community view the police. *Using the response sheet attached on pages 397–400,* put the *number* of the response that you think best describes each group's perception. Remember, give the response based on how *you* feel each group would answer the statements. Use the response sheet attached.

1. In your opinion, how would this group rate the job this police department does? (see response sheet)
2. This group generally cooperates with the police.
3. Overall, this group thinks that _____ police department acts to protect the rights of individuals.
4. This group feels that the current relationship between the police and the community is:
5. Overall, this group feels this department responds to citizen complaints about officers in an objective and fair manner.
6. This group thinks most contacts with police are negative.

The next set of questions ask for *your* opinions about procedures and practices within the police department.

7. Overall, police supervisors in this department respond to citizens' complaints about employees in an objective and fair manner.
8a. Most police officers in this department are sensitive to cultural and community differences.
8b. Most civilian employees in this department are sensitive to cultural and community differences.

Sources: Adapted with permission from the Alameda, California Police Department, March 1993.

9a. This department adequately prepares officers to work with minorities in the community.

9b. This department adequately prepares civilian employees to work with minorities in the community.

10. The police administration is more concerned about police–community relations than they should be.

11a. Special training should be given to officers who work with minority community members.

11b. Special training should be given to civilian employees who work with minority community members.

12. Special training should be given to assist officers in working with the following segments of the community:

13. How often are racial slurs and negative comments about minorities expressed by personnel in this department?

14a. Racial/ethnic minorities in this city are subject to unfair treatment by *some* officers in this department.

14b. Racial/ethnic minorities in this city are subject to unfair treatment by *some* civilian employees in this department.

15a. Prejudicial remarks and discriminatory behavior by officers are *not* tolerated by line supervisors in this department.

15b. Prejudicial remarks and discriminatory behavior by civilian employees are *not* tolerated by line supervisors in this department.

16. Transfer policies in this department have a negative effect on police–community affairs.

17. Citizen complaint procedures in this department operate in favor of the citizen, not the employee.

18. Internal discipline procedures for employee misconduct are generally appropriate.

19. The procedure for a citizen to file a complaint against a department employee *should* be as follows:

20. With regard to discipline for misconduct, all employees in this department are treated the same in similar situations, regardless of race or ethnicity.

21. What kind of discipline do you think is appropriate for the first incident of the following types of misconduct? (Assume intentional.)

This section examines your views about police–community relations training and community participation. PLEASE CIRCLE THE RESPONSE THAT BEST DESCRIBES YOUR OPINION.

22. Do you think training in police–community relations was adequate to prepare you to work with all segments of the community?

23. How often do you have opportunities to participate in positive contacts with community groups?

24. Do you think this department has an adequate community relations program?

25. What subject areas related to community relations would be helpful on an in-service training basis?

26. What do you think is the most important thing that citizens need to understand about the police?

27. How can the police department *best* educate the public about police policies and practices?

28. Listed are steps that police departments can take to improve police services as they relate to community relations.

Attitude Assessment Survey Response Sheet

Place the number that corresponds to your response in each column.

	Business community	Minority residents	Community leaders	Most residents	Juveniles
Question 1:					
(1) Very good					
(2) Good					
(3) Fair					
(4) Poor					
(5) Very Poor					
Question 2:					
(1) Most of the time					
(2) Sometimes					
(3) Rarely'					
(4) Never					
Question 3:					
(1) Strongly agree					
(2) Agree					
(3) Disagree					
(4) Strongly disagree					
Question 4:					
(1) Very good					
(2) Good					
(3) Fair					
(4) Poor					
(5) Very poor					
Question 5:					
(1) Strongly agree					
(2) Agree					
(3) Disagree					
(4) Strongly disagree					
Question 6:					
(1) Strongly agree					
(2) Agree					
(3) Disagree					
(4) Strongly disagree					

Place check in column corresponding to your response for each question.

	Strongly agree	Agree	Disagree	Strongly disagree	Don't know
Question 7:					
Question 8a:					
Question 8b:					
Question 9a:					
Question 9b:					
Question 10:					
Question 11a:					
Question 11b:					

Check one response for each group.

Question 12:	Strongly agree	Agree	Disagree	Strongly disagree
Homosexual community				
Disabled persons				
Elderly				
Vietnam veterans				

Circle your response.

Question 13:   (1)   Often   (2)   Sometimes   (3)   Rarely   (4)   Never

Place check in column corresponding to your response for each question.

	Strongly agree	Agree	Disagree	Strongly disagree	Don't know
Question 14a:					
Question 14b:					
Question 15a:					
Question 15b:					
Question 16:					
Question 17:					
Question 18:					

Circle one response.

Question 19:

(1) Citizen sends complaint in writing to department

(2) Citizen telephones complaint to department

(3) Citizen comes to department

(4) Any of the above are acceptable means

(5) None of the above are acceptable means

(PLEASE EXPLAIN): _____

_____

_____

Question 20:   (1) Strongly agree   (2) Agree   (3) Disagree   (4) Strongly disagree

Check one response for each.

Question 21:

Type of misconduct	Verbal warning	Training/ counseling	Oral reprimand	Formal reprimand	Suspension	Termination
Excessive force						
False arrest						
Discrimination						
Use of racial slurs						
Criminal conduct						
Poor service						
Discourtesy to citizen						
Improper procedure						

Please circle the response that best describes your opinion.

Question 22:   (1) Yes   (2) No   (3) Did not receive training
If No, please describe why the training was not satisfactory:
(PLEASE EXPLAIN):_____

_____

_____

Question 23:   (1) Frequently   (2) Sometimes   (3) Rarely   (4) Never

Question 24:   (1) Yes   (2) No   (3) Don't know
Please explain your response: _____

_____

_____

Question 25: _____

_____

Question 26:   What do you think is the most important thing that citizens need to understand about the police?

Circle one only.

_____

_____

_____

Question 27:

(1) Through patrol officer contacts with citizens
(2) Through public meetings
(3) Through the media
(4) Selected combinations of the responses above
(5) Other (explain):_____

_____

_____

(6) Don't know

Please indicate how important you think each of the following *should be* to this administration by placing the number that best describes your response next to the appropriate question.

Question 28:	1 Somewhat Important	2 Important	3 Not at all important
Hire more police			
Focus on more serious crime			
Improve response time			
Increase salaries			
Provide more training			
Raise qualifications for potential applicants			
Be more courteous to public			
Increase foot patrols			
Reduce discrimination			
Provide dedicated time for community involvement			

Appendix B

CULTURAL DIVERSITY SURVEY:

Needs Assessment*

ANONYMOUS QUESTIONNAIRE

There has been a lot of discussion in recent years about whether the job of police officer has been changing. Some of the discussion involves issues about contact with people of different cultural groups. We'd like to get your frank opinions on these matters. Your responses are anonymous. Do not put your name or an identifier of any kind on these pages. Please check or enter one answer for each question.

1. Comparing the job of officer today with that of officer a few years ago, I think that today the job is . . .
   - ( ) a lot more difficult
   - ( ) somewhat more difficult
   - ( ) about the same in difficulty
   - ( ) somewhat easier
   - ( ) a lot easier

2. When I stop a car with minority occupant(s), I must admit that I am more concerned about my safety than I would be if I stopped a car with the same number of white occupant(s).
   - ( ) strongly agree
   - ( ) agree
   - ( ) disagree
   - ( ) strongly disagree

*Adapted with permission; police department wishes to remain anonymous.

3. If an officer notices a group of young people gathering in a public place and the young people aren't known to the officer, they should be watched very closely for possible trouble.

( ) strongly agree

( ) agree

( ) disagree

( ) strongly disagree

4. If an officer notices a group of young minorities who (s)he doesn't know gathered in a public place, the officer should plan on watching them very closely for possible trouble.

( ) strongly agree

( ) agree

( ) disagree

( ) strongly disagree

5. How often do you think it is justifiable to use derogatory labels such as "scumbag" and "dirtbag" when dealing with possible suspects?

( ) frequently

( ) some of the time

( ) once in a while

( ) never

6. When I interact on duty with civilians who are of a different race or culture, my view is that . . .

( ) they should be responded to a little more firmly to make sure that they understand the powers of the police

( ) they should be responded to somewhat differently, taking into account their different backgrounds

( ) they should be responded to the same as anyone else

7. When I encounter a minority citizen who has committed a violation of the law, my view is that . . .

( ) they should be responded to a little more firmly to make sure they understand the powers of the police

( ) they should be responded to somewhat differently, taking into account their different backgrounds

( ) they should be responded to the same as anyone else

8. When interacting on duty with *civilians* who have a complaint or a question and who are of a different race or culture, I try to be very aware of the fact that my usual gestures may frighten or offend them.

( ) strongly agree

( ) agree

( ) disagree

( ) strongly disagree

9. When interacting on duty with *offenders* who are of a different race or culture, I try to be very aware of the fact that my usual behavior may frighten or offend them.
    (   ) strongly agree
    (   ) agree
    (   ) disagree
    (   ) strongly disagree

10. How often have you run into a difficulty in understanding what a *civilian* was talking about due to language barriers or accents?
    (   ) frequently
    (   ) once in a while
    (   ) hardly ever
    (   ) never

11. How often have you run into a difficulty in understanding what an *offender* was talking about due to language barriers or accents?
    (   ) frequently
    (   ) once in a while
    (   ) hardly ever
    (   ) never

12. How often have you run into some difficulty in making yourself clear while talking to a *civilian* due to language barriers or accents?
    (   ) frequently
    (   ) once in a while
    (   ) hardly ever
    (   ) never

13. How often have you run into some difficulty in making yourself clear while talking to an *offender* due to language barriers or accents?
    (   ) frequently
    (   ) once in a while
    (   ) hardly ever
    (   ) never

14. How important is it that the *xyz Police Department* provide training to make its members more aware of the differences in culture, religion, and race?
    (   ) extremely important
    (   ) very important
    (   ) fairly important
    (   ) not too important
    (   ) not important at all

15. Personally, I believe that the training I have received on group differences is . . .
    (   ) far too much
    (   ) somewhat too much
    (   ) about the right amount
    (   ) too little
    (   ) virtually nothing

16. The helpfulness of the training in the area of group differences has been . . .
    ( ) extremely helpful
    ( ) very helpful
    ( ) somewhat helpful
    ( ) not too helpful
    ( ) not helpful at all

17. My own view is that our department's quality of service could be improved by . . .
    ( ) placing greater emphasis on hiring on the basis of the highest score obtained on the entrance exam, making no attempt to diversify by race or gender
    ( ) placing greater emphasis on diversity by race or gender and somewhat less emphasis on the numerical rank obtained on the entrance examination
    ( ) giving equal weight to both the score obtained on the entrance examination and diversification by race or gender

18. What percent of civilian or internal complaints against members, whether handled in troop or at division level, are adjudicated equitably?
    ( ) over 80 percent of the time
    ( ) between 60 and 80 percent
    ( ) between 40 and 60 percent
    ( ) between 20 and 40 percent
    ( ) less than 20 percent

19. Some civilian or internal complaints are adjudicated more favorably toward minority members than toward nonminority members mainly because they are minorities.
    ( ) strongly agree
    ( ) agree
    ( ) disagree
    ( ) strongly disagree

20. I know that in theory the affirmative action office of our department is available to assist all members, but in actuality it only serves female and minority members.
    ( ) strongly agree
    ( ) agree
    ( ) disagree
    ( ) strongly disagree

21. I think minority members receive preferential treatment on this job.
    ( ) strongly agree
    ( ) agree
    ( ) disagree
    ( ) strongly disagree

22. The racial diversity of my co-workers has made it easier for me to see issues and incidents from another perspective.
    ( ) strongly agree
    ( ) agree
    ( ) disagree
    ( ) strongly disagree

23. To think that minorities receive preferential treatment on this job . . .
    ( ) bothers me because I don't think it is justified
    ( ) doesn't bother me because I think it is justified
    ( ) is fair only because it makes up for past discrimination
    ( ) I don't believe minorities get preferential treatment

24. In certain situations, having a minority partner is more advantageous than having a nonminority partner.
    ( ) strongly agree
    ( ) agree
    ( ) disagree
    ( ) strongly disagree

25. I have received negative feedback from members of the community regarding conduct of other officers:
    ( ) strongly agree
    ( ) agree
    ( ) disagree
    ( ) strongly disagree

26. I have received negative feedback from members of the community regarding the conduct of minority officers in particular.
    ( ) strongly agree
    ( ) agree
    ( ) disagree
    ( ) strongly disagree

27. I have received more negative feedback from members of the community regarding the conduct of minority officers as opposed to nonminority officers.
    ( ) strongly agree
    ( ) agree
    ( ) disagree
    ( ) strongly disagree

28. In terms of being supervised:
    ( ) I'd much rather be supervised by a male
    ( ) I'd somewhat rather be supervised by a male
    ( ) I'd much rather be supervised by a female
    ( ) I'd somewhat rather be supervised by a female
    ( ) It doesn't make a difference whether it is a male or a female who supervises me

29. In terms of being supervised by a male:
    ( ) I'd much rather be supervised by a nonminority
    ( ) I'd somewhat rather be supervised by a nonminority
    ( ) I'd much rather be supervised by a minority
    ( ) I'd somewhat rather be supervised by a minority
    ( ) It doesn't make a difference whether it's a minority or a nonminority who supervises me

30. In terms of being supervised by a female:
    ( ) I'd much rather be supervised by a nonminority
    ( ) I'd somewhat rather be supervised by a nonminority
    ( ) I'd much rather be supervised by a minority
    ( ) I'd somewhat rather be supervised by a minority
    ( ) It doesn't make a difference whether it's a minority or a nonminority who supervises me

Please check the one answer in the following questions that best applies to you:

31. What is your sex?
    male
    female

32. What is your race?
    White
    African American or black
    Hispanic
    Native American
    Asian American
    other

33. How many years have you been employed by the *xyz Police Department?*
    0 to 5 years
    6 to 10 years
    11 to 20 years
    more than 20 years

34. What is your current rank?
    Officer
    Sergeant
    Investigator/Senior Investigator

35. What is the highest academic degree you hold?
    High school
    Associate's
    Bachelor's
    Master's

Appendix C
RECRUITMENT ACTION PLAN

Goal: To recruit, hire, and retain well-qualified personnel and volunteers to provide the most effective police services to the community.

Specific Objectives

1. To maintain our current recruitment standards, which exceed California Commission on Peace Officer Standards and Training employment standards.
2. To emphasize recruitment of minorities, enabling our work force to reflect the ethnic/racial composition of the community.
3. To seek and employ women, capable of meeting or exceeding our basic police officer standards, for the position of police officer.

Standard

I. Sworn Officer Recruitment Team
   A. Team Administration and Logistics
      1. Team composition: volunteers with recommendation of supervisor
      2. Team selection criteria
         .1 Positive role model
            .01 Attitude
            .02 Appearance that reflects good physical condition and businesslike appearance
         .2 Performance: past and present
         .3 Investigative skills/abilities: with appropriate training, the officer is able to complete a concise background investigation
      3. The recruitment program requires a commitment from command staff to release officers from divisional/bureau assignments to complete these collateral functions

    4. Budget: initial budgetary commitments would be necessary to cover the production and printing expenses associated with the recruiting materials although the program is planned to operate without overtime costs by using team members on duty and/or prearranging schedules. Compensatory overtime may be necessary.

  B. Team Functions

    1. Outreach recruitment (mailers, presentations, etc.) not limited to:

      .1 Police academies

      .2 Colleges

      .3 Military bases

      .4 High schools and junior high schools

      .5 Police associations

      .6 Minority organizations

    2. Recontact qualified prior applicants who failed to appear for testing or failed, within reasonable limits, the written or oral

    3. Sit on in-house orals for sworn or nonsworn applicants

    4. Conduct background investigations

    5. Participate in swearing-in ceremonies

    6. Participate in big brother/sister mentor program

      .1 To provide continuing support to new hires

      .2 To provide information to new hires regarding such things as credit union, housing, schools, etc.

II. Nonsworn Recruitment Team

  A. Team Administration and Logistics

    1. Team composition: volunteers with recommendation of supervisor

    2. Team selection criteria

      .1 Positive role model

        .01 Attitude

        .02 Good physical condition and businesslike appearance

      .2 Meets or exceeds standards on performance evaluations

  B. Team Functions

    1. Sit on in-house orals for nonsworn, job-related positions

    2. Participate in big brother/sister mentor program

      .1 To provide continuing support to new hires

      .2 To provide information to new hires regarding such things as credit union, housing, schools, etc.

III. Training

  A. Sworn Officer Recruitment Team

    1. Recruitment processes

      .1 Who are we looking for

      .2 Qualifications and standards

      .3 Team functions and methods

    2. Background investigations

      .1 Examples

      .2 Procedures

    3. Oral boards

      .1 Rules, regulations, and procedures

      .2 Types of questions

  B. Nonsworn Recruitment Team

    1. Oral boards

      .1 Rules, regulations, and procedures

      .2 Types of questions

IV. Recruitment and Orientation Materials
  A. Graphics
     1. 15- to 20-minute orientation video and slides: City of _____ and Police Department
     2. 10- to 18-minute recruitment video and slides
     3. Multicolor trifold recruitment brochure
     4. Recruitment posters
  B. Press Releases
     1. Local media: newspaper, radio, and television
     2. Law enforcement journals/magazines
     3. Minority publications
 V. Incentives
    Recruitment incentives in form of official recognition, comp-time off, money, privileged parking, etc.

Evaluation: The evaluation will take place in _____ to determine the effectiveness of the program. It will measure how many were recruited by team members; how many recruited were hired; how effective the campaign was.

Timing: The recruitment team is expected to be trained and operational by _____ _____. The graphics preparation is expected to be in place by _____.

Value: The expected benefit of this program is that the _____ department will reach more of the persons in the job market to create a broader base of high-quality people to test and hire and they will be from all racial/ethnic groups

Costs: The costs of this program, not counting personnel, are primarily in the area of graphics production: brochures, slides, videotapes, and advertising. The estimated total cost during fiscal year _____ is $_____?.

Accountability: The accountability of each team member for the assigned responsibilities will be established.

Appendix D

TECHNIQUES AND METHODS OF RECRUITMENT:

Expanded Course Outline (24 Hours)

COURSE OUTLINE (ABBREVIATED)

> ***Block 1:***   Introduction (1.0 hour)
>   Registration and Course Overview

> ***Block 2:***   Role of the Recruiter (2.0 hours)

  I. Being aware of department needs
    A. Time frame for hiring
    B. Vacancies
    C. Composition goals: ethnic, gender
    D. Knowing resources
  II. Marketing the job and the department
    A. The recruiter's role in projecting an image
    B. Knowledge of the department: mission statement; salary and benefits; job expectations; promotional opportunities
    C. Knowledge of community/service area: demographics; personal issues (schools, housing costs)
    D. Knowledge of selection process: POST requirements and agency requirements
    E. Assisting candidates through selection process: maintain personal contact; personal counseling; assisting in problem solving; tracking systems

> ***Block 3:***   Ethics (1.0 hour)

  I. Personal, Professional, and Organizational Values
    A. Legal and ethical recruiting practices
    B. Assessing organizational values; communicating values

Block 4:   Recruitment Skills (8.0 hours)

I. Time Management
   A. Organization
   B. Scheduling
   C. Prioritizing
   D. Cost-effectiveness
II. Developing Recruitment Presentations
   A. Match the presentation to the audience: department needs; community needs; play to audience; community, individual benefits
   B. Design: outline; introduction; presentation; application
   C. Presentation aids: recruitment materials; visual aids; personal attributes

This part of the course involves lectures, discussions, and small group exercises where actual presentations are made, videotaped, and critiqued.

Block 5:   Cultural Awareness (2.0 hours)

I. Developing an Awareness of Cultural Diversity
   A. Major ethnic communities and tailoring approaches: strategies for minority recruitment (barriers; successes)

Block 6:   Recruitment Methods (2.0 hours)

I. Great Ideas: Small Group Discussion
   A. Groups meet to formulate the 10 best ways to reach candidates: job fairs, community events, ride-alongs, youth programs, media, etc.
II. POST Recruitment Survey
   A. Learning how people become attracted to law enforcement: personal contact; other means

Block 7:   Legal Issues (3.0 hours)

I. Employment and Discrimination
   A. Federal laws: Title VII Regulations; 29 U.S.C. 706(6); 29 U.S.C. 631 and 1681
   B. Consent decrees and hiring quotas
   C. State laws
   D. Local agency rules

Block 8:   Recruitment Resources (4.0 hours)

I. Agency Resources
   A. Internal awareness; incentive programs; administrative commitment
II. External Resources
   A. Broadcast media and public service announcements
   B. Print media
   C. Multiagency efforts: coordinated testing

Block 9:   Course Wrap-up and Evaluation (1.0 hour)

I. Evaluation of Student Projects
II. Course Evaluation Instruments

Appendix E

SAMPLE AGENCY COURSES

NEW YORK CITY POLICE DEPARTMENT

NYPD Academy

The New York City Police Department Academy is 23 weeks in duration. The course curriculum covers a multitude of subjects that prepare recruit officers for their law enforcement positions. The human relations components include:

- Communications I
- Communications II
- Transactional Analysis I
- Transactional Analysis II
- Personality Socialization
- Personality Attitudes
- Myths and Learned Behavior
- Bias and Prejudice
- Various Styles of Policing
- (1) Legalistic
- (2) Service style
- (3) Order maintenance
- Police Cynicism
- Introduction to Authority and Ethics
- Ethics Workshop

The cultural awareness training blocks are separate from those listed on page 412 although a class in any of those subjects includes material in diversity and ethnic/race relations. For example, a communications class would include discussion and training on how words and terms can damage communications across cultures (e.g., racial slurs, etc.). It would also include a discussion of how perceptions, bias, and prejudice influence communications and behavior.

Training in cultural awareness has been taking place at the NYPD for approximately seven years. In September 1992, the academy course was modified extensively. The original course (used since 1985) was determined to be too cultural specific in content by the NYPD. It consisted of approximately 1½ hours on the:

- Immigration of those major groups who came to New York
- Irish
- African Americans
- Italians
- Jews
- Hispanics
- Asians
- Gays and lesbians
- Poverty in New York

Trainers decided that the academy course lessons on diversity should be more generic/general in nature. Prior to each segment, students would receive an assignment to go into the community to learn about one of the groups listed. The student would be required to report back to the class on what they had learned and observed about customs, food, entertainment, music, and the like. Whether the recruit officer wore a uniform or not was at the discretion of the officer. If they were not in uniform, it was also at their discretion whether or not they identified themselves as NYPD recruit officers. Evaluations of this experimental-type training by the students were very good.

According to Sergeant Kocik of the NYPD Academy training staff, the new course is much more generic. It begins with the New York Native Americans, then the Dutch, who originally settled in that area. The revised course also covers the various other major groups who populate New York City. All lesson plans from other blocks of training incorporate the application of this knowledge. Class members are still given experiential assignments in the community and are required to report back as in the original program. There are four exams that test the recruits understanding of cultural awareness materials.

Unlike most large agency academies where courses have a variety of instructors, an instructor is assigned a class (a number of classes are in progress at one time) and he or she is responsible for all lesson plan presentations and testing. Each instructor attends a two-week Instructor Development Course covering teaching skills. Until recently, the academy assignment was not part of NYPD's career development program. Now there are career path points for the academy assignment; therefore, such a position in the Department has become more appealing.

Sergeant Kocik discussed the influence of "veteran cynicism" on the recruit. The recruit witnesses some of the veteran officers treating people in ways that contradict what the new officer has learned in the academy human relations/cultural awareness courses. In their desire to fit in with their peers, new recruits often imitate the behavior of the veteran "models." To make matters worse, some supervisors condone or purposefully overlook such behavior or actions until they receive a citizen's complaint. To overcome this "modeling" problem, Sergeant Kocik suggests that upon completion of an academy class the instructors be assigned to work with the new recruit on patrol for a few weeks. This would allow instructors to reinforce the values/behaviors desired in terms of public contacts in the "real world." The instructors would, in essence, model the behavior expected while still practicing officer safety. After a few weeks, the recruit would be assigned to a field training officer. Sergeant Kocik's idea would also provide the instructors an opportunity to sharpen and review their own skills when working patrol.

NYPD In-Service Programs

The NYPD Human Relations Training Unit (HRTU) has developed a three-day workshop entitled "Invitation to Understanding," which covers such subjects as racism, sexism, elitism, and cultural/ethnic diversity. The HRTU goes to the various precincts and presents workshops to no more than 16 persons at one time. The precinct commander and his or her staff determines who will attend the workshop. Trainers' guidelines recommend that participants consist of a cross section of ranks and assignments (sworn and nonsworn), and also a cross section of employees by ethnicity and race. The variety of races and ethnic groups stimulates a discussion of differing perceptions and ideas. The workshop can also be modified to deal with specific problems within a particular precinct. Workshops use videotapes, case studies, directed readings, role-playing, small-group discussions, and lectures to impart the material. Following is the outline of the course content.

DAY 1

Formal Introduction
Background and overview; ground rules
Patrol Film
A patrol-related film showing the interrelationship of perceptions, stress, and professionalism
Ice Breaker (optional)
A participative exercise to encourage and enhance communications
Introduction to Stress Reduction
Predictability as a means of reducing stress
Dealing with Stress
An overview of physiological reactions to events; making the distinction between events and our reaction to them

DAY 2

Recap
An interactive summary of communications and stress

NYPD: Historical Perspective
A 1934 and a 1963 film showing an overview of the NYPD

A Tale of "O"
An introductory film on dealing with diversity; individualized methods and techniques for dealing with diversity

Do the Right Thing
A filmed study of a typical day in a Brooklyn neighborhood; intervening in typical police situations

DAY 3

Do the Right Thing (continued)

Use of Strategic Feedback
Techniques and methods for giving and receiving feedback to accomplish patrol goals; a series of filmed scenarios and role plays to practice feedback techniques

Ethnicity
Discussion of a variety of ethnic traits, practices, and traditions and their effect on communications

Course Evaluations

Eyes on the Prize
A film outlining some historic perspectives on current problems

Closing Exercise

This course is still being presented to the many precincts in New York City and the instructors have evaluated it positively.

LOS ANGELES SHERIFF'S DEPARTMENT

The Los Angeles Sheriff's Department (LASD) developed cultural diversity training for recruits and in-service officers. LASD has a Cultural Advisory Committee (CAC) consisting of 45 persons representing the diversity of Los Angeles and members of LASD. CAC meets monthly to discuss methods to improve training and review any proposed cultural training material. LASD receives input and direction for cultural awareness training from the CAC. The classes use trained deputies from various ethnic and racial groups to teach the subjects. They also developed and implemented a 48-hour Cultural Diversity Instructor Class certified by the California Peace Officer Standards and Training Commission. LASD has recruit training workshops and a patrol school course, which are very similar in content and duration and have the same learning objectives.

Recruit Training: Cultural Diversity Workshop

LASD's cultural awareness training in the Academy is 32 hours in length. A 10-hour section entitled "The Prejudice and Discrimination Curriculum" is presented in two segments on back-to-back days. The workshops rely on the active participation of the students, both individually and in small groups. The class is presented by a team of instructors, with a primary instructor (a sworn officer) who is responsible as a team leader for orchestrating the other team members' involvement. Although there is an outline for each session, actual time on a subject varies depending on the participants and the amount of discussion generated. The learning objectives for the recruit workshops are as follows:

- The students will become familiar with the department's policy and philosophy regarding prejudice and discrimination.
- The students will become familiar with the distinction between prejudice and discrimination.
- The students will explore the cause and origin of prejudice to increase their understanding of how prejudices develop.
- The students will explore their own biases as a first step toward developing a more positive attitude which will contribute to their professional growth.
- The students will explore stereotypes associated with gender, sexual orientation, race, ethnicity, and religion.
- The students will learn strategies and skills for addressing personal biases to prevent them from interfering with their work, consistent with department policy and philosophy.

Course Outline: Session I (6 hours)

Introduction (15 minutes)

Policy statement (10 minutes)

Class discussion: Definition of prejudice and discrimination (25 minutes)

Perception exercise (25 minutes)

Stereotyping exercise (25 minutes)

Small group I: race/ethnicity/religion (15 minutes/questionnaire, 40 minutes/group discussion)

Class discussion: race/ethnicity/religion (45 minutes)

Small group II: gender/sexual orientation (15 minutes/questionnaire, 40 minutes/group discussion)

Class discussion: gender/sexual orientation (45 minutes)

Closing (10 minutes)

Course Outline: Session II (4 hours)

Introduction (10 minutes)

Videotape "A Class Divided"* (35 minutes)

Videotape discussion "A Class Divided" (30 minutes)

Traffic stop vignette† class discussion (50 minutes)

Intervention exercise/role-playing‡ (50 minutes)

Policy/philosophy review (20 minutes)

Closing (15 minutes)

---

*A "Class Divided" (also known as "Brown Eyes–Blue Eyes") is a video of a two-day experiment in a midwest agricultural community grade school. A teacher separated her class into "superior" and "inferior" groups based solely on eye color. Blue-eyed children were "superior," brown-eyed children were "inferior." The effects of prejudice and discrimination are observed in the attitudes and behavior of the children in the classroom experiment.

†The traffic stop vignette is a video the students watch and then answer questions on a worksheet. The vignette involves officers questioning two men parked in front of a house. The purpose of the exercise is to lead the class into a discussion of how stereotyping can lead to the differential treatment of groups of people.

The Academy also contains 22 hours of culture-specific training on Latino culture, African American, American Indian, Asian/Pacific Islander, East Indian, gay/lesbian issues, and related subjects. LASD'S cultural awareness classes in the academy introduce participants to the acronym S-I-R, providing the student with a means of remembering important principles when dealing with diverse cultures and individuals:

- S: Safety. Nothing about avoiding discrimination requires compromising officer safety. As a good officer you will be aware of your surroundings and of potential threats to the safety of yourself and others. However, you should also remember that the misunderstandings and escalations that can be created by insensitive or discriminatory acts and words are also threats to your safety and your career advancement.

- I: Integrity. A good officer must operate from and with integrity. Inventing probable cause, falsifying reports, stretching or bending the truth, administering "street justice," and overlooking the illegal acts of fellow officers will all corrode your own sense of integrity. The path to corruption often begins with small transgressions, which become easier and larger as time goes on.

- R: Respect. A law enforcement officer must treat all people with dignity and be guided by a genuine reverence for human life. When you show contempt or act in a discriminatory manner, you are showing disrespect for all people. That disrespect can eventually corrode your own self-respect and your capacity to respect other people, including your family and loved ones.

LASD also implemented a course entitled "Cultural Diversity Workshop—Field Operations." The learning objectives are the same as for the LASD recruit and patrol courses. The course outline for the 16-hour class includes:

Field Operations Workshop: Part I

Introduction (20 minutes)
Policy/philosophy review (30 minutes)
Class discussion: definition of prejudice and discrimination (20 minutes)
Perception exercise (30 minutes)
Stereotyping exercise (50 minutes)
Vignette discussions: "Within the Workplace"* (60 minutes)
Intervention exercise/role-playing† (70 minutes)
Closing and class critiques (60 minutes)

The Field Operations Workshop introduction addresses demographic information, the course objectives, and class ground rules. A department executive

‡The students observe the facilitator's role-playing scenarios that involve officers dealing with or discussing persons from different ethnic/racial, etc., backgrounds in a negative or derogatory fashion. Students can then volunteer to recreate the scenario with how they would have responded or intervened with the officer(s) involved. Discussion explores the consequences of failing to intervene.

*This exercise explores racial and ethnic intolerance and insensitivity in the workplace. Five short video vignettes are shown, and after each, discussion is generated. Facilitators guide the discussion, which is intended to create self-awareness and develop skills.

†See explanation under recruit workshop. Time is extended.

speaks to the class and answers questions about agency policy and philosophy related to the training topics. Part II of the Field Operations Workshop is cultural-specific training that includes an additional eight hours of training, giving a broad overview of the demographics of Los Angeles County, as well as specific information on Latino, African American, and Asian/Pacific Islander cultures.

CONCORD, CALIFORNIA POLICE DEPARTMENT

In 1986–1987, 16 hours of cultural awareness training was provided to all 200 police personnel of the city of Concord, California. The training was included in an advanced officer in-service training block which all uniform division officers are required to attend annually. The training, however, was made mandatory for all police personnel by the chief of police, and four sessions were conducted, with one-fourth of the department attending at one time. The program was developed as follows:

1. Research was conducted by the department on what other police agencies and academies were offering in the area of cultural awareness/diversity training. Instructors were researched as well.

2. The department hired a cross-cultural communications specialist to assist in preparation of the training curriculum and also to serve as a moderator during all the training sessions.

3. Minority-community representatives/spokespersons were asked to assist in the preparation and implementation of training. Meetings with minority-community members were held and the broad goals of the training were established.

4. The cross-cultural specialist and a command staff member of the police department designed a needs assessment survey to disseminate to all police personnel. The minority-community representatives provided input and approved of the survey content. (See Appendix B for survey content.)

5. The chief's office disseminated the survey with a cover letter addressed to all police personnel wherein the chief stressed his desire to have a 100 percent return. The memo also indicated that the purpose of the survey was to determine what training police personnel felt they needed. The survey did not require the name of the person completing it, and it was returned to the cross-cultural specialist so that respondents could be candid without fear of retaliation by the Department.

6. The survey returns were reviewed and tabulated by the cross-cultural specialist. The results were summarized in a report and reviewed by the chief, the department command officer, and the minority-community representatives.

7. Large components of the course were designed by minority-community members on the subjects of which they were to be the presenters. The content, however, was reviewed and approved by the department command officer involved and the cross-cultural specialist. The courses learning objectives fulfilled the training needs as identified by the survey as well as satisfied community needs.

8. The 16-hour course content included:

   (a) Chief of police opening remarks stressing the importance of cross-cultural training.

   (b) Command officer review of general order dealing with policy and procedure of the department's response to crimes motivated by hate/bias.

   (c) Command officer review of department training bulletins regarding hate/bias crime investigations and interpreter system.

(d) Dissemination of Department Cultural Issues Manual, providing personnel with insights into cultural specific information about various cultures/ethnic groups, racial groups, religions, and sexual orientation.

(e) Cross-cultural specialist's presentation of four to five hours (i.e., out of 16 hours) on general cross-cultural concepts, including aspects of communication (verbal and nonverbal) relevant to the law enforcement context.

(f) Open forum and lecturettes by each minority-group instructor team covering such material as:

    (1) History of the ethnic or racial group

    (2) Culture-specific information about the ethnic or racial group

    (3) Games and exercises to reinforce learning objectives: values; power–powerless; communication styles; etc.

    (4) Case studies of police–community interactions

All participants were required to submit an anonymous evaluation of the course prior to leaving the training site. The cross-cultural specialist, command officer, and the minority instructors met following each class to review the comments; modifications were made to improve the next presentation. Overall, evaluations were very good and the program a success. The department continues to this day providing officers with 4 hours of instruction per year on cultural/diversity issues in the in-service, advanced officer training program. The training continues to be mandated and now is presented by minority police officers (from other agencies).

METRO-DADE, FLORIDA POLICE DEPARTMENT

In 1988, in an effort to improve and maintain good rapport with the multiethnic community of Dade County, Florida, the Metro-Dade Police Department instituted a violence reduction program. The program focused on the concept that understanding human behavior would enable officers to improve their interactions with citizens. According to the department, from the time of the program's implementation to its completion in 1990, there was a 24 percent decrease in reported incidents of citizen dissatisfaction.

In July 1993, all sworn Metro-Dade Police personnel received 16 hours of diversity training. All academy recruits complete 24 hours of diversity training. Training is designed around activities and discussion rather than lectures. The time devoted to each subject is flexible, depending on class size and the amount of discussion generated. Instructors are trained and receive an Instructor's Guide which provides them with step-by-step information for conducting each session. The basic recruit class curricula and time allotments are as follows:

Session 1: Introduction (1.25 hours)

Training Perspectives
Session Objectives
What Is Culture?
Cultural Effectiveness Continuum

Session 2: Understanding Culture's Influence (2.5 hours)

Session Objectives
Culture Search
Cultural Background

Session 3: Multicultural Communications (7.0 hours)

PART I: BARRIERS TO CROSS-CULTURAL COMMUNICATION

Stereotypes
Cultural Attributes

PART II: BRIDGING THE BARRIER TO CROSS-CULTURAL COMMUNICATIONS

Listening Gestures
Avoiding Resentment and Distrust
Bridging Barriers
Building Rapport and Trust
Building a Climate That Supports Open Communication
The Cultural Informant
Culture Shock

Session 4: Reducing People Conflicts (6.0 hours)

Session Objectives
Definition of Conflict
Cross-Cultural Conflict Factors
Meeting Control/Power Needs
Three Sources of Power
Levels of Power
Power Relationships in U.S. Society
Conscious and Subconscious Experience of Power
The Code of Silence
Misuse of Power
Hate Crimes
Racism, Sexism, and Misuse of Power
Individual Racism and Sexism
Institutional Racism and Sexism
Effects of Powerlessness
Individual and Community Empowerment
"Shared-Power" Relationships
Effects of Powerlessness
Identifying Ways to Improve Police–Community Relations

Session 5: The Law and the Right to Be Different (3.0 hours)

Examples of Protecting and Limiting the Right to Be Different
Session Objectives
What Is Discretion?
Maintenance of Order
Using Your Discretion

Session 6: Cultural Effectiveness

Session Objectives
Stages of Cultural Continuum
Cultural Effectiveness Continuum
Components of Cultural Effectiveness
Commitment to Combat Racism Inventory
Positive Achievement of Various Cultures
Action Plans for Cultural Effectiveness
Six Qualities of Leadership in Diverse Organizations

Session 7: Reducing Stress Through Cultural Awareness (optional)

Change as the Cause of Stress
Positive and Negative Stress
Effects of Stress
Stress Cycle

Appendix F

GUIDELINES FOR DESIGN OF CULTURAL AWARENESS PROGRAMS

There are eight recommended guidelines for law enforcement agencies considering designing cultural awareness training plans. The recommendations prioritized steps that local agency executives and their training managers should follow before implementing such training. The principles are based on years of study and program development by the California Commission on Peace Officer Standards and Training.

Guideline 1: The law enforcement executive should assess the department's cultural awareness condition.

The executive needs to conduct an assessment of the condition of the law enforcement agency. Before initiating such an assessment, it would be useful for executives to reflect closely on their personal perspectives about cultural diversity and their own communication styles with the organization and the community.

(a) Determine the need for development or revision of the agency policy/value statement relative to cultural diversity, including workplace and community.
(b) Review all training received by all agency personnel concerning cultural awareness, human relations, race relations, and communications.
(c) Review cultural diversity indicators such as rudeness complaints by immigrant and racial groups, lawsuits brought by immigrant and racial minority members of the community, EEO complaints within the agency, and complaints by minority-employee groups.
(d) Involving top management of the agency, develop an action plan to meet the needs as determined by A, B, and C.

Guideline 2:   The law enforcement executive should consider the need for training supervisors in techniques of managing and supervising a diverse workforce.

As law enforcement agencies increasingly reflect the ethnic diversity that exists in our communities, it is important to provide supervision and management techniques appropriate to this diverse workforce.

Guideline 3:   The law enforcement executive should appoint an agency cultural awareness facilitator (CAF).

The law enforcement executive should appoint one officer who is responsible for monitoring cultural awareness training needs and who possesses the skills for working with the community and the agency to provide such training.

(a) The CAF should have good interpersonal communication skills, a strong sense of personal identity, and demonstrated professional growth.

(b) Other considerations for the CAF include voluntary participation in cross-cultural activities, cross-cultural communication experience, self-confidence, training experience, respect within the organization and community, and demonstrated concern for others.

Guideline 4:   The cultural awareness facilitator should receive instruction in cultural awareness training procedures.

These procedures should include:

(a) Elements of cultures
  (1) Components of culture
  (2) Process of acculturation and assimilation
  (3) The dynamics of cultural change
(b) Immigrant and racial minority groups in the state, region, and local community
  (1) Immigration and racial patterns
  (2) How to determine immigration and racial patterns within their agency's jurisdiction
(c) Communication skills
  (1) Personal communication skills
  (2) Classroom communication skills
(d) Perception techniques
  (1) The factors involved in developing one's perception, feelings, bases, and thoughts as they relate to immigrant and racial differences
(e) Cultural experiences
  (1) The benefits of having experienced direct and simulated interaction with various immigrant and racial groups in the community
(f) Hate crimes as they relate to immigrant and racial minority groups
  (1) Understanding of the potential for immigrant and racial groups to be victims of hate crimes
  (2) Current legal issues concerning hate crimes
(g) Community sensing
  (1) Procedures for learning about immigrant and racial groups in the community
  (2) How to develop a cultural awareness needs assessment

    (h) Community training mentor (CTM)
        (1) How to select a CTM
        (2) How to train a CTM
    (i) Selecting appropriate training and program strategies
    (j) Managing dynamics of change
        (1) Assessment
        (2) Design
        (3) Implementation
        (4) Evaluation
    (k) Developing agency cultural awareness vision and goals

Guideline 5: The law enforcement executive should evaluate the need for additional cultural awareness training for the law enforcement agency.

After completing an assessment of the community, the law enforcement executive and the cultural awareness facilitator should determine if there are any opportunities for cultural awareness training.

Guideline 6: A training plan should be developed for the law enforcement agency.

If the evaluation in Guideline 5 indicates the need for additional training, the training plan should include, but not be limited to, the following contents:

    (a) Agency policy/value statement
    (b) Principles of perception
    (c) Demography within the agency jurisdiction
    (d) Patterns of immigration and racial employment in the law enforcement agency and local government
    (e) Communication skills
        (1) Personal communication skills, including active listening and tactical communication
        (2) Cultural communications, including "in-group privileges" and cultural conflict management

Guideline 7: Consideration should be given to various types of training delivery levels.

Consideration should be given to placing training at the following levels within the organization:

    (a) Basic police academy
        (1) Experiential training opportunities for recruit officers
    (b) In-service training
        (1) Roll-call cultural literacy training
        (2) Advanced officer training on cultural awareness
        (3) Supervisory and management training on diversity in the workplace
        (4) In-service training for nonsworn personnel on cultural awareness and literacy
        (5) Executive staff seminars on cultural diversity in the workplace and agency policy/value statements

Guideline 8: An evaluation should be developed for the agency training plan.

An evaluation component for the training program should be included during the design phase of the training plan.

(a) The agency and community assessment studies could provide baseline data. Discourtesy complaints, lawsuits, minority recruiting, EEO complaints, and reduction of officer injuries from public contacts could be considered as indicators.

(b) Evaluation techniques that could be considered include time-series comparisons, key person interviews, and survey questionnaires of the community and agency employees.

CULTURAL AWARENESS PROGRAM WORKSHOP FOR THE LAW ENFORCEMENT EXECUTIVE

This workshop is designed for law enforcement agency chief executive officers. The purpose of the training is to give executives an appreciation of the need for personal leadership to lead effectively their agencies to value diversity, within both the law enforcement agency and the community. Expected outcomes are: appreciating techniques to manage internal diversity; establishing a clear policy/value statement for the agency; careful selection of the cultural awareness training facilitator; and understanding evaluation techniques.

1.0 Overview of Cultural Awareness Program
   Learning Goal: The chief executive officer will understand the POST cultural awareness program.
   A. History
      1. POST role in the development of CA training program
      2. State legislation on CA training
      3. Pilot training program(s)
   B. Components of a cultural awareness program
      1. Three steps of the cultural awareness program
         a. Agency Assessment
            (1) Evaluate existing policy/value statement
            (2) Assess current training levels
            (3) Internal assessment
         b. Community Assessment
            (1) Status of diversity in the community
               (a) Identify pressure/social groups
               (b) Obtain census data
               (c) Contact government agencies for additional data
            (2) Identify community training mentors from:
               (a) Churches
               (b) Social groups
               (c) Human relations commissions
               (d) Chambers of commerce
         c. Development of the cultural awareness training plan
            (1) Training needs assessment of the agency
               (a) Identify existing cultural training
               (b) In conjunction with the community assessment, determine gaps in training by target immigrant/race group

        (2) Select community training mentors to represent target immigrant/race groups

        (3) Train community training mentors

            (a) Agency overview, including appropriate policies

            (b) Develop training strategies

            (c) Communication skills

            (d) Identify instructional resources

        (4) Design cultural awareness training plan

            (a) Submit to CEO for approval

2.0 Chief Executive Officer's Role in Cultural Awareness Program

Learning Goal: The chief executive officer will understand his or her role in managing the cultural awareness program.

  A. Support from chief executive officer

    1. Agency must have a policy/value statement

      a. Review examples

      b. Review, update, or develop with top management team in the agency

    2. Publicize the policy

      a. Use existing channels of communication within the organization

      b. Inform city/county management team

      c. Community awareness via:

        (1) Newspapers

        (2) Speaking engagements

        (3) Neighborhood watch programs

  B. Review employment practices

    1. Equal opportunity activities

    2. Goal of labor force to equate with U.S. Department of Labor statistics standards

    3. Equality in promotions and transfers within organization

    4. Recruitment techniques

  C. Coordinations with chief executive officer

    1. Agency cultural awareness facilitator (CAF) must have access to chief/sheriff, as needed

    2. CEO must have access to CAF

    3. Cultural awareness plan must have progress points requiring CEO approval/agreement

    4. CEO can, and should, open doors to community for CAF

  D. Chief executive officer must manage cultural awareness program

    1. The CEO must prepare the organization for change and understand potential resistance

      a. POA (police officers' association) may object

      b. Some officers may be threatened

      c. Attitudes that agency has gone "soft" on crime

    2. Potential for increased service requests from immigrant and/or racial groups

      a. In the interest of policing priorities, CEO must be prepared to say "no" occasionally to these groups

      b. Increased organization interest in immigrant/racial groups may lead to unrealistic expectations from the community

    3. Care must be taken to ensure that community and organizational expectations are based on realistic goals

      a. If qualified applicant pools for immigrant/racial groups hiring do not exist, reflect that when setting hiring goals

      b. Do not set timetable for training goals until resources are identified to meet training cost needs

    4. Cultural awareness program will follow "stages of change"
      a. "Present state" change includes heightened expectations
      b. "Transition state" includes organizational resistance, confusion, and a desire to return to the past
      c. "Desired state" means that within working the cultural awareness program plan, the goals of the program will be reached

3.0 Implementing a Cultural Awareness Program
Learning Goal: The chief executive officer will understand how to implement a cultural awareness program.
  A. Review cultural awareness facilitator selection criteria
    1. personal attributes desirable in the CAF
      a. Personally and professionally growing
      b. Good interpersonal communication skills
      c. Self-awareness and comfort with personal identity
    2. Other factors to consider
      a. Prior voluntary participation in cross-cultural activities
      b. Training background
      c. Respected inside the agency and in the community
      d. Demonstrated concern for others
      e. CEO has confidence in candidate
  B. Overview of cultural awareness facilitator role and responsibility
    1. Appropriate authority delegated to CAF
      a. How much authority to delegate
        (1) CEO must delegate enough authority to accomplish goals
        (2) CAF must know when limits of authority are reached
      b. CEO must ensure that other staff is not threatened by CAF's access to CEO
    2. Initiate a communication plan
      a. A management information system for the program is a must
        (1) Telephone
        (2) Written reports
  C. Overview of cultural awareness project plan
    1. Draft cultural awareness program checklist
      a. Section 1. Background
      b. Section 2. Approach
      c. Section 3. Assessment
      d. Section 4. Design
      e. Section 5. Implementation Considerations
      f. Section 6. Evaluation

4.0 Evaluating a Cultural Awareness Program
Learning Goal: The chief executive officer will understand how the cultural awareness program can be evaluated.
  A. Major indicators of an evaluation component
    1. Discourtesy complaints
    2. Lawsuits
    3. Minority recruiting
    4. EEO complaints
    5. Officers injuries
  B. Program evaluation methods
    1. Time-series comparison
    2. Key person interviews
    3. Survey questionnaires
  C. Does your cultural awareness program reflect you, chief/sheriff?

CULTURAL AWARENESS FACILITATOR TRAINING*

This course is designed for a law enforcement agency employee selected by the chief executive officer (CEO) of that agency. The course is designed to train that person to serve as the CEO's principal staff person for the program. The training presents the skills necessary to conduct both agency and community needs assessments; the elements of culture; information about immigrant and racial groups in (state, region, local); an understanding of personal communications skills; the selection and training of community members to assist the training function; and the development of an agency cultural awareness training plan. Although most of the training activity takes place in a traditional classroom setting, important activities are conducted by the CAF, in conjunction with the CEO in the agency's setting.

1.0 Introduction
- 1.1 The student will understand the definition of key terms and the legal basis for cultural awareness training.
    - 1.1.1 The student will identify the definition of key cultural awareness terms.
        - A. Cultural
        - B. Cultural awareness
        - C. Cultural literacy
        - D. Cultural diversity
    - 1.1.2 The student will identify the legal basis for cultural awareness training.
        - A. U.S. Constitution
        - B. State constitution
        - C. State laws
        - D. City/county policy
        - E. Agency policy/value statement
- 1.2 The student will understand the need to treat all people with dignity and respect.
    - 1.2.1 The student will identify components of cultural awareness that, at a minimum, will include:
        - A. History
            1. Geography
            2. Intercultural dynamics
                - a. Past
                - b. Present
            3. Gender dynamics
        - B. Customs
            1. Art
            2. Music
            3. Food
            4. Ceremony
            5. Family
        - C. Religion
            1. Practices
            2. Dress
        - D. Values
            1. Biases

---

*Course outline is reproduced by permission of Doug Thomas, senior executive of California Commission on Peace Officer Standards and Training, Sacramento, Calif., September 1993.

       E.   Language
          1. Slang
          2. Trigger words
       F.   Law Enforcement
          1. Attitudes toward law enforcement in native country
          2. Attitudes toward California law enforcement

2.1.2 The student will understand the differences between generations of immigrants and types of immigrant and racial groups in California.
      A.   First generation
      B.   Second generation
      C.   Third generation
      D.   Refugees
      E.   Undocumented

2.2   The student will understand the process of acculturation and assimilation.

    2.2.1 The student will understand the elements of acculturation.
        A.   How a culture is formed
        B.   Environment
        C.   Human activity

    2.2.2 The student will understand the elements of assimilation.

2.3   The student will understand the dynamics of change.

    2.3.1 The student will understand the elements of organizational change.
        A.   System readiness for change
        B.   Process of change
        C.   Roles in the change process
        D.   Handling resistance

3.0 Immigrant and Racial Groups in State

3.1   The student will be familiar with various immigrant and racial groups in the state and their immigration patterns.

    3.1.1 The student will identify immigrant and racial groups in the state. This will include at least:
        A.   Asian/Filipino, Pacific Islander
        B.   Black/African American
        C.   Hispanic/Latino/Chicano
        D.   Anglo/White
        E.   American Indian/Native American
        F.   Middle Eastern
        G.   Eastern Europe
        H.   Caribbean

    3.1.2 The student will identify the state's historical and projected immigration and racial patterns.

3.2   The student will become familiar with the methodology of identifying immigrant and racial patterns within the agency jurisdiction.

    3.2.1 The student will define the immigrant and racial patterns within the agency's jurisdiction.

    3.2.2 The student will define the immigrant and racial patterns of employment within the agency and within the agency's city or county government.

4.0 Communications Skills

4.1   The student will learn basic communication skills to effectively communicate with immigrant and racial groups.

    4.1.1 The student will discuss personal communication skills.
        A.   Knowledge of personal communication style
        B.   Active listening skills

        C.   Verbal and nonverbal communications

    4.1.2 The student will identify elements of cultural communication.

        A.   Cultural communication differences

           1. "In-group privileges"

           2. Inappropriate use by outsiders

        B.   Elements of cultural conflict management

4.2 The student will learn specific communications skills needed in a classroom to communicate effectively with students.

    4.2.1 The students will identify various classroom communications skills.

        A.   How to give and receive information without becoming emotionally involved

        B.   How to interpret negative energy from a student as a request for more information

        C.   How to give and receive effective feedback

        D.   Group dynamics

        E.   How to establish rapport with the class

5.0 Perception Techniques

5.1 The student will understand the factors involved in developing one's perceptions, feelings, biases, and thoughts as they relate to immigrant and racial differences.

    5.1.1 The student will discuss how perceptions are developed.

        A.   Past experiences

        B.   Maturity

        C.   Mental condition

        D.   Emotional involvement

        E.   Physical condition

        F.   Environmental conditions present

        G.   Training

        H.   Cultural and ethnic background

        I.   Personal prejudices and biases

    5.1.2 The student will explain the development of self-cultural perception.

        A.   Understanding the development of one's cultural perception

        B.   How to put a professional face on personal culture

    5.1.3 The student will explain why perceptions are neither right nor wrong.

        A.   One's perception is one's reality

        B.   Others' perception is their reality

6.0 Cultural Experiences

6.1 The student will understand the benefits of experiencing direct and simulated interaction with various immigrant and racial groups in the community.

    6.1.1 The student will identify the benefits of personal interaction with representatives of immigrant and racial groups.

    6.1.2. The student will identify methods for interaction and simulation with immigrant and racial groups.

        A.   Methods for simulation

           1. Videotapes

           2. Simulation games

           3. Computer-based training

           4. Interactive videodisc

        B.   Methods for interaction

7.0 Hate Crimes as They Relate to Immigrant and Racial Groups

7.1 The student will understand the potential for immigrant and racial groups to be victims of hate crimes.

    7.1.1 The student will identify reasons why immigrant and racial groups are hate crime targets.

      A.   Perceived threats

      B.   Stereotyping

7.1.2 The student will identify special considerations for investigating hate crimes.

      A.   Observations (appearance, clothing, language, ethnicities of victims and perpetrators, nonverbal behavior)

      B.   Body language

      C.   Community dynamics

      D.   Circumstances

      E.   Neighborhood/turf

7.2   The student will learn about current legal issues concerning hate crimes.

   7.2.1 The student will identify and discuss current hate crime case law.

   7.2.2 The student will discuss new laws concerning hate crimes.

8.0 Community Surveying

   8.1   The student will understand methods for gathering information about community immigrant and racial groups, and how to develop a cultural awareness needs assessment.

      8.1.1 The student will identify organizations and institutions in the agency jurisdictions that may be used to develop a cultural awareness needs assessment and as training resources.

         A.   Organizations that exist in the community

            1. Community organizations

            2. Human relations commissions and associations

            3. Religious organizations

         B.   Business community

            1. Chamber of commerce

            2. Labor unions

            3. Trade associations

         C.   Units of government

            1. Public and private schools

               a. Local school districts

                  (1) District offices for demographics

                  (2) Local schools for diversity activities

               b. Universities

                  (1) Research and data resources

                  (2) Faculty and student as resource

            2. Planning departments

            3. Public information officers

            4. Bureau of the Census

            5. Recreation departments

            6. Bureau of Indian Affairs

      8.1.2 The student will identify the methods of developing a cultural awareness needs assessment.

         A.   Agency

            1. Survey agency employees to identify local training needs

         B.   Community

            1. Community's perceptions of law enforcement

            2. Development of community support for training

         C.   Survey methodology

            1. How to develop community role/expectations

            2. Survey development

            3. Interview techniques (key person, roundtable, focus groups, telephone)

   D. Development and use of community training mentor

  8.1.3 The student will describe benefits to the community for participating in the agency training program.

   A. Increased safety for neighborhoods

   B. Improved communications with law enforcement

9.0 Community Training Mentors

 9.1 The student will understand the criteria for selecting a community training mentor.

  9.1.1 The student will describe the criteria for selecting a community training mentor, including:

   A. Formal community leaders

   B. Informal community leaders

   C. Prior experience working with law enforcement agency

   D. Prior training experience

10.0 Community Training Mentor Training

 10.1 The student will learn the elements of a training process for the community training mentors from immigrant and racial community training mentor.

   A. Agency familiarization

   B. Agency policy (cultural awareness, affirmative action, values)

   C. Agency training plan

   D. Communications skills

   E. Instructional strategies and resources

11.0 Agency Cultural Awareness Training Plan

 11.1 The student will understand the need for a cultural awareness training plan and how its components relate to all immigrant and racial groups.

  11.1.1 The student will identify the following as minimum components of a cultural awareness training plan:

   A. Agency policy/value statement

   B. Principles of perception

  11.1.2 The student will identify the following subcomponents for a cultural awareness training plan.

   A. Elements of culture

    1. History

    2. Customs

    3. Religion

    4. Values

    5. Language

    6. Attitudes toward law enforcement

   B. Differences between generations and types of immigrant and racial groups

    1. First-, second-, and third-generation immigrants

    2. Refugees

    3. Undocumented immigrants

   C. Patterns of immigration and racial employment in the agency and local government

   D. Demography within the agency jurisdiction

 11.2 The student will understand the need for personal communications skills and cultural communications to be included in the cultural awareness training plan:

  11.2.1 The student will identify personal communications skills.

  11.2.2 The student will identify elements of cultural communication.

   A. Cultural communications differences

    1. "In-group privileges"

    2. Inappropriate use by outsiders

   B. Elements of cultural conflict management

11.3   The student will understand issues affecting cultural awareness training.

    11.3.1   The student will describe the following issues that could impact agency cultural awareness training.

        A.   Support of agency executive as expressed by agency policy/value statement

        B.   Political influence of minority groups

        C.   Percentage of police contacts where cultural diversity is a factor

        D.   Minority-employee associations and their ability to influence agency policy

        E.   Agency history in dealing with immigrant and racial groups

        F.   Level of resistance to cultural awareness training likely to be encountered within the agency at various levels of the organization

11.4   The student will identify methods to evaluate an agency cultural awareness training plan.

    11.4.1   The student will identify major components that may be used for evaluating the agency cultural awareness training program.

        A.   Discourtesy complaints

        B.   Lawsuits

        C.   Minority recruiting

        D.   EEO complaints

        E.   Officer safety

    11.4.2   The student will identify evaluation methods.

        A.   Time-series comparison

        B.   Key person interviews

        C.   Survey questionnaires

12.0   Instructional Strategies

12.1   The student will understand instructional strategies.

    12.1.1   The student will discuss the value of the following instructional strategies.

        A.   Scenarios

        B.   Simulation games

        C.   Direct experiences

            1.   Expert panel

            2.   Field trip

            3.   Use of minority officer

        D.   Multimedia

        E.   Computer-based training

        F.   Interactive video

        G.   Lecture

13.0   Introduction to Resources

13.1   The student will become familiar with human and physical resources available for cultural awareness training.

    13.1.1   The student will identify human and physical resources available for cultural awareness training.

        A.   Human resources (annotated list of professionals available in California)

        B.   Physical resources (bibliography of videos, books, newsletters, and other materials available in California)

        C.   Local community resources

14.0   Application of Training

14.1   The student will develop a cultural awareness needs assessment (8.1).

14.2   The student, working with the executive, will select community training mentor(s) (9.0).

14.3   The student will train the community training mentor(s) (10.0).

14.4   The student will develop an agency cultural awareness training plan (11.0).

Appendix G

CULTURAL HOLIDAYS AND RELIGIOUS CELEBRATIONS

Cultural awareness on the part of the law enforcement practitioner involves a rudimentary knowledge of the various cultural or religious holidays and celebrations. Establishing a calendar is difficult for religions. Actual dates of observation of an historical event will vary because, for example, Muslims follow a purely lunar calendar (based on phases of the moon); the Western world is most familiar with a solar calendar (based on the sun); and Jews, Hindus, Sikhs, and Buddhists employ variations of a lunisolar calendar. Most Canadian and American civic holidays are noted on a calendar, but one seldom finds any reference to multicultural or religious holidays and celebrations. Progressive departments assign a staff member to become and remain informed on cultural and religious holidays and celebrations. He or she is then responsible, via memorandum and/or roll-call briefing information, for making employees of the agency aware of the dates and activities that could be expected. An explanation of a few of the cultural and religious holidays and celebrations follows.

Chinese New Year

A distinctive New Year's celebration occurs yearly in the Chinese sections of our large cities. This is especially elaborate in San Francisco, which has the largest of American Chinatowns. Their festival of several days is held on varying dates between January 21 and February 19.

Cinco de Mayo

The Fifth of May—a very important date in Mexican history. It is not the national independence day, as some think; that day occurs in September. May 5, 1862 was the day when the Mexicans succeeded—if only for a time—in opposing the French invasion of Mexico. To the Mexican people, Cinco de Mayo celebration is a symbol that all people of the world—yesterday, today, tomorrow—will fight curtailment of the most beloved principle of freedom and liberty.

Rosh Hashanah

Rosh Hashanah, meaning "head" or beginning of the new year, occurs on the first day of the Jewish month of Tishri. Its date ranges from September 6 to October 5. Rosh Hashanah marks the beginning of the observance covering 10 days, which is climaxed by Yom Kippur, the solemn Day of Atonement. A devout Jew does not begin a new year with gaiety; to him or her it is not the time for idle festivities but a day for meditation and self-examination—a solemn occasion, although not a mournful one.

Yom Kippur, the Day of Atonement

A time of penitence and fasting—falls on Tishri 10, ten days after Rosh Hashanah, the Jewish new year. Literally, the word *Kippur* means "to cover"; and this holy day is "the day of the covering, the day when He would blot out the sins of the Jewish nation and remember them no more. . . ." No other Hebrew festival is celebrated with such devotion and by so many persons of the Jewish faith.

Hanukkah

Hanukkah, the Jewish Feast of Lights, is an eight-day festival, beginning at sundown; it usually occurs in December (or occasionally in late November). It is celebrated in synagogues and homes all around the world, by religious and non-religious Jews. This observance is considered a feast of liberation, symbolic of the victory of the few over many and of the weak over the strong. The holiday's origin goes back to when Judas Maccabaeus and his band of Jewish warriors recaptured the temple in Jerusalem from the Syrians in 165 B.C., cleansed it, rededicated it, and proclaimed an eight-day dedication of the altar.

American Indian Day

American Indian Day is observed in some states to honor our Native Americans. The first general observance took place in New York State in May 1916. American Indian Day is now set in several states by a governor's proclamation or by legislative enactments. In some states the observance takes place in May and in others, in September (Krythe, 1962).

Other religions/cultures requiring understanding by law enforcement practitioners are described on the following pages.

Buddhism

Knowing Buddhist traditions, holidays, and celebrations can be a difficult task since there is no single Buddhist calendar and there are differences depending on the country of origin of the Buddhist. Historical events of importance, patriarchs (those persons living and dead whom they celebrate), and major divisions exist between the different forms of Buddhism. However, there are certain core celebrations. Of significance to all Buddhists everywhere are the life and teachings of Gotama or Siddhartha, the Buddha of the present era, who lived in India ca. 560–480 B.C.E. Events related to Gotama Buddha may be celebrated at different times in different temples, but the full moon is commonly recognized as the most important day for celebration. Officers working neighborhoods with an established Buddhist group should contact them to determine the dates of significant celebrations for them.

Islam

The Islamic calendar is lunar and since each month begins with the appearance of a new moon, a particular date of any month will fall only once in every 32.5 years on the same date of the solar year. Muslims are commanded in their scriptures, the Holy Qur'an (or Koran) to fast (they do not eat, drink, or smoke) from sunrise to sunset during Ramadan, the ninth month, but because of using a lunar calendar, the actual dates will vary each year. Ramadan is believed to be the month during which the Koran was revealed to Mohammed. Two other months are also special: Muharram, which begins the year, is a sacred month, and Dhu-al-Hijja, the last month of the year, is the time of pilgrimage. Officers working neighborhoods with an established Islamic group should consult with them to learn the dates of significant celebrations for them.

Hinduism

Although Hindus live in many parts of the world, their major cultural heritage is East Indian. In addition to certain annual festivals, Hindus may observe three days in each month: Amavasya (the new moon), Purnima (the full moon), and Ekadashi (the eleventh day). Most Hindu festivals celebrate events narrated in the national epics or classical writings. Such festivals characteristically include fasting, Puja (worship or acts of devotion to a deity), and feasting.

Sikhism

The Sikhs employ a traditional East Indian lunisolar calendar for the determination of their own special festivals. Each of the major Sikh festivals commemorates an important event in the early history of the faith. These include the birthdays of two of the Ten Gurus, the first (Nanak) and the last (Gobind Singh). There are a few other Gurus who are celebrated. All festivals will fall on a different day each year, with the exception of Baisakhi, which always falls on April 13 or 14th. Officers working neighborhoods with significant numbers of Sikh residents should determine what celebrations they observe and when (Canadian Ecumenical Action, 1991).

African American: Kwanzaa

Maulana Karenga, chairman of the black studies department at California State Long Beach, founded the holiday in 1966. Kwanzaa pays tribute to the cultural heritage of African Americans and others of African descent. It begins the day after Christmas and lasts seven days. Kwanzaa is a seven-day holiday that means "first fruits" in Swahili. Based on African winter harvest festivals, Kwanzaa culminates with a thanksgiving harvest feast. It reaffirms rootedness in African culture and the bonds between blacks as a people.

Kwanzaa contains seven principles, borrowed from various aspects of native African culture: umoja (unity), kujichagulia (self-determination), ujima (collective work and responsibility), ujamaa (cooperative economics), nia (purpose), kuumba (creativity), and imani (faith). On each night of Kwanzaa, one of seven candles in a holder is lit. Three red ones on the right represent struggle (blood), three green ones on the left represent the African motherland and hope for the future, and a black one in the middle is for African people everywhere. Families talk about one principle each night, discussing how it can be applied to daily life. Once celebrated primarily by black nationalists, Kwanzaa is now observed by 18 million people in the United States, Canada, England, and many African nations.

Many cities hold community celebrations featuring storytelling, African music and dance, and plays about black history. Many African American families celebrate both Christmas and Kwanzaa. Historically, their culture and their religion have gone hand in hand. Gifts are exchanged during Kwanzaa, but the focus is on education and creativity rather than commercialism (Wozencraft, 1992).

REFERENCES

Canadian Ecumenical Action (1991). *The Multifaith Calendar,* Canadian Ecumenical Action, Port Moody, B.C., Canada.

KRYTHE, MAYMIE R. (1962). *All About American Holidays,*

Harper & Brothers, New York.

WOZENCRAFT, ANN (1992). "Celebration of Kwanzaa," *Contra Costa Times,* Dec. 26, 1992.

Appendix H

MODELS FOR MANAGEMENT*

Effective Date:
Subject: Racial, Religious, and Ethnic Violence
Reference: Hate Crimes

I. Purpose

The _____ Police Department will take a proactive role in promoting peace and harmony within the community and in ensuring that rights guaranteed by state laws and the U.S. Constitution are protected for all citizens regardless of their race, color, ethnicity, or religion [sexual orientation should be included]. When such rights are infringed upon by violence, intimidation, threats, or other harassment, the department will use every necessary resource to identify the perpetrators rapidly and decisively, to arrest them, and to bring them before the court.

All acts of racial or religious violence or threats will be viewed as serious, and the investigations will be given priority attention. Such acts may generate fear and concern among victims and the public and have the potential of recurring, thus escalating and possibly causing counterviolence.

II. Definition

A racially, ethnically, or religiously targeted incident is an act or a threatened or attempted act by any person or group of persons against the person or property of

---

*The model presented here is from the International Association of Chiefs of Police.

another individual or group that may in any way constitute an expression of racial, ethnic, sexual orientation* or religious hostility. This includes threatening phone calls, hate mail, physical assaults, vandalism, cross-burning or destruction of other religious symbols, and firebombing. This list is not all-inclusive. Some incidents may not clearly fit a specific definition. In those cases, a commonsense approach must be used. If an incident appears to be an incident of racial, religious, ethnic, or sexual orientation bias, it should be investigated as such. Verification can be made during the investigation.

Officers must recognize that single incidents such as vandalism or threats may initially appear as less serious when viewed in the larger context of crime. Incident reports should be reviewed for *patterns* of incidents occurring at either the same location or directed at a particular individual or group. Very often, what may begin as a minor incident escalates into a more serious crime.

III. Policy

It shall be the policy of this department to bring the investigative and enforcement elements of the police department into quick action following any and all reported or observed incidents of racial, religious, sexual orientation, or ethnic hatred. There is to be special emphasis placed on victim assistance and community cooperation in order to reduce victim/community trauma or fear. It must be remembered that the actions taken by this agency in dealing with incidents of racial, religious, sexual orientation, and ethnic bias are visible signs of concern and commitment to the community on the part of the government of this city and its police department.

The proper investigation of racial, religious, sexual orientation, or ethnic incidents is the responsibility of all police officers. Each officer must be sensitive to the feelings, needs, and fears that may be present in the community as a result of incidents of this nature.

Note: The International Association of Chiefs of Police models for management continues with procedures to be followed. The procedures are the same as presented in Chapter 13.

---

*The authors have added "sexual orientation" to the wording in this policy.

Appendix I

DIRECTORY
OF ORGANIZATIONS:
ANTIBIAS EDUCATION

American-Arab Anti-Discrimination Committee
4201 Connecticut Avenue N.W.
Suite 500
Washington, DC 20008
202/244-2990

Anti-Defamation League of B'nai B'rith
National Office
823 United Nations Plaza
New York, NY 10017
212/490-2525

Anti-Defamation League of B'nai B'rith
10495 Santa Monica Boulevard
Los Angeles, CA 90025
213/446-8000

Anti-Defamation League of B'nai B'rith
121 Stuart Street
Suite 401
San Francisco, CA 94105
415/546-0200

Asia Society
Southern California Center Arco Plaza, Level C
505 South Flower Street
Los Angeles, CA 90071
213/624-0945

Center for Democratic Renewal National
Office
P.O. Box 50469
Atlanta, GA 30302-0469
404/221-0025
A national clearinghouse that monitors hate groups. Provides victim assistance, leadership training, and education.

Chinese American Planning Council
6569 Listpenart Street
New York, NY 10013
212/941-0920

Coalition Against Anti-Asian Violence
c/o Asian American Legal Defense and
Education Fund
99 Hudson Street, 12th Floor
New York, NY 10013
212/966-5932

Community United Against Violence
514 Castro Street
San Francisco, CA 94114
415/864-3112

Equity Institute
6400 Hollis Street
Suite 15
Emeryville, CA 94608
510/658-4577

Hetrick-Martin Institute
(Lesbian and Gay Youth Social Services
Organization)
401 West Street
New York, NY 10014
212/633-8920

Human Rights Resource Center
30 N. San Pedro Road
Suite 140
San Rafael, CA 94903
415/499-7465
Provides unique historical and current information, technical assistance, and state-of-the-art training programs to law enforcement agencies, schools, and human rights organizations throughout the United States, Canada, England, and New Zealand seeking to prevent and solve various human rights problems within their respective communities.

Institute for American Pluralism of the
American Jewish Committee
165 East 56th Street
New York, NY 10022
212/751-4000

Institute for American Pluralism of the
American Jewish Committee
1100 Main Street
Suite D1
Irvine, CA 92714
714/660-8525

Institute for American Pluralism of the
American Jewish Committee
6505 Wilshire Boulevard
Suite 315
Los Angeles, CA 90048
213/655-7071

Japanese American Citizens League
912 F Street
Fresno, CA 93706
209/237-4006

Japanese American Citizens League
244 South San Pedro Street
Suite 507
Los Angeles, CA 90012
213/626-4471

Japanese American Citizens League
1765 Sutter Street

San Francisco, CA
94115 415/921-5225

Klanwatch Southern Poverty Law Center
400 Washington Avenue
Montgomery, AL 36104
205/264-0286
Provides legal services in discrimination, civil rights, and class action cases. Works to educate the public through films and publications.

National Association for the Advancement of
Colored People
Washington Bureau
1025 Vermont Avenue N.W.
Washington, DC 20009
202/638-2269

National Gay and Lesbian Task Force
1734 14th Street N.W.
Washington, DC 20009
202/332-6483
Provides services for gay and lesbian crime victims.

National Institute Against Prejudice and
Violence
31 South Greene Street
Baltimore, MD 21201
301/328-5170
Conducts research on victimization and provides consultation and training to law enforcement personnel, victim assistance providers, and other agencies and community organizations.

U.S. Department of Justice Community
Relations Service
Refer to Government *section of phone book for local office*

Native American Education Program
Room 507
234 West 109th Street
New York, NY 10025
212/663-4040

Appendix J

HATE VIOLENCE TRACKING FORMS

San Francisco Police Department

Date of Report _____ Referred by: _____

Reporting Party: _____ _____ _____

                  Name   Address   Phone

Date of Incident _____ Time of incident _____ Location _____

Report Taker _____ Phone _____ Agency Code_____

	TYPE OF BIAS		TYPE OF INCIDENT	
			PERSONAL	PROPERTY
___ Racial Anti-_____	___ Elder		___ Slurs	___ Graffiti on Public Property
___ National Origin Anti-_____	___ Disability Type _____		___ Verbal Threat	___ Graffiti on Private Property
___ Religion Anti-_____	___ Gender Anti-_____		___ Threat with Apparent Intent to Carry It Out	___ Crossing Burning

442

TYPE OF BIAS

TYPE OF INCIDENT

PERSONAL   PROPERTY

___ Immigrant   ___ Sexual
Anti-_____   Orientation
Anti-_____

___ Physical Assault   ___ Property
No Weapons   Damage
Public

___ Other _____

___ Physical Assault   ___ Property
Weapons   Damage
Private

___ Physical Injury   ___ Arson

___ Homicide   ___ Explosion
___ Other   ___ Other
_____   _____

OTHER PARTIES
(Code: V=Victim D=Victim's domestic partner W=Witness F=Family O=Other)

CODE	NAME	ADDRESS	DAYTIME PHONE
____	_____	_____	_____
____	_____	_____	_____
____	_____	_____	_____

SUSPECTS

RELEVANT INFORMATION/ AFFILIATION	NAME	ADDRESS
_____	_____	_____
_____	_____	_____
_____	_____	_____

SEND A COPY OF THIS REPORT TO THE INTERGROUP CLEARINGHOUSE, 995 MARKET ST RM1114, SAN FRANCISCO 94103 WITHIN 72 HOURS. IF THIS INCIDENT MAY LEAD TO FURTHER INCIDENTS OR IS CAUS-ING COMMUNITY CONCERN, CALL THE CLEARINGHOUSE AT (415) 896-1355.

RESPONDING AGENCIES

Agency Name	Contact Person	Phone
_____	_____	_____
_____	_____	_____
_____	_____	_____

Narrative: _____
_____
_____
_____
_____
_____

Action Taken: _____

_____

Recommendations: _____

_____

Comments: _____

_____

COMMUNITY DISORDER UNIT, BOSTON POLICE DEPARTMENT, CASE ASSIGNMENT AND CONTROL FORM

CASE NUMBER: _____

Investigating Officer:_____ I.D.# _____ Type of Incident:_____
_____Code: _____
Police Area: _____ C.C.# _____ Date of Incident:_____
VICTIM:_____ Date Case Assigned: _____

_____

_____

PHONE:_____

Interviews

VICTIM: _____   Date of Interview: _____
WITNESS #1 _____   Date of Interview: _____
WITNESS #2_____   Date of Interview: _____
WITNESS #3_____   Date of Interview: _____
WITNESS #4_____   Date of Interview: _____

Door to Door Canvas: Dates Performed   _____ _____ _____ _____

Attempts to Interview (negative results)

VICTIM: _____ _____ _____ _____
WITNESS   _____ _____ _____ _____
Surveillance   _____ _____ _____ _____
Performed: _____ _____ _____ _____

Criminal Civil Rights Charges: YES: NO:
Civil Restraining Orders/Injunctions   YES: NO:

COURT APPEARANCES

CHARGES: _____ District Court Hearing Date: _____ COMPLAINTS:
Granted: DENIED:

_____ OTHER: _____
District Court Trial Date: _____ Results: _____

_____   _____

B.M.C. Six Man Jury Trial: _____   Results: _____

_____   _____

_____   _____

Grand Jury: Date: _____   True Bill: Yes No

Superior Court Trial: _____   Results: _____

_____   _____

_____   _____

Case Status: _____

_____

_____

DEFENDANT INFORMATION

Appendix K

LISTING OF CONSULTANTS AND RESOURCES

There are many consultants who conduct training for criminal justice agencies on cultural awareness/diversity issues. We are unable to include all of them, but we do provide the names of a few. Please note that we do not necessarily endorse these consultants as we are not personally familiar with each of them.

CROSS-CULTURAL DIVERSITY CONSULTANTS
USEFUL TO LAW ENFORCEMENT

Consultant's Consortium (P.O. Box 490255, Miami, Florida 33149). Design and implement training programs on: human relations for law enforcement, intercultural diversity, and ethics for law enforcement.

Council on Education in Management (321 Lennon Lane, Walnut Creek, California 94598, USA—TEL: 1-800/942-4494). Produce human resource management tools such as a Compliance Kit to meet employment provisions of Americans with Disabilities Act, ABRA 2000 HR Information System software, Affirmative Action Planning Manual, Drug-Free Work Place Manual, Employment Law Series, Sexual Harassment Prevention Training Kit with video, Team Building video, and other personnel services material.

CRM Films (2215 Faraday Ave., Carlsbad, California 92008, USA—TEL: 1-800/421-0083). Produce and distribute training films with manuals on conflict, communication, and management.

Cultural Contact, Inc. (P.O. Box 1046, Poulsbo, Washington 98370, USA—TEL: 1-206/779-1843). Offers training seminars on cross-cultural communications and understanding specifically designed for the police audience.

Deena Levine & Associates (P.O. Box 582, Alamo, CA 94507; Tel: 501/947-5627). Co-author of *Multicultural Law Enforcement: Strategies for Peacekeeping in a Diverse Society;* Cross-cultural consulting for businesses and organizations.

Diversity Management (800 Fifth Avenue, #390, Seattle, WA 98104; Tel: 206/392-7323. Individual consulting practice of Chuck Shelton, specializing in cross-cultural programs for managers.

Elsie Cross & Associates (7627 Germantown Avenue, Philadelphia, PA 19118; Tel: 215/248-8100).

George Simons International (740 Front Street, Santa Cruz, CA 95060; Tel: 408/426-9608). Consulting practice of George Simons, leading diversity author and producer of videos and instruments on this subject.

Gil Dean Group, The (13751 Lake City Way, N.E., Suite 106, Seattle, WA 98125; Tel: 206/362-0336; Fax: 206/363-5028). Maintain a computer data bank and referral service for cross-cultural consultants; also operate a book service and publish a newsletter/bulletin on diversity training.

Herbert Z. Wong & Associates (One Kendall Square, Suite 2200, Cambridge, MA 02139; Tel: 617/489-1930; Fax: 617/489-2689). Co-author of *Multicultural Law Enforcement: Strategies for Peacekeeping in a Diverse Society;* management and technical consultants engaged in organizational surveys, cultural audits, and workforce diversity training; specialization in Asian cultures and annual diversity conference.

Innovative Communications (800 K Street, Suite 740, Washington, DC 20001; Tel: 202/408-9632). Consulting group featuring Carmen Vazquez, co-author of *Transcultural Leadership.*

Intercultural Development Inc. (755 San Mario Drive, Solano Beach, CA 92075; Tel: 619/755-3160). Individual consulting practice of Selma Meyers, co-author of *The Diversity at Work Training Series.*

Kochman Communication Consultants, Ltd. (2100 North Racine, Suite 1B, Chicago, IL 60614; Tel: 312/645-1578). Consulting group centered around Thomas Kochman, author of *Black and White Styles in Conflict;* conduct both public/contract seminars on changing pluralism, African American/Anglo, Hispanic–Latino/Anglo, Asian/Anglo, gender, and culture.

LMA Inc. (365 Melendy Road, Milford, NH 03055; Tel: 603/672-0355). General management consulting with specializations in leadership and change.

Lieutenant Ondra Berry, Law Enforcement—Cultural Diversity Training, Reno, Nevada Police Department, 702/322-5519

Managing Cultural Differences (MCD) Authors' Network (2702 Costebelle Drive, La Jolla, CA 92037; Tel: 619/453-2271). Ten authors and editors who produced the seven volumes of MCD Series for Gulf Publishing (1-800/231-6275). All experienced cross-cultural consultants.

New Leaders Institute (P.O. Box 1110, Del Mar, CA 92014; Tel: 619/782-5922, Fax: 619/792-9874). Consulting practice centered around career development of women and minorities by Ann M. Morrison, researcher/author of *Breaking the Glass Ceiling* and *New Leaders.*

ODT Inc. (P.O. Box 134, Amhurst, MA 01004; Tel: 1-800/736-1293). Principal distributor of diversity and upward management materials; consulting network.

Pacific Area Communicators of Intercultural affairs (16331 Underhill Lane, Huntington Beach, California 92647, USA—Tel: 1-714/840-3688). PACIA maintains a cross-cultural clearinghouse and publishes *I.N.N.—Intercultural News Network,* a newsletter edited by Janet Rheinhart which focuses upon cultural diversity in health, education, and public services (e.g., Asian- Pacific ethnic affairs, multicultural women and students, and information resources).

Pelikan Associates (6501 Bannockburn Drive, Bethesda, MD 20817; Tel: 301/229-8550; Fax: 301/229-6609). Helen Pelikan's public and customized training programs on use of the instrument called *The Meyer–Briggs Inventory;* MBTI is a tool for working constructively with individual differences in a multicultural society.

PowerPhone, Inc. (P.O. Box 1911, Madison, Connecticut 06443-0900, USA—Tel: 1-800/53-POWER) Provide a two-day, interactive workshop for law enforcement on race relations and cultural awareness.

Prime Systems Company (P.O. Box 404, Beltsville, MD 20705; Tel: 301/937-4477). Consulting practice of author, Gordon F. Shea, who specializes in HRD, mentoring, conflict negotiating, and building/assessing trust in organizations.

*Simulations Training Systems (210 Twelfth St., Del Mar, California 92014, USA—Tel: 1-619/755-0272). Produce simulation games and videos in cross-cultural and team management based on the research of Dr. Garry Shirts.

SJW Associates (740 Front Street, Suite 335, Santa Cruz, CA 95060; Tel: 408/429-9393). Consulting practice of Sally J. Walton featuring workbook, *The Competitive Advantages of Cultural Diversity in the Workplace.*

University Centers Inc. (1190 South Colorado Boulevard, Suite 201, Denver, CO 80222; Tel: 303/756-4441). Consulting practice of Janice C. Hepworth, focused on her slides and workbooks, *Intercultural Communications* and *Things to Know About Americans.*

White Associates (P.O. Box 60118, Palo Alto, CA 94306; Tel: 415/493-5555). Diversity consulting practice of E. J. White.

Woodrow H. Sears, Ed.D. (2160 Plaza del Amo, No. 163, Torrance, CA 90501; Tel: 301/320-2948). Experienced human relations trainer for criminal justice systems with specialization in public sector courses in practical management.

INDEX